The Age of Progress
A SURVEY OF EUROPEAN HISTORY
from 1789 - 1870

The Age of Progress

A SURVEY OF EUROPEAN HISTORY

from 1789 - 1870

by

IRENE COLLINS

Lecturer in History, the University of Liverpool

LONDON

EDWARD ARNOLD (PUBLISHERS) LTD

© Irene Collins 1964

First Published 1964

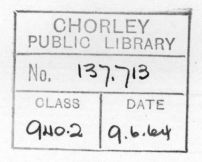
Printed in Great Britain by
ROBERT CUNNINGHAM AND SONS LTD
Alva

Preface

I HAVE tried to write a straightforward account of what happened on the
continent of Europe between the outbreak of the French Revolution and the
downfall of the Second Empire, leaving to others the themes and analyses,
the interpretations and Olympian views. I hope that what I have written
will stimulate and assist further study. Among the many colleagues and
friends who have helped me in one way and another I must thank Professor
Alun Davies for reading the manuscript and making valuable suggestions,
Professor S. B. Saul for guidance in economic matters, Mr A. N. Ryan for
advice on the Continental System, Mr J. Shennan for corrections to the
Russian chapters and my typist, Mrs Ada Jones, for eliminating a host of
small errors in the course of her work. My publishers have been unfailingly
courteous and co-operative, my family forbearing and at times even enthusiastic. If the book has any overall merit I should like it to be a testimony to
my former tutor in Oxford, Dr Hans Schenk, whose learning and humanity
in the field of nineteenth century European studies I have ever since admired.

IRENE COLLINS

Liverpool
September 1963

Contents

Maps

CHAPTER I

The Coming of Revolution in France
1789

I. THE ESTATES GENERAL

IN THE great palace of Versailles, built by Louis XIV as a stage upon which
the king of France could give a dazzling display of power, Louis XVI
welcomed deputies to the Estates General on 2 May 1789. Electoral regulations of 24 January had provided for 300 deputies from the First Estate, the
clergy; 300 from the Second Estate, the nobles; and 600 from the Third
Estate, the commons. All three delegations centred high hopes on the forthcoming meetings, but many deputies found the opening ceremony disappointing. It dragged on for nine hours and the king was plainly bored.
His manner was not unkindly, but the ancient rules of etiquette invoked
for the occasion meant that snubs were inevitably administered to representatives of the Third Estate.

These bourgeois gentlemen had looked forward to a more inspiring
welcome. Because the king had summoned the ancient parliament of the
realm after a lapse of a hundred and seventy-five years, they had imagined
that he was going to break away from the closed world of courtiers at
Versailles and return to the arms of the people. Unfortunately Louis's
intentions were never so straightforward. Good-hearted but dull-witted,
he combined indecision with a peculiar slyness. The Parlement had persuaded him to summon the Estates General because the state was bankrupt
and because the efforts of several ministers to tax the privileged orders had
resulted in a revolt of the nobles (May–June 1788). The Parlement hoped
that the revival of the Estates would secure the triumph of the aristocracy
over the new-fangled absolute monarchy; hence the magistrates' decision,
in September 1788, that medieval procedures should be revived, with three
orders of equal strength voting separately. The bourgeoisie had protested
vigorously against a decision calculated to enable the two privileged orders
to out-vote the commons, and the finance minister Necker had persuaded
the king to mollify angry citizens with a grant of double representation to
the Third Estate. The deputies had thereupon travelled to Versailles expecting Necker to champion their second demand, which was for collective

voting (*par tête* instead of *par ordre*). They were soon disappointed. Necker was not the man to lead a revolution, and Louis had never intended to go over to the commons.

The term 'Tiers État' was a legal concept, including all persons who were not nobles or clergymen – more than 25 million out of a population of 26 million. To this amorphous body the government had granted almost universal male suffrage. With a few exceptions such as actors, bankrupts, domestic servants, and men who were so poor that their names did not appear on tax-rolls, all Frenchmen over the age of twenty-five could vote. Since voting was done in assemblies, however, and the assemblies must be of a suitable size to discuss grievances, the whole process was carried out in stages. In rural areas, primary assemblies chose candidates for a general assembly of the constituency (*baillage*) and election was thus in two stages. In towns, preliminary assemblies of trades and professions increased the number of stages to three, and a fourth stage was added in constituencies which were classed as secondary. The result was the election, almost exclusively, of bourgeois deputies. Illiterate peasants in primary assemblies often chose village schoolmasters or notaries to represent them in the general assembly. These men naturally felt overawed when they came to carry out the important duty of choosing a deputy, and they voted for someone whose social or professional position had attracted attention over a fairly wide area, whose talents would enable him to play a worthy part in national affairs, and whose income would support a journey to Versailles. In the towns these feelings were strengthened by civic patriotism, a desire to send to parliament men who would do well for their home town. Out of 610 deputies of the Third Estate about 400 were lawyers or officials, 80 were financiers, merchants, or industrialists, and another 50 or so were doctors, teachers, or men of letters.

The bourgeosie from which they were drawn formed only a small class in a primarily agricultural population; perhaps a twentieth part of the nation. Within its ranks were many differences of wealth and status. Highest in the social scale came financiers, making fortunes mostly from the state: rich Farmers General who had bought from the government the right to collect indirect taxes, contractors who furnished supplies for the armies and navy, bankers who made the loans which formed the most important item of government finance, and in every provincial town a horde of tax collectors and financial advisers. Next came merchants at the great ports of Marseille, Bordeaux and Toulon and at inland cities such as Lyon and Rouen. Commerce was more advanced than industry. Powerful industrialists were to be found in some textile towns such as Reims and Sedan, and in metal and mining concerns at le Creusot and Anzin, but for the most part industry was in the hands of craftsmen employing only a small number of men. Some master craftsmen qualified by wealth and local status for the name 'bour-geois', but others were scarcely distinguishable from the journeymen with whom they worked. Each profession had likewise its own hierarchy: village notaries were hardly in the same category as judges and barristers, and the local apothecary could not compete in status with the fashionable town doctor.

Contrary to Marxist theory the bourgeoisie was not likely to act as a class even upon vital issues. Upper levels, whose members were prospering and could hope to rise into the aristocracy, were inclined to remain loyal to the *ancien régime*, whilst middle and lower levels, whose members could rise no further and were sometimes afraid of falling, naturally tended to be hostile. Their hostility showed itself in a critical attitude towards government and church, and in resentment at the privileges of the aristocracy. Middling businessmen, small-town lawyers, journalists and the like came upon vexa-tious government activity at every turn, for although the *ancien régime* was by no means an absolutist state petty restrictions were all-pervading. Large numbers of officials, whose posts had been created chiefly to sell for ready money, carried out a daily round of useless activity. The result was a cry of 'despotism', although in fact government control was ineffective in most spheres. Indeed accusations of tyranny were coupled with criticisms of inefficiency, especially at times of crisis. A recession in trade and industry, which began about 1770, was aggravated by the disastrous crop failure of 1788, and many businessmen found their irritation sharpened by anxiety. There was no widespread desire to overthrow the monarchy: the republican ideas of Rousseau were not popular. There was merely a desire that the king should abandon his attempts at absolutism, which had never been effective, and agree to a constitutional régime in which men of talent could co-operate. Most bourgeois were experienced men of affairs, and a moderate parlia-mentary monarchy, although condemned by Rousseau as irrational, seemed to them a means of securing practical reforms advocated by Physiocrats and other down-to-earth writers of the Enlightenment.

Criticism of absolute monarchy had been encouraged during the eight-eenth century by a gradual undermining of the theory of divine right. Unlike some other European rulers, who had bolstered up absolutism with appeals to philosophy, French kings had never abandoned the claim to a religious sanction for their power. It was therefore a matter of serious political importance when philosophers poured contempt on the teaching of the church. It was even more serious, because more widely noticed, when the Parlement fomented discord within the Catholic church and brought about (1763) the expulsion of the Jesuits, the chief defenders of monarchy. The bourgeoisie criticized the church as a political institution, too closely wedded to absolute monarchy, and as an aristocratic institution, corrupted by

privilege. The incompatibility of these two arguments was overlooked, and
the dual function of the Gallican church, which gave divine sanction to the
monarchy while acting as a powerful check on royal authority, was seldom
defined. Most bourgeois had no taste for abstractions. They saw the church
as worldly and intolerant, owning vast estates when purchasers were clam-
ouring for farming land, squandering wealth on aristocratic bishops when
the state was nearly bankrupt, monopolizing education, poor relief, regis-
tration, and other matters which were coming to be regarded as rightly
secular. There was no widespread rejection of Catholic doctrine, but lists of
grievances (*cahiers de doléances*) sent by electoral assemblies to the Estates
General were full of demands that the church should be reformed so that it
could fulfil its Christian duties in a reformed state.

For most of the eighteenth century the bourgeoisie was more articulate
in its criticism of government and church than in its resentment of the
aristocracy. Many a bourgeois could hope to rise into the aristocracy by
marriage or by purchasing a post which carried a title of nobility. As the
century proceeded, however, the aristocracy became more exclusive and
more firmly entrenched in all the most lucrative positions. More and more
young bourgeois, educated in good schools, found no satisfactory careers in
the world. 'The Revolution came and we threw ourselves into it,' wrote
Danton. 'The old régime drove us to it, by giving us a good education
without opening any opportunity for our talents.' Thwarted ambition was
made more galling by social snubs. Barnave remembered all his life the
slights he received from his mother's aristocratic relatives because his father
was a lawyer.

Bitterness smouldered a long time and flared into anger as late as 1788,
when the Parlement made clear its intention that the privileged orders
should dominate the Estates General. Dislike of 'ministerial despotism' gave
place overnight to a fear that the monarchy would resign its power to the
aristocracy. This fear brought the bourgeoisie into action. The campaign
for double representation and for voting *par tête* was more vigorous than the
philosophic movements of earlier years had ever been. Behind the apparently modest demands lay the determination of the bourgeoisie to guide the
life of the community. The most notable of the pamphlets published during
the ensuing months, Sieyès's *Qu'est-ce que le Tiers État?* (January 1789) put
the matter in the form of a catechism: 'What is the Third Estate? Everything. What has it been until now? Nothing. What does it ask? To be
something.'

Unfortunately many nobles, also, were determined to assert themselves.
Ever since the death of Louis XIV the aristocracy had been struggling to
recover the political power which it had lost to the Crown in the seventeenth
century. The Parlement of Paris had led the fight at the centre, ably seconded

by provincial parlements, while Provincial Estates had done battle with the king's intendants in Burgundy, Provence, Béarn, Brittany and Languedoc. Their combined efforts at resisting taxation had obliged the king to summon the Estates General, but the nobles were by no means agreed as to how to use this unique situation.

Glittering nobles who squandered their fortunes and energies at court were only a small fraction of an aristocracy numbering about 400,000. Either from nonchalance, love of intrigue, or real intelligence, the court nobles were usually open to advanced political views, and they despised their country brethren both as reactionary and uncultured. Country nobles, in return, viewed court nobles with a mixture of disapproval and jealousy, knowing bitterly that all the most lucrative pensions and sinecures went to cliques surrounding the queen. Some provincial nobles were fairly well off and had set themselves up as gentlemen farmers, reading the Physiocrats and copying new agricultural methods from England. Others were quite poor, especially in mountainous districts. They had no capital for experiments, and confined themselves to extracting the fullest returns from rents and feudal dues. Poor nobles were usually the most conservative in political views, clinging to tax privileges and to the seigneurial rights through which they exploited their tenants. Others had come to the conclusion by 1789 that tax privileges would have to be abandoned, but they believed that by clever bargaining they could obtain a regular system of Estates General and Estates Provincial, in which their own order predominated and ruled the country. The leading exponents of such a plan were the *parlementaires*, but the alliance between them and the rest of the nobility was one of convenience only. At heart, nobles of ancient lineage despised upstarts who had acquired nobility by purchase.

Not all the 290 nobles who represented the Second Estate at Versailles deserved the title reactionary. About 90 could be classed as liberal nobles who might co-operate with the Third Estate. Among them was the Marquis de Lafayette, reputed to have developed republican sentiments in America, and the Duc d'Orléans, the king's cousin who had distributed model *cahiers* asking for constitutional reform. Ambition played some part in their calculations, especially in those of Orléans, but they were willing to sacrifice tax privileges and feudal rights to obtain a parliament with a Second Chamber. Unfortunately, they were a minority of the deputation. Every noble over the age of twenty-five voted in the elections, and voted directly; the result was an overwhelming majority of provincial nobles, inclined, though in varying degrees, to a more conservative view.

Electoral regulations also affected the composition of the clerical deputation. Every parish priest, as well as every bishop, voted directly, while chapters and communities voted indirectly. Out of 300 representatives for the First Estate, 205 were parish priests, and only 42 were bishops.

The Catholic church was a powerful institution in France on the eve of the Revolution. It levied tithes on all products of the soil and owned land amounting to a tenth of the kingdom. Its buildings had been made more splendid during the eighteenth century; cathedrals and abbeys had reconstructed their fabric on the most elaborate scale. The church was not subject to the ordinary judicial and fiscal systems, but administered its own law in its own courts and gave its own donations to the state, apportioned by its own Assembly. Its social influence was enormous. All births, deaths and marriages must be registered by the church, young people were educated in its schools, large numbers of men and women were employed on its property, and the sick were tended in its hospitals. As the First Estate of the realm the clergy were given precedence at every official gathering. Yet, as Sieyès argued, they were not strictly speaking an estate at all, because they did not constitute a separate class in society.

The upper clergy – bishops, abbots and canons of rich chapters – were nobles who had been given positions in the church to supplement their income. A few of the bishops in the Estates General sympathized with the liberal nobles of the Second Estate. Their motives were mainly ambitious; the group included Talleyrand, the scandalous bishop of Autun, whose open scepticism and careerism brought so much discredit on the rest of the clergy. The others showed no sympathy with advanced political views. In spite of attacks made on the church during the century, the majority of the upper clergy complacently believed that they could obtain even more benefits from the *ancien régime* whose fruits they already enjoyed so lavishly. Meanwhile the lower clergy, including all the parish priests and most monks, were commoners, often from poor families. They resented a system of patronage which handed out the richest rewards of the church as pensions to aristocrats and which allowed privileged chapters and monasteries to alienate a large share of tithes within the parishes. Resentment gave them a fellow-feeling with the bourgeoisie, while poverty gave them sympathy with peasants and workers. The idea that the First Estate would inevitably oppose measures passed by the Third was probably wrong. The parish priests who came to Versailles were anxious to preserve the separate identity of the clerical order, however. It was the alliance of the king with the aristocracy which obliged them to throw in their lot with the commons.

2. THE REVOLT OF THE BOURGEOISIE

The transformation of the Estates General into a revolutionary assembly and a modern parliament can be attributed either to chance or to the extraordinary vitality of the French nation at the time. Curbed but not stifled by a ramshackle absolutism, this vitality had given to France in the eighteenth century a prosperous bourgeoisie, a large class of peasant farmers, flourishing towns, a total population larger than that of any other country in Europe, reforming officials who were gradually changing the structure of the *ancien régime*, political writers known throughout the western world, and an ever-growing belief in the ability of men to improve their condition. The nineteenth-century historian Michelet had some justification for seeing in the events of 1789 the hand of destiny.

At the opening meeting of the Estates General on 5 May, Necker began his eagerly awaited speech with a recital of financial detail in which he made no mention of a need for parliamentary measures. On the crucial question of procedure, he suggested that voting *par ordre* should operate at first, to allow the clergy and nobles to make a voluntary renunciation of their tax privileges, after which the three orders might unite by common consent. This sounded reasonable since many clergy and nobles were willing to sacrifice their tax privileges, but in return they wanted a large share of political power and the maintenance of the old social distinctions. On these points the deputies of the Third Estate were determined to exercise the pressure of their double numbers. Necker gave no promise that the government would help them when the time came, so they determined to help themselves before it was too late, that is, before the voting of new taxes rendered their presence expendable.

Before the Estates General could proceed to business each deputy must verify his credentials. The Third Estate, left alone in the Salle des Menus Plaisirs, refused to carry out even this formal procedure without the other two Estates. For six weeks no petitions could be heard, no reforms discussed, and no money voted. On 3 June the spirit of the Third Estate was stiffened by the arrival of the twenty Paris deputies, elected late. On 17 June the members threw down the gauntlet by declaring that they alone constituted a National Assembly, the final authority in the land. It was the first revolutionary gesture. 'If His Majesty once gives His decided approbation of the proceedings of the Tiers État,' wrote the British ambassador, 'it will be little short of laying His crown at their feet.'

The king would have been well-advised to give his approbation, for his crown would have been safer at the feet of the Third Estate than in the hands of the nobles. But Louis's political sense was even more clouded than usual by personal sorrow (the little Dauphin had died on 4 June) and the advice of courtiers prevailed. Orders were given to prepare the Salle des Menus Plaisirs for a Royal Session. With characteristic inefficiency no notice reached the members of the Third Estate. When, on 20 June, they found soldiers occupying their hall, they assumed, not altogether wrongly, that an attempt was being made to destroy their Assembly. Led by Bailly, their president, they took shelter from the rain in an indoor tennis court, and there swore that since the National Assembly had been elected to give France a constitution they would meet in any place dictated by circumstances until a constitution had been established. It was the second revolutionary gesture, more spectacular than the first; suitably embellished, it gave the artist David a subject for one of his biggest canvasses.

When the king met the three Estates in the Royal Session on 23 June he outlined a plan of reform which might have been copied directly from the *cahiers* of bourgeois electors. But there was no guarantee that the plan would be carried out, for Louis insisted that the orders should sit separately. The members of the Third Estate remained in the hall after the king's departure, whereupon Louis tried to disperse them by force. Mirabeau, in a dramatic speech, inspired his fellow-deputies to resist royal threats. From this moment it was recognized that Louis, far from leading the Third Estate, had thrown in his lot with the aristocracy. A large body of clergy had already joined the Third Estate; this number was now increased to 170. Fifty liberal nobles seceded from the Second Estate. There were rumours that the Paris mob was about to march on Versailles and that soldiers were ready to mutiny. On 27 June the king gave in, somewhat peevishly. He ordered the clergy and nobles to join the Third Estate. A fortnight later the united orders took the title of National Constituent Assembly.

That shrewd observer Arthur Young realized that a revolution had already been accomplished. The bourgeois representatives of the Third Estate had assumed all authority in the kingdom and were about to assign what rôles they pleased to clergy, nobles, and king. 'The whole business now seems over,' Young wrote in his Journal on 27 June. He was wrong. Two revolutionary factors remained to make their force felt.

3. THE REVOLT OF THE PARIS CROWD

Paris in 1789 was at least five times as large as any other city in France. Its ten-foot wall, completed in 1785 to link the customs posts, measured eighteen miles and enclosed a population of about 600,000. Only a minority of Parisians, perhaps a tenth, were privileged or wealthy: they consisted of the clergy, scattered over the older parts of the city in some 140 religious houses, and the nobles and rich bourgeois, vying with each other to build stately mansions in the fashionable western quarters. The vast majority of the population consisted of small shopkeepers and tradespeople, independent craftsmen, workshop masters, journeymen, labourers, apprentices, domestic servants, vagrants and paupers; known collectively as the *menu peuple* (common people), and soon to be given the name 'sans-culottes'.

Among the many types of sans-culottes it is possible to distinguish a class of wage-earners. Most of these were dispersed in small workshops; others worked in factories employing several hundred people, such as the cloth-works in the northern faubourgs and the breweries and glassworks of the faubourg Saint-Antoine. Wage-earners had often struck, during past years, for higher pay or fairer conditions, sometimes emphasizing their demands with acts of violence. These disturbances received a spectacular addition on 27-28 April 1789, when workers sacked the houses of two Saint-Antoine employers (Henriot, a powder manufacturer, and Réveillon, the owner of a wallpaper factory) believing them to have advocated a reduction in wages. It would be wrong, however, to regard the special interests of wage-earners as a dominating factor in the life of the sans-culottes. Wage-earners usually merged with other small income groups in pursuit of common aims. In the old alleys and courtyards of the eastern and southern faubourgs – Saint-Antoine, Saint-Marcel, Saint-Victor, and Saint-Jacques – workshop owners and independent craftsmen rubbed shoulders with journeymen and apprentices in a spirit of comradeship. Luxury trades, so important in Paris, were still organized on a craft basis, and the typical unit of production was the small workshop in which the master worked alongside his few employees. Journeymen often ate and lodged in the house of their master, and in the days to come they were to be found setting out together to form part of the revolutionary crowd or 'Paris mob'. They were joined often enough, by vagrants, paupers, and various undesirable types, but the latter were never sufficiently numerous to form a predominating element.

The sans-culottes looked upon themselves as consumers rather than producers, and the strongest economic bond uniting them was a desire for cheap bread. In normal times, when bread cost 2 sous a pound, it was common for a working-class family to spend half its income on bread, which formed the most important part of its diet. After poor harvests the price was likely to go up to 3 or 4 sous a pound, and at these times the bulk of the lower class was threatened with starvation. Bread riots were more common than wage strikes, and to avoid them the government had long exercised controls on the sale of corn. Statesmen with advanced economic views experimented in free trade in 1763, 1774 and 1787, but the dislocation of prices always led to rumours that landowners and politicians were speculating in corn to the detriment of the people, and riots ensued. Brienne chose a particularly unlucky time for his experiment in 1787. The harvest of 1788 was poor, and the price of bread immediately rose. Necker put back controls and subsidized corn from abroad, but by February 1789 bread in Paris markets cost between 3 and 4 sous a pound. It remained at this level during the opening months of the Estates General. Meanwhile the winter of 1788-9 was the coldest in living memory, and the price of fuel and other necessities rose enormously. Parisians looked with increased hatred at the ring of customs posts where Farmers General took tolls on all meat, wines, vegetables, and livestock entering the city.

In 1789 a special electoral regulation for Paris left the poorest quarter of the population without vote. Consequently no complaints concerning food prices found their way into the *cahiers*. The popular desire for price control was hardly likely to be voiced by bourgeois deputies, believers in the new philosophy of free trade. Nevertheless, Parisian sans-culottes trusted their twenty representatives and looked forward to every kind of benefit. The opening of the Estates General produced a fervent exaltation of spirit, arising not so much from faith in a particular programme as from a joyous feeling that the people were going to count for something at last.

The sans-culottes were not lacking in knowledge of events. Many could read, and the opinions expressed in innumerable pamphlets were rapidly handed round. Hundreds of clerks, journalists, students, and sightseers, jostling each other in the gardens, boulevards and cafés, were quick to spread news and rumours. The Duc d'Orléans had turned the gardens of the Palais Royal into a pleasure ground for the public, with shops, taverns, gambling houses and cheap cabarets under the arcades; and here, of an evening, demo-cratic orators by the dozen harangued the multitude. Some were doubtless in the pay of Orléans, and the Duc's agents almost certainly helped to organize the bands of insurgents which systematically burnt down 40 of the 54 customs posts between 10 and 13 July, but the popular temperature was high enough to rise to fever pitch without much encouragement. Hot weather in early summer had made flour scarcer than ever by drying up rivers so that mills could not grind. The people of Paris would probably have rioted, under any circumstances, for cheaper bread. Their action was given cohesion and political content by rumours that nobles were conspiring to defeat the Third Estate and that the king was summoning armed force to destroy the Assembly.

Not all noble deputies meekly obeyed Louis's order to join the Third Estate. Many continued to meet in ostentatious isolation, tacitly appealing for the king's support. Meanwhile the queen, the Comte d'Artois, and their circle were advising the king to put an end to the National Assembly by force. Louis had already on 26 June called six regiments from the provinces to Versailles. Ten more regiments were summoned to arrive in July. The king explained to the Assembly that vigorous measures were needed to maintain order. Louis had probably not made up his mind what to do; it cannot be said for certain that he was planning an appeal to force. Discipline in the army was breaking down; junior officers, resentful at barriers to promotion, were less willing than ever to obey noble superiors; while the soldiers, who had to buy food from their pay, shared the popular discontent at high prices. The French Guards (the main body of royal troops stationed in Paris) mingled constantly with the townspeople, and officers were toasted at the Palais Royal. Eleven guardsmen, imprisoned for refusing to fire on the people at Versailles on 23 June, were released by a mob on 30 June.

On 11 July Necker was dismissed. This news reached Paris the next day, Sunday, when large crowds were assembled in the Palais Royal. The danger now seemed obvious. So too did the answer; the people must go to the aid of the Assembly. Camille Desmoulins and other orators raised the call to arms, which was answered enthusiastically. During the next two days crowds raided gunsmiths' shops, religious houses, the Invalides – any place where arms and ammunition might be found. The impromptu arming was given a significant degree of organization by the forty Electors of Paris. These men had not dispersed when their official duty of electing deputies to the Estates General was over. They had taken to meeting regularly in the Town Hall, where they were regarded by townspeople as forming a more genuine city government than the Provost and aldermen of the *ancien régime*. On 13 July the Electors set up a Permanent Committee and began organizing a citizens' militia (*milice bourgeoise*). Each of the sixty electoral districts was to provide 200, later 800 persons. The double object of the militia, in the eyes of good bourgeois Electors, was to defend the Assembly against the king and to put a stop to indiscriminate acts of violence. Steps were taken to disarm vagrants and unemployed persons; local rules usually disqualified wage-earners; and the new militia was composed largely of small property owners.

On the morning of 14 July a vast crowd from the faubourg Saint-Antoine gathered outside the Bastille, the medieval fortress whose eight towers and eighty-foot walls frowned over the eastern quarter of the city. Motives in the crowd were mixed. The Bastille had long been hated as a symbol of tyranny; it was said to contain large stores of ammunition; its guns were that morning directed on the narrow streets of the faubourg and numbers of troops were rumoured to be waiting within the walls for a command to massacre the people. There was no immediate intention of attacking the fortress. The Committee of Electors sent a deputation to the governor, De Launay, asking him to surrender his ammunition and lower his guns. The men received a friendly welcome and were invited to dine, but when they did not immediately re-emerge the crowd in the outer courtyard feared a trap. Two dare-devils climbed an unguarded bastion and cut down the drawbridge, over which the crowd surged into the inner courtyard. The garrison – a mere seventy old soldiers and thirty Swiss – panicked and fired and an assault began.

By three o'clock in the afternoon the assailants were losing heavily, when a detachment of rebellious French Guards dragged up five canon from the Invalides. At this point the taking of the Bastille became largely a military operation. Under heavy fire the guards got their guns to bear on the main gate, and the garrison persuaded De Launay to surrender in order to save their lives. He was given a promise of safe conduct, but it could bear no guarantee against an elated crowd. Some of the defenders were slaughtered as they left the fortress; De Launay's head was severed from his shoulders by a cook, Dénot, who afterwards described the murder as 'a patriotic act for which he deserved a medal'.

Ninety-eight assailants were killed in the siege; their bodies were mostly unclaimed and unidentified. Of the 800 or so survivors who claimed to have played an active part in the affair, the majority were respectable sans-culottes, known citizens of the faubourg Saint-Antoine and neighbouring districts, most of whom had enrolled in the *milice bourgeoise*. They were part of a revolutionary force which had accomplished an act of far-reaching importance. The prisoners released from the Bastille were a paltry few – four forgers, two lunatics, and a dissipated young nobleman incarcerated for a term at his family's request – but the political consequences of the assault can hardly be over-estimated. All prospect of a military *coup* had vanished, for the king had lost Paris, and the troops at Versailles could not be relied upon to regain it. The old city government was formally overthrown. The Electors formed themselves into a Municipality, or Commune, and the former Provost, Flesselles, whose head had been stuck on a pike on 14 July because he had refused to give arms to the people, was replaced in office by Bailly, eminent scientist and hero of the Tennis Court Oath, with the title of Mayor. Impromptu governments had sprung up in other towns all over France in the past few weeks; these were now regularized, along with their *milices bourgeoises*, which became the National Guard and elected Lafayette as its commander.

The king's brothers counselled a withdrawal of the court to the provinces, but when the commander of the royal troops, Marshal de Broglie, could not guarantee a safe escort to Metz, Louis submitted to fate with the dignity which he could always muster at the last. Whilst his brothers fled to the frontier, he made a public entry into Paris, where he appeared at a window of the Town Hall wearing a cockade of blue and red, the city colours, henceforward united with the Bourbon white to form the tricolour flag of France. The crowds cheered him wildly, believing that they had reconquered their king from the aristocrats.

The recalcitrant nobles gave up their attempt to meet as a separate estate, and many fled abroad. Royal administration broke down in cities throughout France. The royal army continued to disintegrate, leaving the National Guard the only reliable force in the kingdom. All authority seemed to have fallen to the bourgeoisie, and the National Assembly could go on with its work of reform. The triumph of the people of Paris was to raise insuperable problems for bourgeois governments in days ahead, but this was not yet recognized. At the time another problem seemed more menacing.

4. THE REVOLT OF THE PEASANTRY

The peasants, like other classes in French society, were not a single un-differentiated group. Some were well-to-do farmers who had leased a fairly large plot of land. Others had bought land; about a third of the kingdom belonged to peasant proprietors. Lower in the social scale came the *métayers* (sharecroppers) who farmed land on a produce sharing basis, an arrangement which usually worked unfairly for the peasant. Less fortunate still were peasants who could farm no land at all for their own use, and who, as wage labourers, were only slightly better off than the serfs. Although most aspects of serfdom had disappeared in eighteenth-century France there were still about a million persons to be found, mainly in Franche-Comté and the Nivernais, whose land came under a mainmorte and who could not freely dispose of their goods at death.

The existence in France of a large number of peasant proprietors has caused the condition of French peasants to be compared favourably with that of their English counterparts, who were rapidly being turned into a class of landless labourers by the spread of enclosures. Ownership of land did not necessarily bring wealth, however. A peasant's well-being depended on whether or not he worked a sufficient area of land, either as owner or tenant or both, to provide adequately for his needs, and few did so. The population had increased by almost 50% since the beginning of the century; there was not enough industry to absorb the additional labour; backward agricultural methods, especially lack of knowledge concerning fertilizers, meant that the soil gave only a moderate yield; and the result was a serious land shortage. The vast majority of peasant proprietors were obliged to seek some additional income; they joined the large number of landless peasants in working as labourers for richer farmers or taking in cottage industry. Landless peasants descended on the towns in search of seasonal labour, or lived wild in forests and marshes cutting wood and peat, or roamed about the country begging. In a country where there was no Poor Law, begging was of necessity considered no shame, and at least a tenth of the people – in some areas as many as a fifth – made their living by it. Of some 23 million peasants on the eve of the Revolution, the majority were poor, and a large number destitute. Yet the peasant problem had gone unnoticed by statesmen and philosophers throughout the century. There had been large numbers of peasant riots (*jacqueries*), but no concerted uprising such as could make a serious impression on the *ancien régime*.

When the peasants thought of their poverty they could not be expected to understand intangible economic causes like soil exhaustion and land hunger. Instead they thought angrily of the burdens imposed by manorial lords (*seigneurs*). These burdens had often been increased during the eighteenth century through the ingenuity of paid lawyers, expert in feudal techniques. The right of exercising justice, the essential characteristic of manorial lordship, was found to carry other rights: levying tolls on markets, roads and rivers, demanding watch and ward at the manor house, exacting payments in money or kind from persons domiciled on manorial land, exclusive rights of hunting over peasants' fields and keeping pigeons which preyed on their crops, and maintaining a mill, oven and winepress which all must pay to use. Seigneurial dues, usually newer than the strictly 'feudal' dues exacted by owners of fiefs, involved an element of personal degradation not easily borne by peasants who were free men in the eyes of the law, and many of whom had acquired land for their own use.

Cahiers drawn up by primary assemblies of peasants listed a great many complaints. Landlords were enclosing common land and preventing poor peasants from gleaning and cutting stubble. Tithe paid to the church was especially burdensome when exacted in kind, for produce was of greater value than money in hard times. Indirect taxes bore heavily on articles of common use and made life difficult for the man with a family to support. Taille, the chief direct tax imposed by the state, was levied almost exclusively on the peasantry. These grievances did not concern all peasants equally, however. The most common desire, and the one most commonly expressed, was to be relieved of seigneurial dues. This object alone united peasant proprietors with landless labourers, and gave to the peasant movement the cohesion which the food problem gave to the rebellion of the sans-culottes.

Bourgeois electors in the bailiwick assemblies were torn by conflicting sentiments when they considered seigneurial dues. Many of these electors were country lawyers and doctors who had seen peasant poverty in the course of their daily work, and they were not unsympathetic. For their own purposes, too, they were ready to condemn 'feudalism' in general. On the other hand, seigneurial rights were not confined to aristocrats. During the so-called 'feudal reaction' of the eighteenth century, when manorial lordship was discovered to contain tempting economic possibilities, enterprising bourgeois who bought farmland and vineyards and orchards had taken care to acquire incidental seigneurial rights. These rights were thus a form of property, and to destroy them might set up a dangerous precedent for attacks on other forms of property. Requests for the abolition of seigneurial dues were sometimes transferred from parish *cahiers* to the more general *cahiers*, but usually in less vehement terms and with requests for compensation. In spite of this, the peasants believed that their bourgeois representatives would inaugurate a golden era. The king had asked his people to express their grievances, which surely meant that he was going to propose remedies, and the Third Estate would help him to triumph over selfish aristocrats. Arthur Young, journeying towards Metz in July 1789, met a poor peasant woman who had heard that 'something was to be done by some great folks for such poor ones, but she did not know who nor how'.

Unfortunately the bourgeois deputies at Versailles were extremely hesitant on the subject of seigneurial dues. June passed into July, the Bastille fell, but no joyful news of abolition came to the peasant farmers assembled in the towns on market days. The peasants could attribute this delay to only one cause: aristocrats were deceiving the good king and undermining the work of the Assembly. Rumours of an aristocratic plot, which had already played a part in spurring townspeople to rebellion during the early weeks of July, spread like wildfire over the countryside. They produced peasant risings on a considerable scale in Normandy, Franche-Comté, Alsace and Mâconnais in mid-July.

The news of these risings, spread incoherently by messengers and fugitives, helped to swell another rumour to the effect that huge bands of brigands, in the pay of aristocrats, were descending on farms and villages and terrorizing the inhabitants. Panic seized the peasants over the greater part of the kingdom. The 'brigands', if they existed at all, were probably bands of unemployed labourers seeking work on the harvest, joined by vagabonds and riff-raff who took the opportunity to plunder. The appearance of such bands was an annual phenomenon, but it never failed to frighten peasant farmers, and the latter were the formative influence in peasant opinion. In the overcharged political atmosphere of July 1789 the panic reached proportions which earned it the name of the Great Fear. It resulted in a new and larger wave of peasant risings, in which châteaux were attacked, manor rolls destroyed, enclosures broken down, and stores of grain pillaged. Individuals were rarely attacked, but the breakdown of feudal authority was no less spectacular.

Bourgeois deputies who had applauded the rising of the Paris crowd were horrified at the rising of the peasants. Having planned only political and constitutional reform, they were faced with the prospect of the complete overthrow of the old social system. They thought immediately of restoring order, but National Guards sent out from the towns proved ineffective, and the army could not be used, as Robespierre and Barnave pointed out, without giving a dangerous opportunity to the king. The only alternative was to abolish the hated seigneurial rights legally while there was still hope of achieving compensation for the owners. This conclusion was reached by the Patriot party, a group of about 100 deputies who were vigorous champions of the Third Estate. They held a secret meeting on the night of 3 August and devised what one of their number described as 'a type of magic'. A liberal nobleman, the Duc d'Aiguillon, was to rise in the Assembly towards the end of the next day's session and propose the abolition of privileges and dues with compensation. The more reactionary deputies would probably have gone home, and the rest would be shamed into a sacrificing mood by this example from a great landowner. The plan miscarried in one important respect. When the crucial moment arrived the initiative was seized by a young and landless nobleman, the Vicomte de Noailles, who felt no need for reservations. He proposed unconditional surrender of feudal rights, and d'Aiguillon's speech stressing the need for monetary redemption of seigneurial dues came too late. The Assembly was overcome by a passion for sacrifice, and tax privileges, tithes, feudal and manorial rights, privileges of cities, corporations, guilds and provinces were offered up in mounting hysteria. An entire social revolution was carried out on this one night of 4 August; when the session ended there was very little left of the *ancien régime*.

Self-interest was not entirely absent from the minds of privileged deputies. Serfdom was a wasteful type of labour, and the abolition of mainmorte meant that serf land could be bought up by investors. Parish priests looked forward to a better income from the state than they had received from tithes, and great landowners stood to gain more than small farmers from the abolition of payments to the church. Yet noble deputies had no easy task in writing explanations to their constituents. The sacrifice of tax exemptions was serious indeed, and fief-owners lost a quarter of their income by the abolition of feudal dues. To many provincial nobles, whose seigneurial courts and pigeon-cotes had given them social prestige among their neighbours, the loss of honour was as hard to bear as the loss of income. In the decrees of 5-11 August, giving statutory form to the Assembly's resolutions, an attempt was made to demand monetary redemption of seigneurial dues, but peasants simply refused to pay, and coercion was impossible.

The Marquis de Ferrières thought he could have borne it all cheerfully if he could have been sure that the people would benefit; but in a letter to his wife he confessed his doubts. In the end it was the peasants who were already fairly well off who benefited most. Freed from dues and services they could save money. A few months later, when national land was put up for sale, they could extend their farms to a profitable size. By 1791 they had obtained all they wanted from the Revolution, and formed henceforward the most conservative element in politics. Landless labourers and serfs were freed from personal degradation, but economically they benefited little, and poverty seemed harder to bear when others were enjoying the fruits of reform. The rural poor formed a discontented element which was appealed to occasionally by advanced politicians; but deprived of the leadership of the peasant proprietors they no longer formed a spontaneous revolutionary force. Only in Paris was the lower class still united and threatening.

5. THE TRIUMPH OF THE REVOLUTION

Poets throughout Europe hailed the fall of the Bastille as the dawn of a

new era. Parisians saw the walls of the fortress systematically demolished
by a firm of house-breakers, but it was difficult for sans-culottes to believe
in the birth of liberty when food was scarcer and dearer than ever. At
the beginning of September Paris had only enough flour for ten days'
baking. Thousands of domestic servants and workers in luxury trades had
been thrown out of work by the departure of wealthy citizens in the first
great wave of emigration. Others lost hours of pay in queuing for bread.
A number of trades tested the sympathy of the new Commune by putting
forward wage claims, to no purpose. Hunger and anxiety led quickly to
anger and cruelty. On 23 July the food-controller, Foullon, was hanged from
a lamp bracket (*lanterne*) outside the Town Hall and his head paraded on a
pike, joined by that of his son-in-law Berthier, Intendant for the city. Barbarous attacks were made on bakers suspected of hoarding food and even
Lafayette was threatened. The Commune could do little to restore order, for
its authority was challenged by the sixty electoral Districts which had created
it, and the National Guard sympathized with the sans-culottes.

In the Assembly the left-wing or Patriot party was not sorry to see the
temper of Paris rising. Barnave, who was rapidly emerging as a leader of
this group, condoned the Foullon-Berthier murders as acts of revolutionary
justice: 'Was this blood, then, so pure?' The Patriots had come to feel that
another demonstration of revolutionary strength was needed to deal with
the king, who was proving difficult to handle. While Mounier and his
'English' party strove to provide the new constitution with an Upper House
and a royal veto, Louis demonstrated the use he would make of such power
by refusing to promulgate the resolutions of 4 August. After a series of
stormy debates (28 August-11 September) Louis agreed to publish the resolutions in return for a suspensive veto allowing him to hold up legislation for
two sessions. He never kept his part of the bargain, for he had not yet given
up the idea of force. The Flanders regiment was called to Versailles. Its
officers were welcomed at a banquet on 1 October, and in an exalted mood
of loyalty the king and queen were toasted enthusiastically and the tricolour
cockade trampled underfoot. The Patriot party was not slow to communicate news of these events to its agents in the Palais Royal, who embellished
it for purveyance to angry crowds. Orators of the Orléans faction whipped
up popular fury with stories of aristocratic plots, and dropped hints that the
king must be brought to Paris for safe-keeping. Paid agitators thus helped
to foment the March of the Women to Versailles; but this weird episode
had also its spontaneous aspect, created by the pressing problem of food.

Women of the city had long ago come to believe that only proper
control was needed to provide adequate supplies. From mid-September
crowds of women attacked food convoys and dragged loads of corn to the
Town Hall for distribution. A popular pamphlet, *Quand aurons-nous du pain?*,

blamed the authorities for the food shortage. On the morning of 5 October
a little girl set out from the district of Saint-Eustache beating a drum and
crying for bread. Women of the faubourg – paupers and workers, fishwives
and stallholders from the markets, shopkeepers and neatly dressed house-
wives – flocked to join the demonstration. Similar crowds collected in other
faubourgs, and bellringers were made to ring the tocsin calling citizens to
arms. Encouraged by their menfolk, the women converged on the Town
Hall, demanding that the mayor and commune should give them bread and
arms. Part of the crowd broke into the building, carried out an angry
search, and retired to the Place de Grève shouting threats at Bailly. Someone, unknown, set going the idea of a march to Versailles to petition the
king and Assembly for bread. A leader was found in Stanislas Maillard, a
young man who had already played a spectacular part in the assault on the
Bastille. In the wet, grey afternoon six or seven thousand women marched
twelve miles along muddy roads to Versailles, armed with sticks and pitch-
forks and sometimes with knives slung from their hips.

Arriving in the early evening the women went straight to the Assembly.
They huddled into the benches beside the deputies while Maillard made a
speech demanding bread for the capital and the punishment of the soldiers
who had insulted the tricolour cockade. The Patriot party was willing to
welcome allies, however unorthodox; Robespierre set the tone of co-
operation in which six of the women were chosen to wait on the king. They
were instructed to add to their petition the demand that the king should
sanction the work of the Assembly to date. Louis received the women
kindly, and readily promised food. Other promises came less glibly, but
after waiting five hours the deputies were told that the king accepted their
demands 'without qualification'. He was in fact listening to plans for flight
to Rouen, but his delay in answering the petition meant that the palace was
still surrounded by crowds when, about midnight, Lafayette arrived from
Paris with the National Guard.

The guardsmen had heard the tocsin and had mustered outside the Town
Hall shortly after the departure of the women. They had insisted on being
led to Versailles, not to protect the king but to reinforce their womenfolk.
Lafayette, powerless to resist yet afraid to lead a revolutionary outburst, rode
to and fro on his handsome white horse and made ineffective speeches.
When he finally arrived at Versailles with 20,000 guardsmen, Louis could
not have known whether he was friend or enemy. He brought with him a
further demand, from the Commune, that the king should return home to
his capital.

Nothing could be done till morning. The royal family retired for the
remainder of the night and the women bivouacked with the guardsmen in
the palace yard. The queen had long been unpopular, and whilst Lafayette

snatched an hour's sleep after a distressing day some of the coarser elements among the womenfolk broke into her apartments, causing her to flee in alarm to the king's room. Order was restored by the National Guard, but the incident may have helped to prove to the king that resistance was impossible. On 6 October Louis left Versailles for ever, and drove slowly to Paris with his wife and children, accompanied by thirty thousand of his people, shouting, gesticulating, firing shots into the air, and waving branches of poplar. A marching song was heard: 'Here come the baker, the baker's wife, and the baker's errand boy.' Many believed that the king's presence would ensure bread; aristocratic plots would be foiled; the new era would begin. The people had assuredly conquered their king, and the Revolution could proceed to its triumph.

CHAPTER II

The Revolution at Work, 1789-92

I. PARIS AND THE CONSTITUENT ASSEMBLY

THE Tuileries palace had been deserted by the court for more than a century and its huge apartments occupied by lodgers – retired officers, actors, poor aristocrats, and royal pensioners. Some of these were hastily cleared out to make room for Louis XVI and his family on 6 October 1789. In the shortening autumn days Parisians could flock round the queen as she walked in the garden, and watch the dauphin playing with his little hoe and rake.

The food situation did not immediately improve, and rioting went on for several weeks. Authority was tougher than before, however. The majority in the Assembly had no further use for revolutionary violence, and on 21 October martial law was introduced. Meanwhile Commune and Assembly took vigorous steps to ensure a regular supply of flour to Paris bakers. They were repaid by a period of social calm which was reinforced by a good harvest in 1790 and lasted into the following summer. During these two years the Constituent Assembly carried out its self-appointed task of national reconstruction.

The Assembly declared itself inseparable from the king. Many deputies, either from indignation or fear, retired to provincial homes or fled abroad; 300 had departed by the time the Assembly held its first session in Paris on 19 October. Louis XV's old riding school (*manège*) on the north side of the Tuileries was fitted up as a parliament house, and hundreds of spectators squeezed themselves into the public gallery every day. The features most noticed by English visitors were noise and confusion. Revolutionary initiative demanded that any deputy should be allowed to introduce a bill or propose an amendment, and the clearest of motions sometimes disappeared under a welter of additions and counter-proposals. Any speaker who was hardy enough to defend privilege or impugn the wisdom of the people might raise a storm in which a hundred deputies were on their feet at once, shouting at each other down the long, narrow room. These rowdy sessions were not the rule, however. On most days the deputies listened patiently to long, set speeches, inspired with the belief that they were shaping destiny with their own hands and creating a new civilization for all mankind.

Paris remained very much alive politically, in spite of the social calm.

The Duc d'Orléans withdrew discreetly to England to escape accusations concerning his part in the October days, but the Palais Royal continued to be a centre of political agitation. The Tuileries terrace was opened to the public and attracted large crowds, with the inevitable orators and pamphlet hawkers. Press censorship broke down with the fall of the Bastille, and dozens of newspapers appeared, ranging from Pancoucke's semi-official *Moniteur* to little blurred sheets written and printed by groups of deputies after evening sessions. Pamphlets, posters, caricatures, and even plays and cabarets competed to supply the public with news and views on parliamentary politics.

Interest in the Assembly was so great that a group of Breton deputies, who had formed themselves into a political club at Versailles, opened membership to the public on moving to Paris. The club met in a disused Dominican convent and inherited from the monks the name Jacobin. At evening meetings political speeches were read and important issues debated, sometimes before they were opened in the Assembly. A popular speaker was a provincial deputy, Robespierre, a thin-lipped, immaculate lawyer from Arras, who combined a passionate devotion to Rousseau with shrewd practical insight. The annual subscription of 24 shillings a year provided a solid bourgeois membership, and the opinions of the Jacobin club corresponded with those of the majority of progressive deputies in the Constituent Assembly. A cheaper club was founded on the left bank of the river and given the name Cordeliers from the street in which it met. The subscription of a penny a month opened membership to shopkeepers, artisans, and students, who prided themselves on a sharp and knowing attitude to politics. Favourite orators were men such as Danton and Camille Desmoulins who had made a name for themselves in street politics rather than in parliament. These clubs, and many others less famous, brought the influence of Paris to bear on the Assembly. The deputies were not swayed by 'the mob' as an entity; they scorned intimidation; but they were naturally influenced by the opinions of associates in the club where they spent their evenings.

While Paris influenced the Assembly, the Assembly never succeeded in dominating Paris. The government of the city was officially in the hands of the Municipality or Commune. Between bourgeois councillors and bourgeois deputies there was much similarity of feeling, and Bailly, in his double capacity as mayor and deputy, symbolized co-operation between Commune and Assembly. The authority of the Commune was challenged, however, by the assemblies of the sixty districts. These, too, continued to meet after they had finished their part in the elections to the Estates General; at their sessions any citizen named on the electoral roll could advance views on government. They provided an element of direct decentralized democracy which was always the ideal of the sans-culottes in politics.

AOP C

Meanwhile the government of France was left in the hands of the king, acting through ministers who were his nominees and agents. In England the House of Commons had fought for years for the right to designate ministers and dictate government policy: in France the Constituent Assembly dismissed executive authority from the bosom of the legislature by a decree stating that deputies could not become ministers and ministers could not become members of the Assembly (7 November 1789). The task of the Assembly was legislation, not administration. On 22 May 1790 the deputies took over part-control of foreign policy, by a decree stating that the king could not make war or peace without the ratification of the Assembly; but this was done with considerable reluctance and the precedent was not followed in domestic affairs. Montesquieu had advocated a balance of power, which implies fusion: the deputies preferred separation of powers, because it was more in keeping with the traditions of the *ancien régime*. Government had been the duty of the king from the beginning of the monarchy; the task of deputies was to provide a legislative framework which would prevent government from growing tyrannical.

The effect inside France was chaotic. The wishes of the Assembly were obstructed on every hand by reactionary ministers and unsympathetic officials. In the Assembly itself, separation of powers hindered the development of parties. There was no government party responsible for framing a policy, and no opposition party pledged to constructive criticism. Bills were drawn up by committees of members representing all shades of opinion, and they were presented to the Assembly to be judged on their merits. Deputies prided themselves on keeping an open mind, free from commitment either to a group of electors or to a party. Each deputy believed that he represented the nation and that his whole mind must be at the service of the nation. Though many deputies came in time to engage in group activity they always repudiated the name of 'party', which remained synonymous with 'faction'.

However, the structure of the *manège* gave an appearance of party divisions which was not entirely meaningless. Members faced each other across a narrow gangway, sitting on benches which rose higher from the centre outwards. It soon became customary for moderate members to sit on the low benches near the gangway, acquiring the nickname of Plain or Marsh, while conservative members sat on the Right and progressive members on the Left. A group of extremists on the top left-hand benches came to be known as the Mountain.

Right and Left co-operated to a remarkable degree in the mass of legislation which emerged from the Assembly. Only on the question of royal power was a serious difference of opinion noticed. The Left profoundly distrusted the king. In the famous debates of 28 August-11 September 1789 they attacked the proposal for a royal veto on legislation; on 9 September they succeeded in depriving the king of the right to prorogue or dissolve parliament; and on 30 September they deprived him of the right to initiate legislation. The decree of 7 November, banishing ministers from the assembly, arose partly from their fears lest a clever minister should play upon parliament in the interests of the crown, as Walpole had done in England. Robespierre and Barnave were among the most outstanding speakers of the Left, the former with an unusual mixture of emotion and precision, the latter with a much-envied ability for extempore debate. The Right, meanwhile, disliked the arrogant claims made by the Assembly. A too-powerful parliament could be as tyrannical as a too-powerful monarch. While subscribing to the popular doctrine of national sovereignty, the Right argued that the people had delegated authority to king as well as assembly, and the power of the two agents should balance equally. The obvious implication was that France should have a constitution like the English, but sensible as this may seem to the English mind, the French Right was in a weaker position than the Left from the start. There was a popular dislike of English patterns. Moreover, although Mounier, the leader of the Right during the months at Versailles, was an experienced politician who had taken part in a revolt of the Third Estate in Dauphiné, there was a fear that his policy would play into the hands of reactionary courtiers. The Right's demand for an absolute royal veto had to be abandoned in favour of a suspensive veto allowing the king to hold up legislation for the duration of two parliaments only, whilst the proposal of an Upper Chamber was rejected outright by a huge majority of deputies, who could not trust the French aristocracy to behave like an English House of Lords. Mounier resigned his seat on 10 October 1789 as a protest against the intervention of the mob, and his example was followed by most of the 'English' party. Though justifiable from a parliamentary point of view, this strengthened a suspicion that the Right was afraid of the people and that its members wanted the king to destroy the Revolution.

The suspicion was inapplicable at least to Mirabeau, who remained the most outstanding member of the Right. Mirabeau, although a nobleman, was elected by the Third Estate of Aix en Provence, and he championed the Third on the famous occasion of the Royal Session. His riotous reputation, and his startling ability to express the needs of the moment, loud and clear, won him popularity with the sans-culottes: his popular oratory, and the knowledge that he would take money from anyone foolish enough to pay him, caused Mirabeau to be distrusted by every group in the Assembly, including the one he defended. His political views were based on a sound understanding of parliamentary government. The Assembly, he believed, must be strong enough to guarantee liberty and the king strong enough to guarantee order, a double object which could only be achieved if Assembly and king played a part in both legislative and executive spheres. Mirabeau defended the Assembly against monarchical despotism on 23 June and defended royal power against parliamentary despotism in the debate on the veto. A royal veto, he said, was so essential to liberty that he would 'sooner live in Constantinople than in France without it'. His efforts helped to secure, though not an absolute veto, at least a suspensive veto for the king. He fought hard for deputies to be allowed to become ministers, but in this he failed entirely, and his failure marked the end of right-wing politics as a constructive parliamentary programme.

Perhaps left-wing deputies had Mirabeau in mind when they feared a French Walpole, but it is doubtful whether he would ever have obtained from Louis XVI the support which George II gave to his famous minister. Marie Antoinette distrusted him because of his violent speeches in the Assembly, and her fastidious taste made her recoil from meeting so vicious a man after one disastrous audience. From April, 1790, Louis paid large sums of money to Mirabeau for written advice. More than fifty secret notes were sent to the court, urging the king to flee to some traditionally royalist town such as Rouen and there appeal for a new assembly and a new constitution. The practical difficulties involved in such a scheme are of no more than academic interest. Mirabeau must have known that if the king ever left Paris it would be in an attempt to destroy the Revolution not improve upon it, and this rendered all the notes futile. The advice did no violence to Mirabeau's conscience, however, and the money he received for it enabled him to wear out his life, in April 1791, in a last bout of dissipation. His intellect was that of a great statesman, but popular prejudices against monarchy, along with his own defects as a parliamentary leader, prevented him from securing the type of constitution in which his qualities could have shown to best advantage, and the Revolution found no real use for his talents.

2. REFORM AND RECONSTRUCTION

When the Constituent Assembly began work upon its vast programme of legislation, the deputies were naturally influenced by theoretical knowledge acquired over past years. They were all 'beginners' in parliament. When preparing elaborate speeches with which to regale their fellow-members they drew heavily on classical works studied at school, on rhetorical devices common in the pulpit and at the bar, on the writings of philosophers which had so often provided motions for local debating societies and titles for essay competitions, and on pamphlets which had proved popular in recent months. The incompatibility of some of the grand phrases which they used ('liberty of the individual' and 'national sovereignty' for example) and the difficulty of expressing such concepts in terms of institutions became apparent only gradually. The deputies faced the dilemma with bourgeois commonsense, and it was in an honest attempt at interpretation, rather than from hypocrisy, that the Constituent Assembly again and again adapted ideas to meet circumstances.

The overriding aim of the Assembly was that men should be free to co-operate in forming a more progressive society. The aim was typical of the French bourgeoisie, and might well have gone without formal expression, but in true eighteenth-century fashion the Assembly decided that it must be defined in terms of rights and duties. A long tradition of political thought, stretching back to John Locke and even to medieval times, stressed the idea that man is born with certain rights which the state should guarantee. The legalistic form in which this idea could be expressed, and the use already made of it in the remonstrances of the parlements, appealed to the large number of lawyers in the Assembly, while the analogy with the bills of rights adopted by American colonists gave a happy augury of success. The result was the Declaration of the Rights of Man and the Citizen, adopted on 26 August 1789.

Every person was declared to have a natural right to liberty, property, security, and resistance to oppression (art. 2). The first of these rights was defined (art. 3) as 'liberty to do whatever does not harm another'. No man should be disturbed for his opinions 'even in religion' unless they proved detrimental to public order; every man should be allowed to express his opinions in speech and writing; and no man should be imprisoned without cause shown (arts. 7-11). Recognition of the right to property was not intended to lead to a redistribution of wealth in which all shared alike. The deputies believed merely, as Locke had done, that every man has a right to his own, and no man should be deprived of his property 'except for an obvious requirement of public necessity certified by law' (art. 17). This phrase justified the inroads already made into feudal property, and those about to be made into church property. The fine flourish of article 1 – 'Men are born and remain free and equal in rights' – referred solely to the rights enumerated in article 2. These did not include a right to vote, which was not mentioned in the Declaration. Article 6 said that all citizens have the right to take part in the formation of law 'in person or through their representatives', but nothing was said about the method of choosing representatives. The law was to be administered by men best fitted for the job: article 6 declared careers open to talent.

Later in the Revolution, left-wing politicians pointed out some critical omissions. The Declaration said nothing about a right to subsistence, a right to work, or a right to education, and without these things many men were unable to lay hold on the right to property and the right to compete for official posts. In 1789, however, deputies were more inclined to fear that they had set too high a standard for legislation. The preamble to the Declaration declared that the list of rights was to act as a target for achievement.

The privileges of the aristocracy and the despotism of the king had been shorn away in the first few months of the Revolution, but counter-revolution still seemed menacing. Time only was to show that the greatest threat to the liberties defined in the Declaration came not from aristocracy or monarchy but from a too-powerful democratic state.

The deputies already feared democracy, but for less subtle reasons. They had great faith in the merits of their own class, and they were anxious that future assemblies should be drawn from the bourgeoisie. The surest method, they decided, was to limit the franchise. Left-wing politicians attacked such a notion as contrary to the principle of sovereignty of the people, but political theory was more malleable than such critics would allow. Sieyès pointed out in July 1789 that although all citizens enjoy rights a distinction should be made between civil rights and political rights. The former are possessed by all men from birth, whereas the latter are more in the nature of duties or 'functions' devolving upon men with certain qualifications. Men who have been educated, who are not bound to earn their bread by daily toil, and who enjoy a fair amount of leisure can be reckoned to have acquired political rights; they are, as Sieyès put it, 'the real shareholders in the great social concern'; they can be described as active citizens, distinct from the general body of passive citizens.

Sieyès was probably the only pure ideologist in the Constituent Assembly. The deputies used his theory when framing the electoral law of 22 December 1789, but they defended their work frankly as a piece of class legislation, necessary, they said, for the well-being of France. To qualify as an active citizen a man must pay, in a year, taxes equivalent to three days' wages of a labourer. Four million out of six million adult Frenchmen passed the test, and were entitled to vote, but only indirectly in the first instance. A hundred active citizens must choose one elector, who must be a man paying taxes equivalent to at least ten days' wages. Electors could then choose deputies from a list of men paying taxes equivalent to fifty days' wages, an amount represented by a silver mark. 'In place of Commons, Nobles, and Clergy,' said Cambon, 'we have now the Rich, the Richer, and the Richest.' The disfranchisement of two million 'passive' citizens was justified on the grounds that they were illiterate: only five deputies voted against the clause. The remaining stipulations were more open to attack. Robespierre and Marat accused the Assembly of creating a plutocracy, 'an aristocracy of riches', a new privileged class to replace the old. As a gesture to the opposition the *marc d'argent* was dropped when the electoral regulations were written into the constitution of 1791, and any active citizen could become a candidate for parliament, but the retention of a high property qualification for electors guaranteed a bourgeois assembly. Only 50,000 Frenchmen qualified to vote directly.

The franchise law was prescribed for use in local as well as national elections. Liberty combined with efficiency and guaranteed by bourgeois predominance was to spread to every corner of France. Under the *ancien régime*, liberty of the people at a local level suffered under privileged jurisdictions on the one hand and monarchical absolutism on the other. Provincial Estates, seigneurial courts, and venal corporations, claiming authority from feudal times, preyed upon the people in the interests of the magnates; whilst royal intendants, agents of a centralized monarchy superimposed on an older decentralized system, preyed upon the people in the interests of the state. Oppression existed side by side with chaos: ecclesiastical dioceses, military governancies, judicial bailiwicks, and administrative *généralités* overlapped in bewildering manner, whilst at yet other levels the country was divided into provinces with Estates and provinces without them, regions under Roman law and regions under common law, areas which formed a customs union, the Five Great Farms, and areas outside it. Reform had been suggested by the king's ministers, Calonne and Brienne, in the years preceding the Revolution, but to deputies in 1789 reform was not enough. A framework which had lent itself to privilege, bureaucracy, confusion, and separatism must be destroyed, and a new system devised to express the new spirit animating the French nation.

Tradition was not abandoned entirely, however. It was decided that the new system should absorb the two elements which had obtained an affectionate place in the minds of the people, the province and the parish. Pride in the historic character of Breton, Norman, or Provençal, and passionate interest in the affairs of the village or town in which a man's family had lived for generations, could be valuable assets to the new France. When Thouret submitted a plan for dividing the country into neat rectangles the Assembly modified it in such a way that the old provincial boundaries were retained wherever possible, the bigger provinces being divided and the smaller ones grouped together to form 'departments' roughly equal in area but naturally untidy in shape. When Sieyès and Condorcet proposed an arithmetical division of the departments into cantons, each with 5,000 inhabitants, the Assembly rejected the idea in favour of keeping the old parish units, to be known as communes.

The Assembly's decisions emerged in a series of decrees: 14 and 22 December 1789, 26 February 1790. France was divided into 83 departments, with names taken from geographical features such as rivers and mountains. In each department the active citizens elected a general council of 36 members. Elections were in two stages, and councillors were men paying direct taxes equivalent to 10 days' wages. The general council was responsible for all major decisions concerning the department, but day-to-day administration was entrusted to 8 members who formed a directory. The department was

divided into 6 or more districts, each with a general council of 12 members
and a directory of 4 members. Below the districts came cantons, but these
were merely electoral divisions with no administrative machinery. The lowest
unit of administration was the commune. There were more than 40,000
communes in all, and each one was a natural entity – a village with the valley
in which it was set, or a city with its surrounding fields. All communes,
whether based on tiny hamlets or great towns, were equal in status and were
given the same kind of local government machinery. The active citizens of
the commune chose, by direct election, a general council, a municipal corporation (often known as 'the commune' like the area it served) and a mayor.
The members of the general council were men paying direct taxes equivalent
to 10 days' wages; they made decisions concerning expenses, loans, and
public works, while the municipal corporation wielded executive power.
The municipalities were given the important right of summoning the
National Guard and of proclaiming martial law, signified by flying a red
flag from the Town Hall.

The Constituent Assembly was criticized later in the Revolution for producing too decentralized a system. This was not the intention. The decree
of 26 February 1790 stated clearly that the departments were administrative
not legislative units. Laws were to be made exclusively by the National
Assembly. All local government bodies were subordinate to the king, who
could annul their acts if they appeared contrary to law. Each one was
provided with a *procureur*, a direct representative of the central government.
The directories and municipalities were responsible for carrying out national
as well as local decisions. Their members were state officials, assessing taxes
and selling national land, as well as local functionaries, supervising the
building of roads and organizing civic fêtes.

Unfortunately the system did not work as efficiently as had been expected.
The line between general councils on the one hand and directories and
municipalities on the other had not been clearly drawn, and there were
constant disputes over rights and duties. Directories, elected in two stages,
were composed mainly of wealthy bourgeois, while municipalities, elected
in one stage, were predominantly petits-bourgeois. All local bodies were
short of money. They were expected to perform many public duties, yet
no provision was made for financing them properly. Departments had to
find money for education, justice, prisons, and public works, but until 1791,
when they were allowed to levy an extra 4 sous on the land tax, directories
had virtually no income. Municipalities had to equip the National Guard,
support paupers, and pay for an increasing number of festivities with no
resources beyond a 'sixths' tax levied on sales of national land. In rural
communes there was difficulty in finding suitable persons for office; in
some, not a single person could read. Meanwhile, communes based on

great cities experienced a different problem. In Lyon, Lille, and Toulouse, for instance, the population was divided into sections for electoral purposes. After the elections the 'sections' continued to meet, setting up their own committees and claiming a right to inspect the work of the general council and municipality which they had elected. Paris, on account of its size, was made both a commune, with a municipality, and a department, with a directory; these overlapping authorities were constantly at loggerheads, and both were plagued by the 48 sections of the city. Under these difficult circumstances the *procureurs* failed to maintain cohesion. Although charged with representing the king's government, the *procureurs* were elected by the active citizens of the localities, and their authority was naturally limited.

In its local government acts the Constituent Assembly laid lasting foundations. Through all the vicissitudes of the subsequent century and a half, department and commune remained the two units of administration; equality of status among communes varying in size and population rendered continuous homage to a revolutionary principle; and the practice of carrying out national administration through local authorities proved too useful to be discarded. The Constituent Assembly reaped no immediate reward, however. Local government disintegrated, and the enthusiasm in which the first local elections took place died away in disillusionment. Shortly afterwards the outbreak of war led to a demand for centralization which local authority could not resist.

Judicial reforms were happier in their results. The deputies, 400 of whom were lawyers, tackled the work enthusiastically, and much of the planning was done by senior magistrates and judges. The task was threefold: to establish a new system of courts and judges, to devise a new form of procedure, and to reform the lists of offences and penalties. Under the *ancien régime* there was a superfluity of courts but no justice in the wider sense of the word. A vast number of seigneurial courts exercised civil justice in minor cases, and some still exercised criminal justice though the more important criminal cases had passed into the king's courts. A complicated series of special courts dealt with treasury cases, ecclesiastical disputes, game laws, commercial cases, royal privilege, and many other matters. Over all lay the terrible power of the parlements, the sovereign courts of the realm, in which justice was often subordinated to political ends. Every major court maintained a vast legal personnel. Most of the work was done by underpaid, ill-trained clerks, while rich perquisites went to venal judges. Salaries were small; the fabulous sums of money which most judges paid for their posts were recovered from bribes. Procedure was based on an assumption of the prisoner's guilt; offences were arbitrarily defined and penalties barbarous. No demand was more widespread in the *cahiers* than that for judicial reform.

The Assembly began by placing the parlements, which had thwarted legal reform for half a century, on permanent vacation. It then declared the judiciary independent of the legislature and executive. This statement, made with the parlements in mind, was directed more towards preventing judges from interfering in government than *vice versa*, and the deputies ignored it by proceeding to give judicial powers to the new local government bodies. Every municipality was ordered to choose three to five of its members to form a police tribunal dealing with small offences in the commune. Cases connected with public morals, vagabondage, religious disturbances, and petty larceny were the affair of the canton, and were to be tried by a correctional tribunal of three to six justices of the peace, elected by active citizens from among the wealthier taxpayers. Civil cases were attributed to district courts, where trial was carried out by judges, elected for six years from among lawyers who had completed five years' experience at the bar. Criminal cases were attributed to departmental courts, each with a panel of judges taken by rota from the districts, a public prosecutor elected by departmental voters, and juries of active citizens chosen by lot.

The notorious *lettres de cachet* of the *ancien régime* were abolished: no person could be detained for longer than 24 hours without being charged. Trials were made public, the accused was assumed innocent until he was proved guilty, and torture and other barbarous methods of extracting information were abandoned. Heresy, witchcraft, and all 'imaginary crimes' were abolished, along with mutilation, breaking on the wheel, and other hideous punishments. Robespierre warmly supported a motion for abolishing the death penalty, but the deputies decided on death by decapitation for treason, conspiracy, forgery, arson, and murder. Dr. Guillotin proposed that beheading, which had been carried out expensively with the sword when it was the monopoly of aristocratic offenders, should be done by machine now that it was the privilege of the nation. In 1792 a model perfected by Dr. Louis, Secretary to the College of Surgeons, was brought into general use and became known, misleadingly, as the *guillotine*.

The election of judges was carried out during November 1790, with excellent results. Most of the successful candidates were lawyers known for integrity and progressive ideas. Legal members of the Assembly were in great demand: 'Our deputies are getting themselves elected as judges', wrote the Marquis de Ferrières gleefully, hoping that political debates would be shorter in consequence. Judges in district courts exercised criminal as well as civil jurisdiction until 1792, when the departmental criminal courts were finally organized and the jury system started. Juries were drawn mainly from artisans, shopkeepers, and businessmen of the towns rather than from peasants, who were fertile in excuses and more concerned to obtain justice than to dispense it. On the whole, the principle that justice emanated from the people led to some interesting and worthwhile results. If it later provided an excuse for setting up emergency courts which infringed the most basic rights of the individual, this cannot fairly be laid at the door of the Constituent Assembly.

All this time, financial problems were demanding the attention of deputies whose real interests lay elsewhere. The task here was twofold: to create an annual revenue by devising a new system of taxation, and to meet the enormous deficit bequeathed to France by the absolute monarchy.

Under the *ancien régime*, direct taxes were unfairly distributed, indirect taxes were heavy, and the whole system, or lack of system, aroused bitter resentment without providing an adequate income for the state. The deputies were convinced that moderate taxes, justly apportioned, would meet with co-operation from all citizens; they even believed that people would forestall the work of the legislature and hasten to make voluntary contributions to the Treasury. Disappointed in the latter hope, they persevered in the former, and decreed three taxes, all to be collected without any means of coercion. The basic tax, intended to bring in three quarters of the annual revenue, was a tax on land, which the Physiocrats had believed to be the most important form of wealth. The other two taxes, designed to touch industrial and commercial profits, were exceedingly modest. Assessments for all three taxes were to be made by the municipalities, a job which proved to be entirely outside the scope of untrained men. Citizens did not hesitate to make false declarations and to ignore tax requests, and the revenue for 1791 fell short of the expected figure by one fifth. The deputies were loath to court unpopularity by increasing their demands. The only alternative seemed to be to print more paper money, an experiment which the Assembly had undertaken in its efforts to meet the great deficit.

Before the Revolution, bourgeois critics of government attributed the deficit chiefly to the extravagance of the court. In fact the upkeep of the court accounted for less than 6% of the annual expenditure. By far the largest sum went in interest on the loans by which successive finance ministers paid for France's wars. The deficit could have been reduced to manageable proportions at once by repudiating the public debt, but such a measure would have angered the chief holders of government bonds, the bourgeois class from which the deputies sprang. The respect with which deputies treated all bourgeois investments caused them even to increase the deficit by declaring that former office holders were to be compensated for the abolition of purchase. There seemed to be no reason why worthy property owners should suffer when unworthy ones were at hand.

Many of the *cahiers* had suggested that the state should take over the wealth of the clergy. Radical deputies recalled such suggestions during August 1789, and in December a certain amount of church land was confiscated. It was, however, a bishop, Talleyrand, who first proposed, as early as October, that the lands should actually be sold. In May 1790 a method was agreed upon. Treasury bonds were issued bearing interest at 5%; these 'assignats' as they were called could be exchanged either for 'national land' or for money when the Treasury was sufficiently replenished. Plenty of buyers came forward; nevertheless the sales did not bring in as much money as they should have done and before long the question arose of printing new assignats which would be not Treasury bonds but paper money. There had been a strong prejudice against paper money since the time of John Law. Most of the departmental directories pronounced against the proposal, as did 27 out of 33 cities which the Assembly consulted. Necker observed, sarcastically, that only a paper mill and a printing press were needed to keep France solvent; his enemy Mirabeau rushed to the support of the proposal; and the question rapidly became more political than financial. The Jacobin club declared in favour of new assignats, and opponents became *ipso facto* unpatriotic. On 27 September 1790 the Assembly voted the issue of forty million pounds in assignats; in the following May another five millions; in June, thirty millions more. The situation was fraught with danger, but the Constituent Assembly had secured financial equilibrium for its own lifetime. The first issue of assignats made up for a shortage of currency which had dogged France's economy for the greater part of the eighteenth century. Further issues in 1791 still did not exceed the value of land on the market and the paper money had lost only 8% of its original value by July 1791. It was the issue, in later years, of enormous quantities of assignats to pay for European war which brought catastrophe.

A great deal of national land was bought by middle class speculators, a fact which was often quoted afterwards to illustrate the 'bourgeois' sympathies of the Constituent Assembly. If the Assembly was indeed bourgeois in outlook, the term must not be understood in the Marxist sense. The majority of deputies were professional men, not lords of industry and commerce. Their Declaration of Rights proclaimed the sanctity of property, but this implied merely that every man had a right to exploit his own means, not that rich men had a right to exploit the poor. Interference by the state and control by powerful monopolists were equally deplored. Government regulations regarding trade and industry were abolished, as were guilds and corporations, and the Compagnie des Indes lost its exclusive privileges in overseas trade. Internal customs barriers were destroyed, along with restrictions on the sale of corn in home markets; but free export of corn, which would have benefited big landowners at the expense of small farmers, was forbidden. In economic measures the deputies aimed at an ideal which still seemed attainable in the eighteenth century: a society in which every man owned enough property, be it only a few acres or a small shop, to render him self-sufficient. Unlimited faith in individual capacity prompted the deputies to provide freedom of opportunity, and at the same time prevented them from helping those classes of the population which wanted direct government assistance. Peasant farmers who saved a little money could buy national land by instalments, but peasant labourers with no savings got nothing. The latter wanted land to be held available by the government for cheap and short-term lease-holding; they wished to maintain their rights of gleaning and grazing on the commons; they had long demanded government control of corn prices. The Constituent Assembly sold land freehold, encouraged enclosures, and refused to regulate crop planting and food prices. Similarly, in the towns, small businessmen were freer to improve their income, but wage-earners received no assistance. The Loi le Chapelier of 14 June 1791 forbade all workers' associations, meetings, strikes and picketing. It also forbade associations of employers in the hope that industry would become the friendly concern of equal individuals, but in practice workers were affected more adversely than masters.

3. COUNTER-REVOLUTION

In the summer of 1790 the prevailing atmosphere was one of gratitude and hope. More people than ever before had reason to feel themselves a part of the nation, buying land, electing local officials, choosing J.P.s, and serving in the National Guard. Political enthusiasts did everything they could to embrace the nation. Some 200 political clubs sprang up in provincial centres, many, like that at Bordeaux, opening meetings to the public and corresponding with the Jacobin club in Paris. Newspapers proliferated, and orators in and out of the Assembly addressed their passionate rhetoric as much to the unseen masses as to their immediate audiences. Revolutionary songs formed a new type of folk music, and revolutionary pageants took the place of religious festivals in providing entertainment for the masses. Even artists, under the leadership of David, applied themselves to the task of communicating great experiences in terms which the simplest could understand. French culture was never again to be so truly democratic.

On 14 July 1790 church bells rang all over the kingdom to celebrate the Feast of Federation, and citizens assembled to swear an oath of fidelity to the Nation. To the elated crowds, fraternity seemed to have become a real possession. Political excitement breeds fear as well as hope, however. Émigré nobles were known to be collecting in Brussels, Turin, and the Rhinelands, and appealing to foreign princes for help against the Revolution. The army and navy were riddled with aristocratic officers. A series of mutinies, including a violent upheaval in the Chateauvieux regiment at Nancy, forced the Assembly to give the king exceptional powers to restore order. The Marquis de Bouillé, who marched on Nancy at the head of an army to put down the mutiny, was accused by the Jacobin club of attempting counter-revolution. Rumours of royalist plots were the stock-in-trade of pamphleteers and orators in Paris.

Of all potential enemies of the Revolution the most hated were the clergy. This was not apparent at the opening of the Estates General, but the religious policy of the Constituent Assembly opened a breach which was to complicate French politics for generations to come. The Assembly began reasonably enough. The abolition of tithes and the confiscation of church lands meant that clerical salaries would have to be met by taxation, and the deputies felt that they had a duty to taxpayers to see that their money was spent wisely. The result was an act to reform the church establishment, known as the Civil Constitution of the Clergy (12 July 1790). Dioceses, which had varied enormously in size, were redrawn to correspond with the departments; parishes, which had been too numerous in the old cities, were rationalized. Vacant sees and benefices were henceforward to be filled by election. All bishops and clergy were to receive salaries from the state, and none could be absent from duty for more than a fortnight without permission from the departmental authorities.

The majority of deputies regarded these changes as the logical outcome of the old Gallican position: the state had a right to control the civil establishment of the church while recognizing the spiritual authority of the Pope. Most of the lower clergy were willing to accept arrangements which promised them a better living. The bishops were more hostile, but they obtained no lead from the Pope, who hesitated to antagonize the French Assembly lest it should annex the two papal enclaves of Avignon and the Venaissin. The Civil Constitution would probably have been enacted with nothing more than grumbling had it not been for articles 21 and 38 which required all clergy to take an oath of loyalty to the nation, the law, the king, and the constitution. The deputies appear to have entertained no idea of the opposition this demand would arouse, for the real devotion which existed among the clergy had long been obscured by the notorious scepticism of a few spectacular individuals. When large numbers of clergy hesitated to take an oath which seemed to deny their primary allegiance to the Pope, the deputies accused them of reactionary views. A long acquaintance with the anticlericalism of Voltaire played its part in the Assembly's decision to enforce the oath as a means of weeding out undesirables. A decree of 27 November 1790 required all office-holding clergy to take the oath before their congregations, on pain of deprivation. Out of 160 bishops, only 7 swore; of the lower clergy, about a third.

The 'non-jurors' were replaced by 'constitutional' clergy, but not all parishes were willing to accept the new incumbents. In northern and eastern France particularly, Catholics continued to gather round their former priests, in barns and cellars. Deliberate boycotting of the new priests was encouraged by refractory clergy. Schism was complete when the Pope condemned the Civil Constitution and all the works of the Revolution, in briefs addressed to the French bishops on 10 March and 17 April 1791. All refractory priests were thereafter potential counter-revolutionaries. The loyalty which they could command from devout peasants made counter-revolution for the first time possible, while latent anti-clericalism among bourgeois and sans-culottes, especially in Paris, produced willing hearers for stories of priestly plots and treasons.

It was, in fact, in Paris that fears of counter-revolution reached their height, for here people felt that they had the arch-plotter in their midst. Louis XVI had never whole-heartedly accepted the Revolution, and his dislike of his position increased from the day when he was obliged to sanction the decree enforcing the clerical oath. This action preyed on his mind, for he was a devout man. With the death of Mirabeau there was no statesmanlike influence to compete with the reckless entreaties of Marie Antoinette for possession of the king's slow-moving mind. The queen hoped continually for foreign intervention led by her brother the Emperor. Along with other European monarchs the Emperor declined to intervene, pleading as excuse the fact that Louis lay at the mercy of the revolutionaries. Marie Antoinette, always wilful, decided to force her brother's hand. During the early months of 1791 she elaborated her plans. The royal family would flee to Metz, where the sympathetic Bouillé commanded an army. There the king would call on royalist support against the Assembly. The émigrés would join him. The Emperor and the German princes would send armies and march on Paris if need be. How far Louis shared these intentions is doubtful, but when he was prevented from receiving the ministrations of a non-juring priest he agreed on flight.

The escape from the Tuileries was planned by Marie Antoinette's admirer Count Fersen. He managed to smuggle the king and queen, the king's sister, the two royal children, two waiting-women, and a governess, away from Paris in the midnight hours of 20-21 June 1791. Everything else went wrong. Nothing could inspire Louis with a sense of urgency, and the party moved too slowly to meet the armed escorts which had been arranged along the route. The king incautiously showed himself while new horses were being hired at Sainte-Ménehould, and the posting-master, Drouet, recognized him from his head on the assignats. Drouet was ordered by the mayor to pursue the fugitives, and by a prodigious feat of riding he overtook the coach in pitch darkness at the little town of Varennes. Louis allowed himself to be held captive by a band of peasants. A detachment of hussars, who had been waiting outside the town to meet the king, could have rescued him easily, but Louis would not give the word and none of the officers dared take him by force. The king and queen were led slowly back to Paris under armed guard; they re-entered the Tuileries on 25 June, prisoners in all but name.

News of Louis's flight spread through the capital during the morning of 21 June and angry citizens began tearing down royal arms from public buildings. Everybody, including the deputies, feared immediate invasion by foreign armies. The Assembly took over executive power, closed the frontiers, put the army on a war footing, and asked for an emergency force of 100,000 volunteers. The Paris authorities began distributing gunpowder. When the king was once more in the Tuileries, feeling divided on the subject of his fate. The populace was angry at Louis's treachery and fearful lest he should find further means of endangering the country. Anti-monarchical sentiments hitherto expressed only in extremist papers such as Marat's *Ami du Peuple* and Desmoulin's *Révolutions de France et de Brabant*, began to take root for the first time. The Cordeliers club and its offshoots, the fraternal societies, sent several petitions to the Assembly demanding the deposition of the king, and a great demonstration was planned for 17 July. The Assembly, on the other hand, became more and more impressed with the need for caution. If Louis were deposed the result would surely be foreign invasion. The new constitution, almost completed, reckoned on the king as head of the executive power; without him, the whole elaborate structure would give way to a republic. Hitherto the word 'republic' had been used to describe any state governed in the interests of the people; now the deputies began to think of it as a state governed by hot-heads from the Cordeliers club in the interests of the mob. The Municipality shared these apprehensions. The king's flight to Varennes thus precipitated the first conflict between the sans-culottes and the bourgeois rulers of Paris and France.

On 17 July the Cordeliers club drew up a petition which was placed on the altar of the Champ de Mars to receive signatures. During the afternoon a crowd of about 50,000 people assembled, and 6,000 had signed the petition when Bailly sent 10,000 National Guardsmen to quell the demonstration. Stones were thrown at the Guards, Lafayette gave the order to retaliate, and several volleys were fired into the defenceless crowd, killing 50 persons. Bailly reported the slaughter complacently to the Assembly, which decided on punitive measures to wipe out the whole movement. Ringleaders were arrested along with about 200 sans-culottes who ventured to criticize the Municipality or Assembly, left-wing newspapers were proscribed, and for three weeks the hated red flag flew from the Town Hall. The deputies hurriedly drew together the legislative acts of the past two years to form a constitution; the document received the king's signature on 16 September and the Constituent Assembly dissolved at the end of the month.

4. THE LEGISLATIVE ASSEMBLY AND THE OUTBREAK OF WAR

Criticisms of the constitution of 1791 were rife from the beginning. The most penetrating came from members of the Right, who complained that the king had been declared head of the executive power without receiving the means to govern effectively. More unlikely instruments have been known to work, however. The will to make this one work was by no means lacking. The new parliament was elected by the nation's wealthier tax-payers, who had no desire for further changes. The Legislative Assembly, when it met on 1 October 1791, turned out to have a majority of moderate members, mostly lawyers, with an average age of nearly forty. They hastened to join the Feuillant club, a society of constitutional monarchists formed in protest against the recent republican demonstration. Many of them had had experience of politics at a local level, acting as mayors, councillors, or magistrates. Their most obvious weakness was that they were all new to parliament. On 16 May 1791 the Constituent Assembly had passed a self-denying ordinance whereby none of its members could sit in the next parliament. This had been instigated by Robespierre with the deliberate intention of depriving France's second revolutionary parliament of experienced moderates. New men, he thought, would be more easily swayed by groups of politicians sitting on the left.

About 136 deputies put down their names to become members of the Jacobin or Cordeliers clubs and can therefore be described as belonging to the Left. The Jacobin club, though still drawing its members from the middle class, was more extremist than before. Timid members had seceded after the Champ de Mars affair to form the Feuillant club. Remaining members threw open their meetings to the public and debates began to be influenced to some extent by sans-culottes in the galleries. The clubs did not, however, provide left-wing deputies with a coherent policy. So many shades of opinion were distinguishable that the broad name of 'patriot' was no longer adequate. Each group began to be known by the name of its most forceful member. The group which took the limelight from the beginning was that surrounding Jacques-Pierre Brissot.

Brissot was a new type of politician thrown to the surface by the revolution in Paris. His father, who kept a restaurant at Chartres, had made him a lawyer's clerk at 15, but the young man had found that he could have a livelier time by living on his wits. He wrote pamphlets and newspapers in England, Switzerland, and America, for anyone who wanted a trouble-maker. Money was neither his sole nor his chief object; he liked change, risk, activity, notoriety, and he imagined himself a great lover of mankind. He was an obvious man to enter the service of the Duc d'Orléans in the last years of the *ancien régime*. At the Palais Royal he came into contact with flotsam and jetsam from every revolution in Europe and acquired a facile knowledge of foreign affairs. In 1789 he founded an extremist newspaper, the *Patriote française*, which sold among the Paris crowds. He joined the

AOP D

Jacobin club, helped the Cordeliers to organize the Champ de Mars demon-stration, and was elected to the Legislative Assembly by the active citizens of Paris. Restless and ambitious, with wide experience but no wisdom, he easily impressed the less self-assured deputies from the country. Very few associated with him, but many allowed their votes to be swayed by him.

His most notable adherents were the deputies for the department of Gironde. Vergniaud, Gensonné, Guadet, and their colleagues had been prominent members of the debating society at Bordeaux. They came to Paris with hearts overflowing with virtuous sentiments and minds full of ideas derived from philosophies ancient and modern, but with no policy designed to meet the practical needs of France. Brissot gave them subjects on which to display their superb oratorical gifts, and the Assembly listened entranced while Vergniaud commended, in words fit for a poet, measures totally lacking in statesmanship. To say that Brissot provided his followers with a policy would be to give an exaggerated impression of his quality, for he had no aim beyond that of becoming the leading influence in politics. The surest means of achieving this object was by playing on popular fears and prejudices.

Parisians, conscious that their city presented an easy target for invading armies, watched with alarm the growing number of émigrés who gathered across the frontier during the autumn of 1791. Many were officers who had deserted from the French army. The king's brothers, Provence and Artois, set up their court at Coblentz, and with Calonne to advise them they began arming their followers for the day when they might form the spearhead of an attack on the Revolution. The Brissotins demanded penal legislation. On 9 November the Assembly passed a decree declaring all émigrés who did not return to France by the New Year guilty of treason, their property liable to confiscation and themselves to the death penalty. Louis vetoed it. Meanwhile a parliamentary commission drew up a report on the activities of refractory priests inside France. The Assembly was at a loss to know how to remove the danger without infringing the liberty of conscience promised in the Declaration of Rights. Brissotin orators waved aside such scruples in passionate denunciations. On 20 November the Assembly passed a decree declaring all non-jurors suspect. Louis vetoed this too.

The king was acting on the advice of a group of Feuillant politicians – Barnave, Adrien Duport, and the two brothers Lameth – who told him that he could stem the tide of revolution by a firm use of his constitutional powers. Barnave had been a member of the Left in 1789 but had grown more moderate by 1791. On the journey from Varennes, whither he had been sent by the Assembly to escort the royal fugitives back to Paris, he had been flattered by the queen into thinking that he could save the monarchy. In the ensuing months nearly a hundred letters passed between him and Marie

Antoinette, but she took no more notice of his advice than she had done of Mirabeau's. Far from giving up her schemes for counter-revolution, she continued to intrigue with the Emperor. Information leaked out and compromised the king's position.

Set-backs from Louis gave Brissot further excuses for fanning the flames of war. In the event of war, opponents of the Revolution could be denounced as traitors to the country. Émigrés, refractory priests, royal intriguers, and all who abetted them could be weeded out. Peasants and bourgeoisie would be galvanized into new revolutionary efforts. 'A people which has achieved liberty after a thousand years of slavery needs war', Brissot declared. 'It needs war to consolidate its freedom. It needs war to purge away the vices of despotism. It needs war to banish from its bosom the men who might corrupt its liberty.'

In the early days of the Revolution, Frenchmen imagined that wars were the sport of kings and that in the new era of popular sovereignty France would live in peace and brotherly love with her neighbours. In May 1790 the Constituent Assembly formally renounced all wars of conquest and declared that the French nation would never use its forces against the liberty of any people. By the winter of 1791, however, war had begun to appear necessary in defence of the Revolution. Louis XVI's position after Varennes roused the Emperor and the King of Prussia to a number of strong expressions of sympathy, couched in terms menacing for the revolutionaries. Few Frenchmen realized that the foreign monarchs had no intention of carrying out their threats. More agreed with Vergniaud when he argued, in January 1792, that France should attack the Emperor before he attacked her. The Brissotin Isnard spoke of 'a war of peoples against kings', and Brissot himself confidently believed that French armies would be welcomed by oppressed peoples of Europe. In the Assembly Brissot met with no serious opposition. In the Jacobin club he was attacked by Robespierre in a great debate in January 1792. French armies would receive no welcome in Europe, Robespierre said, for 'no-one loves armed missionaries'. Nor would liberty triumph at home, for war would strengthen the hands of the king and his ministers. Brissot carried the Jacobin club, however, as he had done the Assembly.

On 10 March 1792 Louis appointed new ministers who were connected with the Brissotins. This was an attempt to force the latter into a greater sense of responsibility, but it failed. The Minister of the Interior, Roland, husband of the more famous Manon Roland whose salon provided a centre for the group of intellectuals from the Gironde, was nothing more than a competent civil servant. The Foreign Minister, Dumouriez, a professional soldier, clever and ambitious, believed he could win fame by directing a war against Austria, long hated by the French people. He had established connections with the Brissotins in order to become known as a patriot, but he secretly hoped to work hand-in-glove with the king. Dumouriez tried to break the defensive alliance between Prussia and Austria, but his diplomacy failed and the Duke of Brunswick accepted command of the combined anti-French forces. Louis had some reason to believe that France would be defeated and the Revolution betrayed into his hands. In this false hope he was persuaded by his ministers to propose a declaration of war against Austria. The declaration was approved by the Assembly on 20 April 1792, with only 7 dissentient voices. France entered enthusiastically on a war which was to lead her into dictatorship and alter the whole history of Europe.

CHAPTER III

The Habsburgs and the Defence
of the Old Order

I. THE HABSBURGS AND THE REVOLT OF THE ARISTOCRACY

WHEN France declared war on 'the King of Hungary and Bohemia', Francis II had reigned for little more than a month. His vast dominions in central Europe had no name collectively. Sometimes they were referred to, misleadingly, as Austria, and sometimes, more aptly, as the lands of the House of Austria. The ruling family, the Habsburgs, were a German family whose name derived from their ancestral home of Habichtsburg (Hawk's Castle) in Swabia. Rudolph I of Habsburg, having become Holy Roman Emperor in 1273, bestowed the lands on the south-eastern march of the Empire upon his sons. These Alpine-Germanic provinces – Upper and Lower Austria, Vorarlberg, Tyrol, Styria, Carniola, and Carinthia – formed the 'hereditary lands' of the Habsburg crown. Their ruler held the title of Archduke of Austria and made his capital at Vienna. From this starting point the power of the Habsburgs was extended, not so much by war as by diplomatic skill, strategic marriages, and luck. In 1526 Archduke Ferdinand of Austria became King of Bohemia and King of Hungary. The 'lands of the Bohemian crown' included Moravia and Silesia, those of the Hungarian crown Croatia, Slavonia, and Transylvania. Lombardy and Belgium were acquired in 1713; the greater part of Silesia was lost to Prussia in 1740. Bukovina was taken from the Turks in 1774, and Galicia was acquired in the First Partition of Poland. The empire which resulted had no ethnical justification, for its 24 million inhabitants included many different national groups. In the hereditary lands the people were predominantly German, but the southern half of Tyrol had an Italian population, and there were Slovene minorities in Styria and Carinthia. The lands of the Bohemian crown were predominantly German in the sixteenth century, but Frederick II upset the balance when he stole Silesia; in Bohemia and Moravia at least three fifths of the population was Czech. The peasants in western Galicia were Polish and those in eastern Galicia were Little Russian; landowners and officials throughout the province were Polish. In Hungary the central plain was occupied mainly by Hungarian-speaking people (Magyars), with Slovaks

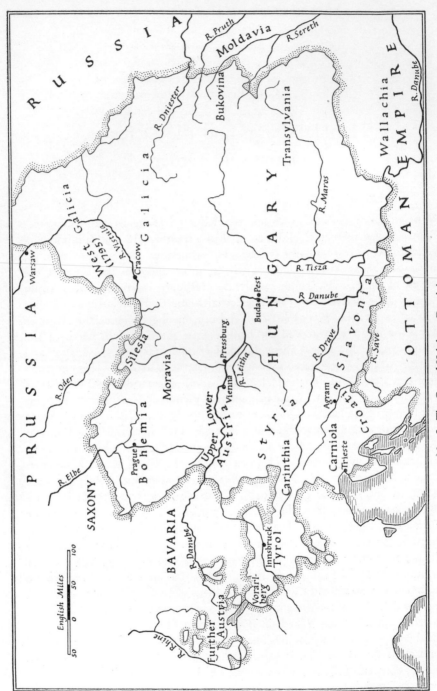

Map I The Central Habsburg Dominions, 1792

in the north, Little Russians in the north-east, Roumanians in the east, and Serbs in the south. The people of Croatia-Slavonia were Serbo-Croat. Boundaries between peoples were not defined; some areas, for instance Bukovina, had a mingled population which could not be described in national terms, while throughout the empire there were islands of German people in the towns. The only exception to the muddle was Lombardy, where towns and countryside were peopled by Italians.

Nationalism, in the sense of an ethnic group claiming the right to control its own destinies and rule its own defined area of land, was unknown in Europe before the French Revolution. The word 'nationalism' had not been invented in any language. Habsburg power was by no means easy to maintain, however. In 1789 intellectual groups made some demands for a new order in government and society. The aristocracy made even more vociferous demands for a return to an older order than that prescribed by eighteenth-century monarchs. These ended in a revolt of the nobles comparable to the revolt which had taken place in France in 1788.

The great landed noblemen, in all the Habsburg dominions except Galicia and Lombardy, owed their possessions and dignities to the dynasty. There were no great aristocratic families, like those in England and France, which could claim to be older than the ruling house and to have derived power from historic sources outside the ruling house. In the hereditary lands, Austrian Archdukes rewarded their followers with estates and titles in the Middle Ages. In Bohemia the native aristocracy was expropriated or driven into exile after the Battle of the White Mountain (1620) and its lands bestowed on courtiers and adventurers – Germans from further north and west, or foreigners like the Wallises from England, and the Taaffes, MacNevens, and O'Kelleys from Ireland, who had given their services to the Habsburgs in the Thirty Years War. In Hungary the old aristocracy was scattered by the invading Turks in 1529. For nearly two centuries its lands lay waste under Turkish rule; when they were recovered by the Habsburgs in the early eighteenth century they were bestowed upon favoured families. Most of these families were of native Hungarian stock, since German, Spanish, or Italian hangers-on had no desire to be presented with miles of wilderness in an outlandish area of the globe; but the Esterházys, Károlyis, Andrássys and Apponyis who received these territories were 'new' nobles in the sense that they now became magnates on an unprecedented scale. The Esterházys alone received nearly 7 million Hungarian acres of land.

The magnates of the empire were more loyal to the dynasty than to the province in which their estates lay. The great noblemen of Bohemia could not speak Czech. Those of Hungary could sometimes speak Magyar but for social purposes they spoke Italian or French like the rest of the aristocracy. Knowledge of German and English was also common; the aristocracy had a surprising linguistic equipment and a truly cosmopolitan culture. Noblemen from all parts of the empire owned town houses in Vienna, spent many months of each year at the Imperial court, and married within their own circle. They provided the high-ranking officers for the Imperial army and filled the most spectacular places in the diplomatic corps. In the eyes of Europe they were the symbol of Habsburg power. Yet even the magnates would oppose the dynasty whenever it invaded their privileges.

Up to the middle of the eighteenth century the lands under the Habsburg crown kept a great deal of their original autonomy and the aristocracy exercised financial, legal, and administrative power through the meeting of the Estates in regular Diets. Maria Theresa was the first Habsburg ruler to decide that her empire could not survive among rapacious neighbours unless she harnessed its resources more effectively to the state. She began a process of centralization, cautiously and with important concessions to the fiercest of the aristocracies, the Hungarian. Her son Joseph, who succeeded her in 1780, speeded up the process and did not envisage concessions to anyone. By 1789 the Habsburg dominions could be regarded as forming four great territorial units: the Bohemian, Austrian and Polish lands, the Hungarian lands, the Austrian Netherlands, and the Italian possessions. Each unit was administered by a governor, with a council of hand-picked advisers and a host of officials sent out from Vienna. Justice in each unit was administered through a threefold hierarchy of courts, civil and criminal cases moving from the manorial and city courts to the royal courts of appeal and thence to the Supreme Court in Vienna. At the summit of the hierarchy sat the monarch, whose word was law. Unlike French kings of the eighteenth century, who were themselves bound by the hierarchy they had created, Joseph II could arrest the bureaucratic machine at any point in its working. He could transmit orders directly to minor officials, or discard plans which had revolved round every wheel in turn. Even the great Diets of Bohemia and Hungary were regarded by him as ciphers. The governmental power of the nobles seemed entirely shattered.

The nobles resented this not merely for its own sake but for the accompanying inroads upon their power over the peasantry. At Maria Theresa's death, serfdom existed in a strict form, with serfs bound like chattels to the land, in Bohemia and Hungary. Joseph abolished this by a stroke of the pen in 1781, declaring the serfs free to marry whom they pleased, free to take up any occupation they pleased, and free to move from manor to manor. Henceforward all peasants were free men, but economically they were still subject to many burdens. The state's taxes fell heavier on the peasants because the nobles were partly, and in Hungary wholly, exempt from taxation. Feudal obligations of many kinds had to be rendered to the lord of the manor, and they fell both on peasants who merely worked part of the lord's estate (dominical land) and on peasants who had rented land (rustical land) on hereditary terms. All had to pay dues in money or kind twice a year, and all had to perform robot, or forced labour. In an edict promulgated on 10 February 1789 Joseph proposed that some, at least, of the rustical peasants should commute their dues and services and become absorbed into a new system of taxation falling on peasants and nobles alike. A new land survey was made, taking into account more than 30% of the productive land of Bohemia which the nobles had hitherto hidden from tax assessments. The new taxes were levied on gross income and were to be collected by state officials. The tax-gatherers would thus join the justices of the peace, appointed by Joseph in 1785, in bringing central government to bear upon the life of the manor.

Joseph was guided not so much by feelings of justice and humanity towards the peasants as by a desire to free peasant resources so that they could be tapped by the state. He intended to reduce aristocratic privileges only in so far as they were a hindrance to the state; the nobles were to him still a superior class in society. The fact that in each province the nobility continued to exist as a separate Estate, proved, in the end, the most serious menace to the reforms, for Joseph lacked the tact necessary to accommodate a feudal society within a modern structure of government. During 1789, as Joseph lay dying, the Estates of the Netherlands repudiated his authority, and groups of noblemen met in many parts of the Habsburg dominions to discuss ways and means of defending their privileges. They cloaked their hostility to social reform by parading historic loyalties. The Crown, they said, had no right to upset the fundamental law of the various lands. They delved into the past to discover constitutional rights long in abeyance. The imported Bohemian nobles learnt Czech in order to make a more impressive claim to the rights which their 'ancestors' had retained when offering the crown of St. Wenceslas to Archduke Ferdinand. The Hungarian Estates prepared for armed resistance and sent Baron Hompesch to the court of Berlin to secure Prussian aid for an independent Kingdom of Hungary. It was hoped that Charles Augustus, Duke of Weimar, the friend of Goethe, would accept the crown.

2. THE HABSBURGS AND THE PEOPLE

As in France, the danger presented to the monarchy by the aristocratic revolt was enhanced by unrest among other classes of society. Joseph II had aroused, by his 'enlightened' policy, many hopes and ambitions which he was unwilling to fulfil. Censorship had been relaxed in order to allow men of letters to attack the political privileges of the aristocracy, but by 1789 writers such as Hoffmann, Riedel, and Martinovics had overstepped Joseph's intentions and were beginning to criticize the existence of an aristocracy of birth. Universities had been patronized as centres of attack upon medieval prejudice, but by 1789 teachers were beginning to question the basis of Joseph's own authority. Martini, Professor of Natural Law, and Sonnenfels, Professor of Political Science in the University of Vienna, claimed that all power derives from the people by the social contract and that the monarch should rule according to a set of principles agreed upon by the people. These ideas were taken over by pamphleteers, who began to popularize them under the relaxed censorship rules. Many people who approved of Joseph's measures did not approve of the dictatorial methods by which he strove to carry them out. Revolution in France was greeted by a flood of cheap political writings in the Habsburg dominions, viewed with alarm by Joseph's Minister of Police, Count Pergen.

Similarly, Joseph's anti-clerical measures had produced among educated classes a more sceptical and irreligious attitude than the monarch was prepared to countenance. Students were particularly affected, and the police were required to keep up a constant search for atheistic works in schools and universities. That a great many atheistic writings continued to circulate was due to the fact that many of Joseph's officials held more extreme anti-clerical views than their sovereign. Joseph was a believing and practising Roman Catholic. He wished to reduce the temporal power and wealth of the church but it was never his intention to weaken the influence of the Catholic faith over his subjects. Indeed he intended to use that faith to create more loyal servants of the monarchy. His edict of toleration was devised solely to bring foreign craftsmen into Austrian industries and foreign settlers into the de-populated areas of Hungary. Its limited clauses, which applied only to Calvinist, Lutheran, and Greek Orthodox religions, and allowed them private but not public worship, were attacked by writers and preachers with advanced views, who demanded full toleration for all non-catholic creeds in Bohemia and Hungary. Enlightened priests regretted Joseph's injunction to speak German, which restricted their influence over non-German communities and discouraged candidates for the priesthood. Men of letters regretted Joseph's attempts to stamp out provincial languages, and men of culture despised his philistine attitude towards the arts. In other words, enlightenment had outstripped the monarch who had sought to use it for his own purposes.

Among the lower classes much suffering was caused when, in 1788, Joseph joined Russia in war upon Turkey. Townsmen and peasants were subjected to heavy taxes at a time when the diversion of foodstuffs to the armies caused a steep rise in prices. As the government's financial embarrassment grew, it ceased to pay compensation to former members of the 'brotherhoods', or friendly societies, suppressed by Joseph; some 20,000 artisans and peasants thus lost their meagre savings. Peasants near the battlefront were forced to send carts, beasts and provisions to the armies and to render increased labour services. Under a new system of recruitment nearly all non-privileged subjects lived in dread of being forced into the army for life. These hardships seemed to have been caused solely by Joseph's lust for military glory, which it was believed that Catherine II had used for her own ends. Police reports of 1788 and 1789 warned Joseph of the hatred which the war had engendered; by early 1790, Count Pergen believed that the unrest constituted a serious threat to the monarchy.

Strange to say, the great edict of 1789 added to the discontent of the peasantry. Peasant farmers objected to the calculation of their tax obligations on the basis of gross income, and many refused to pay the increased amounts involved. Standardization of feudal dues meant an increase of payments in areas where traditional dues had been light, and commutation of services into money payments was disliked in backward areas where money was scarce. Moreover the benefits of the decree did not apply at all to the countless peasants living on dominical land, and among those living on rustical land it applied only to peasants who were wealthy enough to pay 2 florins a year in land tax, perhaps a third of the total number. The peasants had come to expect Joseph to abolish feudal dues and feudal lordship altogether. Many serfs who were excluded from the decree refused to go on rendering labour services, and many of those included in it refused to pay money dues. Joseph II authorized punitive measures. Refractory serfs could be made to work in irons and put on a diet of bread and water. For persistent refusal of dues they could be expelled from their holdings. If a whole village resisted, military force could be used. Bohemia proved to be the most troublesome province; the governor could not send troops to help put down the Netherlands revolt in November 1789 because they were needed to restore order at home. The peasants were encouraged in their resistance by news of the great peasant rising in France. In almost every province of the Habsburg Empire cheap newspapers appeared, addressing the peasants in their own language.

In 1789 Joseph tightened the censorship and allowed Pergen to reorganize the police in such a way as to give them supreme power over all matters relating to public opinion. Pergen, who came himself from one of the great noble families of the realm, urged Joseph to retreat from enlightened despotism into the arms of the aristocracy. Joseph delayed doing so, partly because he could not believe that even the most generous concessions to the aristocracy would induce the latter to give him the taxes he required. The delay lost him the Netherlands at the end of 1789. After this disaster the Chancellor Kaunitz came to believe that large concessions were necessary to prevent the loss of Hungary also. On 30 January 1790 the dying monarch issued a Patent whereby he withdrew from Hungary the edict of 1789 and all other reforms except those on serfdom and toleration.

In France the mere suspicion that Louis XVI was about to submit to the aristocracy was sufficient to provoke rebellion among all non-privileged classes. In the greater part of the Habsburg dominions this did not happen. The middle class and urban populations were too small and too dependent on the state to make a spontaneous revolution, and unrest among the peasants lacked the coherence of the peasant movement in France.

Except for the outlying provinces of Belgium and Lombardy, the Habsburg Empire was predominantly agricultural. The prevailing law of entail (*fideikommis*) helped to preserve large landed estates by fastening inheritance upon the eldest son, and all Joseph's attempts at departing from this tradition were resisted by the aristocracy. The law of entail also forbade mortgages and thereby hindered the aristocracy from obtaining capital. Unlike their English counterparts, few Austrian nobles engaged in commercial and industrial enterprises, which they considered beneath their dignity. Their backwardness in this respect was not yet challenged by a rising class of wealthy commoners, for in the Habsburg empire economic development was constantly subordinated to political considerations.

Bohemia's ancient industries in glass, cloth, and paper sank steadily into depression after the loss of Silesia. The enmity of Prussia and Saxony brought about the closing of the Elbe and Oder to Austrian commerce; Bohemia's exports had to turn south to Trieste, not easily accessible. Money was drained away from Bohemia by the tax demands of Maria Theresa and her successor, who never forgot that Bohemian nobles had been disloyal to the Habsburg crown in 1741. The financial quota previously levied from Silesia was transferred to the rest of the Bohemian lands, and the latter, forming only one tenth of the total area of the Habsburg dominions, provided one fourth of the revenue to the end of Joseph's reign. The high tariff barriers which Maria Theresa and Joseph II erected around their dominions in order to stimulate home industries prevented them from making favourable commercial treaties with other countries. Within the barricade Joseph sought to stimulate industry by allowing serfs to choose their own occupation and by abolishing guilds and corporations. Statistics in 1787 proved to his satisfaction that imports were only a fraction higher in value than exports, but the new industries were of hot-house growth, and the quality of the goods produced was very poor.

Meanwhile Hungary had been punished for her political intransigence by economic repression. She was cut off from the rest of the Habsburg dominions by a tariff wall, at which Hungarian magnates were made to pay heavily for the luxuries which they imported from the west and for their efforts to export their grain. Hungarian landowners, unable to sell more than a fraction of the produce of their estates, consumed the rest themselves: twenty and thirty course dinners were served in castle halls. Exchange of goods for money was rare, so that even owners of large estates had difficulty in paying for more than a short stay in town. Towns remained small and isolated, communications difficult. Peasants gave part of their labour services in the task of carrying travellers in wicker carts. Roads were mere tracks, the approaches to a town being discernible by converging ruts in the soil. Even Budapest had no bridge spanning the Danube, other than a bridge of boats which had to be removed in the winter. To visitors from western Europe, Hungary seemed as strange as China or Tibet.

Towns were few and small in most parts of the Empire. Even in Bohemia, where population was thicker than in Austria or Hungary, barely a quarter of a million people were classed as 'citizens' or 'artisans' in 1790. Moreover, the towns all bore something of an artificial character. Even ancient cities like Prague, Brno, and Zagreb were not in any real sense the heart of the province in which they stood, for their native families had been driven away by the Habsburgs or the Turks and replaced by Germans. The word 'German' came to denote a particular type of activity as much as a nationality. Because many merchants, shopkeepers, artisans, clerks, lawyers, and other essential town-dwellers were German born, the name German was gradually conferred upon the class in general. Czechs, Serbs, and other immigrants from the countryside soon felt obliged to learn the German language, and they became known as German by their neighbours. The towns in Bohemia, Hungary and Croatia became German enclaves in a countryside where the landowners spoke Italian or French and the peasants Czech, Magyar, or Croat. The towns were also the homes of the bureaucrats. The Habsburg dominions produced comparatively few intellectuals, and many of the civil servants needed for the new régime were imported from Protestant Germany. The higher grades were given titles of nobility; the lower grades were often wretchedly paid but they enjoyed a status they would not otherwise have obtained and were encouraged to regard themselves as apostles of enlightenment in dark places.

When Joseph II emancipated the serfs he made special rules ensuring that the poorer peasants would not be driven off the land like so many of their counterparts in France. All land had been registered by Maria Theresa as noble (dominical) or serf (rustical). Joseph II decreed that no nobleman could obtain rustical land and no peasant could obtain dominical land. His main purpose was to prevent the increase of dominical land, which bore privileges with regard to taxation, but his decree produced several incidental results. It deferred the growth of a class of landless peasants which would provide a labour force for industry, and it prevented the growth of hordes of vagrants, whose appearance in France did so much to heighten popular tension in the summer of 1789. The constant division between dominical and rustical serfs, maintained in the edict of 1789, deprived the peasantry of the community of interest which French peasants derived from the common hatred of seigneurial dues. Peasant unrest at the end of Joseph's reign was an incoherent medley of revolution and counter-revolution. The same peasants who refused to render services to feudal lords rioted in defence of religious statues and processions, which Joseph had tried to abolish because he believed them to be a waste of the peasants' money.

3. REVOLT IN HUNGARY AND BELGIUM

Resistance to Joseph II was more strenuous in Hungary than in other central parts of the Habsburg dominions, due to circumstances arising out of the peculiar history of the country. In the ninth century A.D. a band of Magyar warriors from the Pontic steppes settled in the Middle Danube basin. Each member of the band was free, and all were equal. Together they formed the Magyar or Hungarian nation, and they met in conclave to govern their communal affairs. In the year 1000 they accepted a king, Stephen, but only upon recognition of certain rights which were to belong to them and their descendants for ever. Each Magyar 'noble', as a member of the 'nation' came to be called, was to remain a free man, inviolable in person and property. A noble must answer the king's call to war, but he owed no other service to the state, and his land could not, therefore, be taxed. Land which had not been allotted to Magyar nobles was reckoned as belonging to the Crown, and could be let out to slaves or peasant herdsmen. These latter were not part of the Magyar nation and were not entitled to any of its freedoms. The Magyar nation was an equal contracting partner with the king. Decisions affecting the terms of partnership must be taken at meetings of the two contracting parties, gradually assuming the form of a regular Diet. In 1523, when Stephen's line died out, the Hungarian nobles bestowed the crown upon Habsburg Ferdinand, in return for a reiteration of their freedoms. When Joseph II ignored the Hungarian Diet and attempted to tax the nobles, he could be accused of violating a solemn contract made by his ancestors.

In 1790 the Magyars formed barely a third of the population of the lands of St. Stephen. Nevertheless they claimed by virtue of a centuries old tradition that they, and they alone, constituted the Hungarian nation. The Roumanian, Serb, Slovak, and Little Russian peasants were no more part of the nation than the slaves had been of old. Among the constitutional rights which the Magyar nobles claimed was the right to oppress the serfs and place upon their backs the entire burdens of the state.

The Magyars had themselves undergone many changes, as a class, since the days of Stephen. No longer could all Magyars claim to be noblemen, for some of the titles descending from the original freemen had been forfeited by rebellion. Among some 35,000 families which could still claim to be noble, the original equality had disappeared. They now formed three strata. The lowest, comprising 14,000 or 15,000 families, consisted of 'sandalled' or 'seven-plum-tree' nobles: men who owned less than a hide of land, and who could vote in county elections but not sit in county assemblies or take part in the Diet. The highest strata was composed of favoured Magyar families which had received vast estates from the Habsburgs. These titled nobles sat in person in an Upper House of the Diet, designed by the Habsburgs to check the energies of the Lower House. Between the sandalled and the titled nobles came the common nobles, or gentry.

Hungary was unique in all the Habsburg dominions in possessing a gentry. These were the men who were most tenacious of Hungary's historic rights. They preserved the old way of life in their manor houses, where they lived isolated from outside influences. They spoke the old language and wore the old dress. In the county assemblies they continually thwarted crown officials by declaring their measures illegal and refusing to execute them. Thus aristocratic Hungary was kept alive in spite of Joseph's inroads upon the Diet. The gentry were, if anything, more determined than the magnates to preserve robot, for the Turkish wars had so depopulated the country that great landowners would of a certainty entice away labourers from the fields of their less wealthy neighbours if the serfs were freed from their obligations. In 1790 the gentry were ready to fight for the maintenance of traditional Hungary. They were supported by the vast number of lawyers whose main source of income lay in aristocratic disputes concerning the ownership of land. Joseph's Patent of 30 January failed to satisfy them because it fixed no date for the meeting of the Diet. The Hungarian Estates burnt the records of Joseph's government as his body was carried to the tomb.

In the Austrian Netherlands the success of revolt was due to the fact that privileged Estates were joined by a genuine reform party from among the non-privileged orders. The existence of this party owed much to Joseph II, whose changes stimulated political thought in Belgium to a degree unknown for two centuries. Under the lenient eye of his censors, new journals appeared and were allowed to comment on political affairs. In 1785 the *Journal général de l'Europe* was created by the 26 year old Lebrun, son of a poor family of Noyon, whose meteoric career was to make him a minister of France in 1792 and a victim of the guillotine in 1793. Lebrun earned protection from Joseph by attacking the outmoded claims of the Estates of Brabant, and went on to expound the doctrine of popular sovereignty. When the Dutch revolt of 1787 was followed by the outbreak of the French Revolution in 1789, many Belgian newspaper readers identified their own situation with that of their two neighbours, and felt oppressed by a sovereign who would not allow them to develop their own institutions in harmony with traditional ways of living. They began to think that if the Estates were assisted in delivering the Belgian provinces from Habsburg despotism, genuine constitutional reform might afterwards be forced upon the privileged orders.

At the beginning of 1789 a small group of reformers began to meet in Brussels in the house of Jean-François Vonck, a lawyer attached to the Council of Brabant. The group included Vonck's colleagues Verlooy, De Lausnay, and Willems, two more lawyers De Brouwers and Van den Eynde, and a young priest De Broux. In the spring of 1789 they formed a secret society, *Pro Aris et Focis*, whose aims were to build up an army of Belgian patriots beyond the frontiers and to stimulate revolution inside the country by means of pamphlets. It was hoped that the patriotic army would invade the country simultaneously with rebellion in every province.

Success depended largely on Vonck's ability to ally with the more aristocratic rebels, and on the amount of support he could obtain among the non-privileged classes. The nobles and clergy had found a leader in Henri van der Noot, a lawyer from an aristocratic family who had fled abroad in 1788 after a boisterous attack on Austrian despotism. Van der Noot pinned great faith in the possibility of Prussian and Dutch military support, and at first he rejected with scorn the overtures of Vonck, but his negotiations with the Prussian king and the Dutch Stadholder proved futile and he turned to Vonck in the autumn of 1789. The latter had more chance of stirring up the Belgian people when they were no longer seduced by rumours of foreign legions winning their freedom for them. His most enthusiastic supporters were lawyers and professional men who, like himself, came from bourgeois or peasant families and had fought an uphill struggle against wealthier and more privileged rivals. Some support came from financial, commercial, and industrial circles, where enterprising men resented the restrictions imposed upon them by guilds and corporations, and resented too the mercantilist policy of Joseph II.

In the towns there was much poverty, due largely to the fact that industry was too backward to absorb the growing population. In Brussels, Antwerp and Ghent a quarter of the people were registered for poor relief. Vonck had no social programme with which to make an energetic appeal to the masses, however; his views on all topics corresponded to those of the bourgeois members of the French Constituent Assembly. The peasants were on the whole better off than those of neighbouring French provinces. Feudal dues were lighter; in some provinces, notably Hainault and Flanders, they had almost disappeared. Vonck could play on the resentment caused by Joseph's decrees curtailing religious festivities, but this was hardly a sufficient basis for revolution. His justification for unleashing revolt with so little popular support came largely from the inspiration which he received from events in France, convincing him that freedom was dawning for the whole of western Europe, and from the knowledge that the Turkish War would prevent the main Austrian armies from descending upon the Netherlands.

By the autumn of 1789 Vonck had succeeded in smuggling out of the country more than 2,000 patriots and arming them in Holland under the leadership of a disappointed army colonel, Van der Mersch. Revolutionary propaganda inside the country received a serious check when the Austrian authorities succeeded in dispersing the Brussels conspirators. Nevertheless when Van der Mersch invaded Belgium on 24 October he was immediately successful. Soldiers deserted from the Austrian army by the hundred. Ghent fell to the patriots on 17 November; Brussels rose in revolt and was taken on 12 December; the Austrian army retreated in disarray to Luxembourg. The Belgian provinces were delivered from the Austrian yoke; on 10 January 1790 they became the United Belgian States, a republic.

4. LEOPOLD II AND THE POLICY OF COMPROMISE

On 20 February Joseph II died, declaring that everything he had attempted had been a failure. In this he was premature, as usual, for his successor managed to save a creditable amount from the wreck. Leopold II was 43 years old when he succeeded his brother. Like Joseph he was an indefatigable worker, devoted to the ideal of an efficient and resourceful state. For a generation he had been ruler of Tuscany, where he had rehabilitated the finances, reorganized the judicial system, encouraged industry, assisted the serfs, harnessed the church to the service of the state, and in other words conformed to a general pattern of eighteenth-century enlightenment. Unlike Joseph, however, he was not a slave to theory and he cared little for the appearances of power. He foresaw a day when sovereigns would be obliged to co-operate with their people, and he believed that if they acted skilfully they could co-operate to their own advantage. The French ambassador described him as a man who always bowed before a storm. Like a true Habsburg he was determined to keep as much power as possible in the hands of the monarchy. In the circumstances he decided to strike a mean between capitulating to the aristocracy and exposing the Crown to rebellion.

First of all, however, he intended to recover Belgium. He saw at once that divisions between the rebels were widening. Vonck had hoped that in a free Belgium the bourgeoisie and peasant farmers would be represented in an Estates General, endowed with legislative and executive powers wide enough to overcome the narrow conservatism of the provincial Estates. These hopes were quickly squashed. As soon as the Austrians were driven out, Van der Noot established his ascendancy. Everywhere he, and not Vonck, was regarded as the deliverer of the country. Van der Noot's exploits in foreign courts were well known whereas Vonck's work was, of necessity, secret; Van der Noot was boisterous and aggressive whilst Vonck

AOP E

was self-effacing and dogged by ill-health. The nobles, clergy, and trade corporations were increasingly frightened by events in France and were ready to believe that Vonck, like the French revolutionaries he so much admired, wished to overturn the social system and replace a despotic monarch with a despotic assembly. Van der Noot was joined by an ambitious cleric, Van Eupen, and a Jesuit publicist, Feller; between them they succeeded in placing the new Belgium in the hands of the old provincial Estates, rendered stronger than ever by the destruction of Austria's centralizing influence. The new Estates General was composed merely of delegates from the provincial Estates, and its powers were confined to questions of defence and foreign policy.

At first the Vonckists could only protest in pamphlets and posters, but on 2 March they obtained unexpected encouragement from Leopold II. The latter offered Belgium a real constitutional régime in which laws and financial measures would receive the sanction of a representative assembly and government personnel would be drawn from the Belgian people. Leopold as Grand Duke of Tuscany had spoken of a day when kings would be obliged to rule within genuine constitutional limits, but how far he was sincere in offering to patronize the democratic movement in Belgium is uncertain. From a tactical point of view the move was completely successful, for Van der Noot ignored the offer and openly revealed the selfishness of the aristocratic rebels. When the Vonckists protested, bands of hooligans, almost certainly organized and paid by agents of Van der Noot, attacked the houses of the reformers in three terrible days of rioting (16-18 March 1790). Vonck and other democratic leaders were obliged to flee into exile and the Statists, as Van der Noot's supporters came to be called, were left in possession of the Belgian Republic. They were no longer united even among themselves, however. The White Terror which had been unleashed against the reformers brought to the surface the extremists who combined religious fanaticism with a narrow defence of privilege and provincialism. More moderate elements were alienated, especially by the acts of violence committed in the name of law and order. The division between Brabant, where the privileged orders were strong, and provinces such as Hainault and Flanders where the ancien régime had long ago weakened, became more marked.

Leopold, meanwhile, was working for an understanding between Austria and Prussia: no easy task. Prussia expected Austria to acquire new territories in the eastern Mediterranean as a result of the war against Turkey. She sought compensation by meddling in Belgium and Hungary and by amassing an army in Silesia. The Prussian minister Hertzberg dreamed of forcing Austria to restore Galicia to the Poles, who in return would deliver Danzig, Thorn, and Posen to Prussia; Frederick William II dreamed of seizing the

Austrian Netherlands and perhaps even Bohemia. There was thus much more at stake than the memory of old hatreds. Leopold's subtle negotiations eventually succeeded, however. He accepted the good offices of the British government, which informed Frederick William of its hostility to further Prussian aggrandizement. On 27 July 1790 the two continental powers signed the convention of Reichenbach, whereby Austria agreed to withdraw from the Turkish war without major territorial gains, and Prussia abandoned her schemes regarding Galicia and the Netherlands.

The road was now open for the subjugation of the United Belgian States, for the rebels, divided among themselves and divided from the majority of the people, could not stand out against Austrian troops without the help they had come to expect from Prussia. Britain and Holland were desirous, for commercial reasons, that Belgium should return safely into Austrian hands, and France was too much occupied with her own affairs to exploit the situation across her frontier. Leopold's troops entered Belgium in November 1790; by December reconquest was complete. Leopold agreed to restore the political situation which had existed before Joseph implemented his centralizing schemes, knowing, however, that the prestige accruing from recent successes would strengthen the Crown in relation to the Estates. The abandonment of the Vonckists could be excused by references to their failure to win the support of the people; Leopold could argue that Belgians needed to be led along the path of progress by a benevolent despot. Some intellectual groups were bitterly resentful, however, and French revolutionaries were encouraged to regard Belgium as an open field for French expansion.

To stave off the danger to monarchy in the rest of his dominions Leopold made one immediate concession to the demands of the aristocracy. He abolished the edict of February 1789 concerning serfdom and taxation. It was a very great concession. It doomed the Habsburg dominions to a wasteful form of agricultural labour, for Leopold's successors set themselves resolutely against all change, and robot remained alive in the Habsburg empire until the revolution of 1848. No class desirous or capable of great capitalist enterprise appeared in the Habsburg lands. Leopold lost the chance of tapping the wealth of the landowners through regular taxation, and since the aristocracy would never voluntarily make adequate contribution to the finances of the state Francis II was obliged to pay for the wars against France with foreign loans.

In the western half of the Habsburg empire this immediate concession saved Leopold from most of the political demands of the aristocracy. He summoned Diets in every province to formulate claims against the Crown, but by the time they were ready to do so circumstances had changed considerably. The privileged orders soon became alarmed at the progress of revolution in France, and Leopold was not averse to using the ambitions of the Fourth Estate to chasten them into an accommodating mood. He encouraged burghers and peasants to petition for representation in the Diets, and patronized writers who published books demanding popular liberties. Leopold apparently believed the rumours, engineered by French émigrés at Coblentz, that the French government was employing agents to foment revolution throughout Europe, and he expelled a number of foreigners, including Da Ponte, librettist of Mozart's most popular operas, who had hitherto enjoyed asylum in Austria, but this ostentatious sign of panic merely served to stress the dangers threatening the aristocracy. The latter, moreover, suddenly found themselves isolated from the peasantry. The re-establishment of robot at a time when all farmers were busily engaged in work on their own fields caused widespread unrest, as anyone might have foreseen, and the peasants vented their wrath not on the Emperor but on the landlords. The latter met with passive and sometimes active resistance when they tried to extract labour services from village communities; they appealed to the government to proclaim martial law and to send military forces to discipline the peasants but Leopold steadily refused to intervene.

In the hereditary lands Leopold played off one Diet against another and arrived at a lowest common denominator of concessions. From a constitutional point of view he agreed only that the Diets should be summoned regularly to consider the tax demands of the Crown. The nobles of Bohemia were more demanding, but without the support of the peasants who formed nine-tenths of the population they could no longer threaten rebellion. They pressed for recognition of the rights which had belonged to Bohemia in 1745, before the centralizing measures of Maria Theresa, but Leopold insisted on taking as his pattern the year 1764, when the main administrative changes had already been carried out. He agreed to undergo a separate coronation as King of Bohemia, but in doing so he paid no more than lip-service to an illusion of Bohemian autonomy. He refused to grant full legislative powers to the Bohemian Diet. He promised to consult the Diet concerning fundamental changes, but refused to recognize the constitution as inviolable. Hungary with her militant gentry secured more real concessions. In agreeing to be crowned King of Hungary Leopold reiterated the contract with the Hungarian 'nation'. Its ancient freedoms were once more declared inviolable. The Diet was assured of regular meetings, and the county assemblies were allowed to resume control of local administration.

Nowhere were the peasants completely sacrificed to the landowners, however. Leopold saved Joseph's emancipation edict of 1781 and resisted all attempts by the Diets to strengthen the legal jurisdiction of landlords over serfs. Nor were other reforms entirely lost. The threefold hierarchy of law-courts, and the appointment of judges by examination, were retained.

Some concessions had to be made to the Catholic clergy, who had supported aristocratic demands in the Diets. The bishops in all the Austrian, Bohemian, and Polish lands were allowed to present their grievances against Joseph's church measures. In reply to their requests Leopold restored tithes, saved the monasteries which had not already been dissolved, and allowed the church to re-establish seminaries. Religious toleration was maintained, however, in spite of demands by the Catholic bishops for the abolition of Joseph's edict.

Leopold hoped, indeed, to improve upon Joseph's enlightened policy and not only wean educated commoners away from their alliance with the aristocracy but bind them in real affection to the monarchy. The harsher lines of Joseph's policy were soon smoothed away. A chair in the Czech language was established in the University of Prague, and secondary schools in the city were allowed to include Czech in their syllabuses. The fierce punishments prescribed by Joseph's penal code were abolished and the police were instructed that no-one should be imprisoned for longer than three days without charge. Count Pergen resigned his office as Minister of Police after repeated criticism from Leopold and was not replaced. The police fell once more under the supervision of provincial governors and abandoned their interference in politics to concentrate on the detection of crime. Experiments with modern methods to prevent crime were made in Vienna, where each police district was provided with a physician, a surgeon, and a midwife, and more than 16,000 patients received free treatment in the first year of the new régime. In economic matters Leopold moved towards a freer system by reducing import duties on a few essential commodities and working for an understanding with Prussia.

How far Leopold intended to fulfil the ambitions of the Fourth Estate for a share in political power is uncertain. He allowed one non-noble member to sit in the Diet of Styria and began to prepare plans for wider representation in the Hungarian and Bohemian Diets. Time might have justified the liberal hopes entertained by some non-noble members of the Emperor's entourage, but none was granted to Leopold. He died on 1 March 1792 leaving the cares of his vast dominions to his inexperienced son. Among them was the growing menace of revolutionary France.

5. THE HOLY ROMAN EMPIRE AND THE OUTBREAK OF WAR WITH FRANCE

When news of the French Revolution first filtered into the Habsburg Empire, Joseph II's only anxiety was lest discontented groups among his common subjects should draw encouragement from the French example. Police measures were taken but no military precautions were envisaged. The fact that the Revolution would, by releasing popular energies, make France the most frightening military power in Europe was not yet apparent.

Most continental rulers connected military strength with monarchical despotism, and when the events of October 1789 revealed the impotence of the French monarchy Louis XVI's brother sovereigns assumed that France's days as a Great Power were over. Joseph II assured himself that France would not be able to intervene on behalf of her old ally, Turkey, and that the dismemberment of Poland could continue unhindered. A succession of mutinies in the French army in 1789 and 1790 confirmed the opinion that France was finished as a military nation. The French themselves subscribed to the view that war was the preserve of despots. When Louis XVI showed signs of supporting his ally Spain in the Nootka Sound dispute with Britain, the Constituent Assembly held a debate on foreign policy which left no doubt that the deputies believed war to be a weapon designed by kings for enhancing their own power. In deciding that henceforward the king must seek the permission of the Assembly before declaring war, the deputies assumed that the king would always want war and that the Assembly must therefore seek peace. On 22 May 1790 the Constituent Assembly issued a declaration repudiating wars of conquest.

Leopold could not become indifferent to events in France, however. The Habsburgs obtained their title of Emperor not from their dominions in central Europe but from their overlordship of the princes of Germany. Since the fifteenth century Habsburg rulers had been elected Holy Roman Emperors in almost unbroken succession. The power accruing from the title was fast waning, but German princes who chafed at subservience to the Emperor in days of prosperity were likely to call for his assistance in hours of need. To those near the Rhine, the French Revolution brought a greater need than they had known for decades.

In so disunited a country as Germany, the situation created by the French Revolution was bound to differ considerably from place to place. In some of the small principalities which made up the 365 states of the Holy Roman Empire, rulers had patronized the *Aufklärung* in recent years, welcoming philosophers and writers at their courts and carrying out paternal reforms under their guidance. Such was the position in Brunswick, where Duke Charles Ferdinand was visited by French savants and praised by Mirabeau; in Schaumburg-Lippe, ruled by Count William, the friend of Herder; in Gotha, Saxe-Weimar, Anhalt-Dessau, and above all in Baden, where Duke Charles Frederick embraced the doctrines of the Physiocrats, befriended Klopstock, Herder and Jung-Stilling, and employed Edelsheim as his political councillor. The opening scenes of the French Revolution were greeted by leaders of intellectual opinion in a host of German centres. Klopstock wrote an ode regretting that he had not a hundred voices to celebrate the birth of liberty; Herder proclaimed the French Revolution the most important event since the Reformation in the history of liberty. Young men from

German universities visited Paris to see for themselves the new opportunities created by revolutionary equality; gathering around Manon Roland and her talkative friends from the Gironde they sent home enthusiastic reports of intellectual freedom and breadth of vision. Newspapers circulated freely in enlightened states and commented at length on the reforms of the Constituent Assembly; Christian Schubart in Swabia devoted the whole of his weekly *Chronicle* to news from France.

Enthusiasm among intellectuals bore no relation to everyday life in Germany, however. Princes had cultivated the Enlightenment merely as an exotic plant with which to decorate their courts, much as they laid out miniature gardens in imitation of Versailles; it had made no deep impression on the life of the people. Society remained strictly divided into three Estates, aristocracy, commons, and peasantry. The aristocracy retained a traditional right to the chief military and administrative posts, and with them the right to admission at court. Landowners administered the law on their estates and in the surrounding districts. Many nobles were content to remain on their estates, differing little in education from their peasants, striving to become good gentlemen farmers, and presiding over local entertainments such as harvest feasts, hunts, and fairs. These 'junkers' proved for the most part to be conservative in their political views, hating the French Revolution from the start and praising the spirit of obedience which characterized the German peasantry. Other nobles copied French fashions and cultivated a great many social mannerisms; they affected to despise the efforts of the *canaille* and refused to speak seriously of the Revolution.

The commons, as an Estate, embraced all those persons who belonged by birth neither to the nobility nor to the peasantry. The term was usually applied to inhabitants of cities and towns, thereby covering three distinct social classes – upper bourgeoisie, lower bourgeoisie and workers – with very little in common. In imperial cities, subject directly to the Empire, government had usually become the preserve of a few wealthy families which formed a privileged class quite as conservative as the nobles; in provincial towns, subject to the territorial prince, many of the wealthier families had voluntarily surrendered their civic rights and duties in order to obtain privileges from the court. In this way the upper bourgeoisie divided itself off from the artisans, shop-owners, and inn-keepers, becoming a docile part of the *ancien régime*. The lower bourgeoisie, for their part, despised the domestic servants, carters, journeymen, and odd-jobmen who formed Germany's working class. While dramatists such as Lessing and Schiller criticized the arrogance, ignorance, and uselessness of nobles and princes, no bourgeois class arose, as in France, to upset the régime of privilege and despotism, and no class appeared to play the rôle of the Paris sans-culottes. In sleepy little German towns too much depended on patronage from manor house and castle hall. Only in the flourishing port of Hamburg, where merchants traded widely with Europe and America, was there any spontaneous expression of sympathy from the bourgeoisie for the French Revolution. Here in 1790 a large gathering took place to celebrate the fall of the Bastille, and toasts were drunk to 'the German revolution'. Sieveking afterwards created a society for the discussion of foreign news, but the city authorities introduced police measures, and quiet was restored.

The most enthusiastic commentators tended to stress, from the first, the basic differences between France and Germany, and to point out that the French example could not wisely be copied in the Holy Roman Empire. When chaos began to hinder the reforms of the Constituent Assembly, German writers looked with increasing admiration at the despotic methods of their own enlightened rulers. The *Braunchsweiger Journal*, one of the most advanced newspapers in Germany, defended autocracy as the mother of progress; Goethe's *Venetian Epigrams* of 1790 urged princes to save their people from the disasters witnessed in France by taking reform into their own hands. The conservative note was nowhere more insistent than in Hanover, ruled by the King of England. In the University of Göttingen students greatly admired English parliamentary institutions. Brandes and Rehberg asserted the superiority of traditional growth over sudden reform and praised Burke rather than Rousseau. Several translations of Burke's *Reflections* appeared in Hanover and a famous one in Prussia by Gentz. Of all Germany's great thinkers only Kant and Herder, while regretting acts of violence, consistently praised the French Revolution as a step in the liberty of mankind. France, said Herder, was fulfilling her particular destiny: Germany, too, had a part to play, but a different part. German intellectuals were already on the way to developing their own political creed, romanticism; which, while owing much to the French Revolution, became in many hands a repudiation of all western trends of thought.

Eastward from the Elbe stretched the great kingdom of Prussia, where monarchical despotism had reached a pitch of success unparalleled in Europe. Here the resentment felt by the aristocracy at the loss of feudal powers had never reached the point of open revolt, for Frederick II had maintained the policy of co-operation inaugurated by the Great Elector, fitting the nobles into his absolutist state with a degree of tact unknown to Joseph II. The nobility became the officer class and was encouraged to think of itself as possessing superior military qualities. Nobles were also given preferential treatment in the civil service and assured of the highest and most remunerative posts. Provincial diets were allowed to retain wide powers in local administration, resembling those of English justices of the peace, and nobles collected taxes from their peasants and exercised manorial jurisdiction on their estates. Feudal relationships between peasants and landowners were left intact, and the nobles became part of a threefold hierarchy of peasantry, aristocracy, and crown which it was in their own interests to maintain. Alongside the hierarchy, but excluded from it, a small but prosperous bourgeoisie grew up as a result of the Crown's mercantilist policy. Merchants and craftsmen knew themselves to be dependent on the state for advancement in a primarily agricultural community. The chief ambition of the Prussian bourgeoisie in the decades preceding the Revolution was to purchase titles of nobility from the Crown, or to purchase 'noble' land (a procedure forbidden by law but frequently connived at) and thereby enter the hierarchy of state service.

There were some signs that enlightenment had begun to outstrip Frederick the Great towards the end of his reign as it finally outstripped Joseph II. Voices were raised in intellectual circles against the despotism which seemed to be both the means and the end of monarchical reforms. Frederick died in 1786 however, and in ensuing years his successes only were remembered. Frederick William II's weird religious activities roused fears lest Prussia, whose fame had dazzled all Germany in Frederick the Great's time, should sink into obscurantism and disrepute. The French Revolution created an opportunity for Prussian intellectuals, in the salons of Henriette Herz and Rahel Levin, to draw parallels between the reforms of the Constituent Assembly and the reforms of Frederick the Great, and to praise the latter as a warning to Frederick William II not to depart too far from the ways of his illustrious predecessor. In other words, the French Revolution was a stimulus to conservatism in Prussia, and Frederick William II, a vain and weak man, had some excuse for looking upon it as a purely external event which he might use in the interests of his foreign policy. The Convention of Reichenbach was a blow to his pride and a setback to his plan of obtaining a part of Poland. In his vainglorious way he allowed himself to be persuaded by French émigrés that he could recover his prestige by sponsoring a crusade against the French Revolution. At the same time, if Austria could be detached from Russia and persuaded to join in a war against France the two German powers could seize a share of Poland from under the nose of Catherine II.

The biggest obstacle to this scheme was Leopold II. Leopold knew that he had been welcomed by his subjects as a peacemaker; he had no desire to engage gratuitously in a war against France or to enter into dangerous competitions with Catherine the Great. He showed himself to be a true friend to Poland when he recognized the Constitution of May 1791, designed to strengthen the remnant of the country against marauding neighbours. He was distressed by the dangers surrounding his sister, Marie Antoinette, and he believed that the triumph of mob rule in France would constitute a threat to all the crowned heads of Europe, but he felt sure that the best solution to the problem would be for Louis XVI to compromise with the revolutionaries, as he, Leopold, was compromising with rebels in the Habsburg dominions. He urged his brother-in-law to accept the constitution which was being prepared in the Assembly. Émigré princes were cold-shouldered at Vienna, and Frederick William II was obliged to retire into the background, whilst his place as the possible leader of a crusade was taken up by his rival, Gustavus III, King of Sweden.

Among those who were urging the Emperor to intervene against the French Revolution none were more insistent than the princes of the Rhinelands. In their territories, which were easily accessible from France, intellectual leaders were deeply imbued with French ideas. At Mayence, Müller, secretary to the archbishop, and Forster, librarian at the University, were among the first to propagate the idea of annexation of the left bank of the Rhine to France. A foretaste of things to come was presented to those German princes who owned land in Alsace, enclaved in French territory. When feudal dues were abolished by the Constituent Assembly on 4 August 1789, the peasants on these lands refused to continue paying feudal dues, announcing that they were by right French and entitled to the liberties of Frenchmen. The princes protested to the Constituent Assembly, but a committee under the influence of Merlin of Douai announced (October 1790) that the whole of Alsace belonged to France by the will of the people. Mirabeau recognized the threat of war underlying this principle, and sought to placate the German princes by suggesting that they be given compensation for their losses, but the princes would not accept the compromise and referred their case to the Diet of the Empire at Ratisbon. There the matter dragged on, while feeling was embittered on both sides. The ecclesiastical Electors of Mainz, Trier, and Cologne gave asylum to French émigré princes, who began arming their followers for a descent on Paris. In June 1791 tension was increased by the flight of the French royal family.

The recapture of Louis XVI and Marie Antoinette at Varennes and their subsequent imprisonment in the Tuileries seemed to Leopold a fulfilment of his worst fears regarding France: extremists were now in control. No European sovereign could ever again, said Kaunitz, be confident 'that he was bequeathing an undamaged crown to his successors'. Leopold issued an urgent summons to European governments to co-operate in restraining revolutionary forces in France. The only warm response came from the King of Prussia, who met with Leopold to draw up the Declaration of Pillnitz (27 August 1791). The two sovereigns declared that in concert with other European powers they would be ready to restore Louis XVI to a position in which he could strengthen the foundations of monarchy. Leopold must have known that Britain was wedded to peace at this time and that there was very little chance of a concert of Powers intervening in France.

Possibly he hoped that the revolutionaries would not realize the emptiness of his threat and that it would intimidate them into respecting the monarchy. They certainly took the threat seriously, but it had the opposite effect from intimidating them. Marie Antoinette was near to the truth when she said, 'The Emperor has betrayed us'.

Leopold could never undo the impression created by the Declaration of Pillnitz, although he tried. When Louis XVI ratified the Constitution of 1791, Leopold believed that the threat to monarchy had passed and that the time had come for him to co-operate with the new constitutional government of France. In December, 1791, he urged the Elector of Trier to agree to a request from the French government to disperse the armed gathering of émigrés at Coblentz. Nothing could convince the French people that the Emperor was their friend however. Austria had long been hated and suspected. The belief, in France, that the Habsburg monarch was about to send armies to Paris, spearheaded by an émigré force and assisted by a royalist revolt, tempted French politicians to advance their own ambitions by fanning the flames of war. The Comte de Narbonne, created Minister for War on 6 December 1791 at the instigation of the Feuillant group, believed that he could strengthen the power of the Crown by leading a limited war against the Rhine Electors. This scheme was foiled by an announcement from Leopold (21 December 1791) that he would defend the Elector of Trier against French aggression, and Narbonne found himself in alliance with the Brissotins in urging a full-scale war upon Austria. In January 1792 the Brissotins challenged the Emperor to state whether or not he regarded himself as an ally of France by the treaty of 1756. Leopold continued to work for peace, although the Brissotins, with their appeals to popular passion, were exactly the kind of group he had feared to see in France. The Jacobin belief in sovereignty of the people could not be other than totally alien to the Habsburg monarch, whose power rested solely on dynastic right. There is something, indeed, to be said for Ranke's view that war between the new France and the old Europe was inevitable. In February Leopold concluded a defensive alliance with Prussia, hoping against hope that this would deter France from declaring war. On 1 March, the date set by the Brissotins for an answer to their ultimatum, Leopold was dead.

Francis II was young and impetuous, with a taste for military adventure. In a typically Habsburg way he combined a love of chivalry with a desire for aggrandizement. Consequently when Frederick William of Prussia emerged again into the limelight, after the assassination of Gustavus III at a masquerade on 16 March, he found that his schemes concerning France and Poland met with the approval of the new Habsburg monarch. Kaunitz, who had hoped to bully France without fighting her, resigned office and was replaced in Francis's counsels by the more warlike Cobenzl. On 20 April the French declared war on the Habsburg dominions and rushed into the assault. They were easily repulsed, and the road lay open for a counter-attack. In July, Francis II travelled to the free imperial city of Frankfurt to receive the great crown of Charlemagne from the hands of the Elector of Mainz, Arch-Chancellor of the Holy Roman Empire. A few days later he moved to Mainz to meet the King of Prussia and a large assembly of princes, who were to prepare a crusade against revolutionary France. Thus the stage was set for a war which many contemporaries saw as a conflict between the old world and the new, and which some historians have seen as the opening of a long struggle between Germany and France for hegemony in Europe.

CHAPTER IV

The Revolution at War, 1792-4

I. THE SECOND REVOLT OF THE PARIS CROWD

In FRANCE the immediate effects of war were military disaster and economic distress. Lafayette, the commander-in-chief of the French forces, soon found that the regular army was in a state of disintegration. Two thirds of the officers had deserted, the troops were undisciplined, and arms and provisions were seriously short. Volunteers raised by the Constituent Assembly were enthusiastic but untrained, and there was friction between them and the regulars. Convinced that revolutionary enthusiasm would carry the day against mercenary troops of foreign despots, and that the people of Liége and the Austrian Netherlands would welcome French deliverers, Dumouriez planned a general offensive, with three spearheads converging on Brussels. The plan met with total failure. Two columns advancing on Tournai and Mons fled in confusion after the first contact with the enemy, and Lafayette failed to move the main army up the Givet salient in the ridiculously short time allotted to him. In two months all France's hopes were crushed and the frontier lay open to the enemy. Immediate invasion was prevented only by the excessive caution of the Duke of Brunswick, who would not advance until the ripening of the harvest ensured supplies from the countryside.

Preparations for war, though inadequate for victory, were sufficient to strain France's finances, and the assignats began on the downward course which was to bring economic crises for many years. By June 1792 they had declined to 57% of their nominal value. Rural disorder, never wholly cured, became once more rampant. The harvest of 1791 was fair, but peasants were unwilling to sell grain for rapidly depreciating paper money, and bread was dear in the towns. Sugar was scarce, due to a negro revolt in St. Domingo in August 1791. Merchants and shopkeepers were suspected, not altogether unjustly, of hoarding supplies to sell on a rising market, and food riots took place in Paris in January and February 1792.

It was not long before popular agitators began blaming the Brissotins. Marat, in the *Ami du peuple*, and Hébert, in the *Père Duchesne*, hurled abuse at Brissot and his intellectual friends from the Gironde. The latter tried to deflect popular anger on to 'secret enemies'. The king and queen, they said, guided by a sinister 'Austrian committee', were disclosing France's plans to the enemy, and aristocratic officers were leading her soldiers into defeat and desertion. Roland actually sent a letter to the king threatening him with insurrection if he did not mend his ways. When Louis retaliated on 13 June by dismissing the Brissotin ministry, accusations against him were redoubled. The Brissotins thus helped to goad the sans-culottes into another wave of revolutionary activity, which resulted in three great outbursts: the invasion of the Tuileries on 20 June, the attack on the monarchy on 10 August, and the massacre of the prisoners in September 1792.

All three outbursts were fomented in the sections, where economic distress combined with fear and anger provided fertile soil for agitators. On 16 June the two faubourgs of Saint-Marcel and Saint-Antoine asked the Commune to allow them to parade under arms on the anniversary of the Tennis Court Oath. They hoped for support from the mayor, Pétion, who had been elected by the sections in November 1791 to replace the discredited Bailly. Pétion was alarmed, but afraid to lose his popularity, so he temporized until it was too late to make a decision either way. It was thus a disorganized band which gathered on 20 June and presented a petition to the Assembly. In the afternoon the demonstrators turned their attention to the Tuileries and, finding an unguarded door, penetrated to the royal apartments. Until 8 or 10 in the evening a continuous stream of sans-culottes passed before the king, shouting slogans and abuse at him, and making him wear the red cap of liberty and drink the health of the nation. Louis took it all calmly, and when Pétion arrived and harangued the people they agreed to go away.

The Brissotins, like their protégé Pétion, could not be sure whether the insurrectionary forces they had summoned up were friends or foes. Paris was always a doubtful quantity. Patriotic citizens of provincial towns seemed more reliable: in Marseille and elsewhere detachments of the National Guard were attacking counter-revolutionaries with great zest. The Brissotins conceived the idea of summoning guardsmen from the provinces – *fédérés* they were called – to form a camp in Paris for the defence of the Revolution. This was a disastrous miscalculation. As soon as the *fédérés* arrived they were indoctrinated by agitators in the sections and joined forces with the sans-culottes. The marching song of the Marseillais contingent became the theme song of the Revolution.

The courage displayed by the king on 20 June provoked a slight reaction in his favour. Loyal addresses were sent from the departments, and Lafayette arrived in Paris offering to carry out a military *coup* on behalf of the king. Parisians firmly believed that royalists were planning to attack 'patriots' as soon as foreign armies crossed the frontier. On 19 July Austria and Prussia agreed on a plan of invasion. The Prussian army under the Duke of Brunswick was to advance through Coblentz and Verdun, flanked by Austrian armies and supported by émigrés. On 1 August the Duke prepared his ground by issuing two declarations, known as Brunswick's Manifesto, threatening to destroy Paris if the Royal family were harmed.

For weeks it was evident that insurrection was brewing in Paris. Lafayette, whose offer to the king became known, hurried back to camp to escape the fury of the mob. Forty-seven out of forty-eight sections petitioned the Assembly for the deposition of the king, and the faubourg Saint-Antoine warned the deputies that the sections would rise in arms if the petition had not been granted by the 9th. The Brissotins wavered, and the Assembly reflected their indecision. The Assembly admitted passive citizens to the National Guard, agreed that the sections should be allowed to meet at any time, and carried a proposal by Carnot that all citizens should be issued with pikes. Yet it threw out a motion for the impeachment of Lafayette and put aside the petition for the king's deposition. Where the Brissotins and the Assembly hesitated, Robespierre stepped forward. In a speech at the Jacobin club on 29 July he said that a National Convention ought to be elected to consider the deposition of the king.

The Commune, like the Assembly, blew hot and cold, sometimes influenced by Danton, the popular deputy-proctor, and sometimes by Pétion, the Brissotin mayor. On the night of 9 August, 28 sections answered an appeal from the faubourg Saint-Antoine and sent 3 representatives each to form a Revolutionary Commune. All through a hot summer's night the new Commune and the old sat in adjoining rooms in the Town Hall, while crowds gathered in the sections. At seven o'clock on the following morning the Revolutionary Commune announced that it had superseded its legal rival. Shortly afterwards, *fédérés* from the Breton and Marseillais contingents marched to the Tuileries. A column from the faubourg Saint-Antoine brought cannon. The insurgents mustered about 20,000 men, but they were haphazardly armed, and they needed courage to face 900 Swiss mercenaries, 200 knights of Saint Louis, and 2,000 National Guardsmen on duty at the palace. Muddle and treachery came to their assistance, however. Roederer, procureur of the Paris department and official protector of the executive power, advised the king to abandon the palace and take refuge in the Assembly. Always anxious to avoid bloodshed, Louis agreed, but forgot to leave orders for his guards. Mandat, commander of the National Guard, left the palace in answer to a summons from the Town Hall, and the guardsmen fraternized with the insurgents. Only the Swiss put up a hopeless fight. More than 500 died at their posts or were killed in an attempt to reach the Assembly; 60 were taken prisoner and slaughtered by order of the Commune; only 300 survived. The insurgents lost 90 *fédérés* and 300 citizens from the Paris sections. Napoleon Bonaparte, who watched the attack from the safety of a friend's house nearby, ventured to cross the Tuileries gardens in the evening and found them strewn with bodies like a battlefield.

The Brissotins still hesitated, unwilling to recognize the triumph of insurrectionary forces yet afraid to repudiate them. At their suggestion the Legislative Assembly did not depose the king outright but suspended him from his functions and ordered a National Convention to be elected by universal suffrage to draw up a new constitution. A temporary executive council was set up to supervise the ministries. Roland and other Brissotin nominees found places on this council, but a more significant appointment was that of Danton as Minister of Justice. Generous, courageous, and boisterous, Danton was loved and admired by the sans-culottes: and the Brissotins hoped that he would provide a link between themselves and the two bodies which were now supreme in Paris, the sections and the Commune. Each section was given its own battalion of the National Guard, and Santerre, the popular brewer of the faubourg Saint-Antoine, was made commander. The Commune took over the administrative duties of the district and completely overshadowed the department of Paris.

Popular opinion persisted in the belief that there had been a sinister royalist plot, foiled in the nick of time by the patriotic attack on the Tuileries. The anguish of the wounded, and the hardship suffered by families whose menfolk had been killed in the fighting, reinforced the demand for vengeance. The Assembly agreed to the wholesale arrest of suspects. Municipalities were entitled to make security regulations and imprison suspects for a year; in Paris the Commune set up a vigilance committee for the task with the murderous Marat as its leading member. Fear and anger increased when, on 17 August, Lafayette deserted to the Austrians. Meanwhile the Duke of Brunswick was advancing slowly but relentlessly towards the capital. On 20 August he reached Longwy, which capitulated after only three days' siege. Paris seethed with stories of plots and traitors, and the search for suspects was intensified. National Guardsmen were feverishly enrolled for the war. A new fear began to take shape in the sections: a fear that the prisoners would break out, slaughter defenceless citizens while their menfolk were at the front, and open the gates of the city to the enemy. Prison breaks had been known in the past, and the prisons were overcrowded and poorly staffed.

On Sunday 2 September, Paris heard news of the imminent fall of Verdun, only 140 miles from the capital. The Commune closed the barriers and called all citizens to arms. Bells rang in the sections to summon the National Guard. In the Assembly Danton thundered out his historic words, 'The tocsin you will hear today is not an alarm, but an alert. It sounds the charge against the enemies of our country. For victory we must dare, and dare, and dare again. So France will be saved.' At two o'clock in the afternoon, massacres began. A small band of refractory priests, arriving under escort at the Abbaye prison, were lynched by a mob. Another mob broke into the

Carmelite monastery and slaughtered more than 200 priests. During the night the massacre spread to the Conciergerie, the Châtelet, and La Force; on the next day to the Bicêtre, a prison-hospital for paupers and lunatics, and Salpêtrière, a place of detention for women offenders. In some of the prisons, ringleaders among the murderers set up mock tribunals before which the prisoners were led one by one, asked a few questions, and dragged away to be knifed. The massacres went on spasmodically until 6 or 7 September, by which time some 1,000 prisoners, almost half the total prison population of Paris, had been killed. Only a quarter of the victims were priests, nobles, or other political prisoners; the rest were common thieves, forgers, and vagrants.

With a few exceptions, such as the notable Stanislas Maillard, the identity of the murderers is not known. Evidence suggests that they were sansculottes of the militant type who had taken part in the attack on the Tuileries. Responsibility for the ghastly crime must be shared by all persons who were supposed to keep order and who failed to interfere – Danton as Minister of Justice, Roland as Minister of the Interior, Pétion as mayor, Santerre as commander of the National Guard, Marat as leader of the vigilance committee. Marat had long been advising volunteers to slay the prisoners before leaving Paris. His advice would not have been taken, however, if large numbers of persons had not been in agreement with it and if the vast population of Paris had not been willing to stand aside and let the killings go on. From Bordeaux and Marseille there were reports of the lynching of priests and aristocrats, and at Versailles a convoy of prisoners was wiped out by a local mob. These and similar incidents in the provinces, though on a smaller scale than the massacres at Paris, pointed to a common attitude of mind.

Exceptional danger made the killings seem necessary to many people at the time, but to explain is not to condone. Everyone disclaimed responsibility. The Brissotins blamed their enemies in the Jacobin club and made as much as they could of the part played by Marat and Danton. The latter, at least, ignored petty political squabbles in the great work of saving France. In reply to his inspired appeals, volunteers at the rate of 1,800 a day left for the front. Yet is was the old army of the line, with veterans of the American War, which won the first victory. Dumouriez, who had replaced Lafayette as commander-in-chief, withdrew the troops from the Belgian front and turned south, while Kellermann marched from Metz to meet him. They took their stand near the village of Valmy on the thickly wooded hills of the Argonne, intending to face the Prussian advance. They found, however, that Brunswick had out-manoeuvred them, moving his army round the French in an arc so that he stood between them and Paris. Brunswick expected Dumouriez to follow the old rules of strategy and retreat: instead, Kellermann's guns opened fire on the morning of 20 September. The cannonade went on all day. The Prussians lost less than 200 men, but their troops had never been under fire, and they were disheartened at the reverse. Brunswick could not rally them for a new attack, yet he could not advance on Paris leaving the French army undefeated behind him, cutting off his supplies from Verdun. He had no alternative but to retreat across the frontier. France's old royal artillery, reformed in the last decades of the *ancien régime*, had saved the Revolution. Dumouriez could return as a hero to his cherished scheme of invading the Austrian Netherlands, and the Brissotins could claim a little reflected glory with which to face the new parliament.

2. GIRONDINS AND JACOBINS

The National Convention, supposedly elected by universal suffrage, was in fact elected by less than a tenth of France's male population. Large numbers were debarred from the franchise for minor political misdemeanours, such as failure to take the oath to the nation, and even larger numbers stayed away from the polls out of fear or apathy. Many country people had got what they wanted out of the Revolution and were not interested in quarrelling politicians. Elections were indirect, in two stages, and the provinces, at any rate, elected the usual kind of middle class deputy. The majority in the Convention were men of the Plain, uncommitted to any party programme but anxious to defend the solid gains of the Revolution. This meant that they would support the group of politicians which offered the best guarantee against counter-revolution on the one hand and insurrectionary excesses on the other.

They had two groups to choose from. On the immediate left were the Brissotins, hardly a 'group' so much as a loosely-knit connection of some fifteen deputies. Though one or two of these had been elected by Parisian voters their attitude to affairs at the outset of the Convention was so typical of opinion everywhere in France that they won the approval of large numbers of provincial deputies. On the Mountain above the Brissotins sat a smaller but tighter group of radical deputies who claimed to embody the revolutionary ardour of the Parisian sans-culottes – Robespierre, Marat, Camille Desmoulins, Collot d'Herbois, Billaud-Varenne and others. Both Brissotins and Mountain were Jacobins, in the sense that they were members of the Jacobin club or fellow societies. In the Convention, however, the Brissotins and their supporters began to be known as Girondins – chiefly because Robespierre and his associates successfully portrayed them as reactionary provincials – whilst the Mountain retained the name Jacobin. This nomenclature would seem to imply that the Girondins were a large party with a distinct set of principles and a network of societies to support them, which was not so. They were merely a little set of notable individuals within the main body of the Jacobins, and the attacks made upon them by the Mountain arose largely out of personal jealousies.

The deputies united in their first important task, which was to declare the monarchy abolished. France was now a republic, 'one and indivisible' the slogan ran, though unity quickly came to an end among politicians. From September 1792 to June 1793 the Convention was the scene of a venemous campaign by the Mountain to isolate and eliminate the Gironde. Members of the Mountain criticized the Girondins for their conduct of the war and for their failure to quell traitors at home; they accused the Girondins of embittering the provinces against Paris, thereby endangering national unity; and they set themselves up as generous statesmen who would spread the benefits of the Revolution to all classes instead of confining them to the middle class as the Girondins were supposed to be doing. The Girondins, thus goaded, professed to be defenders of liberty against the dictatorial tendencies of the capital. Both sides had some degree of truth in its arguments, but to believe that their contentions arose from convinced policies is to take propaganda for fact.

The Girondins soon showed a lack of tactical sense by their hostility to Danton. The latter was one of the few men in the Convention who stood above personal feuds and factional disputes. 'I am without malice, not by virtue but by temperament', he once said of himself. 'Hatred is unknown to my character.' Roland, however, was bitterly jealous of Danton, and when the latter resigned from his post as Minister of Justice in order to take his seat in the Convention Roland accused him of peculation. It was an obvious accusation for a small-minded man to make, for Danton was never precise in money matters. Roland's spite drove Danton into association with Robespierre, who was himself suffering from attacks inspired by Madame Roland. Instead of taking advantage of the differences of opinion which existed between Danton, Robespierre, and Marat, the Girondins accused these three men of plotting to set up a dictatorship. As late as March 1793 Danton made overtures to the Girondins and was repulsed. The consequences were serious, for Danton was loved by the sans-culottes and admired by the Plain for his efforts in the national defence.

The Girondins were in the saddle when the contest with the Jacobins began. Their nominees held nearly all the places on the executive committee and their general, Dumouriez, was in command of victorious armies. The kind of war Brissot had dreamed of could begin in earnest. Savoy and Nice were occupied in September; Custine invaded German territory and entered Frankfurt in October; Dumouriez crossed into Belgium, won a resounding victory at Jemappes on 6 November, and entered Brussels in triumph. The river Scheldt, closed to all shipping except Dutch since 1648, was declared open. Worldly considerations were present in French minds from the start.

The wealth of foreign despots, and the gifts of liberated peoples, would, it was believed, restore France's finances and support her armies. On 19 November and 15 December 1792 the Convention issued two decrees which outlined for the first time the curious combination of liberty with conquest and enlightenment with plunder which was to characterize French foreign policy for a generation. The first decree, known as the Edict of Fraternity, offered brotherly assistance to all peoples who wished to regain their freedom. The second said that French generals occupying foreign territories must immediately abolish taxes, tithes, and feudal dues, suppress all existing authorities, proclaim sovereignty of the people, confiscate all property belonging to foreign rulers, receive French officials, and arrange for local elected assemblies to co-operate in apportioning the loot and supporting the French armies.

How far could offensive war be justified in the interests of self-defence? A Prussian immigrant, Anacharsis Cloots, had already in 1785 put forward the view that France should expand towards her natural frontiers, the Rhine, the Alps, and the Pyrenees. In January 1793 the doctrine of natural frontiers was proclaimed in the Convention by Danton, regardless of the fact that it was bound to bring Britain and Holland into the war. Brissotin diplomacy had hitherto been directed to keeping these two powers neutral, but Brissotin leaders dared not stand out against popular demand, and on 1 February 1793 Brissot himself introduced into the Convention a decree proclaiming war on Britain and Holland. It was voted unanimously. On 7 March the Convention declared war on Spain. Portugal held to her alliance with England; Sardinia and Naples entered the coalition; Catherine II of Russia, though refusing to declare war, forbade all commerce with France. Only Switzerland and Scandinavia remained neutral among European powers. 'It is all the tyrants of Europe that you now have to fight on land and sea', Brissot told his fellow Frenchmen. The task proved beyond their immediate resources, and the Girondins, who had claimed credit for victory, were held responsible for defeat.

The money taken from occupied territories was a drop in the ocean compared with the cost of war. The Finance Minister Cambon arranged for the issue of new assignats to the value of 40 million pounds, but they had not been printed when Dumouriez began the invasion of Holland. The latter's base of operation, Belgium, was seething with discontent at French exploitation. His troops were unpaid, ill-clothed, badly fed, and demoralized by a few months of inactivity. Discipline among the volunteers had never been strong, and many deserted when the raptures of attack gave place to the boredom of occupation. The men knew, too, that their families at home were not being cared for by the government. Roland, the Minister of the Interior, had no organizing abilities, and was encouraged by his wife to devote his time to party wrangling. Dumouriez himself was no longer the cocksure general who had pulled victory out of defeat in September 1792. Defeated at Neerwinden on 18 March, he evacuated Brussels, and when all his plans for a speedy victory against Austria were crushed he turned on the republican government which he held responsible for his failure. He tried to persuade the French army to march on Paris and restore a Bourbon king, but he failed, and on 5 April he deserted to the Austrians.

The treachery of their best general seriously undermined popular confidence in the Girondins. Parisians already doubted them because of their attitude to Louis XVI. The discovery of the secret 'iron chest' containing correspondence between the king and France's Austrian enemies had placed Louis's guilt as a traitor beyond doubt. The Jacobins, with Robespierre and Saint-Just in the forefront, began pressing for his trial and execution. Every shaft aimed at Louis glanced upon the Girondins. The latter could not defend the king without involving themselves in his treachery, yet they could not agree to his death without alienating provincial voters who feared the extremes to which the Revolution might go if the king were executed. Vergniaud and Brissot tried to evade the issue by asking for a referendum, but Robespierre defeated the proposal. The Girondins could have saved Louis if they had kept together, but they had never really been a coherent parliamentary party. When the final vote was taken they divided, and Louis's fate was sealed by a majority of one. In the Place de la Révolution (Concorde), on the cold morning of 21 January 1793, Frenchmen guillotined their king.

It was now more than ever necessary to defeat counter-revolution at home and abroad, but the Girondins seemed incapable of strong action. On 23 February 1793 the Convention decreed a levy of 300,000 men to be sent at once to the front. In Paris, where the influence of Danton was still vigorous, volunteers answered the call enthusiastically, but in some outlying provinces numbers were less forthcoming. The attempt to enforce the enrolment of 4,000 men on 10 March produced a large-scale revolt in the department of La Vendée. Ancient dislike of military service, which took men away from the fields and left their families succourless, was combined with dislike of interference by government in the life of the peasant. An ultimatum from the rebels demanded 'no enlistment, no forced labour, no requisitioning, no taxation without local consent, no searching of houses, and complete freedom of worship, speech, and publication'.

The revolt of the Vendée was the first of a series of peasant revolts which were to take place against the Revolution in France and elsewhere – in Brittany and Normandy intermittently from 1793 to 1799 (the *chouannerie*); in central and southern Italy between 1796 and 1799; in Belgium, Germany, and Switzerland about the same time. The series was to culminate in the great Spanish revolt against Napoleon. All took place in regions where communications were difficult and new ideas slow to penetrate, where the peasants were very much under the thumb of the landlords and the influence of the clergy, and where there was considerable suspicion of the bourgeoisie, who were known to the peasants almost exclusively as tax-gatherers, land-agents, and usurers. In the Vendée the peasants had welcomed the Revolution in 1789 but had grown disillusioned when it failed to rid them of the burdens imposed by the peculiar land tenures of the region. Aristocratic plots and clerical exhortations found fruitful soil, and the alliance between peasantry and bourgeoisie which had secured the initial triumph of the Revolution failed to last. The government had no force to send against the Vendée other than local detachments of National Guards and a few troops withdrawn from the Belgian front. These proved totally inadequate against an angry and fanatical population scattered in mountain villages and narrow valleys offering every opportunity for guerilla fighting. The Girondins could do no more than isolate the revolt.

In addition to weakening France's military position, the revolt of the Vendée increased her economic difficulties by putting some of the finest stock-rearing areas out of commission. The depreciation of the assignats produced a sharp increase in the price of all foodstuffs in the early months of 1793. In the streets of Paris, popular discontents were taken up by a small group of mob orators, notably a priest, Jacques Roux, and a postal assistant, Jean Varlet, who declaimed against selfish politicians and demanded economic measures – control of prices, requisitioning of food supplies, and legislation against hoarders. For the first time in the Revolution the sans-culottes adopted an economic programme. On 2 May, 10,000 citizens from the faubourg Saint-Antoine paraded before the Convention and demanded price control. To many moderates this demand was reminiscent of the *ancien régime* and seemed nothing short of counter-revolutionary. To the Girondins, economic control appeared both as an infringement of liberty and as a policy bound to alienate middle class voters. They nicknamed Jacques Roux and his associates 'enragés' or wild men, and made only minor concessions to their demands. The sans-culottes came to regard the Girondins as selfish patrons of the monied classes, and rumours of their connections with speculators and profiteers spread through the city.

Girondin leaders, with their usual lack of political tact, combined opposition to the new economic movement with sneering attacks on the presumptuous behaviour of the Paris mob. On 21 May they set up a Commission of Twelve to investigate the activities of the Commune and the sections. It began its work by arresting Hébert, a demagogic journalist and deputy-proctor of the Commune. When the Commune petitioned the Convention for his release, the Girondin Isnard made the threatening retort, 'If the Convention is violated, I tell you in the name of France, Paris will be destroyed; people will search on the banks of the Seine to see if Paris ever existed.' Such ill-judged statements roused the hostility of Paris as a community and enabled the Jacobins from an early date to plant accusations of 'federalism' against the Girondins. When, in the last days of May, Marseille, Bordeaux, Caen, and a number of other moderate municipalities expressed their intention of defying the influence of Paris, the Girondins became associated in the popular mind with separatist revolt.

Insurrection at home and failure abroad increased the fear of counter-revolution. Inside the Convention, deputies began inventing new machinery to strengthen government. They decided to send eighty members as 'representatives-on-mission' to the provinces, endowed with full powers to put down insurrection. On 10 March a Revolutionary Tribunal was set up for summary trial of persons accused of crimes against the state. Military commissions were given power to execute within 24 hours rebels captured under arms, and each commune or section was ordered to set up a 'revolutionary committee' to round up suspects. On 6 April the Convention threw overboard the principle of separation of powers by electing, from among its own members, a Committee of Public Safety to supervise ministers.

The Convention was still influenced to a large extent by the Girondins: during May, four out of the five men elected President of the Assembly were Girondins. The Girondins made the mistake, however, of allowing Jacobins to infiltrate into the new organs of government, thinking that they would thereby be kept too busy to cause mischief. Only in the case of the Committee of Public Safety did the men of the Plain show their growing dislike of faction fights by electing non-party men. The most outstanding member was Danton.

Meanwhile leaders in the sections began agitating for the expulsion of the Girondins from the Convention. On 10 April the Halle au Blé section demanded the arrest of 22 Girondin deputies, and 35 out of 48 sections announced their determination to take matters into their own hands if the Convention would not act. They sent delegates to a meeting at the Archbishop's palace and set up the Central Revolutionary Committee which organized the insurrection of 31 May – 2 June 1793. The committee placed Hanriot, a former customs clerk and a swaggering drunkard, in command of the National Guard. At the same time it decided to raise a revolutionary militia of 20,000 sans-culottes to be paid at the rate of 40 sous a day. On 31 May a petition for the arrest of the Girondins was sent to the Convention. The latter prevaricated by referring the petition to the Committee of Public Safety, but the sovereign people would brook no delay. On 2 June a huge mob of sans-culottes, strengthened by Hanriot's National Guard with cannon, surrounded the Tuileries where the Convention sat. A few of the victims tried vainly to break out; a few others weakly agreed to resign their seats. While the Plain hesitated, two Jacobin members took the initiative: the crippled Couthon asked to be lifted into the tribunal where he proposed the acceptance of the demands of the mob, and Hérault de Séchelles, who had seized the presidential chair, declared the proposal carried without vote. Twenty-nine Girondin members, and two ministers associated with them, Clavière and Lebrun, were placed under house arrest. In the following days many more deputies were proscribed for signifying disapproval. The Jacobins were left without rivals to dominate the Plain.

3. JACOBIN DICTATORSHIP

According to the Jacobins, Paris had once more acted as the worthy instrument of the sovereign people by securing the triumph of popular men. To clinch the argument, the Jacobins at once produced a democratic constitution, confirming universal suffrage and extending the list of man's natural rights to include the right to subsistence. 'In a few days we have reaped the enlightenment of all ages', Barère told the deputies. Reaped, perhaps; but to be stored, not enjoyed. If the Jacobins believed in democratic institutions at all, they believed in them only as an ideal for the future. Three months passed with no attempt to put the constitution into practice. Finally, on 10 October, the deputies agreed to a proposal by Saint-Just that the constitution should be suspended for the duration of the war. 'The provisional government of France is revolutionary until the peace.'

A revolutionary government meant a government organized on lines dictated by expediency rather than by contemporary notions of legality. From July 1793 to July 1794 the Jacobins ruled France by dictatorship and terror, both of which increased in intensity as time went by. The instruments for such rule had been bequeathed to France by the Girondins: they needed only to be given a new inspiration. This inspiration came not so much from new ideas, for Jacobin leaders scarcely differed from Girondins in their views on government and society, but from circumstances, temperament, and sheer personal ability. Foreign armies were invading France on four fronts; the ports were practically closed by the British fleet; a half of France was under rebellion; Paris itself was swarming with radical agitators, army deserters, disguised priests, and spies of every description. On 13 July Marat was stabbed to death by a fanatical young woman from Caen, Charlotte Corday, who travelled to Paris with hatred in her heart for a man she had never seen but whom she held chiefly responsible for the death of her beloved Girondins. The Jacobins were indeed fighting with their backs to the wall, knowing that they could obtain no quarter. The knowledge produced fear and also elation. In a life and death struggle with political rivals the Jacobins had proved the fittest to survive; continuing threats to survival drove them to the full extent of their capabilities. In the first few months of their dictatorship the Jacobins saved the Revolution from certain destruction. The achievement must stand as their epitaph alongside their many and dreadful crimes.

The central organ of dictatorship was the Committee of Public Safety. For a few weeks Danton and other non-party men retained their places, but by the beginning of September they had been excluded, and for almost a year the Committee was firmly Jacobin. The twelve men who ruled France for some of the most decisive months in her history were not all well-known as individuals. Hérault de Séchelles, a pampered aristocrat who had spent most of his life cultivating mannerisms in the hope of impressing beholders, achieved only one moment of real recognition when he played the leading rôle in producing the still-born constitution of 1793. Robert Lindet, a man of forty-six, had been a lawyer all his life when he was put on the Committee with the special duty of supervising commerce, agriculture, and food supplies. Prieur of the Côte d'Or was an engineer officer and Prieur of the Marne a lawyer, both undistinguished men: in their quiet, efficient way they gave useful assistance to Carnot in the organization and supplying of the armies. Lazare Carnot was a professional soldier of forty who had spent eighteen years of his life in dreary garrison duty, a neglected engineer officer barred from promotion by lack of noble birth, devoting his interests to mathematical studies. 'A revolutionary is made, not born,' Carnot once told his fellow-deputies: the desperate circumstances of 1793 brought out his genius as an organizer of armies. Jeanbon Saint-André came from an old and conservative Protestant family; after many years as a sea-captain he became a Protestant pastor; his concern all along was to play a useful part in the community, giving his support to sound government. The Committee gave him the subordinate task of producing a navy out of the disgruntled deck-hands, untrained volunteers, and merchant seamen who were all that remained when the bulk of aristocratic officers had deserted. Barère was rather better known in political circles. He had studied rhetoric for use at the bar, but when the Revolution broke out he used it instead to praise each party which rose to power. He became the chief publicity agent of the Committee, extolling its measures to the bewildered members of the Convention.

Only two members of the Committee can be described as terrorists at heart: Billaud-Varenne and Collot d'Herbois. The former had tried his hand at law, play-writing, and teaching, and had succeeded at nothing, though he was not without talent. At the age of thirty-seven he was full of bitter and violent feelings towards society. Collot d'Herbois shared these grievances, for Collot had spent most of his life as an actor, moderately successful, but at a time when actors were social outcasts. Georges Couthon also became an exponent of terror, but he cannot be described simply as a man of blood. The little crippled lawyer was well liked in his native Auvergne for his gentle, courteous ways and for his sympathy with the poor. His patient endurance of physical suffering brought out an element of stoicism in his character and perhaps helped to make him a devoted supporter of Robespierre. This devotion was shared by Saint-Just, the youngest member of the Committee. Saint-Just had been a selfish, unruly boy in the years before the Revolution; in 1793 he was a ruthless young man of 25, arrogant and coldly fanatical. He spent much of his time on mission to the armies, weeding out traitors and enforcing discipline, arbitrary, brutal, and successful. Ambitious, but not unprincipled, he remained true to Robespierre's ideal of a spartan republic. He was to mount the guillotine in July 1794 with proud disdain for his opponents.

The man who inspired this devotion remains the most enigmatic character of the Revolution, yet no man was more closely identified with all its phases than Maximilien Robespierre. A humanitarian lawyer in the last years of the *ancien régime*, Robespierre won the approval of the citizens of Arras by his virtuous, almost puritanical behaviour, his punctilious manner, elegant dress, and constant application to duty, at the same time winning the love of the poor by his sympathy and respect for them. He dreamed of a society in which snobbery and cruelty were unknown and in which virtue was acknowledged. No-one entered the Revolution with a more sincere belief in the value of mankind; no-one desired more earnestly the good of the people. His lethal failing was his confidence in his own ability to define the good of the people. Coming from a narrow provincial background, and with a precise, almost theological caste of mind, he was sure that he was right. A mixture of idealism and ambition drove him to master the techniques of political opposition, so that from virtual isolation in the winter of 1791 he became by 1793 an essential member of the Committee of Public Safety. In some ways he was the most essential of the twelve, for his oratory could command the support of the Convention when all else failed, and no politician was more trusted by all classes of the population.

Robespierre never exercized a dictatorship over the Committee of Public Safety. The members recognized no chairman; they were jointly responsible for all the Committee's actions; and neither credit nor blame can be allotted to individuals. They were almost all autocratic and fiery-tempered, but they managed at least until April 1794 to hide their disputes from the outside world. The Committee met in a room in the Tuileries at 8 a.m. every day, and remained at work late into the night. A decree of 10 October gave it the task of supervising ministers, generals, and all administrative officials except the police, which remained under the control of the older Committee of General Security. The Committee of Public Safety was theoretically subordinate to the Convention, which elected its members monthly; but month after month the men of the Plain elected the same twelve Jacobins. The Convention was still the legislative authority of the land, but in an assembly purged of opposition members debates were short, and measures presented by the Committee were often passed in a few minutes.

The first task of the Jacobins was to save the country from counter-revolution. The task was many-sided, but it was accomplished between July and December 1793. In September the Convention recognized terror as 'the order of the day' and sanctioned terrorist action against opponents. The rebels of Marseille and Bordeaux were hunted down by representatives-on-mission, Barras, Fréron, and Julien; at Marseille alone 332 persons were guillotined in two months. Sporadic risings in Normandy were crushed easily. Toulon, which had admitted a British fleet, was besieged by an army under the supervision of Robespierre's brother Augustin; it surrendered in December after bombardment by the artillery of the young Corsican Bonaparte; its fortifications were demolished and its armed citizens executed at the rate of 200 a day. A rebellion in Lyon, the second city of France, was attacked by two Jacobin armies; when the rebels finally surrendered after a two months' siege Collot d'Herbois arrived from Paris to set up firing squads. Some of the Girondins proscribed in June had joined these risings; they were rooted out, along with others who had merely gone into hiding, and sent to Paris for punishment. Meanwhile the scattered forces of the Vendéans were defeated by the Army of the West; a punitive campaign lasting throughout the winter culminated in the mass drowning of prisoners by Carrier in the river at Nantes. Over the whole country the number of persons taken as rebels and summarily executed was never known: it greatly surpassed the number of those guillotined more spectacularly in the capital.

In Paris the Revolutionary Tribunal was divided into four sections to deal with the increasing number of persons accused of treachery. The work was speeded up by the efficiency of the public prosecutor, Fouquier-Tinville, who sat all day in the Palais de Justice drawing up lists of prisoners for trial, preparing indictments, and arranging executions. He was a careful civil servant, doing his job for the sake of the salary on which to support his large family. Stories of persons guillotined for private revenge or by mistaken identity originated in sensational gossip and have never been proved. Victims of the guillotine in the early months of Jacobin rule were for the most part recognizable political prisoners: priests, aristocrats, Marie Antoinette (on 17 October, after a long imprisonment and an insulting trial), Philippe Égalité (one-time Duc d'Orléans), Lavoisier (scientist and also, unfortunately, one-time Farmer General), Charlotte Corday, the Girondins, and Madame du Barry. Death was speedy; only half an hour was needed for 31 Girondins. It was said to be painless. Some of the victims died with classic phrases on their lips, like Manon Roland ('Oh, Liberty! What crimes are committed in thy name!'). Almost all died bravely. A Scotswoman, Grace Elliott, who witnessed some of the executions, thought that if more victims had shrieked as hideously as Madame du Barry the guillotining would soon have been stopped by public revulsion. As it was, crowds of citizens watched the heads roll into the baskets, feeling that France was the safer thereby.

For while Sanson, the executioner, was carrying out his daily task, France was fighting a war against foreign armies on several fronts. On 23 August the Convention issued Carnot's famous decree authorizing a *levée en masse*, the mobilization of the whole nation for war. 'All French people, whatever their age or sex, are called by their country to defend liberty', the decree ran. 'Henceforth the republic is a great city in a stage of siege . . . Young men will go to the front; married men will forge arms and carry food; women will make tents and clothing and work in hospitals.' It was the first example of total war. The energies released by the Revolution were harnessed to the national cause, and France's great numerical strength was brought for the first time to bear against Europe.

Recruiting was carried out by *fédérés* under the direction of representatives-on-mission. The first age group alone, those between 18 and 25, produced nearly half a million men, and it was found unnecessary to go further. The astounding speed with which Carnot shaped this vast number of raw recruits into a fighting force was a work of genius. Within three weeks the first levies were engaging the enemy on the field of battle. A few experienced troops were put into each unit to impart rudiments of training to the rest, and new tactics were adopted demanding more numbers and spirit than discipline. By October enemy forces were being pushed back from the frontiers; by the end of the year France had a million soldiers, commanded by young ambitious generals, and Carnot was deploying eleven armies for attack, not defence. A year later, when the Jacobins had fallen and Carnot's fate was being considered by the Convention, an unknown voice rang out, 'He organized the victory', and his life was spared because of it.

There could have been no more eloquent testimony to the triumph of the Jacobins than the law of 4 December 1793, known by the revolutionary calendar as 14 frimaire of the year II. The dictatorship improvised and excused a few months before was enthroned and acclaimed. Administration was centralized to a greater degree than the *ancien régime* had ever known. Departmental authorities, which had grown increasingly unsympathetic to the policy of the government, were suppressed. Districts and communes were given 'national agents' appointed from Paris, and they were ordered to send reports to the capital every ten days. Local officials were warned that 'the piercing eye' of the Committee of Public Safety was upon them and that disobedience could be punished with imprisonment or even death. The 'revolutionary armies,' improvised bodies composed of some 30,000 sans-culottes, which had assisted vigorously in the work of repression and of supplying the troops on the eastern frontiers, were disbanded in the provinces as detrimental to responsible government. The local enthusiasm and initiative which had characterized the early stages of the Revolution died out under this chilling régime. Local affairs passed into the hands of small cliques of Jacobins, regarding themselves as the élite of the nation and willing to tyrannize over their neighbours with the backing of agents from Paris. Even Saint-Just was moved to remark, 'The Revolution is frozen'.

Indeed, when the hectic autumn of 1793 was over and France was no longer fighting for her life, a variety of discontents emerged. The sans-culottes were by no means satisfied with Jacobin economic policy. Jacobin leaders recognized the debt they owed to the mob, and on 29 September 1793 the Convention decreed a General Maximum of prices covering 39 essential commodities, but though the law was greeted with enthusiasm in the sections, its results were disappointing. In Paris a 'revolutionary army' of some 6,000 sans-culottes ensured supplies of cheap rationed bread from the great grain-producing areas of the Pays de France, Beauce, Brie, Vexin, Beauvaisis, Soissonais, and Champagne, but other commodities such as meat, vegetables, eggs, and firewood were never successfully controlled. In the country at large producers and middlemen hoarded supplies to sell on rising markets and entered into illicit deals with retailers, whereupon Paris shopkeepers, having paid too high a price for supplies, recouped their losses at the expense of consumers. Hordes of black marketeers roamed the back streets selling goods at fancy prices, and in various ways the supreme object of a constant supply of food at a reasonable price was defeated. Agitators cried out for fiercer laws of repression and for more 'revolutionary armies' with wider powers. The movement found a leader in Hébert, whose scurrilous *Père Duchesne* was the most widely read paper in the country. Hébert used the Cordeliers club as his headquarters and drew support from a crowd of lesser-known agitators in the outlying sections of Paris. The movement gained even greater popularity in provincial cities such as Lyon and Strasbourg.

Leading Jacobins showed no sympathy with this desire to hand the Revolution over to the lowest classes of society. Most of the members of the Committee of Public Safety were middle class intellectuals, and they believed, as the Girondins had done, in a free economy. In 1793 they had abolished all remaining feudal rights without indemnity and fragmented national land so that it could be bought in ten small instalments: France was rapidly becoming a nation of petty proprietors, economically retrogressive and politically conservative. The constitution of 1793 had reiterated the sanctity of (middle class) property; its recognition of a 'right to subsistence' had meant no more than a promise of poor relief. The Jacobins had never offered to promote the interests of the poor at the expense of other people; they had merely insisted that the Revolution, like Christianity, could be made to suffice for all mankind. The Hébertists threatened to widen the breach between middle and lower classes, both of whom had hitherto supported the Jacobins. By March 1794 it was clear to Robespierre that they must be destroyed.

This seemed all the more necessary since Hébert was giving his support to yet another dangerous movement, that of the dechristianizers. The counter-revolutionary activities of many Catholic priests led to a wave of anti-clericalism during the autumn of 1793. The Convention countenanced a more secular attitude to public affairs by introducing a new calendar, in which the years were numbered not from the birth of Christ but from the proclamation of the French Republic on 22 September 1792, and in which Sunday was eliminated in favour of a rest on every tenth day. Months were prettily named after the weather or crops expected in them. This harmless symbolism was not enough for extremists on the fringes of politics – members of the Paris Commune, leaders of popular societies, commanders of 'revolutionary armies,' and one or two representatives on mission such as Fouché – who took matters into their own hands and encouraged attacks on churches, forbade religious services, and held secular festivals in honour of Reason. Chaumette, procureur of the Paris Commune, hoped to dechristian-ize the capital entirely by closing all its churches. A Festival of Reason was actually held in Notre Dame. On the Committee of Public Safety the only sympathizer with these activities was Collot d'Herbois, whose acting career had given him propensities for appealing to the mob. Robespierre's romantic soul revolted against the narrow Encyclopaedist doctrines embodied in the Worship of Reason and yearned for something more Rousseauesque. The others were afraid that the government would be implicated in the minds of peasants and bourgeois, many of whom had welcomed reform of the Catholic church but would not countenance either a wholesale attack on religion or the relaxation of morals which went with it.

Jacobin rule thus entered on a second phase, the destruction of internal critics. Robespierre's ground against the Hébertists was prepared for him by Danton. Since his elimination from the Committee of Public Safety Danton had left public life for the society of a new young wife. He returned to Paris in November 1793 and began a campaign for clemency. Now that France had defeated her enemies, he said, she should negotiate for favourable terms, so that war and terror could come to an end. Danton's young friend, the brilliant but unstable Camille Desmoulins, launched a newspaper, the *Vieux Cordelier*, in which he made a courageous attack on spies, informers, and extremists who were leading France from horror to horror. The campaign met with much popular support, and the *Vieux Cordelier* so discredited the Hébertists that on 25 March 1794, after the discovery of a plot against the government, Robespierre was able to bring about the guillotining of Hébert and his associates.

The elimination of Hébert did not secure the triumph of Danton. Robespierre was afraid of the man whose popularity and talent made him a serious rival, and he was ready to allow the terrorists to have their way with him. On 30 March Saint-Just acted as Robespierre's mouthpiece in denouncing Danton, Desmoulins, and, with them, Hérault de Séchelles. They were guillotined on 5 April. Like the Hébertists they had been accused of connections with a host of petty offenders, fraudulent financiers, and foreign agents. No-one doubted the wisdom and integrity of the Revolutionary Tribunal which condemned them, but Danton's bravado on the way to the scaffold won admiration to the end. Robespierre might well have reflected on Danton's prophesy that he would follow him along the same road.

Jacobin rule now entered on its third and last phase. In the short period of his supremacy (5 April – 28 July 1794) Robespierre grew more and more isolated from the sovereign people whose will he professed to embody. He easily reconciled his conscience to the lack of democratic institutions, for his reading of Rousseau taught him that the sovereign will of the people can be expressed by one enlightened ruler better than by the sum-total of individuals. On the other hand Rousseau also taught that men are good, and that when the will of the people triumphs in a republic the natural virtue of the people leads society onward to perfection. Circumstances seemed to be disproving this theory, for Robespierre saw all around him corrupt officials, rapacious businessmen, fraudulent financiers, irresponsible agitators, dishonest citizens, liars and intriguers of every description. He came to the conclusion that the souls of these men had been destroyed by long years of tyranny and that their bodies must now be destroyed for the health of society. 'If the basis of popular government in time of peace is virtue', he said on 5 February 1794, 'its basis in time of revolution is both virtue and terrorism: virtue, without which terrorism is disastrous, and terrorism, without which virtue is powerless.' Thus the Reign of Terror increased in intensity. In floréal alone (20 April – 19 May) 354 persons were condemned by the Revolutionary Tribunal. To Robespierre, lack of public spirit, lack of co-operation with the most minor decrees of the republic, was a failing in virtue just as reprehensible as rebellion. This theory was bound to feed a large number of victims to the guillotine, for there were many aspects of Robespierrist policy which provoked opposition.

Saint-Just, Couthon and Robespierre had sponsored a scheme resulting in the laws of ventôse (26 February and 5 March) whereby the property of suspects who were in prison awaiting trial was to be confiscated by the state and used for poor relief. The laws aroused great uneasiness among property owners, who saw a temptation towards wholesale imprisonment. They were greeted enthusiastically by some of the sans-culottes, who envisaged a new distribution of property in their favour, but these hopes came to nothing. The task of assessing the property of 80,000 prisoners and the claims of 40,000 paupers proved too mountainous for the existing civil service. Moreover, Robespierre and his friends, far from wedding themselves to the cause of the poor, disbanded the 'revolutionary army', relaxed the laws against hoarders, and introduced a new Maximum which gave an increased margin of profit. The new Maximum, like the old, controlled wages as well as prices, in an attempt at fairness to all. Workers were angry at not being able to take advantage of the labour shortage caused by the war. A series of strikes during April was dealt with severely by the authorities under the Loi le Chapelier. These measures undermined the loyalty of the sans-culottes without winning the co-operation of peasants and producers. Lack of confidence resulted in a further fall in the assignats to 36% of their face value by July 1794.

Robespierre did not rely on terror alone to destroy corruption. He had some faith in propaganda. The great David, who had already established over French art a dictatorship as rigorous as any the Jacobins could conceive in politics, was engaged to organize patriotic festivals and immortalize the Revolution on huge canvasses. The Committee of Public Safety summoned writers to compose poems and dramas in praise of the republic, musicians to compete with civic songs, and architects to create a new style in public buildings and model farms. The effect was not noticeably successful. A national education was envisaged to destroy illiteracy, the breeding ground of tyranny and fanaticism, and to produce devoted servants of the republic: but though the plans adopted by the Convention proved to be a lasting foundation in the educational field Robespierre's time was too short to see the edifice constructed.

Robespierre had faith, too, in a new form of religion. Unlike the de-christianizers he believed that religion was necessary to keep men faithful to duty. On 7 May 1794 he enacted the Worship of the Supreme Being, modelled closely on the last chapter of Rousseau's *Social Contract*. The only dogma was that of immortality of the soul, and the only commandments were to help the weak, defend the oppressed, punish traitors and tyrants, do good to one's neighbour, and behave with justice toward all men. Denominational creeds were not proscribed: indeed the new religion was intended to absorb, not rival, other religions. It was initiated on 7 June in a magnificent ceremony arranged by David. Robespierre set fire to cardboard figures of Atheism, Egotism, Discord, and False Simplicity, from whose ashes arose a slightly charred image of Wisdom. Dressed in a beautiful sky-blue suit Robespierre headed a procession of deputies carrying bouquets of wheat and flowers to the Altar of the Nation, where the multitude joined in a hymn swearing annihilation to crime and tyranny. Puzzled representatives-on-mission tried to organize similar festivals throughout the country on 8 June. They were not greatly heeded. In Paris Robespierre's enemies began to take heart, for his antics as chief priest of the new religion made him appear more ridiculous than terrible.

Hope was premature, for Robespierre and his friends were preparing to strengthen virtue with a new dose of terror. The law of 22 prairial, known as the law of the suspect, was drafted by Couthon and introduced into the Convention on 10 June. It defined as 'enemies of the people' all persons who worked against republican government, compromised the country's war effort, reduced its food reserves, assisted its enemies, or obstructed its friends. Anyone might fear arrest under so vague a definition of treason. The law further stated that the calling of witnesses was unnecessary and that the only punishment for the guilty was death. Between 10 June and 27 July, 1,376 persons were guillotined in Paris alone.

To most people terror no longer seemed necessary, for France was prevailing over her enemies. Carnot's armies defeated Coburg at Fleurus on 26 June and soon brought Belgium once more under French occupation. Improvisation was less easy at sea, and Saint-André failed to produce a navy capable of defeating the British in battle, but his ships did cunning service as privateers. The British blockade did not succeed in starving France of food from America. A British fleet under Admiral Howe claimed a great victory over the French on the Glorious First of June (1794), but the food ships under convoy by the Brest fleet escaped during the battle and arrived safely in port. If 'enemies of the people' were lurking in France, they were clearly not bringing the country to disaster.

Yet it was not popular revulsion which brought about the fall of Robespierre but enemies in high places. On the Committee of Public Safety Collot and Billaud disliked his sermonizing and knew that he disapproved of their naked terrorism. Lindet disliked the laws of ventôse. Carnot and Prieur of the Côte d'Or objected to the way in which Saint-Just, backed by Robespierre, interfered in military matters. The Committee of General Security, composed almost entirely of pure terrorists and responsible for many of the arrests carried out under the Terror, resented the formation of a new police committee by Robespierre, Couthon, and Saint-Just. In the Convention, men of blood such as Carrier, Tallien, Fréron, and Fouché knew that they had been recalled from their missions and expelled from the Jacobin club at the instigation of Robespierre. These men rapidly came to the conclusion that they must strike Robespierre before he struck them, for

AOP G

the law of 22 prairial made no mention of the usual immunity of deputies, and a speech by Robespierre to the Convention on 26 July threatened enemies numerous and unspecified. Secretly Tallien and Fouché approached members of the Plain. Perhaps because they too went in fear of their lives the Plain agreed to support a conspiracy, hatched by men who were no better than their adversary.

On 27 July (9 thermidor) Robespierre and Saint-Just were shouted down in the Convention and arrested with a small group of friends before they had time to act. The Commune, which remained solidly Robespierrist, sounded the tocsin and called on citizens to defy the Convention. Thirteen working-class sections sent forces, but either because the men were discontented at the new wages scale, or because the Terror had eliminated their leaders, they remained inactive. The National Guard under the drunken, useless Hanriot did nothing. Robespierre and his associates escaped from prison and joined the Commune, but meanwhile the Convention had rallied supporters from the wealthier sections. Robespierre had put two letters of his name to an appeal to the people when a force from the Convention burst into the room and seized him. Couthon was arrested while attempting to escape. Saint-Just stood calmly by, awaiting his captors.

On 10 thermidor Robespierre took the terrible journey to the Place de la Révolution through hostile crowds. He was guillotined along with his brother Augustin, Saint-Just, Couthon, and seventeen of his closest associates. With them died all the initiative of the Revolution.

CHAPTER V

Europe Against the Revolution

I. MOTIVES FOR WAR

WHEN Brissot told Frenchmen that they were fighting against the tyrants of Europe he was not without justification. It is possible to show that in all the countries leagued against France in 1793 privileged cliques were the controlling force in government. This was not only true of the eastern monarchies, Prussia, Austria, and Russia, but of those countries west of the Elbe where economic developments presented a challenge to the old social order. In the Dutch Netherlands, long a republic, a Patriot party desirous of extending political power more widely among the middle classes had attacked the ruling oligarchies of the towns and provinces in 1787, only to be suppressed with the aid of British gold and Prussian troops. In England the Unreformed House of Commons had withstood radical agitation in the seventeen-eighties and defeated even Pitt's modest attempt to extend the franchise. Frenchmen who had helped American colonists to win freedom from British despotism believed that only they and the Americans understood the true meaning of liberty.

To what extent was counter-revolution, consciously or unconsciously, an aim of the allies in the war, however? Among the main combatants the king of Prussia felt no qualms about the possibility of revolution spreading to his own people and never dreamed that the French might one day attack his territories. His interests lay in northern and eastern Europe, and his entry into the war against France was merely a move in a restless campaign to get even with Austria and Russia. Pitt found him unreliable as an ally, because although his sympathies were with the counter-revolutionary cause his ambitions, as he soon realized, were likely to be promoted by the French initiative. To Britain and Austria, on the other hand, counter-revolution was an essential feature of the war because it was allied to their interests. This was no less true because British statesmen did not always acknowledge it and sometimes did not see it. The fact remained that neither Britain nor Austria could make peace whilst revolutionary principles guided French conduct in European affairs. They could make peace only when they saw in Bonaparte a man who seemed capable of negotiating on formal lines acceptable to states involved in the game of power politics.

In Britain, as in most other countries, the French Revolution met with sympathy from the majority of educated and enlightened persons for at least the first two years. Some of these persons were opponents of the established order at home, and the French Revolution was doubly welcome to them as a stick for beating the government. Charles James Fox, returning to the attack on royal power after a number of defeats at the hands of Pitt, described the fall of the Bastille as the greatest event in the history of the world. The dissenters, who had already revived seventeenth-century ideas of natural rights and sovereignty of the people in their opposition to the Test and Corporation Acts, looked with favour on a revolution which appeared to them to be based on these very principles. In addition to controlling important journals the dissenters possessed a rudimentary political organization in bodies such as the London Revolution Society, formed to celebrate the Revolution of 1688. These remained in existence to publish pamphlets, sermons, articles, and letters on the happy sequel in France. The dissenters were allied with the democrats surrounding Christopher Wyvill and Major John Cartwright, and in 1789 they transferred their hopes from Pitt, who had disappointed them as a reformer, to Fox and Sheridan. It was in answer to a sermon preached by one of the more eccentric dissenters, Dr. Richard Price, that Edmund Burke saw fit in October 1790 to denounce the French Revolution in his *Reflections*. Dissenters and democrats persisted in their views, however. The Society for Promoting Constitutional Information, which had been dormant for some years, was revived in 1791.

Up to this point the governing classes showed no great anxiety, but the radical movement soon took a momentous turn. Thomas Paine's *Rights of Man*, containing views of a downright jacobin nature, sold so many copies that it must have been read far outside the circle of educated and 'responsible' citizens. In January 1792 the London Corresponding Society was founded by Thomas Hardy, a shoemaker. Whereas the Constitutional Society had demanded five guineas a year for membership, the new foundation asked for a penny. The members were mainly craftsmen and small shopkeepers. Thereafter British jacobinism, unlike other European manifestations of the movement, was connected with the French by the fact that it appealed primarily to persons of small income. The London Society affiliated with similar groups in provincial centres and developed political and social aims not unlike those of the Parisian sans-culottes, without, however, intending to resort to violence. In November 1792 the Society presented assurances of friendship to the French Convention.

By this time, moderate minded citizens had come to regard Burke's *Reflections* almost as divine prophecy. At first unimpressed by his gloomy prognostications, they came round to his views as soon as blood began to flow in Paris. Thereafter they regarded opinions which were even remotely connected with the French as certain to lead to fearful crimes. Members of popular societies were indicted on charges of sedition and treason and condemned to heavy penalties. Severity increased when war broke out, and reached a pitch of savagery in Scotland where the courts possessed no Erskine to uphold the constitutional liberties of the people. In England an exaggerated charge of high treason brought against Hardy, Horne Tooke, Thelwall, and ten others resulted in resounding acquittals. Pitt decided to regain his ground by legislation. A Seditious Meetings Act prohibited gatherings of more than fifty people without the consent and control of the magistrates, and a Treasonable Practices Act envisaged severe penalties for attempts to coerce parliament or attack the constitution. The measures were accepted complacently by most members of the public, who were horrified at the course which events had taken in France and repelled by the anti-religious views expressed in Tom Paine's *Age of Reason* (1794). The dissenters retired from political agitation and radical societies withered away in an atmosphere of patriotic enthusiasm. Even the sailors who mutinied at the Nore and Spithead in 1797, though tempted by their wretched conditions to listen to political extremists, protested their anxiety to sail against the French. Patrician members of the reform movement made a last stand in 1797. Fox and Grey, advocating an extension of the franchise, defended the French Revolution as a move basically good, and said that Britain should adapt and not reject its principles. The majority of members of parliament agreed, however, with Pitt that the risks were too great. The French Revolution put back reform in Britain for a generation.

Anxiety concerning the possible contagion of French ideas would not alone have led Britain into war against France, however. Indeed British statesmen regarded the French Revolution as in some ways opportune, for they believed that it would withdraw France from the scene of European rivalries for many years to come. Pitt, fearing for Britain's interests in the Mediterranean when the Russians in 1787 and the Austrians in 1788 made war on Turkey, took comfort in the thought that France at least could no longer take part in hostile combinations. The unwillingness of the revolutionaries to allow Louis XVI to stand by his dynastic alliance with Spain enabled Britain, in the Nootka Sound dispute of 1790, to establish a right to exploit fisheries along the Pacific coast of America in spite of Spanish claims to possession of the whole coastline. Pitt could presume also that French designs on the Netherlands were at an end, since the Constituent Assembly renounced territorial ambitions. This, it is true, had the drawback of cooling Prussia's enthusiasm for the Triple Alliance with Britain and the Netherlands. The alliance had been of great service to Britain since it was formed in 1788, enabling Pitt to restore the *status quo* in the Baltic when Denmark answered Gustavus III's attack on Russia with the invasion of Sweden, and enabling him to extricate Austria from the Turkish war without territorial gains. Pitt's foreign secretary, the Duke of Leeds, saw the Triple Alliance as Britain's only refuge from isolation and believed that Britain and Holland should support Prussia in a war against Russia; but although Pitt shared the view that Russia menaced Britain's interests in the east he did not see how a naval war could be waged successfully in the Black Sea nor could he feel sure that the Commons would persist with financial support. Catherine was eventually allowed to make peace with the Sultan on her own terms. The Treaty of Jassy (9 January 1792), conceding to Russia the fortress of Oczakov on the Black Sea and advancing her frontier to the Dniester, could be construed as a blow to British prestige, but Pitt consoled himself with the belief that the actual danger from Russia was remote. In February 1792 he predicted a permanent surplus of revenue over expenditure and informed the Commons that 'unquestionably there never was a time when a durable peace might more reasonably be expected than at the present moment'. Two months later France declared war on Austria and Prussia, but there seemed no reason for Britain to intervene. Prussia could be relied upon to appeal to the Triple Alliance if Austrian ambitions were revived by success over France. No-one suspected that the French would turn their initial defeats into resounding victories.

The situation changed for Pitt as soon as the French began to exploit their occupation of Belgium. The confiscation of feudal and clerical property and the despatch of officials to arrange for elections was tantamount to annexation of the country. The opening of the Scheldt published the fact that the French in control of Belgium would show no respect for the commercial interests of Britain and Holland. In January 1793 France admitted her intention of invading the United Provinces. Economic and strategic considerations were doubtless uppermost in Pitt's mind when he decided that war against France was unavoidable. Britain's Industrial Revolution, after decades of acceleration, had reached the 'take-off' in the seventeen-eighties: hindrances to production had been removed and the chief need now was for markets old and new. To Pitt the Netherlands, along with the Baltic and the Mediterranean, formed one of the nerve centres at which Britain's interests could be touched most disastrously. Yet ideology played a part also. When the French annexed Alsace, Avignon, Savoy, and Nice they justified their action on the grounds of popular sovereignty, claiming that the rights of princes and the terms of treaties held no force comparable to the wishes of the people. When they issued the Edict of Fraternity they spoke to peoples over the heads of governments. Pitt denounced the new procedure as 'contrary to the law of nations' and denied that there could be security for any state in Europe while it lasted. The opening of the Scheldt was of symbolic as well as economic importance. 'England will never consent that France shall arrogate the power of annulling at her pleasure, and under the pretence of a natural right of which she makes herself the only judge, the political system of Europe, established by solemn treaties, and guaranteed by consent of all the powers', Pitt told the Commons on 1 February 1793. These words were no less counter-revolutionary than those of Burke, who described the members of the First Coalition as being at war not against France but against Jacobinism. In October 1793 George III informed his ambassadors and military commanders that, whilst he did not dispute France's right to reform her laws, he insisted that she establish 'some legitimate and stable government . . . capable of maintaining with other Powers the accustomed relations of union and peace'.

Pitt from the beginning of the war regarded Austria as his chief ally. Only Austria had a stake in the war comparable to that of Britain: she stood to lose valuable possessions in the Netherlands and perhaps even Italy if the French persisted in their appeals to sovereignty of the people. In Austria, as in England, the governing classes soon began to take an exaggerated view of political agitation. When Francis II was persuaded in 1792 to make an open rejection of Leopold's 'dangerous' policies, including his hopes of commuting labour services and of increasing representation in the Diets, there was naturally some unrest among peasants and intellectuals. Recruitment for the war against France was resisted in country districts, and defeatist opinions were expressed by writers such as Martinovics, who did not believe that the old type of army could survive the impact of the whole of the French people. The president of the Lower Austrian government, Count Sauer, warned Francis of the need to take strong action against admirers of the French Revolution. In January 1793 the Ministry of Police was made once more into a branch of government whose activities were entirely unaccountable to the public or to other ministers. The jealousies and ambitions of bureaucrats played a part in this reversal of policy, for Count Pergen and his associates now returned to power. A strict censorship was enforced, and governors were told to offer rewards to journalists and authors who 'set forth the evil results of the French Revolution in a manner both lively and comprehensible to ordinary people'. A newspaper sponsored by the government, the *Magazin für Kunst und Literatur* (1793-6), tried to prove that horrifying events such as the September Massacres were the inevitable consequence of undermining the power and privileges of clergy and nobility. The results were disappointing for, contrary to the position in England, the war against revolutionary France never enjoyed popular support in Austria.

Police officials were determined to silence 'insolent critics' of the government by making some spectacular examples, and *agents provocateurs* were employed to produce the necessary criminals. A number of so-called Jacobins were arrested in Vienna, Innsbruck, Upper Styria, and Hungary, during the summer of 1794. Their real offence was that they had met in secret to protest against the enlightened policies of the government and to devise propaganda which might ultimately persuade the emperor to change his course. They had expressed sympathy with the French and had welcomed Austrian defeats as likely to bring an end to the war. Only among the Hungarian 'conspirators', led by Martinovics, had there been plans to overthrow Habsburg rule and set up a republic freed from feudal dominion. Thanks to the courageous efforts of Martini, the emperor declined to set up an all powerful special tribunal to try the prisoners. Every rigour of the ordinary law was brought to bear upon them, however. The indictments made by the police were upheld both in Vienna and Hungary. Sentences of twenty, thirty, and even, in one case, sixty years' imprisonment were passed on the Austrian civilian prisoners, while one Hebenstreit, a soldier who came before a military court, suffered death by hanging. In Hungary, where the death penalty for civilian offenders had been restored in 1793, Martinovics and six others mounted the scaffold in May 1795. Police officials who had taken part in the investigations were promoted to places in the government, whence they influenced Francis II in a number of retrograde measures. The most important was the decision that large urban populations constituted a danger to the state and that restrictions should therefore be placed on the building of factories, the taking on of apprentices, and the employment of foreigners. Efforts to control opinion led to renewed clerical influence over education and to the careful screening of schoolteachers by the police. When the war ended in 1801 the police were satisfied that they had stamped out revolutionary movements throughout the Monarchy.

Austria entered the war nominally for the restoration of the French monarchy, but by 1793 she was fighting, like England, for security. To all the continental allies security was embedded in the balance of power, and the balance seemed to be in even greater jeopardy in the east than in the west. By 1791 Austria and Prussia felt sure that Catherine the Great, while urging them to attack France, would swoop down on Poland as soon as their backs were turned. Leopold II had no covetous designs on Poland: he hoped, rather, to stave off the Russian menace by guaranteeing the Polish constitution of 3 May 1791. To Prussia, on the other hand, annexation of the wheatlands and forests of Poland presented itself as an economic necessity, and pressure had to be imposed upon Frederick William III before he would guarantee the constitution. Leopold in his heart of hearts knew, however, that he would have to fight the French if his threats failed to intimidate them into respecting the monarchy, and in his anxiety to secure an offensive and defensive alliance with Prussia he wavered in his insistence upon the guarantee to Poland. The way was open to Frederick William either to keep

Austria occupied in an attack on France while he partitioned Poland with Catherine II or to make an agreement with Austria detrimental to the ambitions of Russia. Francis II at his accession joyfully accepted the obligation to lead a crusade against revolution and saw nothing to tarnish the lustre of the enterprise in the opportunities presented to him for juggling with the balance of power. He was startled when the French took the initiative by attacking Belgium. The Prussians were annoyed when he sent to the Belgian front some of the forces already allotted for the invasion of France, and they refused to mobilize until Austrian armies were ready to cross the frontier. The offensive was thereby delayed until the end of July, and the French were given three months to prepare for it. During these three months Russian troops invaded Poland and occupied the entire country.

2. THE SECOND PARTITION OF POLAND

At the beginning of the eighteenth century the Polish-Lithuanian state was one of the largest in Europe, stretching from the Oder eastward nearly to Smolensk and Kiev, and from Danzig southward to the Tartar steppe near the Black Sea. Its social and political structure was unique, though Hungary might have developed similar features but for the mixed blessings imparted by Habsburg absolutism. At the top of the social scale some twenty families of magnates, the Potockis, the Czartoryskis, the Radziwills, the Branickis, and a few others owned vast estates and hordes of serfs. Their main strength lay in the eastern and south-eastern parts of the country, in White Russia and the western Ukraine, where they prided themselves on holding the outposts of European religion and culture against the Asiatic barbarism of Russia. Here Prince Karol Radziwill owned estates half as large as Ireland, and Felix Potocki drew from his three million acres an income a third as large as that of the Polish Crown. A few such men could together raise as many soldiers as the king. They built great palaces, employed hundreds of retainers, and disrupted the peace of the countryside with their feuds. Below them some 725,000 lesser landowners claimed noble rank, though a half of them possessed only small farms which they cultivated with their own hands. The members of this class shared not only the privileges of the magnates, which included freedom from taxation without their own consent, but the political powers also. Landowners great and small met in about fifty provincial assemblies (*sejmiki*) to debate local affairs and to consider grants of money and soldiers to the king. Each assembly sent delegates, bound by strict instructions, to the lower house of a national diet (*sejm*), whose upper house consisted of prelates and great officers of the Crown. Since the nobles were unwilling to see power pass from their individual hands into that of the diet they developed a procedure known as the Liberum Veto, which allowed any delegate, acting on behalf of his province, to pronounce a formula which not merely blocked a piece of legislation but dissolved the entire assembly. Since the nobles were also unwilling to see power pass to the king, whom they elected themselves in special conclave, they imposed on each recipient of the Crown an agreement known as the *pacta conventa*, by which he swore to maintain the liberties of the Polish nation. The nation, in this context, did not, of course, include the serfs. The latter numbered about 8 millions, and were owned, body and soul, by about 100,000 nobles. Conditions among them varied, and from the middle of the century the humanitarian influences of the Enlightenment caused some nobles, led by the Czartoryskis, to set up schools and hospitals for their serfs, but generally speaking the standards of living remained low enough to shock and disgust western Europeans who visited the country. Poland was a very poor country, a fact which afflicted peasants and gentry alike, and the former often made their own poverty worse by a mulish refusal to co-operate with their masters.

All members of the Polish nobility or *szlachta* (from a German word meaning noble) were equal in law and supposed to address each other as brother. They were immensely proud of their immunity from monarchical despotism and compared their achievement with that of the English in Magna Carta. If the *szlachta* had been well-educated and public-spirited the system of government which they had established might, perhaps, have given Poland the 'golden freedom' which they extolled. Neither education nor public spirit were common among them, however. The magnates spoke French, went on the Grand Tour, and became acquainted with European enlightenment, but most of the gentry lived secluded in their wooden manor houses, diverting themselves with hunting and feasting, wearing the old Polish costumes, and laughing at the Frenchified manners of the king and his court. Roads were appalling and accommodation for visitors scanty. Not all members of the gentry were brutish and coarse, but the majority in their ignorance of affairs allowed themselves to be led by the magnates, who ruled the commonwealth in their own interests. From the mid-seventeenth century, diets were dissolved more often than not at the word of some obscure country *szlachcic* who obeyed the instructions not of his province but of a Potocki or a Radziwill. The magnates were not averse to seeking foreign aid in their rivalries, and the assemblies which elected the king were notoriously dominated by foreign bribes. In 1764 Catherine II of Russia secured the election of Stanislas Poniatowski, a Polish nobleman who had been her lover. Poniatowski was an intelligent and sensible man who would have raised his country from the welter of anarchy if he had been able to do so, but by then Poland possessed no effective governing body to help him, no civil servants, no trained diplomats, few revenues, and hardly 25,000 soldiers. In 1772 large parts of the country were swallowed up by the rapacious monarchs of Russia, Austria, and Prussia. Russian forces occupied the rest, and Catherine the Great expected the Polish king to rule in her interests.

The shock of the First Partition speeded up a national revival which had already shown flickers of life. The towns played a leading part, especially Warsaw, Cracow, and Vilna. Towns were expanding in size, if only because landowners were entering into a market economy by intensifying their agriculture and exploiting the mineral and forest wealth on their estates. A demand for luxury goods led to the building of factories, though servile labour was used for the most part. Warsaw grew from a dilapidated town of 30,000 inhabitants in the middle of the century to a lively cosmopolitan city of 100,000, open to the latest trends of western thought. An Educational Commission, set up in 1773 to direct the schools vacated by the Jesuits after the papal dissolution of the order, introduced training in citizenship and statecraft to balance the old emphasis on literature and rhetoric. Newspapers were published, and pamphlets on economic and political subjects appeared in large numbers. Two important writers, Stanislas Staszic and Hugo Kollontay, stressed the need for hereditary instead of elective monarchy, for abolition of the Liberum Veto, and for higher taxes, a larger army, industrial development, and emancipation of the serfs. An increasing number of Poles came to think that by gathering strength to resist foreign domination they would lay the basis of a new freedom.

The reform movement found a patron in Stanislas Poniatowski, who was aroused from his naturally defeatist frame of mind by the humiliating circumstances in which Catherine had placed him. Support came from citizens of the larger towns, who resented the fact that only Cracow was represented in the Diet. No movement could hope to succeed without substantial support from the gentry, however. A sufficient number joined the Patriot party to make something of a stand in the Diet of 1788 and to persuade Catherine to withdraw her troops, but more would need to be done if Poland was to withstand the vengeance likely to fall on her when Catherine finished with the Turkish War. Many of the magnates, including the Branicki and Felix Potocki, clung to the old régime and would not allow themselves to be hustled into reform by alarmist talk of Russian aggression. Indeed they thought of Russia as their bulwark against emancipation of the serfs. Other magnates, notably the Radziwills and the Czartoryskis, supported the Patriots in their desire to strengthen government but did not sympathize with the more radical proposals put forward by Kollontay. A year passed in speechifying. News of the fall of the Bastille shocked all but the most extreme reformers and prejudiced the chances of the citizens of 141 Polish towns who, urged on by Kollontay, petitioned the king for representation in the Diet. Reform might have gone no further had not

Stanislas, desperately afraid of Russian interference and mistrusting Prussian offers of help, pushed a measure through the Diet very much as the Patriot party in France pushed abolition proposals through the National Assembly on the night of August 4th.

The resulting constitution of 3 May 1791 was ostensibly based on the model of the French, which Polish reformers were shrewd enough to recognize as a source of strength. A declaration that 'all power emanates from the nation' was intended as a repudiation of foreign aggressors and puppet kings. It was followed by articles separating judicial, legislative, and executive branches of government. Judges were to be elected, and new codes of law were envisaged. Complete legislative powers were entrusted to a parliament of two houses. The executive power was strengthened by the adoption of hereditary monarchy and the creation of a council of ministers. The Liberum Veto was abolished. Self-government was granted to towns receiving a charter from the king. Any burgher who bought 'an entire village' assessed at 200 guilders in taxes could become a noble. Democrats on both sides of the Atlantic were wild in their praise, and it was not until Poland had stolen some of France's thunder that French journals began to point out the essential conservatism of the Polish reform. The serfs got nothing, and the middle class got less than equal rights with the nobles. Property-owning burghers received access to public office and to commissions in the army, but an exception was made of the cavalry, 'the horse', commented Camille Desmoulins, 'being so noble an animal that it can be constitutionally mounted only by a gentleman'. Twenty-one towns received representation in the Diet, but their delegates were described as 'plenipotentiaries' to denote their inferior status and they were allowed to vote only on commercial matters. The nobles were confirmed in 'all their immunities, liberties, and prerogatives', and their power as a body stood to increase.

King Stanislas himself, in an attempt to soothe Russia, denied that anything revolutionary had been done in Poland. 'Our law of 3 May, and everything that has come out of it, are almost the opposite of the French Revolution and keep us very far from democracy, and hence all the more from the Jacobins', he said. But Catherine refused to be placated. 'I shall fight Jacobinism, and defeat it in Poland', she wrote to Grimm. This interpretation was not merely an excuse for crushing a satellite state which showed signs of escaping from her orbit. Jacobinism outside of France made its greatest appeal to aggressive aristocracies, and the Polish example was likely to be more potent than the French in eastern Europe. In February 1792 Catherine hinted to Prussia and Austria that she intended to intervene in Poland. In March Frederick William declared his willingness to compensate himself in Poland for the expenses of war upon France. In the same month Catherine received three Polish traitors, Felix Potocki, Rzewuski, and Branicki, and agreed to aid them in crushing the constitution of 3 May. The Confederation was dated, to save face, from Targowica on 17 May. A day later 100,000 Russian troops crossed the Lithuanian and Ukrainian borders. Two Polish armies together numbered no more than 30,000, and the Polish gentry, so proud of their military tradition, had forgotten how to defend their estates. On 19 June Stanislas begged Catherine for mercy and received the order to submit at once to the Confederation of Targowica. Russian troops thereupon occupied all Poland, restored the old constitution, and drove the leading patriots into exile.

The news of Russia's startlingly rapid success reached Austria and Prussia when they had staved off the first ludicrous offensive by revolutionary armies but had not yet invaded France in their turn. Catherine could have kept all of Poland had she not genuinely wished to encourage her two fellow-sovereigns, with whom she regarded herself as in some sense allied, in their attack upon the French Revolution. She offered them both a share of the spoils, but while Frederick William greedily took all he could get the Austrians vacillated. Francis's ministers disagreed as to whether to take a part of Poland, which they did not really want, or to offer Belgium in exchange for Bavaria with additional indemnities. They were determined to have something which was equal in value to any gain made by Prussia. Negotiations dragged on through the summer weeks, after which the allied invasion of France was turned at Valmy and Austria knew that she would have to defend the Netherlands. In January 1793 Russia and Prussia agreed, the one to take White Russia and the Ukraine, the other Danzig, Thorn, Posen, and Kalish. The Republic was left with a meaningless strip of central Poland and western Lithuania. Russia gained three million subjects and Prussia one. Prussia was committed to continue the war in the west, but Frederick William chose to send most of his troops to Poland and showed little enthusiasm for fighting Francis's battles. Ministerial circles in Vienna were overcome with consternation. The Second Partition of Poland, which might have strengthened the First Coalition, weakened it irretrievably.

3. THE COALITION IN ACTION, 1793-5

The victory of the French at Valmy opened, wrote Goethe, a new era in the world's history. With it the limited and methodical warfare of the eighteenth century gave place to the all-sacrificing effort of a nation in arms. France's opponents did not immediately learn the lesson. Austria and Prussia took comfort in mutual recrimination and suspicion. As the First Coalition assembled in the early months of 1793 the members felt sure of a speedy victory. On paper their forces appeared overwhelming. For naval warfare Naples, Portugal, and Holland could supply considerable numbers of ships and excellent ports and harbours. Spain assured control of the Mediterranean

Map II   The North-Eastern Frontier of France, 1792-4

and furnished, in America, bases for attacking the French West Indies. Spain's navy, though crippled by shortage of money, included some of the most powerful vessels in the world. Britain would be able to put about 100 sail of the line into service as soon as they found crews. France, whose naval officers had been drawn almost exclusively from the old noble families of Brittany and Normandy, could not find replacements for her mere 76 vessels. She could not hope for victory at sea. On land, Prussia's system of cantonal recruitment enabled her to produce 190,000 men. Austria, thanks to conscription, had been able to mass 200,000 men on the Danube at the time of the Turkish War. Spain had 73,000 infantry and 27,000 cavalry; Italy could supply 30,000 Sardinians and as many Neapolitans. Britain's army, reduced

to a mere 13,000 by Pitt's economies on the very eve of war, could be sup-
plemented by 14,000 Hanoverians and 8,000 Hessian mercenaries. Some of
these armies possessed recent experience in the field: the British in the
American War of Independence, the Austrian against the fearsome Turks.
Prussia's army, basking in the glory of Frederick the Great, was accounted
the finest in Europe. Great confidence was derived from the belief that
regular troops were inevitably more effective than volunteers and recruits.

In the concentric assault which was now launched upon revolutionary
France the allies possessed the initial advantage. The Spaniards crossed the
Pyrenees into Roussillon; the Sardinians launched a counter-offensive against
Savoy; the Prussians crossed the Rhine. The Austrians, anxious to free their
hands for dealing with the Prussians in Poland, drove Dumouriez back upon
Brussels, defeated his army at Neerwinden, and advanced towards Valen-
ciennes. France, torn by civil war and faction fights, seemed likely to
succumb to pressure around her frontiers. The allies were already thinking
of what to do with the spoils.

These early successes were not followed up, however. The allies did not
realize that France would have to be totally defeated before she surrendered.
They thought they could bring her to terms by nibbling away at her possessions, thereby combining ultimate success with immediate gain. Austria
wanted to obtain an attractive piece of territory to offer to the Elector of
Bavaria as part of an exchange negotiation: she thought first of Belgium,
then of Alsace, and was finally persuaded by Pitt to concentrate upon French
Flanders. The commander of the Austrian forces, Prince Frederick of Saxe-
Coburg, proceeded thereafter to invest every fortified place in the coveted
area. Pitt thought that Britain's interests required Austria to be established
once and for all in the Low Countries, and in February 1793 he sent three
battalions under the Duke of York to assist in the Flanders campaign. Like
his continental allies he thought also in terms of compensation: having
agreed during the summer of 1793 to pay out huge subsidies to Austria,
Prussia, Sardinia, Hesse-Cassel, Spain, and Naples, he thought that Britain
could reimburse herself from France's overseas possessions. Of Britain's 81
infantry battalions, 17 were reserved for an attack upon the French West
Indies. George III was more interested in taking Dunkirk, and the Duke of
York moved forward to besiege it, but no naval support was given to him.
The British navy divided its attention between the West Indies and Nantes
and Toulon, where anti-Jacobin risings had taken place. Admiral Hood
established an allied force at Toulon in August, but the Austrian troops
expected from Lombardy never appeared.

Meanwhile the Jacobins prepared France's recovery. Victory at Hond-
schoote in September saved Dunkirk from the British; success at Wattignies
in October saved Maubeuge from the Austrians. The Sardinians were pushed

back from Savoy; the Spaniards were held in Roussillon. Revolt was crushed at Lyon and Toulon, and staggering blows were delivered to the Vendée. Danton's peace policy, which raised hopes among the allies that France might surrender, was rejected by Robespierre as unpatriotic: Carnot launched another offensive against Belgium, and after a resounding victory at Fleurus (26 June 1794) the French entered Antwerp and Liége. Except for a few months in 1799 France never again, until 1812, looked like losing.

Her success was better deserved than the allies admitted. The idea that the French simply hurled masses of undisciplined troops upon the enemy was only partly true. Some of the strength of the old army, reformed in the last years of the *ancien régime*, was transferred to the new by the *amalgame*, and a large number of officers, denied promotion by the *ancien régime*, gladly gave the benefit of their training and experience to commanders who offered them rewards at last. Enthusiasm was the decisive factor, among divisions both old and new. The French hardly wavered in their success until the wasting effects of hardship in Spain and Russia undermined the spirit of Napoleon's armies.

On the side of France's opponents the biggest and most lasting asset was British finance. The wars of the revolutionary period, though less costly in lives than those of the seventeenth century had been, were staggeringly costly in money. By engaging to subsidize foreign allies Britain took on the burden of financing not only her own war effort but the greater part of that of other countries too. For the first five years she tried to raise the money solely by loans, and accumulated a mountain of debt. In 1799 she took the momentous decision of paying for the war out of direct taxation, and an income tax was imposed for the purpose. The rapidly increasing wealth of her population enabled her thereafter to meet her expenses out of current income in spite of the fact that by 1815 the wars had cost her at least three times as much as they had cost France. The British public not unnaturally grumbled at the policy of sending good money to foreign allies who often seemed to make ill use of it. Annoyance reached the point of anger in 1794 when Prussia used her regular subsidies not for operations against the French but to strengthen her hold on Poland.

4. THE THIRD PARTITION OF POLAND AND THE COLLAPSE OF THE FIRST COALITION

The Polish revolt of 1794 was the work of the lesser *szlachta*, who had come at last to realize that the magnates had betrayed them to the foreigners. The revolt was instigated by a group of patriots in exile at Leipzig, and the leader whom they chose for the army was, significantly, not one of the great aristocrats but a petty noble, Kósciuszko, honoured for his defence of the Republic in 1792. The revolt began in Cracow in March 1794, and the citizens of Warsaw were emboldened to follow suit. Kósciuszko knew from the start that the position was desperate, for the Prussians marched at once upon Cracow. In May 1794 he called upon the people to rise, and promised what no Polish leader had promised before or was to promise again in the nineteenth century: that the peasants would become free men enjoying the protection of the law. He also appealed to the French for help but was spurned by the Committee of Public Safety, Saint-Just alleging that he remained too closely wedded to aristocratic institutions. In truth Kósciuszko made no attempt to destroy the old economy, for he promised only to alleviate not abolish labour services. 'God sees', he wrote to the Princess Czartoryska, 'that we are not starting a French Revolution.' His policy was in many ways too moderate for the extreme left wing of the reform movement, whose members gained the upper hand for a short time in Warsaw. The bankruptcy of the Republic after the Second Partition had caused severe unemployment in the city, and angry craftsmen were willing to riot for the summary trial and execution of the members of the puppet government and 'the men of Targowica'. Kósciuszko detailed a whole cavalry brigade to restore order, and thereby weakened himself in the face of the enemy. The Prussians were held off after they had taken Cracow, but the Russians could not be defeated. When the Russian army entered Warsaw in November 1794 many moderates as well as conservatives believed that Poland had been saved from Jacobinism. The former continued to hate Russia for her brutality during the assault, but they also continued into the nineteenth century to dread the excesses of revolt.

Whilst the Poles failed to save themselves they helped to save France from the First Coalition. In May 1794 the Austrians thought only of disengaging their army from Flanders so as to restore the balance of power in eastern Europe. The unfortunate Duke of York was involved in their retreat, and the British campaign ended ignominiously when the remains of the expeditionary force, chased into Germany and refused help by Prussia, took ship at Bremen in March 1795 to return to England. Pitt had dropped his subsidies to Prussia in October 1794 and might have known that Frederick William would desert him. A francophile party at Berlin had long been pointing out to the Prussian king the futility of weakening himself by war in the west when his true destiny lay to the east. In November Hardenberg was sent to treat with the French. By the Treaty of Basle, signed on 6 April 1795, Prussia promised France a free hand on the left bank of the Rhine, and France promised Prussia that she would respect the neutrality of north Germany, which Frederick William hoped to take under his protection. By the Third Partition of Poland (October 1795) which obliterated the unhappy Republic from the map, Prussia received the central portion of the great Polish plain from the Niemen in the north to upper Silesia in the south. A million Polish subjects were added to her already large Slavonic population. They benefited at least in the sense that they were brought into the Prussian economic system, and as early as 1796 some Polish magnates were dreaming of restoring the unity of the Republic under Prussian patronage. Had it not been for the interference of Napoleon, Prussia might have become a Slavonic rather than a German power in the nineteenth century.

Prussia's defection exposed Holland to French attack: the new Batavian Republic signed a treaty with France at the Hague on 16 May 1795. The states of southern and western Germany signed a convention the next day, partly from suspicion of Austrian designs on Bavaria and partly in the hope of receiving benefits at French hands. Spain backed out of the war for internal reasons a few weeks later. Large sections of France's frontiers were thus neutralized, and several armies became available for use elsewhere. A general peace seemed possible, and the decision whether or not to continue the war against Britain and Austria rested very largely with the French Republic.

CHAPTER VI

France and the Expansion of Progress, 1794-9

I. THE THERMIDOREAN REACTION

AFTER the fall of Robespierre the immediate object of the men of the Plain was to destroy Jacobinism. To middle class politicians, Jacobinism had come to stand for 'democracy', a term which they construed as government by the mob and control of the economy in the interests of the lower class. The Convention set about its task by dismantling or modifying Jacobin institutions – the Committee of Public Safety, the Paris Commune, the Revolutionary Tribunal, the sections, and the clubs. This was accompanied by an attack on Jacobin personnel, for which the Convention, though it had expunged the word 'terror' from its official documents, did not hesitate to use terrorist methods. Former Hébertists, enragés, and Cordeliers were let out of prison to attack the 'Robespierrist remnant'. More skilled in appealing to the mob than ever Robespierre had been, they knew how to obtain support from the underworld of Paris, from the men who would murder at anyone's bidding for the sheer love of destruction and loot. To these promising types were added young men from the lower ranks of the professions, minor officials, lawyers' clerks, bank clerks and the like, the so-called *jeunesse dorée* with pockets empty and minds full of arrogant ideas. Dressed in silk clothes, wearing blonde wigs, carrying weighted cudgels, and affecting a lisping form of speech, the *jeunesse dorée* gave to the mobs of the Thermidorean reaction a quite different appearance from the mobs of 1789 or 1792, in which the cotton blouse and slacks of the workman had been most conspicuous. Issuing from the Palais Royal the terrorists ranged through the streets dealing out destruction to any who opposed them. Meanwhile a White Terror broke out spontaneously in the Midi and the south, aided by émigrés and refractory priests who were creeping back into France with official connivance.

Extermination of Jacobinism was completed when the sans-culottes played into the hands of the Convention by rising in revolt on 1 April (12 germinal) and 20 May (1 prairial) 1795. The risings had a vague political content, for which Jacobin agitators lying low in the sections were doubtless responsible. On both occasions mobs burst into the Convention demanding 'cheap bread and the constitution of 1793'. The risings were, however, essentially spontaneous protests against suffering caused by the Convention's economic policy. In spite of continuing war and shortage the Convention rewarded its middle class followers, especially large producers and merchants, by liberating the economy from controls imposed by the Jacobins. On 23 December 1794 the Maximum was virtually abolished. Before many months were out the lower classes in cities all over France approached starvation. The Convention promised Parisians a ration of bread and meat at a fixed price, but supplies were not maintained. The sans-culottes found their hardships more difficult to bear in the presence of luxury ostentatiously displayed by the rich. The Jacobins had encouraged an austere mode of living as indicative of republican virtue, but these restraints had broken down and produced a reaction, especially among the *nouveaux riches* of food speculators, army contractors, stock-jobbers, and successful politicians. New salons appeared; the lovely but scandalous Madame Tallien dictated fashion to all Paris; wealthy youths adopted arrogant manners in public. The 'muscadins' (a name previously given to little scented sweets and now applied to the *jeunesse dorée*) particularly angered the sans-culottes. An element of class hatred, which the Jacobins had hoped to destroy, reappeared and played a part in the struggle between the sans-culottes and the Thermidorean Convention.

Minor acts of violence were common from the middle of March 1795 but they lacked cohesion. The day of 12 germinal was itself little more than a riot. The Convention used it, however, as an excuse for condemning Collot, Billaud, and Barère to transportation and for decreeing the arrest of 12 other left-wing deputies. A law passed by the Constituent Assembly to prohibit the army from moving within a certain distance of Paris was suspended to allow troops to be brought to the outskirts, and officers suspected of Jacobin sympathies were purged. The National Guard was reorganized to exclude passive citizens. Nothing was done to improve the food situation beyond a futile attempt to supplement the falling bread ration with issues of rice. Agitation continued in the sections; illicit meetings were held; an anonymous manifesto was spread abroad urging the people to rise. Early on 1 prairial, when the bread ration had fallen to 2 ounces, the tocsin sounded in the eastern sections and women gathered, urging their menfolk to seize arms and follow them in a march on the Convention. The deputies, for the first time in the Revolution, resisted the mob, and after several hours the insurgents were driven back by the National Guard. Next day some 20,000 armed men from the sections surrounded the Convention, which was protected by 40,000 National Guardsmen, the largest display of military force ever seen in Paris since the Revolution began. No shots were fired. Lulled by promises from the Convention the insurgents returned to their sections. On the third day army detachments surrounded the faubourg Saint-Antoine and threatened to starve out the citizens if the rebels did not lay down their arms.

The episode showed clearly that the sans-culottes were no longer the effective insurrectionary force they had been in earlier years. Their leaders had been decimated, partly by Robespierre and partly by the Thermidoreans, and they could no longer rely on the support of a large body of deputies in the Convention or on the support of a radical wing of the bourgeosie. The National Guard, purged of its poorer members, was on the side of authority, and the Convention was willing to use it against the people. The revolutionary fiction of harmony between government and governed was shattered, and the sans-culottes could look upon themselves once more as outcasts. The revolt was followed by systematic repression. Nineteen victims were condemned to death by a military tribunal; most of the remaining members of the great Jacobin committees were arrested; only Carnot was spared. In the sections all former members of Jacobin organizations were disarmed. The companies of gunners, which alone of the National Guard had joined the mob on 2 prairial, were dissolved. The sans-culottes did not re-emerge as a revolutionary force until the eighteen-thirties.

At one time the sans-culottes had provided forces essential for staving off counter-revolution. Now, thanks to Jacobin efforts, counter-revolution seemed only a remote contingency. Belgium and the Rhineland were once more occupied by French troops; the enemy coalition, balked of a speedy victory, was breaking up under pressure of selfish interests; in February 1795 the Vendéan leader Charette signed a pacification with the republican authorities at La Jaunaye and during the next three months the whole of the west laid down its arms. Many people in France wanted the republican government to take advantage of its comparatively strong position to restore a Bourbon king on terms similar to those of 1791 and to make peace with Europe on the basis of a few frontier rectifications. Boissy d'Anglas, whose firmness as president of the Convention on 1 prairial marked him out as a leading politician of the new order, began working cautiously towards these ends. A Bourbon restoration was prevented only by fate and by the stupidity of the émigrés. The little son of Louis XVI, once cruelly ill-treated by the revolutionaries and now the hope of the constitutional monarchists, died of tuberculosis on 8 June 1795. The Comte de Provence became the Pretender, Louis XVIII. He at once issued a manifesto from Verona threatening merciless punishment for the regicides and promising the restoration of all former privileges to the aristocracy and church. Shortly afterwards a force of émigrés was landed by a British fleet on the promontory of Quiberon in southern Brittany. Too late to receive effective help from the Vendéans it was defeated during July by Hoche, and 748 prisoners were shot, including 428 nobles. The constitutional monarchists, including Boissy d'Anglas, drew in their horns, and on 22 August a new republican constitution emerged from the Convention, awaiting only the nation's consent by plebiscite.

The authors of the Constitution offered votes to property owners only. 'We should be governed by the best,' said Boissy d'Anglas, 'and the best are those best educated and most interested in upholding the laws. With very few exceptions you will find such men only among those who, possessing property, are attached to the country containing it and the laws which protect it.' The statement might have been made by any member of the majority in the Constituent Assembly. It was not incompatible with generous hopes for the welfare of the people. Unfortunately the Thermidoreans could not trust all property owners. Indeed they could not, apparently, place perfect trust in anyone but themselves. Priests and former émigrés were disfranchised, along with all arrested Jacobins, and electors were told to choose two thirds of the members of the new legislative body from among the members of the existing Convention. This last injunction very much angered property owners in France, especially in the western sections of Paris. Many, while keeping their faith in the republic, had lost confidence in the Thermidoreans and had no wish to vote them back into power. Anticipating trouble from royalists, the government drafted troops into Paris and even decided to allow former terrorists to vote in the primary assemblies. The hostility aroused by these measures gave a few determined royalists an opportunity to prepare a revolt among property owners, most of whom were not royalists but were, on the contrary, loyal to the republican principle of sovereignty of the people which they believed the Convention to be infringing.

During September the constitution obtained a large majority and the decree of two thirds a small majority of votes in the plebiscite. On 5 October 1795 (13 vendémiaire) revolt broke out in Paris. Food shortage produced some rebels from among the sans-culottes, but the majority came from the upper middle class. Faced with opposition on both sides the Convention had no other course than to turn to the army. Barras, a former infantry officer who had led troops against Robespierre in July 1794, was once more charged with defending his fellow-deputies. He called to his aid the young general Bonaparte and put him in charge of the artillery. Barras's troops were outnumbered 4 to 1 by the rebels, but Bonaparte sent for cannon and used them mercilessly against the civilian enemy, killing some 300 and scattering the rest in confusion. On 26 October 1795 the Thermidoreans resigned their power. The army, which had acted as midwife to the new régime, stayed on to play a decisive part in its life and death.

An important rôle for the army was foreshadowed in the foreign policy of the Thermidoreans. In the summer of 1795 France might have made peace with her sole remaining enemies, Britain and Austria, by sacrificing the revolutionary doctrine of the natural frontiers and abandoning Belgium and the Rhineland. Many members of the Thermidorean Convention believed that the natural frontiers were essential to France's safety, however, and even Carnot could not convince them that France merely needed to rectify her frontier so that it ran along the Scheldt, the Sambre, and the Meuse, with the fortresses of Antwerp and Namur at the extremities. Some members were influenced by political considerations: France's large army could not be disbanded without increasing economic difficulties at home, yet if the army was to be maintained at its revolutionary level it must live off its conquests. In 1793 and 1794 vast amounts of money and supplies had been requisitioned by French troops in Belgium and the Rhineland; indemnities had been imposed by the French government; and the Jacobins had set up 'commercial agencies' to send to France industrial machinery, seeds of interesting plants, specimens of fine horses and cattle, works of art, and any products which might be expected to benefit civilization. Such sources of pride and profit could not lightly be discarded. Some French republicans looked even further than the natural frontiers and envisaged 'sister republics', or satellite states, which would serve as bulwarks against France's enemies, accept French enlightenment, and help to support France's economy. Defence, attack, brotherly love, and self-interest were inextricably mixed in the policy of republican enthusiasts such as Sieyès, Reubell, and Merlin of Douai. Their influence grew greater after the Quiberon affair; Carnot's policy of 'narrow boundaries' was pushed into the background; and on 1 October 1795 the Convention decreed the annexation of Belgium. The Rhineland, on whose value opinion was divided, was declared simply a 'conquered country'. The Thermidoreans assumed that no peace on these terms would be acceptable to Britain and Austria, and they deliberately bequeathed a war against these two powers to their successors.

2. THE DIRECTORY

The Constitution of the Year III was intended to establish liberty on the capable shoulders of France's middle class. The latter, it was believed, would shun Jacobinism, with its undercurrents of socialism and mob rule, and royalism, with its threats of privilege and despotism. In October 1795 a mere 30,000 electors, each possessed of property valued at 200 days' wages of a labourer, chose a legislative body consisting of two houses, a Council of Five Hundred and a Council of Ancients. A large majority of the members could be classed as moderate republicans. The constitution provided a great many safeguards against a minority imposing its will on the body politic. General elections, with opportunities for subversive propaganda, were avoided by a rule that a third of the deputies were to be replaced annually. The two Councils were forbidden to communicate with each other except by written message. The Council of Five Hundred could alone initiate laws, which the Council of Ancients must sanction or reject. Executive power was separated from the legislature, divided between five Directors, and whittled down to a minimum. The Directors could not initiate legislation and could not prorogue or dissolve the Councils. They were chosen by the Ancients from a list drawn up by the Five Hundred; one Director, chosen by lot, must retire each year.

Sandwiched between the Jacobin dictatorship and the Consulate, the Directory appears in historical literature as one of the weaker French régimes of modern times. The weakness should not be exaggerated. The constitution guaranteed a fair amount of continuity in government policy. The large majority of moderates in the Councils of 1795 could not be overthrown in one election. The fact that only one Director could be replaced annually meant that the Councils could only change the political complexion of the government by sustained effort over several years. One of the original Directors, Reubell, managed to maintain his position and impress his views concerning foreign policy upon the government until May 1799. The Directors were endowed with power to appoint ministers, make decrees, conclude treaties, direct diplomacy and war, and choose generals. Although they could not initiate legislation they found that they could give effect to their policy by sending messages to the Councils, while denying responsibility for unpopular laws. Efforts were made also to co-ordinate local government. The independence of the communes was diminished by the abolition of their general councils, the districts were abolished, departmental councils were abolished, and departmental directories could be dissolved at any time by the government. Each department was given a *commissaire*, directly responsible to Paris. Most of the men who held office as Director were men of more than average ability. Carnot was a genius in the administration of war; Le Tourneur was a naval expert; Reubell brought immense energy and knowledge to the conduct of diplomacy; La Revellière had some credit as a scholar and thinker; François de Neufchâteau was a distinguished Minister of the Interior who anticipated many of Napoleon's reforms; Freilhard and Merlin were leading jurisconsults of the day. Even Barras had some talents which were of use to the state, for his life of intrigue fitted him for the necessary job of organizing the police. If the Directory was shackled throughout its lifetime this was not due to any constitutional weakness in the régime or to any lack of ability on the part of the Directors but to financial difficulties.

The Directory opened with a truly dreadful monetary crisis, the culmination of disastrous policies over many years. Assignats nominally valued at 100 francs fell to 15 sous. The government was unable during the night to print enough assignats for use the following day; in less than four months the amount of paper money in circulation doubled. Prices rose hourly. Distress among the lower classes was aggravated by a poor harvest in 1795, followed by a severe winter. The Directory returned to a policy of controlling corn sales: local authorities were ordered to force peasants to bring their stocks into the towns and sell them in the open market. Peasants refused to co-operate, as they had no desire to sell their corn for worthless paper money. Communal authorities were usually under the influence of local farmers and connived at their disobedience; district authorities, which might have been more effective, had been suppressed. Hordes of vagrants roamed the countryside, stealing and pillaging. In Paris the price of bread rose to 50 francs a pound in paper money or 7 sous in specie, a figure much higher than any reached during the famine of 1788-9. Vast numbers of people would have died of starvation had not the government continued the policy of distributing a ration of cheap bread. Even so, deaths in the Department of the Seine increased by 10,000 in the year IV of the republic. The government aimed at supplying each person with a pound of bread a day, but scarcity reduced the ration to a few ounces, and even this amount cost the government 9 million francs a day during December 1795.

In these circumstances it was natural that the ideas of the *enragés* should reappear. They took the form of a primitive kind of communism, advocated by Babeuf, a petty official. Babeuf had long been of the opinion that civil equality was useless without economic equality. Like previous socialist thinkers, he dreamed of a re-distribution of property rather than the abolition of property: the farmer was to work his own little plot of land, but he was to devote the produce to a common market. Unlike previous socialists, Babeuf did not confine his ideas to agriculture: he believed that mechanized industry could be organized for the benefit of the community. And, what was more important, he was not a purely utopian thinker: he had some notions as to how to attain his ends. Mistrusting the ability of the ignorant multitude, and despising politicians, he came to believe that the new social order must be imposed by rebellion and dictatorship, carried out by an enlightened minority. It was this idea of the revolutionary élite, transmitted by Buonarroti and Blanqui, which linked Babeuf with Lenin and gave him his significance in the history of socialism.

His conspiracy was easily crushed. His little band of followers, known as the Equals, joined hands with a few hundred former terrorists and Jacobins who were sworn enemies of the Directory. Government spies were involved from the start, and the conspirators fell a prey to the vigorous anti-Jacobin measures taken by Carnot, one of the first five Directors. Carnot had never believed in the social policy pursued by the great Committee of Public Safety, and his authoritarian instincts rose against conspiracy. In May 1796 Babeuf was arrested with some 200 followers. An attempt was made to raise a rescue party from among the soldiers in camp at Grenelle, but Carnot dispersed the plotters with cavalry, and 30 soldiers were afterwards shot by order of court martial. The other Directors were less vindictive than Carnot, and the trial of the accused was allowed to drag. A time came when honest citizens were more afraid of royalists than of Jacobins, and most of the accused were then acquitted by juries. Some were imprisoned. Babeuf was executed on 27 May 1797.

The Directory made serious efforts to solve France's monetary problems. The first was a proposal to raise a forced loan, payable in specie, corn, or in assignats taken at 1% of their face-value. This was really an attempt at deflation, since assignats were worth much less than 1%. The scheme failed owing to lack of specie for the conversion of assignats. The issuing of assignats had to be abandoned altogether in February 1796, when those in circulation, to the nominal value of 39 milliards of francs, were worth less than the paper they were printed on. The next experiment was devised by the finance minister Ramel, who proposed issuing new paper bills called *mandats territoriaux*, entitling the holder to obtain national land at a fixed valuation. Unfortunately the Council of Five Hundred made assignats convertible into *mandats* at one thirtieth of their face-value, and the *mandats* collapsed as the assignats had done. A decree of 4 February 1797 took all paper bills out of currency.

The Directors knew that a return to a metal standard would be extremely difficult, as coins were rare. Inflation was followed by rapid deflation, aggravated by the abundant harvest of 1796. Bourgeois speculators with a little gold bought up the remaining national land at a low price, while the government lacked means to finance the war and maintain public services. In these circumstances the government was driven, in September 1797, to repudiate two thirds of the public debt. This seriously reduced the nominal income of the *rentiers*, although they could comfort themselves with the knowledge that interest on one third of their capital, paid in specie, was worth more than the gross interest, paid in assignats, had been for a long time. Ramel was able, for the first time in the history of revolutionary finance, to balance the budget. Nevertheless, the faith of the middle classes in the government was shaken. Ramel tried to put national finances on a sounder footing during 1798 by re-organizing the direct taxes and introducing some small indirect ones, but the fruits of his labours were lost in the administrative chaos which swamped the final months of the Directory.

In all this financial turmoil the government could hardly escape censure. War contractors, speculators, and profiteers made huge fortunes; and since these were the new bourgeoisie who formed the social élite of the Directory it was natural that less fortunate classes should suspect government policy of being directed in their favour. A few men in government circles increased their fortunes rapidly, notably Talleyrand, and it was assumed that they had done so by dishonest means. Spectacular scandals concerning the Flachat and Dijon companies of government contractors enhanced the impression that France's rulers were involved in shady transactions. As far as the Directors themselves were concerned the impression was true only of Barras. His corruption was notorious, and since he was the only Director who remained in office from the beginning to the end of the period, his name became a synonym for the moral standards of the Directory.

3. THE ITALIAN CAMPAIGN AND THE COUP D'ÉTAT OF FRUCTIDOR

It was widely assumed at the time that financial motives prompted the First Directory to continue the war against Austria, as an excuse for plundering north Italy. This was an over-simplification. Reubell, the most commanding personality among the Directors, was a whole-hearted supporter of the policy of natural frontiers. His immediate interest lay in annexing the Rhineland to France. He was himself an Alsatian, and he believed that annexation of the Rhineland was the only means of saving northern Alsace from Austria. The latter, disgruntled at the small share she had received in the Third Partition of Poland, was known to be seeking compensation in the west. Very determined, and quite unscrupulous, Reubell would if necessary condemn the whole of Europe to war for the sake of a border province. He was supported in the Directory by La Revellière, a peculiar character, an exponent of the revolutionary cult of theophilanthropy and a fierce enemy of priests and aristocrats. La Revellière believed that it was the duty of France to spread revolutionary enlightenment throughout Europe. In this spirit he had been the chief author of the Edict of Fraternity, and he was a vigorous exponent of the policy of creating sister-republics. The prospect of financial gain was merely an added incentive, but it was sufficient to win the support of Barras. Carnot, still advocating peace on a basis of frontier rectifications, was supported only by his old school-fellow Le Tourneur, a man of small political influence.

At the beginning of 1796 France had little more than 400,000 men under arms, compared with 1,200,000 at the height of Jacobin success. Depletion was not as much due to death, injury and capture, as to desertion. The economic policy of the Thermidoreans was partly to blame, for the abolition of food controls made the feeding of the armies difficult, while the collapse of assignats made payment almost impossible. Even more important, however, was the unfairness of Carnot's *levée en masse*. No limit was set to the length of service of the 18 to 25 class called up by Carnot, and no men attaining their eighteenth birthday after the publication of the decree of 23 August 1793 were called. By 1795 the French armies were virtually professional armies once more, for the volunteers of 1792 had returned home, and of Carnot's levy only those who liked army life saw fit to remain.

There were four French armies. The Army of the North consisted of 25,000 men supported by the Batavian republic in accordance with the Treaty of the Hague. Its men were better clothed, fed, and paid than other French soldiers; discipline was fairly strict but complacency led to a falling off in republican zeal. On the eastern front two armies lived mainly by pillaging the Rhineland. In the south-east the Army of Italy, which had remained inactive since repelling the invasion of 1793, numbered less than 40,000 men and was without doubt the Cinderella of the French armies. Distance from Paris rendered supplies meagre and the poverty of the Alpine country rendered pillage disappointing. Nevertheless it was this dilapidated army which was called upon to swoop down into Piedmont and turn eastward to Milan, the traditional way of attacking Austria. After a demoralizing series of changes, command was given on 2 March 1796 to Napoleon Bonaparte. A few days later the enterprising Corsican cemented his alliance with the Directory by marrying one of Barras's many women friends, the widow Josephine Beauharnais. Napoleon was twenty-six, Josephine thirty-two years of age. After two days of married bliss the bridegroom left to take up his command, and proceeded to conduct one of the most extraordinary campaigns in the history of the Revolution.

Many years later, on St. Helena, Napoleon described how he inspired the men of the Army of Italy with noble words. This was a fabrication. The thought of entering the Promised Land was a sufficient incentive to attack, and Bonaparte's talent for histrionics could be saved for another day. His generals at first had little confidence in their commander, for his youth, his weak physique, and his mere five feet two inches in height were not impressive. They soon changed their minds. He showed his energy and efficiency at once in calling up supplies from Marseille and Genoa. To Carnot's revolutionary tactics Bonaparte added skill as a strategist. His genius in this, as in much else, lay in an inspired use of resources available. In a pitched battle with the whole of the enemy forces he would probably have been defeated, for his men were still badly equipped. By a series of quick marches he was able to fight small engagements with isolated detachments in which he made sure that the French always outnumbered the enemy. His movements were greatly assisted by French sympathies among the people of Piedmont. The Sardinian forces were divided from the Austrians and defeated at Cherasco on 25 April; on 15 May, Victor Amadeus III signed a peace treaty ceding Savoy and Nice to France. Piedmont itself was annexed in 1799.

Discipline was no easy task among soldiers who swooped like carrion crows upon the fallen enemy, yet discipline was essential to further advance. After shooting a few leading offenders Bonaparte replaced private looting with public looting, or requisitioning. Contributions equal to half the pay of the French soldiers were levied upon occupied territory. Towns and individuals were called upon to surrender their richest treasures of art and manufacture to be sent to France. Meanwhile Bonaparte turned his army eastward. No fierce fighting was encountered, for the French outflanked the Austrians at every point. The crossing of the Po was effected by violating the neutrality of Parma. The Duke, unable to resist, sued for an armistice, and paid for it by seeing his art treasures, including some of Correggio's greatest paintings, packed up and sent to Paris. The Adda was crossed at Lodi, where Berthier, Masséna, and other officers led French troops in a dash across a narrow bridge. This small action was exaggerated in contemporary accounts to become a major battle, and Bonaparte was depicted, wrongly, as leading an heroic charge. Embellishments of this kind were hardly necessary, for the incredible speed of the advance was a sufficient testimony to Bonaparte's leadership. In four weeks he advanced 150 miles across the plain of Lombardy, occupied Milan, and drove the Austrians into Mantua and behind the river Adige. Lombardy was his.

Bonaparte wished at this point to cross the Tyrol, join forces with the Army of the Rhine, and attack Vienna, but the Directors had other views. They doubted the ability of French armies to defeat the Emperor on German soil, and they preferred Bonaparte to consolidate his Italian conquests so that they could be surrendered to the Emperor in return for the Rhineland. They ordered him to turn southward to Tuscany, Rome, and Naples. Bonaparte agreed, partly because he could not as yet afford to disobey and partly because he recognized the importance of controlling the ports on the west coast of Italy, from which British ships were menacing communications with France. In central and southern Italy the mere threat of French arms was enough to bring the rulers to terms. The King of Naples asked for an armistice; the Pope agreed to cede Ancona, Bologna, and Ferrara; Leghorn was looted; and within a month Bonaparte was planning once more to invade Germany. He was held up by repeated failures to take Mantua, which did not fall until 2 February 1797; then again by orders from Paris to undertake a punitive expedition against the Pope. The Directors were disappointed with the original armistice signed by Pius VI; they wished Bonaparte to stamp out the Roman religion, which would always be 'an irreconcilable enemy of the Republic'. Bonaparte had no wish to tie up a large part of his army in the Papal States, however. After a lightning descent upon Rome he accepted the Treaty of Tolentino, in which the Pope promised to surrender his claims to Avignon and the Legations, to pay a huge indemnity, and to close his ports to hostile navies.

In the early months of the Italian campaign Bonaparte acknowledged valuable help from the *commissaire* Salicetti, a fellow-Corsican; but when the latter was withdrawn the relationship between the army general and the civilian representatives of government grew strained. Bonaparte increasingly resented instructions from Paris, some of which showed a lack of insight into the position of French troops occupying north Italy. Many Italian patriots had expected to receive freedom at the hands of the French army and would withdraw their support if their wishes were not gratified. The Directors had no desire to commit themselves to a north Italian republic, however, for they intended to barter these conquests in return for the Rhineland. On 15 October 1796 Bonaparte on his own initiative formed Modena and the Legations into a Cispadane republic. On 25 October he ordered the military governor of Lombardy to act without reference to the *commissaires*. On 20 March 1797 he advanced into Austria.

In some ways Bonaparte was right in regarding the time as propitious for a strike towards Vienna. The British fleet had been obliged to leave the Mediterranean subsequent to the signing of a treaty between France and Spain (19 August 1796) and to France's reoccupation of Corsica (October 1796). Britain's finances were strained by the war and she grudged subsidies to foreign governments which seemed to show no return. The new Tsar, Paul I, was unfriendly to the Allies. Among the Emperor's advisers, only Thugut wanted a fight to the finish; others were urging Francis to cut his losses and make peace. Yet the Directors had not underestimated the military difficulties. Bonaparte's left flank was threatened with a new Austrian attack over the Brenner Pass, Venice adopted a hostile attitude, Milan was seething with discontent in the rear, and Genoa threatened to cut off supplies. No help was forthcoming from the German princes. Bonaparte pushed on as fast as he could to Leoben, where he received Austrian envoys and hastened to arrange terms before the accredited agent of the French government could reach the scene.

In the Preliminaries of Leoben (18 April 1797) Bonaparte proposed that France should recognize the integrity of the Holy Roman Empire and that Francis II should cede Belgium and Lombardy in return for a portion of Venice, as yet untouched. On 2 May Bonaparte declared war on Venice, democratic agitators overthrew the Doge and gave entry to the French army, and Bonaparte prepared to carve up the ancient republic as monarchs of the old régime had carved up Poland. He caused a tree of liberty to be planted in front of St. Mark's cathedral and a copy of the Declaration of the Rights of Man to be placed under the paw of the Venetian lion, then stripped Venice of all valuables that could be transported. A year later the four bronze horses from the west porch of St. Mark's were carried in procession through the streets of Paris, bearing the inscription, 'Transported from Corinth to Rome, from Rome to Constantinople, from Constantinople to Venice, from Venice to France, they rest at last upon free ground'.

When the Directory was informed of the Preliminaries of Leoben, Reubell, La Revellière, and Barras declared the terms unacceptable. Bonaparte had not secured the Rhineland, and the Emperor would be more than compensated for the loss of Belgium and Lombardy by receiving an outlet to the Adriatic. Yet on 30 April only Reubell refused to sign a ratification. The Directory could not repudiate the terms without disclosing to the Emperor that Bonaparte was in no position to attack Vienna, and such a disclosure would not help towards the conclusion of a satisfactory final treaty. Barras could console himself with the thought of fifty million francs taken from Italy, La Revellière with a sister republic beyond the Alps. Moreover, the news of Leoben had been received enthusiastically in France. Bonaparte was the all-conquering hero. Behind him stood an army grateful for payment in solid coin, and a host of contractors greedy for further gain. To repudiate such a man would be to repudiate the strongest arm of the republic in face of its enemies.

Enemies were many and near at hand. Financial instability, along with the discovery of the Babeuf plot, brought a reaction in favour of moderate royalism, and the widespread desire for peace laid France open to propaganda by royalists who offered a reconciliation with Europe. In the partial elections of April 1797, constitutional monarchists obtained a majority of available seats. In May their nominee, Barthélemy, replaced Le Tourneur as Director. With sympathy also from Carnot it seemed inevitable that monarchy would triumph by constitutional means. Peace negotiations with the British were already taking place at Lille. Outside observers realized that French royalists were hopelessly divided into moderates and extremists, and that the programme of the émigrés would ruin the cause of monarchy, but the three republican Directors dared take no risks. They decided to carry out a *coup d'état* against their opponents. Defeat in the elections convinced the Directors that there was no question of calling for popular support; the army must be summoned to save the republic. Bonaparte sent his lieutenant Augereau to preside over the business. On 4 September Paris was put under military occupation. Barthélemy was arrested and Carnot fled. The Councils were purged and elections in 49 departments quashed; 177 deputies were eliminated without being replaced. Seventeen leading opponents of the triumvirate, joined by Barthélemy's valet of his own free will, were transported in cages to French Guiana, where the prospect of life was so short that the criminal colony became known as the dry guillotine. Royalists were purged from all administrative bodies. Émigrés were given fifteen days to leave France under pain of death, and a few hundred priests were sent to Guiana. Forty-two newspapers were suppressed and their editors and proprietors deported.

Such was the *coup d'état* of 18 fructidor. The replacement of Carnot and

Barthélemy by François de Neufchâteau and Merlin of Douai brought new support, notably from the latter, to an expansionist foreign policy. New sister republics were created under Bonaparte's aegis in Italy. Lombardy and Modena became the Cisalpine republic, Genoa the Ligurian republic. The Directors wanted to preside over Venice also, and ordered Bonaparte to fight rather than hand it over to the Emperor, but Bonaparte was determined to be the popular peace-maker. The Austrian envoy Cobenzl realized that he would secure more satisfactory terms from Bonaparte than from the Directors, and so hurriedly concluded with him the Treaty of Campo-Formio (18 October 1797). The Emperor promised to allow France to take the left bank of the Rhine if the French government could arrange the transaction with the German princes. He gave up his claims to Belgium and Lombardy and agreed that the Cisalpine republic should absorb the Cispadane republic along with Venetian territory west of the Adige. In return the Emperor was to receive Venice itself, with Istria and Dalmatia, while France took the Ionian islands. The Directors were horrified, but their hands were tied tighter than ever by fructidor.

4. THE EGYPTIAN CAMPAIGN AND THE COUPS D'ÉTAT OF FLORÉAL AND BRUMAIRE

After Campo-Formio only Britain remained at war with France. The chances of Britain striking a military blow were negligible, and there were many people in France who believed that peace could be concluded on terms favourable to the republic. The chances were ruined by the hostility of the Directors to Britain as a commercial rival and by Bonaparte's ambitious schemes.

All French revolutionary governments, while adopting a liberal attitude to economic matters at home, were protectionist with regard to foreign commerce. At the outbreak of war with Britain the Eden Treaty of 1786, which had allowed a modicum of free trade between Britain and France, was annulled. By a law of 31 October 1796 a great many British-made articles were declared contraband in France's territories; shortly afterwards French ports were closed to neutral ships which had touched at a British port. In 1797 the Foreign Minister Delacroix dreamed of a system of commercial alliances whereby all regions of Europe within the French orbit would become a protected market for French goods. The plan achieved only a limited success, but the seed of the later Continental Blockade had been planted. The French government was well aware that the cheapness of British industrial goods, the enterprise of Britain's merchant navy, and the Royal Navy's command of the sea were combining to oust French commerce in America and the Mediterranean. This process would be speeded up if peace were made on a basis of the status quo. It was significant that the negotiations at Lille broke down not over France's claim to Belgium, which Britain was willing to concede, but over Britain's refusal to surrender the colonial conquests she had made during the war (the French West Indies, Dutch Guiana, Ceylon, and the Cape).

The idea of seizing Egypt as a base for attacking British commerce and a stepping-stone towards a French empire in the east seems to have occurred almost simultaneously during 1797 to Talleyrand, France's new foreign secretary, and to Bonaparte. The latter required another sphere for his talents, and the occupation of the Ionian islands turned his thoughts to the Mediterranean. Egypt, ruled by the Mameluke Beys, belonged nominally to France's old ally Turkey, but Bonaparte believed that the Sultan could be pacified with the story that France was merely occupying Egypt temporarily to chastise the Beys for their attacks upon French commerce. The Directors were not greatly impressed by the idea. In November they appointed Bonaparte commander-in-chief of the Army of England and sent him to the Channel ports to consider the prospects of an invasion. He reported unfavourably. He was in no mind to repeat the futile descent upon Ireland carried out in the previous year, and a descent upon England was impossible without mastery at sea. British naval victories over the Spaniards off Cape St. Vincent and the Dutch at Camperdown (February and October 1797) augured ill for France's naval position for years to come. Reluctantly the Directors turned to the Egyptian scheme.

Bonaparte set sail from Toulon in May 1798 with 300 ships, 43,000 troops, and 167 scholars, scientists, and technicians. The destination of the armada, the biggest expedition to cross the Mediterranean since the crusades, was not discovered by the British until the French reached Malta. Bonaparte seized the island from the feeble grasp of the knights of St. John in thirty hours, reorganized everything from government and taxation to street-lighting and postal services in six days, and set sail on 19 June, arriving off Alexandria on the 30th. Meanwhile Nelson, taking a more southerly course in pursuit of the French, had arrived at Alexandria on the 28th, and finding the harbour empty had turned away to the north-east.

In a proclamation to the army, Bonaparte told his troops that they were about to deliver a mortal blow at British power and to bring freedom and culture to a land which for centuries had lain in bondage and darkness. He promised that they would receive inspiration from the monuments of ancient conquest and civilization. The first shock to these hopes came when the French soldiers saw the miserable hovels which stood on the site of the once great city of Alexandria. The ragged population of 5,000 surrendered without serious fighting. Leaving 6,000 men to garrison lower Egypt Bonaparte led the remainder 120 miles over burning sand towards Cairo, the capital city of Egypt and the core of Mameluke power. Carrying almost no

supplies, as was the way with French revolutionary armies, they tried desperately to live off the land. Many died of hunger, thirst, poison, or heat;
many more were killed by Arab marauders; the survivors fought murder-
ously with the Mameluke cavalry before entering Cairo on 24 July. They
found it a city of mud huts and stinking alleys, seething with paupers.

In six months Bonaparte reorganized the government of Egypt and laid
the foundations of the modern state. Knowing that he could only hold the
country with at least the passive consent of the native people he made no
attempt to destroy the Mohammedan religion, for which indeed he had some
respect as a system which had imposed a rule of life upon a wandering people.
He formed consultative bodies, or *divans*, from among the local sheiks.
Above them he acted as a despot, reorganizing taxes, hospitals, and law
courts. He found time for a journey into the desert to investigate the remains
of the ancient canal joining the Red Sea to the Mediterranean, information
which was to form part of the admirable *Description of Egypt* published in
nine volumes by his team of scholars.

All this success ended disappointingly. On 1 August 1798 Nelson came
upon Bonaparte's thirteen ships of the line, anchored in Aboukir Bay, and
captured or destroyed all but two of them. Thereafter the British were able
to blockade the Egyptian coast, foiling Bonaparte's plan of leaving a garrison
in Egypt and returning home with the main army; preventing him, too,
from developing coastal trade with the Aegean islands; and cutting off his
supplies and news from Europe. The appointment of Djezzar-Pacha, a
known enemy of France, as governor of Syria suggested that the Sultan was
planning a counter-attack. On 10 February 1799 Bonaparte left Cairo with
10,000 men on another terrible desert march, this time in biting cold, to
invade Syria. Gaza, Jaffa, and Haifa fell without trouble, but on 20 March
Bonaparte was brought to a halt by the walls of Acre. The siege of Acre
lasted two months. The citadel, surrounded on three sides by the sea and
fortified in recent years by a French engineer, received aid from a British
squadron under Sir Sydney Smith, which captured Bonaparte's siege train
on its way from Jaffa and used the guns against the besiegers. While Djezzar-
Pacha sat in the fortress receiving heads cut from the shoulders of his enemies,
assault after assault was beaten off. On 17 May Bonaparte struck camp and
returned to Egypt. He was justified in abandoning the siege, for in the
course of it he had defeated a Turkish army which was intending to attack
Egypt by land, but Acre was a demoralizing experience for the French
troops. Five thousand were lost, through sickness and wounds, in the Syrian
venture.

Bonaparte returned to Egypt in time to annihilate a second Turkish army
of more than 16,000 men approaching from the sea. A few weeks later he
eluded the British blockade with 400 of his principal officers and landed in

France. He had heard that the republic was in danger from foreign enemies and he hoped to win spectacular victories. The 10,000 survivors from the great army which had sailed so hopefully from Toulon little more than a year before were left behind under General Kléber to garrison Egypt. Kléber was stabbed to death by a Syrian assassin in June 1800. The army held on for another year then surrendered to a British expeditionary force.

Bonaparte arrived in Paris on 16 October 1799 to find the Directors in a position of small political credit but less actual danger than he had hoped. Their dictatorial policy after fructidor had aroused criticism from men of honest, if moderate, democratic views. A majority of the latter had been elected to the Councils in April 1798, only to be dubbed 'neo-Jacobins' and expelled by the Directors on 11 May (22 floréal). This second *coup d'état* had weakened the ranks of the republicans in the face of repercussions following on the Egyptian campaign. On 9 September 1798 the Sultan had declared war on France, bringing with him his new-found friend Tsar Paul I. The latter had reversed his mother's policy of encroaching upon Turkey, to be rewarded by seeing one of his dreams fulfilled: the Sultan had opened the Dardanelles to a Russian naval squadron and Russian troops had established a base in the Mediterranean by seizing the Ionian islands from the French. In the early months of 1799 a Russian army under Suvorov had marched to attack the French in north Italy. Austria had given it free passage and France had declared war on the Emperor (12 March 1799). On 5 September 1798 the Councils of the Directory had passed a law, devised by General Jourdan, introducing permanent conscription. The government was to decide each year the number of men to be enlisted; they were to be drawn from unmarried men between the ages of 20 and 25 starting with the youngest; length of service was to be five years in peacetime. This law, though it was to be of lasting importance to France, had failed to provide the 200,000 men expected in the autumn of 1798, for by this time authority had broken down over large parts of France. Only 79,000 had actually arrived at the dépots. Deserters had formed armed bands to resist capture and were roaming the countryside adding to the terror and chaos. With an army cooped up in Egypt, France had found only 170,000 men to face 300,000 of the enemy. In the spring of 1799 she had been defeated on the Rhine and in the Alps leaving the frontiers once more open to invasion. Fortunately for France the Second Coalition had been weakened by internal conflict. Britain, having agreed to send subsidies to the poverty-stricken Tsar, had refused to allow him to extend Russian power in the Mediterranean by taking Malta, and had ordered him instead to support a futile British descent on Helder, designed to wrest the Low Countries from French domination. Meanwhile Austria, who had been ready enough to see the Russians rescue north Italy from the French but did not want them to rule it, had ordered Suvorov to withdraw to Switzerland where he had been defeated by Masséna in September. Paul I, furious, had withdrawn his contingents from the front.

The threat of invasion had passed by the time Bonaparte arrived on the scene, but France wanted peace at home and abroad and few people thought that the Directory could provide it. The situation was altogether too tempting for Sieyès, who had become a Director when Reubell retired in May 1799. With the extraordinary vanity which was his most noticeable feature Sieyès believed that he could cure all the ills of France and secure immortality for himself by framing a new and perfect constitution. He needed only to get rid of the Constitution of the Year III by a final *coup d'état*. He planned to denounce a new Jacobin and royalist plot and to invite the Councils to abdicate in favour of a provisional government with power to draw up a new constitution. He believed that the majority would succumb like lambs, for public and politicians were haunted by the idea of plots. The only danger spot was a group of left-wing deputies in the Council of Five Hundred, and these, thought Sieyès, could be overawed by the appearance in their midst of a general, hinting at military power. For this rôle Sieyès chose Napoleon Bonaparte.

Bonaparte despised Sieyès but saw how he might use him as a stepping-stone to greater things. Talleyrand acted as intermediary between the two men, and Fouché added subtleties to the plot. On 9 November 1799 the Council of Ancients agreed that in view of exceptional danger the legislative body should be moved from Paris, where Jacobin influence was strong, to St. Cloud. On the next day, 18 brumaire, Bonaparte entered the council-chamber of the Five Hundred and demanded their abdication. Nothing went as planned. Left-wing deputies turned on Bonaparte vehemently and demanded a vote of outlawry. He backed out hurriedly and called on the guards to help him, but the detachments from Paris, strongly republican in sentiment, hesitated to act against the deputies. All would have been lost but for the wit of Napoleon's brother Lucien, president of the Five Hundred. Rushing from the council-chamber he appealed to the guards to save their general from 'the daggers of assassins', whereupon the troops entered and drove out the defenceless deputies by the sword.

5. PROGRESS IN EUROPE

A ridiculous pantomime put an end to France's first attempt at parliamentary government and the memory of the Directory faded into general disrepute. Yet it was during the lifetime of the Directory that French revolutionary ideas made their first real impact on Europe. In these four years Belgium, the Rhineland, Savoy, Nice, Piedmont, and Geneva were annexed to France. France also presided over six sister-republics outside her frontiers: the Batavian, Cisalpine, and Ligurian republics, the Helvetian republic (formed in 1798 from the Swiss cantons), the Roman republic (formed in 1798 when the killing of a French general in Rome led to the entry of a French army and the deposition of Pope Pius VI), and the Parthenopean republic (formed at Naples in 1798 after Ferdinand IV's attack on Rome). All this expansion was carried out by force of arms, but it was justified by the theory that the French people, having won their own freedom by revolution, were duty bound to carry freedom to other peoples of Europe. France proudly claimed the name of *La Grande Nation*, the mother of progress.

France tried to bring her own institutions to the countries under her influence. She was not uniformly successful. Judicial systems were re-organized, but Holland and Switzerland never accepted the jury system and the Cisalpine republic did not complete a new code of law. Taxes were declared equal, but financial re-organization was compromised by military requisitions and people complained that the new demands were heavier than the old. Departments were organized as units of administration, and here France achieved her greatest success, for the French administrative system became widely admired and had a permanent effect on many of the countries which experienced it. Religious freedom, proclaimed but not properly practised in France, was not everywhere carried out in conquered territories. In Belgium, Catholics were made hostile to France by the irreligious activities of the invading army in 1793, and the French government retaliated by keeping priests under surveillance. In the Rhineland a policy of toleration was inaugurated by Hoche, commander of the occupying army, as the best means of obtaining loyalty from the peasants. In Holland the Catholic minority welcomed the French in the hope of obtaining civil equality with protestants, which was duly granted. In Switzerland, the unification of the cantons for the first time emphasized the numerical inferiority of Catholics, who in consequence became hostile and provoked a certain amount of persecution. The Cisalpine republic adopted a settlement similar to the Civil Constitution of the Clergy, which was not unlike the reforms Lombardy had experienced under Joseph II. Elsewhere in Italy, religious settlements were compromised by the hostility of Pope Pius VI, who consistently refused to recognize state claims upon the church. Matters were not mended by the forcible removal of the eighty-two year old Pope to France, where he died in August 1799.

In a superficial sense, social relationships were transformed everywhere by the abolition of aristocratic and clerical privileges and the abolition of feudal dues and tithes. Serfdom was abolished in the few places where it was still found, notably in Switzerland and the Rhineland. On the other hand, no vast transference of land took place, such as was accomplished in France by the sale of national property. In north Italy attempts were made to sell church property, but with limited success. Consequently the social structure was nowhere profoundly altered.

Slavery was abolished throughout France's dominions, after troubles among the slaves in the West Indies. Black and white people were declared equal in rights. A few slaves seized by Genoa from north Africa benefited from these laws, but Holland's colonial possessions were at this time taken by the British, and Britain had not yet abolished slavery in her overseas territories. The abolition movement led in England by Wilberforce received a setback rather than a stimulus from the French example, which seemed to emphasize its revolutionary character.

Sister-republics received their first experience of parliamentary government under French patronage. Sometimes constitutions were drawn up by French agents. Sometimes, as in Holland and Genoa, they were devised by local assemblies. All were more or less closely modelled on the Constitution of the Year III. Legislative power was divided between two chambers; executive power was divided from the legislative and confided to a college, usually of five members. Everywhere the franchise was wider than in France, the Batavian, Helvetian, and Cisalpine constitutions going as far as to establish universal suffrage. These concessions to democracy can be traced to the influence of local enthusiasts. In every country which the French entered they were greeted by small groups of 'patriots' – a name derived from America and bestowed on men who wished to regenerate their country by reform. In Holland, Belgium, and Switzerland many of the patriots were men who had attempted conspiracy and rebellion before the arrival of the French. To this extent there may be said to have been a revolutionary situation already existing in western Europe when the French stepped in and took the lead. Patriots everywhere expected to receive freedom at French hands. To most of them, freedom was defined by the 1789 Declaration of Rights, available in numerous translations. Others admired democratic views embodied in the Jacobin constitution of 1793, and some, without establishing any real contact with the masses, were attracted by the socialism of Babeuf. In Belgium, Holland, Switzerland, and Italy, a desire for a greater degree of unity played a strong part. By no means all of these wishes were gratified.

In Belgium the patriots were a hopeless minority of the population, a few thousand men at most. After the entry of French troops they worked for annexation of their country to France, believing that only thus could they destroy the provincial divisions which crippled reform. Like their former leader Vonck, they were not democrats or social revolutionaries, and they were largely satisfied with the political and social system operating in Directoral France.

In Holland the patriots were more numerous than in Belgium but they weakened their cause by division. One group, mainly composed of wealthy bourgeois, wanted a parliamentary system based on a property qualification and wanted to give large powers to provincial assemblies. Another group, drawn mainly from the lower bourgeoisie and led by Vreede and Valckenaer, took the Jacobin constitution of 1793 as its political ideal and showed strong leanings towards babouvism. This group wanted to weaken provincial institutions, which were a bulwark for vested interests and conservative views, and give supreme power to a National Assembly. The Orangist party, working for the restoration of the Stadholder, allied with the former group, which thereby derived some support from the peasants and fisher-folk. From 1795 to 1798 the Batavian republic was torn by strife between federalists and unitarians, the French ministers supporting the federalists in the earlier years, when Jacobinism was feared in France, and supporting the unitarians from 1797, when royalist views were at a discount. A decision was finally imposed by force. The French army under Joubert carried out punitive measures against the federalists, and a unitarian constitution received a majority of votes in a strictly organized plebiscite (March 1798). The unitarians did not long remain in power, but no subsequent régime in Holland destroyed the unity which they had achieved.

In the Rhineland a small group of patriots under the leadership of Görres worked to achieve annexation to France as a means of obtaining reforms embodied in the Constitution of the Year III. Peasants were either apathetic or openly hostile, not because they wanted their country to remain German (no German 'nationalism' was encountered) but because they had come to connect French government with war requisitions.

In Switzerland the most active patriots, Laharpe and Ochs, were moderates. They welcomed French help in the hope of establishing equality between the cantons and of destroying aristocratic privileges in places where they were strongly entrenched such as Berne and Basle. Other members of the group had more original views. Escher and Usteri spoke of the Swiss people fulfilling their own destiny by their own efforts; while hoping for a democratic constitution they urged the importance of property and believed that feudal dues should only be abolished with compensation. Pestalozzi, the celebrated educational theorist, admired Jacobin ideas and outlined a new agrarian system to increase the number of small proprietors. Ochs was largely responsible for drawing up the unitarian constitution of 1798, which was imposed by French arms. It met with opposition from the smaller cantons, which disliked being merged into larger population groups, and from Catholics. It was abolished in 1803, but it served some purpose in achieving social and political reform.

Italian patriots, though few in number, achieved historical importance by their devotion to the idea of Italian unity. The leading exponent was Buonarroti, an exile from Tuscany who offered his services to the Jacobin government in Paris in 1793 and was sent as its agent to Oneglia. Here he established a centre for propaganda and gathered together Italian patriots from all parts of Italy. The political views of the group were those expressed in the still-born constitution of 1793, with social views akin to babouvism. For the distinct socialist tendencies which he displayed during his mission to Oneglia, Buonarroti was imprisoned in 1795 in Paris, where he met Babeuf and joined the Equals. In 1796 he dreamed of social revolution in France, followed by social and political revolution in Italy. When Bonaparte and Saliceti were sent with an army to Italy he believed that his hour had come, and he addressed a hopeful memoir on Italian unity to the Directors. The latter played for time. Bonaparte was allowed to patronize the patriots in Lombardy, giving them a tricolour flag in green, white, and red, which henceforth became the banner of Italian nationalism. Hopes ran high, and patriotic groups in Turin, Rome, and Naples were largely responsible for the agitations which led to the entry of French troops. By 1799 the whole of Italy, except Venice, was under French dominion, and patriots expected the proclamation of the Italian republic one and indivisible. The French government failed them because it feared their connection with extremist views and because it wished to secure the Alpine passes by annexing Piedmont. From that moment Italian patriots began plotting against the French.

In all the countries under discussion the majority of the population remained inert, seeing in the French dominion not freedom but arrogance, taxes, requisitions, billeting, and sometimes atrocities. However, along with French armies came clubs, newspapers, elections, National Guards, and the formation of local battalions. These increased the number of the politically conscious. More and more patriots turned against French domination as time went on, but they did not necessarily turn against French ideas of individual freedom and self-respect. This seeming paradox was resolved during the reign of Napoleon, when France's naked imperialism was opposed by intellectuals in many parts of Europe in the name of freedom.

CHAPTER VII

France under Napoleon, 1799-1815

I. THE CONSULATE

WHEN Sieyès plotted with Bonaparte to destroy the Directory he had no intention of setting up a military dictatorship. Bonaparte was to be recompensed with a nominal share of power, and France was to be provided with a constitution distilled from Sieyès's political thought over the past ten years; a constitution which distributed power between numerous bodies, checking and balancing each other in the interests of individual liberty. In the negotiations which ensued, Sieyès discovered the consequences of employing a general who had political as well as military ambitions. In the Constitution of the Year VIII, Bonaparte saw to it that he emerged supreme above the interlocking pieces of Sieyès's machinery. Complete executive power, and a large share of legislative power, was attributed to three consuls, elected by the Senate for ten years. Of the three, two had merely a consultative function, and Bonaparte, as First Consul, became the only real power in France. A noticeable departure from the practice of previous years was that the new constitution contained no Declaration of the Rights of Man.

Two years later, the younger Pitt declared that Bonaparte's rise proved to the world that revolutions are inevitably followed by military dictatorship. It would not be true, however, to say that France had been waiting for Napoleon. When the latter returned to Paris from Egypt in October 1799 many people expected him to carry out a *coup d'état*, for his name had become connected with such measures over the past four years, but thoughts concerning the future were mixed. Sincere republicans and revolutionists were opposed to the destruction of parliamentary government. The bourgeoisie and peasant proprietors wanted at last to enter into enjoyment of the gains made during the Revolution. Bonaparte told them that they were about to do so. 'Citizens, the Revolution is stabilized on the principles which began it. The Revolution is over', ran the proclamation which introduced the constitution. But to give real weight to these words administrative order must be restored, royalist and Jacobin hopes crushed, and a profitable peace secured. There was no guarantee that Bonaparte would be able to accomplish these enormous tasks. He had no political experience inside France, and his background did not place him in a strong position for standing firm against Jacobin demands. Parts of the army were Jacobin in sympathy. So, too, were the workers of Paris. The latter were glad to see the Directory go but they could not be expected to welcome a man who was remembered for the artillery attack on the mob in 1795. When the new constitution was published on 15 December 1799 outspoken criticism came only from Jacobin circles in provincial centres such as Metz, Lyon, and Toulouse, and from departmental councils in remote departments, but a plebiscite in which only half the adult male population voted was a sign of acquiescence rather than enthusiasm.

During the three and a half years in which Bonaparte acted as First Consul of the French Republic (December 1799 to May 1804) he worked hard to stabilize his position by giving the bourgeoisie and peasantry the things they most wanted. His achievements caused many Frenchmen in later times to look back upon the Consulate as a halcyon period in which the promises of the Revolution were finally bestowed upon the French nation by a strong and loving guardian. Legend obscured the fact that Napoleon despised human nature and rejected the faith which had inspired the best works of the Revolution. He was fond of saying that men could always be won over by self-interest or fear. The policy of the Consulate was devised in this spirit, and was stamped upon the new coinage in the words *Union et Force*.

For more than six years the western departments of France had been in a state of rebellion. The peasants, as Bonaparte well knew, were backed by royalist agents and inspired by refractory clergy. The First Consul began his attempts at pacification with appeals to self-interest. The massive Breton leader, Georges Cadoudal, refused to be won over by offers of a generalship in the French army, but many of the rank and file proved to be less dedicated to the royalist cause. A proclamation promising a free pardon and liberty of worship to all who submitted encouraged many to lay down their arms. The same proclamation threatened dire punishment for those who continued to 'resist the national sovereignty'. In January 1800 the Army of England marched upon the west. One of the rebel leaders, Frotté, was captured and executed, and similar treatment was promised to any peasant found bearing arms. After three months of ferocious fighting, resistance was virtually defeated.

Meanwhile Bonaparte dealt severely with the brigands who roamed the southern and central districts of France in huge bands, menacing travellers and tyrannizing over farms and villages. More than 5,000 gendarmes were organized into brigades to escort public vehicles and lay ambushes for robbers. Military detachments were sent, with orders to deal ruthlessly both with brigands and with officials who connived at their crime. By the spring of 1800 the main bands had been dispersed.

Surrender did not imply approval, however, and the First Consul could

not be satisfied without applause. He was irritated by criticism from newspapers, however harmless they might be. During 1800, sixty national
newspapers were suppressed and the remaining thirteen were placed under
police supervision. In an atmosphere of enforced calm Bonaparte produced
the great administrative measures for which he was to be honoured by
posterity.

The chief object of the Local Government Act of 17 February 1800 was
to centralize the administration in such a way that the head of the state could
tap the entire resources of the nation. The maintenance of the departments
as the chief units of administration gave a revolutionary air to the new
system, but at the head of each department was placed a prefect, a supreme
government official, who had more in common with the intendant of the
ancien régime than with any agent of the Revolution. The prefects were
nominated by the First Consul, later Emperor, who could dismiss them at
will. Article 3 of the law stated categorically, 'The prefect alone shall be in
charge of the administration'. The General Council of the department remained in existence but the members were no longer elected. They were
nominated by Bonaparte, first for three and later for fifteen years, and they
met for only fifteen days in the year, confining their attention to the assess-
ment of finances. The prefect, meanwhile, exercized complete authority
over sub-prefects and mayors; in communes of less than 5,000 inhabitants
he dismissed officials and councillors at will; in all departments except that
of the Seine he controlled the police; he reported regularly to the Minister
of the Interior concerning public opinion; he was given power to thwart
independent expressions such as clubs, associations, parties and newspapers;
and he was charged with carrying out government policy in the matter of
public works and the establishment of schools, hospitals, and law courts.
It was the prefect's duty, in the words of Beugnot, 'to produce great political
immobility and great domestic activity'. Watching everything, reporting
everything, controlling everything, and supplying everything, the prefect
in his department was the most typical and lasting embodiment of the
Napoleonic idea of government.

The men chosen for such a position must combine immense competence
with a willingness to obey orders. Many of the prefects employed by
Napoleon had been members of revolutionary parliaments or departmental
directories. They were never servile tools of the government, but they were
few enough in number, even when territorial annexations increased the
departments from 98 to 130, to be closely supervised by the Minister of the
Interior. In return for loyalty, Napoleon gave them power to do sound
practical work in their departments and a tenure of office which was immune
from local jealousies and dissensions.

The lowest unit of administration was still the commune, but the communal life which early revolutionaries had regarded as important was stamped out under Napoleonic domination. The mayors were no longer elected. In communes of less than 5,000 inhabitants they were chosen by the prefect, and in larger communes they were nominated by the head of the state. On the mayors devolved all the work attributed to former municipal authorities, and, as the recompense was small, increasing difficulty was found in obtaining suitable men to serve in rural communes. The mayor was assisted by a municipal council, but again the members were nominated and not elected and their functions were purely consultative. In larger towns bourgeois councillors sometimes raised their voices against government demands, but in rural communes, where councils were composed mainly of the mayor's relatives and friends, apathy was the general rule.

Former systems had provided intermediate units, in the shape of districts or cantons, between the departments and the communes. Bonaparte disliked intermediate authorities as being difficult to control. The departments were divided into arrondissements, each with a sub-prefect, but the latter was in effect a mere agent of the prefect, helping to supervise the mayors and local police. Supervision became, indeed, the keynote of the administrative system. From individuals, co-operation was required rather than initiative, and action rather than opinion.

Supervision was likewise the key-note of the new financial system. Under revolutionary governments the peasants, particularly, had evaded taxation either by making false returns or by simply neglecting to pay, and they had got away with it because tax officials were elected. Bonaparte had the officials appointed. While retaining direct taxes in much the same form as those established by the Constituent Assembly he continually increased indirect taxes, which he regarded as a cheap and handy source of revenue. By these means Bonaparte dragged the state out of the morass of bankruptcy. But solvency was not enough. Large sums of money were needed quickly to equip new armies for campaign in the spring of 1800. Private banks, which had enabled a few men to make large fortunes under the Directory, proposed to charge enormous rates of interest on loans to the government. Financial need combined in Bonaparte's mind with anger that a few wealthy individuals should seek to control his policy. The result was the creation of the Bank of France, a typically Napoleonic institution, enormously privileged but wholly dependent upon the government.

Since the time of Voltaire most Frenchmen had thought of good government in terms of law and justice. There was nothing inherently wrong with the law courts created by the Constituent Assembly, but revolutionary justice had been perverted by the Jacobins and had largely broken down under the Directory. In re-establishing a hierarchy of courts, Bonaparte seized the opportunity to destroy the democratic element. All judicial personnel, including justices of the peace, were henceforward appointed by the head of the state or by his subordinates. Judges were ostensibly irremovable during good behaviour, but in fact they could be dismissed at any time during a five year period of 'provisional' office.

More in keeping with revolutionary aims was the production of one uniform code of civil law, mooted by the Constituent Assembly but never completed. Bonaparte set up a commission for the task in August 1800. Valuable help was received from Cambacérès, the Second Consul, who had drawn up a draft code in 1793. The final draft was debated in 102 sessions of the Council of State. Bonaparte presided over 57 of them and astonished even legal experts by his grasp of details and essentials. The 'Code Napoléon', as finally promulgated in March 1804, bore the stamp of the master. Laws and decrees of the Revolution were combined with authoritarian measures drawn from ordinances of French monarchs and the principles of Roman law. Social changes brought about by the Revolution were guaranteed in clauses declaring all citizens equal before the law, requiring civil before religious marriage, and safeguarding the subdivision of inherited estates among all members of the family. Social discipline, often lax during the Revolution, was stiffened by clauses rendering divorce less easy and strengthening parental control over children. Testimony to the emergence of a bourgeois society was found in the clause which defined property as the unlimited right of the individual to enjoy and dispose of his own possessions.

In 1789 bourgeois Frenchmen had believed that liberty would be secured if their own class governed France. To what extent did they govern it now? Under the Constitution of the Year VIII all adult males in possession of civil rights, some 6 million Frenchmen, were given a vote. They met at the chief town of their arrondissement and elected a tenth of their number on to a communal list, from which were chosen justices of the peace, mayors, and other officials of the communes. Men whose names appeared on the communal list then elected a tenth of their number on to a departmental list, from which were chosen prefects, sub-prefects, and members of departmental councils. Men whose names appeared on the departmental list then elected a tenth of their number, some 6,000, on to a national list, from which were chosen the members of the two legislative bodies. The choosing of officials from the lists was done by the First Consul, the Senate, or the prefects. The legislative bodies, a *Tribunat* of 100 members and a *Corps légis-latif* of 300 members, were given strictly limited and divided functions. No member could initiate legislation and neither body could pass amendments. The *Tribunat* could not vote, but could merely discuss bills sent to it by the Council of State and report an opinion to the *Corps législatif*. The *Corps législatif* could not discuss, but could merely vote, silently and secretly, upon measures sent to it from the *Tribunat*. In spite of these limitations Bonaparte distrusted the legislative bodies, which were composed largely of men who had sat in former revolutionary assemblies. He soon began to evade them both, and to govern either through acts of the Senate or by decrees of the Council of State. The Senate was endowed with high-sounding powers. It must choose future Consuls, appoint the great appeal judges, and annul any acts of government which were unconstitutional. The members of the Senate were, however, mainly nominees of Bonaparte. He gradually packed the Senate with distinguished men, mostly elderly, who had reason to be grateful to him for personal and material advancement. In 1804 the Senate took the initiative in making Napoleon Emperor, and for the subsequent ten years simply registered all his measures. The Council of State was a hand-picked body of experts used by Bonaparte to help him in every branch of government.

From a liberal standpoint the Constitution of the Year VIII was a mockery of parliamentary institutions, but most Frenchmen in 1799 were not dis-satisfied with it. Experience during the Revolution suggested that the making of law was less important than the administration of it. Six million Frenchmen now voted in three stages to produce candidates, not members, for an ineffective parliament; but under the system of lists, all voters helped to designate men fit for public office. Frenchmen had tried for ten years to achieve not so much government by the people as government for the people. By the term 'popular sovereignty' they meant that the needs of the people should be of paramount importance in the eyes of the government. Within a few months of brumaire, Frenchmen were beginning to believe that popular sovereignty operated under the strong and skilful guidance of Bonaparte. When law and order at home were followed by peace with Europe, satisfaction was complete.

In the spring of 1800 Austria had two armies in the field. One, commanded by General Kray, was massed at the source of the Danube, charged with defending the defiles leading into the valley of the Rhine. Another, under Field Marshal Mélas, had swept through North Italy and was besieging Genoa. When the town fell, Mélas would cross the French border into Provence while Kray attacked from the east. The French also had two armies engaged. One, under Masséna, was cooped up in Genoa; the other was in a position to advance into Germany before Kray dared leave his defensive station. Bonaparte could not, however, allow Moreau with the Army of the Rhine to strike the decisive blow. In legal matters and financial affairs Bonaparte could seek help from Cambacérès and Gaudin; in the military sphere he must, if he was to make himself indispensable, seize all the credit. So he created a third army, officially a reserve, with which to march into Italy and attack the Austrians upon the scene of his former triumphs. For reasons of expediency, official command was given to Berthier, the Minister of War, but the latter had grown accustomed, as chief of staff, to carrying out Bonaparte's orders. The vivid reports sent to Paris of Bonaparte's exploits in accompanying the army across the Alps left no doubt as to who was the central figure.

The success of the campaign owed much to Bonaparte's legendary good luck. Unaware of the position of the Austrian army Bonaparte detached Desaix across the Po to bar the route southward from Genoa. On 14 June Mélas flung 30,000 men across the Bormida and faced a depleted French army of 22,000 on the field of Marengo. The bulletins which Bonaparte sent to Paris did not confess the confusion into which he had been thrown, nor the debt owed to Kellermann's cavalry attack and to the brilliance of Desaix in bringing his troops into battle. Paris was given the impression that the victory of Marengo was due to the inspiration radiating from the magic presence of the First Consul.

Bonaparte hoped that Marengo would persuade the Emperor to make peace. Francis apparently entertained some thoughts along these lines, especially when Moreau occupied Munich in July 1800, but Thugut strongly opposed the idea of Austria deserting her ally Britain. Negotiations were opened at Lunéville but they proceeded in a desultory fashion, creating the suspicion that the Emperor was merely trying to stave off hostilities until the spring. By November Bonaparte had lost patience and ordered five French armies to attack Austria. He was dreaming of more victories for himself in Italy when on 3 December Moreau totally defeated the Austrians at Hohenlinden and advanced within fifty miles of Vienna. On 9 February 1801 Cobenzl signed the treaty of Lunéville. The Emperor kept the Italian territories he had received at Campo-Formio and France received the Rhine frontier for which she had fought since 1793.

Britain might have been expected to continue war against France. On 5 September 1800 the British navy secured the capitulation of the French garrison holding Malta and thus acquired an important base for naval strategy. The defeat of the French army left behind in Egypt became almost a foregone conclusion: Cairo capitulated in June and Alexandria in August 1801. Meanwhile Paul I of Russia, who had revived Catherine's League of Armed Neutrality in his annoyance at Britain's refusal to restore Malta to the Knights, was assassinated on 23 March 1801 – an event which Bonaparte furiously attributed to British agents. The new Tsar Alexander I was more favourably disposed towards Britain. On 2 April Admiral Parker destroyed the Danish fleet at Copenhagen, and the League of Armed Neutrality could no longer threaten to exclude British ships from the Baltic. From a commercial point of view, seven years of war were not without profit for Britain. European countries which had been accustomed to receive sugar and coffee from the French West Indies were obliged to buy these commodities from Britain's colonies. Manufactured goods sent from England to Germany increased sixfold during the years of war, and France herself imported large quantities of British contraband. Over all, Britain's exports rose from £18,335,000 in 1793 to £25,699,000 in 1801. The financial crisis of 1797 was short-lived, for basically Britain's finances were sound enough to bear the burden of war. Credit was good and the new income tax considerably increased the amount of money flowing into the Treasury.

A few set-backs made the government aware of the country's fatigue, however. The cost of living, which rose steadily as a result of war, rose sharply after bad harvests in 1799 and 1800. Food imported from abroad was costly to purchasers and alarming to English landlords, who could never believe that their country was safe unless she were self-sufficient. Troubles caused by distress among the crowded town populations were attributed to French agents, and discontent in Ireland seemed to offer an open door to the enemy. In March 1801 Pitt gave way to Addington and the peace party; preliminaries were signed in October 1801, becoming on 25 March 1802 the Peace of Amiens.

On 10 September 1801 another kind of peace was ratified, no less desired by most Frenchmen than peace with Europe. A Concordat signed by Bonaparte and Pope Pius VII promised to put an end to the long struggle between revolutionary France and the Catholic church. Napoleon on St. Helena described the securing of the Concordat as the most difficult enterprise of his career. Inside France there were several groups which opposed it: confirmed anti-clericals, especially supporters of the cult of theophilanthropy patronized by the Directory; intellectuals of the *Institut*, who believed that the separation of church and state proclaimed by the Convention in February 1795 would eventually lead to religious freedom; and above all Jacobins, many of them in the army, who equated catholicism with counter-revolution. The majority of Frenchmen still regarded themselves as Catholics, and wanted an end to the experiments and strife of the past twelve years, but they would not countenance a restoration of tithe and church land and a politically powerful clergy. The Pope had never accepted the Civil Constitution of the Clergy or recognized the bishops appointed under it, and whilst he remained adamant, clergy had a constant incentive to preach revolt. Napoleon was no devotee of religion but he recognized the social and political importance of catholicism in France. 'If I were governing Jews, I would rebuild the Temple of Solomon', he told the Council of State. As he was governing Frenchmen, he would rebuild the Gallican church.

An approach to the Vatican was rendered easier by the death of the ill-treated Pius VI in exile and the entry of a new Pope into Rome in July 1800. Pius VII was believed to be a saintly pastor with no subtlety of political views.

Even so, negotiations took a year, for Pius could be stubborn where his conscience was engaged. Ten successive drafts were made before a formula was found which enabled the Pope to communicate with the 'constitutional' bishops and sacrifice former church land. The final text, in 17 articles, recognized the Catholic religion as 'the religion of the great majority' of Frenchmen, and promised that Catholic worship would be unhindered in France provided it conformed to 'such police regulations as are required by public peace'. The Pope was to call upon all existing bishops to resign their sees so that new ones could be nominated by the First Consul and consecrated by the Pope. Bishops were to swear before the First Consul an oath of loyalty to the government and were to appoint to cures 'persons approved by the government'. Pius VII promised that neither he nor his successors would trouble the owners of lands alienated from the church, and in return the French government undertook to restore buildings necessary for public worship and to provide a reasonable salary for bishops and clergy.

After the signing of the Concordat Bonaparte bent his mind to the 'police regulations' mentioned in the text as 'required by public peace'. He produced a list of 77, which he tacked on to the Concordat without the permission of the Pope. The Organic Articles, as they were called, established complete control over the church by the state in France. No Papal bull or any such document could be published in France without permission from the government. No Papal representative could enter or act in France without such permission. No councils or synods could be held by the French church without leave, and no decrees of councils or synods held outside France could be published in the country. Ecclesiastical disputes must be referred to the Council of State. Bishops could not be absent from their dioceses without leave, and they must visit every parish under their care every five years. They could not authorize the use of private chapels or hold out-door services. Parish priests, like bishops, must swear an oath of allegiance to the state, and they must obey the bishops in all things. When the Concordat was published the clergy were exhorted to support the state which had done so much for them. 'See that your teaching and your example shape young citizens in love of our institutions, and in respect and affection for the authorities which have been created to guide and protect them.'

Pius VII never ceased to protest against the Organic Articles. In later years he suffered more examples of Napoleon's arrogance and double dealing, but he believed to the end of his life that Napoleon had done more than any man to restore the worship of the Catholic church in France, and that much else should be forgiven him because of it. Others have argued that devout Catholics were already reviving church worship under the religious freedom allowed by the law of 1795, and that the church lost more than it gained by Bonaparte's interference. It remains true that only a powerful

AOP K

ruler, a familiar type of antagonist, could have brought the Pope to terms with the Revolution, his more formidable foe.

On Easter Day 1802 a Te Deum was sung in Notre Dame in honour of the Concordat and the Peace of Amiens. Bonaparte persisted in decrying Hohenlinden and magnifying Marengo as the victory which had secured the double pacification. He need not have been so ungenerous. Most Frenchmen recognized him as their saviour and were willing to see him rewarded. When a group of Bonaparte's friends in the Senate, overriding the rest of that body, proposed that a plebiscite be taken asking the nation if it wished to make Bonaparte First Consul for life, thirty-five and a half million 'yeas' were recorded against eight thousand 'noes'. The Constitution of the Year X, embodied in a senatus-consultum of 4 August 1802, did more than express the outcome of the plebiscite, for with the life consulship Bonaparte was given the right to nominate the two other consuls and to designate his successor. Further changes were mere commentaries upon a dictatorship which already existed in practice. Electoral colleges of arrondissements and departments were henceforward appointed by the First Consul for life. The *Corps législatif* and the *Tribunat*, reduced in numbers and purged of obstreperous members, virtually ceased to function as legislative bodies.

In a sense the Revolution had been brought to a close, but Bonaparte could not allow its memory to fade. He must always be necessary to post-revolutionary France as a barrier against her enemies. The required symbol was soon found. In August 1803 Georges Cadoudal returned to Paris. Closely watched by the police, his activities soon implicated a score of persons, including Pichegru and Moreau from the higher command. The police suspected that the conspirators were centring their hopes upon a foreign prince, the Duc d'Enghien, grandson of the Prince de Condé. Enghien was forthwith kidnapped while he was staying in neutral territory as the guest of the Elector of Baden, and summarily executed. Twelve of the conspirators were executed, Moreau was banished to the U.S.A., and Pichegru committed suicide in prison. Bonaparte's responsibility for the affair cannot be doubted. No single act of his career brought him more criticism outside France, but inside the country reactions were otherwise. A senatus consultum of 18 May 1804, known as the Constitution of the Year XII, declared Napoleon Bonaparte Emperor of the French. He was thirty-four years old. A plebiscite confirmed the suggestion that the Imperial dignity should be hereditary. 'We wanted to make a king: we have made an emperor', said the condemned Cadoudal.

2. THE EMPIRE

To Napoleon, the title Emperor conjured up visions of the legendary power of Charlemagne. To the French people it was acceptable for its suggestions of commonwealth. The term 'empire' had been used in the eighteenth century to describe prosperous lands with a great future for their people. The senatus-consultum which made Napoleon Emperor charged him with the government of the French Republic. It was believed that he would continue to govern in the interests of the people and thereby fulfil the endeavours of the Revolution. His own astonishing career testified to the tremendous power of human energy and personality to shape events. In this, if in this alone, he could be looked upon as the incarnation of the Revolution.

Years later a famous painting of Napoleon on board the *Bellerephon* created the false impression that he was a taciturn man. People better acquainted with him remembered that he seemed to talk incessantly, without pausing for answers to his own questions or to hear advice which he had solicited. English visitors who flocked to Paris during the brief peace described him as a little man, five feet two inches in height, slightly built, with sallow complexion and piercing blue eyes. Many commented on his extremely mobile features and beautiful smile. A few thought he looked arrogant. None were given adequate warning to leave when war was imminent, and some 700, brusquely rounded up by Napoleon's police, languished in French prisons for ten years. The humble and saintly Pius VII, having agreed for the good of his church to travel to Paris and crown Napoleon in Notre Dame on 2 December 1804, found on arrival that Napoleon insisted on placing the crown upon his head with his own hands. It was a fitting gesture for the most powerful dictator western Europe had ever seen.

One of the English visitors (Lady Elizabeth Foster) who saw Napoleon reviewing his troops during the peace wrote ecstatically: 'It seems to me to be the most worth seeing of any sight I ever beheld – this extraordinary Man in all the simplicity of acknowledged greatness, the creator, the commander, the head of this and innumerable other armies ready to act whatever he commanded, who had acted and executed whatever he had planned, riding from line to line, certain that at a word of his these men would march to the extremity of Europe.' The mutual devotion between Napoleon and the common soldiers of France was a legend which gathered strength after the Emperor's death, obscuring the fact that Napoleon abandoned two armies to their fate, in Egypt and in Russia, and that severe measures were always necessary to prevent troops from deserting. Legend aside, however, the armies of the Empire were among Napoleon's most characteristic achievements. After a decade of revolution, Frenchmen had grown accustomed to improvisation. It suited them that in Napoleon's armies training was reduced to a minimum. Drill was practised during a week in barracks, after which new recruits learnt their trade from older men while on the march. Soldiering was the only profession which brought together all classes of the population in something like equality. A young man from a poor home had as good a chance as others of catching the eye of Napoleon, always on the watch for dash and bravery. Battles were numerous and promotion rapid. Failing other rewards there was always the possibility of loot. The Emperor was never squeamish about the fact that his men fought for personal gain. Many years after Napoleon's death, when France lay once more in the grip of social conventions, young men like Julien Sorel looked back with longing to the Empire as a time when spirit and enterprise were all that was needed to carve out a successful and even glorious career.

The rank and file of Napoleon's armies consisted mainly of recruits enlisted under the *Loi Jourdan* of 1798. This ostensibly fell upon all Frenchmen between the ages of twenty and twenty-five, but in fact many could claim exemption on the grounds that they were married men, supporters of families, or candidates for the priesthood and teaching professions, and others who were rich enough could buy substitutes. Each department had to provide its quota of men, and in some departments escape from service was easier than in others. The unfairness of the system was, strangely enough, one of its most popular aspects, since it allowed room for manoeuvre and for simple good luck. As time went on, however, Napoleon rooted out men who had been passed over in previous years and called up classes which were not due until the following year or later. As campaign followed campaign, and peace seemed nowhere in sight, sheer length of service began to weigh upon the older soldiers. With such men a little personal recognition would sometimes go a long way. Napoleon was in the habit of having veterans pointed out to him by his officers before a parade, so that he could pause and say 'I remember you at Austerlitz'.

Wartime had the advantage of bringing to quite ordinary Frenchmen the feeling that they were needed by their country. Napoleon on the field of battle treated men as cannon fodder, but this did not destroy the illusion that the Emperor valued the services of every one of his subjects. This was why in later years, when the working classes once more felt themselves to be outlaws, Stendhal could describe Napoleon as 'the only king the common folk remembered'. More extraordinary than the satisfactions of wartime was Napoleon's gift of making people feel that they counted in civilian life. He allowed no-one to play a part in framing policy, but he employed vast numbers of persons in running the government. France swarmed with officials in every walk of life, all owing their jobs to the state and acquiring thereby a vested interest in the maintenance of the régime. This was Napoleon's contribution to the art of politics, and it left an indelible mark, for good or ill, upon the countries which came within his orbit.

The officials were always arranged in a hierarchy. The ordering of local government, through the minister of the interior to the prefects, the sub-prefects, and down to the mayors, had its counterpart in the judicial sphere. For summary jurisdiction there were police courts in every group of communes. Above the police courts were correctional tribunals, then assize courts, and finally 29 courts of appeal. The penal code of 1810 coherently classed all criminal offences according to importance and procedure: *contraventions* came under the police courts, *délits* under the correctional tribunals, *crimes* under the assize courts. Procedure under the *Code d'instruction criminelle* (1808) allowed more scope for officialdom than English jurists have thought compatible with liberty of the subject. In all except assize courts, trial was by a panel of judges and not by jury. In spite of the fact that the prefects drew up jury lists Napoleon disliked the jury system, which he regarded as an intrusion by amateurs into what ought to be a strictly professional business. As time went on more and more cases were classed as *délits* and withdrawn from the cognisance of juries. In all cases prosecution was in the hands of a public prosecutor, a state official. The accused was assumed innocent until he was proved guilty, but the public prosecutor was not bound by rules of evidence, and proof of guilt was therefore easier to obtain than it might otherwise have been.

Inside and outside the courts, police were active on a scale unprecedented in Europe. Every large town had its *commissaire de police*, keeping a vigilant eye upon foreigners, vagabonds and beggars, prisons and workhouses, theatres, schools and churches, meetings and newspapers. Each *commissaire* employed a vast number of agents, and local gendarmes also gave assistance. There were special police to prevent smuggling, police to deal with workmen and employment regulations, and political police to repress royalists and Jacobins. The man who directed these vast operations for many years, Joseph Fouché, had himself been a Jacobin. His experience of wielding arbitrary power during the Terror, combined with a subtlety of mind acquired at the Oratorian colleges of Nantes and Paris where he spent his youth, stood him in good stead when he became minister of police, first for the Directory and then, in 1799, for Napoleon. As a revolutionary Fouché stood to lose everything if the royalists returned; as a leading thermidorean he had nothing to hope for from the Jacobins. For all this he never felt any real loyalty towards Napoleon. As a man of independent spirit he disliked Napoleon's calculated pettiness of mind. Napoleon employed Fouché because of his cleverness and as a link with the revolutionaries, but he never really trusted him. When in 1810 he discovered Fouché to be in secret negotiation with Britain he dismissed him for a more rigid and servile tool, General Savary.

The pervasiveness of the police helps to account for a lack of literary achievement during the Empire. Intellectual classes were the ones most likely to feel oppressed by the atmosphere of spying and informing. From the early days of brumaire the minister of police was ordered to read and analyse all books, papers, plays, and even posters appearing in Paris. In 1810 the system was more elaborately organized. Publishers, who must not number more than sixty, were required to obtain a licence from the government, to swear an oath of loyalty, and to send two copies of every work which they handled to a director of publishing. Drama was also supervised. The little theatres, with their melodramas and varieties and farces, had always drawn bigger crowds than the *Opéra comique* or the *Comédie française*, and it was the little theatres that Napoleon most feared, lest they should raise a comment or a laugh against the régime. In 1807 the number of theatres in Paris was reduced to eight, and each one was given strict rules as to the type of performance it might put on. Even the classics were censored. Newspapers were regarded as more dangerous still. By the end of 1800, constant harassing by the police had reduced the number of newspapers in Paris to nine, and the number of subscribers had fallen from 50,000 to 35,000. A decree of 1805 obliged editors to submit copies of their newspapers daily to the police and to pay a tax destined to support a troop of Imperial censors. In 1810, Paris newspapers were reduced to four, and each department was allowed to have only one journal, under the authority of the prefect. Under these circumstances the greatest French literature of the time came from exiles – Chateaubriand, Madame de Staël, Benjamin Constant – and was opposed to the régime. Napoleon never ceased to attribute literary sterility within the Empire to lack of zeal on the part of his officials. 'It is the fault of the minister of the interior', he told Cambacérès. 'He ought to set about getting some decent stuff written.' Meanwhile it was important to train young citizens towards a proper appreciation of their good fortune. Schools were a subject of absorbing interest to Napoleon; he dictated educational policy even from the battlefield.

Revolutionary governments had aimed at a system of primary and secondary education which would be provided free for all children by the state. Little of this had been achieved, but in 1795 the Convention had begun to establish central schools in the larger provincial towns. In spite of economic distress, administrative chaos, and war upon the frontiers, the central schools were providing a worthwhile liberal education when the Directory fell. Bonaparte affected to despise them. His real objection to them was that they taught boys to think, and he had no love of education for education's sake. He believed that the object of a state educational system should be to provide well-disciplined soldiers, civil servants, magistrates, and experts for every walk of public life. The central schools were therefore replaced, in 1803-4, by two types of state school, the *prytanées* and the *lycées*. Here Bonaparte's ideas on education, with emphasis upon the classics, the Catholic religion, and military studies, were developed to the full. In the *prytanées*, or state boarding schools, boys wore uniform similar to that of soldiers, and were marched to classes at the roll of a drum. In the *lycées*, some 3,000 state scholars were given a grounding in reading, writing, arithmetic, Latin, and the use of fire-arms before dividing, at the age of twelve, into civil and military sections. Meanwhile communes and private individuals were allowed to set up secondary schools where reading, writing and arithmetic were taught for a modest fee. By 1805, more than a thousand of these secondary schools had come into existence. Although they obtained no financial support from the state Napoleon expected them to provide a standard form of education. A law of 1806 and a decree of 1808 organized all teachers into a body called the Imperial University. At the head of the University, dispensing teaching diplomas, appointing teachers to posts, dictating syllabuses and prescribing examinations, was a Grand Master, appointed by the Emperor. All teachers were required to take an oath of allegiance to the Grand Master and to obey his orders on pain of imprisonment. An important function of the University was to see that children were taught the catechism, amended by Napoleon in 1806 to stress the obedience owed to himself as the Lord's anointed.

Few people were as docile as Napoleon wished. Within the University it proved impossible to discipline teachers in the communal and private secondary schools, where salaries were low and chances of promotion small. Meanwhile, quite a large number of schools remained outside the Napoleonic system altogether. The education of girls was left to the church, which Napoleon hoped would make them into obedient wives and virtuous mothers. Primary education never exercized the Emperor's mind at all. Provided he got the experts which he required for his army and bureaucracy, Napoleon cared little that the majority of peasants and workers remained illiterate. Such primary schools as existed were mainly, like the girls' schools, in the hands of the church.

Napoleon intended, when he made the Concordat, that the Catholic church should become yet another branch of the civil service, run by a hierarchy of officials in clerical dress. As was his way, he gave enormous power to the highest ranks. The bishops emerged more powerful than ever they had been during the *ancien régime*. They could dispose of nearly all the benefices in their dioceses, instead of the tenth or so which was usual before the Revolution, and they could dismiss clergy from their cures at will. In return the bishops gave to Napoleon a greater degree of loyalty than his subsequent actions warranted. They authorized his catechism for use in all churches, condoned his divorce of Josephine, and made no effective protest against the imprisonment of Pius VII. The lower clergy, on the other hand, came increasingly to resent the authority of the bishops and of the earthly master whom they appeared to serve. From 1801 to the fall of the Empire, parish priests were Napoleon's most constant opponents.

Under these circumstances it was fortunate for Napoleon that anti-clericalism was still strong in France, especially among the bourgeoisie. Napoleon drew his officials from the middle classes, and to this extent he was dependent on them. They, for their part, could be regarded as the chief beneficiaries of the Empire. Never had there been so many jobs for men of talent, great and small. Those who could not find posts at home could often find them in occupied countries, whose civil services absorbed many of the former members of revolutionary communes, departmental directories, and the like. The hierarchical order, which Napoleon was so fond of, catered for the jealousies and snobberies which had been prominent among the bourgeoisie before the Revolution and which a decade of lip-service to equality had never eradicated. The institution of the Legion of Honour, with its graded rewards for public service, could be said to fulfil bourgeois ambitions to become the new aristocracy. Mme. de Staël, trying hard during the early years of the reign to maintain the critical spirit of the eighteenth century, found that the statesmen and generals and officials who frequented her salon and applauded her wit went away only to court more favours from Napoleon.

The lower classes fared less well. Napoleon's policy for workers in Paris and other large towns was to regiment them, either literally by conscripting them for the army, or more originally by subjecting them to strict rules of employment. Every workman had to carry a *livret* (work-book) in which his employer recorded comments on his behaviour. The *livret* must be submitted to the police on request and to the new master when changing employment. The institution of the *livret* was the only direct social measure of the Napoleonic régime. Nothing at all was done for those rural poor who could not find work on the small farms of peasant families and who could not, owing to age or family responsibilities, be conscripted. This may help to explain the fact that highway robbery and violence of every description were endemic in country districts, in spite of continuous repression. The problem was hushed up by the officials of the régime, who prided themselves on maintaining law and order.

In all other spheres Napoleon succeeded in organizing Frenchmen, where previous governments had failed. But to do it he required men to cease thinking and to cease acting spontaneously. No man was persecuted for his past actions. Former royalists and Jacobins could take service under Napoleon as prefects and even as ministers, but to do so they must cease to express any of the opinions which had made them royalist or Jacobin. This was what Napoleon called internal peace. His system, at the time and long afterwards, appealed to men who cared more for efficiency than for liberty. It left a tradition in French politics that, when times are difficult, freedom should be suspended to allow experts to get on with urgent tasks. Under Napoleon, times were always difficult, from the breach of the Peace of Amiens to the final collapse. Few people in France resented Napoleon's dictatorship as such, but many came in the end to resent his wars. Conscription and taxation were merely the most obvious of many grievances. The arrogant and brutal behaviour of the military in Paris and garrison towns, the starving of any personal endeavour which could not be used directly for military purposes, the prostitution of the mind to glorify conquest – these things caused sensitive Frenchmen to see finally that France was descending into barbarism. By 1814 the majority of people had come to think that a man who directed the entire resources of the nation towards satisfying his lust for war could not be ruling in the interests of the people.

CHAPTER VIII

From Amiens to Tilsit:
the Expansion of the French Empire

I. THE BREACH OF THE PEACE OF AMIENS

THE Peace of Amiens between Britain and France signed on 27 March 1802 lasted precisely one year and sixteen days. The basic requirements for a lasting peace were never present. Bonaparte would not accept the idea that the treaty terms defined his position on the Continent unalterably: the British government would not accept the fact that they placed France in a position to renew her commercial rivalry. Bonaparte's insatiable desire for territorial conquest and Britain's unquenchable thirst for overseas markets were not really compatible, as Pitt had implied they would be when, in March 1801, he had spoken of a great land power and a great sea power living amicably together. The clash between the two was to contribute towards the unique tenacity of the Franco-British struggle.

A year before the conclusion of peace Bonaparte had agreed with the Emperor Francis at Lunéville that Austria should keep Venice, Istria, eastern Lombardy and the Dalmatian coast, whilst France should receive the left bank of the Rhine from Switzerland to Holland. The Helvetian, Batavian, Cisalpine (Italian) and Ligurian republics were recognized as independent states. The treaty of Lunéville was not reaffirmed at Amiens, but the British government regarded its terms as an essential basis of peace and looked upon any extension of French power beyond the limits mentioned at Lunéville as an act of aggression warranting British protest. Bonaparte, who must have been aware of this view, provoked British protests on a number of occasions during the summer and autumn of 1802. In August he proclaimed a new Republic of Valais and guaranteed the construction of a military route over the Simplon Pass; in September he formally annexed Piedmont; in October he invaded Switzerland and imposed his own form of government upon her. Bonaparte claimed that these matters were no concern of a third party, and instructed his ambassador Andréossy to prevent the British government from interfering in continental affairs. The British foreign minister, meanwhile, ordered Lord Whitworth, as ambassador to Paris, to 'state most distinctly his Majesty's determination never to forego his right of interfering in the affairs of the Continent, especially in any case which might lead to the extension of the power or influence of France'.

There were other disputes, bearing upon the specific terms of the treaty of Amiens. In the treaty Bonaparte undertook to withdraw French troops from Holland. He failed to do so, explaining to the British minister that they would have to remain until ships could be provided to transport them to Louisiana. While Holland was occupied by French troops, Bonaparte possessed another jumping-off ground for an invasion of England. Even if this were dismissed as a remote possibility, French occupation of Dutch as well as Belgian ports could not be regarded as other than detrimental to British commerce. When people in Britain welcomed negotiations with France in the winter of 1801-2, they did not expect to be confronted with a treaty detrimental to their commerce. They were willing to sacrifice Belgium to France for the sake of peace, but they expected that the treaty would include trade agreements favourable to Britain. On the contrary, the Addington government restored to France and her allies (Holland and Spain) all the colonies which Britain had seized during the nine years war, except Ceylon and Trinidad. Mediterranean bases east of Gibraltar were abandoned, including Malta which was to be restored to the Knights. No trade agreement was secured, and English merchants knew that Bonaparte would continue France's traditional policy of closing markets to British goods.

Signs of France's renewed commercial rivalry were not slow in coming. Bonaparte set in motion a vast programme of naval construction which in a few years time would enable him to challenge Britain on the seas. Already he was able to send an expedition of 10,000 men to San Domingo in an attempt to capture the island from the negro rebel leader, Toussaint l'Ouverture. Louisiana was purchased from Spain. Alarming developments took place in the Mediterranean. Leghorn and Elba were annexed to France; treaties were negotiated with the Barbary powers; a mission to Constantinople secured privileged access to the Black Sea for French vessels. Englishmen began to fear that Bonaparte intended to dominate the Mediterranean, capture Levantine and Russian trade, and ultimately threaten India. The fear was intensified when he adopted a provocative attitude towards Egypt. In September 1802 Colonel Sébastiani sailed from France to Egypt with instructions to report on the position of the British garrisons and the condition of the native population. Four months later his report was published in the *Moniteur*. It described both the British commander and the Egyptian pacha as powerless, and stated that the few troops in the ruined fortifications could easily be overcome by 6,000 Frenchmen. Britain at once assumed that Bonaparte was preparing to occupy Egypt as soon as British troops evacuated Mediterranean bases under the terms of the treaty of Amiens.

There is no proof that Bonaparte intended any such move. His colonial enterprises across the Atlantic might be taken as a sign that he expected peace to be of some duration, for as soon as war commenced he was obliged by difficulties of communication to sell Louisiana to the U.S.A. The publication of Sébastiani's report could have been a piece of bravado designed to compensate Bonaparte for the blow delivered to his pride by the loss of Egypt and for the continual insults levied at him in the English press. Perhaps Bonaparte thought that the report would frighten the British into evacuating Malta. The result was otherwise. If Malta were abandoned, the Mediterranean and the land route to the east would be laid open to France, for Britain could not long maintain an army isolated in Alexandria. The sea route to the east had already been opened to the French by the return of the Cape of Good Hope to the Dutch. Whitworth therefore informed Bonaparte that no evacuation of Malta could be considered until a satisfactory explanation was received concerning Egypt. British troops remained on the island even when, on 4 March 1803, a Grand Master of the Knights of Malta was appointed. Bonaparte could now accuse the British government of breaking the treaty of Amiens. George III's answer was to call out the militia, in view of the 'considerable military preparations carrying on in the ports of France and Holland'.

Negotiations which took place during the next few weeks showed that Bonaparte was ready to compromise on the subject of Malta. There is no reason to suppose that he cherished the hope of perpetual peace, but France was not yet ready for war. If there had been a strong sector of British opinion desirous of peace at any price, such a peace could have been obtained, for a while at least. But there was no party of appeasement. On 18 May 1803 Britain declared war on France.

2. FRANCE PLANS INVASION: BRITAIN FORMS A COALITION

It was not long before both powers experienced the fundamental difficulty which was to prolong the war for more than a decade: the difficulty of a land power and a sea power getting to grips with each other.

Bonaparte's first intention was to transport troops across the Channel. The road leading out of Amiens was labelled 'To England', and a vast army encamped at Boulogne made ready for invasion. The British press poked fun at Little Boney's grandiose schemes, but for more than two years the threat was a serious one, and defence measures were taken on a considerable scale. England lacked military forces adequate to face 100,000 experienced French troops. Twenty thousand of her regular army had to be kept in Ireland to quell rebellion, leaving only 28,000 troops to defend the whole of Great Britian. The government recalled 3,000 troops which had recently been transferred from Egypt to Malta. This left in the Mediterranean only the small garrisons needed at Gibraltar and Malta, and there was no force available to make a landing should Bonaparte decide to attack at any point upon the enormous coastline. Bonaparte was not slow to seize this opportunity for a war of nerves. General Gouvion Saint-Cyr was ordered to march on Taranto with a corps of the Army of Italy. From this central position in Apulia he could threaten Greece, Naples, and Sicily. Sicily supplied grain to Malta, and the harbours and inlets of the island could offer shelter to a fleet operating in the central Mediterranean. No-one knew where Bonaparte might strike next, cutting off supplies from British naval bases and threatening the existence of Nelson's fleet blockading Toulon.

Part of Saint-Cyr's task was to draw Nelson's attention to the eastern Mediterranean while the main French army crossed the Channel. Bonaparte knew that he could not rely on holding the British Isles permanently until he had a navy larger than the British, and this, he reckoned, would take ten years; but a descent upon London, especially if accompanied by a landing in Ireland, would almost certainly cause such a panic that the English would sue for peace. Plans varied during the changing circumstances of two years, but the favourite idea seems to have been that Villeneuve's squadron should make a dash from Toulon to the West Indies, rendezvous with a Spanish fleet, and return in time to hold the Channel for a few days while the Army of the Invasion of England crossed to a point near Chatham for the march on London. Nothing proves Bonaparte's seriousness more decisively than the efforts he made to obtain naval assistance from Spain. Extravagant promises had to be made to Godoy to persuade him to enter the war, and persistent energy had to be employed to galvanize the Spaniards into producing the 57 ships of the line and 38 frigates which formed the official strength of the Royal Armada. Bonaparte was convinced that his troops, once landed on the shore of England, would take the capital within three days. Letters to his admirals poured from his pen. Give him only a few days' protection from the British fleet and 'with God's help I will put an end to the future and very existence of England'.

It was a wild dream, but not too wild for a man who had already evaded a British fleet in the Mediterranean and transported a huge army to Egypt. Yet the plans came to nothing. The flat-bottomed boats needed to transport 100,000 men were never built in sufficient quantity, in spite of constant harrying of the shipbuilders by Bonaparte. This was a minor obstacle. More important was the fact that French and Spanish naval vessels under Ganteaume at Brest, Villeneuve at Toulon, Gravina at Cadiz, and Gourdon at Ferrol were hemmed into their harbours by the British blockade. Villeneuve succeeded in breaking out of Toulon, freeing a Spanish squadron from Cadiz, and sailing to Martinique with a combined fleet of eighteen ships of the line, but when he returned he was driven into Corunna by Cornwallis's squadron cruising off Ushant before Ganteaume could come out of Brest to his assistance. Bonaparte continued to make plans on the assumption that his admirals would elude the waiting British ships, but wind and tide could not be controlled as he would have liked. The tide, especially, irritated him beyond measure: there had been no tide in the Mediterranean. Finally came the news that the Austrians were preparing an offensive. In September 1805 French troops were withdrawn from Boulogne for the long trek into Germany, and the threat of invading England was over.

The younger Pitt, who returned to office as Prime Minister in May 1804, had been working towards a means of attacking France on land. The only possible means was the formation of a Third Coalition, with Britain acting as paymaster to continental armies. The need to subsidize foreign powers in order to secure a land attack upon France resulted for ten years in the curious spectacle of Britain, whose people prided themselves on their liberty, acting as sponsor to some of the most despotic governments in Europe.

The most forthcoming ally seemed to be Russia. Tsar Alexander became seriously alarmed during the Peace of Amiens concerning Napoleon's Mediterranean ambitions. His anxiety increased when war was renewed and Bonaparte violated the neutrality of Naples in order to secure her ports. Almost at the same time the assumption by Napoleon of the title Emperor was regarded by the Tsar as a personal affront. The admiration which Alexander had once felt for the Corsican soldier was badly shaken by the Enghien affair; it weakened even further under the promptings of a new foreign minister, Prince Adam Czartoryski. This great Polish noble, who had taken service under the Tsar, cherished the dream that from a European war Poland would emerge as a united kingdom under the protection of Russia. With Czartoryski's encouragement Alexander sent to London a young diplomat, Novosiltsev, to open negotiations for the formation of a European coalition. Pitt disliked the ambiguous terms of Novosiltsev's instructions and strongly suspected Russia of designs on Turkey. Necessity prevailed, however, and on 11 April 1805 Britain and Russia signed a treaty of alliance which was to become the basis of the Third Coalition. Russia was to request Austria and Prussia to help her in providing 500,000 troops for the war, to be subsidized by Britain at the rate of £1¼ millions for every 100,000 men put into the field.

The task of inducing Austria to enter the war was more laborious than Alexander had anticipated, and did not augur well for the firmness of the coalition. The Emperor Francis might have remained neutral and perhaps even become friendly towards France if Bonaparte had not ruthlessly exploited the position given to him at Lunéville. By the terms of this treaty the German princes dispossessed of property on the left bank of the Rhine were to receive compensation from erstwhile church property in other parts of the Empire. Bonaparte, who was empowered to arrange the transaction through the Diet of Princes at Regensburg, saw his opportunity for becoming a rival power to Austria in Germany. When the final agreement, known as the Recession, was accepted by the Diet of Princes on 25 February 1803, France emerged with a string of client states along the Rhine. Bavaria, Baden, Württemberg, Hesse-Cassel, Hesse-Darmstadt, and Prussia had extended and consolidated their territories by absorbing ecclesiastical states and free cities. Austria had lost her most reliable clients, the ecclesiastical princes, and had lost her electoral superiority, for with the promotion of Baden, Württemberg, and Hesse-Cassel to the dignity of electoral states six out of ten electors were protestants.

Bonaparte's contempt for the Holy Roman Emperor was seen only too clearly in subsequent months. At the outbreak of war with Britain, French troops occupied Hanover and the ports of Cuxhaven and Ritzebüttel at the mouth of the Elbe. In March 1804 French police violated German territory and kidnapped Enghien, a guest of the Elector of Baden. Similar encroachments and provocations were practised in Italy, the second sphere of traditional Habsburg influence. On 26 May 1805 Napoleon had himself crowned King of Italy with the iron crown of Charlemagne. Yet Francis hesitated to join Russia, for he feared Russian designs in the Mediterranean almost more than he feared France. He might have wavered indefinitely had not Napoleon occupied Genoa. It was not until 9 August 1805 that Austria joined the Third Coalition. Negotiations had been carried out with the utmost secrecy, but Napoleon was aware of hostile moves, and it was never his way to wait until he was attacked. By 23 August he had made up his mind to divert his army from England to Germany. By 7 October his troops were encircling an Austrian army in the Danube valley.

Long before hostilities began, both sides realized that Prussia occupied a strategic position in the coming campaign. Francis and Alexander sent insistent requests to Frederick William III, but the latter, though uneasy about Napoleon's ambitions and more than half afraid of him, could not make up his mind to abandon a man who had given him the prospect of equality with the ruler of Austria. Napoleon made a brief attempt to win Prussia to France's side, but he cared too little for her military potentialities to spend much time on her. On 5 October he ordered Bernadotte to march into the Margravate of Ansbach which lay across his line of advance. Ansbach belonged to Prussia, and Frederick William was roused by the insult to his dignity. Even so, a personal visit from Alexander, and the exercise of all the charm and persuasion which the young Tsar could command, were necessary to bring Frederick William to the point. On 3 November 1805 Prussia signed the treaty of Potsdam and became a member of the Third Coalition. Before the tomb of Frederick the Great the two monarchs swore undying loyalty to each other's cause. Unlike his famous predecessor, Frederick William had delayed too long for his own good. A fortnight earlier a large Austrian army had capitulated to Napoleon at Ulm.

3. AUSTERLITZ AND TRAFALGAR

The Austrians entered the campaign of 1805 in a better state of military preparedness than they had known for years, thanks to Francis's capable soldier-brother, Archduke Charles. They were still only half prepared, however. Their main army of 95,000 men, commanded by Charles, lay south of the Alps, and was ordered to join an allied army advancing from Naples to clear the French from north Italy. Pending the arrival of the Russians, the rest of Austria's forces were divided into two in order to fight a defensive war in Germany. Archduke John with 22,000 men was to cover the passes of the Tyrol. General Mack with an army of 52,000 men was to advance up the Danube and take a stand on the Iller river, with headquarters in the fortress of Ulm, to block an expected French advance through the Black Forest.

Napoleon's answer to this challenge was to move at great speed, before the main Russian army of 50,000 men under Kutusov had a chance to come up, and approach the incompetent General Mack from a direction he was not expecting. The French army of 172,000 men, proudly called the Grand Army, marched the four hundred miles from Boulogne to Ulm at the rate of fifteen miles a day. The men advanced in seven columns on roughly parallel routes, so as to draw on different parts of the country for supplies. Each column was commanded by one of Napoleon's already famous marshals – Bernadotte, Marmont, Davout, Soult, Ney, Lannes and Murat. While expecting considerable initiative from his marshals in their own tactical sphere, Napoleon never allowed them to meddle with strategy. On the march from Boulogne they reported to the Emperor every twenty-four hours. Napoleon's personal leadership was worth a force of 40,000 men any day, Wellington afterwards reckoned. As Emperor, Napoleon could ensure that all the resources of the state were directed towards the field in which he commanded, and officers and men were spurred on to their best efforts by the knowledge that Napoleon was at hand to distribute rewards.

On 12 October Mack found himself completely surrounded by the enemy. After a brief assault by the French he capitulated on 20 October with 30,000 men and 60 cannon. The rest of the Austrian army managed to join the Russians and retire safely to where a reserve corps awaited them at Olmutz, thanks to some heroic rearguard fighting by Prince Bagration and a masterly retreating action devised by Kutusov. The latter was a competent and experienced general who had come to see that discretion can be the better part of valour. At Olmutz he thought only of avoiding further battle until Archduke Charles brought up his forces and the Prussians completed their mobilization. His advice was unfortunately brushed aside by the twenty-eight year old Tsar, newly arrived in camp after his emotional meeting with Frederick William III and eager to cover himself with military glory. Napoleon, whose entire strategy rested upon defeating the armies of the coalition piecemeal, began tempting Alexander into battle by feigning a retreat. Encouraged by the Austrian General Weyrother, who knew well how to play on a sovereign's vanity, Alexander decided upon an immediate attack. The Austrian and Russian forces advanced towards Napoleon's camp at Brünn, taking a stand near the village of Austerlitz on 1 December 1805. The battle began in the early hours of the following morning and was all over when the winter sun went down. The allied army, attempting to carry out Weyrother's complicated plan for an encircling movement, weakened its forces in the centre and allowed Napoleon to carry out his favourite move, cutting the enemy in two and defeating each half in detail. It was an overwhelming victory for France, whose soldiers never tired of remembering their Emperor, as the light faded upon the first anniversary of his coronation, riding triumphantly over the battlefield among the 20,000 enemy dead.

Whilst Alexander fled in tears with the remnant of his army, and Frederick William hastened to repudiate the allies he had failed to assist, Francis sued for peace. On 26 December Austria signed the humiliating treaty of Pressburg, by which she lost more than three million inhabitants, all her possessions in Italy, and the strategic territory of Tyrol, Vorarlberg, and Constance commanding the mountain passes into Germany. A further clause by which she agreed to pay an indemnity of £2 millions was calculated to make a military recovery impossible. The Third Coalition was at an end. 'Roll up the map of Europe; it will not be needed these ten years', Pitt is reported to have said when he heard the news of Austerlitz. But if England could see no chance of attacking Napoleon, Napoleon had lost his chance of invading England. On 21 October 1805 Nelson annihilated the combined French and Spanish fleets at Trafalgar.

Part of the agreement between Britain and Russia at the opening of the Third Coalition had been that combined armies should land in Naples. By March 1805 Britain could spare about 4,000 troops for the operation, and this force, under the command of Sir James Craig, was transported at great hazard to the Mediterranean. Napoleon professed contempt for Pitt's habit of frittering away Britain's forces in isolated manoeuvres, but the Naples expedition was not without success, of an incidental kind. Fearing lest the allied expedition should threaten the Grand Army in the rear, Napoleon ordered Villeneuve to break out of Cadiz, whither he had retired when the invasion of England was called off, and to land troops in Italy to reinforce Saint-Cyr. Villeneuve was loath to obey for he knew that Nelson, whom he dreaded, had joined Collingwood's blockading squadron. He sailed from Cadiz with 34 ships of the line on 19 October. Nelson followed in pursuit with 27 ships, and at daybreak on the 21st the two fleets formed for battle off Cape Trafalgar to the north-west of Gibraltar. The French and Spanish ships were extended in a half-moon. Nelson's plan was to divide his fleet into three, two parts advancing in double line to pierce the enemy at two places, and the third acting as a reserve, moving up swiftly to help in the destruction of the scattered enemy. Only a fraction of the plan was carried out. In a fierce fight at close quarters, British gunnery and tenacity won the day. By sunset 19 French ships were captured or destroyed, and the rest never fought again. British losses in killed and wounded were only a quarter of those sustained by the enemy, but they included Nelson, shot by a French sniper from the mizzen mast of *Redoubtable* as he strode across the deck of *Victory* in his glittering orders of knighthood. He left behind him a myth of British invincibility at sea which even Napoleon's self-confidence could never entirely dispel.

Trafalgar meant that Napoleon would have to postpone his plan for invading England for many years. For the rest of his reign he was busy strengthening the Channel ports and building ships. By 1814 he had some 60 ships of the line, 40 frigates, and 800 smaller vessels. They were destined to remain at anchor in the ports of Germany, Holland, Belgium, France, and Italy, while British blockading squadrons cruised outside. There were, how-ever, means of weakening England before delivering a decisive blow, or so Napoleon firmly believed. Britain, he argued, was a commercial country, and the maintenance of her wealth, power, and social stability depended upon the continued pursuit of commerce. If she could be prevented from exporting manufactured goods and making profits in the form of gold, any number of disasters might crowd upon her. The paper money with which she financed her daily affairs would collapse, and the distress which France had experienced with the fall of the assignats would overtake her cocksure enemy. Industry would fall on hard times. Merchants and businessmen would cease to support the government. There would be little money for buying essential commodities from abroad, food would become scarce and dear, and the poor would rebel.

Napoleon was aware that he could not prevent British merchant vessels from sailing the seas. French privateers, who were active throughout the war, might snatch isolated ships, but the British navy could always protect the main convoys, and England would continue to trade with her colonies. Napoleon believed he could, however, close the continent to British goods, or, if not close it altogether, for some types of British manufactured goods were essential for his own purposes, he could impose import duties and exact heavy payments for licences to trade. Ideas of this kind were present in

Bonaparte's mind from at least the breach of the Peace of Amiens. They came almost naturally to a ruler who remembered the long French tradition of excluding British goods from French soil. They were present alongside the scheme for invading England, and took firm root as French troops occupied more and more ports along the Channel and the North Sea. They moved into first place when the invasion scheme had to be pushed into the background. By 1806 they had blossomed into the Continental System or Continental Blockade – not a blockade as British sailors cruising off French ports understood the term, but rather a prohibition of British commerce, growing ever more extensive as French armies marched across Europe. The system supplied, as Napoleon said to his brother Joseph, 'a means of attacking the sea from the land'. It became an added incentive, though never the chief reason, for Napoleon's wars of conquest.

4. FROM PRESSBURG TO TILSIT

After the treaty of Pressburg Napoleon consolidated his position in Germany. His client states received yet more territory. Bavaria, whose ruler Maximilian Joseph was now styled king, could feel that with three million inhabitants, richly varied lands, and a commanding position at the gateway to Italy she had blossomed into a new German power as a result of her friendship with France. The Duke of Württemberg became a king; the Elector of Baden, the Duke of Berg, and the Landgrave of Hesse-Darmstadt became grand dukes. Their territories were freed from all obligation to the Empire and were grouped into a Confederation under Napoleon's protection. Princes of western Germany hurried to join the arrangement, hoping to profit at the expense of their neighbours. Napoleon's cynical foreign secretary, Talleyrand, made a fortune from the bribes offered to him. When the Confederation of the Rhine was completed, on 12 July 1806, it comprised 16 German states stretching from the Elbe to the Bavarian Alps. The members engaged themselves to provide 63,000 troops for any war Napoleon cared to wage on the Continent.

Austrian lands in Germany now formed no more than a third bloc alongside Prussia and the Rhine Confederation. In August 1806 Francis formally renounced the title of Holy Roman Emperor and became Francis I, Emperor of Austria. Prussia had been given a place in the new Germany almost immediately after Austerlitz. Napoleon probably suspected that Frederick William had flirted with the Third Coalition, but it was not in his interests to fight a war against Prussia if he could form an alliance with her on his own terms. Accordingly on 15 December 1805, by the treaty of Schönbrunn, Prussia was promised Hanover in return for ceding Ansbach to Bavaria, and Frederick William III bound himself to an offensive and defensive alliance with Napoleon.

French gains in Italy were also consolidated. The Austrian Queen of Naples, Marie Caroline, had chosen an ill-fated time, a month before Ulm, to persuade her weak-minded husband, the Spanish Bourbon Ferdinand, to open his kingdom to British and Russian armies. Napoleon was unlikely to forgive such treachery on the part of a state which could offer valuable harbours to its allies. Two days after Pressburg he announced that the Bourbons had ceased to reign in Naples. On 6 January 1806 Masséna set out to invade southern Italy, taking Napoleon's brother Joseph with him to be crowned king. Ferdinand and his queen were carried by the British fleet to Sicily, and the Russians retired to their island of Corfu.

When Joseph became King of Naples the French Empire was already on the way to becoming a family concern. Elisa Bonaparte and her husband had been given the principality of Lucca in 1805; Louis became King of Holland in June 1806. Napoleon showed little real affection for his troublesome brothers and sisters except, perhaps, for the beautiful Pauline, but like a true son of Corsica he showered patronage upon them. Caroline Bonaparte and her husband Murat were made sovereigns of Naples when Joseph was transferred to the throne of Spain in 1808. The worthless Jérome became King of Westphalia (1807). Only Lucien, the most capable of all, lived in disgrace because of his refusal to divorce his wife at Napoleon's request. Even Josephine's children by her former marriage came under their stepfather's protection. Hortense Beauharnais was married to Louis of Holland and Eugène was appointed, at the age of twenty-three, viceroy of the Kingdom of Italy.

If Eugène was the only one to be called viceroy the others were expected to fulfil much the same office. Napoleon's vassals were expected to rule in the interests of the Emperor of France, as poor Louis discovered when he was obliged, in 1810, to abdicate his throne for showing too much concern for his Dutch subjects. The same rule applied to the many marshals and ministers for whom Napoleon created dukedoms and principalities in Germany and Italy and elsewhere. Napoleon never expected loyalty to arise from pure affection but he expected to get it unstintingly from persons whom he had benefited in some material way. He was to be disappointed with many of his protégés, and with none more than the treacherous Bernadotte.

When Thiers sought for a turning point at which Napoleon could be said to have taken the road towards disaster he chose a date some few months after Austerlitz. The defeat of Austria and the terms of Pressburg he defended as necessary for the preservation of the natural frontiers. It was Napoleon's further exploits – his attempts to subjugate Prussia and Russia – which deviated from France's true interests and brought about the downfall of 1814. Other writers have seen a turning point at an earlier date, and one statesman ventured at the time to advise Napoleon to pursue a different course. While the capitulation of Ulm was being completed Talleyrand wrote to Napoleon urging him not to humiliate Austria further but to make an alliance with her on equal terms. The existence of Austria, he said, was necessary to civilized Europe, as a barrier against the Russians. The Austrians were the traditional rivals of the Russians in regard to the decaying Turkey: let them keep this unenviable position. Napoleon paid no attention to Talleyrand's advice. After Austerlitz he not only humiliated Austria but took Venice and the Dalmatian coastlands from her and brought himself face to face with the Russians in the eastern Mediterranean. The rebuff did not prevent Talleyrand from accepting the princedom of Benevento when the spoils were shared out but it did make him wonder whether he was backing the wrong horse.

The Peace of Pressburg proved, after all, to be an impossible stopping place. Frederick William III had succumbed to Napoleon from a mixture of fear and self-interest, but even these Napoleonic weapons were turned by the incalculable vagaries of a weak man. Napoleon assumed, reasonably enough, that as Frederick William had failed to fight in 1805, when there were allies in the field, he would never fight after Pressburg, when he was alone. Yet by the summer of 1806 he was obliged to admit that this was precisely what Frederick William was preparing to do. Frightened by French encroachments in western Germany, angered by France's failure to evacuate Hanover, stung by constant reminders of his humiliating position, Frederick William gave in to the pleadings of Queen Louise and the importunities of the war party among the Prussian nobility and began to mobilize his troops. Before he could complete the operation Napoleon, whose Grand Army had not yet left German soil, issued orders for the invasion of Saxony, Prussia's ally and neighbour (6 October 1806).

The French army descending upon Prussia numbered some 195,000 men. Flushed with victory, all ranks were convinced that enthusiastic French soldiers could defeat a cumbersome Prussian army any day, as they had done at Valmy fourteen years earlier. The Prussians were equally confident of victory but with less reason. No improvement had been made in their army since the time of Frederick the Great. All officers were noblemen, promoted for birth rather than for capacity. The rank and file was mainly conscripted from the peasantry, obliged to serve for long years under brutal discipline. Most important of all, the inspiration afforded by Frederick the Great was lacking. Only Queen Louise showed enough spirit to ride before the troops and urge them into battle, a spectacle which Napoleon did not hesitate to deride in the French press.

French troops were soon throwing back Prussia's advance guards in preliminary skirmishes. Fugitives joined the two main Prussian armies, one of which was encamped near the little town of Jena under the command of

Prince Hohenlohe, while the other, under the Duke of Brunswick, retired northwards towards Naumburg. Napoleon surmised that Prussia would concentrate her forces in the region of Weimar in order to safeguard Berlin. Advancing in this direction he blundered upon the army of Prince Hohenlohe; the latter, believing himself to be faced by an inferior French force, prepared to give battle. In fact Napoleon's troops greatly outnumbered their opponents. The battle opened shortly after dawn on 14 October 1806 and soon turned into a complete victory for the French. Fleeing Prussian troops were pursued by Murat's cavalry and hacked down in the streets of Weimar. Prince Hohenlohe himself, escaping northward with a small force of men, met fugitives coming from an opposite direction and learnt that the Duke of Brunswick had been killed and his army routed in a chance encounter with a single French corps under Marshal Davout at Auerstädt. In one fatal day the Prussians lost 27,000 killed and wounded. The rest were mopped up as they fled over the plains of Germany. Demoralization was such that garrisons everywhere collapsed without resistance and city governors handed over their keys to French subalterns. While Frederick William hid himself at Memel, Napoleon entered Berlin. It was just three weeks since the outbreak of war.

The defeat of Prussia gave Napoleon his opportunity to extend the Continental blockade along the whole of the German coastline. From Berlin on 21 November 1806 he issued the decree which could be regarded as the real beginning of the Continental System. Its terms were flamboyant, for it was not only an instrument of policy but a gesture of defiance towards England and a proclamation of dominion over the greater part of Europe. The British Isles were declared to be in a state of blockade. All British subjects found on French occupied territory were to be imprisoned and their property confiscated. Every port on the continent was to be closed to vessels coming from or calling at any port in England or her colonies.

French successes on land during 1805 and 1806 gave Napoleon some reason for supposing that he would be able to enforce the Berlin decree. A British expeditionary force under Sir John Stuart made a landing in the south of Italy, but after winning a victory over the French troops encamped at Maida on 4 July 1806 Stuart judged the general situation hopeless and withdrew to Sicily. The Russians occupied Cattaro and Castel Nuovo, but the French spread along the Dalmatian coast, occupied Ragusa, and isolated the Russian garrison. Alexander tried to extend Russian power over Moldavia and Wallachia, and Britain sent a fleet to the Dardanelles to add pressure to the cause, but the Sultan successfully resisted encroachment on his territory and threatened to make an alliance with Napoleon. A British expedition to Egypt, after receiving heavy casualties in attacks on Alexandria and Rosetta, retired in haste to Sicily. It seemed that all Napoleon needed to do to establish complete mastery over the continent was to bring the Tsar to heel. In December 1806 Napoleon moved to Warsaw, the capital of Prussian Poland. He would have advanced immediately against the Russians had not the unusually wet weather rendered Polish roads impassable. His first encounter with the enemy took place at Eylau in East Prussia on 8 February 1807. The battle was bloody and indecisive. Napoleon claimed the victory because his army was in possession of the town when night fell, but losses on both sides were heavy, and reports sent to Paris had to be embellished with stories of French bravery and of how the Emperor had directed the men in the thickest part of the fight, standing unflinching in the graveyard of the city while enemy bullets whistled round his head and corpses mounted up at his feet. The reverse – for it could just as well be described so – determined Napoleon to direct preparations on the spot for the final encounter. He remained in winter quarters, first at Osterode then at Finkenstein, for four months, summoning Spanish troops to undertake garrison duties in Holland and Germany, calling up the 1808 class of Frenchmen ahead of schedule, supervising the training of recruits, and by various means increasing his fighting strength to 200,000 men.

All the time that the master was away from home the ever-growing empire had to be governed. From 1805 onwards Napoleon was absent from France for more than a third of his time. Ministers were expected to use a great deal of discretionary power and to put up with fearful outbursts of wrath if they did not accurately forecast the Emperor's wishes. To help them a constant stream of letters arrived by fast courier. Wherever Napoleon went his three secretaries travelled with him. As soon as his tent was pitched the business of dictating letters began. The total number of documents despatched has been estimated at 80,000, an average of fifteen a day for fifteen years. No matter was too small or remote for the Emperor's attention. From Poland he wrote to Fouché telling him to dismiss the editor of the *Mercure de France*; from Moscow in 1812 he issued a decree regulating the number of Paris theatres. Napoleon prided himself on being able to concentrate on anything at any time. A treatise on education, a letter of reprimand to one of his brothers, comments to Fouché on the latest novels, and routine measures concerning the army might issue from his fertile brain in the course of a day. The work could have worn out a constitution stronger than Napoleon's. He slept little (a few hours a night), ate his meals hurriedly, and wasted energy on fits of temper. He knew something of everything and trusted his own judgment implicitly. In 1807 he was not daunted by one of the greatest enigmas of the time, the character of Tsar Alexander I.

In May 1807 Danzig fell to Marshal Lefebvre, and Napoleon was given a clear road along the sea coast to Königsberg, the old capital of East Prussia.

To save the city, which sheltered the Prussian royal family, the Tsar ordered an immediate Russian advance against the French. General Bennigsen, with a force of 100,000 men, prepared to cross the Alle river, unwisely choosing as his base the little town of Friedland, nestling in a bend of the river and sheltered by forests. It was at 5 p.m. when Napoleon arrived on the scene, but he saw the enemy hemmed in by trees and water and he ordered his forces to attack at once. When firing ceased at 10 p.m. the Russians had lost 25,000 killed and wounded and almost all their artillery. It was 14 June, the anniversary of Marengo. The campaign was at an end: the remainder of the Russian army could only save itself by flight. Napoleon followed to the banks of the Niemen, and here, on the border of Russia, he granted an armistice.

The subsequent treaty of Tilsit (7 July 1807) was negotiated under circumstances which fascinated all Europe. A raft, carrying a gaily decorated pavilion, was constructed by French engineers and moored amidstream. At precisely one hour after noon, on 25th June, the two Emperors were rowed out simultaneously from opposite banks amid the sound of cannon and the fluttering of flags. They embraced on the raft and disappeared into the pavilion. Immense crowds on both sides of the river watched this beautiful piece of stage direction, but no-one was invited to hear what Napoleon and Alexander said to each other and no minutes were written down. During the next few days, when Alexander moved into the town of Tilsit and met Napoleon regularly, the fate of Prussia was decided without reference to Frederick William, and resolutions public and private settled matters of deep concern to all the world.

Alexander did his best for Prussia, but Napoleon insisted that the territory left to Frederick William should be no wider than fifty leagues along a line running from Königsberg to Berlin. Frederick William lost in all a third of his possessions, including his Polish provinces in the east and his German provinces west and north of the lower Elbe. The former, designed to become a buffer state on the border of Russia, were made into the Grand Duchy of Warsaw and given to Napoleon's latest client, the King of Saxony: the German provinces were merged into the Confederation of the Rhine under the name of the Kingdom of Westphalia. The fact that Prussia was allowed to keep a neck of land stretching up the Oder valley into Silesia and, indeed, the fact that she retained any independence at all, was described by Napoleon as a mark of 'deference to His Majesty the Emperor of all the Russias'. There is no proof, however, that Napoleon originally intended to annex Prussia to France. He could make better use of her as a vassal state. Under the terms of the treaty of Tilsit Prussia was obliged to close her territory to British commerce, to pay a huge indemnity, and to open a military route between Saxony and Warsaw.

The secret clauses establishing an alliance between Russia and France were of more momentous consequence. Alexander promised to mediate between Britain and France. If Britain refused to restore all her conquests and lift her blockade of the European coast, Russia would declare war on her, close the Baltic ports to British commerce, and force Denmark, Sweden, and Portugal to enter both the war and the Continental System. Napoleon similarly promised to mediate between Russia and Turkey. If the Sultan refused to accept his terms, France and Russia would 'come to a mutual understanding for the purpose of liberating all the provinces of the Ottoman Empire in Europe, except the city of Constantinople and the province of Rumelia, from the yoke and vexations of the Turk'.

Alexander's motives at Tilsit remain a subject for speculation. The Tsar was doubtless tempted by the thought of increasing his power at the expense of Turkey, but how far this induced him to accept what appeared in other respects to be a one-sided treaty is not certain. Russia could not continue to fight France, and Alexander was clever enough to make a virtue of necessity. Behind his guileless and even impetuous demeanour his mind was inscrutable to all who knew him. And the treaty was not, after all, completely one-sided. By allying with the Tsar Napoleon sacrificed the real possibility of allying with the Sultan. The treaty of Tilsit did not envisage a complete dismemberment of Turkey, but only that she should cede to Russia the Danubian principalities of Moldavia and Wallachia, nevertheless the suggestion was proudly rejected by Sultan Selim III, and his successors became more anti-French as time went on. From 1807 to 1812 Egypt and the Levant provided important facilities for British commerce, and with no fleet in the Mediterranean comparable to the British under Collingwood there was little Napoleon could do to stop the leakage. A desire to enforce the Continental System does not by itself explain why Napoleon virtually abandoned the Sultan for the Tsar in 1807. Friendship, which looked like subservience, from the ruler of all the Russias was a prize which might have dazzled the most hard-headed. At Tilsit Napoleon caught a glimpse of a power as mighty and more mysterious than his own. The thought of it was to lure him to his ruin in 1812.

CHAPTER IX

Economic Warfare

I. THE CONTINENTAL SYSTEM AND THE ORDERS IN COUNCIL

FROM 1806 to 1814 economic warfare played an important part in hostilities between Britain and France. Both sides had been taking up their positions gradually since the breach of the Peace of Amiens. On 20 June 1803 and 13 March 1804 Bonaparte closed all French ports to British goods and to colonial goods carried in British ships; neutral ships could only be admitted if they produced a certificate from the French representative at their port of origin or undertook to carry back French goods equal in value to the cargo landed. On 28 June and 26 July 1803 Britain declared a blockade of the mouths of the Elbe and the Weser. On 9 August 1804 the blockade was extended to all French ports on the English Channel and the North Sea. Finally, on 16th May 1806, Britain declared a blockade of the entire European coastline from Brest to the Elbe. A blockade on so extensive a scale was bound to be mainly fictitious, in spite of the much vaunted prowess of the British navy: outside some ports there was not a single British warship. Napoleon replied in equally flamboyant style with his Berlin decree. Both sides had still to make their threats effective.

With the death of Pitt at the beginning of 1806, British politics entered a period of confusion ill-fitted to the prosecution of war. The government's immediate reply to the Berlin decree nevertheless showed considerable determination: the first Order in Council, published on 7 January 1807, forbade neutral vessels to trade between one French occupied port and another. In the spring of 1807 a Tory government emerged through the direct intervention of George III, and the True Blue party stayed in office, first under the Duke of Portland, then under Spencer Perceval, and finally under Lord Liverpool, to the end of the war. Alongside a number of mediocre politicians two men of ability and decision rose to posts of importance: Canning as Foreign Secretary and Castlereagh as Secretary of State for War. The new driving force behind British policy soon became apparent. Learning from secret sources that the Danish fleet was about to pass into French hands, Canning ordered a bombardment of Copenhagen (2 September 1807). The city burned for three days, and 18 Danish ships of the line, with frigates, gunboats, brigs, and vast quantities of naval stores, were captured by the

British fleet. From the point of view of international morality the action was deplorable. The Danes immediately declared war on Britain. Napoleon professed himself 'deeply incensed' at the 'horrible crime', and opposition members in the House of Commons accused Canning of 'piracy'. Canning saw only that he had staved off the immediate threat of a hostile fleet blocking supplies of wood, hemp, tar, copper, and iron from the Baltic. This action was followed, in November 1807, by a series of Orders in Council. All countries which excluded British ships were declared to be in a state of blockade. No neutral vessel could proceed towards a blockaded port unless it first of all entered a British port, paid import duties of about 25% on its cargo, and bought a licence.

Before hearing of the new Orders in Council Napoleon issued the first of his Milan decrees (23 November 1807) designed to regulate and extend the working of the Berlin decree. Any neutral vessel which had touched at a British port was declared subject to seizure, and colonial produce was declared liable to be treated as British. The second Milan decree (17 December 1807) came as a direct answer to the British measures. Any ship which submitted to British authority was declared to have lost its nationality and to have become a legitimate prize of war, in port or on the high seas.

By the early months of 1808 the greater part of the continent of Europe had been absorbed into the Napoleonic system. Holland adhered in December 1806, Denmark in October, Russia in November, and Prussia in December 1807. Joseph took the necessary measures in Naples in March 1806; Eugène in north Italy in December; Leghorn and the Adriatic coast of the Papal States were occupied in 1807. Spain promised adherence in February 1807; Portugal was invaded and forced into the system later in the year. Finally Austria submitted in February 1808. The amount of organization entailed was enormous. Prefects, chambers of commerce, leading industrialists, ministers, consuls, and officials were required to submit information constantly to Napoleon. All along the vast coastline of Europe customs officers mounted guard. In 1809 there were 27,000 of them, under a director-general, Collin de Sussy. Later, forty sub-directors were appointed to submit orders to subordinate officials grouped into four great sectors – southern France, northern France, Italy and Switzerland, Holland and Germany. Napoleon insisted that all satellite rulers should allow complete freedom of action to his customs officials. To many fishermen, bargees, warehousemen, and other workers in the lower spheres of trade, Napoleonic domination meant the coast guard and the customs inspector and became a reality for the first time in this form.

Contrary to British expectations continental opinion did not immediately denounce Napoleon's measures. In Germany, especially, the arrogance of British merchants and the selfishness of Britain's commercial policy had long been resented. Newspapers, along with more serious works by Buchholz and Fichte, welcomed the Continental System as the beginning of a new economic régime which was likely to prove advantageous to many European nations. Two benefits especially were envisaged: a more just attitude towards neutral shipping, and the formation of a self-supporting economic unit covering the whole of central and eastern Europe.

The rights of belligerent powers with regard to neutrals were bound up with the rights of warships to seize private cargoes and merchant vessels. Both had been the subject of juridical dispute for more than a century. According to general practice, countries at war seldom respected private cargoes and merchant ships issuing from enemy ports. This meant that neutral ships suspected of trading with enemy powers were also liable to seizure, although the treaty of Utrecht had declared them inviolable. Britain, with her naval superiority, had every incentive for upholding a harsh view concerning private cargoes and merchant vessels: Napoleon, by contrast, proclaimed a view which Italian jurists had been pressing for many years, that at sea, as on land, armed forces had no rights over persons and properties outside the profession of war. With regard to neutrals, Britain's attitude varied with circumstances. The government was aware that neutral shipping rendered important services to the British economy and war effort. Greek ships carried cargoes to and from the Levant; Scandinavian neutrals brought wood and fish; above all, American ships delivered supplies of raw cotton and took back Britain's manufactured goods. In 1806, about 40% of shipping clearing from British ports was under a neutral flag. British shipowners were not slow to complain of rivalry, and their complaints, combined with the exigencies of war, led the government into a policy which was both fluctuating and arbitrary. While the first Order in Council was lenient in its specifications regarding neutrals, the fictitious extension of the term 'blockade' meant that more and more neutral ships were rendered liable to seizure. The rigorous Orders in Council of November 1807 subjected neutrals to a type of British taxation and severely reduced their profits to the advantage of the British treasury. Licences to trade were nevertheless eagerly sought after, but they were granted or refused by British authorities at will. Under these circumstances Napoleon was able to adopt a righteous pose which was never entirely exploded. Writers on the continent continued to look upon him as the would-be defender of freedom of the seas against British tyranny, in spite of the fact that when, in 1807, the Americans sought to bring pressure to bear on both belligerents by placing an embargo on trade, Napoleon merely seized the opportunity to declare that all American ships in his ports became prizes of war.

Meanwhile the vision of a great continental economic unit, enjoying freedom of trade within its own boundaries and negotiating on favourable terms with other economic powers, was discovered to be an illusion. Napoleon's idea from first to last was that France should dominate, economically as well as politically, over vassal states. France's peasants must be able to sell their agricultural produce to France's town labourers, who must derive adequate wages from industry to buy it. To this end, vassal states must supply France with raw materials for industry and absorb her manufactured goods. French industry was increasingly protected by customs tariffs, and treaties favourable to France's economy were forced upon other countries with every political advance. Thus Joseph Bonaparte in Spain was obliged to sacrifice the Catalan textile industry to that of France; the Kingdom of Italy was obliged to give up buying cloth from Moravia, Bohemia, Saxony, and Switzerland; the silk industry of Piedmont was deprived of raw materials by heavy import duties. Of the glorious vision, only one aspect approached reality. To facilitate French commerce, which could not move safely by sea, Napoleon planned a network of roads radiating from Paris to Holland, Germany, Italy, and Spain. His roads, especially those which pierced the Alps at the Simplon and Mont Cenis passes, had a more profound effect on European commerce than any other single development until the coming of railways.

The Continental System never had the disastrous effect upon Britain which Napoleon anticipated. Indeed there were periods when the British economy was completely unharmed, either by the Continental System or by the war. From the promulgation of the Berlin decree in the autumn of 1806 to the defeat of Russia by France in the summer of 1807, economic activity in Britain was almost normal. Signs of serious depression appeared in the winter of 1807-8, but these were followed by a boom which lasted for over two years. Harder times than Britain had yet known came in 1811-12, but these too were followed by a trade revival, and in the last years of the war many businessmen enjoyed a prosperity which could not be sustained with the coming of peace.

Englishmen at the time tended to speak of the invulnerability of the British economy as though it were some divinely bestowed quality which required no further explanation. Outside Providence the British government placed its greatest confidence in smuggling. Dubious practices were widely encouraged, in spite of protests from honest members of the public. British authorities became expert at forging papers to be carried by merchantmen, by which it appeared that they had cleared from a port under French influence or control. Crews were well drilled in substantiating, under interrogation, the details contained in the papers. As time went on, certain continental ports gained new importance as points of entry for British goods. From Amsterdam, goods were passed through Belgium into France, or along the Rhine and through the Grand Duchy of Berg into Germany; from Trieste, goods travelled along alpine roads into Austria, Switzerland, and Bavaria. Cargoes were carried along the Save and the Danube to Vienna; others were deposited at Odessa for collection by Slav, German, and Levantine merchants. International centres of commerce such as Frankfurt, Basle, and the great fairs at Leipzig provided excellent cover for British trade. Napoleon was hampered everywhere by the cupidity of his officials, many of whom were bought over by the enemy, and by lack of co-operation from local authorities.

Smuggling could not have been organized on such a scale without the active support of the British navy, which protected merchantmen from enemy action on the high seas.. Once the merchant ships neared foreign ports, the subtle arts of producing forged papers and bribing officials came into play, but until they reached coastal waters they were dependent upon the Admiralty's convoy system. The many duties of the navy were nowhere more successfully performed than in the Baltic. By 1804, British trade with the Baltic had increased to ten times the amount carried on in pre-war years, partly because of the demand for naval stores from Russia, and partly because, as the Scandinavian states remained neutral or allied to Britain, Baltic ports became the principal channel for introducing British goods into Europe. The alliance between Russia and France in 1807 threatened to put a stop to this trade. The capture of the Danish fleet removed an immediate menace, but the Danes soon produced a fleet of gunboats capable of operating in coastal waters and of attacking shipping in the narrow entrances to the Baltic. The Danes and the Norwegians also equipped large numbers of privateers which lurked in the harbours of Bornholm and the adjacent islets of the Ertholm group, while a number of French corsairs operated continuously from bases on the south coast of the Baltic. From 1808 to 1813 British cruisers patrolled the trade routes to drive off raiders and the Admiralty arranged escorts of warships for merchantmen. During these years there were no glorious actions between battle fleets, but the patient work of defending trade in the Baltic was not without political significance. Many Baltic and also American shipowners came in the end to seek the protection of the British navy in Baltic waters, and thereby developed a vested interest in keeping British influence alive in the Baltic zone.

The volume of contraband fluctuated greatly, however, and at no time can smugglers be given chief credit for the vast amount of British trade which penetrated to the continent. Of greater importance to Britain were the paradoxes inherent in Napoleon's design. The main purpose of the Continental System was to prevent Britain from exporting her surplus produce, namely her manufactured goods and colonial produce. Napoleon's decrees also made provision for preventing Britain from importing raw materials and foodstuffs from the continent, but these clauses were framed only so that such commodities could, when necessary, be directed into

France. Napoleon never made systematic efforts to deprive Britain of raw materials for her industries or food for her crowded population. Indeed he could not have hoped for success in such an enterprise, because he could not prevent Great Britain from obtaining supplies from her colonies, from the Far East, and from America. He hoped, rather, to encourage British manufacturers to go on producing goods which would glut the home market, while the country went on importing raw materials and foodstuffs for which she paid out valuable gold. This meant that ships chartered by British merchants had to be admitted to continental ports to load their habitual cargoes of wheat, raw silk, flax seed, chemicals and naval stores. Often the masters refused to pay gold. If they offered, instead, clothing for French armies, Napoleon allowed his officials to connive at the arrangement. On many occasions, French consuls at the great Baltic and North Sea ports took the initiative in allowing merchant ships to unload cargoes of British manufactured goods. They were not necessarily acting under the influence of bribes in doing so. They were often, rather, acting from a shrewd sense that a certain amount of the old commercial life must go on if the local populace was to survive and the harbours remain open. It was not in Napoleon's interests, in the long run, that the coastline of his empire should be dotted with ghost towns.

2. DEPRESSION AND REVIVAL IN BRITAIN, 1807-10

At the beginning of the nineteenth century, Great Britain was the most advanced of all European countries in the way of large-scale industry, but she was not yet completely industrialized. Her large-scale industry was more or less confined within an area bounded by Preston, Liverpool, Shrewsbury, Droitwich, Coventry, Leicester, Nottingham, and Leeds, with two smaller areas in South Wales and the Scottish Lowlands. In 1806 less than a quarter of the population obtained a living from large-scale industry, and only a third of the nation's revenue was derived from it. Nevertheless, industry was the dynamic element in the nation's life. If Napoleon could cripple Britain's industry he would reduce her to the status of a backward country. An important part of her population would suffer acute distress, and the whole of the national economy would be indirectly affected. To what extent, however, was a closure of continental markets likely to cripple Britain's industry? In the three years preceding the Berlin decree, European countries absorbed only one third of Britain's exports. The closing of continental markets would thus be a serious blow to British industry, but it would only be a mortal blow if it were delivered simultaneously with the closing of another important market.

A potential enemy of Britain in Napoleonic times was the U.S.A. Two subjects were likely to infuriate the Americans into a dangerously hostile

attitude – the impressment of American citizens into the British fleet, and
Britain's attitude towards neutral shipping. The British government maintained that British subjects who emigrated to America remained British
subjects unless they had been inhabitants of America at or before the time
of the separation of that country from the British crown, and British naval
captains were ordered to search American ships and impress 'deserters' who
lurked under the shelter of America's generous naturalization laws. Along
with this indignity and hardship the Americans saw their trade seriously
reduced and a large percentage of its profit diverted to the British treasury
by the Orders in Council. Napoleon's decrees were in essence equally
offensive, but they were less resented because his naval power for enforcing
them was less than that of Great Britain. Moreover, Napoleon had staked
a claim to America's friendship by acquiring Louisiana from Spain and
selling it to the United States in 1803. On this very matter Britain aroused
further resentment among her former colonists by drawing a new Canadian
boundary between the Lake of the Woods and Lake Superior, and thereby,
according to the American senate, prejudicing America's claims to territory
associated with Louisiana.

In the three years before the Berlin decree, continental Europe and the
United States between them took three fifths of Britain's exports. The proportion was higher in some commodities than others. Seventy-four per cent
of Britain's cotton exports and sixty-six per cent of her woollen exports went
to these two markets. British silk, which could not compete with French
silk in Europe, sold well in the United States, which took two thirds of the
total exports. Thus the textile industries, which provided sixty-four per cent
of Britain's export trade, would suffer very heavily indeed if continental and
United States markets were closed simultaneously. Their vulnerability was
increased by certain structural features within the industries at the time. The
cotton industry had expanded rapidly at the turn of the century. Spinning
mills had been started often on insufficient capital, far too many domestic
workers had taken up cotton weaving, and the whole industry was more
open to fluctuation and speculation than others. In addition, a half of the
raw cotton used in Britain came from the U.S.A. In the woollen industry,
which was less mechanized than cotton, there was resentment among workers
at the introduction of gig mills and shearing frames by the more advanced
manufacturers. Thus Lancashire and Yorkshire, the centres of the two main
textile industries, were ripe for social troubles.

Between July and November 1807 almost the whole of continental Europe
was closed by Napoleon to British commerce. Only Sweden remained
faithful to her alliance with Britain. Smuggling had not yet been organized
on an effective scale, no British fleet had been sent to the Baltic, and early
attempts by the British government to find alternative markets in Latin

America met with failure. Following on an expedition under Home Popham in 1806 a force under General Whitelocke was sent in July 1807 to attack Buenos Aires and open up the Plate area, but it soon withdrew in face of local hostility. President Jefferson chose this timely moment to bring pressure to bear on the economic situation. On 14 December 1807 a non-importation law, voted by Congress in the previous year but hitherto suspended, forbade entry into the United States to certain types of British goods. On 22 December a law of embargo forbade American ships to sail for foreign ports without a licence from the President.

The simultaneous closing of continental and United States markets produced in Britain the marked depression of the winter months of 1807-8. Panic, out of all proportion to the actual danger, seized British opinion, and the sort of crisis that Napoleon had envisaged might indeed have ensued if the French had been able to maintain their advantage for a while longer. In May 1808, however, Britain heard news that Spain was in open rebellion against its French king. In July the government lifted its blockade from the ports of Spain which were not occupied by French troops, and commerce began slowly to revive. The insurrection in Spain was soon followed by the liberation of Portugal and the opening of her harbours to British ships. The first breach had been made in the great wall built by Napoleon, and the importance of it, in bringing about the failure of the Continental System, can hardly be exaggerated. Trade with Spain's American colonies received a lively impetus. British goods obtained a wide point of entry into southern Europe, and contraband trade in northern and eastern Europe was facilitated by the diversion of a large French army into Spain. The development of Malta as a base for contraband trade with Trieste encouraged British merchants to look more closely at commercial possibilities in the eastern Mediterranean and, as Russia's ambitions in this area threw both Turkey and Persia into the arms of Britain, flourishing markets were opened in the Levant. It cannot be denied that, as far as the Continental System was concerned, Napoleon made a grave miscalculation when he provoked rebellion in Madrid and started a long chain of reactions. Prior to his dethronement of the Spanish king in April 1808 the Continental Blockade had been enforced more or less effectively by the Spanish authorities.

3. CRISES IN FRANCE AND BRITAIN, 1810-12

In July 1810, the French Minister of the Interior, Montalivet, drew up a report which concluded that Great Britain was not suffering at all from the Continental System, and that France alone was adversely affected by it. French manufacturers, who had at first been grateful for restrictions on British competition, soon began to feel the shortage of raw materials. Raw cotton, especially, was acutely scarce, and many cotton mills closed down.

Map III   Central Europe in 1811

As the British navy deprived France of her colonies one by one, supplies of
sugar, coffee, and soda failed, and attempts to find substitutes were expensive
and unpopular. The gradual impoverishment of the vassal states meant that
the market for French luxury goods steadily declined; by 1809, exports were
valued at only three quarters of the amount recorded in 1806.

An English minister, George Rose, said that Britain and France were in the position of two men who had put their heads in a bucket and were seeing which could keep his head under water the longer. The British device of issuing licences to trade brought welcome draughts of air. Napoleon, who always prided himself on his adaptability, began to copy the system in 1808. He decided that if he could sell French corn and wine to Britain he would benefit the French peasants, who often suffered from a glut. If he could sell permits to the Americans he would attract their raw cotton to French mills. At the same time the high price paid for the licences would benefit France's treasury. In April 1809 Napoleon provided 300 French ships with neutral flags and allowed them to carry French produce to England. The result was unexpected. The owners of the ships, glad to be once more in business, sold their services to the British and failed to return to France. In spite of this check Napoleon persisted with the new policy. It was welcomed by French consuls who began selling licences on a reckless scale at ports and commercial centres all over Europe. Under cover of the licences, smuggling and black marketeering of every kind flourished apace. Napoleon soon realized that his concessions were being abused and that he was benefiting the enemy more than France. In July 1810 he decided that a new system of licences should come into operation, more strictly under his own control and confined to the hands of Frenchmen. By the St. Cloud and Trianon decrees 29 French ports were allowed to sell 200 licences each to French traders. A special concession was made in favour of Americans, who were allowed to land colonial produce provided they took back larger quantities of French goods.

To make the policy effective a new drive was undertaken against smugglers. The Fontainebleau decree of 18 October 1810 set up special courts to deal with infringements of the economic code; vast stores of British contraband goods were seized by Napoleon's police and publicly burned. The policy resulted in a series of bankruptcies among Dutch, German, and French firms which had been heavily involved in illicit trade. The bankruptcies in their turn heralded a general financial crisis. Banks curtailed the amount of credit they were willing to supply to industrial firms, and many of the latter were obliged to close. The failure of the credit system, which had never been more than rudimentary, accentuated the fundamental weakness of the French financial system – shortage of gold – and placed a higher premium than ever on the illicit arts of forging, debasing, and clipping. Meanwhile the Tsar chose the last day of the year 1810 on which to publish a ukase placing an almost prohibitive tariff on French wines and luxury goods imported into Russia. By 1811 the whole of the French empire was suffering under the worst economic crisis of the war years. Napoleon sponsored schemes to provide temporary work for the unemployed in Paris, and granted huge subsidies to the Lyon silk industry. These were relief measures which might stave off popular insurrection but could not cure the deep-seated malaise of the European economy.

Perhaps Napoleon believed that he needed only to gain a little time for victory to be his. In 1811, reports told him that Great Britain, too, was suffering from a severe economic crisis, bringing with it social and political disturbances of a significant nature. The crisis had been brewing up for some time, beginning with monetary troubles. The adverse trade balance with Europe had caused the pound to depreciate in terms of French francs as early as 1808. In the years which followed, more and more British gold crossed the seas, to support armies in Portugal and Spain and to pay for increased amounts of grain after bad harvests. Further depreciation of the pound followed, and the gold reserves of the Bank of England were drained lower and lower. Confidence was already waning when Napoleon's re-newed efforts in 1810 to enforce the Continental System intensified the crisis. Holland was annexed to France; French troops occupied the south-western shores of the Baltic in large numbers; Britain's contraband trade through Amsterdam and Heligoland virtually ceased. In the same year a vast British convoy was delayed by adverse winds at the entrance to the Baltic and 240 ships were seized by the enemy, entailing a loss of £2 million. At the end of the year Sweden was drawn into the Continental System, Charles XIII submitting to a French ultimatum and declaring war on Britain. Napoleon's fierce measures against smugglers acted as a deterrent to illicit traders all over Europe. The financial crisis of 1810-11 reduced the purchasing power of continental countries, and this power decreased even further when Napoleon began to make preparations for his gigantic attack upon Russia. By 1811 British exports to northern Europe had fallen to 20% of the level achieved in 1810.

Again the situation would not have been critical had the closure of Euro-pean markets not coincided with rigorous measures on the part of the United States. In 1809 America had relaxed her Non-Intercourse Act and a flood of trade had opened up between Britain and the U.S.A. This situation was dramatically reversed when Napoleon, who needed the help of neutral ship-ping in his preparations for war against Russia, relaxed his economic decrees in favour of the U.S.A. President Madison judged that the time had come to take a strong line with the British government regarding its attitude to neutrals. He announced that the Non-Intercourse Act would return to life if Britain had not relaxed her Orders in Council by 2 February 1811. The British government remained adamant and the American threat was carried out. Congress, indeed, went further: by the Non-Importation law of 2 March 1811 American ships were allowed to carry American cargoes to Britain but neither American nor British ships could land British cargoes in the U.S.A. In 1810 the United States had taken 17% of Britain's total exports: in 1811 she took only 4·4%.

Beginning towards the end of 1810 a wave of industrial failures spread over Great Britain. Many firms went bankrupt and closed down. Many more cut down the number of employees and put the remainder on short time. The cotton industry suffered most: by May 1811 the majority of mills in Lancashire were working a three day week. At the same time bad harvests made bread dearer than it had been for many a year. In various parts of the country the distressed poor took to rioting. The governing classes began to panic, and there were many well-placed persons who feared a general rebellion of the poor against the rich.

The so-called Luddite riots were the nearest point Britain ever reached to the revolution Napoleon anticipated. At their most dangerous they constituted a revolutionary situation rather than a revolution. The riots spread over a period from March 1811 to July 1812, but within this period outbreaks were spasmodic and limited in area. A mild outburst from the stocking workers of the Midlands took place in March 1811, followed by more serious rioting in the winter months from November 1811 to February 1812. Nottingham was the area chiefly affected: Derbyshire was only mildly troubled, and Leicestershire not at all. By January 1812 the riots had spread to the woollen district of Yorkshire, where they lasted intermittently for six months, Huddersfield being the main trouble centre. The cotton operatives of Lancashire and Cheshire were the last to move. Their riots, which took place in February and the few months following, were limited to the southeast part of Lancashire and the border of Cheshire, centring upon Bolton, Manchester, Oldham, and Stockport. There was practically no trouble in Scotland, nor in the areas around Newcastle and Birmingham, nor in the Black Country, nor in London.

The riots were limited, also, in their nature and objectives. In the Midlands the rioters broke frames not in order to abolish frames, which had long been used in the stocking industry, but as a means of intimidating employers who undercut the market by lowering wages and producing inferior articles. In the West Riding of Yorkshire the rioters broke shearing frames in an attempt to stop factory owners from installing them. In Lancashire and Cheshire the riots mostly took the form of attacks on markets and barns as a protest against the high price of food. There were practically no attacks upon the authorities, the police, or the army, and few acts of violence against individuals. There was certainly no attempt to overthrow the government by a general rising or to massacre the upper classes. This can be attributed in some measure to deliberate restraint on the part of the Luddite leaders. Many of the latter obviously possessed powers of organization, but they used them to direct attack upon well-chosen local targets. The authorities, meanwhile, saw fit to use against the rioters more troops than Wellington commanded in the Peninsular War. Large sections of the public, especially in the Midlands and the West Riding, were sympathetic to the rioters, but the middle classes, whose co-operation alone could have produced a movement worthy of the name revolution, nevertheless helped to put down an agitation which threatened their position as property owners.

The middle classes had their grievances but they expressed them in a different way and concentrated on different objectives. Many industrialists and merchants resented the loss of trade with the U.S.A., and in the winter of 1811-12 meetings were held to frame petitions to the Prince Regent protesting against the maintenance of the Orders in Council. The movement was taken up by the parliamentary opposition and organized by the young Whig politician Henry Brougham. Agitation increased impressively during March and April 1812 when committees were formed in a large number of provincial centres to collect signatures for petitions to parliament. About twenty petitions were submitted, signed by vast numbers from the middle class and from the more intelligent sections of the working class. In the West Riding, 15,000 names were collected; in Birmingham, 14,000; in Leicester, 11,000. The petitions affirmed that, since the Orders in Council had failed to reopen the continent of Europe to British trade, the United States had become the chief outlet for British goods; this market was virtually lost through the obstinacy of the British government in maintaining the Orders in Council; and the inevitable result would be pauperism for the workers and ruin for the middle class.

The campaign against the Orders in Council was potentially dangerous for the government in that respectable merchants and industrialists were willing to back a popular agitation. By no means all the middle class had lost confidence in the government's policy, however. Counter petitions were organized, defending the Orders in Council as essential to Britain's war effort and harmless to Britain's economy. They were backed by London businessmen, by the Merchant Venturers of Bristol, by the West India Merchants and the Canada Merchants, by shipowners, and by groups of industrialists in Birmingham, Liverpool and Glasgow. They represented the views of men who made money from contraband trade with Europe and from trade with the eastern Mediterranean lands, the colonies, and South America. From their point of view trade with the U.S.A., carried on mainly in American ships, was dangerous to Britain's commercial interests and could well be abandoned. Nor would it be true to say that those who petitioned against the Orders in Council were anxious to bring down the government. Some of the leaders of the movement, notably Thomas Attwood, counted themselves as Tories. Many of those who signed were opposed to only one aspect of the government's policy, and that for purely practical reasons. To regard the campaign against the Orders in Council as a struggle for free trade against protection, or as a protest of the new society against the old, is to read too much of the future into it.

Nevertheless, the movement played its part in bringing about the retreat of the government. Retreat was made easier when Perceval, the author of the measures, was assassinated by a madman and replaced as Prime Minister by Lord Liverpool. On 23 June 1812 the government announced that the Orders in Council would cease to have effect on American commerce from 1 August. The decision came too late to mend British affairs with the U.S.A. To many Americans, complaints against British treatment of neutrals had been no more than a legalistic cover for deeper issues, notably for designs upon British territory in northern and western America. On 19 June 1812 President Madison had implemented a Congressional vote and declared war on Britain. The declaration was not revoked when the Orders were withdrawn. The futile and tragic war dragged on when Britain's affairs in Europe mended: in the last months of 1812 Napoleon's invading army was driven out of Russia and the Continental System collapsed.

When the Napoleonic wars ended Britain's economic superiority over France was greater than it had been in 1793. Nevertheless, Napoleon believed to the end of his days that his Continental System was based on sound principles. According to Gourgaud he said on St. Helena, 'England is insatiable and goes on manufacturing goods until she has more than she needs. So her people get accustomed to luxury and, when their produce can find no more markets, they rebel.' If Napoleon had defeated Russia and enforced the System in all its rigidity over a long period the fate of Britain might have been different. In the end, however, the fatal flaw in Napoleon's strategy was that he relied on his armies to enforce his economic measures. Twice they failed him, in Spain and Russia.

CHAPTER X

Spain and National Independence

In 1795 Spain made peace with the French Republic by the treaty of Basle. She abandoned her territory in San Domingo to France and in the following year made an alliance with the Directory. The British fleet withdrew from the Mediterranean but other benefits which France had expected to obtain from the alliance never materialized. The Spanish government would not agree either to invade Portugal or to help in preparations for an attack upon Britain.

When Bonaparte inherited this unsatisfactory alliance he fancied he would be able to turn it to greater profit. His first attempts were encouraging. Spanish statesmen wanted him to give peace to their exhausted country; the Spanish queen, Maria Louisa, wanted him to enlarge the territory ruled by her brother, the Duke of Parma. The situation happened to suit Bonaparte's personal plans. By the preliminaries of San Ildefonso (1800) the French Republic undertook to provide the ruling house of Parma with 1,200,000 subjects in Italy, and Spain agreed to pay for them by ceding Louisiana and six ships of the line to France. Bonaparte found the 1,200,000 subjects in Tuscany whence he expelled the Austrian ruler and installed the Duke of Parma's son Louis as puppet king. By this arrangement Bonaparte extended his own influence over central Italy and over the port of Leghorn.

Napoleon entrusted his affairs at Madrid to the skilful hands of his younger brother. Lucien not only brought off the Parma business with great finesse but succeeded at long last in obtaining Spanish co-operation in an attack on Portugal. In April 1801 a French expeditionary force crossed the Bidassoa and in May a Spanish army began the 'War of the Oranges'. The Portuguese had small hopes of resisting a combined attack without British help, and when no such help arrived the Regent of Portugal came to terms with the enemy. Lucien Bonaparte called off the attack in return for Portuguese gold. He earned thereby the anger of Napoleon, who continued to believe for another seven years that the Spaniards could be made to bully their neighbours into breaking with their ancient British alliance.

Another obvious use for Spaniards, in Napoleon's eyes, was to provide gold for France. When war with Britain was renewed in 1803 Napoleon decided to make Spain pay heavily for permission to remain neutral. He threatened and bullied, and finally Godoy, the power behind the throne, agreed to send a large sum of money to France each month while the war lasted. No-one familiar with Spanish promises was surprised when half the gold never arrived. Only the gravest necessity could have induced Napoleon to continue negotiations with so irritating an ally, but by 1804 he needed ships and he believed that Spain could supply both vessels and crews. He bribed Godoy with promises of a principality in Portugal, and the Spanish fleet was put at France's disposal for the projected invasion of England. Almost the whole of it was destroyed and a thousand men lost in the Trafalgar campaign. This time it was Napoleon's promise to Godoy which was not carried out.

How far Godoy ever trusted Napoleon and how far he was playing cat and mouse with a dangerous neighbour is not certain. By 1806 he had come to the conclusion that Napoleon was planning to annex the whole of Spain north of the Ebro and he asked the allies for assistance. Godoy's suspicions were by no means ill-founded. After Tilsit Napoleon told Portugal to close her ports to British shipping. She refused and French troops under Junot crossed the Bidassoa for an attack on Lisbon. Godoy agreed by the treaty of Fontainebleau (29 October 1807) to their passage through Spain – he could do no other – and he again accepted offers of a principality in Portugal. The French troops strung themselves out, in search of provisions, over the whole of north-western Spain, occupying every town and citadel in their path. The temptation to Napoleon was irresistible. He believed Spain to possess vast potential riches: all she needed was organization.

Napoleon's original plan for imposing suitable organization upon Spain seems to have been to back the heir to the throne, Prince Ferdinand, in his quarrels with Godoy and the king. Ferdinand was popular in Spain and if Napoleon had placed him on the throne the arrangement might have worked to everyone's advantage. Napoleon abandoned this solution, however, and decided to dethrone the Bourbons altogether. In March 1808 he put Murat in charge of the 40,000 French troops in Spain and ordered him to march upon Madrid. On 17 March a popular rising against Godoy so frightened Charles IV that he abdicated in favour of his son. Ferdinand was afraid to take up the Crown and for a month the court was in chaos. At the end of April Napoleon invited father and son to Bayonne, and there both men signed away their claims to the Spanish throne (5 May 1808). They accepted a comfortable exile in France while Godoy went to prison and Joseph Bonaparte left Naples at his brother's behest to become King of Spain.

2. THE CONDITION OF SPAIN

The country which Napoleon proposed to add to his satellite states was different in important respects from any he had yet dealt with. It was his basic mistake that he did not realize this. He believed, and was still believing on St. Helena, that all countries in Europe were fundamentally alike. They all needed social and economic regeneration and they would accept it joyfully from a French conqueror.

To a superficial observer Spain at the end of the eighteenth century might have seemed to possess all the ingredients necessary for revolution. A privileged nobility and clergy, an oppressed peasantry, a growing bourgeoisie, and an enlightened intelligentsia gave Spain some resemblance to France. Between 1723 and 1787 the total population of Spain increased from 6 million to 10½ million. Large parts of the country remained almost deserted, and a traveller in Castile, León, Extremadura, or Aragon might journey for forty or fifty miles without seeing a permanent habitation, but in Valencia and Andalusia and along the north coast the population was growing rapidly. Spain was very largely an agricultural country and by the end of the century land hunger had become a serious problem in areas where farming was aided by sufficient rainfall. Between 1750 and 1790 prices rose about 35%. Rents rose accordingly and land became a valuable source of income.

Much of the profit from the land went into the pockets of the nobility and clergy. Not all Spain's noblemen were wealthy, for any family which owned an entailed estate (*mayorazgo*) could claim nobility. By the end of the eighteenth century Spain had half a million *hidalgos*. Many of them were hardly distinguishable from commoners. They enjoyed a few 'honorific' privileges, such as the right to display a coat of arms and to be addressed as 'Don', but unlike French nobles they were not exempt from taxation. Some were very poor, especially those whose estates lay in barren regions. In Old Castile *hidalgos* could be found working as cowherds. On the other hand there were fortunate *hidalgos* who had been appointed members of military orders. These *caballeros* shared the income from the extensive lands given to the orders at the time when Spain was reconquered from the Moors. Wealthier still were the *señores*. These were men who, in addition to owning large family estates, had been granted rights of lordship over vast areas of land known as *señoríos legos*. All persons living on a *señorío* had to pay dues to the overlord. The church controlled extensive *señoríos* as well as owning land outright in most parts of Spain. The census of 1797 indicated that about 3,000 cities, towns, and villages lay under the church's jurisdiction.

The condition of the peasantry differed greatly from one part of Spain to another. On the whole peasants were better off in the rainy provinces of the north and north-east than in the more arid regions of the centre and south. In Galicia, Asturias, and the Basque provinces, and in Navarre, Aragon, and Catalonia, arable farming lent itself to division of the land into small holdings. In the Basque provinces, and in Navarre and northern Aragon, large numbers of peasants owned their own land. Others had been able to lease land on favourable terms, passing it on from generation to generation and paying a fixed rent. In Catalonia most of the land belonged to *señoríos legos* and *eclesiásticos*, but by long custom the *señorío* was regarded as the private property of the overlord and many *señores* let out pieces of land to peasants on long-term contracts. In Galicia and Asturias, unfortunately, the process of sub-letting had gone too far for the peasants' good. The rents which could be charged by owners of land to tenants had been frozen by law in 1763, but tenants were able to sub-let their holdings to under-tenants without any rent restrictions at all. As the years went by, and prices rose, tenants who paid a comparatively small rent took advantage of the opportunity to let out small parcels of land at high figures. Some lands were sub-let several times over until the tiller of the land found himself paying rent to three or four land-lords. Many peasants, in Galicia especially, were driven off the land alto-gether and obliged to seek a living as knife-grinders or water-carriers in the cities.

Some regions of Spain, such as Valencia, Alicante, Murcia, and Granada, made up for shortage of rainfall by irrigation, an art learnt from the Moors. In these regions also the peasants were comparatively fortunate. The position was far different in Andalusia, Extremadura, Old and New Castile, southern Léon, and southern Aragon. Here the hot, dry land was used in vast tracts for growing grain, vines, or olives, or for grazing sheep. The wealthy nobles employed overseers to run their estates or leased their land to monied men who could afford to rent large areas. These powerful tenants often sub-let the land for very high rents, terminating the leases abruptly whenever there was an opportunity to obtain more rent from a new sub-tenant. The middlemen dominated the local peasantry to such an extent that they became known as *caciques* after the Indian chieftains of Spanish America. The census of 1797 showed that south of Madrid two thirds of the peasants were landless labourers. Many could obtain only seasonal work on the estates of some great *señor*, where they were herded into settlements (*cortijos*) by the overseer and given bread and soup for sustenance and the hard ground to sleep on. For the rest of the year they were reduced to begging in the streets of Seville, Jerez, and Córdoba.

During the reconquest of Spain from the Moors, Spanish rulers had granted extensive lands to cities, towns, and villages. Most municipalities devoted some of this land to common pasture and divided the rest among the inhabitants, redistributing the plots at regular intervals to make sure that everyone took his turn at good and bad. In northern Spain, and in the hilly districts separating the rainy north from the dry areas, the peasants derived much benefit from municipal lands. In Castile, Extremadura, and Andalusia again the position was worse for the peasantry. Towns were larger and more

widely separated than in northern Spain and they were dominated by
wealthy families rather than by peasant communities. The local oligarchies
either kept the best lands for themselves or put the town lands up for auction
and leased them to outside bidders.

Agriculture had thus become thoroughly capitalistic over large parts of
Spain and there was much scope for monied men to profit at the expense of
the poor. A monied class was making its presence felt in the towns also.
The eighteenth century was one of commercial and industrial expansion for
Spain. Seville and Cadiz were no longer allowed to monopolize trade with
the colonies, and in the course of the century Barcelona, Valencia, Alicante,
Cartagena and Málaga on the Mediterranean coast, and La Coruña, Gijón,
Santander and San Sebastián on the north coast of Spain became lively ports.
Industry flourished in three main areas. The kingdom of Valencia had long
produced the best raw silk in Europe, but most of it was sold abroad until the
eighteenth century, when the domestic silk industry grew so rapidly that
Valencia was able to draw trade away from Lyon and to take advantage of
the decline in French manufactures. The Basque provinces became known
all over northern Europe for their ironware. They possessed the most
important shipyards in Spain and they also played a part in developing a
comparatively new industry of the eighteenth century, the manufacture of
paper. Another new industry, cotton manufacture, found a centre in
Catalonia. The most advanced machinery, copied from English and French
models, was installed in Barcelona mills. In 1792 the Catalan cotton industry
employed 80,000 workers and ranked second in Europe to that of England.

Merchants and industrialists formed the nucleus of an audience for writers
who wanted to give their country a place in the main stream of European
development. The works of Buffon and Linnaeus on natural science were
translated into Spanish, and periodicals published in Madrid gave regular
reports on scientific progress in Europe. Political economy became a popular
subject, regarded by many enlightened Spaniards as a panacea for all their
country's ills. Works of political philosophy were less popular, with a few
notable exceptions. Montesquieu's *De l'esprit des lois*, Rousseau's *Émile*, and
the works of the two great Italian jurists Beccaria and Filangieri were known
and esteemed by most educated Spaniards towards the end of the century.
Peasants and labourers, who formed the majority of Spain's population, were
unable to take an interest in new trends of thought, but attempts were made
to spread enlightenment as widely as possible among the literate classes. One
of the most original developments was the formation of societies of *Amigos
del País* (Friends of the Country). The first was founded in the middle of the
century by a group of Basque gentlemen with the purpose of encouraging
progress in agriculture, industry, commerce, and the arts and sciences. Other
localities copied the enterprise until by 1789 there were as many as 56

societies expressing the purpose of regenerating their country. The periodical press supported the campaign. Among the most important journals were *El Correo de Madrid*, which carried a notable series of articles on modern philosophers in the winter of 1789-90, and the *Semanario erudito* (1787-91), whose editor Valladores used the writings of Spaniards from past ages as a means of criticizing contemporary conditions in church and state. Subscribers appear to have been professional men, businessmen, and government officials, with some nobles and clergymen. They formed a minority even of their own classes. The four leading journals of the movement had less than 1,500 subscribers between them in 1789. Subscriptions were costly, especially for readers outside Madrid, but even though each copy of a journal was read by a whole group of persons it cannot be reckoned that more than 1% of the population of Spain came into contact with the press in its attempt to spread new ideas.

Nevertheless when revolution broke out in France the Spanish secretary of state, Floridablanca, thought he should take steps to prevent news of it from reaching the Spanish public. The few journals which had obtained permission to print foreign news were forbidden to mention the Tennis Court Oath, the fall of the Bastille, and subsequent revolutionary events. Frontiers and ports were closed to foreign newspapers and the Inquisition was ordered to assist the government in seizing dangerous publications. In 1791 foreigners were expelled from the country. Floridablanca did not immediately turn against enlightened policies at home, but there were bread riots in Barcelona in 1789 and a rebellion of the peasants in Galicia in 1790 and these events embittered his mind. In 1791 he secured the dismissal from the government of the three most notable advocates of the *luces* – Compomanes, Cabarrús, and Jovellanos. The tragedy of the situation lay in the fact that such measures were completely unnecessary. Spain resembled France in a number of ways but she lacked two ingredients which had been of prime importance in leading her neighbour into revolution: scepticism towards the church and dissatisfaction with the monarchy.

The Catholic church in Spain was by no means exempt from abuses. In 1788 Spain had nearly 200,000 ecclesiastics in a population of 10,000,000. The wealth of the church appeared in startling contrast to the poverty of the countryside, especially in Castile where the soil was exhausted from sheep-grazing and the people were ruined by heavier taxes than elsewhere in Spain. Amid the barren fields and the mud huts of the peasantry the churches, chapels, and monasteries were full of costly jewels and fine vestments. The church owned vast areas of land, which was prevented by right of mortmain from passing to private owners. In some regions large tracts of church land stood untilled while peasants cried out for farms: in others ecclesiastical institutions exploited the peasantry by sub-letting small plots of land at high rents. The money thus extracted from honest tillers of the soil was often bestowed recklessly upon the less deserving poor, for the church prided itself on giving alms to all who begged at its doors. Around every cathedral and monastery hordes of mendicants lived in idleness. The bishop of Granada alone gave daily bread to some five or six thousand persons. Within the church wealth was unevenly divided, the higher clergy enjoying great luxury while parish priests lived in dire poverty. The latter were drawn mainly from peasant families, they were given little education, and in consequence they could only perpetuate the superstitions among which they had been born and bred. Yet the peasants and town labourers remained devoted to the church which provided them with their only advice and consolation and their only excitement and entertainment. Obsessed by nature with thoughts of courage and death, Spaniards were as fascinated by stories of martyrdom and crucifixion as they were by bull-fights. Even the middle class supporters of Enlightenment, who prided themselves on a European outlook, remained impervious to the anti-clericalism of their French neighbours. The writings of atheistic *philosophes* such as Helvétius, Holbach, and La Mettrie were virtually unknown in Spain. Works which appeared dangerous to religion were banned by the Inquisition, but this alone cannot account for the discriminating attitude of middle class Spaniards, most of whom could read French and could obtain clandestine copies of French books. Voltaire was definitely known in Spain but while he was admired in some circles for his sense of social justice he was generally pitied for his errors in religion. Spanish writers who aspired to enlighten their country urged the need for scientific progress, economic change, educational reform, and social justice, but they saw no need to challenge the authority of the church let alone the validity of the Catholic faith in order to obtain these things.

The attitude of educated Spaniards towards the church was due in part to the attitude of the church towards the monarchy. After the expulsion of the Jesuits in 1767 the church ceased to challenge royal absolutism. No serious opposition was expressed when Charles III began to strengthen the discipline of the religious orders and to demand a higher standard of conduct from the bishops. A small group of churchmen, known as Jansenists because of their hostility to the Jesuits, even gave Charles active support in his reforms. The rest of the clergy lacked the intellectual breadth to appreciate the king's policy but they knew that Charles was a devoted Catholic and that he would never harm the church in the supposed interests of the state. They knew too that there would be no popular support for a campaign against the king. From the beginning of his reign Charles strove hard to improve the condition of his country. He tried to cut down the power of *señores* and rural oligarchies and he no longer allowed the Mesta, the hitherto powerful organization of owners of migrant sheep, to prey upon the country's agriculture. He ended the monopoly of colonial trade held by Cadiz and Seville, abolished the restrictive practices of trade guilds, placed protective tariffs on home industries, and built roads in coastal areas. Spain remained backward in agriculture, industry, and commerce compared with France or Britain, but Charles's efforts towards progress won him the respect of the middle classes. When he died in 1788 he bequeathed to his son a united country and a devoted people.

3. GODOY

Charles IV was forty years old when he ascended the throne in the last days of 1788. In the eyes of the court painter Goya he stood before posterity with an amiable but vacant expression, entirely dominated by his vulgar and sensual wife Maria Louisa. When on 28 February 1792 Charles dismissed Floridablanca from office and appointed the Conde de Aranda in his place, public opinion at once attributed the move to the influence of the queen, who hated Floridablanca for slighting her in former days. Evidence suggests, however, that Charles IV was trying to ease the position of his cousin, Louis XVI of France, by appointing a minister who was known to be sympathetic towards the Revolution. The gesture failed: Louis was condemned to death and Charles interceded for his life. On 7 March 1793 the Convention declared war on Spain.

By this time Aranda in his turn had been dismissed from office (15 November 1792). Spaniards heard, to their astonishment and anger, that Manuel Godoy, Duque de la Alcudia, was to become first secretary. Godoy came from a poverty-stricken family of provincial nobles. Since the accession of Charles IV he had risen rapidly to positions of honour and influence in the army, at court, and in the government. The French ambassador described him as having 'a sane mind, an honest and good heart', but his personal qualities were not taken into account by the Spanish public. People knew only that the handsome young guardsman was the queen's lover and that the king accepted complacently a situation which scandalized lower and middle class Spaniards throughout the country.

A member of the French embassy in Madrid said later that the period following the appointment of Godoy was the only time when he felt the possibility of a revolution in Spain. A number of high officials were known to be in touch with French agents. In educated circles, and among army and navy officers, there were many who desired a change of government and some who went as far as to hope for a French invasion. Aristocrats who resented the appointment of the upstart Godoy collected around Aranda, whose outspoken criticism of the régime caused him to be dismissed from the council of state in March 1794. During the following months secret clubs and subversive intrigues were discovered in Barcelona and Madrid.

In July there were demonstrations in favour of the French in the streets of the capital. A group of malcontents led by a teacher, Juan Picornell, planned a rising to take place on 3 February 1795 but the conspirators were betrayed and arrested before the plot could mature. Meanwhile in the universities students read French works clandestinely and a professor at Salamanca, Ramón de Salas, was tried by the Inquisition for writing a popular paper condemning the backwardness of Spain.

Yet these activities were the work of a very small minority. However much the majority of Spaniards may have disliked the situation at court they were far from supporting revolution. Encouraged by their own priests, and by refugee priests from France, they regarded the war against the French Revolution as a crusade and gave it their whole-hearted support. Enthusiasm waned towards the end of 1793, when Spanish arms did not meet with the success that people had expected, but zeal was restored in 1794 when it became necessary to repel French invaders from Catalonia and the Basque provinces. Attempts by French agents to spread revolutionary propaganda in the wake of their armies were entirely without success, even among Catalans who had long grumbled at Castilian domination.

Opponents of Godoy drew on two different sets of ideas. The majority blamed him for degrading the royal family and diverting the king from the path laid down by Charles III. Their ideal was still enlightened despotism. Others looked back into history and decided that Spain had been greatest in the days of her 'ancient constitution' destroyed by Habsburg rulers. From exile in France José Marchena urged Spaniards to recapture their lost liberty not by copying foreign revolutions but by restoring medieval institutions: 'Let Cortes, Cortes, be the universal cry.' In Spain the cry could be uttered only in the secluded atmosphere of academic gatherings, but the idea was to bear fruit in the constitution of 1812, which demanded that the elected representatives of the people should honour 'the ancient fundamental laws of this kingdom'.

Godoy was not, in fact, an enemy of progress. Under his aegis the government resumed many of the policies which had been typical of the Enlightenment, promoting education, patronizing industry, and allowing some freedom of discussion. Godoy could claim with justice that his enemies were not lovers of progress but privileged persons who stood to lose by his enlightened policies and especially by his measures to finance the war. Faced with a large deficit at the end of 1793 Godoy lowered the salaries of high-grade officials, took a levy upon the income of the church, and made the aristocracy and clergy guarantee the government bonds (*vales reales*) which circulated as paper money during the war. Three large issues of *vales* were made during 1794 and 1795. On each occasion money was taken from the church and from the owners of entailed estates to form a fund for the payment of interest and for the eventual redemption of the *vales*. By these means the Spanish government was able to maintain armies in the field without borrowing money from Britain, but influential groups were alienated.

Godoy's reasons for making peace with France in 1795 when he knew that the result would be war with Britain are conjectural. He was given a large estate and the title Prince of the Peace, but these rewards were incidental. He may have thought that Spain, as a colonial power, had stronger reasons for fighting Britain than for fighting France. He almost certainly thought that there was less to be feared from a naval attack by Britain than from a land attack by France. Contrary to his expectations the British navy quickly outmatched the Spanish. On 14 February 1797 Nelson captured four ships of the line off Cape Saint Vincent and proceeded to blockade Cadiz. Local merchants were soon reported to be in distress. Ships in Barcelona harbour were afraid to sail, and the factories of Catalonia were consequently cut off from their supplies of raw cotton and from their American markets. Trade with the Spanish American colonies very soon slipped into the hands of neutrals. Repeated losses of ships carrying specie from America accelerated the depreciation of paper money. Prices rose rapidly, and town labourers who were suffering from low wages and unemployment had difficulty in buying food. Again the government turned to the privileged classes in an attempt to back the paper money. This time it took the unprecedented step of encouraging the sale of property in entail. In 1798 Charles IV decreed that all buildings let out for rent by municipalities were to be sold by auction to private individuals, the proceeds going to the Crown in return for interest paid annually. Owners of *mayorazgos* were permitted to sell land on the same terms. In 1799 a forced contribution of 20 million reales in hard currency was levied on all landowners, and the church was ordered to sell some of its property. These measures did not prevent the *vales* from falling to a half of their face value by April 1800.

In 1797 Godoy made a last attempt to undermine the propaganda of his opponents by appointing to the government a number of leading figures of the Enlightenment. Cabarrús was made ambassador to France, and Jovellanos was recalled from his banishment in Asturias to become secretary of grace and justice with control of religious affairs. As under-secretary for foreign affairs Godoy chose Mariano Luis de Urquijo, previously known for falling foul of the Inquisition by translating Voltaire into Spanish. A few months later Godoy himself retired from the government, bequeathing his place as first secretary to Francisco de Saavedra, a protégé of Cabarrús. The new government committed political suicide by arousing hostility from the church. Jovellanos could not stomach the arrogance of the Inquisition, restored to favour by Floridablanca as a weapon against revolutionary manifestations, and he began to prepare the ground for its abolition. At the same time he persuaded the king to appoint a noted Jansenist, bishop Tavira, to the see of Salamanca. The ultramontane party fought back vigorously. Its leading supporters in the country were some 700 former Jesuits whom Charles IV had allowed to return to Spain when French armies invaded the Papal States. As the war against Britain became more and more unpopular the ultramontane party obtained an increasing hold over the king's mind. Charles IV could not forget that the clergy had roused the people to save king and country when Spain was invaded by republican armies. Towards the end of 1798 he dismissed Jovellanos and Saavedra. The fight against ultramontanism was continued doggedly by Urquijo, now first secretary, but lacking the support of the king it was doomed to failure. Pope Pius VII wrote to Charles IV complaining of the spirit of innovation to be found in some Spanish ministers and bishops, whom he said were encouraging doctrines pernicious to the Holy See. Bonaparte suspected Urquijo of undermining French influence with Charles IV, and brother Lucien was sent to Madrid to procure the dismissal of the offending minister. Charles IV was anxious to keep on friendly terms with Bonaparte lest the fortunes of the Bourbon family in Italy should suffer. In December 1800 Urquijo was dismissed from office. In the same month Charles gave official recognition to the papal bull *Auctorem fidei* condemning Jansenist proposals. The triumph of conservatism was complete. Godoy became once more the guiding spirit of the government but he could attempt no more enlightened policies.

4. THE NAPOLEONIC INVASION AND THE REBELLION OF SPAIN

When Napoleon turned his attention to Spain, monarchy, church, and people were united as never before. Widespread disgust at the influence of Godoy might have given the impression that the Bourbon throne was tottering, but in fact the Spanish people were entirely satisfied when Charles IV abdicated in favour of his son. Even advanced groups believed that necessary reforms would now be carried out, and only a few disgruntled officials, nobles, and intellectuals were ready to accept a French monarch bringing French innovations. Napoleon thought that because Spaniards had accepted a French king at the beginning of the eighteenth century they would accept another. He underestimated the affection which the Spanish people had acquired for the Bourbon dynasty and the abhorrence which Spanish Catholics felt for revolutionary France.

There was little resistance to Murat's troops as they marched upon Madrid, but this was due to a belief that the French emperor was intervening to place Ferdinand on the throne. Murat secretly hoped to obtain the Spanish throne for himself, so he sent home enthusiastic reports of the welcome he had received from the Spanish people. Disorders at Burgos and Toledo were written off as the work of criminals and foreign agents. No such interpretation could be given to a terrible rising which took place in Madrid on 2 May. As soon as Napoleon's real intentions with regard to the Spanish royal family became known the populace ran riot in the streets. The shooting of an aide-de-camp provided an excuse for the French artillery to open fire, whereupon the rioters cried for vengeance and massacred every French soldier who fell into their hands. Murat retaliated on the following day. Military commissions shot Spanish rebels out of hand; French troops pillaged the city; hatred and brutality took possession of both sides and lived to posterity in Goya's portrayals of the scene.

On 20 May the abdication of the Bourbons was officially announced. Immediately revolution broke out in the provinces; first in Asturias, then in Galicia, Andalusia, Catalonia, and Valencia. It was at one and the same time a revolt against the French and against the authorities who were supposed to have accepted them. Savagery was a prominent feature from the first and many civil and military officials were slaughtered without cause. A revolutionary committee which sprang into existence at Seville gave itself the name of 'Supreme Junta of Spain and the Indies', assumed control of the royal armies, and issued a manifesto to Spaniards and Americans promising that Cortes would be summoned to reform abuses and direct the war. Canning hastened to send British supplies, and before many weeks were out rebels were in arms all over Spain. They included priests, nobles, jacobins, anglophiles, and ignorant peasants. In typical Spanish fashion the revolt cut across ordinary distinctions of class and creed. Priests and nobles rebelled because they wished to resist reform, progressives because they wished to achieve reform, and peasants because they combined their love of church and king with a rooted dislike of all authority.

Napoleon continued to misunderstand the situation. He informed Talleyrand that 'the good lesson' given by Murat to the city of Madrid would soon settle affairs in Spain. 'The Spaniards are like other people, and not a class apart. They will be happy to accept the imperial institutions.' He believed that his only serious opponents were the privileged classes, and since he was, after all, more anxious to control Spain's economy than to reform her social system, he decided to pay lip-service to powerful groups. He summoned 120 Spanish notables to Bayonne. Some refused to attend. Others, in Catalonia for instance, were prevented from attending by patriotic fellow-citizens. To the 91 who arrived Napoleon read a constitution which provided for the summoning of Cortes in the old aristocratic manner, the maintenance of the Inquisition, and the preservation of the Catholic religion as the established religion of Spain. Deputations of the nobility, military orders, government councils, and the Inquisition then swore allegiance to Joseph Bonaparte as king.

French armies easily defeated the bulk of the Spanish regular forces at Cabezon and Rioseco. Napoleon, who always thought in terms of regular forces, ignored the possibility of further resistance, and ordered Dupont to march south with two divisions and attack Cadiz, where the rebels had established contact with Lord Collingwood at Gibraltar and forced a French fleet to surrender. Meanwhile Joseph Bonaparte left Bayonne (8 July 1808) to take up his throne. His hopes of a triumphal progress were soon shattered. 'No-one has as yet told Your Majesty the truth', he wrote to his brother from Vittoria. 'The fact is, not a single Spaniard is on my side except the few who are travelling with me.' When he entered Madrid on 20 July he found the streets deserted. Three days later, Dupont's troops capitulated to the Spaniards. The French army, after pillaging Córdoba, had been caught by General Castanos, commanding four divisions of the Army of Andalusia and supported by a vast number of irregulars, and defeated at Bailén. The news gave an immense impetus to the national revolt. The French managed to hold Navarre and Catalonia, but in Aragon they failed to reduce Saragossa in spite of fierce street fighting. Joseph Bonaparte did not want to have to conquer Spain: on 30 July he left Madrid, hoping vainly that his brother would allow him to abdicate. As he retreated northward he learnt that a British expeditionary force under the command of Sir Arthur Wellesley had landed at Lisbon and totally defeated Junot's army in the Battle of Vimeiro (30 August 1808). By the Convention of Cintra French troops evacuated Portugal.

Joseph might have been driven out of Spain at this point if the rebels had been moderately well organized. For a long time local juntas were too jealous of each other to co-operate in organizing resistance. Each one was torn by dissensions between conservatives and reformers, and the latter resented the predominantly conservative character of the Supreme Junta under the presidency of Floridablanca. A council of generals formed a plan for three Spanish armies to converge upon the French, but no one man was appointed to command the operation and the armed peasants of Galicia and Asturias were loath to fight anywhere except in their own mountains. When Sir John Moore arrived at Ferrol with a British expeditionary force he was hindered by the suspicious and jealous attitude of the Spaniards he had come to help. All this gave time for Napoleon to make a swift descent into Spain with the Grand Army. He crossed the Pyrenees in the late autumn, inflicted a few stunning defeats on Spanish armies, and entered Madrid on 4 December 1808. Here he issued a series of decrees which completely reversed the constitution of Bayonne. Seigneurial rights were destroyed, the Inquisition was abolished, and the number of convents was reduced by two thirds. Napoleon hoped by these means to win for Joseph the support of reformers. To some extent he succeeded, but the success hardly improved Joseph's position. The *afrancesados* included illustrious persons such as the poet Marchena and the scholar Melendéz Valdés, but they were too few in number to give solid backing to the régime.

Napoleon would have rendered a greater service to his brother if he had destroyed the British expeditionary forces at this early stage and thereby discouraged further British interference. The British government had frittered away the success of Vimeiro by changing the command of Wellesley's army twice in twenty-four hours. A small if valiant British force, advancing on Salamanca under Sir John Moore, was all that threatened a quarter of a million men of the Grand Army. Napoleon began to pursue Sir John Moore northward, but suddenly he abandoned the command to Marshal Soult and posted back to France. He knew that there was a plot against him in Paris, and that the Austrians were preparing for war. He had known both these things before entering Spain, however, and the real reason for his withdrawal remained a mystery. Wellington always believed that Napoleon withdrew because he could not feel sure of winning a victory over the British troops. The latter, in spite of a demoralizing retreat over 250 miles of mountainous country in bitter weather, were inspired by Moore's personal courage and gifts of leadership to defend Corunna. Sir John Moore lost his life in the engagement, but 24,000 of his 30,000 men were taken off successfully by the British navy. Napoleon never entered Spain again. Although he said on St. Helena that the Spanish ulcer defeated him, he seems at the time to have regarded the business as no more than a nuisance.

In February 1809 Saragossa fell to Marshal Lannes after a bloody siege. Despairing henceforward of winning a victory in regular battle, the Supreme Junta called on all Spaniards to harry the invaders by falling on isolated detachments, picking off sentries, intercepting supplies, and murdering escorts. Many peasants particularly in northern and central provinces neglected their fields in order to engage in plunder and massacre. The zest with which the 'guerillas' pursued their task gave to the Spanish rebellion the air of a great national rising, but the movement had its drawbacks. It hindered the development of regular armies. It gave free reign to the brutality which often accompanies civilian fighting. It encouraged insubordination and hindered the establishment of good government.

The Supreme Junta became thoroughly unpopular with reformers because of its conservative policy and with the people at large because of its failure to secure victory over the French. On 31 January 1810 it dissolved itself, bequeathing its powers to a Regency Council of five members. The latter, after much debate, decided that Cortes should meet in September at Cadiz. Only one chamber was convoked, elected indirectly by universal suffrage, representing Spain and her provinces overseas. In effect the deputies came mostly from the democratic provinces of Galicia, Asturias, and Catalonia.

Elsewhere French occupation rendered elections impossible or futile. Cadiz itself was besieged by land forces and remained open only to seaward. All the most ardent patriots and reformers in Spain had gathered in the city, where there was a strong local junta composed of merchants and seamen with advanced political views. In this little world apart the Regency Council tried to wield executive power and the Cortes tried to establish constitutional rule over Spain and her American colonies.

The Regency Council began its work by sending proclamations to America announcing the change of régime and inviting the Americans to send representatives to the Cortes. Many Americans were unable to believe, however, that the rebellion in the mother-country would sustain itself, and as they neither wished to fall under French domination nor to remain under the sway of Spanish colonial authorities they started to overthrow the latter. Revolt began in Venezuela in April 1810. In the following month the Viceroy at Buenos Aires was deposed. In Mexico the authorities were faced with a rising supported largely by the coloured population. The situation was extremely confused, some areas submitting to the Regency and others rebelling against it. At Cadiz, the Cortes thought only of the money losses involved. Up to January 1810 the colonies had sent large sums to Spain for the expenses of war. To try and subdue Argentina, General Elio with 500 men was sent to Montevideo. The revolt merely grew in intensity. In October the Cortes conceded equality of rights between Spaniards and Americans but the Americans remained irreconcilable. They had long wanted liberty of commerce and the Cortes refused to grant it.

The economic policy of the Cortes was on many grounds the least defensible part of its activity. Nobles throughout Spain were allowed to keep their land, partly because the Cortes needed the support of the aristocracy in the war against France and partly because, in the manner of liberals all over Europe, the deputies regarded property as sacred. This belief did not prevent the Cortes from decreeing that a half of the municipal lands in Spain should be sold to private bidders. Fortunately the decision was not widely implemented, but a foundation was laid for the disastrous liberal legislation of the mid-nineteenth century which deprived poor peasants of rights on the common in order to place private property in the hands of a middle class. The Cortes showed great faith in property owners, to the extent of believing that they would agree to pay a direct tax on land, commerce, and industry. The result of the tax was to alienate property owners from the liberal policy of the Cortes and to produce, in the second elections of 1813, a majority of conservative members.

Meanwhile the Cortes had completed its main piece of work, the constitution of 1812. This provided for a parliamentary monarchy with elections held on a universal franchise from which only negroes, at the insistence of the

American deputies, were omitted. Each province was given a considerable amount of independence in matters of local administration. Seigneurial juris-diction was abolished, Spaniards were declared equal before the law, and the nation was declared sovereign. The men who framed the constitution have been accused of copying clauses verbatim from the French constitution of 1791 without thought for the different conditions existing in Spain, but in one respect at least they showed an appreciation of the temper of the Spanish people: the Catholic religion was recognized as the sole religion practised by Spaniards, to the exclusion of all others.

The constitution was opposed systematically by conservative members of the Cortes, who were given the name *serviles* by their enemies the *liberales*. After the promulgation of the constitution on 19 March 1812 the *serviles* launched a propaganda campaign against it, assisted by two rival authorities to the Cortes, the Regency Council and the Council of Castille. The cam-paign was probably unnecessary as few Spaniards seem to have known or cared much about the constitution. Thanks to the poet, José de Quintana, who was secretary to the Cortes, the press was freed from censorship, but although publishing increased twofold the number of Spaniards affected by literature remained small. The futility of a war which totally lacked the inspiration of high ideals was depicted by Goya in stark and horrifying terms. The only value of the constitution was that it provided a handful of educated Spaniards with an alternative to the reforms offered by the French usurper in Madrid.

Joseph was more likeable than some other members of the Bonaparte clan. He had made himself acceptable to the people of Naples, and Napoleon ex-pected him to succeed at once in governing the Spaniards. Joseph genuinely hoped to carry out reforms which would benefit Spain. He published the Constitution of Bayonne as a pledge, and made a beginning on educational, judicial, administrative, and economic reforms. He went on believing, to the day of his defeat at Vittoria, that the Spaniards would grow to love him. He would not admit that they first had to be conquered, and he gave only fleeting attention to the war, in which he showed little ability anyway. He was bitterly hurt when Napoleon lost patience with his muddle-headed concilia-toriness and set up military governments in the provinces of Catalonia, Aragon, Navarre, and Biscay. He begged to be allowed to abdicate, but after a brief visit to Paris he was persuaded once more to sacrifice his pride to his brother's ambition.

Towards the end of 1810 an Irishman, General Blake, tried to organize Spaniards into armies capable of defeating the French. Thanks to his efforts Asturias was liberated and communications between Navarre and France were threatened. Nothing was done to co-ordinate movements between Spanish and British troops, however, for Spanish generals would not submit to British authority. Blake was eventually defeated in an attempt to hold Valencia, where he capitulated with 16,000 men. Only the guerillas remained, and though the wasting effect of their activities upon the French should not be underestimated they were no match for experienced troops in battle.

5. THE PENINSULAR WAR

Napoleon always believed that the only important factor in the Peninsula was the presence of the British army. It is the more surprising that he waited a long time before making a serious attempt to secure Portugal. When Wellesley made a second landing at Lisbon in April 1809 Soult was no match for him. The French succumbed to a surprise attack and retreated over the mountains leaving Portugal to the British army. Wellesley realized that he could not easily be attacked, for invading armies could only move along the narrow defiles of the Tagus and Douro, but equally he could not easily attack the French in Spain, where 'a small army would be defeated and a large army would starve'. His first attempt, in the summer of 1809, took the form of a surprise assault. It taught him that he could not rely on support from Spanish generals, and though he defeated Joseph's troops in a bloody battle at Talavera in July he retreated to Portugal for the winter rather than face the French under Ney and Soult.

The victory at Talavera aroused great enthusiasm among the British people, and Wellesley was rewarded with the title of Duke of Wellington, but the subsequent retreat brought a corresponding disillusionment. A new Tory government under Perceval was jeered at for wasting money on a pantomime. Only Lord Liverpool at the war office was firmly convinced of the value of the Peninsular campaign. He promised reinforcements, but Wellington knew that he could not rely on promises from a member of a cabinet which was daily expected to fall. Not the least of Wellington's virtues as a commander was a toughness of temperament which enabled him to rise above the weakness of his political chiefs. Calmly and stoically he went on training his 30,000 men until they became the most highly disciplined force yet directed against the enemy.

In the spring of 1810 Napoleon launched the big offensive at last. An army of 70,000 men under Masséna marched upon Portugal. Wellington knew that he could not defeat such an enemy in a head-on collision: his plan was to draw Masséna across the mountains to the sea and there make him wait. The French always travelled light and relied on striking at speed with large numbers of men: a winter in Portugal, deprived of provisions, would weaken them more surely than any battle. Masséna's advance was delayed by the need to capture the three border fortresses of Ciudad Rodrigo, Almeida, and Badajoz. When he eventually entered Portugal in the late autumn he hurried towards Lisbon in the hope of catching Wellington before the winter set in, but he failed to do so. Wellington had long insisted on the importance of good maps. On his arrival in the Peninsula he had set his officers to work on mapping Portugal at four miles to the inch. As a result his army was able to move by the quickest and least hazardous routes over the mountainous interior. Once in Lisbon the French were unable to drive him into the sea. Hillsides had been made more perilous, stone walls had been built across valleys, ditches had been dug, waters dammed, and every kind of natural difficulty had been enhanced to form two parallel barriers stretching across the Lisbon peninsula. An inner line of fortifications protected the harbour. Within the lines of Torres Vedras Wellington had built up supplies which Lord Liverpool courageously refurnished by sea. The French army had lost what stores it possessed at Coimbra through the action of Portuguese guerillas. Unable to obtain food from a hostile peasantry in a devastated country Masséna held on grimly till the spring, when he began to drag his depleted army back over the mountains.

Masséna had lost a third of his men by the time he reached the frontier but his army was still larger than Wellington's. He yearned to collect his forces and deliver a smashing blow at the British. Unfortunately his forces could seldom be collected, for a large army must disperse to live. Wellington had every opportunity to attack isolated portions of the enemy provided that he could keep up with them. If his men were to move fast enough – 15 or 20 miles a day – they could not carry all their provisions. Wellington fell back on the old method of establishing depots for supply. By 1812 he had established thirty-seven depots in the Peninsula, administered by young officers whom he had made for perhaps the first time in their lives to work hard and obey orders. In building up supplies the British were helped by the good will of the peasants. Unlike French generals Wellington paid for what he got. He paid for food and he often received information along with it. His intelligence in consequence surpassed anything which the French could achieve.

Wellington's success in the Peninsula was due to exact planning, patient training, and immense stamina. Nothing came easily. He advanced into Spain in the spring of 1811 but his attempts to retake the three fortresses cost him so many men and so much time that he was obliged to withdraw to Portugal for a third winter. The British public was disheartened, but the Perceval government had by this time made up its mind to give full support to the Peninsular campaign. While the country groaned at the expense of keeping British and Portuguese troops on a permanent war footing at a time of economic crisis the government doggedly sent money to Wellington to pay his men and honour his bills from Portuguese merchants. Equally important it at last sent a siege train. With this Wellington attacked the fortresses in icy weather and took Ciudad Rodrigo for the loss of only 1,000 men, but Badajoz was a more formidable task. Even when a breach had been made in the walls the garrison refused to surrender, and Wellington lost 5,000 men in vain attempts to take the town by storm. The defenders eventually fell to a surprise attack when Picton and the 3rd Division, intending to create only a diversion, scaled the walls of the citadel with twenty-foot ladders. As the bugles sounded for a British victory discipline went to pieces and the Spanish population of the town was made to suffer for the months of hardship endured by the British troops. Rape and plunder went on for three days before Wellington could restore order and collect his men for a march upon the enemy. His first move was to divide Soult and Marmont, who had replaced Masséna, by destroying their bridge of boats across the river Tagus at Almaroz. Next he tried to out-manoeuvre Marmont. For two summer months the armies marched and counter-marched over the scorching plains of the Spanish interior. On 22 July the British formed themselves for battle south of Salamanca. Marmont strung out his forces in an attempt to cut off the British line of retreat to Ciudad Rodrigo. Seeing at once the weakness of the French position Wellington ordered an attack upon Marmont's leading division. The French flank was shattered in under an hour and the centre caved in. Marmont was wounded and the French lost 14,000 men to Wellington's 5,000. This great victory opened the road to Madrid. Joseph Bonaparte retired to Catalonia and the British troops entered the capital amid scenes of popular rejoicing.

Exultation did not last long, however. Wellington knew that if he was to destroy the French armies in Andalusia and Catalonia he must prevent further French troops from entering Spain across the Pyrenees. Leaving his best men to garrison Madrid he marched north-eastward, but his small force outran the transports and failed to capture the castle of Burgos. The French were thus given time to muster their forces and Wellington was afraid that they would retake Madrid and cut him off. Withdrawing his garrison in time to avert the danger he led his troops in weariness and disappointment back to Portugal for a fourth winter. In the general depression of spirits few people in Britain could see ultimate victory as assured. Yet the French had been obliged to give up all of Spain south of the Tagus, and they were no nearer to solving the problem of how to concentrate their forces for a decisive blow. Why Napoleon kept nearly 300,000 troops tied to a hopeless struggle is one of the mysteries of his career. The military and economic consequences of abandoning the Peninsula to the British could have been mitigated by sealing the Pyrenees. Napoleon did, indeed, offer terms in the summer of 1812, but they included the maintenance of Joseph Bonaparte on the throne of Spain, and Castlereagh could hardly have been expected to agree to terms so abhorrent to his Spanish allies. No doubt Napoleon expected his campaign against Russia to decide all. The decision was hardly the one he wanted. By December 1812 he had lost the largest army Europe had ever seen, in a nightmare retreat from Moscow.

Early in 1813 Wellington began his inevitable advance into Spain. He outflanked the enemy at every river crossing and reached the Ebro by mid-June. The French armies of the south and centre took a stand under Joseph Bonaparte and Marshal Jourdan but their last attempt to smash Wellington in open battle failed completely at Vittoria. Joseph fled from the battlefield leaving behind him the carriage containing the masterpieces of Spanish painting which he had torn down from the palace walls in Madrid. The French troops streamed over the frontier at Irun. Soult tried to bar the enemy from entering France but in the autumn San Sebastián and Pamplona surrendered to British and Spanish forces. By November the French army had retreated to Bayonne and the British were encamped on French soil.

The Spanish revolt and the Peninsula campaign had together secured the downfall of French rule in Spain. The contribution made by the former to the eventual collapse of Napoleonic power in Europe is incalculable in the strict sense of the word. Historians can only guess at the hope which the Spanish example brought to oppressed peoples in Europe and the encouragement which it gave to the Russians in their resistance. More measurable is the importance of the revolt in presenting Britain with an opportunity to fight the French on land. Napoleon lost large numbers of men in the Peninsula. Many of his young admirers saw for the first time in Spain the horrors rather than the glories of war. As the wounded were carried continuously over the frontier the people of southern France were reminded that Napoleon was not invincible. The stage was set for the overwhelming news of defeat in Russia.

CHAPTER XI

Russia and the Mission to the West

1. DIPLOMACY AND WAR, 1807-12

THE invasion of Spain by French armies convinced at least one observer that Napoleon's ambition was insatiable. 'The present power in France cannot exist side by side with any other power in Europe', wrote Metternich. 'One has only to look at the map to guess where the next blow will fall.'

In 1807 Napoleon seemed willing to agree to the existence of one other power. The treaty of Tilsit implied that the Emperor of the French and the Tsar of all the Russias would exercise a condominium over Europe. The agreement worked as long as the two rulers were dealing with peripheral matters. Napoleon allowed Alexander to seize Finland for Russia in 1809 whilst fighting a war against Sweden to bring her into the Continental System. Alexander gave Napoleon a free hand in Spain. Friction was felt from the start, however, in matters of mutual concern. Alexander failed to withdraw his troops from Moldavia and Wallachia, thereby retaining a position in the Balkans which Napoleon regarded as a threat to his Mediterranean schemes: Napoleon failed to withdraw his troops from Prussia, thereby securing for the Grand Army a direct route through Silesia and the Grand Duchy of Warsaw to Russia. Napoleon in characteristic fashion tried to strike a bargain on a grand plane. France and Russia would partition Turkey between them. Napoleon would compensate himself in Greece, Syria, and Egypt for Alexander's gains in the Balkans, and the Tsar would send Russian troops from the Danube to join French troops from Dalmatia in a march upon India. Napoleon's reasons for suggesting this scheme, in a letter to Alexander on 2 February 1808, were never clear. He might have been trying to seduce the Tsar with lavish promises; he might have been trying to frighten Britain; or he might have been serious. He asked his agents in Turkey to provide him with information concerning the territories over which his armies would have to pass, and he strengthened his army in Dalmatia and concentrated French squadrons at Corfu. The Tsar made no immediate moves. He suspected a plot to send his army away to distant parts of the earth. Preliminary discussions between the new French ambassador, General Caulaincourt, and the Russian minister for foreign affairs, Count Nicholas Rumyantsev, revealed a fundamental disagreement between the two powers on the subject of Turkey. To Alexander the value of any partition scheme lay in the possibility of obtaining possession of the Straits and thereby ensuring for Russia an outlet from the Black Sea into the Mediterranean. Constantinople itself was less important to him: he was willing to see the city neutralized. Napoleon was determined that Russia should not control the full length of the Straits. Alexander could take the Bosporus but the Dardanelles must belong to France or become part of an autonomous principality. The negotiations showed that both sides were more concerned with the immediate issue of obtaining power in the Mediterranean than with the remoter prospect of absorbing the Sultan's empire. Napoleon intended to strengthen his hand in Mediterranean affairs by a speedy conquest of Spain, and he was irritated when he learnt that Austria was using his preoccupation with the Spanish revolt as an opportunity to re-arm.

On 27 September 1808 Alexander and Napoleon met for the second time to decide the destinies of Europe. The meeting took place at Erfurt in a blaze of splendour. Behind the scenes things were different. Talleyrand, who appeared as the chief agent of Napoleon, sold himself as secret adviser to the Tsar. The Turkish project foundered once more on the subject of the Straits, but this was not the only, and perhaps not even the biggest flaw which had developed in the friendship of Tilsit. Alexander could neither be charmed nor bullied into bringing pressure to bear on Austria, for he had come to regard the sprawling dominions of the Habsburg crown as a barrier between France and Russia.

A war party in Austria, headed by Empress Maria Ludovica, burned to revenge the insult of Pressburg. Emperor Francis was pessimistic about the outcome but he was won over to the idea of waging one more campaign by the argument that his dominions were due to be carved up by Napoleon as soon as the monster's hands were freed from Spain. Other Austrian statesmen besides Metternich had taken the trouble of looking at the map. Among them were the Chancellor Stadion and the Emperor's brother Charles. Stadion believed implicitly that Austria must fight if she wished to save herself, and he came to believe that she might never have a better chance than the one presented by the revolt in Spain. He was assured by Metternich, Austria's ambassador to Paris, that the French people were beginning to turn against Napoleon and that they would give little support to a new war. He knew that Talleyrand, dismissed from his post as foreign secretary in August 1807, had never agreed with Napoleon's policy of humiliating Austria and that he was ready to sell information to Metternich. Archduke Charles realized that Napoleon, even with 300,000 men tied up in Spain, was still a formidable enemy, but he was ready to risk another war. Charles had been engaged since Austerlitz in forming a bigger and a better trained army than Austria had ever had before. He was a good general, the best of the age said Wellington, and with the army under his supreme command it was unlikely that the mistakes of 1805 would be repeated.

Perhaps it was the Spanish war which taught Stadion that a professional army was not enough and that the people of Austria must be roused to support the dynasty. Poets and dramatists were directed to extol Austria's past greatness and glorify the heroic deeds of Habsburg princes.. The operas of Glück were patronized in preference to Italian works. Archduke John commissioned painters and musicians to develop patriotic themes. Stadion sponsored two newspapers and engaged Friedrich Schlegel to translate anti-Napoleonic literature from Spain. In June 1808 a *Landwehr*, or citizen militia, was formed to give short periods of training to all men between the ages of 18 and 42. Stadion placed a great deal of faith in these measures and also in the national feeling which his brother, the abbé Stadion, told him was stirring throughout Germany. He was not dismayed when his envoy to London received only a small subsidy from the British government, nor when the Prussian court decided that it dared not come out into the open against Napoleon. On 8 February 1809 an imperial council decided for war; on 10 April Archduke Charles invaded Bavaria.

In the early stages of the Austrian war Napoleon came as near to disaster as he had ever been, but Austrian irresolution turned the tables and by 12 May he was in Vienna. Eugène succeeded in bringing up reinforcements from Italy, and by the beginning of July Napoleon could outnumber the enemy. After a surprise crossing to the north bank of the Danube he engaged the Austrian forces in a pitched battle at Wagram. Casualties numbered 20,000 on each side. The Austrians were by no means routed, but Emperor Francis lost heart, and Napoleon was able to stampede him into signing the Peace of Schönbrunn on 14 October 1809.

In the event, Stadion's hopes of a popular rising came to nothing. Archduke Charles's appeal to the German nation, 'We are fighting to give back to Germany her independence and national honour', was heard only by a few intellectuals, and isolated disturbances were all that occurred. The enthusiasm which had been aroused in Austria for a war of revenge did not survive desertion by the dynasty. Only in the Tyrol was there a popular movement bearing some resemblance to the guerilla war in Spain. Tyrolese peasants bitterly resented the taxes and military exactions which had descended upon them when the Tyrol was handed over to Bavaria by the treaty of Pressburg. Nostalgic memories of a more lenient Habsburg rule were translated into patriotic terms by the literary efforts of Baron Hormayr. The peasants found a leader in an innkeeper, Andreas Hofer, whose brave stand at Innsbruck against French and Bavarian troops earned him a death penalty when the revolt was put down at the end of the year 1809.

The help which Austria might have expected to obtain from other governments proved equally disappointing. The princes of Germany were either too servile to Napoleon or too jealous of Habsburg power to fight under Austrian leadership. A Prussian officer, Friedrich von Schill, tried to force his government to take part in the war by invading the Kingdom of Westphalia, but he was killed by the French at Stralsund without a move from Prussia. The British government might have commanded support from Prussia if an expeditionary force had landed on the north coast of Germany, but instead the troops were sent to the Netherlands in the hope of taking Antwerp and restoring British trade. Flushing was captured, but only after a fortnight's siege, and in the meantime the defences of Antwerp had been strengthened. The British troops landed on the muddy island of Walcheren in time to hear that the Austrian war effort had collapsed. They clung to the island for a few months in the hope of keeping the river Scheldt open, but as more and more men sickened and died the rest were evacuated at the end of the year.

The terms imposed on Francis at Schönbrunn humiliated the House of Habsburg at Napoleon's hands for the fourth time. Territory had to be ceded to Napoleon's allies: Salzburg and the province of the Inn to Bavaria, a part of Galicia and Cracow to the Grand Duchy of Warsaw, Tarnapol to Russia. The Adriatic coastlands had to be given to Napoleon for purposes of strengthening the Continental System. Austria lost altogether 3½ million people and found herself deprived of access to the sea. In addition she had to pay an indemnity of £3¾ millions, send nearly a thousand books and manuscripts from the Imperial library to Paris, and reduce her army to 150,000 men. Never had Napoleon seemed more brutally successful.

It was the brutality of the success which repelled the Tsar. Like Talleyrand, Alexander came to dislike not so much the unscrupulousness of Napoleon's policy as the violence of his methods and the vulgarity of his mind. Alexander had been disturbed, as early as Erfurt, by a rumour that Napoleon intended to divorce Josephine and marry the Grand Duchess Catherine of Russia. The latter had been somewhat hastily married off to the Duke of Oldenburg, but Napoleon did not forego his intention of marrying into the Tsar's family. An attempt on his life by the Austrian student Staps convinced him that he must have an heir. The birth of a son to one of his mistresses in 1807 proved to him that he was capable of getting a child, but Josephine was 46 and could no longer be expected to fulfil her dynastic duties. In November 1809 Josephine was told that she must consent to a divorce, and Napoleon applied to the Tsar for the hand of his younger sister Anna. Alexander prevaricated until February 1810, when Napoleon demanded an answer. The answer was a refusal by the Tsar to have Napoleon as a brother-in-law.

A fortnight later Napoleon closed with a marriage offer which he had received from Austria. Francis I, remembering the traditions of his family, sacrificed his daughter Marie Louise to the French conqueror in the hope of political returns. Marie Louise was too simple and insensitive to be appalled at her fate. She was nineteen, and bored with life at Schönbrunn; she thought Paris would offer more attractions. The marriage took place at the beginning of April 1810. Napoleon was sufficiently delighted with his new wife's youthful freshness to sustain the part of a lover for the short time that he was with her. In 1811 the required heir was born and given the title of King of Rome.

The Austrian marriage was to a large extent the work of Metternich, who suggested it to Napoleon and pointed out its advantages to Francis in December 1809. Metternich had been appointed foreign minister of the Austrian Empire after Wagram. Francis was by this time disgusted with the 'patriots' who had led him into a disastrous war. He dubbed their ideas jacobinical and transferred his allegiance to the more civilized qualities exemplified in Metternich. Prince Klemens von Metternich was a Rhinelander deprived of his patrimony by French marauders during the Revolution. Until his marriage with Eleanor von Kaunitz he possessed no ties with Austria. A subsequent series of ambassadorial appointments to Dresden, Berlin, and finally Paris taught him that the Emperor Francis was the best employer he was likely to find, and he was ready to place at his service the cultivated manners, the worldly wisdom, and the subtlety of mind which were to make him for several decades the most influential statesman in Europe. The marriage project was a typically two-edged piece of work. It might lead to a real partnership between Napoleon and Francis: it would at least deter Napoleon from obliterating Francis's dominions. It would give time, and time was bound to be on Austria's side. Metternich once described Napoleon as an inveterate gambler: Austria had only to wait for the day when he overplayed his hand.

After Wagram there was only one prize left to play for. Alexander had been sufficiently wary to give only nominal support to Napoleon in the war of 1809. After Schönbrunn the game moved rapidly. First there was the question of Poland. In return for military help from the Poles Napoleon added Austrian Poland to the Grand Duchy of Warsaw. The Tsar would not submit to this veiled threat of a united Poland arising under French protection. He demanded a formal guarantee that Poland would never be restored to the map of Europe. When Napoleon refused to give a guarantee Alexander began to give more attention to the idea, mooted years ago by Czartoryski, of creating a united Poland under Russian suzerainty. Then there was the question of Sweden. The Swedes were so infuriated by the loss of Finland to Russia that they dethroned their king Gustavus IV Adolphus in favour of his uncle Charles XIII. As Charles was an old man and childless the Swedish Estates were required to elect an heir to the throne. They chose Bernadotte, thinking thereby to please Napoleon and earn French support against Russia. No love existed between Bernadotte and Napoleon, but the latter nevertheless expected Bernadotte to make Sweden into a French satellite, and his installation as Crown Prince was rightly interpreted by Alexander as an anti-Russian move. There was also the question of power in the Mediterranean. By 1809 France's tentacles reached as close to Constantinople from the west as those of Russia from the north. A vague understanding between Napoleon and Ali Pasha of Janina seemed to Alexander a dangerous patronage of Balkan national aspirations hardly outweighed by his own understanding with Karageorge of Serbia. After the decline of Austria there was no land power interested in checking French advances towards Turkey. Only the British navy wrested the Ionian islands from France in 1809, and Alexander was given cause to wonder whether he ought to continue to weaken Britain through the Continental System. Tensions arising out of the Continental System were the last straw. Napoleon in his efforts to close the North Sea ports annexed Holland, then the Hanseatic towns, then the Duchy of Oldenburg to France. This last move was not only a personal insult to Alexander but an open breach of the treaty of Tilsit. Napoleon complained that Alexander too had broken the terms of Tilsit by allowing neutral vessels to land cargoes at Russian ports. Alexander not only refused to stop this practice but placed a prohibitive tariff on merchandise entering Russia by land, most of which was French in origin. These measures virtually withdrew Russia from the Continental System. By 1811 both sides were preparing for war.

Instructions given to the new French ambassador to Russia, Lauriston, indicated clearly that Napoleon was not going to make war on Alexander for the sake of the blockade but because he believed Alexander to be overstepping the limits laid down at Tilsit for Russian power in Poland, Turkey, and the Balkans and because he suspected Alexander of planning to make peace with Britain. The instructions amounted to the fact that if Alexander did not toe the line drawn for him at Tilsit he was to be driven out of Europe altogether. Napoleon expressed his purpose in grandiloquent terms as he advanced towards Moscow in 1812. 'I have come to make an end once and for all to the Colossus of the barbarian north. My sword is drawn. These barbarians must be driven back into their Arctic ice-fields. Europe can manage its affairs without them.'

2. THE CONDITION OF RUSSIA

When Napoleon issued his threat no honest observer could deny that Russia differed in many respects from the countries of the west. She was a Christian country, like the rest of Europe, but her Christianity had come from Byzantium. With the fall of Constantinople to the Turks in 1453 Russia became the chief defender of the Orthodox faith, and the vision of Moscow as 'the third Rome' encouraged in Russia the idea that she was destined to save Europe for Christ. Byzantine tradition contributed to the development of a specifically Russian way of life by attributing a semi-divine position to the tsar, who was said to be ordained by God to carry out His will in temporal matters and to protect the people in spiritual matters. In the seventeenth century the hierarchy of the Russian church called upon the state to enforce acceptance of new Greek forms of the Scriptures. Thereafter the union between church and state was overweighted in favour of the state. Under Peter the Great the Orthodox church became a part of the administration. It was governed by a Holy Synod, whose head or Procurator was a civil official appointed by the tsar. The Procurator governed a large bureaucracy which resembled the permanent staff of a ministry. Bishops were chosen by the tsar from a list of three candidates submitted to him by the Synod. They were recruited solely from the ranks of the 'black clergy' or monks. Within their dioceses they were closely supervised by the Procurator, who appointed for this purpose a lay secretary to each diocesan chancery, and they were liable to be removed from one diocese to another at the will of the Procurator. Parish priests were 'secular clergy' and they were obliged to marry before they could be ordained. They were poorly paid and ill educated. Often they were devoted to their parishioners, but they were obliged to act as agents of the government, posting proclamations and decrees in their churches and giving information to the police. Under Catherine the Great and Alexander I a fairly tolerant spirit operated in church and state, but with the advent of Nicholas I reactionary policies were riveted upon the country with the help of the church. Enemies of the government became almost automatically enemies of the church, and all the leading revolutionaries of the nineteenth century were anti-Christian.

Russian rulers were not alone in Europe in their determination to wield absolute authority. The difference between their position and that of aspiring autocrats in the west was that their power was never challenged by an aristocracy acting as an estate. Russian noblemen were powerful individuals, and on a number of occasions groups of them exercised a decisive influence over political events, but they never felt the need to organize their class on a political basis. In the sixteenth entury Ivan the Terrible called into existence for his own purposes an Assembly of the Land analogous to the Estates General of western Europe. This assembly elected Michael Romanov as tsar in 1613 but made no attempt to bind the ruler to formal conditions. The chaos of the preceding years had indicated too clearly the advantages of strong rule over disputing factions. After 1653 the tsar summoned no more full Assemblies of the Land, nor was there any demand that he should do so.

After a brief experience of oligarchy in 1730 the officer-gentry in Moscow conferred upon the Empress Anna 'autocracy such as Your glorious and renowned predecessors had', and until 1825 there was no further challenge to the principle of absolute rule. In 1785 Catherine II issued a Charter establishing the nobility and gentry as an 'estate', but the term held no political significance and the Charter did not legally diminish the sovereign's power.

The nobles allowed power to be exercised by the tsar in return for power over the peasants. Catherine the Great capitulated so completely to the demands of the aristocracy that serfdom became the basis of the whole of Russian society and government. The serfs lived in village communities. They cultivated a part of the land of the village for their own use and the rest was reserved for the landowner. In return for the land which they used the serfs owed money dues (*obrok*) or labour services (*barshchina*) to the landowner. *Obrok* was the less onerous because less fluctuating. Provided the serfs paid their money dues they were left free to engage in whatever occupations they could find. *Barshchina* usually consisted of three days' work every week on the landowner's estate, but sometimes four or even five days were exacted. When there was a shortage of labour, serfs might be compelled to work continuously for the landowner while their own plots were neglected. The serfs had their own social organization, the village commune. The commune from time to time redistributed plots of land among the peasant families in accordance with the number of mouths to be fed and the amount of tax to be paid. The landowner could interfere in the redistribution, however, just as at any time he could increase or diminish the plot of land worked by a particular peasant or the total area of land allotted to the village. A serf was attached to the soil in the sense that he could not leave his holding or leave the estate without the landowner's consent, or earn wages, borrow money, or rent land from any person outside the estate without his master's permission. On the other hand a serf owner could take his serfs off the land and employ them in his house, stables, offices, factory, or mines as he saw fit. He could sell his serfs, or hand them over to another man in payment of a gambling debt, with or without land, individually or by families. Alexander I issued decrees against the sale of serfs without the other members of their families, but the decrees were often ignored. Serfs were frequently advertised for sale, or sold by public auction, the only restriction being that a law of 1771 forbade the auction of serfs without land. A specially onerous type of serfdom ensured labour for factories and mines, whole colonies of serfs being permanently ascribed to these undertakings.

A serf owner's judicial powers were not clearly defined, but they covered most offences other than brigandage and murder. He could impose sentences of flogging so severe that they sometimes resulted in death. He could sentence his serfs to hard labour in Siberia. He decided which serfs were to be sent to the army, where service normally lasted for twenty-five years. He could at any time confiscate a serf's moveable goods. He could forbid a serf to marry or demand a money payment for allowing him to marry. The only obligations he possessed towards his serfs were to give them seed in times of crop failure and food in times of scarcity. There was also a general idea that a landowner must not bring his serfs to ruin or treat them with great cruelty, but as a serf had no means of appealing against his master the safeguards were far from effective.

Serfdom was hereditary. For a long time the only escape from it lay in flight, which gave but a precarious freedom. In 1803 Alexander provided means whereby serfs could buy freedom from their landowner with the latter's consent. The redemption rate was high, however, and no more than 50,000 serfs took advantage of the arrangement during the next two decades. It was said that the serfs of a bad master did not have the money to buy their freedom, whilst those of a good master did not need it. Conditions of serfdom naturally varied a great deal in different parts of the country and under different masters. Many serfs prospered. Many filled responsible posts in their masters' households or in their village communes. It remained true, however, that the personal servitude of one man to another was the great evil of Russian life.

Serfdom operated in full force in Russia long after it had disintegrated in countries west of the Elbe partly, at least, because it seemed at the time the only way of ruling the vast areas of the Russian empire. The serfs themselves, though in a sense abandoned by the tsar to the mercy of the landowners, regarded the tsar as their protector. They believed that all the land of Russia belonged to the tsar and that oppression arose only when the nobles failed to carry out the tsar's instructions. In the peasant revolts which formed a recurrent feature of Russian history the serfs never regarded themselves as rebelling against the tsar but only against his false friends. It was indeed true that on crown lands, which employed about two fifths of the total serf population of Russia, conditions were far easier than among the bonded peasants of hereditary nobles and gentry.

Tsars had once intended that the nobles should pay for their privileges by service to the state, but in 1762 the nobles secured from Peter III the abolition of any obligation to serve at all. Many noblemen were themselves aware that Peter's edict destroyed the formal justification for serfdom. The upper class produced, towards the end of the eighteenth century, some of the most profound critics of social conditions in the empire. This development was partly the result of an unfortunate educational policy. Peter the Great wanted all classes in Russia to learn western techniques and to benefit from western inventions, but his educational innovations resulted merely in an aping of western manners by the aristocracy alone. Catherine the Great deepened the understanding of western culture among the upper classes by advertising the works of foreign writers but she made no attempt to educate other classes to the same level or to alter the framework of Russian society to fit the new ideas. The educated minority was thus cut off from the rest of the people. The 'conscience stricken nobility' formed an isolated section of idealists whose views were divorced from the real conditions of life around them.

Serfdom and autocracy would have been more effectively undermined if there had existed a sufficiently large class of the population whose economic interest lay in disrupting the threefold hierarchy of peasants, landowners, and tsar. Russia had no class comparable to the middle class of western Europe, however. The economy was still overwhelmingly agricultural at the end of the nineteenth century. The peasants needed certain manufactured goods of a simple nature, such as coarse cloth and household utensils, but these were produced by the peasants themselves in their cottages. The aristocracy demanded luxury goods for their manor houses and for their town houses in Moscow and St. Petersburg, but these were mostly supplied by imports from abroad. The merchants who distributed peasant goods were scattered in provincial centres; the rich merchants of Moscow and the Baltic ports who handled Russia's foreign trade formed a privileged clique rather than an independent class. There were some factory owners, but these too occupied a special position and were more dependent on the régime than were their counterparts in western Europe. Peter the Great set up industries designed to meet the needs of the army and navy and ascribed serfs to them as a labour force. Most of his factories and mines were handed over in time to private companies or individuals but they remained dependent on government grants and on a degree of government control. The growth of these so-called 'possession' factories was bitterly resented by the nobles. Many of the latter founded factories on their estates and employed their own serfs in them, but they suffered from the low productivity of serf labour. Gradually a third type of undertaking appeared, wholly private in ownership and employing free labourers. Russia remained far behind western countries in industrial development, however. Internal trade was hampered by the low purchasing power of the masses and by poor means of transport. In 1804 less than 100,000 persons out of Russia's vast population worked in factories: only 1,300,000 people lived in towns. Townsmen were allowed to elect councils for local government but in practice these were completely overawed by the provincial governors.

Control of industry was only one of countless duties which fell to the government in autocratic Russia. The will of the tsar was brought to bear upon the country, with varying degrees of accuracy, by a vast and ever-

growing bureaucracy. Russian officials were on the whole poorly educated
and poorly paid. Their ignorance tended to make them incompetent and
arrogant, their poverty rendered them open to corruption. Oppression
was increased by the fact that administrative and judicial powers were
in the same hands. Procedure in the law courts was antiquated and un-
fair, with emphasis upon formal evidence and confession. The police,
growing in numbers during the eighteenth century, encouraged spying and
informing and created an atmosphere of suspicion and fear. The state's
officials became increasingly divorced from other educated elements in the
community. Even the higher officials such as provincial governors and town
commandants won little respect from the nobility and from the small professional class of teachers, lawyers, and doctors.

Alexander I seemed to be aware that he ought to organize the bureaucracy
into an effective instrument of government, but his steps towards this end
were nullified by his refusal to delegate authority. In 1802 and 1811 he
created departments, each headed by a minister, but the ministers never
acted as a body and the tsar was neither obliged to consult them nor to carry
out their advice. A committee of ministers was set up, the Senate was reorganized, and a Council of State was created, but they were used haphazardly or not at all. Policy was decided not according to any fixed procedure or with reference to any definite body but by any method that
appealed to the tsar at the time. Sometimes a number of bodies were consulted and their opinions balanced against each other; sometimes special
commissions were appointed to advise on particular issues; sometimes
specially qualified individuals or mere favourites were consulted. Alexander I
was fond of conferring with his generals. The whole system, or lack of
system, lent itself to secrecy, jealousy, and intrigue. In the end Russia moved
backwards or forwards according to the whim or determination of the tsar.
The inefficiency of the executive power was the only real check upon his
absolutism.

3. REACTION AND REFORM, 1789-1812

When revolution broke out in France Catherine II was drawing to the end
of her reign. She had tried to make life in Russia less nasty than it was when
she arrived there, and she had tried to win for Russia the reputation of being
a part of Europe, but she had never countenanced revolution and she was
not expected to do so now. French literature was confiscated and Russian
newspapers were forbidden to publish foreign news, but Catherine's subjects
continued to regard her as an enlightened monarch and to dread the reaction
which would take place under her son. Catherine hated Paul as she had hated
her husband. When he grew to manhood she treated him with contempt
and encouraged her favourites to do the same. She would allow him to play

no part in state affairs and she debarred him from a military career on which he was set. She tried to deprive him of the succession and failed only because her grandson refused to ascend the throne before his father. By the time Paul became tsar at the age of forty-two his mind was unhinged to a dangerous degree. A fierce determination to wield power long denied to him was combined with a grandiose idea of his own position. More alarming still was a dark shadow of suspicion and fear which lay heavily upon all his thoughts and deeds.

The few years of Paul's reign (1796-1801) were a period of confusion and terror scarcely paralleled in revolutionary France. His best known acts as tsar were his attempts to abolish French fashions such as top-boots and frock-coats, connected in his mind with revolution, and his insistence that people should kneel in the streets as his carriage passed by. To eradicate offences in matters of dress and etiquette he created a special police department, the Secret Expedition, and thousands of persons were imprisoned or exiled. Yet not all his actions were utterly devoid of reason. His acceptance of the title of Grand Master of the Knights of Malta flattered his insensate vanity but also gave him a claim to a position in the Mediterranean which became a factor in European politics. His withdrawal of the Charter granted by Catherine to the nobility and gentry was prompted partly by a determination to destroy his mother's measures but also by a belief that no-one should enjoy privileges except at the reigning tsar's hands. Paul's arrogant words, 'He only to whom I speak is noble, and for as long as I speak to him', were reminiscent of Peter the Great's idea of an aristocracy. Unfortunately for Paul, the time had gone by for treating noblemen like servants. When he abolished their exemption from corporal punishment they were angry as well as afraid, and groups were soon plotting for his removal. They were joined by discontented army officers. Paul was a great admirer of Prussian military methods, which to him consisted of constant drilling and harsh discipline. He was always on the watch, for he regarded the army as his special concern. High ranking officers were humiliated in front of their subordinates; all went in constant dread of cruel punishment for trivial offences.

On the whole it was the privileged classes in civilian and military life which suffered most at the hands of Paul. He could be aroused to compassion for the multitude and his reign witnessed one or two minor attempts to improve the conditions of the serfs. Decrees were issued against the selling of serfs without their families and against the excessive punishment of serfs by their owners. A ukase of 1797 forbade work on landowners' estates on Sundays and recommended three days as an appropriate amount of *barshchina*. The laws remained without sanction, however. Paul seemed powerless to enforce his more humane policies yet he was vigorous in cruelty.

When peasant revolts broke out at the beginning of his reign he sent troops under Field-Marshal Prince Repnin to suppress the revolts by violent and degrading methods. When house-serfs in St. Petersburg petitioned against ill-treatment by their masters, he had them knouted in the public square. Under these circumstances it would be useless to interpret his attack on the privileges of the aristocracy as a move towards the abolition of serfdom. During his short reign many thousands of peasants were taken from crown estates and given to favourites as bonded serfs.

No-one made awkward enquiries when it was given out that Paul I had died of an apoplectic stroke. In fact he had been deposed, in the time-honoured manner of Russian tsars, by a group of officers and gentry led on this occasion by Catherine the Great's last favourite, Platon Zubov, and the governor of St. Petersburg, Count Pahlen. The conspirators entered the gloomy Mikhailovsky Palace at midnight on 23 March 1801 on the pretext of bringing news to the Tsar. They dragged Paul, gibbering with rage and terror, from a hiding place in his bedroom and having forced him to sign a form of abdication they strangled him. Downstairs, awake and dressed, Paul's eldest son waited for news. The conspirators had taken care to impli-cate the heir to the throne but they had not obtained his permission for murder. Alexander had naïvely imagined that Paul's deposition could be obtained without his death. He was morbidly sensitive for the rest of his life about his responsibility for his father's violent end. He could never like Napoleon because he once referred to it.

Alexander's upbringing had been as unsatisfactory as Paul's. He was Catherine's favourite grandson. She took him away from his parents and supervised every detail of his education herself. In doing so she gave full reign to her penchant for enlightened ideas, and gave Alexander an education totally out of keeping with his surroundings. As tutor she appointed a Swiss, La Harpe, known to her through her acquaintance with Grimm. La Harpe had been brought up on republican and democratic ideas which he could not help but communicate to Alexander. As religious instructor Catherine chose the Archpresbyter Somborsky, a man who had lived in England for many years, married an English wife, and learnt to admire English ways. Both were earnest and upright souls, and they encouraged in Alexander a lofty conception of his duties, but they gave him no practical insight into the difficulty of carrying out those duties. Alexander's friends were equally incapable of giving depth of understanding to his naturally superficial mind. Stroganov had travelled in France in 1790 and become a member of the Jacobin club, an experience which left him with austere moral views and a tendency to adopt attitudes which were more democratic than his policies. Novosiltsev was a member of the enlightened nobility; Czar-toryski was a Polish patriot; Kochubey was a diplomat better acquainted with foreign courts than with Russia. Between them they created in Alexander the illusion that he was in touch with western modes of thought. Vanity was always Alexander's greatest weakness: at the age of 23 he joined in the conspiracy against his father under the impression that he would be able to bring a golden age to Russia.

The beginning was easy, for all he needed to do to satisfy the public was to abolish his father's more tyrannical measures. He banished Paul's favourite courtier and one-time barber Kutaysov, dismissed the leading police officials, and abolished the Secret Expedition. Large numbers of victims were recalled from Siberia, prohibitions on foreign books and foreign travel were rescinded, the ludicrous decrees concerning dress were repealed, and charters were restored to the nobility and towns. This put Russia back to the time of Catherine. Alexander's leading statesmen in these early days were mostly men who had served under Catherine, and a return to her policies was the height of their ambitions for Russia. One of them, Troschinsky, framed a manifesto whereby Alexander promised to govern the people 'after the laws and heart of his grandmother'. The first of the periodical magazines to appear with the relaxation of censorship, Karamzin's *European Messenger*, asserted that all nations of Europe were convinced of the need for firm government and that the autocratic tsar needed only to encourage and follow the free expression of public opinion to be beloved by all his subjects. Enlightened despotism was the ideal of the times.

Alexander soon began to indulge his fancy for setting up new administrative bodies. Within a few months of his accession he summoned a commission to interpret the laws, set up a permanent council to advise on policy, and ordered the Senate to report on its rights and duties with a view to reorganization. This seemed to many Russians convincing proof of the new tsar's enlightened intentions. Alexander had vague notions of altering the structure of government, however. In June 1801 he set up a committee composed of his friends Stroganov, Novosiltsev, Czartoryski, and Kochubey to advise him on radical changes. Characteristically the committee's discussions ranged over a wide area, including foreign policy and serfdom, and Alexander did not hesitate to ask advice from outsiders, such as La Harpe, on matters within the competence of the committee. The members of the committee proved to be less daring when faced with a share of responsibility for the future of Russia than they had been in earlier days. They dissuaded Alexander from issuing a Declaration of Rights on the grounds that the rights would probably have to be withdrawn in the future, and they advised him not to limit royal power until the administration had been tidied up. They noticed a curious trait in the young tsar. Although Alexander had expressed a desire to limit his own power he opposed a suggestion that ministers should report their plans to the Senate; and when the Senate used its new right of remonstrance to protest against a decree concerning army service Alexander said that the senators had exceeded their powers, which allowed them to remonstrate only against the decrees of former tsars.

Numerous plans for emancipation of the serfs were discussed by the committee. Stroganov favoured large-scale measures, but Alexander was impressed by the warnings of Novosiltsev against alienating the landowners while still dependent on them for controlling the vast population of Russia. Alexander placed his hopes on an edict of 1803 allowing serfs to buy their freedom according to mutual arrangement with the landowner. He imagined that this would produce a substantial body of free peasant farmers whose success would prove that serfdom was unprofitable to all concerned. His disappointment in this sphere contributed towards the total disillusionment which came upon him in later years.

After a year or so Alexander ceased to consult the reform committee and it automatically dissolved. For advice on fundamental questions he turned to the committee of ministers, which included Kochubey, Stroganov, and the talented Speransky, the most competent adviser Alexander ever found. Speransky was the son of a parish priest, educated free of charge, as was the right of sons of the clergy, in a church seminary. He had risen by sheer brilliance to a post in the government. His knowledge of living conditions in rural Russia gave a practical bias to his thinking which was of great value. Unlike many of Alexander's advisers Speransky did not start off with glowing hopes which he could not fulfil. Indeed his memorandum of 1803 was distinctly gloomy in character. It recognized constitutional monarchy as the ideal form of government but found popular representation impossible in a country where three quarters of the people were serfs, unaccustomed to accepting responsibility even for their own livelihood. Serfdom ought first to be abolished, but to free the serfs without educating them would be to abandon them to ruin, while to educate them in their position of servitude would be both difficult and dangerous. The enchanted circle could only be broken by slow and persistent efforts.

A beginning was made in the realm of education. Modern education had appeared in Russia under Peter the Great and Catherine, but Alexander's Schools Statute of 1804 was the first attempt to establish a complete system. It envisaged parish and district elementary schools, secondary schools, and universities where members of all classes including serfs would be educated free of charge. The practical achievements fell far short of the plans, for teachers were few and new schools expensive. Nevertheless some thousands of Russians obtained an education during the next few years, many of them non-nobles. Alexander founded two universities, at Kharkov and Kazan, and remodelled two others on German lines. Educational policy aroused considerable discussion in progressive circles, the most advanced views being expressed by a new journal, the *Magazine of Russian Letters* (1804-6). Strangely enough the leading writer in the journal, I. P. Pnin, while deploring serfdom, believed that there should be different schools for peasants', merchants', and noblemen's sons. The magazine advocated the abolition of censorship, a step Alexander was not prepared to take although he recommended his censors to show leniency. Alexander gave generous subsidies for the translation of foreign works into Russian. He also subsidized a journal, the *Northern Messenger*, which described constitutional monarchy on the English pattern as the ideal form of government.

The money for all this activity was hard to find. Since 1769 Russia had lived on an inconvertible paper money system. The paper rouble had depreciated continuously since Catherine's last Turkish war yet Alexander went on issuing new batches of paper money without backing. Danger was averted for a time by an improvement in trade. Paul's embargo on commerce with Britain was repealed, transport was improved by the completion of a number of canals, and the vigorous colonization of the south (New Russia) brought a notable increase in the production of grain. The course of the paper money actually rose from 50 kopecks per rouble to 80 kopecks. but war against Napoleon soon reduced Russia to the verge of bankruptcy. Russia had to recruit and arm 150,000 men for the war of 1805. The subsidy offered by the British government was small for the purpose and a loan was refused by the Ministry of all the Talents in 1806. In the same year Russia suffered an almost total failure of the crops. Economic collapse was without doubt responsible in part for Alexander's decision to make peace with Napoleon at Tilsit.

Peace did not improve the situation for it involved joining the Continental System. Russian landowners and merchants found themselves deprived of their best customer for flax and hemp, iron ore and naval stores. Besides selling to the British, these commodities had in the past been transported in British ships. Too heavy and bulky to travel by land, they were unable to find alternative markets. There was a rapid increase in the production of cotton textiles for the home market but the increase was not sustained. Merchants complained bitterly of the loss of Baltic trade and of the injunction to buy French luxury goods at high prices. Smuggling was rife, but smuggled goods were costly. Between 1807 and 1810 the paper rouble dropped to below a fifth of its nominal value. Along with economic loss there was a feeling of humiliation hard to bear. Alexander's responsibility for the disaster of Austerlitz was well known in military and society circles. The latter had long regarded Napoleon as a barbarian, the embodiment of a crude materialistic outlook on life which had developed in France as the result of the revolution. Alexander himself had done much to encourage abhorrence of Napoleon when, in order to rouse the Russian people against a possible French invasion in 1807, he had ordered appeals from the Holy Synod to be read in all churches, describing Napoleon as a usurper who had trampled on religion in France and plotted to instal himself as the Messiah of Europe with the aid of the Jews. Friendship for such a monster was inconceivable. Napoleon's envoy to the Russian court, Savary, was shunned by the society of St. Petersburg. At the court itself the Dowager Empress Maria Fedorovna and the Grand Duchess Catherine were bitter opponents of the French alliance.

Alexander could not ignore the opinion of the nobility and merchants, which stood for 'public opinion' in Russia. He apparently had some idea of redeeming his character by introducing great measures at home, and in 1809 he again approached Speransky concerning the possibility of constitutional reform. Speransky was less cautious than before. He advised sweeping measures at once, and when Alexander agreed with this on principle Speransky drew up a detailed plan for elected assemblies at both local and national levels. Alexander took fright and without actually rejecting the plan he shelved its major recommendations. This deplorable waste of Speransky's time and mental energies did not deter the tsar from consulting him again in the same year on the nation's finances. Speransky again advised drastic measures: no further issues of paper money, a new tax devoted entirely to reducing the national debt, a new loan backed by the sale of state property, and cuts in expenditure on education and public works. Unfortunately only the last recommendation was fully carried out. A new tax was decreed but the proceeds were used for current expenses and a vast new issue of paper money caused further depreciation. On Speransky's advice Alexander decreed a new tariff in 1810 and withdrew Russia from the Continental System. This staved off total collapse, but Speransky was blamed by the public for failing to restore prosperity. Speransky was never liked in aristocratic circles. As a self-made man he was assumed to be less than a gentleman. Suspicions were confirmed when the tsar issued two ukases, attributed to Speransky, demanding service in return for court titles and requiring a university degree for nomination to the council of state. Speransky was reputed to admire French institutions and to hanker after establishing the *Code Napoléon* in Russia. He was even accused of planning the nation's ruin so as to place Russia at the mercy of Napoleon. In 1812 Alexander sacrificed him to the patriotic fervour of the nobility. He was exiled to Novgorod and all his talents rejected.

4. THE MOSCOW CAMPAIGN

Russian nobles regarded the war of 1805 as useless, for it held no prospect of expansion, the only motive they could have understood at the time. Six years later they saw Russia threatened by a revolutionary tyrant who would destroy aristocracy and free the serfs. Self-interest was connected in their minds with protection of the tsar, of the church, of Holy Russia. They prepared for the new war as for a crusade, mortgaging their estates and pawning their valuables to send gifts to the Treasury.

Napoleon meanwhile was planning the most spectacular war of his career. Russia was to be overwhelmed by sheer weight of numbers. The King of Saxony was told to raise 70,000 troops from the population of 4 million in the Grand Duchy of Warsaw; French troops numbering 200,000 and supported by German battalions of the Confederation of the Rhine were massed along the Elbe and the Oder; a third army was formed in Holland and northern France; Prince Eugène collected units from all over Italy for a march across the Alps. Detachments were summoned from Croatia, Switzerland, Portugal, and Spain. Prussia was bullied into promising 20,000 men, Austria cajoled into promising 30,000. When Napoleon held his last great court at Dresden in May 1812 he proposed to send more than 600,000 men across the Niemen. Reliance on numbers alone was in itself a sign of the deterioration of Napoleon's genius. Two moves were lost at the beginning. Napoleon offered Finland to Bernadotte in return for a military alliance, but the latter chose instead to ally with Alexander in return for a promise of Norway. He offered the Crimea to Turkey in return for a military diversion in southern Russia, but the Sultan was tired of war and preferred to sign a hasty peace with Alexander at Bucharest (28 May 1812) ceding Bessarabia to Russia in return for evacuation of the Principalities. Alexander was thus able to withdraw Russian troops from Finland and the Danube. About the same time Alexander received secret assurances from Austria that her troops would never be brought into serious action against Russia.

Napoleon's forces were nevertheless twice if not three times the size of any that Alexander could put into the field. He was not worried by the fact that the Grand Army contained only a nucleus of Frenchmen, surrounded by Poles, Lithuanians, Austrians, Prussians, Germans from the Confederation, Hungarians, Dutchmen, Italians, Swiss, Croats, Illyrians, Spaniards, and Portuguese, most of whom had no loyalty to France. He was not blind, · however, to the difficulties of leading a vast army into the spaces of Russia. As usual he supplied himself with a library of books describing the topography of the country he was about to attack. He knew that from the banks of the Niemen a relentless plain stretched for five hundred miles to Moscow. Dry dusty soil gave place to marshland and sometimes to forest. Towns were more than a day's march apart, villages were tiny collections of wooden huts surrounded by a few cultivated fields sufficient only to feed the inhabitants. No army could live off such a land in the way that French armies had lived off the fertile valleys of north Italy. Preparations were made accordingly. Huge stores of grain were collected at Danzig, Thorn, Elbing,

and many other depots. Thirty million bottles of wine and spirits were
ordered from Italy. Transports were arranged on a more elaborate scale
than Napoleon had ever envisaged before. In the event circumstances combined to render the preparations ineffective, while improvisation remained
impossible. Heavy rains destroyed many of the transports in the early
stages of the campaign. On the march through Poland vast numbers of
troops deserted, carrying supplies with them, and the disgusting behaviour
of the rest alienated the local population. On the long march through
Russia the baggage trains could not keep up with the rapidly advancing
troops: meanwhile the Russian army scorched the earth over which it
retreated, and nobles and peasants zealously co-operated in the devastation
of their land.

If sheer starvation was responsible for the death of large numbers of the
Grand Army, Napoleon himself was responsible for leading his men further
and further towards their doom. In the early stages he talked of a limited
war: he would conquer Lithuania, establish winter quarters at Vilna, and
approach Alexander with terms. 'My undertaking is of the kind that is solved
by patience', he said. Unfortunately, patience had never been one of his
virtues and by 1812 he was less patient than ever. His dealings with Spain
and his handling of the Divorce showed the growing insensitivity of his
character. Berthier, the incomparable chief of staff, was treated to more
frequent outbursts of temper during the Russian campaign than he had ever
known. More alarming still, Berthier saw the great master, whom he had
thought unshakeable, assailed by doubt. For the first time in his career
Napoleon allowed the enemy to dictate the course of the war.

The Moscow campaign began when the Grand Army crossed the Niemen
on 24 June 1812. Two Russian armies under Barclay de Tolly and Bagration
waited on the opposite bank to discover Napoleon's line of attack, then
retreated by separate roads towards Smolensk. The retreat was dictated more
by necessity than by cunning but it was carried out in an orderly fashion,
very few stragglers falling into French hands, and Napoleon failed to catch
his enemies while they were still divided. He entered Vilna unopposed on
1 July. Vilna was the capital of those Lithuanian provinces of Poland which
had been annexed by Russia in the Partitions. The Poles, who formed a large
part of the population of the city, had many times hoped that Napoleon
would restore Lithuania to a united Poland. They waited now to see what
he would do. He frightened the landowners and clergy with a jacobinical
constitution and alienated the peasantry by demands of military service.
The Grand Army pillaged and looted. Failure at all levels to deal honourably
with the Polish people left Napoleon with an insecure base for further
advance. Eastward the people were predominantly White Russian and less
friendly.

More than a fortnight was lost in Vilna but Napoleon did not despair of catching the Russians before they left Lithuania and inflicting on them a defeat which would bring Alexander to terms. He was seriously shaken when he found the next large town, Vitebsk, undefended and the Russians gone. He nevertheless decided to press on to the borders of Lithuania. He felt sure that he would succeed in bringing the Russians to battle at Smolensk. Smolensk rose on the far bank of the Dnieper surrounded by a high brick wall with thirty towers. It had been many times fought over, and to Russians it was almost a sacred city. Their armies united before the town but Barclay knew that they could not win a pitched battle against the Grand Army. A division under Neverovsky was ordered to man the defences while the main army prepared to retreat along the Moscow road. Napoleon saw the camp fires shining in the city and imagined that he had caught a major Russian force at last. He ordered a bombardment. For two days his guns pounded away at the great walls and every attack was beaten off. When at last the French were able to make a frontal assault Barclay ordered the retreat of the Russian forces (17 August). Junot, who had been sent to cut the Moscow road, moved too slowly and arrived too late. When Napoleon entered the burnt out city he found it piled with dead bodies. Both sides had lost some 20,000 men. No army could be expected to stay here for the winter: the memories were too horrible, the sights too gruesome, the city and countryside for miles around denuded of food. Few of Napoleon's men had heart for going further, but it was not in Napoleon's nature to turn back. He could argue that he had reached the point of no return and that all he needed was one big battle against inferior numbers. 'He tried to make me say', wrote Caulaincourt afterwards, 'that the Russians would hold and fight a battle, which was what he wanted. He was like a man in need of consolation.'

Napoleon was not the only man spoiling for a fight. Bagration disliked Barclay's cautious strategy and chafed under his command when the two armies united at Smolensk. He intrigued against him in camp and at court until the issue was settled by the appointment of the aged Kutuzov as generalissimo with instructions to bring the armies to battle for the defence of Moscow. Kutuzov chose to take his stand near the village of Borodino on the banks of a little river, the Kolotcha, some seventy miles west of Moscow. His position was a formidable one, defended at its northern end by a Grand Redoubt bristling with cannon and at its centre by the fortified village of Semenovskoe, while to the south lay hill slopes heavily wooded. Napoleon spent the day before the battle in a mood of unaccustomed depression. Both sides had about 120,000 men in the field but the Russian artillery was the stronger and the Russian troops would die rather than surrender. The battle opened with a French attack at 6 a.m. on 7 September.

For twelve hours the two armies fought hand to hand with the desperation of starving men, charging and counter-charging around Semenovskoe and the Grand Redoubt with little room for manoeuvre and no heart for quarter. Napoleon watched the battle from a safe distance. Ney and Murat sent desperate appeals to him to use his final reserve, the Young Guard, but he ignored them, saying later that he knew he would need the Guard either to pursue the Russians or to defend himself when the battle was over. Kutuzov, so fat that he had to be carried around the field, saw that he could never again expose his army to such an encounter. The battle came to an end when both sides were exhausted. The Russians had lost 43 generals and 58,000 men, the French 50 generals and 30,000 men. It was the most terrible carnage of the Napoleonic wars.

Napoleon counted Borodino a victory because the Russians lost more men than he did and because they left him in possession of the field. On 15 September he gazed upon the gleaming cupolas of Moscow and knew that he had reached the city of his dreams. When he entered it he found it empty. Kutuzov's army had marched through the streets and away to the south. The civilian population had fled in terror to the countryside, taking with them such valuables and provisions as they could carry. There remained only a few thousand jail-birds and vagabonds looting the wine cellars and scavenging among the deserted houses. On 16 September Napoleon took up residence in the Kremlin to await the Russian surrender which he felt sure would come. In the night, careless behaviour among his soldiers caused fire to break out in the bazaar opposite the Kremlin and in several other parts of the city. The fire engines had been removed when Moscow was evacuated and there were no police or civil authorities to organize the fighting of the flames. Soon the half wooden city was ablaze from end to end. Soldiers tore recklessly through the burning churches and palaces, seizing every valuable object they could lay hands on. The fire raged for five days. When it was over, the Kremlin stood safely within its circuit of walls but three quarters of the houses were burnt to the ground.

Napoleon blamed the Russians for the fire. He said that Rostopchin, the eccentric governor of Moscow, had left incendiaries behind to destroy the beautiful city. The Russians blamed the French and execrated them for their vandalism. Whoever was responsible, the great fire was the most decisive event of the campaign. The city could no longer provide winter quarters for Napoleon's army. There was plenty of strong drink in the cellars but no food anywhere. Peasants in the surrounding countryside would not sell their meagre stocks to the vandals who had profaned their churches and who offered them, besides, false rouble notes printed in Paris. Alexander must be bullied into sending his submission quickly so that the Grand Army could find comfortable quarters before the winter set in.

Napoleon stayed in Moscow for five weeks, waiting for a Russian surrender which never came. Three times he sent messages to the Tsar in St. Petersburg but they were ignored. Alexander had vowed that he would make no agreement while the Grand Army remained on Russian soil. Sometimes Napoleon talked of marching on St. Petersburg, but he knew at heart that he would have to retreat by the shortest possible route to a friendlier place once the winter came on. The season was unusually mild and he lingered in Moscow longer than was wise. On 13 October a little snow fell and he knew that he could wait no longer. In his anger he ordered Mortier to blow up the Kremlin when the army had left the city. The mines were badly placed and the main buildings escaped destruction but this last act of barbarism increased the hatred of the Russian people.

Of the army which had marched upon Moscow only a third remained. The problem of finding food for even 100,000 men was enormous, however. They left Moscow on 19 October, laden with precious ornaments and costly raiments but with provisions for only a few days' march. Napoleon hoped to return to Smolensk by a more southerly route not previously ravaged by starving armies, but when his advance guard lost 10,000 men in a fierce encounter with the Russians at Malo-Yaroslavets he turned northward towards the old road. It was the beginning of the end. The battlefield of Borodino struck horror into the French army. When men fell out of line exhausted with hunger they were murdered by Russian peasants or captured by Cossack horsemen. Kutuzov would not risk his army in a large scale encounter, but rearguard actions took heavy toll of the enemy. 6,000 were killed or wounded at Vyazma on 3 November and 2,000 taken prisoner.

Napoleon reached Smolensk on 8 November, but far from finding a haven for his army he discovered that the garrison was waiting for him to deliver the city from starvation. Food supplies had been stolen by deserters or used up by the sick and wounded as they straggled homeward. On 17 November the weary march was resumed. Harried mercilessly by the Russians, the French were held up at the Dnieper and the Beresina by the need to build bridges, for the autumn had been so mild that the waters were only just beginning to freeze. At the Beresina about half the army only had crossed when the Russians came up and opened shell-fire on the rest. In the stampede which followed men were trampled down by their fellows, crushed under the wheels of carriages, or thrown into the icy water. When Napoleon saw that he could no longer defend the bridges against the advancing Russian infantry he ordered them to be burnt, leaving 10,000 of his own people, mostly wounded men and civilian followers, at the mercy of the enemy.

The fighting at the Beresina (27-29 November) was the last major action of the war. After it the Russians held back their forces but the elements

AOP P

brought their fiercest weapons to bear. The temperature fell to 30 degrees below zero and a cruel wind lashed at Napoleon's broken army. Thousands lay down in the snow and ice to die. Many used their last ounce of strength in fighting each other for a pair of shoes, or for the meat of dying horses, or even for human flesh. Forty miles short of Vilna Napoleon deserted his army and sped back to Paris in relays of comfortable equipages to save his government from a republican plot. According to Caulaincourt who travelled with him he gave no thought to the desperate men who fell like savages upon the town of Vilna, beating their way into the houses and grasping ravenously at the meagre stores of food. After two days Murat, now in command, was obliged to order evacuation. Marshal Ney fought a series of stubborn rearguard actions to save the few thousand tattered and half demented men who trudged over the frozen Niemen to find refuge in Germany. The 350 who battled at his side were the only effective fighters remaining from the great force which had entered Russia six months before. Of the 600,000 troops used by Napoleon in the campaign, only 30,000 survived.

To the makers of legend, disaster on so fantastic a scale increased the grandeur of Napoleon. Nature herself, it seemed, had warred against the greatest conqueror the world had ever seen. Yet in truth the Grand Army was defeated long before the winter set in, and the thrilling epic became a ghastly crime to anyone thinking in terms of the human sorrow and suffering which surrounded the death of more than half a million men. Napoleon on St. Helena admitted his responsibility but without remorse. Indeed he thought of it with a strange pride. To have returned safely to Paris after so enormous a catastrophe seemed to him a sign that he was protected by Providence.

On the other side the Tsar too was impressed by thoughts of a more than human encounter. A strong vein of mysticism had always been present in Alexander's character. As a boy he had been attracted by the teaching of the freemasons, who attacked the loose living of Catherine's circle and pleaded for a new religious zeal and a new sense of duty towards humanity. The experiences of 1812 caused Alexander to see himself as the leader not only of a vast national rising against invasion but of a crusade against the embodied evil of the times. The unseasonable weather and above all the great fire of Moscow were signs to him that mysterious powers were fighting on his side. Napoleon became the anti-Christ, Alexander the chosen instrument of God.

Kutuzov, like his sovereign, had prayed to God, but only for the deliverance of Russia from human enemies. When Kutuzov saw the Grand Army retreating from Moscow he was not concerned to destroy it or even to capture Napoleon, though he might have done both at the Beresina. He was concerned only that the invader should leave Russia with the minimum number of Russian lives lost. When the Grand Army crossed the Niemen

Kutuzov saw the war as ended. Napoleon, he believed, would be willing to make peace with Russia and grant her the line of the Vistula as compensation for her losses. To Alexander in his growing messianic mood, however, the liberation of Russia was not enough, and negotiations with Napoleon were unthinkable. The tyrant must be driven from Europe and his hold over men's minds destroyed for ever.

Alexander knew that the triumph of Spain and of Russia had been achieved through the efforts of the whole people. If victory was to be complete other oppressed peoples must rise also. In February 1813 he issued a proclamation pledging himself to bring 'peace and independence to nations prepared to face sacrifices to achieve this end'. The appeal to national spirit had revolutionary implications, but Alexander was not thinking of the democratic nationalism which had appeared in France. He was thinking, rather, of loyalty to ancient traditions and institutions such as had inspired Spaniards and Russians to defend their country. Significantly he addressed his proclamation chiefly to the Prussia of former times: 'for it is the intention of His Imperial Majesty . . . to give back to the kingdom of Frederick the Great its former frontiers and lustre.' Thus Alexander, with a fighting force of only 40,000 men, prepared to enter Germany in fulfilment of a mission to the nations of Europe.

CHAPTER XII

Germany and the Rejection of the Universal State

I. THE UNIVERSAL STATE

IN EXILE on St. Helena Napoleon claimed that he too had pursued a mission towards the nations of Europe. 'There are in Europe more than thirty million French, fifteen million Spanish, fifteen million Italians, and thirty million Germans. I would have wished to make each of these people a single united body.' The claim does more credit to Napoleon's shrewdness as a propagandist than to his veracity. There were times when he conjured up nationalist illusions, by creating, for instance, the Kingdom of Italy, the Grand Duchy of Warsaw, and the Illyrian provinces. On these occasions he played upon nationalist feeling much as he played upon other jealousies and rivalries latent in mankind for his own purposes. He never fulfilled any of the nationalist hopes he might have aroused. The Kingdom of Italy was truncated by the annexation of a large part of the Italian peninsula to France when this seemed necessary in the interests of war and of the Continental System. The Grand Duchy of Warsaw was created only because Tsar Alexander would not take Poland and give Napoleon Silesia. It was bestowed upon Napoleon's ally Frederick Augustus of Saxony and not upon the gallant Polish patriot Poniatowski, and it was never restored as 'Poland' to the map of Europe even after Napoleon had ceased to respect Alexander's wishes on this subject. The Illyrian provinces were given only an artificial unity, achieved by administrative organization on French lines. Their name was derived from Roman origins, and the language prescribed for official use was not Croat but French.

Elsewhere in Europe Napoleon looked coldly upon nationalist aspirations which he could not use. When Karageorge appealed to him to help the Serbs against the Turks he neglected even to answer. The great Serbian leader had already built up a military position which would make him a difficult protégé, and Napoleon always wanted to be the patron not the ally. Moreover Napoleon was afraid to weaken the power of the Sultan in the Balkans lest he should open the way for Russia. Appeals from Greek tribal leaders were ignored. Friendly overtures to Ali Pasha of Janina were prompted not by interest in Albanian independence but by the desire to warn Alexander against renewing Catherine's dream of a Russian protectorate over the Balkans.

To suppose that Napoleon wished to create a Europe composed of autonomous states is to suppose that he wished France to lose her primacy. This supposition finds no support from the history of Napoleon's empire. 'It was a fine empire', he said wistfully on St. Helena. 'I had 83 millions of men to govern, more than half the population of Europe.' By 1811 his dominion outside of France extended over four different types of territory. First were the lands which had been annexed to France and were administered directly from Paris: a third of the Italian peninsula (Savoy, Genoa, Piedmont, Tuscany, Parma, Piacenza, and Rome), a third of Germany (the left bank of the Rhine, Hanover, Oldenburg, and the Hanseatic towns), the Belgian provinces, and the Kingdom of Holland. Secondly there were provinces which, though not formally annexed to France, were administered by prefects sent from Paris: the Illyrian provinces and the four Spanish provinces of Catalonia, Aragon, Navarre, and Biscay. In a third category were the vassal states: the Kingdom of Italy, Naples, Spain, Westphalia, and the Grand Duchy of Warsaw. Lastly can be reckoned the states of the Rhine Confederation and the Swiss Confederation, which accepted Napoleon as protector and pledged themselves to furnish quotas of men for the imperial armies. Napoleon never made any long-term plans for the organization of this empire, but he was determined that no section of the population should escape from his dominion. It seemed unreasonable to him that any should wish to do so. Insubordination was a sign of ignorance and backwardness to which force was the only suitable reply.

On the few occasions when Napoleon gave his attention to the government of the Empire he showed that he was a true son of the eighteenth century. He believed that the *ancien régime* had been disrupted by enlightened despots and that he needed only to clear away the débris to produce a flat surface over which to operate the universal principles of the French Revolution. These principles, as interpreted by Napoleon, amounted to the right of all men to civil equality, which would have the practical advantage of weakening the aristocracy and clergy, whom he regarded as enemies, and rallying the bourgeoisie and peasantry, whom he persisted in seeing as friends. Hence he made some efforts to recommend the *Code Napoléon* to vassal kings and confederate rulers. The efforts were singularly feeble, for at heart Napoleon cared little whether his puppet rulers carried out reform or not provided they collected taxes and conscripted army units. There were some parts of the Empire where the *Code* never penetrated at all, notably Spain, Bavaria, and Württemberg. Other regions adopted it late in the day and with modifications: Naples in 1810, Frankfurt in 1811, the Illyrian pro-

vinces as late as 1812. In Poland the *Code* was promulgated by Frederick
Augustus in 1808, but nobles and bishops took a stand on the Constitution
of 1791 and contended with army officers, government officials, and members of the bourgeoisie to limit its application.

Changes in social structure depended, as Polish aristocrats saw only too
well, on the extent to which the *Code* was applied. On the left bank of the
Rhine, privileges and seigneurial dues were abolished totally and without
redemption, giving rise to a prosperous class of peasant proprietors and a
bourgeoisie predominant in economic and administrative affairs. In Westphalia, Berg, and the Illyrian provinces, personal dues were abolished but
real dues were declared redeemable. In Naples, owners of feudal rights were
indemnified. Tithes remained in existence in Holland and Frankfurt.
Bavaria abolished serfdom but retained forced labour services and tithes in
a limited form. Württemberg and Baden kept tithes, forced labour services,
and feudal dues. In Poland, serfs were emancipated by article 4 of the
constitution, but a decree of 21 December 1807 said that if a peasant left his
master he must forfeit his house, land, and farming implements. Opponents
of the *Code* were thus able to show that the peasants were worse off than
before, and social changes were held up.

Local variations were always greater than Napoleon bargained for, and
so, too, were local loyalties. In some parts of the Empire, notably Spain and
Tyrol, devotion to traditional forms was strong. In other parts, if there was
no real affection for the old ways there was no respect for the new. Provinces which had suffered exploitation at the hands of French revolutionary
armies were not likely to love French rule. Cities which had been obliged
to send their art treasures to Paris were not likely to regard the imperial
capital as a centre of civilization. Napoleon's régime was judged entirely by
utilitarian standards. When taxes, conscription, and the requirements of the
Continental System pressed heavily on the people they were resented more
bitterly than the older burdens imposed by legitimate rulers. No region of
the Empire, with the doubtful exception of Naples, attempted to defend the
Napoleonic régime when the crash came in 1814.

Equally, however, very few regions made an active attempt to get rid of
it. Napoleon's admirers might have claimed that he had nurtured the spirit
of nationalism, albeit against his will, if groups of people under his rule had
risen against him with new feelings of nationhood. That this was not so can
be seen clearly in the cases of Italy and Germany.

Under the Napoleonic system Italy was divided (or, as the Emperor would
have preferred it, collected together) to form three units. French Italy ran
down the western side of the Appenines to include Rome; the Kingdom of
Italy stretched along the Po valley and down the eastern side of the Apennines beyond Ancona; and the Kingdom of Naples covered the southern

half of the peninsula. 'One of my grandest ideas was agglomeration', Napoleon is reported to have said at St. Helena. 'As regards the 15 million Italians, agglomeration had already gone far; it needed only time to mature. Every day ripened that unity of . . . thought and feeling, which is the sure and infallible cement of human societies.' This was hardly true, even within the separate units. Tuscans regarded themselves as the purest bred of all Italians, sought to subject the Italian language to standards set up by the Academy of Florence, and despised writers from Piedmont. Romans could not submit with dignity to the status of citizens of the chief town of a department. Neapolitans nursed pretensions over the former Papal States. A few intellectuals tried in vain to imbue Italians with a feeling of brotherhood. Cuoco at Milan edited a newspaper, the *Giornale italiano*, which ransacked past ages for inspiring examples of national greatness, and wrote a novel, *Platone in Italia*, designed to 'form the national feeling of the Italians'. The masses, however, remained inert.

A semblance of uniformity was given by French administrative and legal reforms. All Italy came under the same master hand, for Eugène Beauharnais as Viceroy of the Kingdom of Italy and Joseph Bonaparte as King of Naples were almost as strictly supervised as the prefects of the trans-Alpine departments. Eugène received twenty-one letters of advice from his step-father in his first week of office. The Kingdom of Italy was given decrees confiscating church land, dissolving monastic orders, introducing the French civil and commercial codes, ordering the building of roads and canals, stabilizing the coinage to match the French franc, and proclaiming a constitution designed to act as a symbol of popular sovereignty. In Naples Joseph decreed the reduction of clerical privileges, the reform of taxation, and the codification of the laws. Reorganization was nowhere fully carried out, however. In the Kingdom of Italy, once the Cisalpine republic, overthrown in 1799, reconstructed in 1800, renamed the Italian republic in 1802, and given Napoleon as king in 1805, there was a feeling of impermanence which weakened the new régime from start to finish. The men who most welcomed Napoleonic institutions – the young Italian volunteers whom Eugène chose as officers for the army – regarded French hegemony as a mere expedient and looked forward to independence in the future. In the south, Joseph's rule was hampered by guerilla warfare in Calabria and by the menace of a British landing from Sicily or Capri. Joachim Murat, who succeeded to Joseph's throne in 1808, lessened the danger from the British by leading a lucky assault on Capri, but Murat was not the man to consolidate French reforms. Resentful of orders from Napoleon, and more concerned with political schemes than with administrative detail, he encouraged a few freemasons, members of secret societies, ambitious government officials and discontented army officers to indulge in schemes for proclaiming him king of all Italy. The conspiracy was never solidly grounded. As a cavalry leader Murat placed his reliance upon the army, only to discover that the French units and French officers with which the Neapolitan army was liberally endowed remained loyal to the Emperor.

Perhaps the main reason why French reforms failed to take root was the absence of any social development similar to that of France in the eighteenth century. Italy had no large and ambitious middle class anxious to take advantage of new institutions. Nor had she a large class of peasant proprietors resentful of feudal privilege. In Italy the most powerful of the privileged classes was the clergy, and the reduction of their privileges by paper reforms failed to destroy their all-pervading influence. The secular spirit of the French Revolution could thus make little headway among the Italian people. It could serve neither to engender loyalty to Napoleon in the name of progress nor to rouse hostility to him in the name of freedom.

The burdens which Napoleon imposed on Italy were unevenly spread but everywhere heavy. The ports and coastal regions suffered most from the Continental Blockade. Lombards believed at first that their textile industry would benefit from the exclusion of British competition, only to find that their whole economy was sacrificed to that of France. The low import duties on French manufactures discouraged industry in backward areas such as Naples. The benefits which should have resulted everywhere from improved communications, more efficient administration, and simplified laws were offset by heavy taxes and by military conscription. Napoleon's financial demands increased annually. In 1806 the Kingdom of Italy was sending a fifth of her revenues to the imperial treasury and contributing further sums to extraordinary military expenses. By 1812 she was sending two thirds of her revenues to France, and taxes, which started by being twice as heavy as those levied by Austrian rulers, increased 20% before the fall of the Empire. In Naples Napoleon's exactions absorbed two thirds of the income which Joseph had planned to use on improving the impoverished kingdom. Conscription in Italy was less heavy than in France, but greater difficulties were experienced by those trying to carry it out. Demands rose from 30,000 men in 1807 to 90,000 in 1812, but at least a half of the men deserted before they crossed the Alps. Among those who served in the armies, however, the death rate was very high, for Napoleon cared less about his Italian conscripts than about his French soldiers.

All these burdens aroused no more than sporadic protests. The Italians prepared to change their allegiance to Austria when war broke out in 1809 but relapsed into subservience when they heard the news of Wagram. Desertions from the army were occasioned more by Italian indolence and insubordination than by hostility to Napoleon – there was an equal lack of zeal when armies were needed for the Risorgimento. Even when the Empire was tottering the Italians made no impressive move to throw off the foreign yoke. A Milanese mob lynched the finance minister, Giuseppe Prina, but otherwise Italians simply waited for the French to go. The hostility expressed by a few intellectuals, such as Foscolo and Alfieri, did not betoken a great national rejection of foreign tyranny.

More notable still, in view of clerical influence with the peasantry, was Italy's lack of protest at Napoleon's ill-treatment of the Pope. Conduct which might have been expected to antagonize the whole Catholic world produced hardly a ripple on the surface of Napoleon's power in Italy. When Pius VII travelled to Paris to crown Napoleon the latter took the gesture as a sign of weakness and virtually discounted the Pope from then on as a factor in the political situation. A Concordat was very soon introduced into the Italian dependencies, followed by a statute on the lines of the Organic Articles and a decision to introduce the Civil Code. The latter, with its provisions for divorce, was as much of an affront to Papal authority as were the new catechism and the addition of St. Napoléon to the Calendar. If the spiritual functions of the Pope were usurped by Napoleon the temporal power was unlikely to remain sacrosanct. Within two years of the coronation Napoleon was describing himself as a new Charlemagne and referring to Papal lands as the gift of the Emperor. 'The Emperor . . . does not really want to take anything away from the Pope, but his intention is to include the Pope in his system,' wrote Napoleon in January 1808. This meant that the Pope must join in the Continental Blockade. When Pius failed to show 'accommodation' General Miollis was ordered to seize the Papal States and enter Rome. Under the shadow of French guns Pius VII issued the bull *Quam Memoranda* excommunicating the authors of attacks upon the Holy See. Napoleon, triumphantly established in Vienna, ordered the immediate arrest of the Pope, and as French troops repulsed the Austrians at Wagram the mild old man who had dared to defy the Emperor was hurried into exile at Savona. When Pius VII advertised the breach with the Emperor in letters to the bishops, exile was turned into imprisonment and eventually into solitary confinement. Pius retaliated by refusing to institute bishops to vacant sees. Napoleon was sure that a victory in Moscow would bring the Pope to heel, and Pius was installed at Fontainebleau to be ready for the final submission. No victory was achieved, and the Continental System collapsed, but Napoleon was determined to have his way with the church. Pius was bullied into agreeing that investiture would pass, after six months' delay, to the Archbishop of Paris, but he recanted twenty-four hours afterwards. A victory in Germany was meant to secure Pius's submission, but again no victory was achieved. The Pope returned to Rome in the spring of 1814 amid the rejoicing of his subjects. Equally the former Austrian rulers of north Italian states and even the abominable Spanish Bourbon rulers of

Naples were greeted with enthusiasm by their people. Politically the Italians were as uneducated and indiscriminating as when French revolutionary armies first crossed the Alps.

In Germany during the Napoleonic era some pretence was made at emancipating the population in the manner of the French. The peasants were found to be labouring under a variety of burdens. In the south and west conditions were similar to those in eighteenth-century France. Peasants who bought or rented farms had to pay dues in money or kind to the manorial lord and to perform labour services on his estate; land became scarce as the population increased, and the small peasant farms became economically less capable of bearing the manorial burdens which were exploited more elaborately than ever before. East of the Elbe the peasants were worse off. The sandy plain was profitable to the great landowner selling corn to the west, so the noblemen of East Prussia, Pomerania, and Mecklenburg absorbed the holdings of the villagers and reduced the peasants to serfdom. In the intervening lands between the Elbe and the Weser the peasants were better off than anywhere else in Germany. Large estates were not uncommon but they could not expand at the expense of the villager who was protected by custom and law. Since conditions were not favourable to large-scale agriculture many noblemen let out their estates in small lots to peasant proprietors. Even here, however, land hunger on the one hand and exploitation of manorial dues on the other led to complaints from peasant farmers.

Enlightened princes of the eighteenth century made some attempts to improve the lot of the peasantry, but with the notable exception of the Margrave Charles Frederick of Baden they merely tinkered about with the old system and shrank from fundamental changes. Not until French armies advanced into Germany did German princes embark on large-scale measures. While peasants of the Rhineland and of Hanover became free citizens of the French Empire, rulers of other states began to emancipate their serfs and to dissolve manorial rights. Bavaria, Nassau, Hesse-Darmstadt, and the Kingdom of Westphalia took the lead in commuting labour services into rents and arranging, even, for the liquidation of rents by mutual agreement between landlord and tenant. At the same time German industry began to escape from the stranglehold of the guilds. The French system of laissez-faire was extended first to the left bank of the Rhine, then, as Napoleon absorbed more and more of northern Germany, to Hanover, Oldenburg, and the Hanseatic cities. Between 1808 and 1810 the King of Westphalia and the Grand Duke of Berg abolished guilds. Princes of the Confederation of the Rhine followed suit in varying degrees. The King of Bavaria reduced the power of the guilds by restricting their right to license tradesmen; the Duke of Saxe-Weimar revised guild statutes to allow free trade within his tiny dominion.

The object behind these measures was to produce a population free enough to use its energies in the best interests of the state. The reforms owed little or nothing to popular initiative: they were bestowed by enlightened rulers. Benevolent despotism remained the ideal of the best German minds. Even Beethoven, who came to regard Napoleonic rule as stark tyranny, caused the prisoners in his opera *Fidelio* to receive their freedom at the hands of a loving prince. Demands for self-government were unlikely to appear in Germany until there was an ambitious and sufficiently powerful middle class, and in spite of economic reforms no such class emerged. Even after Napoleon's reorganization, Germany remained too fragmented to flourish economically. The Continental System put a brake upon the commercial development of Prussian and north coast ports, and shortage of raw materials starved the Silesian cotton industry. Germany's total population ought to have given her a position among the great powers of Europe, but her largest city, Berlin, was barely a third of the size of Paris, and her resources in man-power and money were hopelessly scattered.

Long accustomed to limited fortunes, the middle classes of Germany bolstered up their pride by cultivating moral worth. Performance of duty to friends and family, pursuit of quiet respectability, insistence upon complete integrity in personal and business matters became the supreme end in view. Nowhere in Europe, until the Victorian age in England, were bourgeois virtues so exalted. Whereas in Victorian England, however, the middle class became more ambitious and self-confident as a result of pride in godliness, the German middle class revenged itself upon fortune by rejecting worldly ambition. Until the middle decades of the nineteenth century the German bourgeoisie remained more docile in political affairs than any class of comparable size and talent in Europe.

Since the middle class, which suffered most from an economic point of view, took no lead in protesting against the fragmentation of Germany, there was unlikely to be a very strong nationalist movement to trouble the princes. In Germany, as in Italy, 'agglomeration' had by no means reached the stage which Napoleon boasted of. Within each Napoleonic unit local loyalties and hatreds remained as strong as ever. Bavaria, anxious to set herself up as a centre of German culture, invited Hegel, Schelling, Jacobi, Feuerbach and Savigny to teach in its universities, only to find that these northerners and protestants angered native scholars by adopting an air of superiority. 'It is difficult to describe the degree of jealousy and animosity which reigns between the different governments of the Confederation', wrote Napoleon's representative from Munich. Under these circumstances the mounting hostility to Napoleon frittered itself away in petty scenes. Princes who paid lip-service to the conqueror were cold-shouldered in their own court circles, much as French diplomats were isolated in their legations. Professional soldiers, who at first welcomed the chance to serve in Napoleon's armies but later resented the subordinate positions to which he confined them, vented their feelings in slipshod service and insubordination. No attempt was made to rise against the princes who had consigned Germany to her humiliating position. In 1814 the majority of Germans simply waited for news of allied victories to force their self-seeking rulers to change sides. The peasants, who had given an overwhelming impetus to national risings in Spain and Russia, did not move in Germany.

2. GERMAN ROMANTICISM AND THE RISE OF PRUSSIA

The majority of mankind will accommodate itself to circumstances it cannot alter, and comfort itself by grumbling. In Germany, however, a few second-rate minds had long sought to escape from stark reality by inventing a mystical form of nationalism. They wished to prove that Germany was a great nation in spite of appearances; that she was superior, even, in essential ways to those nations of the west which played a part of superficial brilliance upon the European stage. In 1783 Herder's *Ideas upon the Philosophy of the History of Mankind* rejected traditional conceptions of the politico-juridical state and spoke instead of the folk-nation, an organic historical growth. Climate, education, tradition, and heredity were said to have produced the different folk-nations, each with its own merits. Germans should be proud of their history and culture; they should seek to purify their language of French accretions. In Herder's thought, romanticism, which rejected the Enlightenment and its emphasis upon reason, rejected also the prevailing cultural subservience to France. His pride in the German folk-nation was tempered by warnings against extremes, but the warnings were not always heeded by subsequent generations. While earlier romantics such as Schiller, Novalis, and Friedrich von Schlegel kept something of the cosmopolitan outlook of the eighteenth century, later writers in their search for a typically German spirit came to glorify the militaristic and authoritarian traditions of Prussia and to express a barbaric hatred of the foreigner.

Events in Prussia were therefore of immense significance not only for the immediate future of Germany but for her subsequent development as a nation state. If Prussia, in order to equip herself as the leader of a national rising against Napoleon, had reformed her institutions in such a way as to become the home of a free community there would have been less chance of Germany following the autocratic path which she took under Bismarck. Ironically, the greatest of all Prussian statesmen during the Napoleonic era had exactly this aim in view. When Karl Freiherr vom Stein became chief minister to Frederick William III in October 1807 he planned to replace the slovenly bureaucratic régime which had existed before Jena with a system in which 'all strata of society participated in the life of the state'. But though

Stein was the most admired of all Prussian statesmen before Bismarck, his aims were only fully appreciated by his opponents, who succeeded in thwarting his policy.

Frederick William III had seen for years that all was not well with Prussia. He had toyed with ideas of reform from the time he ascended the throne, but his good intentions had always been balked by fear of weakening the monarchical power and by a profound dislike of making decisions. His behaviour towards Stein was characteristic of his attitude in political affairs. Stein was a native of the Rhineland who had been attracted to the Prussian civil service by the fame of the great Frederick in the last years of the latter's reign. Frederick William III could recognize a conscientious and imaginative official, and in 1804 Stein was called to Berlin as minister. For the next two years he laboured at economic reform, but he saw that Prussia would never be able to survive the threat from France if she remained under a régime which had grown too decadent to harness the resources of the country. In the time of Frederick the Great all important decisions had been made by the king himself: now they were made by the king's secretaries, a set of irresponsible favourites. The ministers who were officially charged with carrying on the government were treated as mere agents, and their effectiveness was further reduced by the division of ministerial duties into provinces rather than departments. One minister would be expected to understand all the problems of one province, perhaps Westphalia or Silesia, but no one minister was allowed to take an overall view of the country's agriculture or finances. Stein urged the king to form an effective council of ministers, but Frederick William was too timid to make so radical a break with the system of his illustrious predecessor. He still wanted to make use of Stein, but the latter refused to remain minister unless his plans were fully adopted, and in January 1807 the king petulantly dismissed him for disrespect and insubordination.

The reappointment of Stein only a few months later was a sign of Frederick William's deep humiliation and of the country's desperate position after Tilsit. The king never liked Stein, for he was never comfortable with persons of strong will and superior intellect, but he dismissed his favourite counsellor, Karl Friedrich Beyme, and for a short time gave Stein a free hand to try and build a new Prussia.

If all strata of society were to participate in the life of the state the first step must be the emancipation of the serfs. Only a small minority of Prussian peasants were free men. The great mass lived in both personal and economic bondage. They were legally bound to the land on which they lived and hence to its owner: they could not move elsewhere, could not marry without their lord's consent, and could not bequeath their land to another. They held their small farms under various kinds of lease, and for rent they were obliged to pay dues and render services. Sometimes the obligations were light, but more often they were heavy. There were even peasants who were compelled to work on their master's land for six days a week with only Sundays and moonlight nights to cultivate their own fields. Custom dictated that the lord should maintain peasant cottages, provide food at times of scarcity, and pay taxes if the peasants defaulted on them, but custom was not invariably obeyed. The state prevented landlords from evicting peasants and absorbing their land, but in all other respects the feudal lord exercized unlimited sway over his domains. His position was buttressed by political power: in rural areas local government, including supervision of police and administration of justice, was carried on by landed noblemen. Men from other classes were normally prevented from buying land and thereby aspiring to the privileges of the nobility. These privileges included freedom from taxation, whose burdens in consequence fell heavily upon the peasants.

The Emancipation Edict of 9 October 1807, produced within a few days of Stein's appointment, abolished personal servitude and declared land a free commodity which any man could purchase regardless of class. The glorious simplicity of these two clauses was marred by ambiguity in the rest of the text. The Edict had been drawn up at speed; moreover two other men, Schroetter and Schön, had worked at the draft before Stein's arrival and had disagreed as to the ends in view. The peasants were freed from such dues and services as were based on personal servitude but no-one knew how many of the obligations based on the tenure of land were to remain in force. The peasants were not given plots of land in freehold but remained leaseholders as before. Did this mean, since land was declared to be a freely marketable commodity, that the landlord could evict his tenants and absorb their holdings? It was conceivable that the peasants might be worse off as freemen than they had been as serfs. Schroetter had been prepared to see this happen, for he believed that the productivity of the land would be increased by the elimination of small peasant holdings. Schön had hoped, rather, that the smallest holdings would be combined to make sizeable peasant farms, and Stein, for moral and political reasons, agreed with Schön's view, but no clauses in the extremely short Edict could be said to embody the idea.

On 14 February 1808 Stein issued a supplementary decree which went a little way towards creating an independent peasant class. The decree said that provincial governments could grant permission for the absorption of peasant leaseholds if the landlord was prepared to let out, on free and hereditary tenures, sizeable plots of land equal in total area to the amount of land he had absorbed. The decree applied only to East Prussia, the only province remaining directly under the king's control. Here it met with bitter resistance from the nobles, but Stein refused to be either bullied or cajoled into making bigger concessions to the landlords. He was equally firm in his dealings with Silesian noblemen, who had long subjected their peasants to the most onerous forms of servitude and who now tried to conceal the Emancipation Edict from them. Noblemen throughout Prussia were instinctively hostile to Stein's measures as an attack on feudal privileges, yet some of them were at the same time glad to see serfdom abolished for they knew it to be a wasteful form of labour. They resolved the paradox by trying to exploit the Emancipation Edict to their own advantage. Stein worked tirelessly to reach an understanding with the nobles and to instruct government officials in the spirit of the Edict, but he achieved only piecemeal success.

To Stein, emancipation of the serfs was merely a first step in the regeneration of Prussia. He pictured local self government in both town and country, an elected assembly in each province, and finally a national assembly working alongside a fully responsible government. His greatest success was in establishing self government in the towns. In the countryside the nobles clung to their administrative powers, and Stein had merely begun to undermine their position by proposing to abolish their rights of justice over their tenants when he was dismissed from office. The only step he was able to take towards the creation of provincial assemblies was the restoration, with a slightly enlarged membership, of the aristocratic Diet of East Prussia. All other provinces lay under French occupation. This blight had its uses, for it enabled Stein to secure the dismissal of all ministers in charge of provinces other than East Prussia and to divide their powers between five functional departments. This was the nearest he got to replacing absolutism with responsible government. A national assembly never materialized.

Stein's dismissal on 24 November 1808 was brought about by Napoleon, who discovered him to be planning a revolt of the people. The great reformer had been opposed all along, however, by large sections of the population. Prussian noblemen suspected him of working towards the creation of a new Germany in which Prussian institutions would be overwhelmed. Civil servants resented his attacks on the old bureaucratic system which gave them their livelihood, and resented too his insistence that the government be moved from Berlin to the remote town of Memel, as far away as possible from French interference. These resentments were shared by the bourgeoisie as a whole, whose outlook was too narrow to allow them to sponsor the kind of reform which had appealed to the English and French middle classes. Intellectual support for the movement was almost totally lacking. Pamphlets and journals for the most part made no mention of the reforms. Görres in his journal the *Rheinische Merkur* and Schleiermacher in his sermons were almost alone in trying to arouse interest in political and social reconstruction among the people of Prussia. Even Hegel had not so much as heard of the reform movement as late as 1809. Under these circumstances it would be false to ascribe too much influence to the lectures delivered by Fichte in Berlin in the winter of 1807-8. In the *Reden an die deutsche Nation* Fichte ascribed the disaster of Jena to indolence and lack of morale on the part of the people. He pointed out the need for a new system of education to transmute subjects into citizens, independent and self-reliant. The lectures did not create the stir which was afterwards attributed to them by nationalist historians. Fichte himself failed to realize the affinity between his own ideas and those of Stein, and he made no attempt to assist the cause of political and social reform. He expressly stated his belief that education was the only field in which the state could usefully act.

Stein was, moreover, hampered by lack of co-operation from reformers whose ideas were different from his own. Since he was obliged to spend many weeks at a time in Berlin negotiating with the French for the payment of indemnities and the withdrawal of occupying armies his rivals found many opportunities for obtaining the king's ear. Hardenberg in particular was able to persuade the king that the summoning of a national assembly would merely call down the wrath of Napoleon upon Prussia. When Stein went into enforced exile there was no-one to carry on with his programme. His immediate successors, Altenstein and Dohna, made laudable efforts to extend the Emancipation Edict to provinces which escaped from French occupation, but they did not understand Stein's larger aims. The educational programme begun by Humboldt in 1809 came nearest to fulfilling Stein's dreams, but the development of a spirit of independence in schools and universities was unlikely, in the absence of any corresponding development in social and political spheres, to lead to anything but the isolation of scholars and teachers from the life around them. Finally Hardenberg, who became Chancellor in June 1810, gave a new twist to the reform movement. His views bore no more than a superficial resemblance to those of Stein, although the latter had long regarded him as an ally.

Baron Hardenberg had entered the Prussian civil service many years before Jena. What he most admired in Prussia was the absolutism which Frederick II had imposed upon the feudalism of former times. He saw that the country needed to find new fervour to withstand the threat from Napoleon, and he believed that just as France had derived vigour from revolution, so Prussia must be given it by a purposeful state. All prejudices and institutions which hampered the progress of the state must be swept away. Individuals and classes must be organized in such a way that they gave their best service to the state, and for this purpose there must be free trade, free transactions in land, and complete freedom of occupation. 'Our objective, our guiding principle must be a revolution in the good sense of the word', he wrote, 'leading directly to the great goal of increasing the dignity of human life by the exercize of wisdom in the government and not through the pressure of violence either from within or without.' Where Stein aimed at self government, Hardenberg aimed at efficient government. Where Stein would have given new meaning to old institutions such as provincial Diets and trade guilds, which he regarded as a part of the nation's personality, Hardenberg wished to sweep them away as irrational. Where Stein hoped to educate the nobles to play a leading part in a reformed Prussia, Hardenberg seemed to wish to abolish aristocracy altogether. Where Stein pictured a national assembly endowed with governing powers, Hardenberg believed that the nation should elect representatives to act merely in an advisory capacity. 'Democratic principles in a monarchical government: this seems to me the mixture appropriate to the present *Zeitgeist*', he wrote. It was the mixture Napoleon had applied to France.

Hardenberg achieved a considerable amount of success in economic spheres. The need to find money for war indemnities enabled him in October 1810 to create a new tax upon all land, and thereby to end the ancient tax exemptions of the nobility. Financial needs also provided him with an opportunity to attack guilds. After imposing a new tax on trade and manufacture, Hardenberg arranged that persons could enter any employment they chose if they paid a fee and produced evidence of sound character. In 1811 guild membership was made voluntary and the privileges formerly bestowed by guilds upon their members were abolished. Corporate direction of trade and industry was thus destroyed and individuals were free to stand or fall in economic affairs. Hardenberg hoped to achieve a similar result in the agricultural sphere. An Edict of 14 September 1811 aimed at producing a free, landowning peasantry by declaring that peasants could buy their release from labour services and buy a clear title to a half of the land they had leased as serfs by surrendering the other half to the landlord. The Edict would doubtless, if carried out, have created a class of peasant farmers whose property was too small to provide a decent livelihood. Fortunately the unsettled conditions of the war years prevented most peasants from taking advantage of the Edict. Meanwhile Hardenberg's proposal was attacked vigorously by the nobles, who had no wish to see their former serfs established as neighbouring landowners.

Hardenberg was attacked by the aristocracy throughout his career. They hated him more than they had hated Stein. Whilst the majority of Prussian noblemen were conservative, wishing to maintain the Frederician system which gave them the highest places in the bureaucracy and army, some were reactionary and aimed at restoring the power of the aristocracy as it had existed in feudal times. The latter found a leader in Ludwig von der Marwitz, whose efforts were mainly responsible for thwarting Hardenberg's liveliest attempt at political reorganization. In 1811 Hardenberg proposed to summon an Assembly of Notables to consider the tax laws of the previous year. He carefully explained that the Assembly would not be an elected body and that it would have no legislative power. The members were to be nominated by the king and their function would be to explain royal policy to the people. In other words the Assembly was designed to strengthen the monarchy. In spite of Hardenberg's attempt to appease the aristocracy by packing the Assembly with nobles, Marwitz led the Brandenburg aristocracy in protesting to the king against the creation of an unconstitutional body. Marwitz claimed that the legitimate representative bodies of the realm were the provincial Estates, whose powers were older than those of the monarchy. Prussia thus experienced during her era of reform an aristocratic resurgence such as had taken place in France, Austria, and Hungary more than twenty years before. Hardenberg soon found that in summoning an Assembly of Notables he had created an obstreperous body, and he dissolved it after a few months.

In opposing Hardenberg, members of the aristocracy were able to present themselves as defenders of native traditions and values against Frenchified innovators. They made common cause with an intellectual group calling itself the *christlich-deutsche Tischgesellschaft*. The leading member of the group, the poet Kleist, was a fanatical German patriot with a romantic attachment to Germany's remote past: in his journal *Berliner Adenblätter* he castigated all departures from German tradition. Arnim, another poet, specialized in collecting German legends and folklore. Adam Müller formulated a theory of conservatism worthy of a place alongside that of Edmund Burke. The state, he argued, is a living organism which cannot be cut off from its roots without endangering its life. Past, present, and future witness a continuous growth, and the past must live in the present and the future. The past life of the state is represented by the nobles, who fill this rôle by virtue of their historic connection with the land. Agriculture is the most continuous and natural element in the life of society, and the aristocracy which perpetuates it fulfils a moral function. Other nations of Europe have cut themselves off from their past: Prussia must not follow the deplorable example of France simply because she lies under the heel of the French conqueror. These arguments lacked conviction in the years when Hardenberg was striving to keep the French conqueror at bay, but they gained ground after Waterloo. By 1819 Hardenberg had been defeated as completely as Stein. Only the aristocratic and military traditions of Prussia remained as an inspiration to the rest of Germany.

The connection between the aristocracy and the army was one of the things the reformers – in this case Scharnhorst, Gneisenau, Clausewitz, and Boyen – had hoped to destroy. They were not entirely successful. Their plans were threefold: to abolish the exclusive right of the aristocracy to officer commissions, to end a system of recruitment for the rank and file which fell entirely upon the peasantry, and to create a type of militia to act as a bond between the army and the civilian population. Stein delegated the military side of his programme to Scharnhorst, who at once proposed to open military careers to the bourgeoisie. In spite of vigorous protests from aristocratic officers such as General Yorck, the king decided in 1808 that commissions were henceforward to be awarded on grounds of ability and bravery. Universal conscription was Scharnhorst's most cherished aim and he laboured until 1812 to achieve it. He was opposed throughout by aristocrats who described his plan as a part of 'the French fraud about freedom and equality', and in the end he failed to win the support of the king. Napoleon had ruled that the Prussian army should be limited to 42,000 men, but he had not stipulated as to how the 42,000 were to be obtained. A decree of universal conscription would have created a reservoir of manpower which could be tapped when Prussia eventually went to war against Napoleon. In the end Scharnhorst adopted the Krümper system whereby men were passed quickly through the army into the reserve. He won great fame by it, but the adoption of the system was to him an acceptance of failure, for it did not abolish exemptions from service and its military effectiveness was doubtful. Without universal conscription the creation of a militia was out of the question. A *Landwehr* came into being almost spontaneously in 1814 as the result of the pressure of war, but the king never liked the idea. Attempts by Scharnhorst's successor Boyen to create a permanent *Landwehr* in the period after Waterloo succumbed to the attacks of the aristocracy.

In rejecting the liberalism of Stein and the egalitarianism of Hardenberg Germany turned her back on the mainstream of European development. Her intellectuals came not only to hate French imperialism, as Stein and Hardenberg had done, but to despise all western values. Theories of the German folk-nation became more and more aggressive. Fichte advanced the thesis that German culture was more primal and fundamental than western civilization and that it was 'unquestionably equivalent to have character and be a German'. The poet Arndt claimed that the German fatherland extended wherever the German tongue was spoken and that the Rhine was Germany's river. A curious individual known as Father Jahn coined the phrase *Deutsches Volkstum* and asserted the racial superiority of the Germans. He believed that German youth should train itself for future domination by means of physical culture, and he held gymnastics classes to the accompaniment of barbaric war songs by Kleist, Körner, and Arnim.

Anti-westernism was to have its effect on the future history of Germany. The posturings of cranks and hysterical poets did not herald a great armed rising against Napoleon, however. Stein could find no support for a people's war on the Spanish pattern in 1808 nor did Germany rally to the side of

Austria in 1809. Prussia alone made noteworthy efforts to throw off the French yoke in 1813, and even in Prussia the bulk of the fighting was done by the professional army. A call for volunteers from the rest of Germany produced negligible results.

CHAPTER XIII

The Fall of the Napoleonic Empire

I. THE CAMPAIGN OF 1813

MANY people in Britain thought that the crossing of the Niemen by the Russians was a sign for Europe to rise against Napoleon. Walter Scott thought he saw 'the old bones of the Continent . . . warm with life again.' In Paris itself the régime seemed to totter when early in December 1812 a quixotic general called Malet succeeded for a short time, after announcing that Napoleon was dead, in proclaiming the Republic. Yet appearances were deceiving. The Malet conspiracy taught Napoleon not that France was about to reject his war policy but that she needed his presence to stir her to renewed war efforts. Even before his carriage drew to a halt at the Tuileries in the late hours of 18 December he was dreaming of a new army. He imagined that the remnants of the Grand Army would amount to 150,000 men; that the 1813 class of recruits would give him 140,000 more; that the National Guard, reconstituted for home defence when the Grand Army set out to invade Russia, could be made to provide 100,000 men for foreign service. The figures were too optimistic. As the early months of 1813 brought darker and darker news from Germany Napoleon schemed more ways of obtaining troops. He called up men who had escaped enlistment in previous years and boys who would become eligible in the following year. He withdrew veterans from Spain, took 3,000 officers from the gendarmerie, and drafted several thousand gunners from the navy into the army. Men shirked the call-up or deserted from the depots; nevertheless Napoleon had raised his fighting force in Germany to 226,000 by the spring.

If Napoleon had been less enamoured of warfare the campaign of 1813 might have been limited by diplomacy. Frederick William of Prussia was pushed into an alliance with the Tsar when General Yorck marched the Prussian army into the Russian camp, but at heart he feared a new war. Metternich, for Austria, would have accepted any terms which restored the *status quo* in Germany, for he was horrified when Stein, who had entered the service of the Tsar, drew up a proclamation calling upon every German to help in liberating the fatherland. Metternich had no desire to see Russia advancing westward or Prussia setting herself up as the champion of Germany, and he deplored appeals to the masses under any circumstances. Napoleon

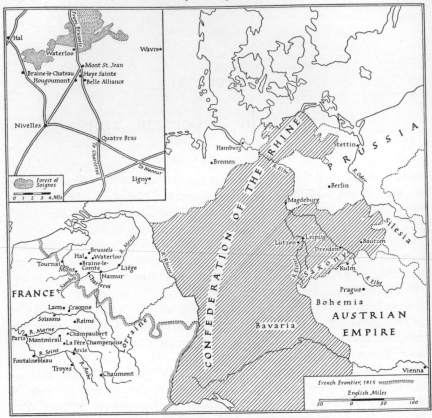

Map IV   The campaigns of 1813-15, with *inset*, the
Neighbourhood of Waterloo

would not abandon his empire in Germany, however. He was convinced
that new military successes were necessary to preserve his dynasty and that
buffer states were needed to preserve the Rhine frontier.

As the Russians and Prussians advanced towards the Elbe Napoleon planned
to sweep northward through Stettin and Danzig and carry war into the
heart of Prussia. By May, however, he knew that he would have to abandon
or at least postpone this plan, for he could not rely on the princes of the
Confederation to support him in the rear. With his army centred upon
Magdeburg he turned south-eastward to Leipzig and Dresden, upon which
allied armies were converging. His forces outnumbered the enemy by three
to two, and in former times he might have secured a speedy victory, but
conditions had changed since Austerlitz. Armies had grown too large and
theatres of war too extended for Napoleon to direct all troop movements
himself, as he insisted upon doing. Moreover he had lost most of his cavalry
horses in Russia and replacements were not easily secured. On 2 May he

forced the allies to retreat after a general engagement at Lützen; the news brought Saxony into the war on the French side and Napoleon gained sufficient confidence to launch a frontal assault on the enemy forces at Bautzen (21 May); but though he again forced a retreat he could not engage in pursuit, for his own losses were heavy and his young recruits could not sustain long marches. On 4 June he accepted an armistice at Pleiswitz.

Napoleon used the armistice to increase his forces in Germany to 470,000, including 40,000 cavalry. He also managed, however, to increase the enmity of Britain and Austria. Castlereagh, like Metternich, held no brief for Russia: he would have accepted terms which guaranteed a balance of power in Europe. It was Napoleon's intransigence which caused Britain to add her subsidies and Austria her armies to the Fourth Coalition. When the campaign reopened in the autumn Bernadotte brought 39,000 Swedes into the fight against his former master.

The allies advanced in three armies of mixed nationality. Napoleon won a brilliant tactical victory against the largest of these armies in the suburbs of Dresden (26-27 August) but his advantage soon evaporated. On the advice of Moreau, who had returned from America to serve the Tsar, the allied leaders decided never to fight against Napoleon if they could help it but only against his lieutenants. Napoleon exhausted his troops in vain attempts to get to grips with the enemy while detachments of his army suffered defeat at many places on a large semi-circular front. At last he heard that the allies were advancing towards Leipzig. As he concentrated his forces for a decisive battle he heard that the Bavarians had gone over to the enemy. The Battle of the Nations opened on 16 October with 200,000 allied troops converging on Napoleon's 160,000 in a city whose antiquated fortifications had been prepared only to withstand local attacks by Cossack raiders. The first day's fighting was indecisive but on 18 October Bernadotte brought his troops into action, the Saxons deserted to the allies, and the French began to retreat from Leipzig. As night fell, indescribable confusion reigned. The French were penned into the city by lack of bridges over the streams which ran alongside the western suburbs. As the shells of the enemy fell among the wounded and dying, and the soldiers still unhurt struggled with women and children to escape from the carnage, Napoleon and the Old Guard crossed safely by the only serviceable bridge over the river Elster. The bridge was then blown prematurely leaving a fifth of the army, with thirty generals and most of the guns and transports, to fall into the hands of the enemy. Napoleon recrossed the Rhine with barely 60,000 men. Twice in twelve months he had lost nearly half a million. Germany was lost, Spain was lost, Fouché abandoned Illyria, Murat prepared to steal Italy, and even the cautious Dutch welcomed Bernadotte's troops. Of all France's great achievement, only the Rhine frontier remained.

2. THE CAMPAIGN OF 1814

When Napoleon re-entered the palace of St. Cloud in November 1813 there was still a good chance for him to treat with the enemy. Britain and Austria were more than ever anxious to put an end to the war so that Russia would have no further excuse for interference in the west. Their vague offer of the natural frontiers in December 1813 was not genuine, but even after fighting had recommenced they were willing to concede the frontiers of 1792. Napoleon could not bring himself to accept. 'He could not forget that he had once dictated to Europe', wrote Caulaincourt. 'He could not bear having an inexorable *sine qua non* written at the foot of every article of a treaty which he had to sign at such a time on such a day.' He preferred to stake everything on a last military throw. On 1 March 1814 the allies signed Castlereagh's treaty of Chaumont agreeing to fight if necessary for twenty years.

Napoleon's hopes of victory were not altogether fantastic. During the bitter cold winter which followed the retreat from Germany desperate measures produced a little more money and a few more troops. All the *octrois* in the country were confiscated and Napoleon's private treasure was at last sacrificed. Taxes were increased and army contractors were paid with bills of credit until the money came in. Boys of the 1815 class were called up along with married men of the 1803-8 classes, and guards used by the prefects to grace civic ceremonies were drafted into garrison duty. By the end of January there were 120,000 French soldiers to use against 300,000 of the allies. They were ill-armed and untrained, but they derived some enthusiasm from the thought that they were defending their future against the repressive forces of old Europe.

The allies advanced in two armies, under Blücher along the Marne and under Schwarzenberg along the Aube. Napoleon's strategy was more brilliant than it had ever been since 1796. His plan was to act against the flank and rear of the enemy, keeping them apart and drawing them back from Paris. The impetuous Blücher, spurred on by the Tsar, pushed his advance corps too far ahead for safety, and with his army strung out in a great arc he suffered 15,000 casualties at Napoleon's hands in the battles of Montmirail and Champaubert (9-14 February). He pressed on to Soissons and would have been caught between two French armies had not General Morreau, commanding at Soissons, lost his nerve and capitulated. The fall of Soissons was described by Thiers as the worst disaster in French history next to Waterloo. It forced Napoleon to fight two costly battles at Craonne and Laon (7 and 9 March) to prevent Blücher from reaching Reims. At this point Napoleon heard that the slower-moving Schwarzenberg was at last advancing on Paris. He turned to make a flank attack while the enemy line was strung out for the march, but the Austrian commander managed to draw in his men, and on the second day of the Battle of Arcis (20-21 March) 27,000 Frenchmen fought against 100,000 men of the allied army. A desperate rearguard action enabled Napoleon and a defeated French force to recross the Aube and disappear under cover of night.

Napoleon's plan now was to withdraw to Lorraine and call the fortress garrisons to his assistance. As he had hoped, Schwarzenberg and Blücher turned to pursue him. They were carrying out the manoeuvre when a Cossack corps captured despatch riders who were on their way from Paris to Napoleon, and the allies learnt of the demoralized state of the capital. Hitherto they had assumed that Paris would defend itself, and they knew that they could not afford to halt outside the city while Napoleon remained at large in their rear. Now they were persuaded by the Tsar that if they marched straight on the capital they would be able to enter it before Napoleon caught up. On 25 March the advance began. On 27 March Napoleon heard what had happened and hurried to the rescue of Paris, but when he arrived at the outskirts he learnt that the city had capitulated a few hours earlier.

Napoleon's excuse all along for fighting another campaign had been that the French people would resent an inglorious peace and that they would rise to defend their homeland. There may have been times when he deluded himself into believing his words to be true, but there were clearly others when he knew that they were false. When advisers spoke to him of reviving the patriotic spirit of 1793 he replied, 'Rouse the nation, when the Revolution has destroyed the nobles and priests, and I myself have destroyed the Revolution?' In December 1813 the Senate appealed to him to make peace. The *Corps législatif* in even stronger terms urged him to curb his ambitions and abandon the empire. Napoleon forbade the publication of the incriminating appeal and prorogued the legislative body, but he could not stifle the opinion of the people. The twenty-three agents whom he sent to the provinces to stir up local patriotism warned him that the nation would not or could not fight. Only from the border provinces of Champagne, Lorraine, Alsace, and Dauphiné and from the coastal regions of Brittany were officials able to report some stirrings of ancient hostility to the foreigner. Elsewhere the people yearned for peace. In Paris the highest officials of the régime lost confidence in the future. Even the schools and colleges ceased to echo eulogies of the Emperor. The bourgeoisie obeyed orders in a carping spirit: the lower classes waited in a state of dull despair to suffer whatever the fortunes of war might bring them. On 25 March the corps of Marmont and Mortier were routed at La Fère-Champenoise and pushed back towards the city. As Joseph Bonaparte tried to improvise the defence of Paris the two marshals drew up their forces for battle at the foot of Montmartre.

When fighting reached the streets of Belleville Marmont carried out Joseph's instructions and negotiated an armistice with the Tsar. On 31 March the allied armies marched into Paris. That same night the allied leaders issued a Declaration refusing to treat with Napoleon and promising to accept a constitution drawn up by the French people.

3. THE BOURBON RESTORATION AND THE FIRST TREATY OF PARIS

The political and moral breakdown of the imperial régime played an important part in the fall of Napoleon but no-one could say that the French had overthrown their Emperor. They had simply allowed him to be defeated. Their spirit of resignation was not a promising foundation on which to build a new political structure. The British government had thought since at least 1800 that the restoration of a Bourbon king would give the best guarantee of peace if the French people would agree to it, but the royalist cause was at a low ebb in France. A secret society calling itself the Knights of the Faith had persuaded the mayor of Bordeaux to declare for Louis XVIII when Wellington's troops entered the town, and this had created enough of a sensation for Castlereagh and Metternich to drink to the health of the Bourbons, but Alexander, advancing upon Paris with Schwarzenberg's army, had not committed himself even to that extent. The Tsar did not like the Bourbon princes, whom he believed were too insensitive and illiberal to rule over post-revolutionary France. He imagined himself placing on the throne a citizen-king, perhaps Bernadotte or Eugène Beauharnais, and earning the undying gratitude of the French people. Once he had entered Paris he became dangerously sympathetic to the 'fallen' Napoleon. On 2 April he told Caulaincourt that he would sponsor a regency for the King of Rome.

In the event it was Talleyrand who took it upon himself to persuade Alexander to accept a Bourbon king. Whatever personal motives Talleyrand may have had for playing a leading part in the creation of the new régime his decision to bring it about as soon as possible served the best interests of France, for Napoleon had merely retired to Fontainebleau and was planning a counter-attack. On 2 April Talleyrand summoned a meeting of available senators and persuaded them to nominate himself and four of his friends to a provisional government. Most of the senators could hope for little from the Bourbons but they were led to think that if they co-operated in effecting a restoration of the monarchy they might secure guarantees for themselves. Accordingly they proclaimed the deposition of Napoleon and agreed that Marshal Marmont, commanding Napoleon's troops on the road to Fontainebleau, should be invited to surrender in order to avoid civil war. Marmont hesitated, but on 6 April the generals of his corps marched their men to the allied headquarters at Versailles. Only then did Alexander agree that Bonapartism was a lost cause. Talleyrand persuaded him that France would never accept a puppet king such as Bernadotte: the restoration of the Bourbons was the only alternative. On the evening of the same day (6 April) the Senate adopted unanimously a constitution which declared, 'The French people freely summon to the throne Louis-Stanislaus-Xavier de France, brother of the last king, and after him the other members of the house of Bourbon in the old order'. It was the first time in history that European powers in concert had sought to eliminate a European menace by presiding over a change of political system.

Tsar Alexander, basking in the rôle of European arbiter, could not envisage further danger. On his own initiative he promised Napoleon the island of Elba in full sovereignty for the rest of his life. Some people thought the promise too generous, others thought that Elba was too near to France to be safe. *The Times* thought that Botany Bay would be too good for the scoundrel; Talleyrand suggested the Azores, Metternich the Atlantic island of St. Helena as a suitable domicile for the incorrigible warmonger. Alexander said he would give Napoleon a home in Russia if he could find nowhere else; Napoleon said he would most of all like to live in England. In the end the allies reluctantly honoured Alexander's promise of Elba in the treaty of Fontainebleau (12 April). They agreed that Napoleon should receive 2 million francs a year from the French government and that he should be allowed to keep a bodyguard of 400 officers and men and the corvette which carried him to Elba. Marie Louise was given the duchy of Parma and members of the Bonaparte family were given pensions. Napoleon at first took no interest in the arrangements. In the early hours of the next morning he tried to commit suicide but the attempt failed and after this he recovered his self-confidence and zest.

Alexander's generosity to his former foes was a thing that Frenchmen wondered at. The young Charles de Rémusat, brought up under the deadening influence of Napoleonic officialdom, decided afterwards that it was the sight of Alexander's gracious countenance as he rode in triumph through the streets of Paris which first kindled in his heart the love of freedom. Alexander had promised before entering Paris that the allies would respect the boundaries of France as they had existed under her kings. 'They may even do more, for they profess always the same belief, that it is necessary for the well-being of Europe that France should be great and strong.' These words aroused in some quarters the hope that France might be allowed to keep the natural frontiers formed by the Rhine and the Alps, or at least that she might be allowed to keep Belgium; but Talleyrand, negotiating peace between France and the allies, found Castlereagh inflexible. The First Treaty of Paris signed by France and the four Great Powers on 30 May 1814 allowed for a few minor frontier rectifications to the north-east, the retention of a part of Savoy, and the recognition, in spite of protests from the Pope, of the annexation of Avignon and the Comtat-Venaissin. Britain restored to France the colonies she had taken from her during the war, except for St. Lucia and Tobago in the West Indies and the Île de France in the Indian Ocean; Sweden restored Guadeloupe and Portugal French Guiana. France restored to Spain her former territories in St. Domingo and received Britain's permission to try and re-establish French authority over the negro rebels in the rest of the island. The allies undertook to withdraw their troops from France and to forego any claims to war indemnities. Six 'separate and secret' articles provided that the débris of Napoleon's empire in Europe should be sorted out by an international congress according to general lines agreed upon by the Great Powers.

The First Treaty of Paris was a more generous settlement than any which Napoleon had bestowed upon countries unfortunate enough to lose in battle. Nevertheless the French were not disposed to accept it gratefully. They had already begun to lay the blame for wanton aggression upon Napoleon and to expect Europe to pay tribute to the inherent greatness of a revolutionary nation. Talleyrand saw with his usual perspicacity that a great deal of tact, and perhaps a little hypocrisy, would be needed to help the French people to adjust themselves to the position of a second-rate power. He pretended that the opening of the Rhine to international shipping was adequate compensation for the loss of Belgium. He suggested that France's experience of freedom and responsibility would win influence and respect for her in Europe. The allotting of territories once dominated by Napoleon soon stimulated jealousy and rivalry between the Great Powers. France might once again figure as the protector of weak and oppressed nations and as an essential member of a western bloc allied against the menacing power of Russia. Talleyrand had begun to practise the rôle at the Congress of Vienna when the escape of Napoleon from Elba altered the entire scene.

4. THE HUNDRED DAYS AND WATERLOO

Napoleon landed on the south coast of France, between Fréjus and Antibes, at three o'clock in the afternoon of 1 March 1815, with less than a thousand armed men. Only ten months before he had journeyed through France to take ship from the same spot in fear of his life, disguised in clothes borrowed from his alien captors. Now he promised his 'handful of braves' that 'he would be in Paris without firing a shot'. He cannot have believed that things had changed so drastically in ten months. Indeed it was because he knew that they had not changed that he decided to avoid ultra-royalist Provence and take the mountain road to Grenoble. He knew that Louis XVIII and his ministers had made a number of false moves. They had insisted on levying all the former taxes and on maintaining the hated *droits réunis*, although the Comte d'Artois, who entered France before Louis, had specifically promised that the latter would be abolished. In the interests of economy they had cut down salaries and pensions and deprived 15,000 bourgeois Frenchmen of jobs in the civil service. They had failed to prevent émigrés from staking awkward claims to their former land. They had held elaborate services for Louis XVI and Marie Antoinette, calling upon the nation to expiate the guilt of regicide. They had axed 300,000 men from the army and placed 11,000 officers on half-pay, at the same time reinstating émigré officers who had never seen service on any battlefield. They had humiliated the former Imperial Guard and recreated the Household Guard, giving high rank, fine uniforms, and generous pay to 6,000 court favourites at a cost of 20 million francs a year. Most insensitive move of all, they had abolished the tricolour and imposed on France the white flag of the Bourbons, the flag of counter-revolution and foreign invasion. These mistakes were not sufficient in themselves to shake the foundations of the Bourbon régime, but they had raised a flicker of life in feelings which had lain dormant, giving Napoleon the chance to appeal once more to the self-centredness of the bourgeoisie, the prejudices of the peasantry, the pride of the army, and the bravado of a revolutionary nation. Rather than work for a solid and sober future under the unlovable Bourbons the French people sacrificed themselves once more to 'the streak of divine folly' in their favourite son.

The march from Fréjus to Paris gave Napoleon the most dazzling personal triumph of his career. At a critical moment before Grenoble, where the garrison was commanded by a determined royalist, Napoleon advanced alone towards an infantry battalion which blocked the road, inviting the soldiers to kill him if they wished: ignoring all commands to fire, the men swarmed round him with shouts of '*Vive l'Empereur!*' From Grenoble the march became almost a triumphal procession. The Comte d'Artois was obliged to flee from Lyon as Napoleon approached. Marshal Ney, commanding the army in Franche-Comté, defected to Napoleon when he received an emotional appeal from his old master. Louis XVIII quietly and unhurriedly left the Tuileries accompanied by a few horsemen. He presented himself first at Lille, but the garrison there proving hostile he crossed the frontier to his second exile at Ghent. Napoleon was carried up the steps of the Tuileries by a wildly cheering crowd on the evening of 20 March, not twenty-four hours after the old king had left it.

Napoleon was under no illusions about the nature of his position. An upsurge of emotion had carried him to the Tuileries but it would not keep him there. In former years Napoleon's authority, however burdensome, had seemed irreplaceable, but by 1815 France had sampled an alternative régime. Support from the French people would depend, as it had done during the Consulate, on Napoleon's ability to embody and guarantee the traditions of the Revolution. These traditions were now believed to include representative government, and Napoleon felt obliged to court the favour of the middle classes by convoking the electoral colleges and employing the clever but volatile Benjamin Constant to draw up a constitution to rival the one recently applied by Louis XVIII. The electoral colleges were the unrepresentative bodies of 1802, and the constitution, nicknamed the *Benjamine*, received a lukewarm response when submitted to a plebiscite. Napoleon described the *Benjamine* as an 'Additional Act to the Constitutions of the Empire' and pretended that representative government was the logical outcome of the imperial régime, but this fiction hoodwinked nobody. It was of a piece with other humiliating shams – the fulsome addresses of loyalty sent in by officials who had despatched similar testimonials to Louis XVIII less than twelve months before, the artificial display of patriotism at the Champ de Mars when dignitaries who had twice in a single year forsworn their loyalty to their sovereign took an oath to the new constitution. Few could believe that Napoleon would long confine himself to the rôle of constitutional monarch. When the Chambers met in June their criticisms were rudely brushed aside by the Emperor, who was wholly engaged in preparing once more for war. Throughout the Hundred Days which sufficed to bring about Napoleon's second abdication there was a crippling sensation of impermanence and unreality. Fouché, once again Minister of Police, calculated that the régime would last just long enough for an experienced intriguer to make himself indispensable to all parties. Carnot apparently believed that there was a chance of consolidating the gains of the Revolution, for he emerged from retirement to become Minister of the Interior, but even sincerity could do little against mounting odds. The allied leaders meeting at Vienna refused to be placated by the woolly statements in which Napoleon purported to have abandoned aggressive designs. They needed only a few days to patch up the quarrels which Napoleon had thought would immobilize them, and to take the unprecedented step of declaring their former foe 'outside the pale of civil and social relations'. After this they reconstituted the Grand Alliance and prepared to defeat Napoleon all over again.

5. THE WATERLOO CAMPAIGN AND THE SECOND TREATY OF PARIS

In France the preparations for war were carried out against a background of disloyalty among imperial officials and resentment among large sections of the population. Taxation, conscription, and the threat of invasion by overwhelming enemy forces showed once and for all that Napoleon could not give French peasants and bourgeoisie the one thing that they insisted on having, secure possession of their land and jobs. Napoleon made no attempt to arouse popular fervour: there were sufficient resources left over from a decade of imperial warfare to fight one more campaign. By the end of April he could put 123,000 troops into the field.

The allies had nearly 800,000 men under arms, but only a mixed force of 93,000 Belgian, Dutch, Hanoverian and British troops under Wellington and a Prussian army of 117,000 under Blücher were near enough for immediate action. All the allies assumed that Napoleon would fight a defensive campaign as he had done in 1814. Wellington said later that lack of patience drove Napoleon to take the offensive, but other factors were more decisive. Napoleon had to show the French people that he could beat off the enemy, and his best chance of doing this was to separate Wellington and Blücher and defeat them in detail before the Austrians and Russians could come up. He left the most skilful of his marshals, Davout, with orders to defend Paris if the offensive move should fail, but Davout himself protested, 'Sire, if you are the victor, Paris will be yours, and if you are beaten, neither I nor anyone else can do anything for you'.

In 1815 Napoleon and Wellington fought against each other for the first time. Napoleon's strategy was as brilliant as ever whereas Wellington was clearly out of touch with the situation until two days before Waterloo. The subsequent defeat of Napoleon led to the conclusion that the greater of the two commanders went down before the lesser and that genius was finally eclipsed by commonsense. Napoleon blamed his defeat on his subordinates, second-rate men forced on him by circumstances. As chief-of-staff there was Soult, who could not send a comprehensible order; on the right-wing there was Grouchy, skilled as a calvary officer but totally inexperienced in independent command; on the left-wing there was Ney, brave but so thickheaded that according to Napoleon he was no more able to grasp a general design than 'the last-joined drummer boy'. Wellington was no better served, however. He described his polyglot army with its large numbers of raw recruits as 'the worst equipped army, with the worst staff, ever brought together'. In the Battle of Waterloo Wellington's tactical skill, his courage, and the discipline which he imposed upon the lines were worthy of greater admiration than Napoleon gave them.

When Napoleon left Paris on 12 June the two allied armies in Belgium were spread out in lines which converged towards the French frontier but did not quite meet. Blücher's Prussians stretched along the banks of the Meuse and Sambre from Liége through Namur to Charleroi; Wellington's force was strung out from Brussels through Braine-le-Comte to Mons. Napoleon's plan was to prise them apart from the point between Charleroi and Mons where they almost met. Behind this point a high-road ran from Namur to Braine-le-Comte. The road was intercepted at three places, Nivelles, Quatre-Bras, and Ligny, by other roads running north-east, any one of which Napoleon might take in advancing towards Brussels. By 15 June the allies were aware that they would need to defend themselves somewhere along the Namur–Braine-le-Comte high-road but they were still unaware at which of the three cross-roads the attack would come. Wellington seemed to favour Nivelles, and took up a curved position from Brussels accordingly. It was not until midnight on the 15th that Wellington, who was attending the Duchess of Richmond's ball in Brussels, learnt that he would have to defend himself at Quatre-Bras on the following day while Blücher took a stand at Ligny. The order to concentrate forward was carried out in extreme confusion in the early hours of the 16th, many of the officers still in ball dress and some having no idea what was happening.

In the battles fought at the two cross-roads Napoleon assumed that if he could force the enemy to retreat they would fall back on their bases, Blücher towards Liége and Wellington towards Brussels. They would then be far enough apart for him to ignore the one while he crushed the other. His success in the two battles was remarkable and might have been greater but for a series of errors and mischances. Napoleon saw at once that the major effort must take place at Ligny, where two-thirds of the Prussian army faced him. Commanding the French forces himself he launched so vigorous an assault that Blücher's centre was completely shattered and his right-wing severed from his left. If any part of Ney's army, repeatedly summoned from Quatre-Bras, had been in the rear, the Prussians would have been annihilated as they retreated from Ligny. Unfortunately Ney so grossly mishandled the battle at Quatre-Bras that he was unable to obey Napoleon's orders. He managed to hold Wellington's forces in check, however, and both sides resumed at night the position they had held at the beginning of the day.

News of the Prussian retreat reached Wellington early the following morning and convinced him that he must retire from Quatre-Bras before he was attacked by combined French armies. If Ney had fallen on him at once and pinned him down until Napoleon arrived nothing could have saved him. Ney made no move during the morning, however, and Wellington began his retreat unmolested. Napoleon arrived at Quatre-Bras at 1 p.m. and furiously ordered the pursuit of the enemy, but a torrential storm prevented the French army from cutting across country and allowed Wellington to take up a new position at Mont St. Jean as the sun set. Before leaving Quatre-Bras he had sent a message to Blücher to say that he would stand at Mont St. Jean and give battle to the French if he could be sure of help from one Prussian corps. The reply came at dawn on the 18th: not one Prussian corps, but two would march to his assistance. To the north of him, on the main road to Brussels, lay the village of Waterloo.

The position of the Prussians turned out to be an important factor in the Battle of Waterloo, but opinion has differed as to whether it was decisive. After Ligny Napoleon was so sure that he had finished with the Prussians that he sent Grouchy to pursue them towards Liége. In fact they were not retreating on Liége but on Wavre, whence they could keep in touch with their allies. Grouchy's 33,000 men never arrived at Waterloo in time to take part in the battle. Their loss to Napoleon was partly offset, however, by the loss of Prince Frederick of the Netherland's 17,000 men to Wellington. The latter was so afraid of being turned by way of the Tournia-Brussels road that he left this strong detachment, a fifth of his total force, out of reach during the whole day at Hal. The numbers engaged when the Battle of Waterloo commenced were thus 68,000 on Wellington's side and 72,000 on Napoleon's. The French were greatly superior in cavalry and artillery. The Prussians moved with incredible slowness along the ten-mile road from Wavre to Waterloo. The French attack on Wellington's centre had been in progress for two hours before Napoleon needed to divert 10,000 men to hold off the first corps, and even then there were still fourteen battalions of the Guard in reserve for the grand assault. These had been beaten off by British troops before the second Prussian corps under Ziethen arrived.

The battlefield of Waterloo was very small even by the standard of the times. Thousands of men fought hand to hand for six or seven hours on a front which was restricted for most of the time to 1,000 yards and sometimes to less. 'Never', said Wellington, 'did I see such a pounding match.' From north to south the battlefield was cut in two by the Brussels-Charleroi road. From east to west, three quarters of a mile south of the village of Mont St. Jean, a road from Wavre to Braine-le Château ran along a low ridge. Wellington's line stretched for about a mile and a half along this road but the bulk of his forces were placed on the rear slope of the ridge so that they would be protected by the ground from the enemy's guns. In front of their centre lay the farm of La Haye Sainte and a large sandpit: in front of their right flank rose the château of Hougoumont surrounded by orchards and gardens. Half a mile south the French were drawn up on the parallel ridge of La Belle Alliance. Napoleon believed that Wellington had blundered in taking up a position in front of heavily wooded ground which would break up his army if the line retreated. Consequently he decided to waste no time in manoeuvring against the flanks but to batter at the enemy centre with massed columns. Some of his lieutenants who had fought against Wellington in Spain reminded him of the tremendous fire-power which the British derived from their ability to remain in line as enemy columns advanced towards them, but all he would say was, 'I tell you that Wellington is a bad general, that the English are bad troops, and it will be a picnic'.

Napoleon opened the battle with the usual cannonade and with a demonstration against Hougoumont calculated to draw in the enemy lines. The cannonade did little damage to the sheltered allied army, and at Hougoumont Jérome Bonaparte foolishly engaged in an all-out attempt to take the château, drawing in the French lines and wasting many lives. At half past one d'Erlon's infantry advanced against Wellington's centre in heavy columns. When they approached the top of the ridge the enemy rose from behind it and delivered a crushing volley on their heads, and Uxbridge's cavalry swept the disordered columns pell-mell down the slope. This initial triumph for Wellington turned to bitterness, however. The cavalrymen failed to check their horses when Uxbridge sounded the retreat, and two English brigades thundered across the narrow valley at full speed into the teeth of the French battery.

At 3.30 p.m. Napoleon ordered Ney to occupy La Haye Sainte as a base from which to launch a grand assault on the enemy centre. Ney had so much difficulty in detaching men from Hougoumont that he could send only two divisions to attack the farm and they failed to take it; nevertheless he was so carried away by excitement that he launched 5,000 cavalry upon Wellington's unbroken infantry squares. When Napoleon saw what was happening he ordered Kellermann to support Ney rather than demoralize the whole army by ordering a retreat. The sacrifice of Kellermann not only deprived the Emperor of his last cavalry reserve but so crammed the field with horses that manoeuvre was impossible. Some 12,000 horsemen attacked on a front of 500 yards between Hougoumont and La Haye Sainte, unsupported by infantry. Assault after assault was driven off, though with severe strain to the allied line. At 6 p.m. Napoleon ordered Ney to take La Haye Sainte at all costs. He succeeded when Baring's detachment, which had defended the farm all day, ran out of ammunition. Ney was then able to set up a battery within 300 yards of the allied position and gain a footing on the Wavre road, in the very centre of Wellington's line. Wellington's personal courage at this critical point prevented immediate panic, but if Napoleon had sent Ney only a half of the forces he still had in hand the victory might have gone to the French. Napoleon failed to recognize the decisive moment, however; the reserves were used to drive back the Prussians on the right flank; and by the time Napoleon mounted the final assault Wellington had patched up the breach in his lines.

The assault began as the sun was going down. The grenadiers of the Old Guard advanced in close column diagonally across the slope between Hougoumont and La Haye Sainte towards the enemy's right centre. They halted for a fatal moment as Maitland's Guards sprang up from behind the crest to meet them and were mown down by terrible fire. The chasseurs of the Middle Guard attacked only ten minutes later and were faring better when they were dispersed by the Light Brigade in a courageous counter-attack. Meanwhile Ziethen's corps had at last arrived from Wavre. Riding forward to the top of the ridge Wellington waved his hat in the air and 40,000 men poured down the slope. Among many eyewitness accounts that of Colonel Frazer strikes a typical note of confusion and exhilaration: 'I have seen nothing like that moment, the sky literally darkened with smoke, . . . the indescribable shouts of thousands, where it was impossible to distinguish between friend and foe. Every man's arm seemed to be raised against that of every other. Suddenly, after the mingled mass has ebbed and flowed, the enemy began to yield; and cheerings and English huzzas announced that the day must be ours.'

Casualties were heavy on both sides: the battlefield was said to be piled with bodies like a breach taken by assault. Wellington lost at least 15,000 men, Blücher 7,000, and Napoleon 25,000. Wellington afterwards admitted that he had never been so near to defeat: it was 'a damned nice thing', he told Creevey the next day, 'the nearest run thing you ever saw in your life'. He must have known, however, that defeat, for the allies, would not have been decisive. Within weeks their armies would have invaded France and the work of 1814 would have been repeated. For Napoleon the case was otherwise. True, he would not admit the finality of defeat. On the very next day after the battle he was telling Joseph that all was not lost; that there would be 150,000 men when he reassembled his forces; that the National Guard would provide 100,000; that he would 'organize a mass levy in Dauphiné, in the Lyon district, in Burgundy, Lorraine, Champagne, and overwhelm the foe'. When he arrived in Paris he described his plans so eloquently to the Council of State that Fouché confessed himself afraid that the wars were going to start all over again. Napoleon's career had already cost France nearly 900,000 lives, a half of them the lives of young men in their twenties: the nation wanted no more war. Someone in authority needed the nerve to say so, however. Fouché put the necessary nerve into the elected representatives of the nation by warning them that Napoleon was about to set up a dictatorship to produce another army. The deputies declared both Chambers in permanent session and demanded the abdication of the Emperor. Napoleon could only have evaded the demand by raising civil war; he had always hated the idea of leading a rabble and there was no certainty that an attempt would succeed; on 22 June he abdicated for the second time in favour of his son. The Chambers ignored the proposal to set up a regency for the King of Rome. Blücher was advancing furiously upon Paris, refusing even an armistice until Napoleon left Malmaison. Fouché with half promises persuaded Napoleon to withdraw to Rochefort; on 4 July Paris surrendered to the Prussians; on the 8th the Bourbon king re-entered his capital.

The terms of the Second Treaty of Paris were harsher than the first. France was reduced to the frontiers of 1789, with the additional loss of a few small areas on the borders of the Netherlands, Germany, and Italy for strategic reasons. The departments of the north and east were to be occupied by 150,000 allied troops for a period of three to five years, the cost of the occupation (150 million francs a year) being charged to France. An indemnity of 700 million francs was also imposed, and the royal government was told both to pay the debts which Napoleon had contracted with individuals in other countries and to return the works of art stolen from foreign cities.

Napoleon imagined that he was going to be able to retire unmolested to America, but after waiting for several days at Rochefort for a safe conduct which never arrived he surrendered himself to the captain of a British ship, the *Bellerophon*. Again he imagined that he might be allowed to live as a country gentleman in England, but the British government, with the approval of the allies, shipped him off to the island of St. Helena. There he lived for nearly six years, a prisoner, and died on 5 May 1821. He was fifty-one years old. On St. Helena Napoleon repeatedly complained that his conditions were intolerable, but in fact he lived in reasonable comfort, the officious behaviour of the governor, Sir Hudson Lowe, being his only real cause of complaint. His friends asserted that the tropical climate of the island was injurious to health, but there is no reason to suppose that Napoleon suffered from it or that it hastened his death. His was not the temperament to show resilience in captivity, and if anything hastened the progress of the disease which killed him it was most likely the lack of any further will to live.

As a prisoner Napoleon thought mainly of his past career and of the use which might be made of it by some future restorer of the Bonaparte dynasty. He saw that nationalism and liberalism were the forces of the new age, and he pretended that he had fostered the one and cherished the hope of the other. 'If I had won in 1812 my constitutional reign would have begun.' This 'legend', transmitted to posterity in Napoleon's writings and recorded conversations, had little or no effect on the future generations to whom it was addressed. It is doubtful whether anybody ever believed it. But neither France nor Europe forgot Napoleon. Generation after generation of young men admired his audacity and his wondrous successes. Frenchmen remained proud of a man whom all Europe had feared, and during times of hardship, disillusionment, humiliation, and despair there grew up another legend of a man of the people who had never accepted fate but had fought and shaped destiny with his own hands. The effect of this legend cannot be calculated in definite political terms, but it was probably more important than the roads and bridges, the street lighting and vaccination, the bureaucracy and police, and all the other concrete steps which Napoleon took towards the modern world.

CHAPTER XIV

European Management, 1815-25

I. TREATIES AND ALLIANCES

IN 1815 four powers claimed to have rescued Europe from the tyranny of Napoleon, but the claims of two of them were scarcely valid. Austria had never been able to bear the brunt of war, and Prussia had not played an effective part in anti-French coalitions until 1813. Napoleon had in truth been defeated by Britain and Russia. Moreover neither Austria nor Prussia were Great Powers (a term just coming into use) except by courtesy, for Austria's vulnerability was chronic and notorious, while Prussia's assets depended very much on the gains she was able to make from the peace settlement. Britain, on the other hand, had emerged from the Napoleonic wars the greatest economic power in the world, and Russia as the most renowned military power. Neither Britain nor Russia occupied a central position in Europe; neither had ever done more than intervene at moments of crisis in European affairs. Both had grown up different in many ways from countries which lay nearer to the heart of Europe, and both possessed major interests in a wider world. Neither of them, moreover, looked back upon the old European order with enthusiasm. Englishmen, while fighting to defend their interests and at times their homeland from the threat of Napoleonic domination, had deluded themselves into thinking that they were fighting to rid Europe of a terrible tyrant. The politically minded classes which read the newspapers and voted at elections had despised the petty despots of old Europe, mocked at their feeble resistance to Napoleon, attributed England's tenacity to her superior political system, and adopted a patronizing attitude towards popular efforts in Spain and Prussia. They would lose face if, after all, their statesmen merely restored the old régime. In Russia the landowners and peasants, while fighting to defend their traditional way of life, had given a new spirit of exaltation to the nation. The Tsar had come to believe that he was destined to regenerate the peoples of Europe. His reading of politico-religious writers such as Novalis and Franz von Baader, and above all his friendship with the religious revivalist Madame de Krüdener, had helped to convince him that a new faith in Christ must lead men to produce a new form of society, a new political structure, and a new concept of peace.

Yet in political terms at least the old order was restored to Europe, with only a few inescapable modifications. The responsibility for this must rest with British statesmen who in the event cared more for Britain's interests than for public sentiment or for duty towards Europe. Castlereagh and Wellington were aware that Britain had experienced great difficulty in defeating Napoleon and that she could not hope to carry out a policy entailing constant interference on the continent. The landed gentry who dominated the House of Commons would not welcome expensive commitments in foreign affairs. Industrial and commercial groups were only moderately interested in European countries as a market for textiles and industrial machinery. They were more interested in building up connections overseas where rivals were negligible and Britain's naval supremacy could be used to advantage. With India not yet totally subdued, Australasia largely unexplored, and Africa unexploited save for coastal belts, vast opportunities were available to an enterprising nation. The English public as a whole did not care about colonial expansion, but Castlereagh was not the man to be influenced by public opinion. His policy at the Congress of Vienna was to reject any spurious political triumphs in Europe, make a few additions to Britain's overseas possessions, and keep a free hand for the future.

This last resolve entailed a modicum of regard for the fate of Europe, in a negative way. Britain must not allow one power ever again to aspire to hegemony lest that power should plunge Europe into war, close European markets, build a navy, and embark on overseas ventures. Among the members of the European community in 1815 there seemed to be two powers with dangerous tendencies: France, and, significantly, Russia herself. No-one could be sure that the restored Bourbons would curb France's revolutionary traditions abroad; and as for Russia, Castlereagh had become personally acquainted in 1814 with Alexander's desire to superintend the affairs of western Europe. He was more irritated than alarmed by a meddlesome attitude which seemed remote from Russia's real interests, but from 1815 onwards he was aware that the Tsar's newly-won confidence might lead him to interfere also in the affairs of eastern Europe where valuable prizes were to be gained. The decrepitude of the Turkish empire presented Russia with an obvious opportunity for pursuing a policy of expansion, territorially or morally, in the Balkans.

Castlereagh devised a number of ways and means for hemming in France and Russia, but the most important was his willingness to allow Austria to assume a dominant position on the continent. He knew that Austria's very existence depended on her ability to prevent the territorial expansion of France and Russia and also to combat the nationalist ideas which they were believed to favour. The Prince Regent described himself as 'an Austrian, body and soul'. Unfortunately Austria was wedded not only to containing

France and Russia but to maintaining the *ancien régime* politically and socially in all areas where her influence could penetrate. Metternich, created chancellor of Austria in 1815, believed that to maintain the Habsburg dynasty he must extinguish every ember of revolution throughout Europe.

The Congress into whose hands had been assigned the fate of territories rescued from Napoleon met at Vienna in September 1814 and produced a settlement in June 1815. It was not technically a peace conference, for peace between France and her victors had been made by the Treaty of Paris. It was, rather, a conference for the settlement of general European issues, and as France was once more supposed to be a respectable European power her representative, Talleyrand, was admitted to discussions. His intervention was important in the tricky affair of Poland and Saxony, but otherwise results depended on the attitude of Russia, Austria, Britain, and Prussia. A multitude of smaller states sent representatives, but plenary sessions merely registered decisions which the Great Powers had arrived at by private negotiation. Metternich, who acted as host to the Congress, claimed that business was despatched more quickly by this method than could ever have been the case if formalities had been observed. He neglected to point out that the method lent itself to secrecy and intrigue which formed his own natural element. While arranging lavish entertainments and adopting an air of insouciance Metternich organized an elaborate system of spies and secret agents to sow suspicion and discord among the more important delegates. There is no reason to suppose that he gained more for Austria in this way than he would have obtained by open discussion, but it was the way he liked to work. Among the precepts on which he prided himself were those of never trusting to luck and never relying on the goodwill of others.

The Congress agreed to restore the old rulers wherever it was feasible to do so. The restoration of the Bourbons to the throne of France seemed to be the best way of obtaining peace in that quarter: by analogy the same device might be valuable elsewhere. So the Bourbon Ferdinand VII was established on the throne of Spain while a third branch of the Bourbon family returned to the throne of Naples. The duchies of Modena, Tuscany, and Parma were given once more to Austrian rulers, and Piedmont to the princely House of Savoy. For want of a theoretical basis for these restorations now that divine right was discredited and benevolent despotism suspected the Congress gave a half-hearted approval to the doctrine of legitimacy, invented by Talleyrand to express the advantages of the Bourbon restoration in France. The people, it was said, needed an object of loyalty to stabilize their affections after years of upheaval, and none would satisfy them so well as the ruler who could claim legal possession. As a doctrine legitimacy was a poor thing to set beside sovereignty of the people. The Congress itself ignored legitimacy when it wished to honour an older conception, that of the right of the victorious to the spoils of the vanquished. Bernadotte wanted a reward for entering the coalition against Napoleon and for resigning Finland to Russia. Sweden was therefore allowed to take Norway from Denmark, which had remained on Napoleon's side too long. In Germany the land could hardly have been divided once more into several hundred small lots in order to restore all the princelings, so Napoleon's state boundaries were for the most part retained and thirty-nine German princes were established on their thrones.

Castlereagh did not place much faith in legitimacy as a means of confining France within her frontiers. He preferred to create barrier states by strengthening a chain of small neighbours. Belgium was not restored to the Habsburgs, who preferred to compensate themselves with Venetia, but was added, with Liége and the Duchy of Limburg, to Holland to form a Kingdom of the Netherlands. Luxembourg, though enjoying the status of independence, was united with the crown of the Netherlands and given a Prussian garrison. The Rhineland was handed over to Prussia, who alone in Germany could be thought to have the military power to defend it. Bavaria and Baden received land on the French frontier; Switzerland was enlarged and neutralized; and Genoa and a part of Savoy were added to Sardinia. Behind this 'arc of containment' three of the Great Powers were placed in positions of strategic significance. Britain could strengthen the line in the north through her old association with Hanover, whose territories were enlarged so that she controlled the lower Ems as well as the lower Weser and Elbe. Prussia's new western territories were of such a shape that she could back up the Netherlands as well as gain direct entry into France. Austria through her acquisitions in north Italy could support Sardinia from Lombardy and threaten the French island of Corsica from Tuscany.

The trickiest feature of the whole settlement was the position of Prussia. Frederick William had played a part in the last campaigns against Napoleon and could claim his reward. His ambition was to obtain, in addition to the Rhineland, the lion's share of Saxony, whose northern and eastern regions possessed not only some of the richest agricultural land in Germany but some of the most advanced industrial centres in Europe. Metternich and Castlereagh were anxious to make use of Prussia's military potentialities but they were not happy about the political condition of the country. Metternich dreaded the prospect of the Prussian king establishing a representative assembly, and Castlereagh complained to the British ambassador of the prevalence of revolutionary ideas. More suspicious still, Prussia had been adopted by Alexander I, who had signed a treaty with Frederick William at Kalisch in 1813. The Tsar duly produced the kind of suggestion the other two leaders had feared: that Napoleon's Grand Duchy of Warsaw should form a Kingdom of Poland ruled by the Tsar as a constitutional monarch, while Prussia received compensation at the expense of the King of Saxony. The opposition of Castlereagh and Metternich to this scheme was encouraged by Talleyrand, who had no desire to see Prussia enlarged at the expense of France's possible ally Saxony, and who saw at once the chance of driving a wedge between the Great Powers. On 2 January Castlereagh agreed to a proposal by Talleyrand that Britain, France, and Austria should form a secret alliance, pledging themselves to provide 150,000 men each for war should Russia and Prussia persist in their plans. The existence of the secret treaty soon became known to the Tsar, who backed down, for he did not wish to fight. Talleyrand's manoeuvre merely resulted, therefore, in the rapid solution of a problem which might otherwise have estranged the Powers for a long time. Poland was divided more elaborately than ever. Russia kept her former share; Austria recovered most of Galicia; Cracow was made into a tiny free state; Prussia recovered Posen, Thorn, and Danzig; and only the remaining portion of the Grand Duchy of Warsaw became Alexander's Kingdom of Poland. The greater part of Saxony was absorbed by Prussia, the southern portion only remaining under the king who had been too loyal to Napoleon.

Alexander's behaviour over the Polish affair illustrated the rights and wrongs of his entire position at the Congress of Vienna. That he was sincere and generous in his intentions over Poland, as over the rest of Europe, there can be little doubt. He imagined that if the large area covered by the Grand Duchy of Warsaw became a Polish kingdom under his protection it might expand to absorb even Lithuania, which Russia had ruled as an integral part of her empire ever since the Partitions, and acquire real meaning for the Poles. Castlereagh and Metternich were wrong in suspecting Alexander of sinister designs, but they were probably right in doubting whether his fair promises would ever be carried out. The majority of Russian statesmen disliked the idea of the Tsar acting as foster-father to a Polish nation and they had no desire to let go of the 'western lands'. Alexander's ideals did not always triumph over realities, nor was his word binding on his successors. The constitution which he gave to the Kingdom of Poland was designed more to placate the landowners than to benefit the peasants, and even this was soon withdrawn. Western statesmen could claim that their suspicions were vindicated; yet a larger kingdom might have fared better. 'Congress Poland' satisfied neither the Tsar nor the Poles from the beginning. Alexander needed encouragement and support if he was to do his best and he did not get these things either from the Congress or from Polish leaders.

The treatment of Poland at the Congress of Vienna was bitterly criticized by a later generation which regarded nationalism as an imperative right of mankind. It is fairer to remember that Polish nationalism was virtually confined to the lesser *szlachta*, for the magnates were willing to co-operate with the Partitioning Powers in order to safeguard the old social system, and the peasants were either aloof or hostile. A Polish state based on such flimsy foundations could not have been relied upon to maintain its independence. The treatment of Norway and Belgium was also criticized by devotees of nationalism, often again without regard to the circumstances of 1815. The wishes of the people of Norway were not taken into consideration when the Great Powers decided to transfer their country from Denmark to Sweden, but Norway was given its own government, parliament, army, and navy, and these institutions stimulated national feeling in a country which had not been a separate kingdom since 1397. Belgium received more anxious attention because of its proximity to France. The Belgians had asserted their independence in 1790, but memories of the experiment were not such as to encourage statesmen at Vienna to repeat it. The Belgians had shown no real will to resist the French. Belgian troops fighting under Wellington in the Waterloo campaign had not proved very satisfactory allies. Taken all in all there was little to suggest that Belgium in 1815 could be made into an independent state strong enough to withstand French aggression. By 1830 the situation had changed in many ways: the brief life of the Kingdom of the Netherlands was not in itself a condemnation of the work of the Congress of Vienna.

The Congress in its dealings with Italy and Germany was later accused of sacrificing national feeling to the political expediency of enlarging Austria. The gift of Lombardy-Venetia to Austria, which exposed the whole peninsula to the baleful influence of the Habsburgs, certainly came to be resented in Italy, but it is doubtful whether more than a small minority of the Italian people, composed mainly of army officers, wished in 1815 for the creation of an Italian national state. As for Germany, members of the Congress readily made some concessions to national feeling in order to prevent a head-on collision between Austria and Prussia. The thirty-nine states were bound into a Confederation of Germany and required to send representatives to a Diet sitting at Frankfurt and presided over by Austria. Each state remained fully sovereign, however. The members of the Diet were bound by instructions from the ruler of their state, the Diet was given no executive authority of its own and no army, and the president was endowed with no more official power than the chairman of a meeting. In subsequent years German rulers pursued completely independent policies inside their own states and quarrelled with each other at meetings of the Diet. This caused Germans to complain of the powerlessness of the Bund, as though the latter could have been made to express strong German feeling regardless of the members who composed it. Nationalists argued that if the governments in the thirty-nine states had been freely elected they would have sent representatives to a Diet which was more devoted to German interests. The argument was not borne out by experience. Moreover the Congress cannot fairly be blamed for the reappearance of despotic governments in Germany, since the Act setting up the Confederation required rulers to establish constitutions.

If the Congress laid itself open to criticism from nationalists, it earned respect from internationalists in two spheres. The establishment of international control over the main rivers of Europe played an important part in opening the continent to trade, and the abolition of the slave traffic was a step which humanitarian opinion had long demanded. Britain was the leading champion of both these arrangements, and her detractors lost no time in pointing out how much she gained by the former and how little she lost by the latter. Unfortunately, slave trading continued to thrive illegally for several decades, for Britain did not abolish slavery in her colonies until 1834 and France (after her first attempt in 1793) until 1848.

Among contemporary critics of the Congress of Vienna Tsar Alexander was the most pronounced. In May 1815 he informed his ambassadors that the needs and wishes of the people of Europe had been ignored at Vienna. About the same time he drew up the draft of a treaty which he hoped would be signed eventually by all his fellow monarchs. The treaty said that the rulers of Russia, Austria, and Prussia were convinced that the principles of the Christian religion must henceforward guide all their relationships, and that therefore:

'. . . the subjects of the three contracting parties will remain united by the bonds of a true and indissoluble fraternity, and considering each other as fellow-countrymen they will, on all occasions, and in all places, lend each other aid and assistance. The same will apply to the respective armies which will equally consider themselves as belonging to the same army which is called upon to protect Religion, Peace, and Justice.'

Metternich described the religious element in the proposal as 'high-sounding Nothing' and decided that if it came to mean anything at all it would be useful as a means of distracting the Tsar from thoughts of Russian expansion. Castlereagh similarly described the proposal as 'a piece of sublime mysticism and nonsense' but advised the Prince Regent to express sympathy with it in a letter to the Tsar. 'The fact is', Castlereagh confided to the Prince, 'that the Emperor's mind is not completely sound. Last year there was but too much reason to fear that its impulse would be to conquest and dominion. The general belief now is, that he is disposed to found his own glory upon a principle of peace and benevolence. . . . It is, at all events, wise to profit by his disposition as far as it will carry us.' Metternich was worried, however, by the democratic implications of the Tsar's proposal. To destroy these he persuaded Alexander that the draft of the treaty needed a few verbal alterations. The 'subjects of the three contracting parties' was replaced by the

'Three contracting Monarchs'. The reference to armies was almost obliterated. In its place the three contracting monarchs, 'regarding themselves towards their subjects and armies as fathers of families', promised to 'lead them in the same spirit of fraternity with which they are animated to protect Religion, Peace, and Justice'. Metternich, for all his dislike of Russian interference, could not forget that the Tsar was the greatest autocratic ruler in Europe and that his help might some day be needed in the conservative cause. In its new form the 'Holy Alliance' was ambiguous enough either to be ignored or to be invoked for putting down revolutions. The rulers of Russia, Austria, and Prussia signed the treaty in September 1815 and the Tsar then submitted it to all European states with the exception of Turkey. The invitation to join the alliance was accepted by the rulers of Württemberg, Saxony, Sardinia, France, the Netherlands, the Hanseatic towns, Spain, and Switzerland. Castlereagh pleaded protocol and said that the Prince Regent could not sign. The Pope refused to sign because he disapproved of the Tsar's religious views. The Sultan, although not a Christian, resented his exclusion and was inclined to think that the Holy Alliance cloaked sinister Russian designs on Turkey, although Alexander had offered to include the Sultan's dominions in a general guarantee issued by the Congress of Vienna.

The Congress did not, as a matter of fact, guarantee any of the frontiers which it arranged, except those of France. The Tsar proposed in October 1815 that the Four should mutually guarantee each other's possessions, but even this was rejected by Castlereagh, presumably because he believed he could rely on Austria to hold back Prussia and Russia without placing Britain under any obligation. More was needed, Castlereagh felt, to hold back France, and on his initiative the Four signed on 20 November 1815 a Quadruple Alliance which was virtually a renewal of the Treaty of Chaumont. They agreed to form 'a permanent league' to ensure the maintenance of the second Treaty of Paris and they undertook, should 'revolutionary troubles' again 'rend France and menace the peace of other states . . . to concert together and along with His Most Christian Majesty the measures that they judge necessary for the safety of their respective states and for the general tranquillity of Europe'. The engagement was never acted upon. With very minor exceptions (the separation of Belgium from Holland, the creation of the tiny Kingdom of Greece, and the disappearance of the free city of Cracow) the frontiers arranged in 1815 remained fixed for forty years, and until the middle of the century neither France nor any other country provoked a general war in Europe.

This was not entirely due to the wisdom of the work accomplished at Vienna, although it is only fair to point out that the Treaty did not create any subject of discord, as Utrecht had done and Versailles was to do. More important was the fact that many responsible statesmen belonging to the leading powers of Europe wanted peace and worked hard to get it. The ruling classes everywhere had come to connect modern warfare with the intervention of the masses in politics, and in this threatening situation they no longer contemplated war for mere dynastic purposes or short-term ends. Castlereagh and Alexander I while extolling respectively the economic and religious motives for peace were never blind to its enormous social implications, and Metternich saw perhaps more clearly still that peace and conservatism were locked together. Personalities played a part, especially in the case of Tsar Alexander, who derived a feeling of satisfaction from negotiating at a personal level with other rulers in Europe. Metternich should be given credit also among the peace-makers for skill in handling situations which might easily have led to war though nobody wanted it. As a practitioner of diplomacy there was none to rival him.

2. THE CONCERT OF EUROPE AND THE POLICY OF INTERVENTION

As the Congress of Vienna drew to a close Alexander I proposed that the Great Powers should decide upon a line of conduct to be followed in all matters likely to lead to dispute. Castlereagh rejected the notion as foolish and dangerous. The Powers could and should, he believed, devise only a form of procedure which would enable them to hammer out decisions when the need arose. He accordingly created what came to be known as the Concert of Europe. Article 6 of the treaty of 20 November 1815 said that the sovereigns of the four Great Powers, or their ministers, should meet from time to time to discuss matters of common interest and to consult each other concerning measures necessary for the maintenance of peace. Four conferences were held: at Aix-la-Chapelle in 1818, at Troppau in 1820, continued at Laibach in 1821, and at Verona in 1822. After this the undertaking to meet regularly was abandoned, but the idea that there existed a Concert of Europe which could be summoned at times of crisis influenced most statesmen until the Crimean War.

The Tsar had hoped that the Great Powers would undertake to maintain the governments established in 1815. He believed that these governments were newly inspired with Christian zeal which would cause them to promote the eternal welfare of their subjects. Castlereagh rejected the proposal only because he was averse to committing Britain to a part in continental affairs when their relevance had not been proved. He was not opposed on principle to the idea of intervention in the affairs of other states. He intended the Powers to intervene in France should any bonapartist or revolutionary movement assume threatening proportions there. He realized that the undertaking entailed a fairly detailed supervision of French affairs: for three years the ambassadors of the Great Powers met weekly in Paris to discuss, among numerous matters, the bills about to be submitted to the Chambers, the conduct of elections, and the collection of the war indemnity. Article 6 of the treaty of Quadruple Alliance implied that Castlereagh was also willing to countenance intervention by the Powers in countries where revolution seemed likely to disturb the peace of Europe. He was prepared even to consider unilateral intervention in cases where special interests were at stake: he agreed that Austria had a right to put down a Piedmontese rebellion which threatened to affect Lombardy-Venetia in 1821, and evidence suggests that in the same year he was considering sending Hanoverian troops to put down a rebellion by anti-British elements in Portugal. The point at which he differed from the Tsar was when the latter seemed to favour setting up a species of international organization whose recognized duty was to prescribe intervention in the domestic affairs of individual states. Such an organization would in itself, Castlereagh believed, constitute a threat to European peace. To him there were European needs and European problems but there could be no European government. He disliked revolution but until it proved dangerous to another state or to the peace of Europe he saw no reason for outside interference. A chronic danger of revolution might even have its uses, to distract the sovereigns from wars of aggression.

Metternich was less addicted to intervention than his critics have allowed. He was afraid of revolution, but he was even more afraid of the extension of Russian influence in Europe, and the fear played a part in all his decisions with regard to counter-revolutionary action. These decisions appear to have been singularly inconsistent for a man who prided himself on working always according to fundamental principles. Metternich joined the Quadruple Alliance and thereby threatened to intervene in France; he sent Austrian armies to Naples and Piedmont in 1821; he proclaimed at Troppau and Laibach the right of monarchical governments to put down revolutions. Yet he opposed the idea of French intervention in Spain in 1822, and he declared himself averse to any kind of intervention against the July Revolution in France in 1830, though he regretted that Prussia had not attempted to quell the Belgian revolt of the same year. Explaining himself in a letter to Ficquelmont in October 1830 he enunciated a principle which was not far from that held by Castlereagh. When a state, he wrote, is so shaken by revolution that it cannot fulfil its treaty obligations with other states, the latter have a right to interfere in their own interest, as have also any states whose safety is threatened. In no case should intervention be attempted unless it is absolutely certain to succeed.

Intervention became a topic of discussion with the Powers in 1818, when the French foreign minister Richelieu complained that allied interference in French affairs was making the Bourbon monarchy unpopular with the majority of Frenchmen and encouraging ultra-royalists to believe that they could pursue reactionary policies without danger of revolution. Richelieu wanted the Powers to withdraw their army of occupation after the minimum period of three years stipulated by the Treaty of Paris and to admit France to the Concert of Europe. The commander-in-chief of the army of occupation, Wellington, believed with Richelieu that evacuation would ease Louis XVIII's difficulties. At the Congress of Aix-la-Chapelle the Powers accepted Wellington's advice and agreed to evacuate France as soon as the indemnity was paid, but Richelieu's second request produced more agitated under-currents. Castlereagh wanted to keep France out of the Concert of Europe because he feared that if she were admitted she would collaborate with Russia. Metternich thought that France ought to be brought into the Concert because if she were kept out she might make a secret alliance with Russia. Alexander wanted to have France in the Concert to balance the weight of Britain and Austria. On 12 October 1818 a compromise was arranged. France was declared eligible to send representatives to future congresses but at the same time Britain, Russia, Austria, and Prussia secretly renewed the Quadruple Alliance against her.

In 1820 a revolution in Naples succeeded in forcing a constitution upon the king Ferdinand. Metternich was determined to obtain permission from the Concert to crush the revolution, and determined also to evade any suggestions of joint intervention. Only if Austria alone restored the absolute authority of Ferdinand I would Austrian influence continue to be held supreme in Italy. Moreover a joint expedition would entail the unwelcome sight of Russian troops marching across Europe and ensconcing themselves near the Mediterranean. Alexander had already offered 100,000 troops in support of joint intervention, disclosing later his intention of obliging Ferdinand to rule through a parliament. Metternich managed the tricky situation with great success when he summoned the Concert to meet at Troppau and Laibach. Austria, Prussia, and Russia proclaimed the right of the Powers to defend monarchy against rebels everywhere, and were thereafter known in England as the 'Holy Alliance Powers', but with this famous proclamation their unity ended. Metternich outmanoeuvred Alexander and obtained permission for Austria to intervene alone in Italy. Although Castlereagh in a State Paper of 5 May 1820 said that intervention in the domestic affairs of states other than France lay outside the scope of the Quadruple Alliance and that Britain could take no part in crushing liberal movements he changed his tune once the threat of Russian intervention was eliminated. On 21 February 1821 he told the House of Commons that he was willing to tolerate an Austrian expedition to Naples because the revolution there had been effected by a military *pronunciamento*. The Austrian army re-established the authority of Ferdinand at the end of February 1821, then turned north at the request of the king of Sardinia to crush a rebellion in Piedmont.

Meanwhile in January 1820 Spanish rebels forced the king Ferdinand VII to accept the constitution of 1812, and Tsar Alexander demanded concerted intervention. Castlereagh was even more hostile to the idea of intervention in Spain than in Naples, for commercial relations with Spain's American colonies were at stake. In the State Paper of 5 May 1820 he expressed the view that revolution in Spain was no concern of the Quadruple Alliance. The French foreign minister also put up a show of detachment to hide domestic interest: he saw no reason for alienating liberal opinion at home by joining cause with the Holy Alliance Powers. Metternich was as usual unwilling to encourage Alexander in projects involving Russian military assistance, and the question of Spain was therefore allowed to slide at Troppau and Laibach. Tension was unfortunately renewed when France changed her policy. Among the ultra-royalists who came to power with Villèle at the end of 1821 a vociferous group believed that Louis XVIII ought to restore the prestige of the Bourbon monarchy by sending an expedition to defeat the rebels in Madrid. They believed, however, that their aims could only be achieved if France intervened on her own initiative and not under instructions from the Powers. When renewed troubles in Spain caused the whole question to be brought before a congress at Verona in the autumn of 1822 the French government instructed its plenipotentiaries to avoid receiving a mandate from the Concert. They failed to do so, partly because Mathieu de Montmorency bungled his mission, and more because France came to see that she needed the approval of the Concert to protect her from the hostility of Britain.

The latter was no longer represented by Castlereagh, who had committed suicide just before the Congress met, but by George Canning, a more wilful and less sensitive man. Canning was no more sympathetic to democracy than Castlereagh had been, nor was he averse to intervention when it seemed desirous in the interests of Britain or of his own popularity. The difference between the two men lay mainly in their manner of proceeding. Where Castlereagh could dissent from the decisions of the Concert and still remain on negotiating terms with the other Powers, Canning washed his hands of the whole set-up. When Canning informed the Powers at Verona that Britain refused to give her support to intervention in Spain he virtually told them that Britain had broken with the whole continent. For the preservation of peace he turned once more to the old game of the balance of power, which he praised in the House of Commons on 29 April 1823 as 'the only safeguard of nations, the protection of the weak against the strong, the principle by which small states flourished in the vicinity of great ones'. He might also have said that it was the only means by which England could shelve her obligations in Europe and pursue her interests elsewhere. As he put it on another occasion, 'Things are getting back to a wholesome state again, every nation for itself and God for us all'.

3. THE INDEPENDENCE OF THE SOUTH AMERICAN COLONIES

When French troops crossed the Bidassoa to put down the rebellion in Spain the Congress System was virtually at an end. Disagreement upon the rights and wrongs of intervention was not the real cause of its disruption, however. Canning even saw some advantage in the French action, for it enabled him, as he explained to one of Britain's ambassadors, to appear as the friend of the liberal cause while making certain that the rebels would be punished. Canning's real objection to the expedition arose from his fear that France would secure influence over Spain's American colonies. The British ambassador in Paris, Sir Charles Stuart, warned Canning on 10 February 1823 that French intervention in Spain might result 'in rendering France the protectress of Spain, with Cuba as a new Jamaica, and an enfranchised South America as her grateful client'.

Spain's colonies in South America had been in a state of rebellion since 1810. Ferdinand VII had made military efforts to regain the colonies after his restoration to the throne of Spain but the insurgents had received so much help in the form of arms and volunteers from almost every country of Europe that by 1819 Argentina, Chile, Venezuela, and Colombia had been liberated. Peru was holding out as the centre of Spanish resistance when revolution broke out in Madrid and for three years the Spanish government was unable to send forces to South America. The rebels made use of the respite to prepare their great offensive. The defeat of the Spanish army at Ayacucho in 1824 guaranteed the success of the movement for independence.

The complete break between the colonies and the mother-country which ensued was partly due to the intransigence of Spain. Many of the rebel leaders would have liked the new states to become monarchies ruled by Spanish Bourbon princes, but Spanish governments, royalist and liberal alike, persistently refused to treat on these terms. The Portuguese government in its relations with Brazil proved to be more reasonable. When the colony in 1822 seized the opportunity presented by a rebellion in the mother-country to declare itself an independent empire under the rule of the king's eldest son, the government at Lisbon accepted the *fait accompli*. It is true that John VI of Portugal could expect no help in recovering Brazil, whereas Ferdinand VII of Spain was led, by Russia's proposals for joint intervention in 1817 and 1818 and by France's policy in 1822-3, to hope for foreign assistance. Only Britain was interested in Brazil, where she had obtained commercial concessions in return for defending Portugal in 1810,

AOP S

and Canning brought pressure to bear on the Portuguese government to recognize the independence of the colony in 1825.

The future of Spain's colonies was complicated by rival economic interests. Austria, Russia, and Prussia were largely disinterested, but the Atlantic powers were far from being so. Britain had obtained permission to trade with Spain's colonies during the Napoleonic wars. Now that the wars were over she was anxious to preserve and develop the markets she had opened in South America, especially as other channels of trade proved disappointing. European countries, impoverished by Napoleon, could not buy the vast quantities of goods which Britain had accumulated, nor did they wish to do so. Many of them imposed tariffs to protect their own new industries. The United States showed the same tendency. West Indian trade had lost some of its importance with the introduction of beet sugar into Europe during the Continental Blockade, and Eastern trade showed no signs of rapid increase. British merchants vied with each other in trading with South American regions as they escaped one by one from Spanish domination. The textile industries benefited most from this trade, though monied men began also to invest capital in agricultural and mining concerns. By 1824 British trade with South America was booming. Investment in South American loans also reached a peak, much of the money going to support the rebels in their resistance to Spain. British trade and speculation were thus thriving during, and sometimes because of, hostilities between the colonies and the mother-country, but the activity of pirates in southern and central American waters made British businessmen desire a legal sanction for their trade. In 1824, 113 business houses signed a petition asking the government to give official recognition to those colonies 'which had in fact established independent governments'.

French industrial development was far behind that of Britain, but the French Government from about 1820 was aware of the potential value of South America as a market for silks and wines. On three occasions French missions were sent to South American ports to enquire into the prospect of commercial exchanges. France certainly did not want Britain to obtain a monopoly of trade in South America, nor did the U.S.A. As far as the latter was concerned, South America offered the prospect of important markets for raw cotton, timber, and cereals. Moreover the merchant ships of the U.S.A. could look forward to playing an important rôle in the commerce of Mexico, Central America, and Venezuela. In 1822 the U.S.A. recognized the independence of Colombia, Chile, Argentina, and Mexico. In 1822 the French government accepted from Chateaubriand the idea that Spain's American colonies should become independent monarchies ruled by Bourbon princes and that France should send ships, money, and 'a few soldiers' to South America to enforce this solution. Castlereagh and Canning were sympathetic towards the monarchical proposal because there would be less chance of the new states falling under the influence of the U.S.A. if they rejected the republican form of government, but the thought of French armed intervention aroused their immediate hostility. Villèle dropped the proposal, but British fears were by no means allayed. When French troops prepared to cross the Bidassoa a year later Canning took it upon himself to threaten war if France intervened in the New World.

From then on Britain was disposed to recognize republican governments in South America, relying on her reputation as the 'saviour' of the colonies to oust the influence of the U.S.A. Canning even suggested that Britain and the U.S.A. should co-operate in guaranteeing the independence of the colonies, but Adams, the Secretary of State, had no desire to see the U.S.A. become a satellite of Britain. He believed that President Monroe could safely issue a unilateral guarantee, for although the United States military resources were quite inadequate to protect South America from France or Spain, Britain could always be relied upon in the event of any serious threat to send her navy to protect her trade. Monroe accordingly enunciated in his Message to Congress on 2 December 1823 the famous Doctrine, that any move by Spain or by any other European country to reduce the independence of Latin America would be regarded as an act of hostility towards the U.S.A.

The immediate result of the Monroe Doctrine was to strengthen Canning's determination to recognize the independence of the colonies before it was too late to bring them under British influence. That he regarded both the U.S.A. and France as dangerous rivals is shown by his memorandum to the Cabinet on 30 November 1824:

'The views and policy of the North Americans seem mainly directed towards supplanting us in navigation in every quarter of the globe, but more particularly in the seas contiguous to America. . . . Let us remember that peace, however desirable, and however cherished by us, cannot last for ever. Sooner or later we shall probably have to contend with the combined maritime power of France and of the U.S.'

Less than a month later Canning was able to write, however, 'Spanish America is free, and if we do not mismanage our affairs sadly, she is English'. At the beginning of 1825 Great Britain recognized the independence of Argentina, Colombia, and Mexico, and signed favourable commercial treaties with them. Twenty states were eventually formed from the débris of the Spanish and Portuguese empires. The U.S.A. hesitated to form close ties with them because she dreaded the contagion of the liberal policy they had adopted towards their negro slaves and because she looked upon Mexico

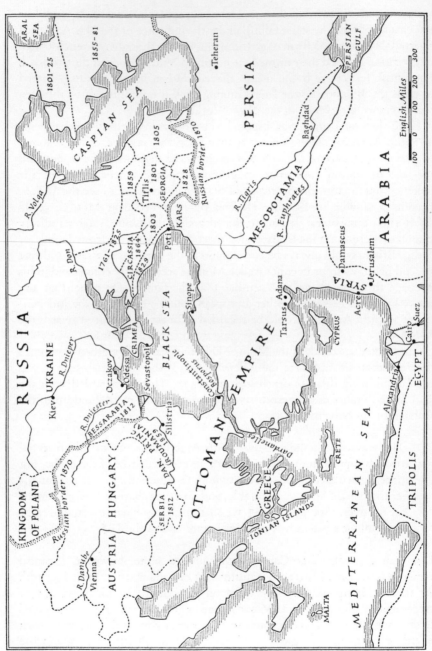

Map V Aspects of the Eastern Question, 1789–1870

ARAL SEA

1801–25

1855–81

CASPIAN SEA

•Teheran

PERSIA

PERSIAN GULF

1805

R. Volga

1859

Tiflis•

1801

GEORGIA

Russian border 1810

Baghdad

1828

KARS

R. Tigris

MESOPOTAMIA

R. Euphrates

ARABIA

R. Don

1761–1825

1803

CIRCASSIA

1864

1829

Poti•

•Sinope

Damascus•

Jerusalem•

SYRIA

Kiev•

UKRAINE

R. Dnieper

Ozakov•

Odessa•

CRIMEA

Sevastopol•

BLACK SEA

Constantinople

Bosporus

Adana

Tarsus•

•Acre

Cairo•

Suez

R. Dniester

BESSARABIA

1812

Silistria•

OTTOMAN EMPIRE

CYPRUS

Alexandria•

EGYPT

KINGDOM OF POLAND

Russian border 1870

PRINC.

DAN.

ROUMANIA

1859

Dardanelles

CRETE

MEDITERRANEAN SEA

TRIPOLIS

AUSTRIA HUNGARY

SERBIA

1812

GREECE

IONIAN ISLANDS

R. Danube

Vienna•

MALTA

English Miles

0 100 200 300

and Colombia as rival claimants to Cuba, the only important possession re-maining to Spain in the New World. There was consequently no-one to challenge Canning when he said that it was he who had 'called the New World into existence' and no country to rival Britain's commercial influence. By 1830 British trade with South America outweighed that of the U.S.A. three or four times over.

4. THE EASTERN QUESTION

In the Mediterranean and the Middle East rival imperialisms as well as rival commercial interests caused tension between the Great Powers. In 1799 the three-cornered struggle between Russia, Persia, and Turkey for the possession of Transcaucasia reached a turning point with the Russian occupation of Tiflis. In 1801 the whole of the Georgian kingdom passed from the suzerainty of Persia into the hands of Russia. Alexander I felt qualms of conscience about annexing Georgia but he overcame them, and in 1804 Russian troops invaded Persian territory and waged war inter-mittently for nine years. By 1813 they had acquired Baku and most of eastern Transcaucasia, which the Shah ceded to Russia in the Treaty of Gulistan. On both sides the treaty was regarded as an armistice only. Russia's command of Caucasian territories made possible two expansionist drives, the one south-eastward towards the Indian ocean, the other south-westward towards the Levant. Both were regarded by British statesmen as threats to British trade and as threats to Britain's position in India.

Shortly after Tilsit the Governor-General of the East India Company, Lord Minto, suggested that Persia, Afghanistan, and the Punjab should form a cordon to protect British India from Russia. The idea was never followed up, but the British government came to pay increasing attention to events in Persia. In 1809 the Shah signed a treaty with Britain in which he promised to prevent any European force from passing through his territories towards India. Britain in return promised to protect Persia from foreign invasion, supplying her with arms and military forces and sending subsidies. British officers and gunners thereafter played an active part in Persia's war against Russia and continued to do so even when Napoleon's attack on Moscow made Britain and Russia allies in Europe. The anomaly was prolonged in 1814 by the Treaty of Teheran, which provided that Britain should send money or troops to assist Persia in an attack from Russia even if Britain and Russia were at peace. Members of Alexander's government strongly re-sented such interference and hinted that Russia had as much right to expand into Asia as Britain had to conquer India. British statesmen were unlikely, however, to feel safe with spheres of influence, for British territory in north-west India had not yet reached the mountain barrier of the Karakorum. In 1822 Russian officers in disguise were rumoured to be working on the north-west frontier of British India in large numbers. A few years later Lieutenant-Colonel de Lacy Evans, in a pamphlet entitled *On the Designs of Russia*, wondered 'whether Russia, if suffered to proceed in her career, . . . may not shortly acquire a degree of intercourse with India . . . whereby India must become untenable or unworthy of further retention.'

Meanwhile Russia under Catherine II had annexed the northern shore of the Black Sea from the Dniester to the Kuban. The colonization of New Russia proceeded energetically and the Black Sea steppes became an important wheat growing area during Alexander I's reign. The value of grain exports rose to a level second only to that of flax and hemp. Odessa, founded in 1794, grew rapidly under the direction of the French émigré Duc de Richelieu, and all Black Sea ports became increasingly important when trade in the Baltic was hampered by the Continental Blockade. The acquisition of Transcaucasia gave Russia supremacy over Turkey in the Black Sea, but the narrow bottleneck which connected the Black Sea with the Mediterranean was still controlled by the Sultan. Russia had obtained the right of sending merchant vessels through the Straits of the Bosporus and the Dardanelles by the Treaty of Kutchuk Kainardji in 1774, but their safety was by no means guaranteed. Throughout Alexander's reign the Sultan was likely to requisition at will cargoes passing through the Bosporus. Meanwhile Russia failed to obtain lasting permission to send warships through the Straits. The Sultan granted her the right in 1799 but withdrew it in 1812 when the Tsar was obliged to come to terms hurriedly. Without warships in the Mediterranean Russia could not defend her commerce against pirates. Paul I and Alexander I tried during the Napoleonic wars to establish claims to Malta or the Ionian islands as naval bases, but in 1815 both these strategic positions passed to Britain.

When in 1815 Turkey's powers could be seen to be waning Russia could be expected to encourage the process. By extending her patronage to Balkan rebels, or by partitioning Turkey, or simply by bringing pressure to bear on the Sultan, Russia might succeed in dominating the Straits. Unfortunately any power which dominated the Straits would also be likely to dominate Constantinople and with it the whole of the Turkish Empire. Hence Britain in a treaty of 1809 obtained from the Sultan a pledge that the Straits would remain closed to warships of all nations in time of peace. Castlereagh inherited from the younger Pitt the idea of 'bolstering up the sick man of Europe' as a barrier against Russia. In pursuing such a policy he could expect to find an ally in Metternich. Austria's main strategic highway, the Danube, ran through the Balkans into the Black Sea. Russia had obtained Bessarabia from Turkey in 1812: one step further down the eastern Balkans and she would control the mouth of the Danube. Russia, on the other hand, might one day find an ally in France, who had little chance of reviving her commerce in the Mediterranean while so much depended on the Sultan.

Friction between the Great Powers over the Eastern Question bedevilled the Concert of Europe almost from the beginning. Alexander's scheme for founding a maritime league to crush the Barbary pirates was rejected by Britain because Castlereagh thought that Russia intended to create satellite states along the African coast. Rumours of Russian designs on Minorca in 1817 aroused protests from the Austrian ambassador, who was told by Alexander's foreign minister, 'I don't know why England should have the exclusive privilege of occupying islands in the Mediterranean'. Alexander's plans for joint intervention in Naples and Spain aroused opposition partly because of the proximity of these lands to the Mediterranean. Tension reached a climax in April 1821 when the Greeks rebelled against the Sultan and Europe waited to see what Alexander would do.

As soon as the revolt broke out Castlereagh and Metternich feared that commercial and political interests would compel Alexander to support the Greeks. Russia's trade in the Mediterranean was carried on largely by merchants and sailors from the Greek islands, who now ceased their activities. Russian intervention in the Balkan peninsula had been known in the past. Catherine II assumed the rôle of protector of Orthodox Christianity and launched revolts in Greece during her first Turkish war. The subsequent Treaty of Kutchuk Kainardji (1774) gave Russia special rights in the Princi-palities of Moldavia and Wallachia and gave the Tsar the right to make representations on behalf of the members of the Greek Orthodox church at Constantinople. The precise meaning of the treaty was obscure, but Russian rulers up to the time of the Crimean War were able to claim that it gave them a right to interfere throughout Turkey on behalf of the Orthodox. Alexander I asserted his claims to the Principalities in 1806. The Russians were assisted for the first time by a serious popular movement, the Serbian peasant rebellion led by Karageorge. Russian agents were active among the Serbs, and even though Alexander abandoned the latter to the mercy of the Turks when he made peace with the Sultan in 1812, Russia continued to arouse hopes among Balkan patriots. During the Congress of Vienna Alexander's foreign minister, the Corfiot Capodistria, and a group of his friends revived the pro-Hellenic society known as the *Hetairía Philiké* with the object of raising the cultural standards of modern Greece. Shortly afterwards a secret society of a political nature was founded under the same name by Greek merchants at Odessa, and Alexander was widely believed to be in sympathetic contact with it.

The British merchants who traded in the eastern Mediterranean under the direction of the Levant Company were friends of the Porte in normal times, but they soon became anxious to see legal status given to the Greek rebels in order to put an end to the depredations made by pirates upon their commerce. British financiers sided with the Greeks because of the high rates of interest they offered on loans. Material interests eddied in the wake of a tremendous surge of emotion. Englishmen who loved the classics saw the revolt as an attempt by modern Greece to recover her ancient glory; others saw it as a bid for liberty by an oppressed minority; still others saw it as a fight for the Christian cause against the Muslim. Castlereagh in his anxiety to hold back Russia described the revolt in a letter to Alexander as 'a branch of that organized spirit of revolution' which could be seen all over Europe, but he knew well enough that the Greeks could claim more sympathy in England than the Spaniards or Italians. He was himself not averse to the creation of an independent Greece if such a state could be guaranteed against the encroachment of Russia. Metternich held a very low opinion of the Greek rebels. He believed that philhellenism was based on gross ignorance of the situation, and he was cynically surprised to see liberals supporting Christianity in a fight against Islam. He did not believe that the Greeks were capable of forming an independent state but he cared little what happened to them as long as a solution was reached before Alexander moved. On 22 October 1821 Britain and Austria declared their intention of opposing armed intervention by Russia.

Political circles in Russia did not take the threat very seriously. They believed that a Russian expeditionary force could easily turn the scales in the Morea and that Alexander should move at once in Russia's interests. In March 1823 Canning submitted to popular pressure and recognized the Greeks as belligerents. He was hailed throughout Greece as a patron and he could hardly, thereafter, attack the Russians if they too began to support the rebels. Madame de Krüdener added her entreaties to those of Greek patriots and Russian expansionists, but Alexander held firmly to his principles. He dismissed Capodistria and turned to the Concert for a solution. 'Everything with my Allies and nothing without them', he told the French ambassador. He hoped that united diplomatic pressure would be brought to bear upon the Sultan to give the Greeks some degree of freedom under Turkish suzerainty. His efforts were undermined by the individual policies of Britain, Austria, and France, the first working for a fully independent Greece, the second combatting Russian initiative, and the third pursuing private ambitions in the Mediterranean by aiding Mohammed Ali of Egypt in his projected attack upon the Morea. By 1825 Alexander had despaired of the Concert. He instructed his ambassadors in Vienna and Paris not to enter into any more negotiations about the Eastern Question with the governments to which they were accredited. In December 1825 Europe heard the news that Tsar Alexander was dead.

CHAPTER XV

Metternich's Europe, 1815-35

WITH the collapse of the Congress System peace depended on the efforts of individual statesmen either to maintain the status quo or to adjust it without war. The central position was occupied by Metternich, who guided the policy of the Austrian empire from the Congress of Vienna to the death of Francis I. Contemporaries were inclined to see the influence of Metternich behind government policies everywhere in Europe and to refer in consequence to his 'system'. Metternich denied that he had a system and said that he only had principles. These he enunciated at greater and greater length as the years went by until his verbosity became a joke in diplomatic circles. He did not claim to have invented the principles: he said that they were deep immutable laws which he had discerned beneath the surface of society.

According to these principles the chief duty of government was to preserve order. The type of government most likely to fulfil its duty was monarchy, for a king could unite his subjects by a common bond of loyalty. The king must have sole responsibility for policy but he must delegate authority to ministers standing at the head of each branch of administration. He must not on any account delegate power to a representative assembly for this would encourage the pernicious doctrine of sovereignty of the people. Kings who possessed supreme authority were often referred to as absolute monarchs, but in fact all monarchies were constitutional monarchies for they existed by consent of landed aristocracies, of urban corporations, and of the people. This consent was natural because it derived from deep-seated material interests: revolutions were usually stirred up by irresponsible persons either from a desire to obtain property rightfully possessed by others or from a desire to wield power which did not belong to them. In contemporary society the 'agitated classes' were the upper middle class (bankers, capitalists, large-scale industrialists) and the lower middle class ('paid officials, men of letters, lawyers, and individuals charged with public education'). These persons often professed to speak for the public through journals and pamphlets. Hence the press ought to be censored, for though public opinion was an extremely valuable guide the government must be sure that it was genuine. In particular governments ought to silence propaganda concerning social equality and nationality. The only justifiable form of equality was equality before the law, and common interests stronger than those created by community of language and race were necessary to form the basis of a state.

A superficial observer might have wondered why Metternich persisted in viewing all forms of intellectual activity with suspicion, for the bulk of such activity in the years following Waterloo was directed towards criticizing the social forms and mental attitudes fostered by an era of revolution. Romanticism, which dictated the mood of the period, has with some justice been called the swan-song of the European aristocracy, for though its most inspired performers were often of non-noble birth the yearning of youth and genius for recognition in a society which seemed heedless of their superiority found a common cause in the protest of aristocratic writers against a society which had rejected their caste. Thus Friedrich Schlegel, Schelling, Coleridge, Scott, and many another romantic of middle-class origin inveighed as passionately as a Chateaubriand or a Lamartine against the levelling tendencies of the French Revolution and complained as bitterly of the premium placed on mediocrity in a democratic age.

Romanticism developed simultaneously in Britain and Germany in the last years of the eighteenth century. In 1798 the *Lyrical Ballads* of Wordsworth and Coleridge sounded the death-knell of Augustan poetry: in the same year the brothers Schlegel founded their review the *Athenaeum* and consorted with Novalis, Schelling, and Tieck to propound a new philosophy. France in the throes of Napoleonic sterility lagged behind: Benjamin Constant's *Wallstein* achieved only a restricted effect in 1809. Chateaubriand had opened the century with his *Atala* and *Génie du christianisme*, but Chateaubriand was in exile. However, Frenchmen were awakened to romanticism with a shock in 1813 when Madame de Staël translated Wilhelm Schlegel's study of the drama. Thereafter they could not escape the challenge to classicism, for the émigrés who returned from Britain and Germany were full of the new fervour.

After 1815 romanticism fanned out from Britain, Germany, and France over the greater part of Europe. The novels of Scott and Mérimée, the poetry of Byron and Leopardi, the plays of Grillparzer and Dumas, the painting of Constable, Géricault, and Delacroix, the music of Schubert, Weber, and above all of the dying Beethoven proclaimed the mastery of romanticism over the majority of the creative arts. Only sculpture and architecture, less likely to be fed from popular sources than poetry or music, remained strongholds of classicism. In sculpture the Italian Canova wielded the kind of dictatorship which David (now banished to Brussels) had once enjoyed in painting, whilst in architecture the neo-Roman style favoured for public buildings was challenged only in industrial countries by the functional beauty of the new bridges, viaducts, and mills. Romanticism was not confined to the arts, however. Its influence pervaded every branch of mental activity from philology to religion. It flowered so profusely in Germany (known to western Europe largely through Madame de Staël's *De l'Allemagne*) that an irascible French newspaper of left-wing views accused the Germans of inventing the whole movement deliberately in an attempt to conquer an intellectual empire equivalent to the territorial achievements of Napoleon.

Definitions of romanticism abound in the works of romantic writers, but their meaning has remained obscure to the most diligent seekers after the truth. The romantics were incapable of expressing themselves clearly on so important a subject as the content of their creed, partly, no doubt, because they deliberately rejected the rationalism of the eighteenth century. They condemned the laws and definitions pursued so inexorably by preceding generations as bumptious attempts to reduce a mysterious universe to the limits of man's paltry intelligence. Their bugbear was Newton, whom they regarded as the founding father of the age of reason. To the mechanistic interpretations advanced by Newtonian science they opposed a 'natural philosophy' which was emotional and intuitive, expressing the unity of all creation and the force of the world spirit. Yet despite much unintelligible rhapsodizing the basic desire of the romantics was patent to all: the wish to assert the overriding importance of individual personality. In painting, music, and literature the romantics protested against forms which had cramped the artist in his yearning for self-expression. No common standards, no professional rules, no public requirements should confine the creative soul in its instinct for communication. Keats at the age of twenty declared that he would accept nothing but 'the holiness of the heart's affections and the truth of imagination'. Thus the romantics invented the concept of the genius, the final assertion of triumphant individuality, the supremely gifted person who must be allowed to present his unique message to the world in his own terms.

When the French Revolution attacked despotism in the name of individual freedom the men who were later to launch the romantic movement greeted it with enthusiasm. Wordsworth, Southey, Blake, and Coleridge, Novalis, Friedrich Schlegel, and a dozen others hailed the dawn of a new age. Their expectations were disappointed, and with the fading of their hopes they lost faith in the efficacy of reason. It was not only the bloodshed and tyranny which disillusioned them: these alone might have been simply deplored as human shortcomings and the whole endeavour begun again. It was the very achievements of the Revolution which sickened them. The soulless machine of democracy required all men to be reduced to the same level, for which purpose it was necessary to depersonalize them and isolate them one from another. The romantics became obsessed with the notion of human 'alienation', and they searched feverishly for a means of uniting the soul of man once more with the world. In doing so they explored a variety of conservative, not to say reactionary paths which governments after 1815 sometimes pretended, at least, to follow.

The most obvious means of reconciliation and harmony lay in a return to Christianity. Not that many people had ever completely left it: the majority of the French bourgeoisie had retained a saving belief even during the Revolution, and the polite indifference which had reigned among the upper classes in the hey-day of Enlightenment had allowed room for a more fervent faith in harsher times. The fact remained, however, that the French Revolution had been based on a secular ideology. It was no accident that Novalis founded German political romanticism with a plea for the regeneration of society through Catholicism (*Christendom or Europe*, 1799). The aspects of religion which appealed to the romantics varied according to taste and temperament. Novalis was influenced by pietism, the revivalist movement which hung heavily over Germany at the turn of the century, inspiring preachers such as Jung-Stilling and Madame de Krüdener to speak prophesies and see visions. Schleiermacher and Chateaubriand stressed the civilizing influences of Christianity, the German theologian seeking to show that mysticism was compatible with scientific culture (*Addresses on religion to the educated who despise it*, 1799) and the French poet attributing to Christianity every sign of progress in the modern world (*Génie du christianisme*, 1802). Others were attracted by the authoritarian potentialities of religion, for they believed that repression alone could save an erring generation. Zacharias Werner announced to huge congregations in Vienna at the time of the Congress that only the Pope and the executioner could rescue Europe from the impious legacy of the French Revolution. The same theme had been propounded more voluminously by the Frenchman Bonald and the Savoyard De Maistre during the emigration. Bonald's tedious works were little read, but De Maistre's later work *Du Pape* (1819) achieved sufficient notoriety in Restoration France to provoke ridicule by Stendhal in *Le Rouge et le Noir* (1829). Bonald and De Maistre decked out their argument with a formidable apparatus of reasoning but in this they were untypical. More popular writers such as Chateaubriand relied on appeals to emotion, as Rousseau had done in the Savoyard Vicar. To many devotees, sentiment became a substitute for faith, and the content of belief became less important than the sensation of believing. 'I do not know exactly what we must believe, but I believe that we must believe!' wrote Madame de Staël. 'The eighteenth century did nothing but deny. The human spirit lives by its beliefs.'

Friedrich Schlegel was the most outstanding of many romantics who imagined that a satisfying faith had pervaded Europe in medieval times. It was not only religion, however, which attracted the romantics to the Middle Ages. Chivalry provided them with an example of the natural superiority of historic nobility. The supposedly idyllic life of village and market town enabled them to denounce the Industrial Revolution (a product, like the French Revolution, of the age of reason) for having uprooted men from the shelter of home and cast them defenceless upon a greedy world. The medievalism of German lyrics and of the ubiquitous historical novel owed something, too, to the romantic love of the picturesque as an escape from the dullness of modern life. A short step led to admiration for the institutions of medieval Europe – the Holy Roman Empire, the guilds, the Estates. A few romantics – Schleiermacher and Stein in Germany, Madame de Staël, Benjamin Constant and in a qualified sense Chateaubriand in France – remained faithful to the ideal of free government, but the majority, in the decade after Waterloo, became advocates of authority. They appealed constantly to history, which was a popular and developing subject in this period. Improving upon Edmund Burke, whose *Reflections* were the fountain of most of the conservative doctrine flooding the continent, they came to regard tradition as another manifestation of personality and to believe that it merely had to be elucidated to become indefeasible.

Akin to the romantics in criticizing the bourgeois creeds of the eighteenth and nineteenth centuries were the German 'idealist' or 'classical' philosophers. As early as 1781 (*Critique of Pure Reason*) Kant found that morals and faith were superior to reason as guides to the truth. He never lost the love of individual freedom which caused him to welcome the French Revolution, but in his latest works he argued that the individual can realize himself only through society. Schelling developed the theme until he dreamed of a world order in which the individual was submerged altogether. The poetry and mysticism of Schelling's work endeared him to the romantics, but Hegel's *Natural Law and Political Science* (1821) represented a more monumental achievement. After welcoming the French Revolution Hegel became disillusioned more quickly than most. The state came to play a more fundamental part in his philosophy than in that of Kant. He saw the individual as existing only through the state, and the state as a natural organism representing a necessary phase in world development.

Metternich never tried to make use of these intellectual excursions, except for allowing his secretary Gentz, another disillusioned romantic, to give a running commentary on his own more realistic brand of conservatism. He preferred to rely on the immovability of the masses. After all, the overwhelming majority of the population of Europe was illiterate. In a sense his aloofness was vindicated, for romanticism and its offshoots held strains which were inimical to the status quo. The concept of human alienation played a part in the development of utopian socialism; idealist philosophy lent itself to the advance of Prussian militarism; and Hegel's theory of progress through the repeated resolution of contradictions (the dialectic) profoundly influenced Karl Marx. More immediately, romanticism fostered the growth of nationalism, which became a force in Europe for the first time during the twenty years of Metternich's supremacy.

Up to 1815 nationalist feeling in a modern sense had been more or less confined to France. After 1815 it was deliberately cultivated elsewhere by scholars and literary men who resented most bitterly the deadening effect of the restored order. They had seen from the French Revolution what powerful results could be achieved by popular enthusiasm for the cause of fatherland. Poets, dramatists, historians, journalists, and others whose nature or calling equipped them to appeal to the public adapted the symbols of the French Revolution – the national flag, the national song, the national festival, and the National Guard – to fit the cause of Serbs and Greeks fighting against Turkish domination, of Italians protesting against foreign influence, and of Germans trying to find strength through unity. Romantics were attracted to nationalist movements both by the spirit of adventure and by a sentimental attitude to history. They assumed that the peasants and craftsmen of a preindustrial era embodied the simple virtues which created harmony in the world, and they devoted themselves enthusiastically to the collection of folksongs, folktales, folkdances and other manifestations of the true spirit of the people. Appeals to tradition were not necessarily conservative in tendency: they possessed revolutionary implications in countries where the folk now lay under alien domination. Romantics threw their hearts into the first great liberating movement of the post-Napoleonic age, the revolt of the Greeks. In 1824 Byron gained the halo of martyrdom by dying in the cause. The stage was set for a new phase of the romantic movement.

2. THE AUSTRIAN EMPIRE

Metternich's principles provided a perfect justification for the preservation of the status quo in the Austrian empire, and critics concluded that the verbiage was a smoke-screen covering a policy which was essentially opportunist. The implied conflict did not exist in Metternich's mind. His devotion to the Habsburg Monarchy arose from his fondness for the way of life which it symbolized. He belonged to a world of aristocratic salons: his intellectual outlook was that of the French *ancien régime*. He did not venerate kingship, but he was willing to court it for the sake of the things that went with it. He could see faults in the institutions which he supported, but they had stood the test of time and were bound to be more serviceable than anything new. Though shatteringly proud of his own intellectual capacities, he was cynically aware of human deficiencies in general and he did not think that men were capable of great constructive achievement. He was therefore conservative but not reactionary: he could no more appreciate a fervent belief in Divine Right than he could sympathize with ardent democrats. The perpetual compromise and manoeuvre to which the Habsburgs were driven was his whole idea of government. He was particularly incapable of understanding nationalism. A Rhenish émigré, he belonged to a class, not a country. He carried out his daily work in six languages. In 1824 he told the Duke of Wellington that Europe had long been his fatherland.

The vehemence with which Metternich rejected the validity of the new faith damned him in the eyes of a generation of historians. His rôle as an opponent of nationalism should not be exaggerated, however. In the Austrian empire nationalism had scarcely awakened. Count Istvan Széchenyi gave a year's income to endow an academy for the Hungarian language; Dobrovsky and Jungmann studied the Czech language and Palacky sought to arouse pride in Bohemia's past; Shashkevych and Holovatzki collected Ruthenian folklore; the poet Vodnik adopted Illyria as a patriotic ideal and another poet Gaj tried through his *Short Outline of Croat-Slovene Orthography* to instil into fellow-Croats a feeling of community with Slovenes. Sometimes these scholarly efforts were almost single-handed, like that of Kopitar to lift the Slovenian tongue from a peasant dialect to the status of a literary language. Metternich, although he knew that he was playing with fire, was not afraid to patronize nationalism in its early stages. He saw that national pride among the Czechs, Roumanians, and southern Slavs might serve as a weapon against the nationalism he most feared, that of the Germans and the Magyars.

Nationalism in the Austrian empire undoubtedly contained the seeds of much evil. The Germans had been able to claim since the time of Joseph II that their culture was superior to that of other people. National pride of this kind puffed up the ambition of many Germans to dominate the empire, an ambition strongly resented by other national groups and in particular by Magyars, Poles, and Italians. A few Germans believed that the empire ought to be divided, the western half becoming part of a new and stronger Germany arising from the ashes of the Confederation; but even this ambition could only be achieved by submerging the Czechs and abandoning the German communities enclaved in Hungary and Transylvania. Hungarian nationalism held the threat of Magyar domination over the Roumanian and Slav peasantry and of a cut-throat struggle between the Magyar and Croatian nobility. Under these circumstances Metternich could claim that the House of Habsburg had a mission to provide a home for the peasant peoples of central Europe.

Unfortunately neither Metternich nor Francis I worked hard to fulfil the mission, partly because they were afraid of rousing democracy and partly because they were too ready to make concessions to dominant groups. Metternich realized that the Emperor was dependent on the Germans. The latter provided the empire with business men, merchants, and civil servants, and although they formed only a third of the population they paid two thirds of the taxes. Moreover of all national groups they were the least likely to disrupt the empire, for without their connection with a numerous non-German body they could not hope to rival the claims of Prussia to hegemony in a new Germany. Metternich would not sponsor the ambition of the Germans to control the empire, for this could only be achieved through a parliamentary system with the franchise based on property or education, but he was willing to allow the Germans to continue exploiting the Czechs in Bohemia. He understood also that the Emperor was dependent on the Magyars, who were the greatest landowners of the empire and the most important suppliers of conscripts for the army. He had no intention of submitting to the greatest ambition of the Magyars, which was for legislative power in Hungary, but he was ready to allow them to continue exploiting the Slavs. In other words Metternich was willing to keep in force all over the empire the labour services and feudal dues which Joseph II had tried to abolish, and to maintain the Diets by way of a guarantee. The Hungarian Diet, dissolved in 1811 for opposing the Emperor's fiscal policy, was restored in 1825. Metternich hoped that concessions to the Magyars and Germans would keep the two, if not moderately happy, at least only moderately discontented, while the peasants would be unlikely to join them in national agitations. The hopes were fulfilled until the eighteen-forties.

Metternich thus held a balance of power within the Habsburg empire much as he tried to hold a balance of power in Europe. Constructive policies seemed unnecessary to him and government became a matter of administration. The governmental machine had been inherited from Joseph II. The ministers who stood at the head of each department were seldom asked by Francis to give advice on policy: the Conference of Ministers created during the Napoleonic wars fell into disuse and Francis acted on his own initiative in all matters great and small. Each office employed an enormous staff, the number of civil servants amounting to more than 140,000. Most of them were industrious, but their tasks were meaningless to them. Their salaries were low and the cost of administration already overburdened the state's finances so heavily that there was no chance of an increase. The civil service did not attract the best brains: if it contained men of imagination they were unable to rise above the routine duties which weighed upon them. Metternich was well aware that a centralized bureaucracy needed intelligent direction and that Francis was not the man to supply it. The latter's experiences during two decades of upheaval had left him without a policy except that of resisting foreign enemies, repressing internal critics, and refusing to make innovations. Metternich was not dissatisfied with the policy but he saw that Francis's stupid refusal to delegate authority even in the most trivial matters resulted in slowness and inefficiency. He repeatedly requested the formation of a Council of State, but without result.

The bureaucratic machine did no more than lumber on, but Metternich believed he could rely on the inherent conservatism of the masses to stave off revolt. Traditional respect for the monarchy was strong among the peasants. It was especially strong among the Catholic population which saw a religious sanction in the dynasty. Metternich was not a zealous Catholic but he was willing to support the claims of the church for purposes of state. In 1820 Jesuits were re-admitted to the country. The church obtained a monopoly of education in schools, and even in universities students were obliged to attend lectures on Catholic theology however remote it may be from their special subject. Writings which were hostile to Catholicism were banned by the censors even if, like the works of Voltaire, they had been tolerated by Joseph II. A number of converts from Protestantism to Catholicism were given senior posts in the civil service, though the most famous of them, Friedrich von Schlegel, knew that the government's zeal was put on for political reasons. The attitude of the government was shared by the upper classes, whose recognition of the social value of religion caused them to repent of their former scepticism. The sermons of the religious revivalist Zacharias Werner became the talk of Viennese salons.

The imperial régime was not noted for cruelty or reprisals. The most serious evils were the refusal to improve the status of the lower classes and the denial of scope to men of ability.

The condition of the peasants varied from province to province and even from village to village but all were subject to forced labour services and all had to pay dues to landlord, state, and church. Peasants in Bohemia owed half their working time to the landowner: those in Hungary owed more. All peasants had to surrender a part of their crops, varying from a twentieth to a tenth, to the landowner, and a share of their animal products and poultry. They were required to pay a substantial sum of money when land changed hands. To the state the peasants paid tax amounting sometimes to 24 per cent of the net proceeds of the land. They provided horses and conveyances for government officials, quartered soldiers in their cottages, and helped to build roads and bridges. At times of exceptional hardship such as 1816, when bad harvests ruined half of the peasant farmers in the empire, the government distributed subsidies and relief, but the effect was superficial.

In Austria the industries which had developed under cover of the Continental Blockade suffered severely when the war ended. Metternich did his best to hamper large-scale enterprises because he feared the ambitions of the men who ran them and feared the effect of gathering large numbers of workers together in one place. Petty restrictions were imposed on the position and size of factories and the number of houses that could be built. The government began once more to support guilds. Industry was confined for the most part to small workshops and rural cottages, neither of which could withstand competition from foreign goods. Every employee in a factory was out of work for three months in each year, and peasants who wove cloth in their cottages received only a pittance for a fourteen hour day. Yet Metternich remained confident that the poor would not rebel. 'The labours to which this class – the real people – are obliged to devote themselves are too continuous and too positive to allow them to throw themselves into vague abstractions and ambitions', he wrote to Alexander. His secretary Gentz confessed to Robert Owen that the government's neglect of the lower classes had a positive political aim. 'We do not by any means desire the great masses to become wealthy and independent, for how could we govern them?'

Of all people Metternich most distrusted 'savants' or intellectuals. The efforts of the police were chiefly directed towards thwarting their activities. Only official newspapers, sponsored by the government and partly written in government offices, were allowed to circulate. No printed matter of any kind could appear before the public without passing through the hands of censors who could alter it at their discretion. Detailed syllabuses were laid down for schools and universities, the Emperor explaining to a group of teachers at Laibach, 'I want not scholars but good citizens. It is your duty to educate youth in this direction. Whoever serves me must teach according to my orders. Whoever is not able to do so, or starts new ideas going, must go or I will eliminate him.' Metternich delighted in collecting information about every person employed in a position of responsibility great or small. This was a facet of government which he had observed in France under Napoleon, and it pleased him that Austria's minister of police, Count Joseph Sedlnitzky, had been a pupil of Fouché. Spies were introduced into schools, lecture rooms, theatres, churches, and government offices. The whole of the expeditionary force sent to Naples in 1821 was kept under observation by the police. To all treaties with foreign states Metternich appended a clause directing their postal services through Vienna so that letters could be opened in his offices. The correspondence even of members of the imperial family was investigated. The atmosphere of spying and informing disgusted intelligent citizens, especially as the means were out of all proportion to the ends. In the greater part of the Austrian empire there were no plots to discover. Only Italy provided some justification for the régime in the shape of conspirators.

3. ITALY

Metternich knew that if Austria was to maintain her hold over Lombardy and Venetia she must keep Italy divided. He proclaimed the task to be an easy one. He described Italy as nothing more than a geographical expression and the Italians as having no more than local loyalties. The view was shared to some extent by men as different as Napoleon, Cobden, Lamartine, and Niebuhr. Fascist historians have claimed that there was a re-birth of national feeling among Italians in the eighteenth century but the claim cannot be substantiated. A few Italian writers in the seventeen-seventies were calling for a renewal of national vitality, a *risorgimento*, but the only discernible developments owed their appearance to European Enlightenment and the French Revolution. Even these developments were few and problematical. The administrative and economic reforms carried out by enlightened rulers in Tuscany, Lombardy, and Naples increased the number of officials and therefore increased the number of persons who thought about public affairs, but there is no evidence that they thought beyond the achievement of good government in their several states. It can be argued that the demand for unification was implicit in their ideas but it was certainly not explicit. The revolutionary and Napoleonic period produced a turmoil of ideas and feelings but only a small proportion of the population was affected and the impulse towards or away from the French was always important. Metternich could well assume that without the French factor the Italian cause was reduced to negligible proportions.

Again, historians have discerned glimmerings of national feeling in Italy in the decades following Waterloo. Different regions have been credited with making different contributions to the national heritage. The salons and theatres of Florence provided audiences for the works of Alfieri, Foscolo, Leopardi, Niccolini, and Manzoni; Lombardy was the scene of agricultural reforms carried out by paternalistic landowners such as Lambertenghi and Confalonieri; Naples in her secret societies gave an example of political action; Piedmont first saw the importance of fighting Austria. These regional manifestations did not at the time add up to a national awakening, however. No theory of Italian nationality came into being; no ideas about Italian *Volk* or Italian superiority were expressed in Italian literature. Censorship was only partly to blame. The forces working against nationalism were very great indeed. Italians of north and south were virtually unknown to each other; even members of the aristocracy spoke mutually unintelligible dialects.

The king of Sardinia and the Pope foiled Metternich's attempts to make Austria the head of an Italian confederation, but the princes of Italy supported Austrian policies in the main. The old balance of states was not restored in 1815: only Sardinia and Naples were capable of pursuing an independant foreign policy and Naples was eliminated in 1821. Sardinia could no longer play off France against Austria, and in any case Victor Emmanuel's ambitions were curbed by his fear of revolution. Not all the princes were as reactionary as Victor Emmanuel, who forbade recognition of any change made in the kingdom since 1770, but reforms in Rome and the Duchies were paternalistic rather than liberal, and rulers would inevitably turn to Austria in the event of revolution.

The greatest danger to the restored régime in Italy as in other parts of Europe came from irresponsible sections of the community which might start rebellions for selfish reasons. The ending of a long period of warfare brought inevitable problems of readjustment. Armies had to be cut down to a peace-time size. Large numbers of discharged soldiers were faced with the difficulty of finding jobs in countries impoverished by French exactions, ravaged by war, and poorly endowed with industry. Young men were suddenly deprived of the easy career they had expected to pursue in the army. Many of them had grown accustomed to exercising authority and carrying responsibility beyond their years and qualifications, and they were not willing to accept the drudgery of peace-time soldiering or face competition in civilian employment. Grievances were often aggravated by the manner in which governments handled the situation. Restored monarchs discriminated against officers who had earned distinction under French command. Arrears of pay were seldom made up and discharged soldiers were given no help in rehabilitating themselves to civilian life. Nothing was done to soften the blows which armies received to their pride or to make life bearable for officers and men confined to dreary barracks in provincial towns. In 1820 a chain of military revolts started in Spain and spread across southern Europe, welcoming any support that offered itself.

The leader of the revolution in Spain was an army colonel, Riego, who had been taken prisoner during the Napoleonic wars. His experience as a member of a foreign secret society gave him a wider vision than most of his associates, who mutinied simply to avenge personal grievances. The army and navy suffered badly from the financial disorganization of Ferdinand VII's government. Most officers were ill-paid and they were forbidden by decree to submit complaints. The king's personal guards were treated munificently while soldiers in Madrid barracks were obliged to sleep on bare earth. The government's habit of getting rid of disgruntled regiments by sending them to fight in America only increased the discontent. The revolt of the military provided an opening for the re-emergence of the liberals driven underground by Ferdinand. The Constitution of 1812 was proclaimed, but its only real supporters came from the small and weak middle class. Not a single village declared spontaneously for Riego, and little resistance was offered to the French invaders in 1823. The only lasting gift which the revolt bestowed upon mankind was the method by which it had been carried out, the military pronunciamento. This not only became a permanent feature of revolts in Spain, Portugal, and Latin America, but was immediately borrowed by the Neapolitans, a fact whose significance Castlereagh did not fail to note.

Ferdinand I of Naples behaved in general in a less brutal way than his nephew of Spain but he too distrusted the army. The men were subjected once more to corporal punishment. Officers who had fought under Murat suffered a sharp reduction in pay and even the reduced sum often failed to reach them. The corruption which Metternich described as 'an incurable evil' of Naples resulted in the frequent embezzlement of army pay by civil servants. The revolt of 1820 was planned by General Pepe commanding the third military division at Avellino and Foggia. The government had ordered Pepe to raise a militia of 10,000 men to help in suppressing brigands: he decided, however, to use the militia to force the king to grant a constitution. The original plan misfired but the flag of rebellion was raised by two lieutenants, Morelli and Salvati, acting independently. Pepe remained unsuspected by the government and was able to persuade the latter to mobilize the militia, with which he promptly marched on the capital. Three generals who ought to have barred his way found that they could not trust their men, and on 9 July the rebels defiled before Ferdinand who proclaimed the Spanish Constitution of 1812 and summoned a parliament.

The revolt in Naples was given a special character by widespread support from the upper classes. The aristocracy found to its disappointment that revolutionary measures carried out by French governments in the matter of land ownership were not annulled by the restored king. Entails and feudal tenures disappeared in 1819. This led to the rise of a new class of smaller landowners but they too nursed grievances. They were afraid lest former ecclesiastical land should be restored to the church and irritated by the government's policy of importing cheap corn from the Crimea. Meanwhile the small commercial bourgeoisie found itself hampered by customs barriers and inefficient absolutism. The greatest common cause of complaint lay in the government's policy towards brigands, which was both humiliating and ineffective. Brigandage, always a popular occupation with the peasants of Naples, became more widespread than ever after 1815 when large numbers of unsavoury types were let loose from the army. Brigands could live with comparative safety in the mountains whence they descended upon farms and even upon towns. Bands under the leadership of one Annichiarico were reported to be 50,000 strong. The minister of police, Canosa, offered bribes to anyone who could poison brigands and formed gangs of ruffians to attack them. Austrian troops were used to provide escorts for travellers until

1818 when the government decided to form a militia. Pepe found that his recruits for the militia were mostly landowners and wealthy persons, large numbers of whom were members of the Carboneria.

A society calling itself the charcoal-burners appeared in Naples during the reign of Murat and seems to have acted at first as an association for mutual assistance among officers of lower rank. About 1811 British agents in Sicily established contact with the Carboneria whose activities thereafter became increasingly political. Members were recruited from the petty bourgeoisie and lower clergy, the classes most interested in conspiring against French rule. After 1815 members were drawn predominantly from the upper classes. Secrecy and lurid symbolism appealed to the Neapolitans, and societies such as the Sanfedisti and Apostolati, similar in form but conservative and Catholic in tendency, met with equal success among the peasantry. Many peasants were worse off after 1815 as a result of exploitation by the new gentry, a fact which drove them away from the Carboneria into the arms of the absolutist régime. Bands of brigands made alliances with both sides.

Pepe wrote afterwards in his memoirs, 'I had succeeded in forming ten thousand of the most wealthy landowners into companies and battalions adhering to the most rigid discipline.' In another passage he claimed, 'I was ready to form the nucleus of a revolution either in the immediate Kingdom or all over Italy.' Discipline was not strong enough to hold the militia to the fight against Austria, however: the rebel forces melted away after the first clash at Rieti and the Austrians entered Naples unopposed in March 1821. Nor were aspirations to Italian independence visible in the events of the revolution. Requests from the two Papal enclaves of Pontecorvo and Benevento to be incorporated into the state of Naples were refused.

Three days after the defeat of Pepe's army a revolt broke out in Piedmont. The ringleaders acted under the influence of Count Santorre di Santarosa, a highly placed government official who believed that King Victor Emmanuel could be persuaded to declare war upon Austria under the banner of reform. Subversive propaganda won over half the army. The military conspirators were supported by secret societies such as the Federati which were predominantly aristocratic in membership. On 21 March the garrisons at Alessandria and several other towns mutinied, demanding war with Austria and the proclamation of a constitution. When the government hesitated the garrison at Turin threatened to bombard the city. The Powers meeting at Laibach threatened intervention if any constitution were granted and Victor Emmanuel, faced with the alternatives of civil war and foreign invasion, abdicated in favour of his brother Charles Felix. An agitation stirred up by the secret societies persuaded the Regent, Charles Albert, to proclaim the Spanish Constitution of 1812. For this he was ordered into exile by the king, who petitioned Austria for help. The rebels, deserted by the

dynasty, were easily scattered by Austrian troops returning from Naples.
The revolts gave Metternich an excuse to intensify the régime of police and
spies in Italy. The result was not to destroy conspiracy but to change its
character. The exile of hundreds of Italian suspects meant that conspirators
worked from foreign centres where they were more out of touch than ever
with the feelings of the masses and where they too readily came to think in
terms of help from foreign governments. Their biggest effort, which raised
simultaneous rebellions in the Duchies and Legations, achieved a temporary
success in 1831 but collapsed when France failed to send help and when rebel
cliques in the towns of central Italy failed to unite in the face of the Austrians.
Among the exiles after this last affair was Guiseppe Mazzini, a young
Genoese. In the bitterness of his heart Mazzini decided that Italy would
never prosper until her cause was removed from the hands of 'sects'. The
Carbonari and Federati demanded only partial liberties instead of total independence; they emphasized secrecy and therefore encouraged vagueness;
and they relied too much on aristocracies and governments. Leaders and
people must be educated towards a national effort. In July 1831 Mazzini
gathered forty exiles in Marseilles and formed a society called Young Italy.
The members dedicated themselves to the cause of revolt throughout the
peninsula. The society abandoned secrecy except for the names of members
and devoted a large part of its funds to propaganda. In the six numbers of
the society's newspaper and in many subsequent writings Mazzini tried to
inspire the people of Italy with his own fervent desire for independence,
unity, and liberty. The latter he believed could only be achieved in a
republic, whence the Italian nation would emerge.
Mazzini gave new meaning to the concept of nationality. He believed that
a nation had a moral purpose, as well as a linguistic basis and a political heritage. The nation, he explained, meant 'the totality of citizens speaking the
same language, associated together with equal political and civil rights in the
common aim of bringing the forces of society . . . progressively to greater
perfection'. The perfection of humanity became Mazzini's ultimate goal
and he believed that it could be achieved by forming a brotherhood of
nations in Europe. He summoned the youth of each nation to help him,
founding in 1834 another society called Young Europe. This was suppressed
by the Swiss authorities in 1836, but Mazzini's call to the nations to fulfil
their mission reverberated down the years. It caused Metternich to describe
Mazzini as the most dangerous man in Europe.

4. THE PAPACY

If by 1831 nationalism had become a revolutionary religion, catholicism
had become a bulwark of conservative policy. The two developments were
not unconnected. In 1815 even enlightened churchmen believed that

possession of a strip of territory across the centre of Italy was necessary to the independence of the Holy See. Under these circumstances the Pope was obliged to fight against Mazzini's vision of an Italian republic one and indivisible. The necessity to protect the Papal States has been seen by some historians as the root of all Papal utterances condemning revolutionary movements in Europe. Popes themselves conceived their policy in wider terms, however. Gregory XVI and Pius IX insisted that in attacking revolutionary ideas they were fighting against the greatest evil of their times.

When Pius VII returned to Rome in 1814 there was no certainty that he would recover temporal authority over all the former possessions of the church. Metternich wanted to see an Austrian puppet ruler installed in the Romagna, which was connected culturally, geographically, and economically with Lombardy-Venetia. The Great Powers were on the whole unheedful of the rights of small states and unwilling to restore ecclesiastical possessions. Rulers north of the Alps did not see any need to secure the support of the Pope. They were willing to take advantage of a renewed religious fervour among their subjects, but they hoped to keep the church in a subordinate position. The Catholic King of France recognized Napoleon's Concordat; the Catholic Emperor of Austria was openly Josephist. Monarchs were alarmed rather than gratified when Pius VII re-established the Society of Jesus in August 1814. However, a settlement of the Papal question was precipitated by Napoleon's escape from Elba and the rebellion of Murat. On 9 June 1815 the Final Act of the Congress of Vienna restored the temporal power of the Pope as far as the right bank of the river Po.

The Pope's representative at Vienna, his secretary of state Cardinal Consalvi, was congratulated even by his enemies on the success of his diplomacy. The recovery of the Romagna turned out to be a mixed blessing, however. The four Legations were the most prosperous, indeed the only profitable part of the Papal dominion but they were also the most difficult to rule. For seventeen years they had been joined with Lombardy under French administration. They lay far away from Rome, cut off by the Apennines. Their principal town, Bologna, was proud of its cultural tradition and resented domination from Rome. Wealthy inhabitants disliked the idea of returning to the incompetent rule of priests. All the troubles of the next forty years were to begin in the Romagna.

Consalvi saw the need to win respect for Papal government at home and abroad by combining moderation with efficiency and by introducing a lay element into the administration. Unfortunately a number of reactionary measures had been carried out by his colleagues before he returned from Vienna. Mgr Rivarola had dismissed from their posts all officials who had served the French and evicted from their benefices all clergy who had taken the oath of loyalty to Napoleon. Cardinal Pacca had destroyed the French codes of law and abolished street lighting and vaccination. Consalvi on his return to Rome worked out a plan to reconstruct the entire system of government. Cardinal-legates in the four Legations and bishop-delegates in the thirteen Delegations were to be assisted by committees of four laymen. Justice was to be separated from administration and placed in the hands of lay magistrates. An element of lay government did not mean, however, that there were to be concessions to representative ideas. Consalvi was no liberal. The lay committees were to be nominated by the government and were to act in a purely advisory capacity. In fact only a few materialized, for Consalvi's plans were undermined from the first by reactionary members of the Curia. In Rome, power was concentrated in the hands of the cardinal secretary of state and the eight or nine ecclesiastics appointed by the Pope to direct government departments. Municipal liberties were not restored, to the disappointment of the citizens of Bologna, Ravenna, and other towns of the Romagna.

During his eight years of office as secretary of state Consalvi tried to govern well. He was hampered by a growing number of reactionary cardinals and bishops, some of whom had to be appointed to leading posts in the administration. He was weighed down by the financial burden of compensating owners of land confiscated by the French. Under these circumstances his achievements were creditable. He introduced a new code of civil procedure, new measures for regulating roads and water supplies, and a new system of higher education. He replanned Rome, and reorganized taxation in order to relieve poorer communes. He failed, however, to create lasting prosperity by finding work for a rapidly growing population. His efforts to subsidize the textile industry and to embark on new agricultural ventures petered out for lack of capital. Agriculture and craft industry prospered in Umbria and the Legations, while an increasing number of tourists brought business to Rome, but poverty remained widespread over the western coastal region, in the Marches, and on the barren slopes of the Apennines. Beggars and brigands roamed the country. Their depredations angered the wealthy, particularly in the Legations, and gave them another motive for joining subversive societies. The cardinal-legates at Forlí and Ravenna imitated the bad example set by the government of Naples and formed voluntary bands, known as Centurions, to combat secret societies.

Metternich was afraid that revolutionary disturbances would break out in the Romagna and threaten the peace of Lombardy. He tried again and again to persuade Consalvi to enter into an alliance which would allow Austria to intervene in the Papal States at her discretion and in the rest of Italy with the Pope's blessing. Consalvi resolutely protested the neutrality of the Pope, though he could not render it effective. Without an army the Pope could not prevent the passage of Austrian troops through his territory to Naples in

1820. Without an adequate police force Consalvi could not guarantee order in the Papal States and eliminate the threat of Austrian intervention. Fortunately no serious revolt occurred at the time of the Neapolitan and Piedmontese troubles, a fact which Metternich attributed to Consalvi's enlightened rule. In 1823 however, Pius VII died and Consalvi was dismissed from office.

Pius VII's successor must bear some responsibility for the discontent in the Papal States culminating in the rebellion of 1831. Leo XII owed his election to the fact that he had been an enemy of Consalvi and could be relied upon to keep Papal government in the hands of priests. During his short reign (1823-9) he managed to remove from laymen the only effective power they had obtained since 1815 by restoring the old judicial system. Discontent reached dangerous proportions in the Legations and was aggravated rather than allayed when the Pope gave his blessing to the Centurions. In 1825 Leo appointed the intransigent Rivarola as legate at Ravenna and allowed him to carry out a brutal policy of repression. The Carboneria nevertheless grew apace and a few months of milder government under Pius VIII were powerless to undo the mischief. When the cardinal-legates were summoned to Rome to elect yet another Pope conspirators in Bologna seized the opportunity to rebel. They succeeded in setting up a provisional government to which almost all the cities not only in the Legations but in Umbria and the Marches gave their allegiance. The revolt was led by professional and aristocratic citizens whose chief complaint was the Papacy's refusal to allow men of their kind to play a part in government. Little support was obtained from the poorer inhabitants of the towns and no attempt was made to appeal to the countryside. The revolt was nevertheless too stubborn to be put down by Papal troops. The new Pope Gregory XVI had the alternatives of negotiating with the rebels or calling in the aid of the Austrians.

The demand of the rebels for lay government could only have been met by removing priests from all political, administrative, and judicial posts. The demand for elected government was less explicit but could be regarded as implicit in the revolutionary programme. The Pope would have needed to set up elected councils in the cities and provinces and probably in Rome itself. He would have been required to reign but not rule over a federation of papal states. Comparable solutions to the papal problem were suggested on several occasions later in the century. The men who suggested them were, like the rebels of 1831, members of the Catholic church: they believed that the spiritual authority and independence of the Pope could be guaranteed if he allowed his political affairs to be guided by a Catholic assembly. There is no evidence that Gregory seriously considered such a solution. The vested interests of the cardinals and bishops would have caused them to fight against relinquishing a traditional source of profit and power even if there had not been more sensitive reasons for opposing change. Most of the Pope's advisers thought back to the successive stages of the French Revolution and could not believe that rebels would remain content with reorganizing the temporal activities of the Holy See. Even if liberals were modest in their conscious aims their demands rested on the belief that sovereignty belonged to the people, whereas to the Pope it belonged to God and under Him to the church. Even the mildest liberal aspirations could be construed as a rejection of the church's teaching concerning man's fall from grace and his need of redemption.

On 15 March 1831 Gregory appealed to Austria for help and the rebellion was crushed by Austrian troops. This did not end the Pope's difficulties, however. Without substantial concessions to public opinion the Pope's authority must continue to rest on foreign bayonets. The Austrians withdrew in July 1831 only to be recalled in January 1832. Their occupation of Bologna provoked the French into occupying Ancona. France offered to protect the temporal power if reform were carried out but Gregory preferred to cling to the old régime. As he told the Prussian ambassador, he regarded even an advisory lay council as 'the beginning of a representative system, which is incompatible with Pontifical government'.

The moral support which Metternich had wished since 1815 to obtain from the Pope was at last acquired. Gregory before he became Pope adopted an uncompromising attitude towards the Belgian revolt, exhorting Belgian clergy to remain loyal to the King of the Netherlands. In the early months of his pontificate he adopted a similar attitude towards the Polish revolt, exhorting Polish clergy to preach filial obedience to the Tsar's government even though Nicholas I had pursued anti-catholic policies in Poland for many years. In 1832, when Polish rebels were suffering the harshest repression, Gregory ordered Polish bishops to remain submissive to the powers ordained by God and to endeavour to safeguard their flocks against the error of new ideas.

In Belgium and Poland Gregory foresaw two dangers: that the clergy would support revolution for the sake of achieving independence for the church, and that they would come to believe in the principles preached by the rebels. A French priest, Lamennais, showed that only a step was needed to move from one position to the next. In the early days of the July Monarchy Lamennais joined left-wing critics of Louis-Philippe in demanding more extensive liberties than the bourgeois monarch seemed prepared to grant. He argued in terms of expediency: the Catholic church must free itself from control by a king who was openly indifferent to religion and obtain more elbow room for converting an irreligious generation. In August 1830 he founded a daily newspaper, the *Avenir*, to campaign for freedom of education, freedom of the press, freedom of association, and freedom of worship. From demanding liberty as a weapon for Catholics against a wicked world Lamennais came to regard it as a part of Christ's gift to His people. He became so sure that his beliefs belonged to God's truth that he determined to appeal to the Pope against the hostility of the French hierarchy. In November 1831 he travelled with his young friends Lacordaire and Montalembert to Rome. Gregory spoke to them graciously but without mentioning the object of their visit. On their way home through Germany they were overtaken by the bull *Mirari vos* (1832) which condemned any notion that the church should take over the liberties demanded by revolutionary politicians. Lamennais gave up publishing the *Avenir* but he could not give up his opinions. The fate of the Polish exiles inspired him to write a book, *Paroles d'un croyant*, which was condemned by the Pope in 1834 as 'false, calumnious, rash, tending towards anarchy, contrary to the word of God, impious, scandalous, and erroneous'. The breach between the religion of Rome and the religion of liberty was complete.

5. THE CONFEDERATION OF GERMANY

The condition of Germany was extremely confused after 1815. Some of the tiny pieces which had made up the patchwork of the Holy Roman Empire were sewn together to produce thirty-nine states but the seams were by no means strong. The two largest states, Austria and Prussia, lacked internal cohesion. Prussia's eastern provinces were divided from her western provinces geographically by a string of sovereign petty states. Her people were divided also by acute differences in outlook. The junkers of Brandenburg and Pomerania were less educated and more narrow in their interests than the upper classes of the Province of Prussia, of Silesia, and of the west. A German historian has described the 'colonial tone', military and bureaucratic, which came from the east and pervaded the entire state of Prussia, to the annoyance of people in Saxony, Westphalia, and on the Rhine. Prussia found her Rhineland provinces especially difficult to assimilate, for the people were Catholic and they had long been influenced by French ideas.

The aggrandizement of Prussia caused considerable resentment in Germany and nowhere more than in Bavaria. The latter was developing into a Great German Power in Napoleonic times but her ambitions were frustrated in 1815. Her territories in Franconia pointed westward along the Main but she did not receive Frankfurt or Mainz. She secured the East Rhenish Palatinate but failed to connect it with her central dominions and achieve a dominating position on the Rhine. Her rulers claimed superiority over a host of petty princes by emphasizing the exclusively German and Catholic nature of Bavaria, but her total population was smaller than the German population of Prussia, and as a Catholic leader she could not compete with Austria. King Ludwig I at his accession in 1825 tacitly confessed the impossibility of wielding political power in Germany by beginning to sponsor scholars and musicians and to deck out Munich as the cultural centre of Germany. He continued, however, to claim a right to the West Rhenish Palatinate, which cut Bavarian territories in two and had been given in 1815 to Baden. The narrow strip of land which formed Napoleon's Grand Duchy of Baden was one of the most artificial states in Germany. Its people were of mixed origin. Their livelihood came from the Rhine, which caused them to turn away from south German neighbours towards the west and north. Their rulers were at loggerheads not only with Bavaria but with Württemberg. King William I of Württemberg had won military honours under Napoleon and was dissatisfied after 1815 with his little state.

Other petty states could also be grouped geographically, and might have been able to fulfil a useful function in Germany if their rulers had deigned to do so. A north-western group might have crippled the policy of Prussia, whose territories they divided, if they had co-operated under Hanover. A Saxon-Thuringian group in central Germany might have acted as a barrier between Prussia on the one hand and Austria and Bavaria on the other, but Thuringia had always outdone the rest of Germany in a capacity for splitting into fragments. There were still ten rulers in Thuringia, each insisting on a portion of rich country to balance the poor, a tract of woodland and an area of pasture. Thus the Grand Duchy of Saxony-Weimar-Eisenach consisted of two principal parts and eleven enclaves, Altenburg of one main part and five enclaves. A Partition Commission set up in 1826 failed to simplify the muddle.

It would be useless to pretend that the German people burned collectively with a desire to abolish the ludicrous divisions. Germany was still overwhelmingly agricultural and the peasants who formed the vast majority of her population were too ignorant and depressed to think in political terms. Many peasants were worse off after 1815 than they had been before. A more selfconscious nobility attacked or exploited the half-hearted measures of emancipation carried out during the French era. In some states, notably Württemberg and the two Mecklenburgs, nobles continued to exact feudal dues; in others, peasants were driven out of their small holdings by capitalist landowners. In Prussia Hardenberg succumbed to the pressure of the aristocracy and allowed the Edict of 1811 to be modified to the detriment of the peasants. The Declaration of 29 May 1816 said that only restricted categories of peasants (i.e. those who possessed draft animals and paid land tax) could obtain release from feudal services. These measures coincided with a severe agricultural depression throughout Germany. Britain had become more self-supporting during the war and no longer needed to buy large quantities of food from Germany; the result was a sharp fall in Germany's exports and hence in prices. Many small farmers were unable to maintain themselves. The harvest of 1816 was the worst of the century, and

peasants in some parts of Germany were reduced to making bread from the
bark of trees. No work was to be found in factories, for the dislocation
which took place in German industry after the ending of the Continental
Blockade coincided with an influx of labour from disbanded armies. A
local historian described the poor people of Mecklenburg as so restricted in
outlook that they had no fatherland but only a father village. The same was
found to be true of the poor throughout Prussia when an enquiry was made
into their political opinions in 1817. Germany might have meant more to
them if the *Bund* had done anything for them, but a proposal by a sub-
committee at Frankfurt that food supplies should be allowed to circulate
free of duty at times of scarcity was resisted by Austria and Bavaria as an
encroachment on the sovereign rights of the component states.

Political ideas were to be found only among the aristocracy and intelligentsia. The former gave allegiance to the princes and hoped to recover the
powers and privileges lost in previous years. The educated middle class was
more obstreperous. Its members resented most bitterly the stuffy atmosphere
of the petty states, the gossip and intrigue which dominated the life of the
miniature courts, the necessity to bow and scrape to lordlings whose patronage governed the community, the inability to escape from soldiers and
officials with nothing to do but bully and interfere. Political ideas were
confused and ill-defined, however. Some Germans came to think that a
written constitution would safe-guard them from the licentiousness of their
particular ruler. When efforts to secure parliamentary rule failed they came
to wish for a national state to overawe the petty tyrant. This brought them
into contact with romanticism, which in Germany continued to follow the
undesirable trends springing from the theories of Herder. While many
Germans admired the medieval Empire, others saw in Prussian authoritar-
ianism the most remarkable expression of the German spirit. Political theory
gained support from the philosophy of Hegel, which idealized the state based
on power and represented Germany as driven by historical necessity to form
such a state. Indeed, Hegel envisaged the emergence of an all-powerful Germany as the final phase in world history. His *Philosophy of Right* had no
counterpart in English or French writing, a feature which enhanced its popularity among a generation of German readers who rejected the influence of the
West. Among Germany's great writers only Goethe continued to speak of
the debt which he owed to French culture and to deplore the arrogant and
exclusive character of the new nationalism. A wave of anti-semitism was
one of the most startling features of the time. Aggressive attitudes were
encouraged by Father Jahn, who remained influential among the youth of
Germany. His demands for racial purity grew more and more hysterical as
he urged Germans to prepare themselves for a great war against the West.

The complications embedded in Germany's political thinking were either lost upon or ignored by Metternich. To him all agitators were liberals and all liberals nationalists. Perhaps he felt that by presenting them in this way he could most effectively use them to frighten the princes. After 1815 the rulers of Bavaria, Baden, Württemberg, Hesse-Darmstadt, and Saxe-Weimar had obeyed the injunction implicit in article 13 of the Federal Act and had granted constitutions to their subjects. Their elected assemblies were more like medieval estates than modern parliaments but Metternich regarded them as dangerous. He was also alarmed at the freedom allowed to universities by princes such as the Duke of Saxe-Weimar who liked to think of themselves as patrons of learning. Events in Germany played into his hands. On 18 October 1817 a large gathering of university students celebrated on the Wartburg the tercentenery of the Reformation. A bonfire was built and a few relics of French domination such as a corporal's cane and some books hostile to German nationalism were consigned to the flames. This piece of adolescent bad taste was exaggerated by Metternich into a sign that desperate doings were afoot in Germany. Then in the spring of 1819 a German student, Karl Sand, assassinated a writer of reactionary propaganda, Kotzebue. Metternich could scarcely conceal his joy. In August the representatives of nine German states joined him in framing the Carlsbad Decrees, which were ratified later by the Federal Diet. Strict censorship was prescribed for almost all publications, inspectors were allotted to universities, and informers were introduced into lecture rooms and churches. Gentz expressed his satisfaction at 'the greatest retrograde movement that has taken place in Europe since 1789'. In the following year Metternich persuaded the Diet to limit the number of subjects which might be discussed in elected assemblies. 'I have become', he said, 'a species of moral power in Germany'.

Metternich's most strenuous efforts were directed towards enticing Prussia away from reform. Frederick William III had promised four times since 1810 that he would grant a constitution and in his slow-moving way he seemed to be progressing towards fulfilment of his promise. In spite of the reactionary influence of members of the aristocracy and of writers such as Ancillon and Schmalz, he appointed a determined reformer, Humboldt, to an important place in the government in 1819. Metternich worked steadily upon Frederick William's mind, however, through an agent, Wittgenstein, who secured a post in the Prussian government. The chancellor Hardenberg proved to be a broken reed to the reformers. He wanted to crown his career by giving Prussia a constitution but he was more anxious still to remain in power, and because he wished to hush up his own connections with patriotic societies in earlier days he joined Metternich in the hue and cry against them. It was in fact Hardenberg who, in a meeting with Metternich at Teplitz, set in motion the chain of proposals which culminated in the Carlsbad Decrees. In the same meeting Metternich succeeded in persuading Frederick William III that representative institutions were incompatible with monarchical government. Prussia abandoned not only the path of constitutional reform but the attempts made by Scharnhorst and Boyen to integrate the army into civilian life. Boyen had succeeded in 1815 in establishing universal conscription but he failed in 1819 to prevent Frederick William from modifying the *Landwehr* out of all recognition. He resigned office along with Humboldt at the end of the year.

Metternich failed to see that Prussia under an authoritarian and military régime would one day become a greater rival to Austria than she had been in her era of reform. Admittedly the danger was a long way off, for Hardenberg had openly subordinated Prussia to the will of the Austrian chancellor. When revolutionary events in Europe stimulated a new outburst of radical feeling in Germany in 1832 Prussia co-operated with Austria in persuading the Diet to re-enforce reactionary measures. The works of the exile Heine and of other writers calling themselves Young Germany were banned by the Prussian government in 1835.

The 'system' appeared to be supreme in Germany, yet Metternich himself lamented that the first nail had been driven into the coffin of the German Confederation. He referred to the formation of a Customs Union under the leadership of Prussia. The Union was a product of the efforts made by the government and the business community of Prussia to drag their country out of the depression into which it sank after 1815. The Napoleonic wars had left heavy debts, only a few of which were recovered from the French indemnity. Various industries such as ironworks which had been stimulated during the war could not immediately reorganize themselves to meet peacetime needs. Other industries were almost swept away by the influx of British manufactures, particularly of textiles and hardware. Former export trades in cereals, timber, wool, and linen could not easily be recovered in view of the customs tariffs imposed by most of Germany's neighbours. A number of natural difficulties stood in the way of economic development. Large areas of sandy heath and marshland were unsuitable for agriculture and unable to produce food for large urban communities. Coal supplies were to be found only on the periphery of the country, in the Ruhr and Saar, in Saxony and Silesia, and could not be utilized fully without railways. Germany's North Sea ports were less favourably situated than French, Dutch, and British ports for trading on the North Atlantic route in days of sail. Some other hindrances could be removed, however. The sovereign rights of the component states of Germany allowed each prince to erect customs barriers. The result was that goods travelling through Germany were held up at every state frontier and at innumerable provincial boundaries and city gates where they were obliged to pay dues and tolls which rendered them extremely expensive. Merchants complained of a life spent among

RUSSIA

AUSTRIAN EMPIRE

R. Dniester

BESSARABIA

R. Pruth

MOLDAVIA

Jassy

Odessa

R. Sava

WALLACHIA

BLACK
SEA

BOSNIA

Belgrade

Bucharest

SERBIA   Vidin   *R. Danube*

BULGARIA

ROUMELIA

MONTE-
NEGRO

A D R I A T I C   S E A

THRACE   Constantinople

Bosporus

ALBANIA-EPIRUS

MACEDONIA

Janina

Corfu

SOULI

THESSALY

Dardanelles

ÆGEAN
SEA

Chios

ANATOLIA

ROUMELIA
Missolonghi

Corinth   Athens

MOREA

Tripolitsa

Navarino

English Miles

50   0   50   100   150   200

CRETE

The terms *Albania* and *Epirus* were
interchangeable at this time.
The term *Roumelia* was used by the Turks to denote their European
provinces and by the Greeks to denote merely Central Greece.

Map VI   The Balkans, 1815–21

stupid customs officials, and industrialists found that accumulation of capital
was impossible.

In 1818 Prussia accepted Maassen's reformed tariff for all her provinces.
Raw materials were freed entirely from duty, manufactured goods were
subjected to a duty of only ten per cent, and transit duty on goods crossing
Prussian territory was radically reduced. Prussian statesmen then began to

negotiate commercial treaties with other states on the basis of the reformed tariff. Progress was extremely slow. A petition by Friedrich List to the Federal Diet produced no result. Persistent efforts built up the German Customs Union (*Zollverein*) by 1834, however, only a few states remaining aloof.

Prussia could now begin to take over the economic leadership of Germany. Her acquisitions in 1815 had given her control over the main coalfields and over important industries in Saxony, Westphalia, and the Rhineland. She commanded the most important commercial routes along the Rhine, Elbe, Oder, and Vistula, and she could build roads and railways easily across the north German plain. She probably had no political aim when she made the *Zollverein*, which was in a sense a concession to disunity, a means of obtaining commercial regeneration whilst respecting the political sovereignty of the petty states. The political significance of the move was none the less obvious to Metternich.

CHAPTER XVI

The Wind of Change

I. THE BALKAN TURMOIL

IN 1815 the continuation of Turkish rule in the Balkans seemed to Britain and Austria a necessary if deplorable barrier to the expansion of Russia. Yet from the time of the French Revolution there had been no-one in the Balkans, not even among the Turks, whose interest lay in maintaining the status quo. Ottoman rule was characterized not only by a complete indifference to the needs and wishes of conquered peoples but also by a total neglect of the resources of conquered regions. Government was decentralized to the point of feudal anarchy. Each province was ruled by a pasha who was nominally the representative of the Sultan, but the pashas were in fact local chieftains enjoying almost complete independence. Each sought only to enlarge his pashalik at the expense of his neighbours, the results of continuous intrigue and local warfare being simply registered each year by the Divan when it renewed the titles of its supposed servants. The people of the Balkans became poorer and poorer, for the peasants ceased to cultivate the fields, which were ravaged continually by passing armies. Thousands sought to escape the extortionate demands of their local potentate by fleeing to the mountains. Huge bands of brigands, owning no government save the power of their chief to impose his will, were regarded as heroes by the wretched people of the plains simply because they plundered the rich. To this state of anarchy must be added wholesale corruption, for every pasha enhanced his fortunes by selling offices large and small to the highest bidder.

Under these circumstances rebellion was endemic. Nationalism, however, was scarcely discernible. Revolts were more often directed against local tyrants than against the Sultan: often they were stirred up by one pasha against another. A characteristic if extreme case was the turmoil out of which Ali Pasha, the 'Lion' of Janina, carved himself an empire in the early years of the nineteenth century. This prodigious personage, of unbounded cruelty, duplicity, greed, and vindictiveness, won the gratitude of the Porte for his relentless attacks on the Souliots, a group of clans which had flourished in the mountains of Epirus since the beginning of the seventeenth century, maintaining themselves by preying on the people of the valleys and on the traffic passing between Janina and southern Greece. Having reduced the

Souliot Confederation to ruins in 1803 Ali proceeded to build a reputation for good government in Janina, encouraging commerce, organizing a police force, protecting scholars, and (since he was himself an atheist) distributing posts and favours (for cash) to Christians and Moslems alike. At the same time he stopped neither at theft nor murder to increase his horde of wealth and extend his power at the expense of his neighbours. By 1817 he and his son Veli controlled in the name of the Sultan the whole of Albania, Thessaly, western Macedonia, and central Greece. In 1821 Ali chanced his arm against the Sultan, promising the people a constitution if they would aid him in rebellion. He even allowed the Souliots to return from exile in Corfu to their mountain fortresses. He and they were attacked by Turkish armies under the capable and zealous Kourchid Pasha of the Morea. After fierce fighting Ali's double dealing came home to roost: his followers deserted or turned traitor and he himself met his death at the hands of Turkish troops whom he believed had come to treat with him. The only significance of the affair from a nationalist point of view was that by keeping Turkish armies occupied for the whole of the year 1822 Ali allowed the Greek revolt to gain ground.

The first Balkan revolt to assume anything like a nationalist character was the Serbian revolt which began in 1804, though even this was directed in the first place against local oppressors (the Janissaries stationed at Belgrade) rather than against the Sultan. The Serbs were almost all peasants. They had retained the rudiments of local administration, each village possessing a headman, but they had no bourgeoisie or aristocracy. Faint glimmerings of national culture reached them from Serbian writers such as the historian Obradovitch in southern Hungary, but their leader in revolt was a man who could neither read nor write, the heroic Kara or Black George, a pig-dealer. Sultan Selim III gave his tacit consent to punitive measures against the unruly Janissaries; but when the Serbs, flushed by their victories, demanded a semi-autonomous position he sent armies against them. The revolt thus became a war of independence. The Serbs received little or no support from other Balkan peoples: the Greek officials who meddled in the revolt in the early stages backed out when they could no longer hope to obtain princely positions in a tributary state. Karageorge fought desperately, but with the ending of the Russo-Turkish war he realized that the cause was hopeless and in 1807 he fled to Hungary. Three Turkish armies descended upon Serbia and carried out a terrible vengeance. Even families which had played no part in the revolt feared extermination, and on Palm Sunday 1815 they launched a second rebellion, under the equally illiterate but more astute Miloch Obrenovitch. Within two years, without foreign aid, the Serbs triumphed over Turkish arms. Many more years of patient negotiation and subtle manoeuvre were needed on the part of Obrenovitch before Serbian autonomy and his own title of hereditary prince were recognized by the Porte, but by 1834 the task was complete and Serbia free to govern herself. The triumph of the Serbs revealed as nothing else had ever done the military weakness of the Turks. Members of the Turkish government at Constantinople were not altogether complacent, but most of them hesitated to copy ideas from the infidel. The Sultan himself, Selim III, knew no such qualms. Coming to the throne in 1789 in the middle of a war against Austria and Russia he at once launched a series of reforms calculated to modernize the army on western lines, harness the financial resources of the Empire to the service of the state, and transform the Divan into a committee of ministers with executive power. He met with stubborn and even violent resistance from every group whose interests were threatened: from the great Moslem landowners and military fief owners, from the leaders of the church, and above all from the Janissaries, the immensely privileged and by now ungovernable regiments of guards. Resistance found a leader in Osman Pasvanoglou, a bandit chief who so terrorized the Sultan that the latter made him pasha of Vidin and allowed him to dominate the greater part of Bulgaria. Here Pasvanoglou maintained himself for many years by adopting the devise of 'liberty and equality', by reducing the taxes of the Moslem population, and by granting toleration to the Christians.

Meanwhile Selim III became more and more unpopular through his attempts to levy troops for his new model armies. Finally in 1807 he was forced by a palace revolution to destroy his great reforming edict, the *Nizam-i Djedid* of 1792, and abdicate the throne. His successor Mahmud II was a less dedicated but more successful reformer. He persisted, though in a more dissimulating manner, with his uncle's projects, until in 1826 he felt obliged to take the terrible step necessary to make them really effective: the wholesale slaughter of the Janissaries. By this time, however, Ottoman rule in the Balkans was facing a greater threat than it had ever known.

Against a general background of chaos and neglect the social and political situation in the Balkans differed from province to province. The Albanians were for the most part primitive tribesmen, continually warring against each other or serving as mercenaries under warring pashas. Some had become converted to Islam and acquired important posts under the Sultan: these were looked at askance by the Christians who were, however, content to remain under Ottoman rule as long as it did not interfere with their turbulent behaviour. The Bulgars were equally primitive. Living near to Constantinople they had borne the brunt of Turkish oppression. They were peasants, mostly serfs, working for great Turkish landowners. Commerce in Bulgaria was in the hands of Greeks, the towns were predominantly Greek, the schools were Greek, and most positions in the church were held by Greeks. A few monasteries sheltered the flame of native culture, kindled in the late eighteenth century by the historian Paissy, but many decades were to pass before the light penetrated to the people. The entire province was ravished by bandits, the Kirjalis, who attacked and destroyed whole towns with impunity.

The Serbs were slightly more advanced, if only because a large part of their country had been occupied by the Austrians in the eighteenth century. The Roumanians were even more privileged, for the provinces of Moldavia and Wallachia were mere tributaries of the Porte, which appointed their prince or hospodar. The peasants were exploited by a native nobility, the boyards, who owned most of the land and did no work. Among the boyards French culture was considered a sign of good breeding, and a superficial attachment to French revolutionary ideas spread rapidly. The peasants hated the boyards without realizing that they in their turn were exploited by two classes of Greeks: the merchants, and the officials appointed by the prince. The latter was himself usually a Phanariot Greek. Having paid heavily for his throne he reimbursed himself pitilessly at the expense of the people. Nevertheless the Principalities owed to the Phanariots, who were a highly cultivated class, their first written laws and considerable advances in art, education, and letters. Roumanian as well as Greek schools were founded, and the standard of education in them was often higher than that found under the Austrians in Transylvania.

The Greeks possessed a highly complicated social structure and the unique position of having penetrated every part of the Balkans save Montenegro (which remained fiercely independent not only of Greek influence but of Turkish domination throughout the Ottoman era). Most illustrious of the Greeks were the Phanariots, privileged officials from the *fanar* or Patriarch's quarter of Constantinople. Since the middle of the seventeenth century Phanariots had occupied nearly all the leading positions in the service of the Sultan. Ambitious, unscrupulous, and greatly talented, they intrigued continually against the Sultan without, however, wishing to destroy the Ottoman Empire. Their object was to change it into a modern state in which they could expect to hold the most lucrative and important posts. Next to the Phanariots the dignitaries of the Greek church played the most direct part in political life. The Porte did not recognize different nationalities but only different religions, hence the Patriarch of Constantinople was regarded as the representative of the 'Roman people' at the court of the Sultan, and bishops occupied a similar position in relation to the pachas. Ecclesiastical posts, like all others, were sold to the highest bidders, and many bishops were from a religious point of view unworthy of their sees. They carried out administrative and judicial duties with some credit, however. Bishops were usually employed by the Turks to govern towns and villages situated on imperial fiefs, and they also dispensed justice to Christians and, on demand, to Moslems. Whilst sharing Phanariot dreams of transforming the Empire they were rendered cautious by the knowledge that reprisals would fall most heavily on them in the event of a revolt. Merchants, on the other hand, were enthusiastic and impatient supporters of Phanariot schemes, not because they wanted power but because they wanted liberty of commerce. They travelled a great deal, maintaining contact with Greek colonies in foreign countries as well as with Europeans of all nations domiciled in Turkey. The ideas which they brought back to Greece were spread along the coast and throughout the interior by hosts of seamen and muleteers. Seamen were especially important in the islands of the Aegean, where the Ottoman governor, who was also commander-in-chief of the Ottoman fleet, interfered little with the local oligarchies. The decline of French commerce in the Levant during the Napoleonic wars gave Greek ship-owners an unrivalled opportunity to build large merchant fleets, equipped with guns for the purpose of warding off pirates and breaking the blockade. Greek peasants, like their counterparts all over the Balkans, were ground down by depradations and exactions, but they enjoyed a few crumbs of education which fell to them from the lavish expenditure on schools and colleges by the Phanariots and the church. The Greeks were a quick-witted people, and even the humblest of them seized hold of the idea that they must drive the Turks away from the homeland and set up some sort of constitutional government which would win them support from a Great Power. Their ultimate aim was to restore the Greek medieval empire at Constantinople.

The people of the Balkans were extremely diverse, in both religion and nationality, and the boundaries between the groups were in no way defined. Surprisingly, in these circumstances, a few idealists dreamed from time to time of rousing combined action against the Turks and setting up some kind of a pan-Balkan state. The first to do so was a writer known as Rhigas, whose plans for a Balkan Republic on the lines of the French earned him a martyr's death at the hands of the Turks in 1798. Rhigas was best known for his patriotic songs, one of which was an adaptation of the *Marseillaise*. Whether he ever founded a secret society is doubtful, though such societies flourished in Greece from at least the end of the eighteenth century. The most successful was the *Hetairía Philiké*, revived by Greek merchants at Odessa in 1814. Members were drawn mainly from the Greeks engaged in commerce and administration all over the Balkans and in many parts of Europe and Turkey. Indeed by 1818, when the headquarters of the society were transferred to Constantinople, almost all Greeks of importance had been initiated. Efforts were made to extend membership to other Balkan nationalities, for the society aimed ultimately at the expulsion of the Turks from the entire peninsula, but the greatest faith was clearly placed in the Greeks, who were expected to form the first independent state. The leader chosen by the society after early years of indecision was a Greek prince, Alexander Ypsilanti, son of one of the Phanariot hospodars of Moldavia.

Ypsilanti was a general in the Russian army. Unlike most members of the *Hetairía* he was not entirely confident that he would receive Russian help, but in his proclamations he hinted at the possibility of such help in order to attract rebels to the cause. On 22 February 1821 he crossed the Pruth with a handful of followers and called upon the people of Moldavia to expel the Turks. His preparations in the Principalities had been minimal, partly because he assumed that the Roumanians and Greeks were ready to rise as one man and partly because he merely intended to pass through the Principalities into Serbia and Greece. Contrary to his expectations the Moldavian boyards greeted him with sullen hostility, for they hated all Greeks. He managed to raise an army of some three thousand Greek students only, and with this he advanced upon Bucharest. A rebellion was already in progress in western Wallachia, led by an adventurer Theodore Vladimirescu who had launched a peasant *jacquerie* against the Roumanian nobility. The two rebel leaders agreed at first to act together against the Turks, but Vladimirescu soon began negotiating with the Sultan in the hope of getting himself appointed prince of Wallachia. Ypsilanti thereupon had him beheaded at the hands of the *Hetairía*, a typically unwise action which increased Roumanian hostility to the Greek cause. Isolated in the Principalities, forsworn by the Serbs who were at this time trying to get the Sultan to recognize their independence, and repudiated by the Tsar, Ypsilanti suffered final defeat at the hands of the Turks on 7 June. The most important result of the whole abysmal adventure was to stimulate revolt in the Morea.

Greek peasants fell upon their Turkish overlords with tremendous fury, murdering all who could not take refuge in the walled towns. The Turks retaliated on Easter Day by hanging the Greek Patriarch and three archbishops outside the church at Constantinople. The act aroused the horror of the Christian world, and marked the beginning of an ever-growing philhellenist movement. The revolt was characterized throughout by horrible butchery. The Turks committed the worst single atrocity when they slaughtered the Greek islanders of Chios in 1822, but the Greeks were not lacking in brutality, especially the brigands (klephts) who played a leading part in the fighting. The Turks were at first too much occupied with Ali Pasha to give adequate attention to the Greeks, and the latter obtained striking successes. On land they captured the fortresses of Navarino, Tripolitsa, Missolonghi, Athens, and Corinth, whilst at sea their armed merchant fleet sank the most formidable Turkish vessels and drove the rest into the Dardanelles. In January 1822 a national assembly met at Epidauros, proclaimed the independence of Greece, and promulgated a constitution. The Greeks seemed incapable of uniting in constructive government, however. The constitution, drawn up by a few westernized Greeks from American and French models, meant nothing to the bandits, who set up rival authorities, while civil war raged in the Morea between the islanders and the people of the mainland. No decisive blow was delivered at the decrepit power of the Turks, and the latter were able to hold on grimly until 1825, when Mahmud II invited Mohammed Ali, pasha of Egypt, to come to his assistance.

With the disciplined forces of Mohammed Ali overrunning the Morea the Greek cause took a new turn. The whole of the western world believed that Nicholas I of Russia, who had succeeded Alexander in 1825, would now intervene to save the Greeks. Nicholas was an autocrat by nature, but he was not as doctrinaire as Alexander, and there was good reason to believe that he would combine repressive measures at home with a forward policy abroad, giving useful occupation to his disgruntled army officers. Canning could hardly shatter his reputation in the liberal world by depriving the Greeks of Russian help, and in any case the danger from Russia was now overshadowed by another menace, from Mohammed Ali himself. The latter had agreed to help the Sultan only on condition that he be allowed to govern Crete and that his son Ibrahim be made governor of the Morea. As one fortress after another was wrested from the Greeks it appeared that Ibrahim, who was commanding the Egyptian armies, intended to exterminate the Greek population and settle the Morea with colonists from north Africa. Canning therefore entered into an agreement with the Tsar in the hope of controlling his influence (4 April 1826). The two powers offered to mediate between the Sultan and the Greeks to secure an autonomous Greece under Turkish suzerainty. When the offer was refused by the Sultan they undertook, with French aid, to procure an armistice by blockading the Morea. This tricky operation resulted, shortly after Canning's death, in an 'unauthorized battle' in which allied squadrons destroyed the Turko-Egyptian fleet in the bay of Navarino (20 October 1827). The event signalized the breakdown of British policy, for war between Turkish and Russian troops in the Principalities became inevitable. The war which began in the spring of 1828 was not as shattering as Britain feared, however. The Tsar was discouraged by failure to win a quick victory and agreed that French troops should act on behalf of France and Britain in clearing the Egyptians from the Morea. All three powers were subsequently able to arrange the future of Greece which became an independent kingdom (1830) under the constitutional rule of a Bavarian prince, crowned Otto I, King of the Hellenes, in 1833.

It soon became obvious that constitutional government in Greece was a travesty of that known in the west. The liberation of Greece had, however, made an ineffaceable impression all over Europe. When in 1830 the Restoration settlement in France also collapsed, the world of conservatism and the balance of power seemed shaken indeed.

2. THE JULY REVOLUTION IN FRANCE

In 1814 Napoleon I was sent into exile but his followers remained behind to organize the next régime. At the end of May nine members of the *Corps législatif* and nine members of the Senate met with three agents of the king to draw up a constitution. The Napoleonic notables represented, in a general sense, those classes of the population which had done well for themselves during the last quarter of a century, namely the landed peasantry and the middle and upper levels of the bourgeoisie. Their minds were obsessed with the thought of benefits to be preserved: land ownership free from dues and tithes, economic enterprise unshackled by privileged corporations, the highest ranks of the professions open to men of humble birth, jobs in the civil service available to young men of education, and social prestige accruing to anyone with wealth or public position. They were also mindful of dangers which might threaten beneficiaries of the Revolution: a return to aristocratic and clerical privilege, possibly through the agency of a despotic monarch, or the rise of democracy and socialism, following from further revolutionary upheavals. Conservatism thus dominated the production of the Charter proclaimed to the people as the hallmark of liberty on 4 June 1814.

The first three articles were designed to ward off aristocratic privilege by declaring all Frenchmen equal before the law, all liable to taxation according to income, and all eligible for civil and military posts according to their talents. National land was declared an inviolable possession of those who had bought it. The Catholic religion was declared to be the state religion, but the maintenance of the Concordat and the Organic articles indicated the subordinate position it was intended to hold. Popular rights were embodied in articles guaranteeing freedom of opinion and freedom from arbitrary arrest, and stipulating the regular summoning of a parliament endowed with legislative and financial powers. The parliament was to consist of a Chamber of hereditary Peers nominated by the king (into which Napoleon's titled followers would be absorbed) and a Chamber of Deputies elected from the departments. Deputies were to be at least 40 years of age and possessed of property taxed at 1,000 francs a year; voters were to be at least 30 and taxed at 300 francs a year. In the interests of law and order the king was declared sole head of the executive power and was given the sole right to initiate legislation, an absolute veto on laws passed by parliament, and the right to prorogue and dissolve the Chambers.

The Bourbon Restoration lasted only 15 years, even when it was given a new start after the Hundred Days. There is no reason to believe that it was doomed to failure from the beginning, however. There were many people on both sides who were willing to accept a compromise between the old France and the new. Louis XVIII did not like constitutional government, but he saw that his loving subjects would not have him without it. He was too cynical to crusade against it and too sensible to run it deliberately on to the rocks. He contented himself with briefing his three agents so well that the Charter gave him more power than he had seen in the hands of the king of England. Most members of the nobility found themselves in a similar position. Few liked the Charter in the first place, but they soon realized that it gave them political power such as they had tried vainly to obtain at the beginning of the Revolution. The Chamber of Peers was merely the most obvious gain. The Chamber of Deputies was elected by some 90,000 wealthy persons, scarcely 10,000 of whom were qualified to stand as candidates. Voters and 'eligibles' were mainly landowners, not only because agriculture far outweighed industry in the national economy but also because direct taxes which carried eligibility to political rights fell most heavily on land. Provincial noblemen sat in large numbers in all the parliaments of the Restoration and succeeded in dominating most of them.

On the part of the new France there was no enthusiasm for Louis XVIII, who had been a stranger to his country for twenty-five years and an enemy in the wars. Dreams of a gallant figure from the pages of romance were dispelled by the first sight of Louis, fat, gouty, and disdainful. Nor were the courtiers who returned from exile or emerged from seclusion any more attractive, with their self-righteous airs and fulsome praises of the royal family. Intelligent observers realized, however, like Charles de Rémusat, that in return for recognition of the main revolutionary achievements an effort should be made to put up with the forms and pantomimes attending hereditary monarchy. They included in this category the curious preamble to the Charter, in which Louis announced that he was 'granting' liberties to his subjects of his own gracious will. Madame de Staël was about the only person who took serious exception to the preamble at the time. This formidable lady began work at once on her *Considerations on the principal events of the French Revolution*, vindicating popular sovereignty as a centuries-old tradition, but her book received a lukewarm response from the liberal press.

The liberal party which emerged in the early parliaments of the Restoration remained conservative from beginning to end. It achieved its greatest influence over government between 1817 and 1819 when the king's minister Decazes thought of broadening his popularity by co-operating with a little group of academic liberals known as the Doctrinaires. The most notable adherent of the group, Guizot, although not yet a member of parliament, had a hand in producing the three most important liberal measures of the period, the electoral law of 1817, the recruitment law of 1818, and the press law of 1819. The first guaranteed the existence of a freely elected Chamber but confined political rights within the narrow limits laid down by the Charter, the Doctrinaires rejecting a suggestion put forward by royalists that poorer persons might be given a share in elections at a lower level. The recruitment law embodied the liberal idea of equality by abolishing aristocratic privileges in the matter of army promotions. The press law established a system of trial by jury for press offences and was regarded by the Doctrinaires as fulfilling the promise of freedom made in the Charter. Their pride in it was not diminished by clauses requiring large sums of caution money from editors, a device intended to place newspapers under the direction of property owners. Benjamin Constant was one of a very few liberal deputies who protested against caution money and the only prominent liberal who ever advocated extending the franchise. The most eminent theorist of the Doctrinaire group, Royer-Collard, openly defended the right of the wealthiest property owners to monopolize seats in parliament which, however, he believed should confine itself to critical and legislative functions. The idea that a majority in parliament should be able to force the king to dismiss his ministers was resisted by liberals until 1830, when Guizot and Royer-Collard accepted it as a desperate expedient for getting rid of Polignac.

From early days there were fanatics on both sides who worked to destroy the Restoration compromise root and branch. A group of bonapartists founded a newspaper, the *Bibliothèque Historique*, in December 1817 to foster the Napoleonic legend. Secret societies of a republican character were active from 1818. Lafayette gave his august patronage to the formation of the *charbonnerie* in 1821, and a series of plots followed rapidly at Saumur, Belfort, Toulouse, Brest, Nantes, and La Rochelle. The Knights of the Faith remained in existence until 1828, scheming feverishly to restore absolute monarchy. Bonald published a journal and De Maistre some weighty tomes denouncing the evils of popular sovereignty. The number of fanatics was small, however, and their activities contributed little towards the destruction of the régime. The majority of politically-minded Frenchmen devoted themselves with enthusiasm to getting as much as they could out of the parliamentary system, believing that it gave them all the advantages of the famous English constitution without the accompanying defects of an illogical franchise and a barbarous penal code. A great deal went wrong. Ministers sometimes acted arbitrarily from sheer inexperience of constitutional government, as Beugnot did in 1814; some illustrious politicians, notably Chateaubriand, were unsuited by temperament to the conditions of parliamentary life; statesmen blundered; Charles X made grave tactical errors. Even the cumulative effect was not decisive, however. The Revolution of 1830 was brought about because of an intense fear on the part of large sections of the population that aristocrats and priests were going to destroy the fruits of the Revolution. Suspicions were aroused by the reaction which followed the Hundred Days. The government accepted the aid of royalist committees and secret societies in carrying out a purge of the administration, in which large numbers of bourgeois Frenchmen who had elbowed their way into prefectures and mayoralties during the Empire lost their jobs to aristocratic favourites. The number has been estimated at something between 50,000 and 80,000, constituting a quarter to a third of all the people employed in administrative posts. Meanwhile elections held according to rules devised by the king produced a Chamber of Deputies dominated by zealous royalists, known thereafter as 'ultras'. Liberal propaganda soon obscured the fact that more than half the members of the 'Chambre Introuvable' were of bourgeois origin and that its repressive legislation, of a temporary character only, was accepted as necessary by orderly citizens. By the summer of 1816 the existence of the 'Chambre Introuvable' was arousing such intense fears that foreign observers forecast another revolutionary outburst.

Louis XVIII wisely dissolved the Chamber on 5 September and secured the election of a majority of deputies with moderate views but, although tension was relaxed, suspicions still existed. They centred upon the fact that Élie Decazes remained in office as minister of police, becoming minister of the interior and virtual head of the cabinet when Richelieu resigned office in December 1818. It is not at first sight easy to see why liberal leaders so much distrusted Decazes. He professed moderation in politics. He was instrumental in persuading Louis to dissolve the 'Chambre Introuvable'; he persecuted ultra-royalist societies and dealt severely with ultra-royalist newspapers. He married into the Doctrinaire circle and took a member of the Doctrinaire group, De Serre, into the ministry in 1819. His unpopularity arose from the nature of his position, which was altogether remote from a parliamentary régime. He was the king's favourite, and the king had enormous power. Decazes owed his appointment not to the leadership of a moderate party in parliament, though such a party at first supported him, but to the king's liking for his conversation. He toadied to Louis on every occasion: Talleyrand said that the first time he saw Decazes he thought he was a hairdresser. There was a well-grounded fear that if aristocrats ever prevailed upon Decazes to attack the Charter, Decazes would prevail upon the king.

In their efforts to pull down Decazes, left-wing politicians and journalists whipped up a feeling of injustice among two sections of the community, the old soldiers of Napoleon's armies and the owners of one-time national land. Reminiscences of famous battles encouraged disbanded warriors to feel that they had rendered great services to their country which were now ignored by the government. Officers placed on half-pay and tied down to a fixed abode were made to feel that they ought to have been treated as the cream of the nation. Some dabbled in conspiracy; many more placed their faith in left-wing deputies elected in larger numbers every time a fifth of the Chamber was renewed. Liberals directed their annual election campaigns in large part at the new class of landowners, who were constantly reminded of the insecurity of their property. Émigrés had been given no compensation for the loss of their land; their reasonable complaints were easily interpreted as demands for full restitution; and fear that the government would one day give in to the émigrés caused former national land to fall in value. All these grievances were blamed by means of dark hints upon scheming aristocrats and priests, and the most widely-read liberal newspaper of the time, the *Constitutionnel*, spread rumours that Jesuits had already obtained a hold over the government.

Meanwhile ultra-royalists, ninety of whom were re-elected to the Chamber in 1816, accused Decazes of running the country headlong into revolution by flirting with left-wing ideas. As more and more radicals succeeded at elections the ultras pressed for a revision of the electoral law. Both Richelieu and Decazes came to the conclusion that the ministry could only survive by seeking allies from Right or Left: Richelieu wanted to take the former course and resigned office when Decazes's fancy for an open alliance with the Doctrinaires won the favour of the king. The ensuing press law widened the opportunity for critics on both sides to hurl abuse at Decazes. The hysterical attitude adopted by the extreme Left alarmed the Doctrinaires as well as the ministry, and the election of abbé Grégoire, a notorious member of the Convention, to the Chamber of Deputies in September 1819 convinced even Royer-Collard that the electoral law would have to be modified. The projected swing to the Right had not, however, been completed when on 13 February 1820 a madman named Louvel murdered the Duc de Berry, second in succession to the throne and the only prince of the older Bourbon line capable of begetting a son. Ultra-royalists at once connected Louvel with the Left and blamed Decazes for failing to curb revolutionary elements. Some even accused Decazes of complicity in the murder. Security measures were at once presented to the Chamber but the hue and cry continued. Neither the dismissal of Decazes nor the re-appointment of the once respected Richelieu satisfied the ultras, who made use of revolutionary disturbances in many parts of Europe to arouse fears among France's property owners. In December 1821 Villèle became chief minister with a large ultra-royalist majority in the Chamber of Deputies.

Villèle was not a fanatic anxious to destroy the Charter. He was merely determined that his own party should run the government and that his own followers should receive the perquisites. Events played into his hands in discrediting the liberal party. The audacity with which liberal politicians encouraged conspiracies and then repudiated all connection with them when they proved abortive disgusted large sections of the public. The satisfaction with which liberals hinted at sedition in the army was destroyed when a French expeditionary force loyally put down a rebellion in Spain in 1823. Villèle himself proved to be both unscrupulous and ingenious in obtaining his ends. The administration was purged of 'doubtful' elements to make room for hopeful young men of noble family. A new press law of 1822 gave libel so wide a definition that liberal newspapers were almost silenced for two years. When the *Constitutionnel* and the *Courrier français* found a means of evading restraint, Villèle countenanced a deplorable scheme for buying up all opposition newspapers and placing them under the direction of a royalist committee. An entirely new Chamber of Deputies was elected in 1824 in accordance with a law passed shortly after the murder of Berry. The new procedure, which gave a double vote to the wealthiest quarter of the electorate, was combined with every sort of government pressure to produce a Chamber in which the liberal opposition was reduced to a mere nineteen deputies. This Chamber proceeded in June 1824 to prolong its own expectancy of life by passing a Septennial Act.

In these circumstances liberal journalists and politicians felt justified in resorting to irresponsible methods. They took the line that the conspiracy to restore the reign of privilege was now in full swing, and for six years they presented every one of Villèle's measures as a step in the counter-revolution. Saint-Marc Girardin afterwards confessed that he and his friends knew these accusations to be false. Villèle, he said, was a sound parliamentarian, but his intention was 'to liberalize the monarchy without the liberals', and this was what liberal leaders would never forgive.

One of the most successful efforts at misrepresentation was made during the session of 1824, when Villèle introduced a double scheme to indemnify the émigrés for the loss of their land and to obtain the money, not by new taxes, but by converting five per cent government bonds to a lower rate of interest. Louis XVIII hoped in this way to 'heal the last wounds of the Revolution', and Villèle looked forward to uniting all landowners in a great conservative party. However, liberals in and out of the Chamber denounced the proposal as an attempt to ruin millions of small investors for the benefit of the aristocracy, and Villèle's sensible measure was thoroughly blackened in the eyes of the nation when it became law in 1825. A further outburst against aristocratic designs took place in 1826, when Villèle proposed to restore, in a mere 80,000 families only, the pre-revolutionary rule of primogeniture in the inheritance of landed property.

For long intervals, however, liberals curbed their bitter feelings towards the aristocracy, for the simple reason that the most effective opposition to Villèle came from Napoleonic peers in the Upper Chamber and from noble

magistrates of the royal courts who fancied themselves in the rôle of *parlementaires*. In the drama of advancing counter-revolution the lead was
ascribed not to wicked aristocrats but to scheming priests. Liberal daily
newspapers created the impression, by means of a continuous series of small
news items, that over-zealous priests, home mission societies, charitable organizations, and above all the Jesuits were working under the cloak of a fanatical
religion to restore the *ancien régime*. Hints and rumours were intensified
when Charles X succeeded his brother in 1824, for the new king was known
to have atoned for a rakish youth by turning religious bigot in middle age.
Charles X was accredited with a number of disparaging remarks about the
Charter, and though there is no serious reason to believe him fool enough to
have planned its total destruction, there were well-grounded reasons for
thinking that he would use every ounce of royal power to favour the
aristocracy and church.

Villèle was no *dévôt*, but he knew that religious feeling had revived among
the aristocracy in days of suffering, and he believed that he must make concessions to the horror felt by many noble families at the voltairian spirit which
pervaded France. Hence he turned a blind eye to the fact that the seminaries
which the church was allowed to establish for the preparatory training of
priests took more and more lay pupils until they rivalled the state secondary
schools. Hence also he appointed Bishop Frayssinous Minister of Education
in 1824 and hoped he would modify the fiercely secular régime imposed by
the University upon state schools and colleges. The relationship between
Villèle and Charles X was not as intimate as people imagined, but to please
the king Villèle agreed in 1825 to put forward a bill to make sacrilege punish-
able by death. All these developments were decried by liberals as a sign that
Jesuits were returning to the country in large numbers, spreading their
pernicious doctrines among the youth of the nation, and worming their way
into the councils of the state. Whatever else people had remembered or forgotten about the Jesuits it was well known that they had worked in secret,
and the name Jesuit became a useful label for liberals to attach to anyone
whom they wished to accuse of sinister political designs. They described as
Jesuits the evangelists of the *Missions de France* who held open-air services and
dramatic prayer meetings in provincial centres. They attributed to Jesuits the
leadership of the Congregation, a Catholic society widely supported by the
aristocracy, and pictured them placing its members in strategic positions in
government offices. They mentioned regretfully in the same category as
Jesuits the young priests who were inspired by Lamennais (at this time an
ultra-royalist) with a burning zeal for missionary work and an intense devotion to Rome. By directing their attack upon the Jesuits, liberals were able to
present themselves not as opponents of religion but as defenders of the gallican
tradition against an ultramontane conspiracy to sell France to the Pope. This

halo of respectability commended their propaganda more widely to peasants and bourgeois, who combined anti-clericalism with a respect for the orderliness and decency which the Catholic church had restored to public life after the licentiousness of the Revolution.

The popularity of the anti-clerical campaign showed that fear of priestly rule extended far beyond the boundaries of the narrow political class. No grievances of a social or economic nature provided a comparable field for political agitation. No industrial revolution had as yet taken place, for though the Revolution had destroyed medieval restrictions on trade and production French businessmen seemed to lack the initiative to take full advantage of the new freedom. In business circles there was little opposition to the government's old-fashioned economic policy, which imposed high tariffs on foreign imports in order to protect French manufactures from British competition and maintain wartime grain prices in face of possible supplies from Russia. An economic crisis which began in 1826 caused doubts to arise among winegrowers and shipowners; J.-B. Say began to obtain a hearing in parliament for his theories of free trade; among bankers, who constituted the élite of the business world, a few such as Jacques Laffitte and Casimir Périer regarded the government's financial policy as unimaginative; but Villèle would never have been defeated in parliament if his own party had not proved disloyal.

The great government party of 1824 began to break up almost as soon as it was formed. Chateaubriand defected after a few months because the king did not show him sufficient gratitude for instigating the Spanish campaign. Most of the younger and more romantic members of the ultra-royalist party followed him into opposition, for they felt that he gave more lustre to the royalist cause than Villèle, whose talents lay exclusively in the field of finance and whose outlook on government was that of an accountant. Religious issues caused further dissensions. An ultramontane group inspired by Lamennais resented the subordination of the church to an unpopular government, while a gallican group, voicing the age-old jealousy of aristocrats for priests, supported the Comte de Montlosier in denouncing the influence of Jesuits. Villèle's last important measure, a press bill designed to destroy the greater number of national newspapers in existence, was defeated in parliament by an alliance of liberals and dissident ultras in 1827, and Villèle resigned office after failing to win a majority in the elections at the end of the year.

Liberal politicians seem to have hoped that Charles X would choose ministers from their ranks, but they could not have been more wildly deceived. Charles regarded all liberals as potential revolutionaries and would not even speak to them willingly. He appointed the persuasive Martignac in the hope of reviving the ultra-royalist party of 1824. When this proved impossible and Martignac fell back on reviving Decazes's centre policy of 1819 the ministry was doomed, for Martignac could offer the liberals only legislative concessions, not places, and they would not support him on those terms. Nevertheless tension in the country relaxed. Martignac appeared so much less dangerous than Villèle, and Thiers's assertion that he ought to be attacked simply because he was the personal choice of a dangerous king fell on deaf ears. The temper of the public could only be roused by the news that on 8 August 1829 the king had dismissed Martignac in favour of three men reputed to hold the most reactionary views in France: Polignac, son of the princess whom Marie Antoinette had loved, Bourmont, traitor to Napoleon before Waterloo, and La Bourdonnaie, exponent of reprisals after the Hundred Days. Even now few people denied the right of the king to make a personal choice of ministers. Of the 54 persons who had held portfolios since the Restoration only 15 had been deputies. Horror was aroused only by the nature of the king's choice, which seemed to imply that he was going to attack all the achievements of the Revolution.

Whether Charles really intended to destroy the Charter is doubtful. He had come to believe during the ministry of Martignac that the liberals were trying to diminish royal power, and he seemed ready to take as ministers any men who would stand firm against liberal demands. Months passed and the *coup d'état* predicted by the liberal press did not come. In January 1830 Thiers, Mignet, and Carrel began publishing a new daily paper, the *National*, hinting that the king's choice of ministers should be dictated by parliament. This was tantamount to a rejection of the Bourbon dynasty, for ministerial responsibility was the one thing which Charles X would never concede. In March the Chamber voted an address describing the ministry as obnoxious to the wishes of the people. The liberal lawyer Dupin denied that the address constituted a demand for ministerial responsibility, but Charles X took it as a challenge. When new elections failed to produce a ministerial majority, and the seizure of Algiers failed to dazzle the public, the king determined to carry out the long expected *coup d'état*. Even then he persuaded himself that he was defending the Charter, not attacking it, by resisting an unconstitutional assault on the royal prerogative. In a strict sense he was right, as Thiers afterwards admitted. The Ordinances of 25 July which dissolved the new Chamber, deprived bourgeois electors of the vote, and suspended liberty of the press were issued by virtue of article 14 of the Charter entitling the king to rule by decree at times of crisis.

The July Revolution was begun by newspaper editors and their employees who resisted a threat to their livelihood. The building of barricades was organized by republicans from secret societies. The parliamentary leaders of the Left, Laffitte and Périer, were more alarmed than gratified at the turn of events, for popular insurrection did not come within their programme, though their propaganda had done much to stimulate it. Eventually they intervened to forestall the republicans, and at Thiers's suggestion they invited the Duc d'Orléans to become king with a slightly modified Charter. They tried to pretend that nothing much had happened, that Louis Philippe was simply another and a better Louis XVIII, but they were wrong. The Citizen King owed his throne to ideas of popular sovereignty which Restoration liberals had denounced as jacobinical. From 1830 liberals were increasingly on the defensive against democratic forces which they had done much to arm.

3. THREATS TO THE BALANCE OF POWER

When Metternich heard the news of the July Revolution he collapsed on his desk crying, 'My life's work is destroyed.' The new king, Louis-Philippe, was expected by left-wing elements in France to revive Jacobin foreign policy and become the patron of freedom throughout Europe. No-one, least of all Metternich, could know that he was ready to disavow his revolutionary origins. When revolt broke out in Belgium, traditional sphere of French expansion, the danger to European stability loomed immense.

In 1815 there seemed little likelihood that the Belgian people would unite in protest against union with Holland. Walloons and Flemings were divided both in language and outlook. In Flanders, where the peasants were devoutly Catholic, the clergy fanned a smouldering opposition to the rule of a protestant government: in the more sophisticated French-speaking Walloon provinces the bourgeoisie resented the political preponderance given to the Dutch, who formed only a third of the population of the Netherlands but were allotted a half of the seats in the Estates General and four fifths of the posts in the government. Union between the religious fervour of the Flemish clergy and the liberal tenets of the Walloon bourgeoisie was not easily achieved, for the Walloons were anti-clerical. Opposing views on education for a long time presented an insurmountable barrier. About 1828, however, a section of the Flemish clergy came under the liberal influence of Lamennais, whilst a younger generation of Walloon liberals decided to place political ideals before religious prejudices. The two groups united in pursuit of liberty of education, liberty of the press, and electoral reform. Economic factors helped to range Belgians against Dutch rule. Belgian industry was the first after 1815 to copy English methods. King William I patronized and subsidized the development but the Belgian bourgeoisie, far from accepting his help meekly, decided that their new economic position gave them a right to political power. Discontent reached a head in the spring of 1830 when the textile industry at Verviers, Liége, and Tournai suffered a crisis due to over-production. Business circles were by no means unanimous in desiring a complete break with Holland, however.

At Antwerp businessmen were satisfied with a union which secured freedom of commerce on the Scheldt; at Ghent, merchants were afraid of losing Dutch colonial markets. Most of them wished Belgium to remain united with Holland under the House of Orange though separated politically and financially. It was William I's intransigence which destroyed the Kingdom of the Netherlands.

The first outbreak was in the nature of a social protest. Between 1824 and 1830 Belgian peasants suffered from a series of poor harvests while in the towns the workers saw a rise in the cost of living without a corresponding increase in wages. A demonstration in Brussels on 25 August secured the withdrawal of the Dutch garrison, whereupon bourgeois leaders, partly to suppress social disorder, took control of the situation and demanded a separate parliament for the Belgian provinces. The king refused to accede to the demand and ordered Dutch troops to retake Brussels. Their failure to do so marked the triumph of the rebels who proceeded to declare the independence of Belgium (4 October 1830).

Metternich wanted to see the revolt crushed at once and gave moral support to the idea of intervention by Russia and Prussia. The latter hesitated, however, before a threat from France. Louis-Philippe announced that although he would not gratuitously fight for Belgium he would be obliged by French public opinion to intervene if the Prussians invaded. Fearing for his own throne in such a contingency Louis-Philippe sent Talleyrand to London to work for an international agreement. Metternich still wanted a joint expedition to restore the Kingdom of the Netherlands but Palmerston took the lead in demanding the creation of an independent Belgium mapped out and guaranteed by the Great Powers. A rising in Poland diverted the attention of the eastern powers and made them ready to compromise over Belgium. France made difficulties at the last moment by intriguing to secure the throne of the new kingdom for Louis-Philippe's son, but Palmerston's threats of war brought the French government to heel, and the London Conference accepted Belgium's choice of Leopold of Saxe-Coburg as king of a parliamentary state.

Metternich was thus indebted to Britain for the creation of a new barrier against France. He never liked it, though it proved more effective than the old, and he distrusted Britain only slightly less than he distrusted France. His efforts to co-operate with both over the affairs of the Middle East were to drive him eventually into the arms of Russia, whose expansionist tendencies he so much feared.

Russia had made considerable advances as a result of her intervention in the Greek affair. In the Treaty of Adrianople (1829) which ended the Russo-Turkish war she had obtained a protectorate over the Danubian Principalities, acquired the port of Poti on the Black Sea, and extended her territory in the Caucasus. Metternich, like Wellington, was greatly dismayed and came to the conclusion that a more closely united policy on the part of Austria and the western powers was vital for the preservation of the Turkish Empire. In 1832 he warned Britain and France of the need to take collective action against Mohammed Ali, pasha of Egypt, the Sultan's most formidable foe.

The career of Mohammed Ali was of great significance in the history of the Middle East, and might have been even more important but for interference from European powers. Mohammed Ali was not a nationalist, though nationalism grew, at a much later date, out of the seeds planted under his rule. He was merely a usurping autocrat, like Ali Pasha or Osman Pasvanoglou, who needed to find ways and means of preserving and if possible extending his power. He began his career as an Albanian soldier, employed by the Turks in driving off the Mamelukes when the latter sought to recover Egypt in the confused period following the expulsion of Napoleon's army. Mohammed Ali did the job so well that he was given the position of pasha by a reluctant but intimidated sultan (1809). His ambitions were obviously far-reaching. Expeditions into the Sudan and against the Wahhabis secured him control of the Red Sea and the Arabian coasts. Perhaps he dreamed of an Arab empire. If only for security he needed a strong army and navy, and he was astute enough to see that they must be modelled on western lines. In 1819 he set up an officers' training corps at Assuan and shortly afterwards began to conscript the fellaheen and townsmen into the army by ballot. By the 1830s he could boast of more than 100,000 regulars. He established a modern naval base at Alexandria and built up a navy which included eleven ships of the line. It was to obtain the money for all this that he devoted himself to the economic regeneration of his country.

When Mohammed Ali established his rule over Egypt, centuries of neglect had caused the famous irrigation system of ancient times to fall into decay, allowing the desert to encroach upon the cultivated land, bringing plagues and famines and decimating the population. Mohammed Ali's earliest efforts were directed towards restoring and extending irrigation, with such success that the cultivated area rose from about two million acres in 1821 to more than four million at the time of his death (1849). Wherever possible he substituted perennial irrigation for basin irrigation, allowing two or even three crops to be grown each year. He then began producing cotton, which had long been known in Egypt, on a large enough scale for the world market. At a time when Lancashire's mills were insatiable for raw materials, Egypt's cotton became her leading export, offering her an assured, if secondary place in the economy of the modern world. To Mohammed Ali this was not enough. He asked himself why the West was progressing while the East declined, and found the answer in science, technology, and industry.

He proceeded to send young Egyptians abroad for training, to establish schools and technical colleges and, most striking innovation of all, to set up factories. By the 1830s a quarter of Egypt's cotton crop was going into domestic spinning and weaving, which employed nearly 40,000 hands. Richard Cobden was horrified at the waste, for he believed that the raw cotton could have been put to better use in England and that the Egyptians ought to work on the land. The ultimate threat, that Egypt might be the first of many Asian countries to adopt European techniques for the purpose of rejecting the influence of the western world, was not formulated at the time. Perhaps Mohammed Ali's industries would not have been sufficiently successful to constitute such a threat. Like his great enemy and rival Sultan Mahmud II, who also set up industries by decree a decade or so later, Mohammed Ali believed that technical skills were the only things worth importing from the West and that they would work the oracle without changes in society and government. Mahmud II's industries died a natural death. Mohammed Ali's were nipped in the bud by Britain when she made a trade agreement with the Sultan in 1838, opening Egypt to British competition, and by the European powers in concert when they forced Mohammed Ali to reduce his army in 1841, thus taking away his incentive to industrialize.

Mohammed Ali was dependent on the European powers all along. He turned most naturally to France, for it was Napoleon who had given Egypt the first push towards the modern world. Soldiers, scientists, doctors, engineers, surveyors, and technicians of every kind were imported by Mohammed Ali from France, and it was to French lycées and colleges that he sent his first large batch of students in 1826. One of the scientists who had been attached to Napoleon's expedition, François Jomard, served as adviser to Mohammed Ali in education; a French engineer Louis Alexis Jumel, who had come to Egypt to supervise woollen mills, experimented with various types of cotton plant and developed the strain which bears his name. Yet Mohammed Ali would only use France for his own purposes. He kept on moderately good terms with all the European powers and waited for the day when he might be able to play off one against the other. Thus he withdrew from Greece with only a show of fighting when the western powers intervened in 1828, and refused to alienate Britain by invading Tunis and Tripoli, as Polignac suggested, when France attacked Algiers in 1830.

Late in 1831 he believed that the time had come to extend his power over Syria. Manufacturing a dispute with the pasha of Lebanon he sent an army under his son Ibrahim to invest Acre. Mahmud II denounced him as a rebel and tried to crush him, but by December 1832 his troops were overrunning Asia Minor and threatening Constantinople. The French rejected Metternich's plea for collective action because they saw Mohammed Ali as a possible counterweight to British preponderence in the Mediterranean. Britain was equally cool because although Palmerston was at this time interested in developing his own route through Syria to the East he would not fall in with any initiative from Metternich. The Sultan, in his extremity, turned to Russia for aid, and in February 1833 Russian troops landed at Scutari and a Russian fleet anchored off Constantinople. The Sultan himself was not a little alarmed at the proportions of the Russian force. He hastily came to terms with Mohammed Ali, allowing him Syria, Adana, and Tarsus, and paid for Russian help in the Treaty of Unkiar Skelessi (8 July 1833). This famous treaty bound the Sultan for eight years to accept Russian assistance in the event of aggression and to close the Dardanelles to foreign vessels whenever Russia was at war. Palmerston jumped to the conclusion that Turkey had become a satellite of Russia and blamed Metternich for not informing the British government of the Tsar's intentions. Metternich made the best of a bad job by seeking the friendship of the victorious power. Nicholas was ready to accept a friend, for the furor created by Palmerston convinced him that he would never be able to make use of the Treaty of Unkiar Skelessi. At Münchengrätz in September 1833 Nicholas and Francis agreed to act together against revolutionary movements which threatened each other's power, to give joint assistance to monarchs who asked for it, and to respect each other's interests in Turkey.

The agreement of Münchengrätz might have had unhappy results. Palmerston retaliated with a Quadruple Alliance between Britain, France, Spain, and Portugal (April 1834) which threatened to divide the western powers from the eastern powers in hostile array. Fortunately the Quadruple Alliance was never a serviceable instrument. The entente between Russia and Austria, on the other hand, lasted long enough to bring Russia in 1849 to the aid of Austria in her darkest hour.

CHAPTER XVII

Nationalism and Revolution, 1830-51

I. THE GROWTH OF IDEAS

DURING the last years of the reign of Francis I the cause of nationalism received a stunning defeat in Poland. A revolt in Russian Poland was crushed by Nicholas I with immense ferocity in 1831. The intellectual élite of the nation was scattered when 10,000 exiles, mainly nobles, gentry, and bourgeoisie fled to western Europe. In subsequent years the Prussian and Austrian governments pursued a more vigorous policy of germanization in Posnania and Galicia.

The fate of Poland contrasted sharply with the fortune of Belgium and Greece and seemed to prove that nationalism could only triumph if the Great Powers failed to agree on any other solution. In Poland no conflicting interests were at stake. The eastern powers carried out repressive policies with mutual approval while the western powers watched inertly. Similarly in the Danubian Principalities Russia stifled the growing nationalist feeling among upper class Roumanians while Britain congratulated herself on having found a harmless occupation for Nicholas. No Great Power seemed likely to sponsor nationalist causes among submerged peoples for ideological reasons. Austria and Russia were multi-national states which could not afford to encourage subversive ideas. Britain prided herself on liberal institutions but clung to existing treaties and the balance of power as the best means of securing peace in Europe. France under Louis-Philippe rejected all invitations to fight crusades for European liberty. Patriots were driven by necessity to listen to Mazzini's exhortations to the people of each nation to help themselves.

During the eighteen-thirties and 'forties nationalism strengthened its hold over European opinion. Exiles in London, Brussels, Geneva, and Paris fostered the cause through patriotic societies and conspiracies. Great writers such as Michelet, Quinet, Browning, and Lamennais brought intellectual argument and artistic emotion to bear upon the movement. Two great poets from central Europe, Petöfi and Mickiewicz, found in Hungarian and Polish patriotism the true outlet for their genius. The romantics became more fervently committed to nationalism as a new generation grew up which had not experienced the disenchantment of 1793. To the disciples of Byron and

Shelley the French Revolution was a liberating fire whose flame should be carried to all the peoples of Europe. The rôle of the revolutionary was itself romanticized, the classic figures which David had depicted giving way to ardent youths who fought with the workers in Delacroix's *Liberty on the Barricades* (1831). The growth of nationalism cannot be explained in terms of propaganda by an intellectual élite, however. Only a complex series of sufferings, frustrations, hopes, and ambitions could account for the growth of a mood of nationalism among whole classes of people such as the aristocracy of Poland, the gentry of Hungary, the bourgeoisie of Germany, and the peasantry of Ireland. Increasing numbers of people came to think that they would personally derive greater satisfaction, more confidence, and wider scope for action if they were recognized as members of a community bound by the same traditions, the same language, the same blood, and the same homeland. No longer would they be oppressed by alien governments, stifled by petty despots, or exploited by unfeeling overlords. Nationalism would burst all artificial bonds and supersede all unworthy attachments, raising human personality and comradeship to the heights of power.

In a state such as Austria, where national groups overlapped each other and where some groups could claim to possess a nobler culture or a more impressive history than others, nationalism was bound to lead to conflict. Eventually it led to aggression on the part of the more powerful groups. These sinister implications were not manifest in the period leading to the nationalist revolts of 1848, however. Even in Germany the new generation of nationalists played down the hostile attitude which romantics had shown towards the West. At the Hambach Festival of 1832 a spirit of comradeship with liberal France was widely felt, and the organizers refused to publish a suggestion made by one of the speakers that unification of Germany would require the restoration of Alsace-Lorraine. By 1848 many nationalists believed that the creation of nation states would lead to universal brotherhood.

Nationalism required in many cases the breaking of a foreign yoke or the destruction of vested interests. In this sense the fight was for freedom, and it was easily connected in men's mind with the fight for another sort of freedom, that of the individual within the community. Nationalism and liberalism came to be regarded by many people almost as one and the same thing, and even the events of 1848 did not succeed in convincing everybody that nationalism carried overtones of power which could be totally destructive of liberty of the individual.

Liberalism on the continent of Europe derived its inspiration chiefly from France. The most advanced formulations of liberal ideology were to be found in Britain, but the extreme rationalism of Jeremy Bentham and James Mill was not widely copied even in England, and the political economy of Adam Smith and David Ricardo was not easily acceptable in countries economically less advanced. French publicists of the eighteenth century, particularly Rousseau, were more attractive to the underdog. Although some of their ideas had fallen into disrepute by the beginning of the nineteenth century their most comforting theme, that men were born good and needed only to be given the right institutions to progress towards perfection, continued to echo in the minds of people less self-confident than the British middle class. The search for the right type of institution led a number of notable political theorists in Restoration France to favour a system which gave the maximum amount of scope to the individual to bring his gifts to bear upon the common weal. The individual must have freedom of speech, freedom of religion, freedom from arbitrary arrest, freedom to enter any trade or profession according to his ability, freedom to acquire property, and freedom to choose a government and to make his wishes felt by its members. The liberalism thus developed by Benjamin Constant and the Doctrinaires laid so much stress upon the individual that the community could not be regarded as anything more than the sum-total of individuals. Rousseau's attempt to invest the community with a life distinct from that of the individuals who formed it was denounced as jacobinical. Nationalism, on the other hand, implied that nations continued to exist even when their members were scattered and that the brotherliness which lay at the heart of the community would triumph over individual self-seeking. The connection between the liberalism which triumphed in France in 1830 and the nationalism which inspired many people in Europe in the next two decades rested on an imperfect understanding of the reticences of the former and an imperfect recognition of the implications of the latter. In this connection, more attention was paid to memories of the early years of the French Revolution, when free institutions had given Frenchmen a deeper sense of brotherhood and a greater feeling of strength, than to the sobering example of French parliamentary politics under the July Monarchy.

Liberalism appealed most strongly to professional men and businessmen who could most easily believe in their ability to benefit themselves and their fellow men by their own efforts. It was found in its most complete form in regions which possessed a bourgeois class comparable to that of Britain and France: Belgium, *par excellence*, and western Germany. It was denounced by socialists as a cloak for the selfish ambitions of the middle class, and the behaviour of liberals in countries where they were able to exert influence over government policy gave support to the indictment. French liberals during the reign of Louis-Philippe adopted an aloof attitude towards the lower classes, refusing to extend the franchise to include them and neglecting to carry out social legislation to benefit them. They defended their attitude on the grounds that universal suffrage would give votes to an ignorant multitude and that social measures would place power in the hands of the state, both policies leading directly to dictatorship. They believed that only those persons whose wealth betokened education and experience could be regarded as individuals capable of exercising political functions, and that as long as they maintained freedom of speech, freedom of religion, freedom from arbitrary arrest, and above all freedom to amass property, social and economic conditions could be expected to improve of their own accord. Their greatest writer, Alexis de Tocqueville, was profoundly disturbed by the more democratic régime which had developed under President Jackson in the U.S.A. While liberal governments attacked democrats and socialists, however, the condition of the workers in French cities grew more and more deplorable. Belgian liberals were equally exclusive, and because Belgian industry was the most advanced on the continent the wretchedness of Belgian factory workers compared only with that of their counterparts in Britain.

Meanwhile the problems created by largescale industry met with sympathetic attention from several other quarters. The new generation of romantics turned from denouncing the horrors of the French Revolution to depicting (who better than Daumier in his republican youth?) the bitterness of life among the rejected masses. For the most part the romantics could see, however, no solution other than a return to the rural idyll. A new school of socialist writers distinguished itself by a frank acceptance of the Industrial Revolution, attributing the evils which had arisen from it entirely to the capitalist system under which it had developed. This system, they argued, could be replaced. Early French socialists believed, as Robert Owen believed in England, that workers could be raised from their degradation and masters saved from their wickedness by substituting co-operation for competition as the mainspring of production. Saint-Simon believed that if men were directed towards tasks for which they were fitted by nature and rewarded in accordance with their contribution to the community wealth and happiness would increase together. Charles Fourier envisaged people working and living in small communities, each man investing a part of his income in the communal enterprise and receiving a share of the produce sufficient to free him from anxiety. Etienne Cabet imagined that a benevolent dictator could set up an ideal community. That these schemes were utopian in the strict sense of the word was demonstrated when one after another of their progenitors tried and failed to set up little colonies which would convince the world.

Louis Blanc intended to be more practical in his *Organization of Labour* (1839). He advocated government action to set going a new system of production which would gradually supersede capitalist industry. The state needed only to advance money for co-operative workshops, which would soon become so successful that capitalist undertakings would be driven from the field. This plan to fight the bourgeoisie on its own terms seemed not merely futile but immoral to the most earnest of all French socialist writers, Proudhon. Unlike most other socialist leaders Proudhon belonged himself to the ranks of the workers. His tremendous love of humanity led him to believe that men could devise an economic system in keeping with moral law and that all classes of society could be drawn together in operating it. His work was denounced by Karl Marx as sentimental and petit bourgeois. German socialists rapidly came to the conclusion that neither co-operation between workers and masters nor a fusion of proletariat and bourgeoisie could be regarded as anything but illusory: the two classes were destined to fight to the death. In the eighteen-thirties a group of German exiles dedicated themselves to the ideals of Babeuf and formed a society called the League of the Just. Meeting in Brussels in 1846 to decide on 'a common tactic for the working class movement' they re-christened themselves the Communist League. Karl Marx became a member in 1847. In conjunction with Friedrich Engels he published the *Communist Manifesto* in London in February 1848, calling on the workers of the world to unite in bringing about the destruction of the bourgeois order by revolution.

Combining Hegel's dialectic with British classical economy and French socialism, Marx came to the conclusion that the whole of history was the history of class struggles. Each class as it rose to predominance set up the type of society which answered the needs of its own day, but each contained 'internal contradictions' which eventually made it a barrier to progress and caused it to be superseded. Thus aristocracy inevitably succumbed to the onslaught of the bourgeoisie as it had already done in Britan and France and as it was about to do, Marx was convinced, in Germany. With the downfall of the aristocracy and the triumph of the bourgeoisie, exploitation 'veiled by religious and political illusions' gave way to exploitation which was 'naked, shameless, direct, and brutal'. But retribution was at hand. The bourgeoisie in the course of its rise inevitably forged the weapons for its own destruction. With the triumph of the proletariat socialism would prevail; for just as capitalism was the inescapable creation of the bourgeoisie so the communist state was the only milieu answering the needs of the working class.

The *Communist Manifesto* heralded one of the greatest intellectual achievements of the nineteenth century. Thanks to Marx, socialism could claim to be not only desirable but inevitable. From a practical point of view the *Manifesto* was of no immediate significance, however. Its diagnosis of the condition of the times was false for the greater part of Europe if not for the whole of it, and its message was meaningless to all but a minority of the labouring poor. Industrialization had only just begun to affect the continent by mid-century. At a time when population was growing more rapidly than industry the most depressed sections of humanity were to be found not in factories but in the cottages of the countryside. Here more and more peasants strove to eke out a living from the crumbs of labour which fell to them as a result of the survival of the putting-out system. To these people socialist writings said little and meant even less. Socialist ideas had some circulation among workers in France, but the effect is by no means clear. When the Paris workers joined in the revolution of February 1848 they merely transferred their allegiance from one set of bourgeois politicians to another which promised more generous measures. Outside of France, only Belgium among continental countries could be said to have experienced the evils described by Engels in 1845 in his *Condition of the Working Class in England*, and Belgian workers, like their counterparts across the Channel, did not rebel in 1848. Industrial concentrations were to be found in Berlin and Vienna, in the Rhineland, Thuringia, Saxony, Silesia, and Bohemia, but poverty and wretchedness in these regions could be blamed like everything else upon despotic governments. When the workers of Germany and Austria rose in 1848 they placed their trust in bourgeois liberals who promised a golden era as a result of freedom and nationality. Their illusions lasted just long enough to secure the triumph of the liberal revolution.

The existence of socialism nevertheless helped to drive liberals into the shelter of monarchy. Liberals in France at the height of their success in 1830 recognized the need of a monarch to save them from excessive demands by the mob. Liberals in Germany, Austria, and Italy hardly dreamed of overthrowing monarchs who had long held the loyalty of the peasantry. Liberals aimed, therefore, not at destroying monarchy but at persuading and if necessary forcing kings and princes to surround their thrones with free institutions. The shining example was not Louis-Philippe, who manipulated parliamentary machinery in the interests of his own power, but Leopold I, king of the Belgians, guide and mentor to the young Queen Victoria. In 1848 liberals in many parts of Europe sought to combine individual freedom with monarchical government by adapting portions of the Belgian constitution of 1831. Some wished to give freedom to localities as well as individuals by devising a federal system for the nation. These found that the constitution of the United States publicized, if with adverse criticisms, by De Tocqueville in his *Democracy in America* (1835) offered suitable features.

Many nationalists shelved their liberal principles when their loyalties were put to the test in 1848. Some nationalists, notably Kossuth, had never done more than use liberal weapons for illiberal purposes. One great nationalist spurned the liberalism of his generation from the start. Mazzini's doctrines exalted the community above the individual; his political creed was democratic and his ideal form of government a republic. Democracy and republicanism were not incompatible with liberalism, but they had parted company with it during the French Revolution. They continued to take a separate course in France when the revolution of 1830 secured the triumph of liberalism. An increasing number of radicals rejected the monarchy of Louis-Philippe in the name of a wider conception of freedom. Yet in Germany and Austria members of the lower middle class and especially students in the universities were attracted to democratic ideas without thinking in terms of a cleavage with liberals. All rebelled together in the halcyon spring of 1848, but by the end of the year divergence was complete. Mazzini's republic enjoyed a brief life in Italy when the liberal revolution was over.

2. FRANCE: EXAMPLE OR WARNING?

With the overthrow of the Bourbon monarchy in July 1830, bourgeois liberalism triumphed over aristocratic reaction in France. Most members of the aristocracy withdrew from political life to nurse their injured pride in country châteaux or in the salons of the faubourg Saint-Germain. A few 'legitimists' remained active in the newspaper press, where their wealth and talent gave them an appearance of authority far greater than the number of their adherents. An attempt by Berry's widow to raise the Vendée in 1832 on behalf of Henri V, the 'miracle child' born a few months after the death of her husband, was a fiasco. Thereafter legistimist opposition was an embarrassment but not a serious menace to Louis-Philippe.

With the elimination of the aristocracy the upper middle class assumed the dominating position in social and political life. The class included great financiers such as Rothschild and Périer, great business entrepreneurs such as the brothers Schneider, great academic figures such as François Guizot and Victor Cousin, and great political tacticians such as Thiers. Anybody who could rise into a high income group could enter the social and political élite. The milieu exactly suited the new king, Louis-Philippe, who prided himself on his ability to consort with persons of enterprise and scholarship but who nevertheless regarded wealth as the hallmark of talent. Louis-Philippe had never been fully accepted in aristocratic circles, not so much because of the republican adventures in which he had engaged as a young man as because of a natural lack of dignity in his behaviour. His acquisitive instincts and his combination of private thrift with public display seemed so precisely typical of the *nouveaux riches*. He possessed a good deal of common sense and was quite knowledgeable about European affairs, but these solid virtues were often hidden by petty faults.

The upper bourgeoisie showed no inclination to share political power with the lower ranks of their own class. An electoral law of February 1831 placed the property qualification for voters at 200 francs and for parliamentary candidates at 500 francs. A few deputies of the extreme Left tried from time to time during the eighteen-forties to extend votes to members of the professions regardless of income, and Thiers decided for tactical reasons at a late hour to support a campaign to enfranchise the middle sections of the bourgeoisie, but such ideas were steadily resisted by most members of Orleanist parliaments. This determination to restrict the franchise produced an anomalous situation in which the upper bourgeoisie exercised governing functions with the aid of a parliament composed predominantly of land-owners. Of some 240,000 electors in the eighteen-forties 82-90 per cent obtained a livelihood from agriculture. Among 4,000 persons who sought election to parliament during the reign the high proportion of agriculturists owed something to the fact that landowners were willing to leave their estates in the hands of agents, while few industrialists were willing at this time to absent themselves from their firms.

Since most of the deputies drew their economic experience from agriculture, and most of the ministers chosen by Louis-Philippe came from academic circles or from the army, the economic policy of the reign was understandably prosaic. The only direct contribution made by the government towards the growth of trade and industry was in the improvement of communications. A law of 1836 concerning country roads greatly accelerated local transport and widened the area over which producers could sell their goods. More than 2,000 kilometres of canals were built. Railway development was held up for nearly ten years whilst the Chambers considered the relative merits of national and private ownership, but the subsequent Railway Law of 1842, establishing a partnership between public and private enterprise, led to a boom in construction. By 1847 France had nearly 2,000 kilometres of railways in operation, and Paris was linked with Rouen, Le Havre, Orléans, and Lille. In other respects the government thought only of allowing businessmen to go ahead with their own affairs without interference. They did not move very fast, partly because they encountered technical and structural handicaps. France possessed a large population, labour was cheap, and the introduction of machines was not a pressing necessity. Some of France's coal deposits remained undiscovered, and imported coal was dear. Banking remained in the hands of a few great families, which gave credit only to the safest borrowers, and capital was not properly mobilized for large-scale investment. Production and trade increased steadily in the eighteen-forties but nothing like a complete industrial revolution was experienced. Large industrial plants were rare and the most modern methods were introduced only in the textile industry of Alsace and Roubaix and the ironworks at Le Creusot and Hayange. The outlook of the business class itself was to some extent responsible for the slow progress. Businessmen thought of preserving rather than creating wealth, business families hesitated to expand their concerns for fear of losing control to outsiders, and entrepreneurs were stifled by the feeling that industry was socially inferior to finance. Few businessmen criticized the tariff policy of the government, which maintained the high barriers created during the Restoration. Most were satisfied with the low level of taxes, which fell heavier on land than on other forms of property.

The narrowness of the franchise produced parliaments in which most of the members thought alike on subjects of social and political importance. Only a few deputies on the extreme Left voiced the grievances of the republicans at the beginning of the reign and demanded the extension of the franchise, the appointment of Lafayette as minister, and the launching of a crusade on behalf of liberty in Europe. They reminded Louis-Philippe that he was the son of Philippe Égalité and that he had won his greatest renown in the battle for freedom at Jemappes. Louis-Philippe knew, however, that he had been put on the throne by a conservative class and that the electorate would not want to pay for foreign adventures. He told republican delegates that their hopes of changing society overnight were foolish dreams, and his ministers offered the warmongers nothing more than co-operation with Britain in Belgium, a firm stand against the Austrians in Italy, and an extension of French activities in north Africa. Charles X had never intended to colonize Algeria, but Louis-Philippe decided to cling to a coastal strip chiefly because the British wanted to get him out, and the need to defend the possession resulted in the gradual conquest of the interior. Success in colonial fields aroused no enthusiasm in France, however.

The republicans were merely a nuisance in parliament, but outside they were something of a menace. Their leading newspaper, the *Tribune*, repudiated the monarchy when the rigid Casimir Périer was appointed chief minister in March 1831. Republican organizations, semi-secret, with headquarters in Paris and branches in provincial cities, worked to co-ordinate propaganda and action. Adherents were not numerous but the leaders were experienced in revolutionary techniques. Between 1831 and 1834 they promoted or adopted a number of violent disturbances in the two chief cities of France. Events in Lyon illustrated the confused relationship between political agitation and social distress. Workers in the silk industry found their earnings cut down to a bare subsistence level by small masters facing competition from Switzerland and Britain. In defiance of the 1791 Loi le Chapelier they grouped together and negotiated a minimum wage scale, but many masters were encouraged to repudiate the agreement when Périer announced that no such scale could be binding. In November 1831 the enraged weavers rose in a body, declaring that they would live by work or die by combat, and descending in force from their hovels on the hill of Croix-Rouge they gained control of the city. The political aims of the rioters were obscure, but the government took fright, and Marshal Soult overawed the city with a force comprising nearly a tenth of the whole French army. The Chamber of Deputies ignored Périer's recommendation to study the root causes of industrial unrest, with the result that republican propaganda was received more sympathetically by the distressed workers. A cheap republican newspaper, the *Glaneuse*, discussed workers' problems, and the republican society of the *Droits de l'homme* established connections with workers' mutuals. A strike among the silk weavers in 1834 gave the republicans a chance to arm their sections, and in April a savage battle with the government troops raged for five days before order was restored. Among the thousand casualties suffered by the insurgents only a hundred were silk workers. The patronage given by republican societies to newspapers of a socialist nature, such as Cabet's *Populaire*, did not alter the fact that the republicans thought mainly in political terms and rested their hopes chiefly upon the political ambitions of the petty bourgeoisie.

The Lyon affair left a permanent impression in the minds of the Orleanist governing class that the workers were docile unless roused by ambitious factions, and that when so roused they could be quietened again by a whiff of grapeshot. A revolt in the eastern faubourgs of Paris, raised by the *Droits de l'homme* in sympathy with the Lyon revolt, left the further impression that republicans were irresponsible fanatics whose propaganda was a crime against humanity. A series of measures to repress republican newspapers and societies culminated in the laws of September 1835 which virtually silenced republicanism until the eighteen-forties. Attempts by Louis Napoleon Bonaparte to appeal to republican sentiment as the heir of the Little Corporal ended in ludicrous failure at Strasbourg in 1836 and Boulogne in 1840. Discontent remained unchannelled and leaderless, breaking out only in lunatic attempts (ten in as many years) on the king's life.

Deputies who thought the same on important issues might have been expected to produce harmonious parliaments, but such was not the case. Parliamentary life was disfigured for a decade by an acrimonious fight for places. Since there were no clearcut parties the deputies divided into amorphous groups. Governments depended on uneasy coalitions, and Louis-Philippe was able to indulge his penchant for cabinet-making much as George III was obliged to do in mid-eighteenth century England. There were sixteen ministries in the first ten years of the reign. Instability can be blamed in part upon Louis-Philippe, whose determination to dominate the government led him to appoint nonentities whenever possible. There were ludicrous incidents, such as the appointment in 1834, after a prolonged crisis, of a ministry which lasted only eight days; there were discreditable manoeuvres, such as the formation in 1839 of an unholy alliance between Thiers, Guizot, and Barrot to pull Molé down. Most of the ministries came from the Right, whose members pretended to approve of royal government, but on two occasions a Left-Centre group led by Adolphe Thiers forced itself on the reluctant sovereign and tried to establish the rule that the king should reign but not govern. On both occasions Thiers hoped to

AOP Y

make himself indispensable by prosecuting a dazzling foreign policy, but his proposal to intervene in Spain on behalf of Queen Isabella in 1836 caused him to be dismissed at once by Louis-Philippe, and his patronage of Mohammed Ali in claims upon Egypt and Syria in 1840 ended unhappily. Thiers was not alone in overestimating Mohammed Ali's military strength, for Louis-Philippe and the greater part of the French public made the same mistake, but Thiers's belief that Britain and Russia were bluffing when they threatened to intervene on behalf of Turkey was not shared by the king. Rather than risk a general war Louis-Philippe dismissed Thiers and appointed a minister who would pay court to Palmerston.

In François Guizot Louis-Philippe at last found a minister with whom he could identify himself completely. Guizot admitted that his authority emanated from the king and that his rôle in parliament was to secure support for the king's measures. For eight years he played the rôle so successfully that the Orleanist system seemed petrified beyond all hope of peaceful change. To liberals his leadership must have seemed inevitable, for his intellectual attainments were staggering and he had long played an eminent part in many walks of public life. His outlook on society and politics was shared by a great many bourgeois voters. He believed, as they did, that the upper bourgeoisie formed an intellectual and spiritual élite whose duty was to guide the masses. His grave sense of responsibility, strengthened by his calvinist upbringing, appealed to old provincial families like the Périers where the influence of Jansenism was still discernible. Even among the Parisian bourgeoisie a revival of Catholic faith inspired by the preaching of Lacordaire had softened the voltairean spirit of destructive criticism. Yet very few people who knew Guizot really liked him. Nobody could say what things he genuinely cared for. Some people were impressed by the air of authority with which he spoke on all subjects; many more were irritated by his contemptuous manner; a few were inclined to think that he was a fraud. Nobody denied that he was personally incorruptible, but political opponents tried vainly to convince him that he was morally wrong in offering material rewards to supporters of his government.

Guizot and his subordinates spent a lot of time and money on electoral manipulation and parliamentary management. The electoral law of 1831 had created a great many colleges in which voters were so few that each one could be known personally by the authorities. Qualifications for the franchise had to be submitted to so many officials that the names of undesirable claimants could easily be omitted from the final list. Official candidates were allowed to use the civil service machine and to draw on government funds. Inside the Chamber potential supporters of the administration were offered salaried posts. These methods were not new: in the hands of skilful practitioners such as Decazes and Villèle they had not always yielded government majorities. Armand Marrast, the democratic editor of the *National*, tried to give his readers the impression that Guizot's success in elections was entirely due to corruption, but constituencies where opposition groups were lively continued to return opposition candidates. The importance of place-men in the Chamber seemed to be admitted by Guizot when he resisted eighteen successive bills to render their election illegal, but their numbers were never sufficient to guarantee the passage of the king's measures.

The most obvious fields for criticism were the exclusion of many educated property owners from the franchise and the distressing condition of the working class. Guizot insisted that the upper bourgeoisie adequately main-tained those liberal institutions which allowed individual talents to flourish, and that freedom could not be improved upon merely by increasing the number of voters. He believed that his great elementary education act, passed when he was minister of public instruction in 1833, completed the grant of equal opportunity to the lower classes; if they failed to make good the reason must be sought in their natural limitations. That a great many did indeed fail to make good was not unknown to him. In the chief cities of France the majority of working class families did not earn enough to keep themselves alive, even when the children worked for long hours in the mills. If charity was unobtainable crime became the only alternative to starvation. Housing conditions were shocking; drunkenness and promiscuity were rife; undernourishment, cruelty, disease, and neglect made nine out of every ten young men called up for the army from manufacturing districts unfit to serve.

Even critics of the régime had to admit that peace and stability benefited property owners in town and country and that the number of property owners increased. Yet even beneficiaries of the régime were sometimes ashamed to defend it openly. They could not deny that the garrulous old king was as pear-shaped as Daumier depicted him. They were uneasily aware that the *entente* with England, though sensible, required humiliating surrenders to keep it alive until 1846, after which it was thrown away by Louis-Philippe's inordinate haste in marrying his youngest son to a Spanish princess for the sake of a Spanish dowry. Finally they were forced to admit that corruption existed in high places. A series of scandals involving ministers and peers in 1847 so shocked the public that notable supporters of the government attended reform meetings to prove to their neighbours that they held no brief for immoral practices.

The July Monarchy suffered more, in the end, from the inertia of its friends than from the determination of its enemies. Though discontent was widespread in the last years of Guizot's ministry no revolutionary movement was discernible. Bonapartist sentiment inspired crowds to file past Napoleon's tomb in the Invalides, but Napoleon's heir was allowed to remain in the fortress of Ham until 1846, and even after he escaped to England his active supporters in France could be numbered on the fingers of one hand. Secret societies formed by the few remaining republicans of a militant type were riddled with police spies. Democratic politicians drew up petitions to parliament, but their demands for universal suffrage met with little support from the masses. Their two national newspapers, the *National* and the *Réforme*, possessed only a few thousand subscribers between them. They were notoriously divided on the subject of social policy, the *National* remaining entirely aloof and the *Réforme* adopting a vague humanitarian programme. The workers themselves remained remarkably docile. Unskilled labourers in factories and mines, most of whom were illiterate, possessed little knowledge of socialist views. Skilled workers in craft industries, to whom Louis Blanc addressed his *Organization of Labour*, were willing enough to strike for isolated and limited objectives but showed little capacity for combined action. Danger arose only when normal difficulties were increased by food shortage. A poor harvest in 1845 followed by a mediocre one in 1846 caused food prices to rise to a prohibitive level during the ensuing winter. The agricultural depression produced repercussions in industry, unemployment increased, and there was no poor law to tide distressed families over the crisis. Fortunately the harvest of 1847 was abundant and prefects assured the minister of the interior in July that tension had relaxed. In the same month two moderate left-wing groups led by Odilon Barrot and Thiers co-operated with democrats in launching a public campaign in support of electoral reform. There seemed to be no other way of dislodging Guizot, which was their only ambition. To evade the law restricting public meetings they adapted an English device explained to them by Richard Cobden, holding banquets at which speeches were made and toasts drunk. The banquets were intended to be respectable gatherings, demanding only a modest extension of the franchise. When democrats such as Lamartine and Ledru Rollin made excitable speeches the leaders of the moderate Left rejected a suggestion for holding a final banquet in Paris.

Though Alexis de Tocqueville warned the deputies in January 1848 that they were moving towards a social upheaval he did not really expect that revolution would break out in the very next month. He decided afterwards that the catastrophe was brought on by 'general causes impregnated by accidents'. A demonstration planned by radical elements in Paris was banned by the government. Students took the lead in deciding to go on with the demonstration on 22 February, and desultory rioting took place in the streets. Louis-Philippe could have restored order easily by vigorous military action, but he hesitated to be responsible for bloodshed. At the end of a second day of rioting the king dismissed Guizot, and the British ambassador thought that danger was over. Unfortunately a clash between demonstrators and troops outside Guizot's residence aroused popular anger, and men from the republican societies began building barricades. On the morning of 24 February Louis-Philippe reviewed the National Guard with the intention of putting heart into the forces of law and order, but when he discovered that the guardsmen shared the desire of the petty bourgeoisie for electoral reform he apparently felt that his régime had failed, and in a spirit of dejection he agreed to abdicate in favour of his little grandson. Crowds which collected at the offices of the two democratic newspapers would not hear of a Regency, however. Inundating the Chamber of Deputies they gave Lamartine his most dramatic opportunity to speak for the people, whereupon they carried him in triumph to the Hôtel de Ville and proclaimed the Second Republic.

In spite of the slovenly way in which the July Monarchy was overthrown the Second Republic began life in an atmosphere of exaltation and enthusiasm. Hundreds of political clubs were formed in a month; dozens of new journals appeared every day. Almost all articulate sections of the community expressed the belief that an era of universal happiness was about to commence. The phenomenon can only be attributed to the influence of socialists, novelists, and religious revivalists who had insisted for years that the world's problems would disappear if brotherly love were allowed to blossom.

The eleven members of the Provisional Government were chosen by a process which can best be described as haggling between three self-important groups – the left-wing deputies in the Chamber, and the staffs and supporters of the two democratic newspapers, the *National* and the *Réforme*. The chosen were 'consecrated', however, by the acclamation of such parts of the sovereign people as happened to be present, either thronging the Chamber of Deputies or milling outside the Hôtel de Ville. They included one workingman, known to everybody as Albert, which was his Christian name. His presence was regarded as symbolic by the remaining ten, who were all professional men. There were several lawyers, and the eminent mathematician and astrologer François Arago. At the head there was, officially, Dupont de l'Eure, whose long life of devotion to the republican cause entitled him to honour. The real leading light was Alphonse de Lamartine, France's most gifted poet.

Lamartine was born an aristocrat, but like so many romantics he turned from conservatism in the eighteen-twenties to liberalism in the eighteen-thirties, ending in the eighteen-forties as a democrat and nationalist of fervent if ill-defined views. Like all the prominent artists of the period he was wholly committed to whatever political line he chose to follow and regarded his art as a part of his politics. He was more ambitious than most, for he thought that he ought to be recognized not only as a greater poet but as a greater politician than Chateaubriand. In spite of his unique literary genius he can almost be said to have embodied the virtues and weaknesses of the Second Republic. His illusions about brotherly love were genuine, but he displayed them so ostentatiously that they sometimes seemed manufactured. He had written a false and moving account of the great Revolution (*Histoire des Girondins*, 1847) which he enacted in 1848, glorying in the leading rôle. His immense popularity, which was based not on his poetry but on his political oratory of purple and gold (the description is Louis Blanc's) was so wholly undeserved that he did not realize that the measures needed to sustain it were almost impossible of fulfilment. He was so staggeringly proud of his own abilities that a great many contemporaries and most historians came in the end to value them at less than their worth. His noble courage in standing by his republican convictions in the disillusionment which ended the year 1848 was widely and wrongly attributed entirely to lack of sense. With all his political failings he possessed a kind of merit which made his fate more saddening than absurd.

The success of the Second Republic depended on the ability of the government to satisfy or at least pacify the workers, who made great demands upon it, without alienating the middle classes, who merely welcomed or accepted it. The workers had played little part in setting up the Republic but they expected it to put an end to poverty and social degradation. On the first day of its life an armed man, described by Louis Blanc as handsome, pale, and savage, with the people's fire in his eyes, burst into the government chamber and demanded the *droit au travail*. When he was informed of the difficulty of organizing labour overnight he said that the people would place three months of hardship at the service of the Republic. After this they would add up the reckoning.

The government was divided between those who believed that the democratic republic could and should of itself suffice for all men and those who advocated a policy of social welfare. Even the former (the seven deputies chosen in the Chamber, along with Marrast of the *National*) were willing to make some gestures of sympathy with workers' problems, and the government at once proclaimed the right to work, allowed trades unions to appear, and set up a labour commission, containing twice as many workers as employers, to sit at the Luxembourg under the direction of Louis Blanc and recommend useful social experiments. The trouble arose over what, if anything, to do next, for the workers were clearly not satisfied that matters would now mend of their own accord. The social democrats in the government consisted merely of Louis Blanc, Albert, and Flocon of the *Réforme*. Their ideas were mild compared with the attitude adopted by the revolutionary societies of the capital under the guidance of Auguste Blanqui. This sinister personage, recently released from one of his many long spells in prison, was more fanatically devoted to the class struggle than Karl Marx himself. The right wing decided to stand by its principles: Louis Blanc's plan for national workshops was rejected as alien to the spirit of brotherhood, and schemes for large public works were resisted throughout the lifetime of the Republic as an unwarranted encroachment by the state upon the rights of individuals. The only acceptable solution to the needs of vast numbers of men who remained unemployed in Paris and all the large towns of France was to herd them into ateliers, called National Workshops as a gesture to Louis Blanc, and either employ them on road-sweeping jobs and similar occupations or to pay them a dole. By June about 120,000 were in receipt of a miserable pittance, and many thousands more had to be turned away with nothing.

Wretched as they were, the National Workshops cost ruinous amounts of money. The government was informed on the best financial authority that its position was hopeless. The imperturbable Garnier-Pagès, as minister of finance, decreed an extra 45 centimes on every franc paid in land tax during the previous year, but so many persons were exempted on pleas of hardship that the yield was only a half of the estimates. Even so the peasants became bitterly hostile to the Republic, which had presumed to take away some of the benefit they had derived from the first and greatest of revolutions in an attempt to give a miserable share to the city mob. Disillusionment on both sides caused class hatred to rise to a pitch never before experienced in Paris. As early as March there were demonstrations of hostility between the old propertied regiments of the National Guard and the newly-enrolled working class élite. By April De Tocqueville was describing society as 'split into two: those who possessed nothing united in a common greed; those who possessed something in a common fear. No bonds, no sympathies existed between these two great classes, everywhere was the idea of an inevitable and approaching struggle.'

The Provisional Government clung doggedly to a decision to hold elections as early as possible, though it feared the conservative instincts of the peasant masses. Ledru-Rollin as minister of the interior repudiated all forms of electoral pressure and tried to win a radical victory purely by propaganda. Unfortunately he was the most tactless of men. Though possessed of the mildest social views he had long ago gained a reputation for 'red' republicanism. His chief helper at the ministry, George Sand, did not improve matters with her vividly worded bulletins. The agents whom he sent to the provinces in the manner of representatives-on-mission to galvanize republican zeal, though aided by the schoolteachers, were outdone by the clergy, who fought republicanism with a cry for freedom of education. Out of nearly 900 deputies elected on the momentous Easter Sunday nearly 700 would have fulfilled the electoral qualifications of the July Monarchy. The majority were local notables with very moderate republican views and a substantial minority were monarchists. The Assembly followed the chairman of its Labour committee, the Comte de Falloux, in deciding to close the National Workshops and get rid of a dangerous mob by drafting unmarried men into the army and sending the rest to drain pestilential swamps in the provinces. The result was the rebellion of the June Days.

In this desperate action only about a tenth of the workers of Paris took part but the class character was evident from the start. The workers fought not for any particular programme but out of bitterness and anger. They began, on 23 June, by building barricades, knowing that their temporary immunity was not due to any sympathy or faint-heartedness on the part of the middle class but to the desire to bring up sufficient troops and ammunition to attack in force, and with cannon. Lamartine argued all night before the new ministry that it would be more humane and civilian to attack each barricade as it was built, but General Cavaignac, who was to command the government forces, would not move until he could attack all vital points at once. Cavaignac had been a republican all his life, and the social disadvantages he had faced in consequence had helped to harden his heart. He regarded the insurgents with the same mixture of fear and contempt which had been inspired in him by the natives of Algeria, where he had won his military fame. His opinion of their barbarism was shared by property owners all over France. Sentimental ideas about the noble workers and the brotherhood of man were gone: in their place was terror and hatred. An appeal by Ledru-Rollin for help from the country brought National Guards, peasants, shopkeepers, businessmen and great landowners pouring into Paris to attack the 'anarchists'. On the last day of the insurrection they were coming from 500 miles away.

The fighting was savage, with atrocities on both sides. The insurgents held on desperately until their last stronghold in the faubourg Saint-Antoine fell on the sixth day (30 June). Punitive measures carried out afterwards in the name of law and order were of such ferocity that no-one who took part in them was ever the same again. The whole bloody episode shook the foundations of Europe in the golden days of revolution. If sophisticated French liberals could not stave off the horrors of working class rebellion and class war what hope was there for others, save in a speedy return to the arms of authority? Even for social democrats, was it not better to leave the workers in the slough of suffering than to raise their spirits and call down savage retribution? Herzen described the shock which had been inflicted upon sensitive minds: 'Half of our hopes, half of our beliefs were slain; ideas of scepticism and despair haunted the brain and took root in it. One could never have supposed that, after passing through so many trials, . . . we had so much left in our souls to be destroyed.'

The Second Republic survived the June Days by permission of the army. Cavaignac's principles would not allow him to exercise a military dictatorship, and he faithfully protected the Assembly until it finished its task of constitution-making in November 1848. In spite of fear and hatred of the mob the republican deputies clung to the principles which had emerged in February and placed political power in the hands of the sovereign people. An assembly with supreme legislative power and a president with supreme executive power were to be elected separately and directly by the whole nation. The deputies were warned that the nation might elect a president who was incapable of working with the Assembly, but they agreed with Lamartine that 'something must be left to providence'. In December 1848 Louis Napoleon Bonaparte was elected President of the Republic by an overwhelming majority. Lamartine polled less than 18,000 votes in the whole of France.

The nephew of the great emperor had not made much of a mark in French politics when he presented himself as a candidate for the presidency. His political writings were not widely read. His election to the Assembly earlier in the year had been the work of two devoted agents, Persigny and Ferrère, and had been likened by a reputable newspaper to the sudden appearance through the boards of the demon in a pantomime. His *gauche* behaviour in parliament had stifled fears concerning his dictatorial ambitions, and Odilon Barrot and Thiers had even thought of pushing him forward so that they could exercise power in his name. Yet the news of his election to the presidency was interpreted throughout Europe as the death blow to the revolution. Karl Marx for once expressed the common opinion when he said that the election was due entirely to the passionate desire of the bourgeoisie and peasantry for law and order. Louis Napoleon's agents had certainly been busy, in the months following the June rebellion, stressing this aspect of the Napoleonic Legend: cheap bonapartist journals circulating among the poor had offered relief to the sufferers rather than leadership in the class struggle. Yet the Marxian thesis ignores the fact that the wealthiest voters in town and country supported Cavaignac, who polled a million and a half of the seven million votes, and that the middle and lower sections of the bourgeoisie whose members helped to give Louis Napoleon his five million had long wanted a more dynamic policy than they had experienced since Waterloo.

If bourgeois Frenchmen had only wanted a conservative policy they would surely have applauded the Assembly elected in May 1849. This authoritarian body supported an expedition against Mazzini, passed an education law (the *Loi Falloux*) allowing the church to establish secondary schools, restricted freedom of assembly and freedom of the press, and deprived one in every three Frenchmen of the right to vote. Yet according to the British ambassador the majority of people wanted Louis Napoleon to destroy the Republic. Law and order was apparently not enough, as bonapartist candidates must have known when they presented themselves at elections as advocates of progress. Louis Napoleon ostentatiously worked with the Assembly until December 1851, when he destroyed it in a single night's *coup d'état* for refusing to allow him to run for a second term. By this time he had collected so much evidence of his own popularity that he was able to accuse the deputies of thwarting the will of the people. The *coup d'état* was opposed only by small groups of radical republicans who built barricades in Paris and led riotous crowds against the police in a few provincial towns. These disturbances could easily be written off as 'demagogic' and their true character smothered in a short burst of anti-socialist repression: no-one could have guessed that they would haunt Louis Napoleon for the rest of his life. On 14 January 1852 the latter published a new constitution giving himself, on Lord Normanby's reckoning, more power than any other ruler in Europe except the tsar of Russia. He remained President of the French Republic, but not for long. On 2 December 1852, after a triumphal tour of France, he took note of what he called the nation's wishes and proclaimed himself Emperor Napoleon III.

3. THE AUSTRIAN EMPIRE

An explosive situation was developing in many parts of Europe during the eighteen-forties. In consequence the news of a revolution in Paris in February 1848 met with an immediate response in Germany, Hungary, and Italy. The result would, however, have been doubtful had there not been a gradual winding down of conservative power in the Austrian empire since the death of Francis I.

With the accession of the Emperor Ferdinand I in 1835 supreme power over the Habsburg dominions fell into the hands of a half-wit. Ferdinand had suffered for years from epileptic fits which had shaken the health of body and mind and left him at the mercy of anyone who could guide his wavering hand as he wrote his name on the numerous documents which thereby became law. Francis had confided this unfortunate son to the care of Archduke Louis, who became the head of a council of state with Metternich in charge of foreign affairs and Kolowrat in charge of home affairs. Archduke Louis lacked talent and decision and the two ministers were deadly enemies. Kolowrat was supported by ambitious court cliques in posing as a 'liberal' opponent of Metternich, and the latter retaliated by defeating even the smallest suggestions for change. Government drifted into a state of inertia, finances fell into chaos, censorship became totally inefficient, and police control grew more and more haphazard. Criticism which would have been silenced in Francis's day increased in volume annually.

Opposition developed at a great many levels. Archduchess Sophia intrigued in court circles for the dismissal of Metternich whom she regarded as the chief obstacle to her plans for placing her son Francis Joseph on the throne. Members of the aristocracy saw a chance of increasing their own power at the expense of the Crown by proposing pseudo-liberal measures. The Estates of Lower Austria emulated those of Bohemia and Hungary in requesting wider powers for existing local assemblies. Members of the Diet established contact with the professional and business world of Vienna through a variety of clubs, but found that their motives were distrusted by all but the most conservative citizens. The majority were inspired by the exile Schuselka, whose pamphlets advocated a representative system in which the middle classes played the leading part. More radical views found a hearing among the 2,000 students in the University of Vienna, many of whom were extremely poor, living in dark, damp cellars and supporting themselves on meagre fees received for tutoring. More than their physical hardships the students resented the dreariness of a University syllabus drained of life by censorship and government regulation. They longed to play a part in public affairs and especially to take a hand in ameliorating the lot of the working class.

Vienna had nearly doubled its population since 1815, mainly by immigrants from the countryside. Impoverished peasants and handicraft workers sought employment in the new textile and paper factories of the eighteen-forties but found openings too few for their numbers. Women and children were employed in preference to men because they could be given a pittance for a fourteen hour day. The bad harvests of 1845 and 1846 raised the price of common necessities to a prohibitive level, while the financial crisis of 1847 caused 10,000 factory workers in Vienna alone to be sacked from their jobs. The suburbs of Vienna, where the factories and working class hovels were situated, became dens of drunkenness, prostitution, robbery, and murder. Respectable citizens became more than ever thankful for the broad green belt and the high city walls which divided them from such horrors. The starving wretches in the suburbs had no political ideas, no leaders, and no knowledge of the socialist literature which sometimes penetrated Austria from Germany and France. They would support anyone who promised them a fair deal or merely gave them an opportunity for revenge and plunder.

The decrepitude of the old régime was responsible for creating a dangerous situation in which subversive literature could be read in secret by people who were unable to test it in the light of experience. When news of the Paris revolution reached Vienna every section of the population clamoured for action but few knew precisely what to ask for and no-one could envisage the effect which ideas from France and Germany would have on the conflicting nationalities of the Habsburg empire. Petitions poured into the authorities, from businessmen asking for increased credit, from booksellers requesting the abolition of censorship, from a self-styled 'party of progress' demanding arms for the people, from the Estates asking for a united diet, and from students demanding freedom of speech, freedom of religion, and universal representation of the people. On 13 March, when the Estates of Lower Austria opened their session, a demonstration planned by students led to a clash with the troops and an uprising of the workers. Panic seized the court, and Ferdinand agreed to prod the insufferably composed Metternich to resign. Rumours that the court, having attained its object in the removal of Metternich, intended to turn the army on to the city aroused further demonstrations, and on 15 March the Emperor granted freedom of speech, set up a council of ministers, and promised a constitution.

The fissures which were to bring about the collapse of the revolutionary edifice soon began to appear. All the revolutionaries hoped to work amicably with Ferdinand, who was universally beloved, but his mind could not encompass faithful adherence to promises. The ministers whom he appointed were elderly bureaucrats who had won a reputation for liberal views simply by opposing Metternich; they encouraged Ferdinand to play for time before making even the most moderate concessions. A fresh revolt was needed to procure the publication of the promised constitution. Although this turned out to be one of the most liberal in Europe it was disliked by the students and the lower middle classes because it had not been drafted by a freely elected assembly. The liberal aristocracy and the more prosperous bourgeoisie on the other hand were well satisfied with it and wanted to bring the revolution to a close in order to put a stop to mob violence and social disorder. There had already been looting and burning in the suburbs: shops had been plundered, large houses stoned, customs posts destroyed, and factories gutted. Industry had suffered severe dislocation and hordes of unemployed labourers presented a menacing aspect in the streets. The men showed respect only for the students, who set up advisory committees and undertook social work among them. On 15 May workers armed with shovels and spades flocked into the city to aid the students in a radical demonstration. They forced the ministry to agree that a parliament representing the western half of the empire should be elected by universal suffrage to draw up a new constitution. Another demonstration a few days later forced the government to set up a Committee of Public Safety composed of radical members to be responsible for law and order in the city and for finding work for those in need.

The revolutionary events of May 1848 were the peak of radical success. The task of finding work for thousands of labourers flocking in from the countryside proved too great for any committee. Clashes took place between the disillusioned workers and the National Guard which had hitherto displayed radical sympathies. Meanwhile the Emperor Ferdinand deserted his bewildered capital to spend three months at Innsbruck where he was more closely in touch with the forces of counter-revolution. These consisted chiefly of the army and the peasantry. The army had a vested interest in the maintenance of the old régime and began working towards a restoration of monarchical power without waiting for orders from the government. The Bohemian national movement received a severe setback when Field-Marshal Prince Windischgrätz put down a revolutionary outburst in Prague and subjected the city to martial law (June 1848). The Italian nationalist movement was deprived of its early victories when Field-Marshal Count Radetsky drove the Piedmontese army out of Lombardy-Venetia and established a military dictatorship (August 1848). The twenty-six million peasants of the empire showed no great interest in the revolution which, in Austria as in most other parts of Europe, was an entirely urban affair. The peasants had long regarded the Emperor as their ally against rapacious landlords. In 1846 the peasants of Galicia, rising in the greatest *jacquerie* known in Europe since 1789, had helped the imperial authorities to put down a Polish national revolt in return for the abolition of robot, and aristocratic patriots in Galicia were obliged to remain quiet in 1848. In the early weeks of the Vienna revolution Ferdinand's ministers promised that dues and services should cease throughout Austria within a year, and the loyalty of the peasantry was thereafter assured. The Parliament which met in Vienna in July tackled agrarian problems too late to win the peasants to the side of the revolution. The Emancipation Act of 7 September was the greatest achievement of European liberalism in 1848 but it was put into effect by imperial officials who gave the impression that it was the gift of the Emperor. The civil service, like the army, worked almost automatically on behalf of the old order from force of habit and the pressure of vested interests.

Peasant opinion played its part in the confusion of nationalities which did so much to destroy the revolution. In the spring of 1848 two mighty nations, the German and the Hungarian, seemed about to emerge from the ruins of the empire. Slav peasants on both sides of the Leitha preferred, however, to restore the old, more impartial despotism than to fall a prey to German and Magyar domination. Meanwhile the national problem confronted liberals and radicals in Vienna with complications they had not anticipated. The Viennese rebels were almost all Germans and they assumed that free Austria would become a part of the free Germany which liberals from all over the Confederation were trying to form. They assumed also that this free Germany would be great and powerful. They soon disagreed among themselves as to the form the new Germany should take, however. Liberals wanted it to become a loose confederation of provinces so that the German parts of the Austrian empire could be included without severing their connections with the non-German parts. Radicals wanted it to become a strong federal union, and they were willing to see the German parts of the Austrian empire separated from the Polish, Italian, and Hungarian lands. Liberals and radicals were at one, however, in resenting the anti-German movement which sprang up among the Czechs. To all of them Bohemia was a German province and the Czechs who formed two-thirds of the population were expected to welcome the opportunity of becoming absorbed by the superior German race.

Czech nationalism, which began as a revival of Czech culture, had been patronized by Metternich as a counterblast to German nationalism. He knew that the Czechs, being a small people, could not endanger the Austrian empire unless Russia helped them, a contingency which was eliminated when Nicholas I promised at Münchengrätz to respect Habsburg interests. In any case the Czech leader, Palacký, dreaded the Russians almost as much as he hated the Germans. In April 1848 Palacký rejected an invitation to attend the German National Assembly on the grounds that his people were not a part of the German nation and that the creation of a united Germany would disrupt the Austrian empire, which protected not only Slavs but the whole of Europe from Russian aggression. His first demand, backed by a petition from the Czech bourgeoisie and students of Prague, was for the Czech language to be put on an equal footing with the German in Bohemia and for a separate administrative system to be created for the province. Later the support of Czech workers in Prague encouraged him to extend his aims and he came to think that the happiest future for his people would be secured by the union of Bohemia, Moravia, and Silesia (the lands of St. Wenceslas) to form a Czech-dominated unit in a federated Austria. This new Czech programme exacerbated the Germans in the three provinces concerned, especially in Silesia where the Germans outnumbered the Czechs, and infuriated the Viennese. The Emperor, however, cultivated the favour of the Czechs from the beginning and promised them that a Bohemian Charter would be drawn up by the Austrian parliament convened for July. Palacký tried to strengthen the position of the Czechs by arranging for a Slav Congress to meet in Prague on 2 June to consider what position the Slavs should occupy in a federal Austria. The meeting of the Congress increased political excitement in the city and encouraged more radical politicians than Palacký to put forward demands. Clashes between Czech workers and German masters ensued and gave Windischgrätz, the imperial general in Prague, an opportunity to subdue the city in a five-day battle. Even this episode did not destroy the loyalty of Czech leaders for the Habsburg dynasty. They disliked the socialist nature of the riots which had taken place in June and they deluded themselves into thinking that Windischgrätz's victory would keep Bohemia's record clean until she could receive a Charter from the Austrian parliament. In fact Windischgrätz intended to reduce the parliament to impotence.

Palacký's attempt to achieve solidarity among the Slavs in the Austrian empire was wrecked by an initial failure to make Polish aristocrats of Galicia co-operate on an equal basis with peasant peoples. The Poles regarded themselves as one of the master nations. Their sole interest in attending the Slav Congress was to see that it did not suggest equality of rights between themselves and the Ruthenians in Galicia. Their aim in 1848 was to secure autonomy for a Polish-dominated Galicia within an Austrian federation. The aim met with sympathy from most revolutionaries in Vienna, the radicals even going as far as to suggest that Galicia should be given complete independence so that she would protect Austria against Russia. The prospect aroused the stolid antipathy of the peasants of Galicia, whose representatives in the Austrian parliament relied entirely on the guidance of their patron of 1846, the imperial governor Count Francis Stadion.

Palacký extended the hand of Slav brotherhood to Slovaks and Croats, although by doing so he courted the disfavour of the Magyars on whom he largely relied to keep revolution alive in the empire. Magyar nationalism proved to be the most stubborn of the movements which took the field against Habsburg absolutism in 1848. When Metternich patronized the Hungarian Diet in the last decade of Francis's reign Magyar nationalism seemed to be a controllable force. The leading figure in the Diet, Count István Széchenyi, was a member of the great landed aristocracy whose views Metternich could appreciate. Széchenyi had no sympathy with the ignorant lesser nobility buried away on their country estates. He believed that Hungary could be made into a modern state only if the educated aristocracy sacrificed feudal privileges and co-operated with the bourgeoisie in securing economic improvements. He preached Magyar regeneration to inspire the aristocracy and bourgeoisie, not to reject the Habsburgs, whose support he hoped to obtain. In the pre-March period Széchenyi made friends with Metternich and persuaded him to think of lowering the tariff wall between Austria and Hungary and of extending the Austrian railway system beyond the Leitha. Progress was bound to be slow, for Széchenyi was relying on an urban class which numbered only half a million in 1848. His programme would ruin the lesser nobles, who were far more numerous. These facts account for his displacement by Kossuth in the eighteen-forties.

Louis Kossuth was a journalist from a petty noble family. Though he owned no land he was anxious to be classed as a Hungarian gentleman, so with the bravado of his profession he declared that the criterion was not the possession of land but devotion to the Magyar nation. He captured the support of the backward country gentry by assuring them that they, and not the clever people of the towns, had saved the Magyar nation and that their privileges embodied the Magyar tradition. His triumph was marked by the stages in which Hungary cut herself off from western Europe by insisting on a language which no-one else could understand: in 1840 the Diet declared that only Magyar could be used for official purposes and in 1844 that only Magyar could be used in schools. In 1847 the Diet itself was conducted in Magyar, even King Ferdinand having been coached to make a little speech.

Kossuth devoted all the arts of a brilliant demagogue to arousing Magyar national passion. His policy became expansionist: the Magyar nation must absorb all the lands of St. Stephen. It became culturally arrogant: the Magyar nation must be recognized as superior to the Slovak, Ruthenian, Roumanian, and Serb nations which formed the majority of the population in the lands of St. Stephen, and superior even to the Saxons of Transylvania and the native nobility of Croatia. The latter were warned by the language law of 1844 that they stood in greater danger of absorption by the Magyars than of encroachment from the Habsburgs. Lest the dynasty should desert them in their hour of need they turned to the Illyrian nationalist movement which young men like Tkalac had been promoting for some time, and in 1847 the Diet at Agram declared the Croatian-Slovenian language to be its official tongue.

Kossuth was enjoying his first session as a member of the Hungarian Diet when the news of the Paris revolution reached him. On 3 March in one of the most famous speeches of the century he demanded free institutions for Hungary and Austria under the Habsburg crown. On 15 March a group of students in Budapest unwittingly revealed the limitations of Kossuth's programme by storming the streets with demands for universal suffrage, equal representation of nationalities, and abolition of the robot; on the same day Kossuth damped down these extremes by beginning to pass the March Laws through the Diet at Pressburg. These joined Hungary, Transylvania, and Croatia into a single state under the Habsburg crown, with a separate parliament, ministry, and budget. Magyar speech was an essential qualification for election to parliament, and robot was abolished only with compensation. Ferdinand gave his approval to the March Laws on 11 April.

Kossuth was acclaimed as a hero by half the population of Europe. The first people to lose their enthusiasm for him were the Viennese liberals, who began to suspect that he intended to separate Hungary from the rest of the empire altogether. Court circles had suspected this for a long time and in characteristic fashion they had turned to a smaller nation for help. In March 1848 Ferdinand had appointed Jellačić to the position of viceroy at Agram. This tough Croatian soldier owed his career to Habsburg militarism but he was willing to pose as a Croat patriot in the exigencies of the time. He encouraged Croat nobles to reject the authority of the Hungarian parliament and even to adopt a brotherly attitude towards the Serbs, who created their own Diet at Karlovci. Early in September he crossed the Drave with a Croat army and invaded Hungary. A Slovak rising in the north, a Serb rising in the Voivodina, and Roumanian resistance in Transylvania meant that Hungary was beset on four fronts. Kossuth believed that the time had come for the master nations to stand together, and he appealed to the Austrian parliament, which he assumed to be German, to help save the Magyar nation from the dynasty and the Slavs. The proposal was defeated by German liberals in alliance with Czechs, Slovenes, and Ruthenians. At the beginning of October the Austrian minister for war, Count Latour, ordered grenadiers from Vienna to march to the assistance of Jellačić against Kossuth.

Latour's order provoked a desperate rebellion in Vienna by students and other radicals who believed that the Habsburgs could only be held to their promise of free institutions if the empire were divided between the four master nations. On 6 October a radical mob lynched Latour and ran riot in the streets. After this most middle class citizens were willing to welcome the authority of the Emperor. At the end of October imperial armies under Jellačić and Windischgrätz closed in upon Vienna. By November the revolution was over.

On 21 November Felix Schwarzenberg, the brother-in-law of Windischgrätz, became Prime Minister. Schwarzenberg belonged to one of the greatest families in Austria yet he had no respect for aristocracy or tradition. He possessed a powerful intellect but he distrusted ideas. He was a man of violence who believed that all life's problems could be answered by force. His first step was to remove the Austrian parliament to the remote Moravian town of Kremsier where it could debate in harmless seclusion. The subsequent Kremsier constitution showed that Germans and Czechs were willing to compromise with each other to save the dynasty, but its proposals were useless to Schwarzenberg because they left the Hungarian problem untouched. On 2 December poor Ferdinand, who was bound to an autonomous Hungary by his acceptance of the March Laws, was persuaded to abdicate in favour of his nephew Francis Joseph. On 5 April 1849 Austrian delegates were withdrawn from the German National Assembly whose schemes had threatened to cut the Habsburg empire in two. Italian nationalism was defeated in a renewed war. Against Magyar nationalism, which Kossuth had whipped into a frenzy by unleashing civil war against the Slavs, Schwarzenberg accepted an offer of help from Russia. In August 1849 the Hungarian army surrendered to the Tsar at Világos. The ground was cleared for the greatest centralizing experiment the Habsburgs had carried out since the days of Joseph II.

4. GERMANY

'Wealth and speed are the things the world admires and for which all men strive', wrote Goethe in 1825. Industry was already bringing wealth to new classes of the population in Germany, and industrial enterprise increased enormously during the two decades which followed. In 1827 Alfred Krupp began to build his great industrial empire at Essen; in 1837 August Borsig founded his famous machine works in Berlin. Mechanization came most quickly to textiles and mines. Old established concerns in Saxony and the Rhineland were transformed by the introduction of spinning machines, power looms, and steam pumps; new centres developed in the Prussian capital and in southern towns such as Mannheim, Ludwigshaven, Esslingen, Augsburg, and Nuremberg; and a new importance was given to Westphalia and Silesia as producers of yarn and coal. An immense impetus was given to industry by the building of railways. The first line, opened in 1835, ran a distance of only 7 kilometres from Nuremberg to Fürth, yet by 1850 the railway system connected outlying coalfields with central towns and linked industrial regions with northern ports. Ironworks increased their output to provide rails, and collieries expanded to provide fuel. The first locomotives were supplied by Britain, but production was soon taken over by Borsig and other German firms. Steamboats also came originally from Britain, but before long they were being produced at Ruhrort and were plying on all the main rivers.

Germany was not, however, an industrial country when revolution broke out in 1848. Even though town populations increased twice as fast as country populations between 1815 and 1845, three-quarters of Germany's 35 million inhabitants still lived by agriculture. Moreover, of those employed in industry only one-third worked in factories. The rest were artisans working in cottages or small shops and striving by hand production to compete with machines. Handicraft workers watched with fear and bitterness the destruction of the old corporate system of production which had safeguarded their livelihood and status. Governments in some states protected guilds for political reasons after 1815, but an increasing number were seduced by the financial and military advantages of the factory system into framing industrial laws which allowed greater freedom. Even in states such as those of Thuringia which maintained guild authority into the eighteen-forties the handicraft worker could not escape from competition, for the *Zollverein* brought an influx of cheap goods from Prussia. Artisans pleaded with the authorities, threatened the owners of mills, and occasionally broke into violence. In 1844 some 5,000 weavers in Silesia destroyed machines, sacked manufacturers' houses, and looted shops for food. The revolt was put down by troops and the leaders were sentenced to floggings and long terms of imprisonment.

Peasants on the land also suffered in the new age of freedom and competition. In the north and east the division of common land gave the peasant a plot too small to compensate him for the loss of meadow and forest rights. Sinking further and further into debt he was forced in the end to sell out and become a day labourer on the estate of a nobleman. Wages for agricultural labour were so low that women and small children were obliged to work in the fields alongside their menfolk. In the west and south, population grew too rapidly to be absorbed into industry, and as there were few large estates to employ labourers peasants divided their land until holdings became too small to provide a livelihood. Most peasants lacked the capital to commute manorial services and dues, which remained an added burden upon their meagre income.

Compared with artisans and peasants the factory workers were well off. Those employed in making locomotives and industrial machinery enjoyed steady work and high wages, while even the less skilled workers in textile factories earned five times as much as hand weavers. Yet they had their grievances, consisting of long hours, employment of women and children under degrading and unhealthy conditions, the imposition of fines by employers, and the use of the truck system of payment. So, too, had the businessmen, who were rapidly coming to think of themselves as the élite of the nation. They complained of the backwardness and prejudices of governments wedded to aristocracy and agriculture. Above all they complained of the lack of a central authority to curb the intransigence of princes. The *Zollverein* was a step towards economic unity, but each state in Germany could still coin its own money, promulgate its own business laws, and maintain its own weights and measures. Even the establishment of postal services and the building of railways required persistent negotiation between numerous authorities.

The bourgeoisie found an answer to its desires in the liberalism of the French July Monarchy. This promised an escape from absolutism without the dangers of mob rule. Princes would share their authority with aristocracy and middle class, and since the middle class was the more numerous its wishes would predominate. Leading liberals from all over Germany, such as Pfizer and Rümelin of Württemberg, Laube and Biedermann of Saxony, and Camphaussen and Mevissen of Prussia, agreed that the lower classes were too ignorant to be admitted to the franchise. They agreed, too, that the community could benefit only if men of initiative were free to develop industry and commerce to its fullest capacity and sentimental notions of protecting peasants and artisans were swept aside.

Businessmen were not the only Germans who embraced the liberal cause. Men in the higher ranks of the professions were equally attracted to a creed which offered wide opportunities to men of talent. The lower middle class of petty merchants, small businessmen, lawyers and teachers moved further to the left, calling themselves democrats and adopting a creed which offered a wider franchise. They, too, had no intention of placing political predominance in the hands of the workers, however, and although they admitted the need for government measures to aid the distressed they by no means advocated the abolition of private property. In their ideas they were more akin to the Jacobins of 1793 than to the Communist League. Karl Marx had scarcely any following at all inside Germany, and his propaganda made no impression on the events of the revolution of 1848.

Liberals and democrats agreed that a new system of government in the individual states of Germany must be safeguarded by a new federal bond and the creation of a central parliament representing the people. This was as far as most people's nationalism went, though a few writers expressed the view that the German fatherland existed wherever the German tongue was spoken. Economic argument was brought to the support of political theory by Friedrich List, whose *National System of Political Economy* asserted that Germany should extend her dominion over Denmark and Holland in order to obtain fisheries and naval power, maritime commerce and colonies. Publications of a left-wing nature had little difficulty in appearing in Germany, for censorship was lax in some of the smaller states and clandestine distribution was well organized. Yet in spite of impressive protest and propaganda liberals and democrats made no inroads into the old system of government for a quarter of a century after the promulgation of the Carlsbad Decrees. A few of the constitutions granted in earlier years remained in existence, but Hanover's was withdrawn in 1837 when Victoria's uncle Ernest Augustus became king, and further grants were inhibited by federal decree. Liberal hopes ran high in Prussia when the talented and sensitive Frederick William IV ascended the throne in 1840, but the new king's romantic and religious soul yearned after medieval revivals rather than modern innovations. The United Diet which he convened in 1847 was nothing more than a glorified meeting of Estates, and liberal hopes that its nature might be transformed by a written constitution were dashed when Frederick William opened the session with the words, 'Never will I permit a written sheet of paper to come between our God in heaven and this land, as if it were a second Providence, to rule us with its paragraphs and supplant the old sacred loyalty.'

Constitutionalism came to Germany in the spring of 1848 when princes gave in to liberals and democrats from fear that they would use force. The use of force became a possibility as a result of the depression which hit Germany in the middle years of the decade. A decline in overseas trade beginning about 1844 was rendered disastrous by the potato blight of 1845 and the grain failure of 1846. As thousands of workers were thrown out of employment the cost of daily necessities doubled and starvation faced the lower classes all over Germany. Large-scale riots took place in almost every state during the worst times, yet they remained undirected and without political content. The poor themselves had no political ideas beyond appeals to the princes to better their lot, and the middle classes were so afraid of mob violence that they supported the authorities in suppressing the riots. Only in 1848, when princes were weakened by the frightening news that Louis-Philippe had been overthrown, did middle class agitators dare to take over the leadership of the distressed multitude. By then the worst of the depression was over, but enough bitterness remained to make the poor ready to place their faith in promises of a new order.

News of revolution in Paris gave the signal for artisan riots in many parts of Germany. In Westphalia and the Rhineland mobs set fire to mills and stoned the houses of millowners. In Thuringia and Saxony artisans wrecked machines, while in Berlin manufacturers maintained a private militia to ward off attack. Teamsters and freightmen tore up railway lines in Nassau, and boatmen, stevedores, and towers attacked the steamships of the big companies on the Rhine. Meanwhile the peasants of Baden attacked castles to destroy manorial rolls and compel the owners to promise concessions. From Baden the *jacquerie* spread northward into Darmstadt, Nassau, and the Rhineland, and eastward into Württemberg, Bavaria, and Saxony. In the north and east disorder was less spectacular, but even Prussia suffered some intimidation of landowners in Brandenburg, Pomerania, and Silesia. As news of upheaval in town and country spread through Germany, princes began to dismiss conservative ministers, appoint well-known liberals, and summon elected assemblies. In Prussia the king tried to placate the liberals with meaningless concessions, but news of the fall of Metternich fired the temper of the people. Barricades were erected in the streets of Berlin and citizens fought fiercely against regular troops until Frederick William withdrew the garrison. During the next few days the king was forced to grant freedom of the press, the convocation of a united assembly, and the formation of a liberal ministry. Rulers in Saxony, Hanover, and central Germany followed suit. By the end of March the old order was in disarray in every state of Germany. Moreover a beginning had been made upon creating a new order not merely for individual states but for the German nation. On 31 March, as the result of invitations received from a group of liberals in Heidelberg, progressive politicians from all over Germany met in a preliminary parliament at Frankfurt to make arrangements for the creation of a National Constituent Assembly.

The Pre-Parliament stipulated that direct elections on a basis of universal suffrage should be held within a few weeks. In fact, governments in all but a few small states held indirect elections in order to dilute the influence of the lower classes, but the subterfuge was probably unnecessary, since half the people enfranchised were not sufficiently interested in nationalism to go to the polls. The results were similar to those which France experienced in

1789: members of the German National Assembly came mainly from the
professions (more than 200 were lawyers) with 90 liberal noblemen, 30
merchants and industrialists, 4 artisans, and 1 peasant. The Assembly brought
common sense and worldly experience to bear upon the constitutional
problem, and accomplished its task of constitution-making with considerable expedition. The moderate centre, with well-defined liberal views, soon
triumphed over the aristocratic right and the radical left. By the end of the
year it had produced a list of individual liberties which were to be the
foundation-stone of the new Germany: freedom of speech, freedom of
religion, equality before the law, abolition of servile obligations, sanctity of
property, and maintenance of parliamentary government. The Declaration
of the Fundamental Rights of the German People was designed to act as a
guide to constitution-makers in the several states of Germany while the
Frankfurt Assembly turned its attention to the constitution of the united
fatherland. For this the first draft was made by the historian Friedrich Dahlmann, one of seven liberal professors dismissed from Göttingen by King
Ernest Augustus in 1837. The final form preserved the political identity of
member states in a federal union whose government consisted of a central
judiciary, a freely elected parliament, and an emperor whose executive
power was entrusted to the hands of responsible ministers.

The constitution was ready by the end of March 1849, yet the ten months
which sufficed to complete it sufficed also to render it worth less than the
paper on which it was written. The Frankfurt Assembly possessed no
executive organs through which to enforce its decisions; everything depended on the willingness of the separate state governments to put the constitution into effect; and long before the spring of 1849 the revolution
collapsed in kingdoms and principalities throughout Germany. Critics as
diverse as Karl Marx and Bismarck poured scorn on an assembly of pedants
which talked instead of acting and thereby let the golden moment pass, but
their contempt was wide of the mark. The policy of liberals in and out of the
Assembly, and not the mere passage of time, was responsible for damping
down revolutionary enthusiasm.

From the earliest days of the revolution the lower classes pressed their
claims upon state governments and National Assembly. Factory workers
were the least demanding. In spite of the efforts of Karl Marx in the *Neue
Rheinische Zeitung* (founded in June 1848) the industrial proletariat refused to
proclaim the class war. Regarding themselves as the élite of the lower class,
factory hands clung to their jobs and attempted to negotiate at a parliamentary level for the improvement of conditions. Some 12,000 supported the
moderate socialist programme put forward by Stephan Born, forming
workingmen's clubs in Berlin, Breslau, Munich, Leipzig, Hamburg, and
Cologne and petitioning the Frankfurt Assembly for universal suffrage,

trades unions, and factory legislation. Handicraft workers adopted a more threatening attitude and announced that they would 'no longer endure the yoke of slavery imposed by the money interests'. Delegates from handicrafts associations all over northern Germany met in Hamburg at the beginning of June and declared themselves 'firmly opposed to industrial freedom'. An Artisans' Congress representing the whole of Germany met in Frankfurt on 15 July and drafted a Charter demanding the control of production by guild associations. Journeymen who were excluded from the Artisans' Congress by the master craftsmen held a General German Labour Congress and pronounced themselves equally hostile to economic freedom. Peasants failed to produce a national organization but they petitioned state governments for the abolition of all manorial fees and rents and for assistance in the creation of a landowning peasantry. A Silesian democrat, Adolf Rössler, warned fellow-members of the Frankfurt Assembly, 'The peasant war stands without the gates. Think of that, gentlemen.'

Liberal governments in a few of the smaller states made concessions to the social problem, but the Frankfurt Assembly clung to liberal orthodoxy. Members could not bring themselves to restrict individual freedom in order to legislate for factory workers, to slow down the rate of industrial progress in order to accommodate artisans, or to encroach upon the sanctity of private property in order to establish peasants on the land. The task of framing an industrial code was never completed, but innumerable speeches from the floor of St. Paul's Church, as well as the publication of a report by the economic committee, made clear the Assembly's intention of establishing a system of *laissez-faire* as undiluted as that of the French bourgeois monarchy. The agrarian problem was met with a compromise which had long since been found unworkable in France: an attempt to distinguish between dues rooted in personal servitude, which were abolished, and dues originating in property rights, which were to be commuted. To the peasants this was a continuation of the old régime.

Disillusionment arising out of the economic policy of the liberals provided support for radical politicians when they rebelled against the Frankfurt Assembly in September 1848. The radicals themselves were stirred by political rather than by social grievances, however: they had come to regard the liberals as failures in the great cause of German nationality.

In the early days of the revolution, invitations to the Pre-Parliament were sent out on the assumption that the new German empire would cover the same area as the German Confederation, with extensions in favour of the province of East and West Prussia and the duchy of Schleswig. The assumption aroused protest in two quarters, the Germans of Posnania resenting exclusion and the Czechs of Bohemia resenting inclusion. The Pre-Parliament, in the first flush of enthusiasm for the idea of Europe dominated by

Map VII   The German Problem in 1848

master nations, declared the restitution of Poland to the Poles to be 'a holy duty of the German nation' and ignored appeals from the Germans of Posnania. Even Prussia, fearing intervention by the Tsar, proposed to make concessions to the Poles. A more aggressive spirit soon gained the upper hand, however. Clashes between German and Polish troops exacerbated feeling on both sides, and when the fear of Russian intervention had passed the Prussian government suggested dividing the province. The Frankfurt Assembly accepted the proposal and drew a demarcation line greatly in favour of the Germans, who were described as a nation superior in culture to the Poles. Meanwhile the Czechs steadfastly refused to elect representatives to the Frankfurt Assembly. The latter declared by a vast majority that German deputies elected in Bohemia must be regarded as fully representing the province, and the victory of Windischgrätz over Czech nationalism was thoroughly applauded.

It was the affair of Schleswig which quickly stemmed any pan-German enthusiasm among the Frankfurt liberals. In March 1848 no German could see why Schleswig, though populated mainly by Danes, should not join Holstein in becoming a part of the new Germany. The two duchies were historically and constitutionally connected, and though both were possessions of the Danish crown the Danish succession was in doubt. When on 18 March the people of the duchies rebelled, volunteers from Germany flocked to assist the Prussian army in repelling Danish troops. The economic and strategic importance of the duchies was not lost upon German liberals; nor, however, was it lost upon Great Britain. In August 1848 the Assembly heard that Frederick William had succumbed to pressure from Palmerston and signed an armistice with the Danes at Malmö. The liberal majority in the Assembly felt obliged to endorse the armistice on 16 September, whereupon radical orators raised rebellions in Frankfurt and Cologne. The Assembly called upon Austrian and Prussian troops to restore order, and the dependence of the National Assembly upon the two Great Powers was advertised to all Germany.

This dependence had been inevitable ever since the Assembly rejected the idea of 'mediatizing' the petty states in order to form independent blocs in central Germany. Particularism proved to be as strong among elected representatives of the people as among princes, and liberal fears of encroaching on the property rights of the rulers helped to perpetuate the old divisions. In the early days of the revolution the majority of deputies sought protection for their new Germany under the wing of liberal Austria, but the refusal of the government at Vienna to sever its connections with Hungary delayed a definitive arrangement. The restoration of the Emperor to Vienna in October and the determination of the Schwarzenberg ministry to reconquer Hungary reduced the numbers of the Greater Germany party in the Assembly until by February 1849 they were outnumbered by those who, like Dahlmann and Heinrich von Gagern, sought to exclude Austrian territory from a Lesser Germany under the guidance of Prussia.

Events in Prussia were therefore once more of paramount importance for the future of Germany. In March 1848 Prussia was given the second chance in her history to reject militarism. Unfortunately the bourgeoisie of Berlin, like the bourgeoisie of Vienna, came before many months were over to welcome the return of militarism for the sake of suppressing the mob. Democrats obtained an ascendancy over liberals from the start of the revolution because they were able to call on a large force of discontented workers in Berlin. Elections to the Prussian Assembly met with a larger poll than elections to the National Assembly, and democrats obtained a majority of seats. Their social policy was no more adequate than that of liberals, however, and before very long the forces of reaction were able to gather strength. A propaganda campaign devised by General Joseph von Radowitz promised upper and lower classes a just solution of their grievances at the hands of an enlightened monarch. A few timely concessions by landowners to their tenants appeared in favourable contrast to the harshness of the revolutionary government, which suppressed a mob riot arising out of workers' grievances in October. News of Ferdinand's restoration to power in Vienna heartened Frederick William, and on 2 November he placed the ruthless Count Friedrich von Brandenburg at the head of the ministry. As repressive decrees rained down upon the capital 13,000 troops under General Wrangel marched upon the city. They were received without a shot.

On 28 March 1849 Frederick William was elected Emperor of Germany by the Frankfurt Assembly. After a month's delay he scornfully refused 'the crown from the gutter', and the Frankfurt liberals returned to their homes defeated. Only the radical minority, which had always preferred the idea of a republic, made a bid to establish the constitution by force, but the spring rebellion of 1849 could not rally the support which the spring rebellion of 1848 had used to such effect. The militant petty bourgeoisie of Saxony, Baden, and the Palatinate fought for a few days, but peasants, artisans, and workers remained unmoved. The risings were put down by Prussian troops and the old order returned to Germany. The Diet of Princes recommenced its sittings on 23 August 1851.

5. ITALY

Italy in the eighteen-forties produced a more impressive array of nationalist writings than any other country in Europe. The writers of the so-called Moderate school were stimulated chiefly by a desire to distract Italians from a suicidal devotion to Mazzini. They produced two alternative plans whereby Italy could achieve nationhood: by joining her existing states into a confederation under the presidency of the Pope, or by dividing the country between large units which would then form a confederation under the presidency of the king of Piedmont. Both plans envisaged the co-operation of princes and ruling classes and the rejection of Mazzini's faith in mass revolution on the grounds that it produced only sporadic risings which were put down with needless suffering. The Moderate movement in its opposition to Mazzini's democratic programme bore some resemblance to liberal-nationalist movements in Austria and Germany, but the comparison cannot be carried further. The importance attached by the Moderates to free institutions was always doubtful. The two most influential writers, Gioberti and Balbo, were extremely hesitant in putting forward liberal demands, the former probably because he was appealing to an audience of priests, the latter because he was trying to 'manage' King Charles Albert. Both decided that initiative must remain with the princes, Gioberti advising only consultative assemblies and Balbo going as far as to say that independence could be achieved without representative institutions if the princes wished it so. D'Azeglio wrote of free institutions as a prerequisite of independence but did not define their content, and Rosmini envisaged political power divided among landowners in accordance with the extent of their property.

Vincenzo Gioberti set out to win princes and priests to the cause of Italian nationality. In a pamphlet published during his exile in Brussels in 1843, *On the Moral and Civil Primacy of the Italians*, he described his fellow-countrymen as a nation capable of resuming leadership of the civilized world. Their strength lay in their possession of Rome, selected by God as the seat of the Holy See, and in their devotion to the Catholic religion, without which there could be no progress. The cause of the Italian people and the cause of Papal authority had been welded together when Popes Alexander III, Innocent II, and Julius II led the national effort against foreign emperors. The Guelph tradition, the only national tradition Italy possessed, could be revived by making the Pope the head of a confederation of Italian states. Pope and princes would retain their sovereignty while brotherhood blossomed anew under the only common allegiance Italians could ever accept.

Gioberti made no mention of the future of Lombardy-Venetia. He seemed to assume that the Austrians would need to be driven out by force, and he ended his pamphlet with an ambiguously worded appeal to the king of Piedmont to use his sword in the nation's cause. Cesare Balbo rectified the omission in his pamphlet of the following year, *On the hopes of Italy*, by deciding that Lombardy-Venetia and possibly the Romagna would need to be annexed to Piedmont to form a barrier kingdom. The king of Piedmont was clearly intended in Balbo's scheme to play the leading rôle in a future confederation of Italy. This idea received support from Massimo d'Azeglio's pamphlet of 1846, *On the recent events in the Romagna*, which gave the impression that the papal government was too backward ever to take the lead in Italian affairs, though representative institutions would enable the Papal states to become part of a free Italy.

The moderate movement made nationalism into a respectable cause which could be embraced by churchmen, landowners, government officials, and princes, much as reform had been a respectable cause in the age of Enlightenment. There is no reason to believe, however, that it appealed to wide sections of the community. Nationalist fervour remained confined to small groups among the governing classes and among young men from professional and middle class homes. These small groups had now three programmes to choose from: the neo-Guelph, the Piedmontese, and the Mazzinian. No one of the programmes promised to raise the peasants from their poverty or to lead businessmen to an industrial heaven. The events of 1848 showed that nationalism had not yet moved whole classes of the population in Italy. Constitutionalism was more popular, for rich and poor regarded the mere promise of representative government as a cure for all ills. Revolts were widespread in 1848 but they were stimulated by local grievances and the rebels aimed, for the most part, at local remedies. Larger aims emerged only in the north, and even there rebellion had been in progress for some time before the leaders took to the idea of uniting north Italy under Piedmont. The subsequent belief that inspiring national efforts were made in 1848 belonged to myth rather than reality.

The revolutions of 1848 began with a rising in Palermo. A movement for Home Rule had been simmering among the upper classes in Sicily since 1815, becoming more heated when Ferdinand II replied to demands for autonomy by fusing the Sicilian and Neapolitan administrations. Some members of the aristocracy were convinced by Ferdinand's brutality after the revolt of 1837 that insurrection ought to be abandoned in favour of peaceful persuasion, but others continued to favour Mazzinian methods. When a group of Mazzini's adherents boldly advertised the fact that a demonstration was to be made at Palermo on 12 January 1848 they found plenty of people ready to join them in the streets, for the poor had nothing to lose by menacing the authorities. The demonstration turned into an insurrection, and when success was assured the wealthier malcontents came out into the open and proclaimed the aristocratic constitution of 1812.

The revolution in Sicily had very little to do with Italian unity. Some of the aristocratic conspirators were federalists, with distant ideas of uniting Italy under the presidency of the Pope, but in the event they employed their energies in attempting to keep Sicily independent of Naples. When Ferdinand hastily offered a constitution to the whole of his dominions on 29 January the Sicilians rejected it. The significance of the revolt for the rest of Italy lay in the fact that Ferdinand's surrender convinced hesitant rulers in Sardinia, Tuscany, and Rome that they too must swim with the liberal tide.

Sardinia had been chosen by Balbo and d'Azeglio to lead a movement for independence and unity because it alone among Italian states possessed an army capable of fighting the Austrians in Lombardy-Venetia. Otherwise there was little to commend the kingdom for leadership of the Italian cause. The people were mainly French in language and culture and they formed only one fifth of Italy's population. With the restoration of Victor Emmanuel to the throne in 1814 Sardinia became one of the most backward states in Europe. The aristocracy exercised feudal rights over the peasantry; internal customs barriers and provincial currencies hampered economic developments;

a confusion of antiquated customs and decrees replaced Napoleon's codes of law; and education fell once more into the hands of the church. Acquisition of the coastal province of Liguria made the kingdom into a potential maritime and industrial power, and gradually the wider interests of the merchants of Genoa began to compete with the narrow outlook of the court nobility for the direction of government policy, but progress was rendered precarious by the unsatisfactory character of successive rulers. Charles Albert was ambitious, but even his ambition could not hold him to a consistent course of action, for he would trust no-one. He believed that the liberals had played him false in 1821, so he went to the other extreme when he became king in 1831, refusing to include his former associates in the amnesty granted according to custom at the beginning of his reign and repressing a Mazzinian conspiracy with startling severity in 1833. In foreign policy he hoped to continue the expansionist traditions of his house by using Austria against France. To fit the kingdom for foreign adventures he began to introduce practical reforms. Recruitment and equipment of the army was improved, restrictive tariffs were lowered to foster trade, a few railways and canals were constructed, the port of Genoa was modernized, and the legal system was tidied up. No political reforms were contemplated, however. The church enjoyed greater power in Sardinia than in any other part of Europe outside the Papal States. Censorship was so rigorous that d'Azeglio could not publish even his historical novels in Turin. The only outlet for discussion was an Agricultural Society founded in 1842. Charles Albert imagined that economic progress had no connection with political freedom, but in Sardinia, as in Lombardy and Tuscany, the promotion of new methods in agriculture led to demands for a new social, economic, and political structure. The Agricultural Society with its 2,000 members became thus an important liberalizing influence.

During the eighteen-forties Charles Albert lost his hopes of obtaining territory from France and began to think instead of taking Lombardy from Austria as Habsburg power declined. By 1845 he was willing to listen to federalists who urged him to attack Austria, and he even dropped hints that he might one day do so, but he still did not trust the nationalists. Since 1821 he had regarded nationalism as a revolutionary movement designed to weaken monarchy. He preferred to find dynastic and Catholic reasons for attacking Austria. When in 1847 Metternich sent Austrian troops to check revolutionary symptoms in Modena and the Papal States, Charles Albert could legitimately protest against the threat to the balance of power and the violation of Papal neutrality. Even when Balbo warned him that the Pope and the Duke of Tuscany were outbidding him for Italian leadership he merely tried to thwart his rivals' plans for a customs union and then to buy popularity cheaply by relaxing the censorship and reorganizing local government. He swore that he would never grant a constitution, and stuck to his oath in the teeth of journalistic pressure from Cavour, rioting in Genoa, and appeals from the city council of Turin. He gave in as late as March 1848, and even then the *Statuto* enfranchised only 2½ per cent of Sardinia's population and gave the king as much power as George III had exercised in eighteenth century England.

It is hardly surprising that among neighbouring states there was a growing tendency to despise Sardinia for the backwardness of her institutions and to fear her because of the ambitions of her king. Tuscan liberals such as Montanelli, Capponi, and Guerrazzi, though dissatisfied with the half-hearted concessions obtained from Duke Leopold, looked forward in 1848 to the emergence of progressive states in central Italy, and as soon as they had obtained a constitution for Tuscany they opened negotiations with the Pope for the creation of an Italian League. To many people in Italy events in Rome were more stimulating than those in Sardinia. In 1846 the election of a Pope who was reputed to have progressive ideas aroused wild hopes that Gioberti's dream would be fulfilled. An amnesty which restored 1,200 political exiles and prisoners to freedom in the Papal States was interpreted as a sign that Pius IX sympathized with liberal and nationalist views. Metternich was right when he said that a pardon, requiring repentance, would have been more appropriate than an amnesty, ignoring the existence of guilt, for Pius IX could never believe in liberal doctrines nor, in the circumstances of the time, could he lead a nationalist campaign to fulfilment. Pius IX was a kind-hearted man, anxious to show respect for his subjects. He was willing to build railways, introduce gas lighting, lower tariffs, sponsor agricultural societies, relax censorship, and finally, in October 1847, to summon an elected assembly for consultative purposes, but he announced that he did not wish to go further. He believed, as Gregory had believed, that representative government was incompatible with papal authority. When he discovered, however, that many of his subjects were more liberal than Gioberti, his unwillingness to forego the rôle of *Papa Angelica* led him to make concessions against his better judgment and finally, on 15 March 1848, to grant a constitution. Meanwhile the nationalist tide was also swelling. Pius at his accession was attracted towards Gioberti's idea of a confederation of states under papal leadership, and in August 1847 he proposed the formation of a customs union as a step towards it. Only at this point does he seem to have discovered that Italian nationalists expected him to bless a future war between Piedmont and Austria, a thing which he could never do.

War against Austria was eventually sparked off by events in Milan. That there would be a revolt in Milan was by no means a foregone conclusion, for there were many Lombards, including some liberals like Cattaneo, who believed that there was more to be gained from Austria than Piedmont.

Under Austrian government Lombardy was more advanced from an economic point of view than any other state in Italy. Her educational system was the best in the peninsula, and censorship was lax. Discontent was aroused by particular grievances such as the employment of Germans as well as Italians in the civil service, the use of revenues outside the kingdom, and the existence of Austrian monopolies in tobacco and brandy. The inflexibility of the Austrian system was such that protests were met by repression, and discontent grew to anger. A demonstration by Milanese citizens against the tobacco monopoly in January 1848 was handled so roughly by the military that 61 people were killed. After this, anger turned to hatred. News of the fall of Metternich inspired all classes of the population to rise and expel the Austrian garrison in five days of furious fighting (17-22 March). The barricades were manned chiefly by artisans, some 300 of whom were killed, but social as well as political order was restored as soon as the Austrians had left. The old town council under the mayor Casati formed a provisional government with the economic theorist Cattaneo as the most notable member. Venice liberated herself from the Austrians without bloodshed. The patriot Daniel Manin, imprisoned by the Austrians for demanding Home Rule, was released by an angry mob composed chiefly of workers from the arsenal, but Manin succeeded in restraining the revolutionary forces and in using them simply as a threat to secure the withdrawal of the Austrian garrison and fleet. By the end of March all the cities of Lombardy, Venetia, and the Duchies had driven out the troops.

The revolt in Milan found Charles Albert totally unprepared for war, but he eventually marched to the aid of the rebels partly to outbid Tuscany, whose government had already declared war, and partly to prevent Lombardy from becoming a republic. He advanced so slowly that the Austrians were able to re-group in the Quadrilateral. Charles Albert was not popular in Milan, where Cattaneo denounced him as a traitor to the liberal cause, nor in Venice, where Manin had restored the ancient republic, but he insisted that Lombardy, Venetia, Parma, and Modena should vote themselves into the kingdom of Sardinia, and local patriots agreed for the sake of prosecuting the war. They soon discovered that they had overestimated Charles Albert's military value. Detachments from Naples and Rome brought Italian strength up to nearly 100,000 as against 70,000 of the enemy, but Charles Albert was no match for the 82 year old Austrian commander Radetsky. The latter succeeded in holding Verona until a relief column arrived from Vienna, whereupon he concentrated his forces and pierced the Piedmontese front at Custozza. The Lombards were anxious to invite aid from France, but Charles Albert preferred to abandon Lombardy and accept an armistice from the Austrians (9 August 1848). He advanced once more on Milan in the following March, but the Lombards did not stir, and on 24 March the

Piedmontese army was defeated decisively at Novara. Charles Albert abdicated the same night.

By the summer of 1849 revolution had collapsed all over Italy. In Naples the liberals were never firm enough in their attitude to the king, because they were too anxious to recover Sicily and too interested in posts and favours. Their refusal to pass agrarian reforms involved them in peasant risings, and the army rallied to the side of the king who was able to bombard Naples, restore order, and revoke the constitution after less than four months (May 1848). Ferdinand then withdrew Neapolitan contingents from the Austrian war. In the Papal States the difficulties of parliamentary government commenced when the liberal ministers sent an army to help Charles Albert and Pius IX disowned the war in an allocution of 29 April. Pius's popularity fell like a stone. The ingenuity of the liberal minister Mamiani saved papal authority for a few months, but radical agitators found a ready audience when thousands of disillusioned troops returned to Rome after Custozza. Mamiani's successor Rossi tried to keep the radicals at bay and paid for his courage with his life at the hands of assassins in November 1848. The Pope fled to Gaeta, whence he called upon Catholics to abandon the revolution. People of moderate views abstained from voting in the elections for the Constituent Assembly, which declared the temporal power abolished and on 29 March 1849 appointed Mazzini triumvir of a Roman Republic.

The significance of the Roman Republic for the Italian Risorgimento is not easily assessed. Mazzini afterwards wrote of it as an attempt to destroy catholicism, which he regarded as the great barrier to progress. In his opening address to the Roman Assembly, on the other hand, he spoke in terms of an example: the city which had twice led the civilized world should proclaim the new faith in 'God and the People'. In the event little was achieved. Time was short; Mazzini's doctrines were understood only by a few people and shared by even fewer; and radicals were hampered by moderates who feared disorder and social upheaval. Mazzini had never defined a social policy, because he did not recognize the existence of different classes with different needs and did not think that men's material condition was relevant to the activity of the human spirit. He carried out one or two obvious measures of social justice but beyond these he preached self-sacrifice, hard work, and devotion to duty, and his words had little attraction for labourers and peasants. These two were the only classes which did not answer Garibaldi's call for volunteers to defend the Roman Republic against four foreign armies which bore down upon her in answer to the Pope's appeal. Noblemen fought side by side with craftsmen in the most heroic episode of the Risorgimento but they fought for the independence of their city and the safety of their homes and families, not for Italian unity or European progress. When Rome fell to French troops in July 1849 and Mazzini and Garibaldi fled, no-one cherished the ideals for which the Republic had stood.

The Sicilian revolution was weakened by local rivalry and class selfishness. Messina would not accept the predominance of Palermo, and aristocratic liberals would not carry out agrarian reform. When peasants in some communes invaded the demesne lands and demanded their division they were promptly evicted. In May 1849 the island was overrun by Ferdinand's troops. In Venice Manin, with scarcely any help from the rest of Italy, defended his republic and created material for a legend to rival that of Rome before the Austrians regained control. Only Piedmont retained her parliament in the reaction which followed revolution, and its spontaneity was curbed as much as possible. Radetsky had no desire to subjugate Piedmont, but at the same time he did not wish the kingdom to become a seed bed of revolution. He therefore conceded a lenient peace to the new king Victor Emmanuel so that he could silence the radical war party and re-establish royal authority within the parliamentary system.

CHAPTER XVIII

A New Outlook, 1850-70

I. FROM REVOLUTION TO REALPOLITIK

WHEN the great upheaval of 1848 was over little, at first sight, seemed to have been achieved. The abolition of guilds and feudal servitude in central Europe had set craftsmen and peasants free to move wherever fate or fortune called them, but the tremendous changes which would be wrought by this emancipation lay in the future. For the time being it was clear only that the lower classes in town and country had failed to obtain the social justice for which they had hoped and for which some of their brethren had died. The middle classes were faced with an even more dispiriting record. Countries which had avoided revolution could boast a greater increase in freedom than those which had expended many lives and much emotion in the endeavour: Belgium, for instance, where the liberals elected to power in 1847 had absorbed the impact of democracy by extending the franchise to the limits allowed by the constitution, and Switzerland, where the Protestant and Catholic cantons had emerged from the civil war of 1847 in time to take advantage of the paralysis of their neighbours and create a federal state, guaranteeing democratic institutions and ending the strife of centuries.

In Austria and Germany the middle classes had failed to obtain the parliamentary and civic liberties on which they had pinned their faith: or rather, having obtained them in the early days of revolution they had failed to succour and support them, which was worse. There were many senses in which men were less free in 1851 than they had been before the revolution. They had learnt in 1848 that freedom brought its responsibilities as well as its gifts: notably the responsibility for dealing with the illiterate, the hungry, the selfish, and all whose mental, physical, or moral condition rendered them incapable of appreciating freedom. Most liberals in central Europe had shirked these responsibilities, casting them back upon the old rulers. Frenchmen had started out with a longer experience of freedom, but they too had become more aware of its responsibilities during 1848. The French peasantry and the French army had been thought of as bastions of freedom ever since 1789 and 1792, because they owed so much to revolution, but when in 1848 a new kind of revolution had appeared in France, the social revolution, both peasantry and army had fought against it. The whole of Europe had seen that the legacy of the greatest of revolutions was grown conservative, if not reactionary, and the desire for further progress had been weakened in consequence. Other countries besides France had begun to experience social tensions by June 1848, but no government had given in so completely to class hatred as the French government was to do at the end of the month. It was the show-down in Paris which gave all the others confidence to crush the workers with the aid of public opinion.

Failure leads to more enquiry than success. Most of the revolutionaries themselves sought an explanation in terms of individual culprits, men whose policy or lack of policy could be said to have betrayed the hope of 'the springtime of the nations'. As each new batch of refugees crossed the Channel (for only the most harmless were allowed to stay in Belgium or Switzerland) a little world of the past perpetuated itself in London. Herzen described its thousands of members in 1852, holding on to their illusions by indulging in personal recriminations. Among a wider public Lamartine, Ledru-Rollin, and other members of the French Provisional Government became the most popular scapegoats, whose failure to steer the democratic republic clear of the rocks and shoals of social anarchy was denounced as fatal to the whole of revolutionary Europe. Friedrich Engels, writing articles for an American newspaper over the signature of Karl Marx, was the first to point out that no nation can be betrayed unless it is in a condition for betrayal. According to his brilliant analysis (*Revolution and Counter-Revolution*) the situation which gave the initial impetus to the revolution also caused its defeat. Every class possessed grievances and aspirations for which it was prepared to support or accept the revolution, but no one class was capable of sustaining the revolutionary effort by itself. Under these circumstances the conflicting needs of classes led to total disaster.

In February 1848 both Marx and Engels had believed that the bourgeoisie would carry the day. After the revolution their bitterness centred upon this self-same bourgeoisie, whose failure to march with history meant that the whole process would have to be begun again. Their denunciations, particularly of the Frankfurt Assembly, lent themselves to the notion that 1848 was 'the bourgeois revolution', and that to the bourgeoisie must be attributed both the early success and the final failure of the revolution. According to this popular and long-lived interpretation the bourgeoisie was stripped of its illusions and pretensions in 1848 and revealed to itself and others in its true colours. In fact all classes were shown for what they were. In particular the old régime was seen to possess more strength and versatility than anyone had supposed. In future years it was to produce its finest flowering in Bismarck.

None of the events of 1848 caused more heart searching than those in Germany. Later generations, embittered by German aggression in two world wars, were convinced that Germany in 1848 had fluffed her finest chance of establishing a civilian, liberal régime and had doomed herself to the militaristic, authoritarian rule of Bismarck's Prussia. In the years immediately following 1848 no such catastrophe was perceived. The behaviour of Frederick William IV in the early stages of the revolution, his apparent willingness to dismiss his garrison and his apparent spontaneity in declaring Prussia to be merged in Germany, obscured the fact that Prussia was inherently opposed to liberal solutions. In 1866 and 1871 German liberals genuinely believed that they could mould Bismarck to their own pattern. The readiness of liberals to make terms with Bismarck unfortunately gave support to another adverse criticism, that the liberals of 1848 were chiefly concerned with nationalism and that in their aggressive Pan-Germanism they were forerunners of Hitler. The charge is not unfounded but it exceeds the evidence. A few writers of the pre-revolution period sowed giants' teeth, but most members of the Frankfurt Assembly thought of nationalism in the way that Frenchmen or Belgians thought of it, namely, in terms of citizenship. They hoped to create a German state which conformed, more or less, to the boundaries of the old Confederation, the traditional, internationally accepted Germany. Their small excursions outside this conception owed more to political and strategic motives than to ideology, and they were not prepared to pursue them against reason. No claims were made to include Alsace, or the Flemings, or the Germans of Switzerland in the new Bund. Some members of the Frankfurt Assembly even preferred Lesser Germany from the start, and tried to win the democrats to the cause by conceding universal suffrage. If in subsequent years German liberals still hankered after a more powerful Germany than the restored Confederation supplied, this was not because a demon had taken possession of their souls but because an adequate amount of power seemed to be an elemental need of humanity.

In the decades which followed 1848 European opinion eventually moulded itself to an attitude which both explained the past and confronted the future. The attitude involved a rejection of philosophy, which came to be regarded as the universal culprit of the preceding era. There had been, it was thought, too much theorizing, too much faith, too much idealism. Every philosophy had been greeted with bated breath, as though it were likely to shake the world. Rapturous acclaim had been given to the many philosophies based on the assumption that men were born good and could progress towards perfection. On these had been based the disastrous illusion that appeals to humanity would burst the bonds of class hatred and liberate the spirit of brotherhood. The experiences of 1848 seemed to have shown not only that most of the philosophies were false but that all philosophies were powerless. In future the universal search must be for the facts of human behaviour. On the results of this search must be based the efforts of reformers and the policies of governments.

In many specific senses men still wanted the things they had wanted in 1848: this was the triumph of the revolution. Liberals still believed that educated and experienced sections of the community should be allowed scope to develop their talents and ambitions; humanitarian thinkers were still absorbed with the evils of poverty and ignorance. Only the target was less advanced. Liberals in most countries were willing to accept a sphere of influence arrived at by negotiation with established authority. They were willing to accept from illiberal governments the practical measures which they themselves had striven to effect in 1848, as Austrian liberals accepted bureaucratic centralization from the Habsburgs in the eighteen-fifties and German liberals accepted legal reform from Bismarck. Few people thought any more of eliminating class distinctions: they hoped merely to avoid class war. Increasingly this was believed to be possible through the creation of nation-states.

Nationalism was no less predominant in the eighteen-fifties and 'sixties than it had been in the 'forties, only again the results which men expected from it were less heavenly. They believed that membership of a nation-state would give people an illusion of equality even if the reality escaped them, and that it would give them a status which was not measured in terms of material wealth. Napoleon III still believed that nationalism would promote universal peace, but in this he was untypical of his generation. That there would be strife between nations, especially in central Europe, was taken for granted and even condoned as a means of forging loyalties. Again, conviction was drawn from past experience. Hungary in 1848 had evaded the social problem within her borders by fighting a racial war against culturally inferior groups: the French Republic might, as the British ambassador saw, have avoided the June Days by sending armies into Italy. War between nations came to be regarded as an alternative to war between classes, and only Karl Marx preferred the latter.

At the same time people no longer thought that the nations would rival each other chiefly in the contribution which each wanted to make to civilization. Almost everyone expected nations to fight for their own interests, a concept which horrified Mazzini. Already in 1848 revolutionary governments had spurned the idea of crusading for liberty: Lamartine had refused to intervene in Italy for fear of Britain, the Frankfurt Assembly had abandoned Poland to the Great Powers, and the much canvassed 'united front' of revolutionary nations against absolutism had never been a reality. The revolutionaries had weakened their domestic position by adopting traditional foreign policies, but in subsequent decades nationalists succeeded in making such policies acceptable to the masses. Dynastic interest was translated into national interest and made to seem democratic. By 1870 advanced opinion, as expressed for instance by the Russian Danilevsky, was already moving towards a pseudo-scientific nationalism which described nations as doomed to an internecine struggle for the survival of the fittest. The theory gained much ground after the Franco-Prussian War.

For all their boasted realism, nationalists would probably have been no more successful after 1848 than before if the international situation had not changed. In 1848 groups of men far removed from the lofty realms of diplomacy and war had believed that they could change the map of Europe by their own amateur and civilian efforts. They had failed. They now looked for a statesman to fulfil their aspirations (there was a great longing, after 1848, for strong leadership) and they thought once more in terms of help from a Great Power. The most promising Great Power was, for a long time, France under her new Napoleon.

There was a great deal about Napoleon III which his closest acquaintances could not fathom, but the motive force of his career was apparent to all: a determination to be worshipped by the French people as the greatest ruler France had had since Napoleon I. The heir to the Napoleonic Legend would never achieve his ambition until he had rescued France from a position of tutelage by the signatories of the Quadruple Alliance and made her not only respected but envied and perhaps feared throughout Europe. Frenchmen would never be satisfied until they had made startling revisions in the treaties of Paris and Vienna. They would not be fobbed off with colonial expeditions, with widespread prosperity, or with fine attitudes, as the successive fates of Charles X, Louis-Philippe, and Lamartine had shown. Napoleon was endowed with the gambling instincts of his breed: he could reasonably feel that since several cautious governments had come to ruin his best bet was to strike out a new line.

Inside this broad framework his policy was opportunist, fluctuating, and often contradictory. He was a lover of peace, but only because he was more interested in the arts of peace than the arts of war: he would go to war if it suited his purposes. He had a genuine sympathy for oppressed nations, but would only indulge it if their fortunes ran parallel to his own. In the early years of his reign he probably had no more startling object in mind than to reverse the position of 1815 by making a real friendship with Britian. His attempts to co-operate with the British government in the diplomacy of the Middle East led him, however, irresistibly into the Crimean War against Russia. The defeat of the greatest reactionary power in Europe sounded the death-knell of the old order and gave unprecedented opportunities for re-drawing the map of the continent.

2. REALISM

The realism of the 'fifties and 'sixties was not only or even chiefly a reaction against the past. Had it been so, either fear or cynicism would have undermined constructive forces, which was by no means the case. On the contrary the attitude of the times was one of growing confidence, which brought with it a vigour and enthusiasm scarcely paralleled by the idealists of the previous generation. Nowhere was this more obvious than in the sphere of economics.

In the two decades before the revolution, even those liberals who were most dedicated to classical economy began to feel doubts about the effectiveness of capitalism. Not only were they unable to escape the conclusion, once denied, that whilst the rich grew richer the poor grew poorer; they began to wonder whether the motive power which drove the economy forward was running down. After the first dynamic sweep of the Industrial Revolution in Britain there had not always been equivalent advance. Critics began to detect cyclical fluctuations; Engels analysed 'internal crises' which manifested themselves in the form of periodic slumps. In 1839-41 Britain, and in 1846-8 the continent experienced the worst crisis of early industrialism; socialists predicted the breakdown of capitalism at the very moment when liberals began their assault on the absolutist order. But the crisis passed. By mid-1848 the middle classes had recovered faith in their own economic system, a factor which contributed to their desire for renewed social discipline. Capitalism thereupon entered its most intensive phase of development.

In 1851 Britain was already 'the workshop of the world'. Her rapidly expanding industrial production drove her to seek for wider and wider markets and sources of supply. Her colonial empire, which had grown enormously since 1815, grew even larger, but this was only one aspect of her expansion. Britain's supremacy was such that she hardly needed to take on the trouble of ruling further territories in order to obtain the advantages she wanted. Nowhere was this illustrated more forcibly than in the Far East. Up to the eighteen-thirties China was virtually closed to the commerce of western nations, her rulers being blissfully unaware that she needed anything from the West. The tea, silk, nankeens, and other products which western nations required from her had to be paid for in silver until the British found an illicit substitute in opium, smuggled in from India. In 1839 the emperor Tao Kwang tried to uproot the opium trade, whereupon Britain revised the whole situation in favour of the West by means of a few gunboats and a few thousand troops. The 'Opium War' of 1839-42 revealed so conspicuously the naval, military, and technological inferiority of China that she could no longer maintain her isolation. The subsequent treaty of Nanking was the first of a series of 'unequal' treaties regulating China's relations with foreign powers, admitting their trade through ever-widening channels, and eventually allowing them to establish permanent diplomatic relations with the Son of Heaven. Thereafter foreign imports into China doubled and trebled and domestic industries were ruined. After this rapid subjugation of an empire which was believed to be the mightiest in the East, Japan and Siam were impelled to open their doors to western penetration.

The challenge which Britain presented to other nations of Europe in the middle of the nineteenth century was that of eddying in her wake and seizing a few scraps from the enormous haul which she obtained. This necessitated building up their own industries, a process which Britain was more than willing to assist by investing her capital in their concerns and sending out her entrepreneurs, her engineers, and her skilled operatives. Britain's supremacy was, again, such that she could envisage nothing but gain to herself from the progress of other European countries, with which she would then be able to do business. Her lofty attitude in this matter gave a semblance of internationalism to a period which was otherwise one of growing national dissension. Napoleon III's dream of rivalling it by presiding over a European community of nations was doomed to a rude awakening.

In the two decades which opened in 1850 new company laws in France and Germany facilitated the corporate ownership of big business; new types of banking in Belgium, France, and Germany encouraged investment and expanded credit; a network of free trade treaties centring upon France enlarged the area of business enterprise; and monetary reform in most countries moved towards the standardization of the means of payment. Businessmen everywhere enjoyed unparalleled prosperity and influence. Not only were they free from legislation which would have hampered their activities but, in some large-scale enterprises, they even received government aid. The guarantee of railway dividends by the state in France and several other countries was partly responsible for the increase in the world's railway mileage from 23,000 in 1850 to 130,000 in 1870, a figure constituting one sixth of the mileage the world was eventually to possess. At the same time business men evaded all responsibility for the thousands of men and women who were thrown into unemployment as a result of the world economic crises of 1857 and 1866. These crises, far from shattering confidence in the capitalist system as previous, less extensive crises had threatened to do, merely forced its adherents to introduce greater flexibility into business organization, and introduced the satisfying notion that profits were justified by risk.

No-one could say that Europe was industrialized by 1870. France lagged curiously behind Germany, where really big business got a start only in the late 'sixties; Italy was dragged down by the backwardness of her southern states; Russia awaited the long-term results of peasant emancipation. The fact that there was still much scope for development gave entrepreneurs their vigour: the fact that industrial goods were new gave the French middle classes of the Second Empire, for instance, their appetite for them. People were happier to believe that they were living in a world of their own making because men's devices had not yet proved their ruin; they were more ready to ascribe happiness to an increase in commodities because familiarity had not yet bred contempt.

In this world of man-made things there was a passionate desire among intellectuals to understand men and their activities. Literature dedicated itself to the exploration of reality, not merely by describing everyday life and exposing crudities and horrors, for both these things had been done from the time of Chaucer, but by trying to penetrate and explain in rational terms the mysteries of living. Though Matthew Arnold believed that poetry alone could interpret life, and poetry remained predominantly romantic, novelists set out to address a newly literate public in a new manner. Stendhal, Balzac, Flaubert, George Eliot, Tolstoy, and Dostoyevsky each brought their zeal to the contemplation of reality. Especially were the novelists absorbed by such contemporary problems as the fate of human relationships in a society dominated by thoughts of money and power, and the effect upon impressionable souls when ideals proved inapplicable to daily life. The realist novel was very often the psychological novel, in which the author pursued and analysed the motives and reactions of his hero in the toils of society. From Stendhal's Julien Sorel to Dostoyevsky's Raskolnikoff the heroes in such novels were increasingly unheroic in the traditional sense, being merely characters singled out by their authors to highlight the relationship between man and society. Realism invaded even the historical novels of the period and indeed reached its highest pitch of artistry in Tolstoy's *War and Peace* (1865-9). Subsequent developments in Tolstoy's own life underlined for many critics the weaknesses of the realist movement, however. For Tolstoy believed that literature, being concerned with life, could have nothing to do with ultimate religious demands, and he abandoned it when he was converted to religion in 1880. Whilst the masterpieces of realism succeeded in combining a subtle critique of contemporary society with acceptance of it, there was an insistent pull towards pessimism which led Goncharov at the end of the period to portray life in the person of his hero Oblomov as utterly meaningless.

Realism in the visual arts escaped this pessimism. Painting was dominated by the big, boisterous, self-confident Courbet, who prided himself on portraying life in the raw and saw nothing cheap in the emotions which much of his work aroused. His demonstrative nudes flouted the conventions of fashionable art and aroused a vigorous controversy over the opposing merits of realism and idealism. The latter school was persistently favoured by the Salon juries, which distinguished themselves by following popular taste rather than by detecting works of genius. For Courbet was, in spite of his vulgarity, a very great painter. His first important work, the *Stonebreakers* (1851), took away from the portrayal of peasant life the sentimentality which Millet had unconsciously given it, yet presented the reality in a form equally monumental and inescapable. In 1863 Courbet embraced a new devotee, the young Eduard Manet, whose *Déjeuner sur l'Herbe* was rejected by the Salon in striking contrast to Cabanel's *Birth of Venus*, which was admired and bought by Napoleon III. Manet, like Courbet, believed that he must paint what he saw, and he not only saw subjects which seemed unartistic to fashionable painters but painted them in an equally unorthodox manner. His direct colours were regarded as crude, his huge canvasses too grandiloquent for what were described as 'petty' subjects. In 1867 Manet made one of his famous, if rare excursions into political art by painting in terms of stark honesty the *Execution of the Emperor Maximilian*. Both Courbet and Manet held extreme left-wing views in politics. Realism in art was directed against the artificiality and hypocrisy of middle class society: its most popular exponent was Daumier, whose penetrating caricatures reached a wide public through the medium of the press and the cheap lithograph. Daumier, too, was a radical, and not only because Napoleon III was a dictator.

Artists of the realist school were automatically associated in the popular mind with socialism. Millet was at pains to repudiate the suggestion; Courbet embraced it with his usual flamboyancy. In France it was still possible to interpret socialism simply as a desire for justice for the people. To Courbet, socialism meant Proudhon, whose figure he placed in representative fashion in the painting he made of his own studio. Since in France industrialization was not very far advanced at mid-century, Proudhon could think in terms of obtaining for labour a share in the exploitation of the new steam-power. His schemes for productive co-partnership and decentralized government appealed widely to French artisans, who did not think of themselves as proletarians in the Marxian sense but as individuals worthy of an equal opportunity with others. The chief demand of French labour under the Second Empire was for free, compulsory, and secular education. In spite of the June Days, antagonism was directed less against property owners than against priests, whose alliance with authority under Napoleon III brought out all the latent anticlericalism of the French urban workers.

The Proudhonist type of socialism was almost everywhere destined to be outdone by that of Marx, however. In France the influence of Proudhon continued to permeate the labour movement to the end of the Second Empire, but a sharp turn towards Marxism resulted from the fortuitous events of the Commune of 1871. In Germany the movement for co-operation between artisans and small businessmen, organized by the economist Schulze-Delitsch in the early 'sixties, was rapidly displaced in popularity by the programme of Ferdinand Lassalle, who insisted that nothing could be achieved without help from the state. From this a comparatively short step led to Marx's belief in the need to capture the state, especially as Lassalle, like Marx, advocated strong, centralized government. After the death of Lassalle in a duel in 1864 his leading disciple Liebknecht associated with Auguste Bebel to form, in 1869, the Marxist inspired Social Democratic Party. In a wider sphere the success with which Marx, between 1864 and 1872, eliminated his rivals from the International Working Men's Association illustrates the way in which European socialism moved from doctrines of co-operation and bargaining to those of class conflict and violence.

Marxists prided themselves on being more 'realistic' than their 'utopian' predecessors, but they gave little thought to the complexity of human behaviour, which was the most important aspect of study to realists in art and literature. To Karl Marx the vagaries of human nature were not so much non-existent as irrelevant, for in *Das Kapital* (1867-94) he proved to his own satisfaction that the history and structure of any society, even its arts and sciences, were determined by the ownership of the means of production. The proletariat simply needed to take over the existing industrial plant to bring about the socialist state. He believed that the bourgeoisie had destroyed once and for all the varied human relationships of former times, leaving 'no other nexus between man and man than naked self-interest, than callous cash-payment' (*Communist Manifesto*). The world was irretrievably dominated by commodities; value inhered in commodities; and the ultimate source of value, labour, was itself a negotiable object.

Marx claimed for his sociology the exactness of a science. His deterministic laws resembled Newton's mechanics; his dialectic materialism evinced the growing knowledge of evolution which culminated in Darwin's *Origin of Species* (1859). Science (as distinct from technology) came into its own for the first time in the mid-nineteenth century as a subject worthy of popular interest and serious academic study. While books such as Humboldt's *Cosmos* (1845-62) and Büchner's *Kraft und Stoff* (1855) kept a wide reading public informed of the latest theories and discoveries, scientific subjects acquired a larger place in university syllabuses, and state aid was successfully solicited to provide the large laboratories and expensive apparatus which were increasingly regarded as essential to research. Responding to a new sense of importance, scientists broadened as well as deepened the range of their enquiries. Relating the various branches of science to each other they defined matter, energy, and ether as the ultimate constituents of the universe and produced the great synthetic concepts of thermodynamics and evolution. Each of the four major countries of western Europe could boast of a leading contribution: France of the development by Pasteur of the theory of bacteria, Germany of the first complete account by Helmholtz of thermodynamics, Britain of the exposition by Darwin of the theory of evolution by natural selection, and Italy of the establishment by Cannizaro of the force of the molecular hypothesis. Germany, however, was generally regarded as having assumed in science the overall intellectual ascendancy previously possessed by France. Scientific education was more advanced in Germany than any-where else in Europe. Britain prided herself on her long-standing empirical genius which showed to the greatest advantage in physics, Michael Faraday being one of the most brilliant experimenters of all time.

Later generations might have expected a country which remained far and away the greatest industrial power in the world to be the most advanced in the pursuit and application of scientific knowledge. In fact the connection between industry and science was of late growth. Most of the inventions which produced the Industrial Revolution in Britain – the flying shuttle, the spinning jenny, and the mule, for instance – were the simple devices of in-genious craftsmen. Even the steam-engine was based only on primitive science, for it was not until 1824 that the Frenchman Sadi Carnot developed the principle upon which motive power was obtained from a source of heat. As late as 1851 the Great Exhibition at the Crystal Palace showed that although science was beginning to play a part in industry the part was small compared with that of empirical technology. In 1856 Bessemer illustrated the surviving genius of technology with his process of obtaining steel, soon to replace coal as the backbone of a new industrial age. When the second World Exhibition was held in Paris in 1867 science had clearly enlarged its rôle, but it operated chiefly in new enterprises where there was no strong technological tradition, such as photography and electric-telegraphy, the preparation of rubber and other vegetable products, the synthetic-chemicals industry, and the aniline dye industry (stemming from the accidental dis-covery by Perkin of the first aniline dye, mauve, in 1856). The economist Michel Chevalier who, like all Saint-Simonians, was particularly interested in science, could claim in his report on the Exhibition that scientific progress was responsible for increased productive power, but the time which nor-mally elapsed between scientific discovery and industrial application proved that few people shared his enthusiasm.

The contributions made by science to the arts of healing were more ob-viously revolutionary, though their progress was hindered by conservatism and ignorance on the part of doctors and nurses who should have welcomed them. The discovery by Pasteur that germs were responsible for disease was to have far-reaching consequences, on which work was beginning as the period ended. One of the earliest converts to the theory, Joseph Lister, began in 1865 to use carbolic acid systematically as an antiseptic in operative surgery, and the spread of his methods meant that by 1870 surgery was some-thing more than a last resort from which 50% of patients might expect to die. The general practice of medicine benefited little from science, however. There were few drugs of real effect. Sodium salicylate was prepared in 1860 but the medicament aspirin was not marketed until the end of the century. Hospitals were noisome places, and the pioneer work of Florence Nightingale had not yet produced a general training of nurses. Public Health and improvements in the standard of living waited on such things as common-sense, hygiene, tariff reform, better communications, humanitarian efforts and town planning rather than on science.

Yet the middle decades of the nineteenth century were truly an age of science as the early decades were an age of philosophy. For if science as yet played little part in the daily round and common task, every branch of thought was affected by it. Auguste Comte had already, in the age of philosophy, argued that scientific knowledge was the only certain type of knowledge, and that scientific method ought properly to be applied to all branches of study including sociology (a word he invented about 1830). Classical economists in Britain had always mopped up whatever scientific works they could lay their hands on, but on the whole Comte's teaching had been slow to catch on when scientific knowledge was uncoordinated and scientific methods primitive. In the 'fifties and 'sixties, however, 'scientific' thinking acquired a vogue never equalled in western Europe again. Classical economy received a new injection of science from the work of John Stuart Mill; socialism grew to maturity under a regimen of science; while a host of popularizers, of whom Herbert Spencer was the archetype, sought to give every scientific discovery the status of fundamental truth. It was in prescribing an antidote in the form of Christian faith and revelation that the Roman Catholic Church renewed its reputation for obscurantism.

3. TEEMING POPULATIONS AND A WIDER WORLD

Between 1850 and 1870 western Europe reached the zenith of its power. A period of prosperity, stimulated by an increased supply of precious metals, opened for those countries which had secured a place in the world economy. The industrial revolution extended its sway over Germany, Scandinavia, northern Italy after 1860, Austria and Bohemia after 1867. Everywhere it found a surplus of people hungry for jobs, for the population was rising as never before.

A rapid increase in population had been one of the most important features of European history in the decades preceding the French Revolution. After the Napoleonic wars the increase had gathered momentum, until by mid-century the population had risen from something like 187 million in 1800 to over 270 million. In the next two decades, still greater increases resulted in a figure of over 400 million at the end of the century, in spite of a relative decline which set in about 1875. As early as 1799 Malthus believed that the population would inevitably outrun the means of subsistence. Forty years later the Belgian Quételet arrived at the more comforting conclusion that population growth was reaching a limit: a conclusion not unlike that of Guizot, who decided that evolution was nearing its terminus. The terminus was, by inference, the domination of the world by western Europeans. For though the rise in population affected the whole of Europe, it brought power only to those nations which could find enough raw materials, enough capital, and enough inventive genius to employ the masses.

Reasons for the increase cannot be given with any certainty. A few factors only are discernible from the evidence. In spite of shocking conditions in industrial towns, people had a better chance of surviving in them, because of better chances of obtaining employment, than in the poverty-stricken countryside. Epidemics, especially of cholera, became less frequent from the middle of the century. Increases in population in industrialized countries probably owed more, therefore, to falling death rates than to rising birth rates, whereas the contrary applied to the overwhelmingly agricultural countries of central and eastern Europe. Bourgeois families were everywhere smaller than working class or peasant families, the growing numbers of the bourgeoisie being composed less of sons than of newcomers from other social classes.

Within a general pattern of increase, France stands out as inferior to her neighbours. In the first half of the century her population increased by only 30% compared with Europe's average of 40% and Germany's 50%. Her urban populations increased, but mere rural centres often gained more than industrial centres such as Lille, which meant simply that peasants were flocking in from the countryside without much prospect of employment. The economic crisis beginning in 1846 produced more serious demographic effects in France than in any other country: annual population growth sank to 2·2 per thousand, the lowest figure hitherto recorded, and there was actual decline in some rural areas. Symptoms of chronic weakness were hidden from contemporaries by the recovery which took place in the eighteen-sixties, but the recovery was only partial and it was not maintained. By 1914 Frenchmen were very much outnumbered by Germans.

France was not the only country from which a mass emigration (comprising in her case more than a quarter of a million persons) took place during the crisis of 1846-51. Europe had long been accustomed to losing Irishmen, Castilians, and certain other traditional migratory groups, and since 1800 there had been a notable departure of Britons for North America, but 1846 saw the beginning of those massive shipments of Europeans which caused the population of North America to double and treble itself by 1870. Between 1850 and 1875 an average of nearly 300,000 emigrants a year, mostly British and German, left their homeland for overseas territories. Less spectacular but no less significant in the long run was the migration of Russian peasants eastward to populate the vast stretches of Siberia. Emigration, like population, was conditioned by many factors, only imperfectly known. Poverty in the homeland was probably the most important single factor, but the positive attractions offered by the New World counted for something, as did geographical position (working in favour of maritime countries as points of departure and of North America rather than Australia as a point of arrival), along with official attitudes and so forth. Whilst the British government and most German governments encouraged the poor to emigrate, the French legislated against foreign emigration in 1855 and 1860 and hesitated even to populate Algeria.

For France, with her demographic problems, this attitude was probably realistic. As far as Europe as a whole was concerned, however, the huge losses of population seemed to detract nothing from her strength. On the contrary, emigration could be regarded as an aspect of Europe's power, for it spread her influence over the world without causing any sign, as yet, that other continents would rise and overshadow her. Europe in the middle of the nineteenth century was truly the Europe which General Smuts could still see in 1918, 'the mother of civilization, the glory of the human race'.

CHAPTER XIX

The Defeat of Autocratic Russia

1. THE POLICE STATE

IN 1819 Metternich prided himself on having convinced the Tsar of the universal danger of liberal ideas, and Alexander I entered upon what has been called the reactionary phase of his reign. Censorship became stricter and the activities of secret police more ubiquitous. Officials from St. Petersburg invaded schools and universities and warped the curricula to serve the obscurantist purposes of the official church. The brutal Count Arakcheyev was made responsible for all the Tsar's routine administrative functions and given almost complete control over the military colonies. These had been established in 1816 as a result of Alexander's interest in the schemes of Prussian army reformers. They appealed to the Tsar as a cheap means of keeping an army near the western frontier, and they were intended to improve conditions of service among peasant conscripts by allowing them to live with their wives and families and devote a part of their time to agriculture. Under Arakcheyev's jurisdiction, however, discipline was harsher than in penal settlements. Young officers complained bitterly of the humiliating conditions, but a revolt which broke out in the Chuguyev colony merely led to fiercer repression.

Whether there had ever been any real chance of Alexander transforming government and society in Russia is open to doubt. Napoleon had once said that there was a piece lacking in Alexander's make-up, and the difficulties and dangers attending large-scale reform would probably always have deflected a character so devoid of application. To the weaknesses of Alexander's nature were added the enticing prospects of exerting over the destinies of Europe the redeeming influence which fell upon such stony ground in Russia. These factors were stronger than the persuasions of Metternich, which never wholly directed Alexander's fleeting mind. In the last years of the reign Novosiltsev was encouraged by the Tsar to elaborate a scheme for transforming Russia into a confederation of constitutional states; Arakcheyev was asked to draw up a plan for emancipating the serfs; and members of secret societies never entirely gave up hope that Alexander would initiate reform. Secret societies were denounced by the police, but Alexander declined to take action against men whose hopes he had encouraged.

Only when Nicholas I was proclaimed Tsar did despair result in rebellion.

When Alexander's death was announced in St. Petersburg in November 1825 the circumstances were so peculiar that rumour, not entirely discounted even by members of the imperial family, suggested that the Tsar had not died but had retired to a monastery where he could devote the remainder of his life to Christ. Confusion was prolonged by the fact that Nicholas did not know, or would not believe, that his elder brother Constantine had renounced his right to the throne. A reluctant decision by Nicholas, after a three weeks interregnum, to demand an oath of loyalty from the army aroused something like horror among officers who knew him best. Many of them had become acquainted with western Europe during the invasion and occupation of France. Their patriotic yearning for reforms which would modernize their country could expect no fulfilment from Nicholas, who clung by instinct to authoritarian rule, whether for the army or for Russia.

A rebellion by a few Guards regiments in St. Petersburg on 14 December was easily suppressed by loyal sections of the army, and an attempt to raise mutiny among regiments stationed in the south petered out a few days later. The conspirators hoped for vast changes, such as the emancipation of the serfs and the destruction of autocracy, but their aims lacked precision and unity. Some talked of constitutional monarchy and others of a republic. The soldiers who mutinied at the behest of their officers were inspired for the most part by mistaken notions of loyalty to Constantine, whom they believed to be the rightful tsar. A rebel colonel in the Ukraine told his men that a republic would give them unlimited rights to do as they pleased. Personal grievances and ambitions played a part, as they had done five years earlier in southern Europe, and the British ambassador concluded that Nicholas would have done well to ignore 'the fantasies of a handful of young subalterns'. Repressive measures were indeed much lighter than liberal legend would allow: only five rebels were executed and a few hundred exiled to Siberia under conditions less onerous than those usually imposed upon political prisoners. Nicholas by no means underestimated the significance of the episode, however. The Decembrists had challenged the principle of autocracy for the first time in nearly a hundred years. Most of them were of noble birth; some of them had been his friends. The army and the aristocracy to which they belonged were essential props of tsardom. Nicholas was determined to find out why they had rebelled.

Prolonged enquiries, many of which he conducted personally, led Nicholas to conclusions which guided much of his policy for the rest of his reign. He decided that revolutionary sentiments were to be found mainly among young men who imbibed ideas from western Europe without fully understanding them and received an education out of keeping with their surroundings and opportunities. Henceforward the literate classes must be protected from

AOP 2B

influences which might lead them into error. At the same time the grievances which had justified rebellion must be removed. Government must be rendered more efficient so that the tsar could provide for the needs of the people.

Nicholas was not as firm a character as his behaviour over the Decembrist revolt might suggest. He possessed more courage than confidence and more nervous energy than strength of purpose. His appearance and personality enabled him to play the rôle of father of his people with distinction, and his conscientiousness won respect from all who knew him, but his command over himself and others was never sure. He was often seized by morbid fears, and when revolution broke out in Poland in 1830 and in many parts of Europe in 1848, panic led him to demand harsher measures than his temperament or his means could sustain.

His professed purpose in the field of education was to provide the army with efficient officers and the civil service with competent officials. As far as Nicholas was concerned the serfs could be left uneducated. They were allowed to attend the parish and district schools provided by local initiative but they could not graduate from them to secondary schools. The latter were regulated according to a statute of 1827 in such a way that 'nobody should aim to rise above the position in which it is his lot to remain'. The intake of pupils from lower middle class homes was reduced as much as possible by raising the fees. On the other hand the sons of poorer members of the aristocracy were assisted financially by accommodation in hostels. In 1839 university fees were also raised. Under Count Uvarov as Minister of Education (1833-49) universities were brought more closely under the control of the state. Professors could be appointed to vacant chairs by the government, and the conduct of teachers and students in class was superintended by government officials. From 1850 all rectors and professors were appointed by the government with strict attention to their political and moral views. Philosophy courses were abolished because they were believed to encourage political speculation, and the teaching of logic was entrusted to departments of theology.

In spite of the atmosphere of mental oppression, secondary and university education reached a high standard. In education as in all other spheres the government's methods were crude, its machinery cumbersome, its agents insufficiently ruthless, and its whole policy ineffective. Graduates emerged from the universities not only with scientific knowledge and technical skill but with an awareness of political theory and philosophic ideas. Few educated Russians could ignore the deplorable wastage of human ability and the appalling degradation of the mass of the people in a country which might otherwise have aspired to lead all Europe. Some were willing nevertheless to give loyal service to the régime. More became tacitly hostile, refusing to help the government though not actively conspiring against it. A few were ready to criticize and oppose the régime in any way possible.

Criticism was driven by censorship into literary channels. The censorship decree of 1826, revised in 1828, established boards of officials in cultural centres to examine all writings before publication and prune them of references detrimental to religion and tsardom. The censorship was designed by Nicholas to destroy 'the pernicious luxury of half-knowledge', and he tried to take a pride in the fact that writers of real genius could find ways of expressing their feelings. The novels of Gogol, though not intended as attacks upon the régime, echoed its dreariest tones down the years. Men profoundly concerned for the future of their country turned to literary journals such as the *Contemporary* and the *Muscovite* to air their views. The publication in 1836 of a 'Philosophical Letter' by P. Chaadayev, declaring that Russia had contributed nothing to human thought and progress, led to a Great Debate between groups described as westernizers and slavophiles. The former claimed descent from Pushkin and followed the Decembrists in believing that Russia must learn from western Europe. They longed for political freedom and constitutional government. A few advanced thinkers among them, notably Herzen, Bakunin, and Belinsky, were aware of the social evils which accompanied liberal institutions in the west but believed that the remedies, too, were to be found in western thought. From contact with left-wing Hegelianism they came to admire French utopian socialism and German communism. The slavophiles, on the other hand, believed that Russia had suffered already from the devotion of Peter the Great to an alien tradition. Khomyakov, the brothers Kireyvsky, and several other outspoken publicists joined in describing the social evils of western Europe as incradicable effects of a civilization based on rationalism and individualism. They boasted that the Russian people cherished a deeper Christian faith and a stronger feeling for the community than did the people of western Europe, and they exalted the national church, the village commune, and the craftsmen's co-operative as distinctive expressions of the Russian spirit. They proposed the revival of the old Muscovite consultative assemblies (Zemsky Sobor) instead of experiments with western types of constitutional government as a means of bringing the minds of the people to bear upon the problems of contemporary life.

The slavophiles never lost sight of the fact that Russia was an integral part of Europe. They believed that when the decrepit civilization of the West had died away Russia would play her part in a new creation. They did not rejoice in a barbaric rejection of the West, as some extreme nationalists such as Glinka and Karamzin had done during the Napoleonic wars. Their emotional attitude to the West expressed hatred but also fascination and something akin to love. They believed that Russia instead of slavishly copying the nations of the West should 'teach the world some serious lessons'. Nicholas also believed that Russia possessed a duty to the rest of Europe, but to the anger of the slavophiles he interpreted the duty as that of defending monarchical government against revolutionary doctrines spreading eastward from France. The triple formula of 'Orthodoxy, Autocracy, and Nationality' proclaimed by Uvarov in 1833 stood for an extremely conservative doctrine in which religion and national consciousness were completely subordinated to the needs of tsardom. Nicholas replied to outbursts of European revolution in 1830 and 1848 with stronger doses of repression, believing that the maintenance of autocracy in Russia might one day save Europe from final disintegration. Tsardom thus came to hold a symbolic position throughout Europe as the barrier to all western forms of political progress.

The slavophiles were right in complaining that Russia would never be able to teach Europe the lessons of spirituality and comradeship while the country groaned under serfdom and oppression. Their ardent desire for the emancipation of the serfs was shared not only by the westernizers but to some extent by Nicholas, who once described serfdom as 'the indubitable evil of Russian life'. The ownership of one man by another was rapidly becoming untenable on moral and humanitarian grounds in Russia as it had done elsewhere in Europe. The economic disadvantages of serfdom were also becoming every day more apparent. During Nicholas's reign the government made an effort in a simple mercantilist way to foster industry. Subsidies were granted to manufacturers, model industries were established, technical schools were founded, and until 1852 tariff barriers altogether forbade the import of foreign metal goods and textiles. The production of pig iron increased greatly and the manufacture of textiles doubled, but the effect was scarcely noticeable in vast agrarian Russia. Factory owners employing free wage labour complained of the difficulty of obtaining hands, those employing serfs complained of their technical backwardness, and all bemoaned the low purchasing power of the Russian masses. Landowners in the south and the middle Volga regions, growing wheat for export, were persuaded by English economic theories and finally convinced by practical experiments that mobile wage labour was more profitable than serfdom. Yet Nicholas did no more than tinker about with the old system, trying to encourage landowners to free their serfs with land in return for temporary labour services, allowing owners to free domestic serfs without land, and regulating the amount of service rendered by Russian serfs to Polish masters in the Ukraine. Nicholas sympathized with the serfs and tried to wipe out notorious abuses such as the sale of serfs without land, but he dared not contemplate wholesale emancipation. In spite of startling increases in the number of local peasant risings he continued to regard serfdom as the only reliable means of governing large and sparsely populated areas of Russia. His chief of police defined his view, 'The landowner is the most reliable bulwark of the sovereign. No army can replace the vigilance and influence which the landowner continually exercises in his estates.'

In Nicholas an earnest desire to do good was almost always combined with a fear of doing harm, and pride in the strength of autocracy never mitigated a feeling of insecurity. The paradoxes were demonstrated quite disastrously in the development of the police system. In 1826 Nicholas decided to reinforce and reorganize the political police, which had come into being during the last years of the previous reign, by placing them under a Third Section of the Imperial Chancellery, immediately subordinate to the tsar. The political police would thus be distinguished from the gendarmerie or semimilitary police and from the ordinary local police and could be made into special agents of the tsar in acting as a beneficent but severe father of his people. The members were instructed that one of their chief tasks was to break through the web of bureaucracy which divided the sovereign from his people and to carry 'the voice of each citizen to the throne of the tsar'. A general clause in the original statute authorized the political police to 'report on all events', to protect the people from bureaucratic abuses, and to recommend worthy officials for reward and promotion. At the same time the Third Section was authorized to regulate the activities of religious sects and of foreigners residing in Russia and to deal suitably with persons suspected of crimes against the state. The latter could be subjected to 'administrative arrest' and dealt with outside the ordinary processes of law. Under the direction of General Benckendorff the activities of the Third Section produced an atmosphere of spying, denunciation, sententious interference, and petty tyranny which became a legend. The members of the Third Section not only issued orders to the gendarmerie and the local police but used unknown numbers of secret agents. Russia under Nicholas came to be thought of throughout Europe as the police state *par excellence*, a factor which had some bearing upon the righteous anger with which Englishmen went to war against Russia in the Crimea.

2. ALLIANCES AND ALIGNMENTS, 1833-51

The idea that East and West might fight a war about Turkey never occurred to Metternich. The danger as he saw it was that Austria and Russia might fight a war about the Balkans. Such a war would inevitably unleash revolution in the Habsburg empire and destroy the European civilization which Metternich cherished. He therefore persuaded Nicholas at München-grätz, as he had once persuaded Alexander at Troppau, that the rivalry between Austria and Russia in the Balkans was of small importance compared with their common antipathy to revolution.

Even to Metternich the new alignment had its drawbacks. He did not wish to encourage Nicholas to go crusading against France, whose 'revolutionary' government the Tsar abhorred. Nor did he wish to encourage Nicholas in any idea that the two eastern powers might make a deal over Turkey. Metternich hoped to retain Münchengrätz as a purely defensive arrangement. He was thrown into it largely by the obtuseness of Palmerston, who so wholeheartedly despised Metternich's pettifogging persecutions at home and so much resented Metternich's managerial attitude to European affairs that he lost sight of the natural affinity between the policies of Britain and Austria with regard to Turkey. Palmerston replied to 'the Holy Alliance of the East' with 'a formal union of the four constitutional states of the West' and boasted that 'the moral effect . . . must be by no means inconsiderable'. In fact the moral effect was negligible. The young Queens Maria of Portugal and Isabella of Spain could be described as liberal only because their thrones were being attacked by wicked uncles whose reactionary views were approved by Metternich. Civil war continued for years, and the ultimate triumph of the queens preserved merely the forms of constitutional monarchy. Meanwhile Palmerston stressed in vain to his envoys abroad the importance of Britain not only getting on well with the French government but appearing to all Europe to do so. Industrial and commercial rivalries led to open disputes between the two governments on the subject of tariffs, and Louis-Philippe seemed more anxious to win recognition from the Emperor of Austria than to subordinate himself to the British foreign minister.

The lack of cohesion on both sides of the European divide was seen in the Near Eastern crisis of 1838-9, when Mohammed Ali announced his independence of the Sultan and inflicted shattering defeats upon Turkish forces. Palmerston at once feared that the Tsar would act upon the treaty of Unkiar Skelessi, and the time seemed to have come to bring the Quadruple Alliance to bear, but after a first flourish of trumpets Palmerston was more ready to draw Russia into a general European agreement than to marshal the forces of the West against her. Metternich seized the initiative in the summer of 1839 and arranged in Vienna a conference of ambassadors which informed the Sultan that the five Great Powers were preparing to intervene on his behalf. Metternich was horrified when the Tsar announced that the decision had been made without his knowledge and indicated that he resented Austria's participation in an anti-Russian move. Nicholas had no desire to become isolated, however. He retaliated upon Metternich by opening his own negotiations with London, offering to co-operate in depriving Mohammed Ali of most of his gains and afterwards in replacing Unkiar Skelessi with a general agreement to close the Straits. Nicholas was aware that an attempt to secure concerted action over Mohammed Ali would isolate France, for the French government looked upon the Egyptian viceroy as a client. When Thiers resisted all Palmerston's efforts to bring France into a five-power agreement the British cabinet allowed itself to be bullied by the foreign secretary into signing a Quadruple Agreement with the representatives of Russia, Austria, and Prussia on 15 July 1840.

The aggressive attitudes of both Palmerston and Thiers prolonged the danger of war between Britain and France for several months after the signing of the Quadruple Agreement. Metternich suspected both Palmerston and Nicholas of actually wanting a war against France. Nicholas certainly went as far as to invite Palmerston to translate the Quadruple Agreement into a permanent undertaking to quell any revolutionary dangers emanating from France. Palmerston could not accept such an invitation, but all Metternich's skill was needed to open a way for France, under a new ministry, to join the Great Powers in signing the Straits Convention of 13 July 1841.

The British government under Sir Robert Peel made an effort to keep on good terms with France in the early 'forties. The close friendship which grew between the two foreign ministers, Aberdeen and Guizot, could not, however, dissolve the antagonism which seemed to exist throughout the diplomatic corps of both nations nor lessen the suspicion with which the English and French peoples regarded each other. Disputes over rights in Tahiti and Algiers kept hostility alive until 1846, when Palmerston returned to office in time to make a complete break with Louis-Philippe over the Spanish marriages. The French king had promised not to marry his son to the sister of Queen Isabella until the latter had produced an heir; his failure to fulfil the promise naturally provoked sinister interpretations. Britain's relations with Russia, on the other hand, remained remarkably cordial. Nicholas paid a visit to London in 1844 and spoke enthusiastically to Peel and Aberdeen about the possibility of Anglo-Russian co-operation over Turkey. Palmerston returned to power with every intention of resuming the unprejudiced attitude he had adopted towards Russia when he left office.

Two years later, revolutionary outbursts disrupted the greater part of the continent. Though the sympathies of Palmerston were on the side of the rebels and the sympathies of Nicholas on the side of the kings, both arrived at the necessity of restraining ambitious designs on the part of the new republican government of France and of localizing the revolutions in the interests of peace. Unable to work together, they nevertheless left each other alone to work from different ends towards the same object, and divergent ideologies were ignored in pursuit of a common policy. Palmerston indicated to Lamartine that Britain would restrain reactionary powers from attacking France provided France refrained from attacking them. He forestalled French intervention in Italy by arranging for Anglo-French mediation and later by persuading Schwarzenberg to grant Piedmont a lenient peace. Meanwhile he relied upon the Tsar to use methods barred to himself in restoring the balance of power in eastern Europe. The Russian expedition against Kossuth was carried out with the approval of Palmerston, though the latter afterwards protested against Austria's persecution of the rebels. In 1850 the Tsar threatened to join Austria in war against Prussia if Frederick William IV persisted in a plan devised by Radowitz to unite the German princes under Prussian leadership. Austro-Russian forces could probably not have defeated the Prussian army, but Frederick William took fright and agreed at Olmütz in November 1850 to restore the old Confederation. The Prussian government also gave in, eventually, to the pressure of British and Russian interests in the Baltic, and agreed that the duchies of Schleswig and Holstein should return to the Danish crown.

3. THE CRIMEAN WAR

By an irony of fate, factors which preserved peace during the greatest upheaval since the French Revolution tempted the Tsar into war only five years later. Nicholas reopened the Eastern Question in 1853 on the assumption that Britain appreciated his special interests in Turkey, that she would allow him to defend those interests when he thought they were threatened by France, and that she would co-operate with him in partitioning Turkey in accordance with the balance of power.

In 1850 Louis Napoleon put himself forward on the side of the Latin Christians in their disputes with the Greek Orthodox over the administration of the Holy Places at Jerusalem and Bethlehem. In doing so he was merely breathing new life into France's time-honoured rôle as protector of the Latin Christians, hoping thereby to please Catholic opinion in France and win prestige by vigorous diplomacy. He did not intend to spark off a war against Russia, but he was willing, when the Tsar protested against any diminution of the prominent position obtained by Orthodox monks at the Holy Places, to back up his negotiations at Constantinople with threats of naval action. Nicholas attributed the worst intentions to Louis Napoleon, especially when the latter had assumed the title of Emperor. He certainly believed that French agents were inciting Turkish politicians to repudiate Russia's rights under the treaty of Kutchuk Kainardji.

Nicholas decided that the time had come to specify those rights and to insist on a detailed recognition of them by the Sultan. The outbreak of yet another revolt in Montenegro, combined with the inability of the Sultan to settle the dispute over the Holy Places, convinced Nicholas that Turkish power was collapsing and that he must either establish Russia's claim to a protectorate over Balkan Christians or provide for Russia's interests in some other way. He therefore despatched Prince Menshikov to Constantinople (February 1853) with instructions amounting to a demand that the Sultan should recognize the Tsar as arbiter in all matters relating to the Orthodox throughout Turkey, and at the same time he opened conversations with the British ambassador at St. Petersburg, Sir Hamilton Seymour, with a view to partitioning the Sultan's territories.

Nicholas believed that he had reached an agreement with the British government on the main lines of his Turkish policy when he visited London in 1844. Lord Aberdeen, who had been foreign secretary then, was Prime Minister now, and Nicholas never doubted that an understanding between gentlemen possessed enduring value. Unfortunately, any hopes which Peel and Aberdeen might in 1844 have held out on the subject of Anglo-Russian co-operation in the event of Turkey's collapse were vitiated by the unwillingness of British statesmen at any time to agree with the Tsar that the event was imminent. Lord John Russell, Britain's foreign secretary at the beginning of 1853, pointed out to Nicholas that any co-operation which took place between Britain and Russia must be directed towards maintaining the status quo in Turkey and not towards devising tempting plans for the division of the Sultan's possessions. Nicholas protested his desire to maintain the status quo in Turkey as long as possible, but neglected to make clear that the status quo in his eyes included a wide definition of the terms of Kutchuk Kainardji. Nicholas did not realize that there was any misunderstanding on this point, for Russell in a despatch from the foreign office referred to the Tsar's rights of 'exceptional protection' in Turkey. In fact, however, the British government regarded Menshikov's requirements as an unwarrantable encroachment on Turkish sovereignty.

Nicholas was prepared to back up Menshikov with threats of force in the recent French manner, and he was prepared to contemplate a sudden attack on Constantinople if Menshikov's mission failed. The Romanovs had fought eight wars against Turkey in less than two centuries, and Nicholas did not imagine that a ninth would rouse western Europe to arms. When Menshikov secured the dismissal of the Turkish foreign minister Fuad Pasha (March 1853) Napoleon III ordered the French fleet from Toulon to Salamis, but Nicholas was not alarmed. The British government showed its detachment from the French move by overruling Rose, Britain's chargé d'affaires at Constantinople, when he took it upon himself to summon the British fleet from Malta. As for Austria, Nicholas felt that she was in no position to restrain him now that Metternich was gone. Russian troops had saved the Habsburg Empire from Kossuth only four years before, and Nicholas looked on Francis Joseph as a protégé.

The Sultan, on the other hand, very quickly came to think that Britain and France would support him in resisting Russian demands. On the advice of the British and French ambassadors he gave Menshikov satisfaction over the Holy Places but rejected his major requirements. Believing that Russia would now certainly resort to armed pressure, the British and French governments ordered their fleets to the Dardanelles (June 1853). Nicholas ordered Russian troops to occupy the Principalities until the Sultan accepted Menshikov's last and greatly modified note. Britain was not prepared to see Russian influence extended in the Balkans and Asia Minor; Napoleon III was determined to stand by Britain for the sake of the British alliance; Nicholas would not abandon rights which he believed Russia to have possessed for three quarters of a century. No government wanted war, however. When the Austrian foreign minister Buol arranged for the representatives of France, Britain, and Prussia to join him in devising a settlement, Nicholas accepted the result of their deliberations (28 July 1853). Peace would undoubtedly have been secured if popular passions had not gained the upper hand in Britain. The self-confident Victorian public, spoilt by years of Palmerstonian bravado, would accept nothing short of abject surrender from the Tsar. The Vienna Note was denounced as a Russian concoction, and Aberdeen and the Prince Consort were accused of selling British interests to Russia. The restraint which Nicholas had practised in foreign affairs all his life was forgotten; the 'old Nick policy of aggression and aggrandizement' was said to be in full swing; the pacifist influence of Cobden and Bright was brushed aside; and public and press supported Palmerston in believing that tough attitudes were needed to bring Nicholas to heel. News of these developments added fuel to the flames in Constantinople, where the populace burned with nationalist and religious zeal, and extremist politicians were able to persuade the Sultan to ask for better terms. Nicholas was inclined to accept even a modified Vienna Note, but slavophile elements would not allow him to do so. On 4 September the Sultan announced war against Russia if her troops did not evacuate the Principalities within a fortnight.

On 23 October 1853 the Turks began hostilities on the Danube and in the Caucasus. British public opinion would not allow Aberdeen to give Nicholas a promise of neutrality, but the British and French governments undertook to keep their fleets out of the Black Sea if the Russians remained on the defensive north of the Danube and refrained from attacking Black Sea ports. Nicholas accepted these requirements, but on 30 November at Sinope a Russian squadron destroyed a Turkish flotilla and two transports believed to be bound for the Caucasus front. This perfectly legitimate action was denounced by Britain as a treacherous and brutal massacre and the whole of the British press howled for war. Napoleon III interpreted the outburst in Britain to mean that war was inevitable, and since he could not allow the British government to acquire all the credit for the greatest conflict since

Waterloo he rushed to take the initiative. On his suggestion the fleets were sent to close the Black Sea to Russian naval operations. When his officials throughout the provinces told him that the French people were averse to war and bitterly hostile to the English alliance he tried to back out, but prestige was now too deeply involved on both sides. On 28 March 1854 Britain and France declared war on Russia. It was the first time in history that democratic opinion had altered the published course of governments in foreign fields.

Mismanagement doomed both sides to a costly yet indecisive struggle. The Russians, who had weakened their forces at the outset by dividing them, spent useless months besieging the Danubian town of Silistria. The allies, who had expected the Russians to move rapidly on Adrianople, spent equally useless months wondering whether to concentrate for the defence of Constantinople or for the liberation of the Principalities. In August the Russians withdrew from the Balkans leaving the allies without further need to defend Turkey in Europe at all.

After this the war took on its true colours and became a punitive expedition against the Tsar. The sea powers could not easily find a point of contact with Russia: the original idea of a joint advance with Turkey from the Danube delta had to be abandoned because Austria, who feared the growing strength of Roumanian nationalism, moved her troops into the Principalities as soon as the Russians moved out. No contact *via* Poland was possible without Prussia's support, and none *via* the Baltic without Sweden's. The only answer seemed to be a naval expedition to the Crimea. The campaign was launched under the false assumption that the allied fleets would be able to isolate the Crimean peninsula by dominating the isthmus with their guns whilst allied troops seized Sevastopol and deprived Russia of her only naval base on the Black Sea. In fact the waters on either side of the isthmus were too shallow for ships to close within range. The incompetence of Menshikov as commander-in-chief of the Russian forces saved the allied armies from slaughter during the five days of landing, but equal incompetence on the part of the British and French commanders saved Sevastopol from seizure during October when the garrison was small and the defences unfinished. At Balaclava on 25 October the heroism of the light brigade brought fame to a wasteful action which defeated the Russian field army but left the enemy in command of the only metal road between the British camp and the port of supply. A surprise attack upon the allies by Menshikov at Inkerman on 5 November was beaten off, but not before the Russians had destroyed the allied preparations for an assault on Sevastopol. All three armies were condemned to a winter in the Crimea for which they were totally unprepared. Sickness and privation killed thousands of British and French troops and rendered many more unfit for service. Russian losses were heavier still and reinforcements struggling to reach the Crimea lost two thirds of their numbers through sickness and hunger.

The 1855 campaign opened with no greater successes on either side. Eventually, however, changes in the British and French commands (the appointment of General Simpson after the death of Lord Raglan and the replacement of Canrobert by Pélissier) coincided with the arrival of the Sardinians and produced results. On 16 August the French and Sardinians defeated the Russian field army at the Chernaya; on 1 September the French seized the Malakov fort; and on 9 September the Russians left Sevastopol. The next move seemed uncertain. The taking of Sevastopol was not, after all, an overwhelming victory, and the allies might well hesitate to advance into the unknown spaces of Russia. Palmerston, who had become Britain's Prime Minister when the coalition government succumbed in February 1855 to an outcry against mismanagement of the war, thought that the Russians had 'not been beaten half enough' and continued to look for action in a variety of fields to contain the Russian menace once and for all. He hoped that an alliance between Britain, France, and Sweden formed in November 1855 would lead to the destruction of the Russian forts on the Aaland islands; he planned a new campaign to capture the Russian naval base of Cronstadt and secure the independence of Circassia. The French people were bent on peace, however. They had sent to the Crimea more than three times as many men as Britain, and the false casualty lists published by the government had not succeeded in hiding the appalling waste of life and health. The Russian 'bully', Nicholas, had died in March; the taking of the Malakov fort had satisfied French pride; there seemed no further reason for fighting Britain's battles. Prefects and procureurs informed Napoleon III that the people wanted if possible an honourable peace and in any case peace. The Duke of Cambridge, in Paris on a military mission, wrote and told Queen Victoria that although the Emperor of the French could do as he liked in many things he could not stand out against so pronounced an expression of opinion. Napoleon III was not altogether sorry at the turn of events. He imagined himself playing the arbiter between Britain and Russia and presiding over a new dispensation to the nations of Europe.

No ruler of France could have conceived such notions if Austria and Russia had remained united in defence of the status quo on all fronts. Austrian diplomats had failed, however, to prevent Nicholas from waging war on Turkey, and the Metternich system embodied in the terms of München-grätz had collapsed to the ground. Austria's most obvious need at the outbreak of war was to hold the Russians back from the lower Danube, and this she succeeded in doing by allying with Prussia in an armed threat to Russia to evacuate the Principalities. The Sultan agreed that Austrian forces should occupy the Principalities for the duration of the war. Buol would have liked to give full support to the western allies but he was too much afraid of Russian counter-measures to make a decisive move. He therefore antagonized Russia without winning the friendship of the West. The news of Balaclava led him to believe that allied arms were in the ascendant, and there was a short time in November when Francis Joseph almost declared war on Russia, but the moment passed with the news of Inkerman. Shortly afterwards Buol signed an alliance with France and Britain, but his chief object was to obtain a guarantee from Napoleon III of the integrity of Austria's possessions in Italy. A series of peace negotiations began in Vienna in March 1855 but nobody expected them to produce results, and Austria disappointed the French by failing to declare war on Russia when the negotiations broke down. It was not until December 1855 that Buol presented allied terms to St. Petersburg as an ultimatum expiring on 18 January. By that time neither side trusted or respected Austria. By trying to get something from everybody she emerged with nothing. In all her future troubles she was to remain isolated in Europe.

Two of these troubles were already foreshadowed in the new relationships which emerged during the war. At the beginning of 1856 the Prime Minister of Sardinia, Cavour, succumbed to pressure from his king and signed a military alliance with France and Britain. The immediate advantages were not great, for Austria was also allied with the western powers and had obtained from France a guarantee of the status quo in Italy. Cavour failed to obtain Parma and Modena at the peace congress and was obliged to be satisfied with a statement from the British foreign secretary, Lord Clarendon, deploring the condition of Italy, but he came away convinced of Napoleon III's inherent hostility to Austria. Prussia, too, played her cards well during the war. Though Frederick William supported Buol in putting pressure on Russia in 1854 he did so chiefly to restrain Austrian ambitions and he never seriously endangered Prussia's relations with the Tsar. Consequently when Frederick William supported the ultimatum to St. Petersburg in the last days of December 1855 Alexander II was able to welcome the intervention. The Tsar wanted peace lest further disasters should befall Russia, but he did not wish to humiliate his country by submitting to Austria. Prussia's move gave him the opportunity of accepting the mediation of a friend. Alexander agreed to the ultimatum on 16 January and a peace congress opened in Paris in the following month. When the immediate crisis was over and Alexander could think of restoring Russia's weight in Europe he remembered Prussia, and regrouped the eastern powers round a Russo-Prussian rather than a Russo-Austrian alliance.

Meanwhile, however, the Tsar could look only to France to save Russia from the harsh demands of Britain. Napoleon III's prestige had climbed to a pinnacle with French military achievements, with his successful insistence on peace, and with the choice of Paris as the place for the peace congress. The magnificent Russian Prince Orlov arrived in Paris with the deliberate intention of wooing both Napoleon III and the French public, a task which he accomplished so successfully that he was soon working hand in glove with the French foreign secretary, Walewski, to prevent the full realization of Palmerston's policy at the peace congress. Disastrous parts of this policy were nevertheless implemented by Clarendon and Cowley, the British representatives, for Napoleon III was not prepared to throw the English alliance completely overboard. Turkey, on the slender basis of a promise to deal fairly with the Christian subjects, was declared to be a fully sovereign member of the concert of Europe with whom no power had a right to interfere. On the presumption that Russia was not likely to honour a guarantee of Turkish integrity special measures were taken to disable her. Southern Bessarabia was incorporated in Moldavia to push Russia back from the Danube mouths, and the Principalities were placed under European protection. More important, the Black Sea was neutralized so that Russia could not keep more than a few light vessels in the ports along her thousand miles of coastline. The closure of the Straits was maintained whilst the Porte was at peace, but there was nothing to prevent the Sultan in time of war from summoning allied fleets into the Black Sea to attack his defenceless enemy.

The treaty of Paris proclaimed in several of its clauses the notion that there existed a community of European Powers capable of regulating matters of common concern. Theoretically the inclusion of Turkey in the community was a step forward in the pursuit of peace, for previous writers on the subject of international systems, from William Penn to Rousseau, had assumed that there was a natural state of war between Christendom and Islam. The terms of the treaty implied however, that Russia was not a responsible member of the community. A tripartite agreement was patched up between Britain, France, and Austria to provide protection for Europe against Russia. Under these circumstances neither the treaty nor the concept of European community could last for long. The Black Sea clauses were so detrimental to Russia's prestige and safety that the Tsar would be obliged to repudiate them as soon as he gathered strength to do so. Russia of necessity abandoned the defence of the status quo which had been her rôle in Europe since 1815 and became a disruptive force, ready to exploit the tensions which lay only slightly beneath the surface of Europe. With France also determined to throw the old Europe into the melting-pot the stage was set for an era of wars.

CHAPTER XX

Towards a New Europe

I. PROGRESS IN RUSSIA

IN THE bitter years which followed defeat at the hands of the western powers Alexander II sought to rediscover and reassert the vitality of tsarist Russia by rectifying the defects which had crippled her war effort. He did not intend to make a complete break with the past, nor to reproduce in Russia the society and institutions of western Europe. His programme was one of renovation not revolution. He began by emancipating from the shackles of serfdom the twenty million or more peasants who were owned by private nobles and gentry.

On 30 March 1856 Alexander declared in a speech to the Moscow nobility, 'It is better to abolish serfdom from above than to await the time when its abolition would begin from below without action on our part'. This signified an appeal for the co-operation of the 250,000 serf-owning nobles, on whose support tsardom would continue to depend, in a reform which the government had decided was necessary in the interests of the state. The appeal failed. Most serf-owners could not believe that the state would give them adequate compensation for the losses incurred by emancipation, and the only group which accepted the Tsar's invitation to propose a measure of reform, the Lithuanian nobles, suggested that the serfs should be emancipated without land. The Tsar insisted that they must be allowed to buy land, and he invited committees of noblemen in each province to discuss details on these lines, but the majority remained hostile. Those who came from the black-soil regions of the centre and south, where the land was fertile, demanded a high price for its alienation: those who came from the non-black soil regions of the west and north, where serfs paid valuable *obrok* derived from industrial earnings, demanded a high price for their manumission. Reform would never have taken shape but for the enlightened work done by members of the court and civil service, above all General Rostovtsev, the head of the drafting commissions, and N. Milyutin, assistant minister of the interior. Some concessions were made to the views of the nobility in the draft which finally made its way through Alexander's 'secret' top-level committee, but the nobles never reconciled themselves either to the methods or to the results of emancipation. They were brought into closer contact

with the hated bureaucracy than ever before by the government's decision
to advance four fifths of the compensation due to them for the loss of land
and labour. Many were deeply in debt at the time of emancipation; the
ready money received from the government was swallowed up in mortgages; few could find capital to invest in farming the demesne land, formerly
worked by serfs with their own implements and stock. The Tsar thus lost
the devotion of the nobility and gentry without, unfortunately, winning the
gratitude of the peasantry.

The great emancipation edict of 19 February 1861 gave the peasants the
minimum of civil rights to make them free men. Henceforward they could
marry, enter trade or industry, own property, sign contracts, and prefer
lawsuits. They had expected much more than this, however. As serfs they
had believed that the whole of the land belonged to the tsar, who would
one day give it to the village communes to be divided among the peasantry.
They had certainly assumed that the small plots of land which they worked
for their own livelihood were owned by the commune, and they had never
thought of regarding as 'rent' the labour services and dues which they rendered to the landlord. They were consequently bewildered when they
found that the landlords were allowed to keep all the land which had not
previously been allotted to the communes, and allowed to exact labour
services and money dues to help them run it for the next forty-nine years.
They were astounded when they found that they had to pay for the plots
they had worked as serfs and which they thought they owned, in a sense,
already. The plots had seldom occupied them for more than three or four
days a week, and many were now made smaller, for the emancipation edict
stipulated a minimum allotment which was smaller than the average area
formerly cultivated by the serfs, and in fertile regions the nobility seized the
opportunity to resume as much of the land as possible. The peasants were
ordered to pay to the government annually, for forty-nine years, redemption
sums which were calculated on the capitalization of labour services and were
therefore far greater in amount than the market value of the land. In non-
black soil regions, landlords foisted off on to the peasants the maximum
allotment of land permitted by the law in order to obtain redemption dues
which amounted to twice the market value of the land. Until 1870 no
peasant could refuse to take an allotment. He could escape payments and
obligations only by agreeing to accept an allotment which was a quarter of
the standard size, and many did this, though the so-called 'charity' allotments
were a bad bargain in regions where population was dense, land dear, and
extra work hard to obtain.

For some time the peasants believed that the landlords were concealing or
misinterpreting the Tsar's law, or that the edict was a temporary measure
which would be followed by real emancipation. Wild rumours circulated:

the Tsar was said to be sitting on a golden throne in the Crimea distributing land to any peasants who could reach him. A wave of disorders spread over Russia, increasing in desperation as the peasants learned the true position. By 1863 order had been restored, and the results of emancipation began to emerge, but another eighteen years passed before redemption was enforced. A more generous land settlement was extended to state peasants; also to Polish peasants as a bid for their support against the seditious landowners. Serfs in Transcaucasia, on the other hand, were made to suffer in an attempt to conciliate the nobility. Over the empire as a whole the peasantry slowly divided into three classes, consisting of the richer *kulaks* who made headway at the expense of their less clever, less ruthless, or simply less fortunate neighbours, the middling peasant families, and the village poor who worked as farm labourers or domestic servants for a pittance to add to the income from their dwarf holdings. That the process of differentiation did not proceed quicker was due to the power given to the communes.

The emancipation edict granted land not to peasants as individuals but to peasants organized in the village commune (*mir*). The commune retained all their former duties, which included minor police functions, relief measures, and collective responsibility for taxes. They continued to control meadowlands, pastures, and forests used by the peasants, to determine the crop-cycle employed in the open fields, and to divide the fields between the peasant families. To these duties were added collective responsibility for redemption annuities and, therefore, for tying the peasants to the land. A group of communes formed a new unit called the canton (*volost*) whose duties included larger police functions, control of peasant movement by means of passports, and organization of law courts for the judgment of minor disputes and misdemeanours. The hold which commune and canton possessed over each peasant was almost as great as the hold previously possessed by the landlord. They could, and frequently did, recommend transportation to Siberia for peasants who refused to co-operate. This new form of despotism was justified by reformers on the grounds that a considerable degree of self-government existed within the localities, the heads of families in each village electing their chief communal official or elder, and the elders electing the headman of the canton. Slavophiles had long praised the *mir* as a unique emanation of the Russian spirit. The slavophile theorist Samarin had played a leading part in drafting the emancipation edict, which Ivan Aksakov described as a 'product of fundamental slavic principles' introducing a land settlement 'broader and more liberal than the western'. Even Herzen, in a manifesto *To the Young Generation* (1861), found common ground with the slavophiles in respecting the communes, which he believed could be used to socialize Russia.

Herzen in his newspaper the *Bell*, published in London and smuggled into

AOP 2C

Russia during the early years of the reign, welcomed the initiative of the
Tsar in carrying out reform but continued to believe in the need for democratic institutions. His desire for constitutional reform at a national level was
shared, probably, by the majority of educated Russians in the eighteen-
sixties, the minority including the Tsar. In February 1852 Alexander actually
imprisoned a group of noblemen from the province of Tver for expressing
liberal convictions. Alexander was prepared to make radical changes in
administration, partly because they seemed necessary once the serfs had been
emancipated and partly because he shared the faith of the new generation in
government measures, but he would not contemplate the diminution of
royal power. He knew that the peasants were almost totally illiterate, he
believed that the nobles were almost entirely reactionary, and he might well
doubt the ability of a middle class which was both small and inexperienced
to guide Russia along fruitful paths.

The inadequacy of mere administrative concessions was rapidly demonstrated in Poland. The Marquis Wielopolski, representing a moderate
section of the Polish aristocracy, failed to convince reckless patriots such as
Mieroslawski, returning to Poland as a result of Alexander's amnesty, that
anything worth while was to be gained by co-operating with the tsarist
régime. A conscription order sparked off the inevitable revolt in 1863. Yet
the rebels were hopelessly divided. The 'reds', who courted the peasants
with promises of social reform, were feared and hated by the 'whites',
mostly serf-owning gentry, and inter-faction feuds aided the Russian troops
in their task of repression. Tsarist retribution was fiercer than in 1831.
Executions were accompanied by deportations, confiscations, and fines, and
followed by repression of the Polish language and culture. In 'the western
lands', where a few patriots had joined the Polish revolt and a few others had
made a bid for Lithuanian independence, the national culture which had
begun to revive forty years before was made to suffer. Intense russification
was carried out by the provincial governor, the ruthless Muravyev.

In Russia itself, administrative reform continued in spite of and in a sense
because of the Polish episode. The patriotic indignation aroused by the
behaviour of the Poles, particularly by their demand for the eastern border-
lands, persuaded Alexander that the time was ripe for his next measure. A
decree of 1 January 1864 set up elected councils (*zemstva*) in districts and
provinces. Each district council was elected by three separate colleges, the
first composed of all the rural property owners, the second of all the town
property owners, and the third of peasant representatives chosen by the
headmen of the communes and cantons. Delegates from the district councils
formed the provincial councils. Each body met for only a few days annually
to supervise paid executives whom it appointed for a three-year term.
Although noblemen greatly outnumbered townsmen and peasants, parti-

cularly on provincial councils, the local executives whom they appointed were drawn increasingly from the professional classes. The duties which the latter carried out included road-building, famine relief, provision of medical services, and supervision of education. In all these spheres they did work of great value to the community, but a feeling of frustration was nevertheless common among them. Alexander thwarted all the efforts of the *zemstva* to organize nationally, forbidding them to communicate with each other and subordinating their authority to that of the provincial governors. Town councils (*dumy*) created in 1870 were a less dynamic force, for the richer citizens favoured by the electoral system were more conservative in outlook than the provincial noblemen of the *zemstva*.

The reform of justice carried out at the end of 1868 bore the greatest resemblance to western patterns and gave the most satisfying effect of modernization. In place of the old class courts with their closed proceedings, inquisitorial methods, corrupt hierarchies, and endless references to other courts, 'the mere recollection of which', wrote Ivan Aksakov, 'makes one's hair stand on end and one's blood freeze', judges of assize, appointed by the government but irremovable during good behaviour, gave trial with the aid of juries to all types of criminal offenders. Civil cases, tried without jury, were subject to appeal before judicial chambers. Judges were paid a salary high enough to rescue them from corruption, and the Russian bar soon gained a name for independence and brilliance. Even this reform was marred, however, by Alexander's unwillingness to commit himself to democratic principles. In spite of the appointment of justices of the peace, elected by the *zemstvos* to try minor offences among all classes of the population in the countryside, the communal and cantonal courts created by the emancipation edict were allowed to remain in existence, administering to the peasants law based on custom rather than on the great code drawn up by Speransky in 1833. Alexander's persistence in regarding peasants as a different kind of human being from other men was illustrated by the maintenance of corporal punishment for them long after it had been abolished for others. Equality between peasants and others was embodied only in the army reform of 1874, which fixed compulsory service for all classes at six years with the colours followed by nine with the reserve. The irony was hidden by memories of previous systems under which peasants had served for sixteen and, before 1861, twenty-five years while other men frequently escaped.

Russia differed from other European countries in that the distressing condition of the peasantry attracted more attention from intellectuals than the political starvation of the educated classes. Under these circumstances the initiative was bound to fall to extremists, for the failure of the emancipation edict to integrate the peasantry into the community seemed to prove that the peasant problem was insoluble by all but the most drastic methods. In the eighteen-sixties a movement away from the romantic exiles of the eighteen-forties and from the patient socialism of Herzen began with the writings of Chernyshevsky in St. Petersburg. In his periodical *Sovremennik* (The Contemporary) Chernyshevsky denounced liberalism and embraced democracy, which he defined as a concern for the material welfare of the people. Like Herzen he believed that the communes could be used as breeding grounds for the true spirit of association, and in his novel *What is to be done?* written during his imprisonment in the fortress of St. Peter and St. Paul in 1863 he pictured ideal communities similar to the phalansteries of Fourier. Unlike Herzen, Chernyshevsky did not, however, believe that the desired transformation could be achieved by peaceful means. He almost certainly sympathized with the revolutionary exhortations published in a series of illegal pamphlets during the autumn of 1861, and the police took the opportunity of arresting him along with other radicals when a number of alarming fires broke out in St. Petersburg.

Chernyshevsky was typical of a new generation of radicals whose members were mostly of non-noble origin (*raznochintsy*) and who set about their chosen task with a ferocity unknown to their more urbane predecessors. Their capacity for destructive criticism was satirized by Turgenev, whose model revolutionary Bazarov in the novel *Fathers and Sons* (1862) was convinced that 'every single convention of our present day existence, in family or social life, calls for complete rejection'. Most members of the left repudiated the accusation of 'nihilism' which Turgenev levelled at them, but a new writer in the journal *Russkoye slovo* (Russian Word), Pisarev, acknowledged and rejoiced in the imputation. The times, Pisarev said, required 'realistic thinkers' who devoted themselves body and soul to the one worthwhile end of 'solving for ever the unavoidable question of hungry and naked people'. Renouncing all aesthetic values Pisarev scorned both art and the humanities and advocated education based on science. Renouncing also the accepted teachings of morality he urged men to follow their own desires, believing that they would find gratification only in the service of the community. Pisarev made no contribution towards the organization of the revolutionary movement which gathered momentum in the eighteen-seventies in Russia, but he contributed very largely towards the attitude of puritanical utilitarianism which characterized the revolutionaries. Other tendencies introduced themselves later in the 'sixties. Under the influence of Bakunin complete licence with regard to values became an end as well as a means, and nihilism turned to terrorism. Dostoyevsky probed some of the perversions of the revolutionary spirit in his novel *The Possessed* (1871), a frightening denunciation of 'godless' socialism.

In 1866 enquiries which followed the attempt by a student upon the life of the Tsar led the government to take the old-fashioned view that radical tendencies in the modern generation were due to the educational system. Experiments with a more liberal régime had begun in the universities as recently as 1863. These were not precisely abandoned, but the replacement of the liberal minister of education Golovnin by the reputedly reactionary Count Dmitri Tolstoy presaged a new attempt to direct education in the interests of autocracy. Tolstoy relied chiefly upon changes in the curricula of schools and universities, limiting the teaching of science, which was believed to possess affinities with extreme left-wing politics, and encouraging study of the classics. Censorship had been relaxed early in the reign but had never been abandoned. In 1865 a typical reform had released journalists from the necessity of submitting copy to censors before publication but had rendered them liable to penalties imposed by a government office after publication, even though the offending words might also have been cited as libellous in a court of law. During the next few years controls were tightened and press offences were relegated to chambers of justice where trial was without jury.

Opposition from intellectuals did not suggest to Alexander that his reforms had failed, for he looked upon the merchant class as the real representatives of the new era. Although trade and industry surged forward in the eighteen-sixties, however, many restraints remained upon production, and nothing like an industrial revolution could be said to have taken place in Russia until the last years of the century. The growth of population and the failure of many peasants to prosper as independent farmers created a potential labour force for industry, but the peasants were reluctant to migrate to the towns and work in factories. Many who did so returned home when they had earned a little money and employed their new-found knowledge in rural crafts, which actually expanded in Russia during the decades following emancipation. Illiterate peasants in any case provided only a poor type of labour for factories, a defect not easily overcome by the usually inexperienced and inefficient factory owners. The steps taken towards an industrial revolution were due in large part to government initiative in attracting foreign capital to Russia, most of which came from France and went into the mechanization of the cotton industry and above all into the building of railways. Russia had fought the Crimean War with only one railway line of any importance, connecting the two capitals. By 1870 she had nearly 11,000 kilometres of railways, built mainly by private companies but with state guarantees on a scale which imposed severe strain on the budget. A number of vicissitudes prevented the government from reaping immediate rewards. The out-put of pig-iron from the Urals temporarily declined as the former 'ascribed' serfs drifted away from the mines and foundries; the cotton industry suffered from the scarcity of raw materials caused by the American Civil War; and intermittent famine was rendered more acute by the backward methods of agriculture, still based on the strip system, used by the peasants in the communes. A foundation had without doubt been laid, but in 1870 a British traveller, Sir Donald Mackenzie Wallace, could describe all but a few Russian towns as 'little more than villages in disguise'.

The eighteen-sixties were nevertheless a period of expansion for Russia. With the release of peasants from the land and the building of railways Russia was able to integrate and expand her Asian territories to an extent never before envisaged. The defeat in 1859 of the guerilla leader Shamil after a quarter of a century of stubborn fighting and the subsequent pacification of Transcaucasia freed Russian armies for a policy of expansion in Central Asia and the Far East. Driving south-eastward of the Caspian Sea, the Russians subjugated the three Mohammedan states of Kokand, Bokhara, and Khiva to meet the British in India. Meanwhile the governor-general of Siberia, Muravyev, pushed eastward towards the Pacific, obtaining from the Chinese the cession of territory north of the Amur river and between the Ussuri river and the Sea of Japan. Here in 1860 Russia founded the port of Vladivostok, 'Ruler of the East'.

These successes were gratifying to Russian pride, but several decades elapsed before they formed the basis of a new ideology. In the eighteen-sixties Russians could think of no greatness outside of Europe. The repudiation of Russian sovereignty by the western powers in the treaty of Paris merely brought a more aggressive strain into slavophile thought. The idea that Russia would one day provide Europe with a new civilization was superseded by the idea of an inevitable conflict between western Europe and Russia, out of which Russia would emerge victorious. In preparation for this war she must cement her union with other Slav peoples. In 1869 the Pan-Slav theory was systematically developed by Danilevsky in a book entitled *Russia and Europe*. Pan-Slavism played an important part in Russian foreign policy only in the eighteen-seventies, but a foundation for it was laid, almost unwittingly, in the previous decade. The aggressive nationalism which was stimulated by the journalist Katkov at the time of the Polish revolt conditioned the public mind to the idea that Russia was the natural leader of the Slav world and that the refusal of any Slav group to accept her domination could only be regarded as an abberration. Even earlier than this, Alexander's foreign policy turned attention to the Balkans and laid the seeds of Russia's 'mission' to liberate the Slavs from the grasp of Turkey and Austria. At the insistence of Napoleon III, Alexander's new-found friend, the Sultan was obliged in 1859 to concede self-government to the two Danubian Principalities, which subsequently became Roumania. Russia found that her influence was by no means impaired by this development, and she was encouraged to extend her patronage to other emergent nationalities. Her hopes centred upon a half-forgotten people in the eastern Balkans, the Bulgars. Bulgarian nationalism had been revived in the early decades of the nineteenth century by the efforts of a single Slovak scholar, Venelin, to whose work must be ascribed the subsequent endeavours to establish Bulgar education and an independent Bulgar church. In 1870 Russia secured the first triumph for her new Balkan policy when she forced the Sultan to set up a Bulgarian exarchate independent of the Greek Patriarchate at Constantinople.

Bulgarian ambitions were clearly incompatible with those of Serbia and Greece, though patriots from all three nations imagined for a brief moment in 1867 that they might form a South Slav federation. The rivalries and turmoils which continually rent the Balkan peoples formed a hornets' nest which could not be disturbed without fear of war. This was a prospect which had not occurred to Napoleon III who, in his pre-1848 fashion, imagined that the formation of nation-states would promote peace in Europe. Even Napoleon was willing to use means incompatible with his imagined end, namely, war against the only power still vitally concerned to maintain the status quo in Europe. In 1858 he told Cavour that he would support Sardinia in a war against Austria, provided that the war could be justified in the eyes of Europe. In March 1859 Alexander promised Napoleon not only that he would refrain from helping Austria but that he would move Russian troops to divert Austrian forces, in return for help from France in revising the Treaty of Paris.

2. THE UNIFICATION OF ITALY

When Napoleon III made the famous statement that he would 'like to do something for Italy' he was not thinking of uniting the peninsula. He would have been even more unrealistic than usual had he done so, for Italians who passionately wanted unity were hardly more numerous in the eighteen-fifties than they had been a decade earlier. The war of liberation in 1848 and the defence of the two republics in 1849 touched wider sections of the community than the ideas leading up to them, but the myth of great endeavour for the national cause lay dormant until it was deliberately exploited in 1859 and 1860. Peasants and artisans were awakened by the upheavals of 1848 to a glimmering sense of their social wrongs, but no political leaders seemed anxious to release this latent source of energy. The Risorgimento consisted mainly, as it had done before, of a desire on the part of enlightened groups to improve the condition of their region of Italy by means of liberal reform. In the Duchies and Legations the reformers became convinced after years of reaction at the hands of pro-Austrian rulers that their wishes could only be realized with the aid of Piedmont. The price to be paid to

Map VIII   Italy after 1815, with *inset* the Stages of Unification

Piedmont was, however, a very high one, for the framer of Piedmontese policies in the eighteen-fifties held no brief for Italians from other parts of the peninsula.

Count Camillo di Cavour was a gentleman farmer who did not enter political life until his late thirties. He shared all the views which had been current among the progressive nobility of Lombardy in the two decades before the revolution, concerning the value of scientific knowledge, administrative efficiency, and economic expansion. Among English politicians he admired the practical men such as William Pitt and Sir Robert Peel. When he acquired office under the Marquis Massimo d'Azeglio in 1850 he found a social and economic revolution already in progress in Piedmont, for the reforms of Charles Albert's reign, culminating in the establishment of constitutional government, were causing the old reactionary aristocracy to withdraw gradually from public affairs in favour of a rising bourgeoisie, including exiles from Lombardy and other parts of Italy. D'Azeglio had been appointed premier by Victor Emmanuel in 1849 with the express purpose of reviving the reform movement and restoring the prestige of the monarchy after Novara. He contributed to the process of change by introducing democratic reforms into the army and lowering some of the barriers which the church held in the way of sound administration and good husbandry. The Siccardi Laws of 1850 abolished ecclesiastical jurisdiction, limited the number of recognized holy days, and prevented ecclesiastical corporations from obtaining unlimited amounts of land in mortmain. Cavour supported these measures without qualms of conscience, for he was a rationalist in religion, but he was not directly responsible either for them or for the army reforms. His special task was to find money to clear off wartime deficits and to pay for army measures and railway building. He increased taxation enormously and borrowed heavily without ever succeeding in balancing the budget either now or later. He increased the nation's productivity, however, by encouraging French speculators to invest in Piedmontese industries and railways, and by negotiating commercial treaties with France, Britain, and Austria. He was one of the very few continental liberals to believe in the free trade principles so dear to the Manchester School.

Cavour's liberalism consisted otherwise of a belief in parliamentary institutions as the proper means of obtaining and wielding power. He knew that without parliament he would neither have risen to high office nor enjoyed much prospect of staying there, for his enemies were great and numerous. The king could not like him because he was neither a courtier, a soldier, nor a sportsman, and because his policy was too subtle. The aristocracy disliked him for presiding over changes which drove them further and further into the backwoods. The bishops abhorred him for enabling Rattazzi and the Left to pass a bill abolishing the monasteries in 1855. The common people groaned under his taxes and resented his treatment of their hero Garibaldi. By contrast Cavour came increasingly to represent the moderate liberal views of the upper middle class which alone sent deputies to the Chamber. This does not mean that he exercised an unquestioned sway over members, but merely that he was dealing with men of his own kind, playing a game in which he was master of all the strokes. His technical skill was demonstrated at an early stage in the manoeuvre by which he obtained the premiership at the end of 1852. Drawing d'Azeglio away from his right-wing supporters into an alliance between the right-centre and the left-centre, Cavour afterwards neglected to defend him when a civil marriage bill met with opposition from the king. Cavour was very proud of this *connubio*, which illustrated his belief in governing through an amalgam of groups rather than through a consolidated party. The amalgam enabled him to shift his policy to right or left as strengths in parliament changed, and saved him from being opposed by a united party with an alternative programme.

Critics accused Cavour of a complete lack of principle in the struggle to retain office. They had much evidence to support the accusation. Not only did Cavour employ the civil service to secure election of government candidates and use secret funds to bribe newspapers (methods familiar to the most illustrious of French liberals) but he quashed parliamentary elections, overrode cabinet decisions, held as many as five or six portfolios himself and gave the remaining three or four to nonentities, stampeded parliament by presenting it with *faits accomplis*, and suppressed Mazzini's newspaper, *Italia del Popolo*, by methods unknown to the law. These practices, defended by Cavour as exceptions at times of crisis, came to be regarded by his successors as normal, and liberal constitutional government suffered enormously in consequence. Yet Cavour deserved credit for the fact that parliamentary institutions survived at all. In spite of good work by d'Azeglio the Chamber was not a serviceable instrument when Cavour took it over. He painfully set the example of speaking in Italian, studiously avoiding rhetoric which could all too easily produce disorderly debates. He was efficient in the conduct of business, and he tried to be good humoured. Most Piedmontese, including the few who were allowed to vote, were not interested in parliament, but Cavour taught them to regard it as indispensable and, what is more, he persuaded Victor Emmanuel that parliament ought not to be destroyed. He bequeathed to his successors the firm conviction that free discussion should nurture the government of Italy. The achievement placed his statesmanship in a different category from that of Bismarck, with whom he might otherwise have been fruitfully compared.

When Cavour entered d'Azeglio's ministry there is no reason to suppose that he thought of Italy outside Piedmont. He certainly did not reform Piedmontese laws and revitalize her economy with the deliberate intention of fitting her for the leadership of a nationalist movement. He disliked the nationalists, in and out of Piedmont, because most of them were fusionists whose policy would submerge Piedmont in Italy, and the most notable of them were democrats and republicans. To Cavour Mazzini was at one and the same time an irresponsible agitator whose abortive schemes aroused the disapproval of foreign governments and a dangerous demagogue whose appeal to the illiterate masses could only lead to dictatorship. In time Cavour came to see that the nationalist movement, though it had grown independently of himself, could be used for the advantage of Piedmont. His skill in adopting it was the measure of his genius. His policy was always one of annexation, however, never of fusion. It put the radical Crispi in mind of a prince of the House of Savoy who once said to a courtier at dinner, 'I shall take Italy leaf by leaf, as I now eat this artichoke'. Determined annexationism and uncompromising liberalism contributed to Cavour's success in uniting Italy only twelve years after others had failed, but they also prevented him from embracing all the political energies of the nation and from cementing the affections of all classes of the people.

Nationalists such as the exiled Manin began to have hopes of Cavour for the first time in 1856, but they were warned even then that his nationalism was not like theirs. Cavour was already thinking of a future war with Austria for the possession of north Italy when he annulled the election of conservative deputies in 1857, but he regarded the support of Napoleon III as essential and therefore began immediately afterwards to move towards the right. The Emperor of the French must be assured that Piedmontese policy bore no relation to revolution. Mazzini was once more condemned to death and the anti-clerical Rattazi was made to resign from the ministry. When an Italian radical named Orsini made an attempt on Napoleon's life in January 1858 Cavour took ostentatious measures to wipe out conspiracy. Yet the initiative came, eventually, from the French emperor himself. Cavour travelled to Plombières on 21 July 1858 to meet Napoleon without informing his cabinet and without knowing what sort of an offer he would receive. He was surprised at its boldness, though of course Napoleon III could not have found a better sphere than Italy for venting his spleen against Austria, breaking up the settlement of 1815, and claiming the inheritance of his uncle's prestige. The two leaders arranged that Sardinia should provoke Austria into war in the following spring, whereupon Napoleon III would assist the oppressed peoples of Lombardy and Venetia to find freedom through annexation to Piedmont. The Duchies and Legations might form an autonomous unit with the prospect of becoming part of an Italian federation under the presidency of a reforming Pope. Napoleon had no intention of presiding over the creation of a strong Italy on his south-eastern border. The unification of north Italy would probably arouse quite enough opposition in France, but Napoleon thought he had reinsured himself against this by signing with Cavour in January 1859 a formal treaty allowing France to take Savoy and Nice if Sardinia acquired northern Italy as far as the Adriatic.

Cavour's aims were wholly Sardinian, but during the early months of 1859 he deliberately exploited nationalist fervour by calling for volunteers from all over Italy and by talking of the coming war as though it were to be a decisive national event. Among those whom he convinced must be numbered Austria's foreign secretary, who rushed Francis Joseph into war in April 1859 to defend the idea of the multi-national state. Nationalist propaganda did more than this, however. It enabled Cavour afterwards to claim that Italy had won her own rewards and owed nothing to Napoleon III. The claim possessed no foundation in fact. The Piedmontese army was too small to beat the Austrians, and volunteers from the rest of Italy were negligible in numbers. When Napoleon III backed out of the war in July 1859 with only half the promised gains Cavour urged Victor Emmanuel to continue fighting alone, but the counsel was one of despair and the king rejected it. Sardinia received Lombardy at the hands of the French emperor without being asked to cede Savoy and Nice.

The fighting against the Austrians was harder than Napoleon had imagined. In spite of the use of railways the French moves were slow and clumsy. A victory at Magenta on 4 June was not followed up, the Austrians were allowed to withdraw for a breathing space to the Quadrilateral, and both armies advanced to collide head-on at Solferino on 24 June. Victory went to the French, but only in the sense that they were left in possession of the field. Napoleon III was sickened by the bloodshed. It was not squeamishness which caused him to sign an armistice at Villafranca on 11 July, however. He knew that Prussia was massing troops on the Rhine for a hostile purpose. He had heard, too, that Cavour was sending agents to Florence and Bologna to prepare the ground for the annexation of central Italy.

The outbreak of war against Austria had provoked rebellions in the Duchies and Legations. The rebels had invited Victor Emmanuel to assume dictatorial powers for the duration of the war, but there was every reason to believe that they would seek autonomy once the threat of Austrian domination was removed. The Sardinian government was determined to thwart this end, though Cavour had agreed to it vaguely at Plombières. The crucial task was that of Baron Ricasoli in Tuscany, where the desire for autonomy had survived the disappointments of 1848 and where distrust of Sardinia was profound. Ricasoli's achievement in persuading the peasantry to vote for annexation to Piedmont was a personal triumph which no-one could have foreseen. It inspired Cavour to return to office (he had resigned after Villafranca in order to dissociate himself from the apostate Emperor of the French) with an offer of Savoy and Nice to France if Napoleon III would allow Sardinia to annex central Italy.

Napoleon III could not, in fact, have interfered to prevent annexation without admitting that his pro-Italian policy had been a blunder and without challenging Britain, whose fears concerning French influence in Italy had been aroused by the war. He thought he was justified in accepting Savoy and Nice, but he found that he sacrificed the gratitude of Italian patriots and provoked angry protests from Britain. The transaction was made to depend on plebiscites in Savoy, Nice, the Duchies, and the Legations, but they were taken in the presence of French and Piedmontese troops and few people besides Cavour could pretend that they were genuine expressions of opinion. Cavour on this occasion abandoned his belief in elected assemblies, which would have accepted only conditional annexation, and insisted on taking the votes of the ignorant multitude. He thus deprived Italy of the support of many enlightened sections of opinion in Tuscany and the Romagna and gave Mazzini grounds for denouncing the degrading dependence upon France. Garibaldi had to be prevented by force from smashing the ballot boxes at Nice, which was his birthplace. Cavour hurried to arrange the cession of the two provinces before parliament met, because he might have kept them if he had been willing to agree to a loose federal bond with Tuscany and he dared not let the deputies know that there was a choice. He admitted privately that his action was sufficiently unconstitutional to warrant impeachment.

By March 1860 the kingdom of Sardinia covered more than a third of Italy and included nearly a half of the population. Cavour did not envisage further moves in the immediate future, for the sacrifice of Savoy and Nice had rendered his position as Prime Minister precarious. When Sicilian autonomists approached him for his terms should they succeed in stirring up revolt in the south he gave them no encouragement. He hoped, after consolidating his northern state, to enter the field of European diplomacy once more for the acquisition of Venice and possibly the Papal States. The goodwill of Napoleon III, whose troops had occupied Rome since 1849, seemed indispensable still.

Events would not await Cavour's diplomacy, however. The Sicilian masses, always on the verge of starvation and long possessed with a fierce hatred of the Bourbons, rose in revolt on 4 April. Mazzini's agents had been active on the island for some weeks, for Mazzini hoped to regain in the south the initiative he had lost to Cavour in the north, but the revolt was essentially the work of peasants who knew little or nothing of political aims. Leading families in the villages were loath to help the Bourbon authorities to suppress the revolt, so that in a very short time government and society dissolved throughout the island. Landowners soon recovered from their initial hesitation, however, and their dislike of social upheaval brought them round to the side of law and order. The revolt was on the point of collapse when it received an entirely new impetus from Garibaldi. The latter, though he had become a great admirer of the soldier-king Victor Emmanuel still revered Mazzini as the prophet of the national movement, and he saw in Sicily a chance to prove that popular initiative was more effective than foreign aid. He accordingly collected the famous Thousand volunteers, mostly from Lombardy and Venetia, and set sail for Sicily in May. Cavour did everything he could to stop him, for he could see nothing but harm resulting to the Piedmontese liberal monarchy whether Garibaldi succeeded or failed, but public opinion throughout Italy was so deeply engaged that Cavour did not dare to arrest the expedition. Garibaldi landed on 11 May. His sincerity, courage, and simplicity soon won him the devotion of the peasants, and as one village after another received him joyfully the landowners came to regard him as their best hope of law and order. He captured Palermo on 27 May and assumed a temporary dictatorship of the island.

The future of Sicily thereafter became a bone of contention between rival politicians. Two groups were eliminated at an early stage: Sicilian separatists accepted the fact that total independence was impracticable, and Mazzini realized that he had failed to convert more than a handful of men to republicanism. The issue finally lay between the annexationists, who demanded the immediate and unqualified surrender of Sicily to Piedmont, and the unionists, who wished to use Sicily as a base for forming an entirely new kingdom of Italy. The annexationists were led at a distance by Cavour, who had been persuaded after the capture of Palermo that more leaves of the artichoke were ready for the taking. In June he sent an agent, La Farina, to Sicily to work for a plebiscite. This tactless and ambitious man was soon at loggerheads with Garibaldi's chief minister Francesco Crispi. The latter was willing to accept the dynasty of Savoy but only when Garibaldi had swept through Naples to Rome and could offer the crown of a united people to Victor Emmanuel. Antagonism between annexationists and unionists was thus accentuated by hostility between liberals and democrats. Garibaldi's unrivalled influence over the people of Sicily enabled him to sway the issue whenever he intervened, but more often than not his natural diffidence and his concentration on military problems caused him to leave decisions in the hands of subordinates. Garibaldi's hatred of Cavour did not blind him to the fact that Piedmont and her statesmen were necessary for Italy, but he was determined to resist handing over Sicily until he had carried revolution to the mainland. Cavour tried to steal his thunder by fomenting a revolution of his own in Naples, but this extraordinary venture failed and Garibaldi entered the city as a conquering hero in September. He aimed to march on Rome at once, before the November rains approached, and to make possible the complete unification of Italy. Cavour had hitherto avoided an open breach with Garibaldi but he could prevaricate no longer if he was to prevent the headstrong leader from challenging Napoleon's troops guarding the Holy City. On his advice the Piedmontese army invaded the Papal States, defeated Papal forces at Castelfidado, and confronted Garibaldi in Naples. The latter had no alternative but to hand over his conquests to Victor Emmanuel regretting that they did not include Rome. The natural dignity of the great fighter gave the occasion more grace than anyone could have expected. When his request to serve the new régime as viceroy in the south was rejected he retired to the island of Caprera.

After the usual plebiscites Sicily, Naples, and the Papal States were annexed to Piedmont, and Victor Emmanuel II was proclaimed King of Italy in 1861. Venice remained in the hands of Austria, to be received as yet another diplomatic gift from Napoleon III in 1866; Rome remained in the hands of the Pope until the French garrison was withdrawn in 1870. To most Italian politicians the need to rid the peninsula of the Austrian menace and the desire to place the centre of government at Rome overshadowed all other tasks. D'Azeglio more accurately pin-pointed the central problem facing the kingdom when he said to Victor Emmanuel, 'Sire, we have made Italy – now we must make Italians'. The peasants who formed nine tenths of the population knew and cared nothing about Italy. The upper classes, who might easily have been convinced of the desirability of nationhood, had been alienated by the lack of good faith which characterized the taking of the plebiscites. The élite which had taken part in the Risorgimento had been inspired less by national consciousness than by hatred of petty oppression and alien domination, and once these were removed they thought of themselves first as Lombards, Tuscans, or Sicilians and only second as Italians. Regional pride which in the past had made Milan, Florence, Venice, and a host of small cities equal in creative genius to Rome was a source of potential energy to the nation, but in 1861 it was unchannelled by any desire to co-operate. Under these circumstances the politicians who had played a leading part in the creation of the kingdom felt that they ought not to give any encouragement to local aspirations. They began at once to extend the Piedmontese administrative system, based on the French, over the rest of the kingdom. Cavour had given Neapolitan and Sicilian leaders the notion that annexation would be followed by a large measure of autonomy. He salved his conscience for his change of mind with the thought that deputies from the south were present in the Chamber when the passing of Minghetti's laws (March 1861) sanctioned the process of centralization. The people of the south could argue reasonably, however, that their interests were not adequately represented in a parliament elected on an extremely narrow franchise. Along with the Piedmontese administrative system the Piedmontese *statuto* had also been extended to the rest of Italy. Property qualifications enfranchised only 600,000 people in a total of 27 millions. Only a half or a third of the 600,000 could overcome their religious scruples or their apathy and go to the polls, and the majority of these came from the north.

Parliamentary government suffered a severe blow when Cavour died in June 1861 at the age of fifty. His ascendancy in politics had been so complete that even his enemies were at a loss without him. He had never encouraged a two-party system with a responsible opposition, and after his death there was an increasing tendency for deputies to form shifting groups, continually coalescing or dissolving into new forms. Ministries were unstable; there were nine premiers in as many years. All came from the groups on the Right; the differences between them were personal rather than political. Deputies were drawn from so narrow a section of the community that they tended to think alike on important subjects. Devout Catholics abstained from politics in their horror at Cavour's attack on the Papal States, so that there was no clerical party to bring a real issue into parliamentary life.

Neither the Left nor the Right was equipped with a social or economic programme to meet the needs of the centre and the south. Orthodox liberal tenets led the deputies to extend free trade from Piedmont to the rest of Italy, with the result that struggling industries in the south were depressed. Agriculture needed capital expenditure to compete in foreign markets. The special needs of Sicily and Naples were overlooked in the general need to raise money for the national treasury. In 1862 government receipts were found to meet only a half of government expenditure. A rapid succession of finance ministers tried to economize, but union meant inevitably a demand for railways, roads, and harbours and for an army and navy. Heavy loans were contracted: interest on the national debt accounted for more than a quarter of the government's expenditure. Currency was debased, church property was nationalized, and taxes were increased until Italians became the most heavily taxed nation in Europe. In 1868 an excise duty was placed on all corn passing through the mill. The price of bread rose and many people in the south were reduced to starvation level. Hatred of taxes combined with hatred of conscription to intensify the old problem of brigandage in Naples and Sicily. Sixty battalions of troops had to be kept in the south for four years to quell civil war.

The 'problem of the south' was doubtless accentuated by a lack of sympathy and understanding on the part of politicians, but in truth the problem was very great. The vast majority of people in Naples and Sicily were illiterate. In supplying them with civil servants from northern Italy the government gave them an administration endowed with greater efficiency and integrity than they had ever known. Even Piedmont, which was popularly supposed to have derived all the benefits of unification, felt its burdens. People were appalled when they discovered for the first time the backward state of large parts of the country. They were disappointed by Italy's failure to play the part of a Great Power in 1866, when war against Austria led to the defeat of the army at Custozza and the navy at Lissa. They were ashamed that their government, to prevent attacks on the French garrison, should have felt obliged to wound and capture Garibaldi in 1862 and send troops against his volunteers in 1867. Even the eventual entry into Rome, sheepishly, on the heels of the departing French, was an anti-climax to the glamorous episodes of earlier years. Yet they cherished the new gospel of nationhood and appeared as a shining example to neighbours in Germany.

3. TOWARDS THE UNIFICATION OF GERMANY

In 1849 Bismarck, the future creator of the second German Reich, spoke with horror of an attempt 'to force on Prussia the rôle which Sardinia had played in history'. He referred to a plan devised by General Joseph von Radowitz to exploit the German nationalist movement in the interests of the monarchy. Maintaining a modified constitution in Prussia itself, Frederick William IV coaxed or bullied twenty-four lesser princes into joining a Union of German states with a parliament elected on a limited suffrage and armed forces under Prussian control. Bismarck no doubt disliked the plan because it was put forward by Radowitz, of whom he was unreasonably jealous, but he might also have seen that the circumstances were against it. Schwarzenberg returned to the task of restoring Habsburg supremacy in Germany as soon as he had quelled the Magyars. Claiming that the German Confederation was still in being and promising that its Diet would be reformed, he managed to detach the more important member-states from Radowitz's Union before the congress which was to draw up its constitution had met at Erfurt in May 1850. A few months later he found an opportunity for a show-down. The elector of Hesse appealed to the Federal Diet for help in crushing his liberal opponents, and Austria sent troops. Hesse had formerly promised to become a member of the Erfurt Union, and since Prussia was vitally concerned to control a state which divided her own territory she too sent troops. The Tsar decided the issue by threatening to intervene on Austria's behalf. Radowitz resigned, the Erfurt Union collapsed, and Prussia's new Prime Minister Manteuffel submitted to Schwarzenberg at Olmütz (29 November 1850).

Otto von Bismarck was born at Schönhausen in Brandenburg on 1 April 1815. Though the family estates lay only a little to the east of the Elbe Bismarck prided himself on belonging to the Junker class such as held feudal sway in Pomerania and Silesia. He idolized his dull-witted aristocratic father and disliked the ambitious, intellectual activity of his mother, who came from a family of untitled bureaucrats. In fact he owed a great deal to his mother. He was never content to remain in the backwoods. Though he said, and probably believed, during his long period of office that his greatest wish was to return to country solitude, he felt nothing but frustration during the eight years which he spent as a squire cultivating his estates. He possessed all the arrogance of the Prussian Junker with none of the aloofness. He was a masterful man, driven by a desire to dominate other men and to bend circumstances to his will. He entered politics more or less by accident, but they proved to be the perfect sphere for his genius. In 1847 his fellow

AOP 2D

squires sent him to the United Diet in place of a member who had fallen ill.
He immediately won a reputation for harsh reactionary views. By defending
the 'historic' rights of the aristocracy he was able to attack both the absolutist
state, which he had learnt to despise during a brief spell as a civil servant, and
the liberal majority, which he regarded as a hive of ambitious bureaucrats.
When the United Diet collapsed he returned to Schönhausen but did not lose
his taste for politics. As liberalism advanced he became reconciled to the
monarchy, though he never respected it. In 1848 he hurried to Berlin to
advise Frederick William IV to rally the peasantry to the cause of counter-
revolution. In 1849, when a restricted electorate made him a member of
parliament, he opposed the Erfurt Union on the grounds that it gave
dangerous opportunities to liberalism. Prussia, he said, should co-operate
with Austria against the forces of disorder.

In reality Bismarck was devoid of conservative feelings. Frederick William
IV called him a revolutionary. In 1851 he entered the service of the Prussian
state as representative to the Federal Diet at Frankfurt, and he immediately
began to think of increasing the power of Prussia 'according to the principles
of Frederick the Great'. These principles justified the use of any weapons,
however mean, violent, or two-edged, provided they served the immediate
purpose. The Crown Prince described Bismarck as an evil man, because he
was unscrupulous in the fight for power. Personal humiliation at the hands
of the Austrian representative at Frankfurt encouraged him in a determination that Prussia should be recognized as the equal of Austria in Germany.
He thought in terms of spheres of influence, with Prussia predominant over
the states north of the Main. The aim was wild enough in the years which
followed Olmütz. Whilst Russia stood beside Austria, Frederick William
would not dare to challenge the supremacy of Francis Joseph in Germany.
The position changed only with the Crimean War. Bismarck then saw
Alexander II of Russia and Napoleon III of France united in a desire to
change the map of Europe. He believed they would succeed in a matter of
years. Both were hostile to the Habsburgs, but they might nevertheless
create a united Germany under Austrian leadership, Alexander to distract
Francis Joseph from the Balkans and Napoleon in return for territorial
compensation. Bismarck urged Frederick William to turn danger to advantage by allying with the two restive powers. The king was simply
shocked at the suggestion that he should bargain with Napoleon III.

Frederick William had long been overwrought by political pressures
which he could not control and, succumbing at last to nervous prostration,
he signed away the royal power to his brother William in 1858. William
was duller in intellect and tougher in temperament than his brother. His
instincts were those of a soldier. Though he smarted under the humiliation
of Olmütz he believed that his duty as a good German was to seek recovery

through 'moral conquests' rather than by open hostility to Austria at a time when she was in trouble in Italy. He therefore appointed a moderate liberal ministry at home and withdrew his anti-Austrian delegate from Frankfurt. Bismarck was sent as ambassador to St. Petersburg, but he continued to give advice unsolicited on questions of foreign policy. In 1859 he urged William to seize power in north Germany whilst Austria was engaged in war against France. The Regent revolted against such a course, which would have shocked opinion throughout Germany. He wanted to help Austria, and mobilized his forces with the intention of doing so, but held back again and again as Francis Joseph refused to allow him to command all German forces north of the Main. William's object was, after all, the same as Bismarck's, but he would not admit that it could only be obtained in defiance of Austria.

William was driven to take Bismarck as his Prime Minister by a constitutional crisis at home. Liberals in the Prussian parliament were disappointed when they found that William's interests were wholly absorbed by the army. Weaknesses revealed by mobilization had led him to appoint General Albrecht von Roon as war minister at the end of 1859 and to back him in a number of plans for army reform. Basically the bill placed before parliament at the beginning of 1860 proposed to strengthen the regular army at the expense of the Reserve. The liberals were not opposed to army reform as such, for they too wanted Prussia to appear mighty in Germany, nor were they opposed to universal conscription, which the French Revolution had taught Europe to regard as moral and educational, but they resented the attack on the *Landwehr*, the treasured relic of the era of reform. In 1860 and again in 1861 they passed only compromise military budgets, giving the government money for immediate necessities but not for large-scale reorganization. At the end of 1861 and again in March 1862 general elections produced liberal majorities which were even more recalcitrant. By now, constitutional principle was at stake, for Roon's neglect of conditions laid down by previous parliaments raised the whole question of control over expenditure. William, who had become king in January 1861, sought for ministers who would placate the opposition but he could find none. Bismarck was several times mentioned as a man who would ignore the opposition, but William did not take him until his appointment seemed the only alternative to surrender. He became Prime Minister on 22 September 1862 and Foreign Minister also a fortnight later. He was forty-seven years old.

Bismarck's experience of parliamentary politics hitherto had consisted of a brief period following the revolution when he had engaged in factious criticism of the government without attempting to win support. As a minister he was obliged to state his policy to the Chamber and to allow members to question him but he need not listen to their criticisms. He was always infuriated by opposition. He neither liked nor disliked parliament, however: he thought only how he could use it. In 1863 he had to find money for the army reforms, not because he wanted them but because William had appointed him to secure them. He first of all tried to deflect the deputies from their opposition by offering them a greater Prussia: 'Germany does not look to Prussia's liberalism' he told the finance committee, 'but to her strength. The great questions of the day will not be decided by speeches and resolutions of majorities – that was the mistake of 1848-9 – but by blood and iron.' If the liberals had passed the army reforms and given him a free hand in foreign policy he could have ignored the king. When they failed to rise to the bait he ignored them. Taxes which had once been voted could be collected until they were actually repealed, an extreme measure which the liberals shrank from taking. Expenditure of money without consent of parliament was unconstitutional, but the deputies possessed no powers of impeachment. Bismarck could not be overthrown by parliament, but without its support he was wholly dependent on the uncertain favour of the king.

Bismarck's aim as Foreign Minister was still that of extending Prussia's predominance over the states north of the Main. Though his diplomacy did not follow unerringly the master plan once detected in it by historians no-one could deny that it worked wonderfully towards success. For this Bismarck became admired throughout Germany. Many people criticized his goal, for the wish to turn Germany into a federation of equal parliamentary states was still widespread, but only a few isolated individuals such as Paul de Lagarde, Constantin Franz, Ludwig von Gerlach, and August Reichensberger criticized his methods. Bismarck was no more Machiavellian than Talleyrand or Metternich or Cavour, but he brought to diplomacy a greater coarseness and brutality than would have been acceptable in circles where hypocrisy rendered tribute to virtue. His arrogance probably did more damage in the end than his wars, which were fought on a limited scale for strictly defined objectives. Unlike Napoleon, Bismarck turned to war only when diplomacy had failed. He disliked war because it involved risks and because he had to leave its conduct to others.

At the beginning of his ministry Bismarck believed that he would be able to push Austria out of north Germany by ruthless diplomacy. To orthodox weapons he was willing to add the force of nationalism. Many Germans had been stirred during the Crimean War and the Italian War to a renewed consciousness of the futility of the Bund. A German National Association founded in September 1859 had acquired some 25,000 members by 1862. Most of them came from northern and central states and they looked to the formation of a lesser Germany under the leadership of a liberalized Prussia. In southern states a Reform Association founded at Munich in 1862 supported the idea of a greater Germany under a liberalized Austria. Francis

Joseph was half-persuaded that he could exploit the movement in the interests of the Habsburg monarchy, and in the summer of 1863 he invited the princes of Germany to a conference at Frankfurt to consider the reform of the Confederation. Members of the lesser Germany movement doubted the ability of Austria to satisfy popular demands for free government, but it was not this which wrecked Francis Joseph's scheme. Bismarck with appeals, threats, tears, and tantrums persuaded William not to attend, and without the co-operation of the king of Prussia no reform of the Confederation could be carried out. Bismarck countered with a proposal to divide power in Germany between Austria and Prussia and to base it on a popularly elected assembly. The princes shied at so radical a suggestion and nationalists could not trust Bismarck without evidence.

This was supplied very soon afterwards by the war against Denmark to secure the Duchies. Bismarck fought the war simply to outbid the Confederation – 'It is no concern of ours whether the Germans of Holstein are happy', he said privately – but this was ignored or forgotten in the flush of success. Hoping to fulfil one of the dreams of 1848 and bring the Duchies into complete union with Germany the Federal Diet at the end of 1863 sent troops into Holstein to defend the claims of Frederick, Prince of Augustenburg, in the disputed succession to the throne. Bismarck sent Prussian troops after them, but he took care to associate Austria with the dangerous move, and he assured the Powers that he was intervening only to prevent Christian IX of Denmark from breaking the treaty of 1852 by incorporating Schleswig in the new unitary Danish state. A brief war persuaded Christian IX to sign away his claims to the Duchies, leaving Bismarck with no applicable plans for their future. His ultimate object was to annex them to Prussia and thereby assert the latter's predominance in north Germany. Austria put up a barrier, not because she wanted the Duchies but because she recognized the principle involved. Declaring her right to act on behalf of the Confederation she kept her troops in the Duchies along with those of Prussia, pending a decision by the Diet. The stages by which Bismarck drove her out of this position marked the defeat of her claims to supremacy in Germany.

This supremacy was rapidly being undermined by the force of economic change. Industry had expanded in the Ruhr and in Silesia and Saxony during the 'fifties; Germany had outstripped Belgium and France in the building of railways; and the *Zollverein* had secured the profits. Austria had made one or two attempts to join the *Zollverein* but Prussia had refused to admit her. Bismarck recognized the existence of economic forces but he did not place much reliance on them. During 1865 he hovered between diplomacy and war. He described the Convention of Gastein, signed in the autumn, as 'papering over the cracks' between Prussia and Austria, but in fact it brought them a stage nearer to the final contest. Francis Joseph could no longer claim to be defending German nationalism against Prussian particularism, for he had agreed to take over the administration of Holstein whilst Prussia took over that of Schleswig. Austrian behaviour in Holstein gave Bismarck a pretext for war whenever he cared to use it.

During 1865 Bismarck carefully added up his forces, foreign and domestic. The Franco-Russian alliance on which he had once placed high hopes had broken down when Napoleon III expressed sympathy with Polish rebels in 1863: the two powers would now have to be approached separately. Alexander II had been irritated by Bismarck's high handed offer of help in the Polish crisis and could be relied upon only to remain neutral. In conversations with Napoleon III at Biarritz Bismarck discovered for the first time that the French emperor did not want another war: the most he would offer was neutrality in return for territorial concessions. Bismarck hinted at rewards west of the Rhine, without catching Napoleon as historians once believed. At the last moment Napoleon gave his promise of neutrality to Francis Joseph in return for an offer of Venice. The only positive gain on Prussia's side was an alliance with Italy in April 1866. In Germany most of the small states of the north and centre were bound to Prussia by military conventions, but their forces were negligible. Austria could expect more valuable support, directly from Saxony, and indirectly from Bavaria, Württemberg, Hesse-Darmstadt, Hesse-Cassel, and Hanover. Bismarck made efforts to win popular support against hostile governments but his success was limited. His offer in April 1865 to summon a German assembly based on universal suffrage met with suspicion. Working class leaders in the north were persuaded by Ferdinand Lassalle to support Bismarck in the hope of social legislation, but those in the south remained aloof. The *entente* with Lassalle did not improve Bismarck's relations with the liberals. Only individual members of the Prussian Progressive party moved towards the idea of condoning Bismarck's behaviour in the event of success. German liberals who met at Frankfurt under the presidency of Rudolph Bennigsen of Hanover promised simply to await the outcome of war. Bismarck would not have dared to fight if Roon and Moltke, the Prussian chief of staff, had not regarded the risks as reasonable.

Prussian troops invaded Hanover, Saxony, and Hesse-Cassel on the night of 15-16 June 1866. Moltke made use of all available railways to deploy his armies on a very wide front and prevent encirclement by Austria's allies. His plan to push quickly through the mountain barrier and concentrate his forces in northern Bohemia was thwarted by the king's unwillingness to appear as the aggressor against Austria, but the enemy commander-in-chief, Benedek, failed to take advantage of the central position which he achieved during Prussia's delay. He was attacked near Königgrätz on 3 July by the Prussian centre under Prince Charles Frederick, who managed to hold on long enough for the Prussian left, under the crown prince, to arrive on the Austrian flank. Throughout the action the Prussians derived great advantage from their breech-loading rifle, which gave much quicker fire than the Austrian muzzle-loading rifle and also allowed the men to load and fire while lying flat on the ground, thus presenting a much smaller target to the enemy. The Prussian victory at Königgrätz decided the issue of the Seven Weeks' War. Bismarck accepted the mediation of Napoleon III, arranged for him to receive Venice on behalf of Italy, and secured thereby the terms he wanted from Austria.

The Peace of Prague (23 August 1866) constituted an advance on Bismarck's original aim of dividing Germany into spheres of influence for Austria and Prussia. The rulers of Hanover and Hesse-Cassel were deposed, and their territories, along with Schleswig-Holstein and the free city of Frankfurt, annexed to Prussia to give her for the first time a continuous boundary across northern Germany. Other states north of the Main, and Saxony, were united with Prussia in a North German Confederation. The Federal constitution, agreed upon early in the following year, set up a parliament with a lower house elected by universal suffrage and endowed with significant powers in the realm of finance and military control. Austria was pushed out of Germany altogether and the four states south of the Main (Württemberg, Bavaria, Baden, and Hesse-Darmstadt) received independence under conditions which rendered their union with Prussia at a later date probable. These terms represented the extent to which Bismarck had succumbed to popular and nationalist pressures. He had hoped simply to harness the force of nationalism to the old state system, for he disliked theories of the folk and demands for living space, with their threats of unlimited war. Now, while many old-fashioned conservatives broke with him over his 'theft of the crowns' of Hanover and Hesse-Cassel, and resented the powers given to the German parliament, a large section of the Prussian liberal party, including some of its ablest leaders such as Forckenbeck and Twesten, joined in voting a law to indemnify Bismarck for his years of unconstitutional rule. Soon they were to join with other liberals outside Prussia to form the National Liberal party and help to found a German Reich in a war to the death with the French Empire.

Francis Joseph never completely accepted his defeat in Germany. In 1870 he was still dreaming of a war of revenge. Though he, like Bismarck, distrusted the idea of a Greater Germany, with its revolutionary implications, he would have continued to toy with it but for the stranglehold which the Magyars obtained over him in 1867. In the end the most effective barrier against greater German nationalism proved to be not the particularism of Prussia nor the enmity of France but the creation of the Dual Monarchy.

4. THE CREATION OF THE DUAL MONARCHY

In the aftermath of the revolutions of 1848 Francis Joseph believed that he could rule the empire of the Habsburgs without reference to national divergences. Palacký's dream of a federation of national groups had faded before the ambitions of the master nations: the radicals' plan to divide the empire between the master nations had foundered on the imperialism of the Germans and the resistance of the subject peoples. The dynasty survived because an heir could be found who had not committed himself to nationalist solutions, as Ferdinand, for all his wavering, had done when he sanctioned Hungary's March Laws. Francis Joseph at his accession issued a manifesto informing his subjects of his intention of 'uniting all lands and peoples of the monarchy in one great state'. By union he meant uniformity and by greatness he meant armed power and prestige. The aim had proved too ambitious even for Joseph II, and Francis Joseph was only 18 and of commonplace ability. Like all the Habsburgs, however, he believed that he was born to rule. He was neither worried nor dismayed by difficulties, but merely annoyed. He did not imagine that he had any duty towards his subjects: they existed to contribute to his power, and if they would not co-operate they must be forced or cajoled. He was thick-skinned enough to hang on to his old-fashioned empire long enough for his opponents to sort themselves out, whereupon he compromised, in 1867, with the only formidable forces in the field.

The new centralism was defined in the constitution drawn up by Count Stadion and issued by decree on 4 March 1849. There was to be one citizenship and one law throughout 'the single and undivided Empire of Austria'. The 'historic units' were restored for administrative purposes only, and those which contained mixed populations were divided into crownlands. Thus the Greater Hungary which Kossuth had taught the Magyars to regard as their birthright disappeared: Hungary, Croatia-Slavonia, and Transylvania became crownlands entirely independent of each other and equally subordinate to Vienna. Galicia, which Polish aristocrats had hoped to dominate in 1848, became two crownlands by virtue of the large Ruthenian population. This last innovation was the personal work of Stadion, who had been a warm patron of the Ruthenes as governor of Galicia. Stadion was allowed to introduce a number of liberal ideas into the constitution of 4 March, for a liberal façade was thought to be necessary at the time. He decided that elected assessors should help officials in the localities and that a parliament based on universal suffrage should sit at Vienna. The government, chosen by the Emperor, was to act under a Prime Minister and be responsible to parliament. Unfortunately the façade was erected not to please the Emperor's subjects but merely to tempt the princes of Germany away from Radowitz's

Union. One month after the surrender of Prussia at Olmütz constitutional government, which had never come into operation, was officially abolished. Even before that time the ministers were deprived of responsibility to any-one but the Emperor. Francis Joseph was persuaded by conservative advisers, chiefly one Kübeck, that the office of Prime Minister implied a collective responsibility detrimental to royal authority, and when Schwarzenberg died suddenly in April 1852 no successor was appointed. Francis Joseph acted as his own Prime Minister to the end of his reign.

The ministers who inaugurated the centralist régime were revolutionary in their way. Even Schwarzenberg, though an aristocrat, showed scant respect for the feudal ideas which had dominated the old Diets. The rest – Bach, Bruck, Stadion, Schmerling, Krausz, and Thun – had all played parts of some prominence in liberal circles in 1848. They had come to believe, however, that they could achieve the most worthwhile aim of 1848, the modernization of the empire, by the effective use of governmental power. A central parliament elected by universal suffrage would merely strengthen their hands. Awaiting it, they went ahead as best they could. The revolutionary edict emancipating the serfs was implemented by a land settlement which created over three million peasant farms and required the recipients to pay only a third or less of the compensation to the previous owners (in Hungary they paid nothing). Seigneurial jurisdiction having been abolished, an entirely new system of justice was created with public examination of witnesses and trial by jury for all major offences. Secondary schools were reformed, universities freed from controls, and technical education developed. Railways, which covered only 248 miles in 1847, were taken over by the state and rapidly expanded; roads were improved; postal services were re-organized. Chambers of trade and industry were founded and efforts made to increase exports. A decree of 1850 casually abolished the trade barriers which had divided Austria and Hungary for more than a century. The Habsburg empire was thereafter the biggest free trade area in Europe outside of Russia, and Baron Bruck, as minister of commerce, hoped to make it the predominant economic factor on the continent. He dreamt, indeed, of creating an 'Empire of seventy millions' by pushing the whole of Austria-Hungary into a new German Confederation under Habsburg leadership. Though the German princes rejected the idea when Schwarzenberg presented it to them in a conference at Dresden in 1851 it lived on among German-Austrians for more than a decade.

The economic validity of the Austrian empire was based upon Hungary as a grain producing area and Bohemia and Vienna as centres of industry. Hungarian magnates benefited by receiving compensation for out-moded labour services: the enormous estates between the Danube and the Tisza became more efficiently organized. Money was invested also in saw-mills, paper-mills, and sugar refineries. Smaller men were driven to exploit the difficult and sparsely populated plain of central Hungary, the Alföld. Gradually acacias were planted to fix the shifting sand, and the region became fertile and profitable. Industry in Bohemia and Vienna was assisted by the last considerable coal supplies between western Europe and the Donetz basin. Transport proved to be a major problem, however. The Danube, the only important European river flowing from west to east, provided cheap transport between Vienna and Budapest, but otherwise its drawbacks were insurmountable. The upper reaches suffered from low water in summer and the lower reaches from ice in winter; currents were swift at narrow places; and, more important, bulky agricultural produce had to struggle upstream at great cost to reach industrial towns. Transport difficulties played their part in driving Austria out of northern and western European markets. Exclusion was intensified when Prussia succeeded in keeping Austria out of the *Zollverein*. A treaty of 1853, allowing her the position of 'most favoured nation', was hardly compensatory, and even this was withdrawn in 1862 in favour of France. The prosperity which smiled on the Austrian empire in the early 'fifties never fulfilled its promise.

Deprived of all hope of a parliament the ministers resigned one by one. Bach stayed on the longest, determined that Austria should have improvement from above if she could not have reform from below. As soon as he took over the ministry of the interior from Stadion in June 1849 he applied himself to the task of enlarging and organizing the bureaucracy. A vast host of civil servants, known as the Bach Hussars, was sent from Vienna to Hungary. Bach could see no sense in Magyar patriotism which left Hungary one of the most backward areas in Europe. He felt no qualms about backing up the bureaucracy with soldiers and gendarmes. Law and order reached such a pinnacle among his preferences that he even supported Francis Joseph in making a Concordat with the Holy See in 1855. This gave the Pope greater power over the Austrian church, and the bishops greater power over education, than they had had since the days of the counter-reformation.

Though absolutism was now naked and complete, no serious opposition raised its voice in the western half of the empire for some years. Bohemian aristocrats resented control by lower middle class bureaucrats, but there was no nationalist movement which they could exploit. Czech workers benefited from the boom in industry, and young men from middle class homes spoke enough German to get jobs as Bach Hussars. The intellectuals who had led the nationalist movement in 1848 were disillusioned, and the mild forms of repression to which the government subjected them were hardly necessary to quell their activities. In the German lands opinion was dominated by the monied classes which shot into prosperity in the early years of the decade. Industry began for the first time to operate on a credit basis; Viennese speculators made large fortunes; many small investors drew pleasing dividends from shareholding companies. The state, in vain endeavours to find money for the bureaucracy and army, floated loans at high rates of interest and sold crown property and even state railways to credit companies on easy terms. To these sources of profit the régime added one immense source of pride: the subjugation of Hungary to the status of an administrative zone.

The centralist policy pursued by the government was not in theory a German nationalist policy, and in fact the largest contingent of Bach Hussars was Czech, but at least Vienna could for the first time claim predominance over every other city in the empire. This fact, which so much pleased the Germans, infuriated the Magyars. Hungarian magnates still hoped to bargain with the dynasty for pre-1848 terms, but the gentry were uncompromisingly aloof. Passions were sharpened by material losses, for the smaller landowners had relied on the services and implements supplied by their peasants and they suffered accordingly by the emancipation edict. At the same time the state tried to impose on them the unaccustomed burden of taxation. They simply refused to pay. So too did the peasants, who were willing to support the gentry in boycotting the Viennese administration now that the barrier of serfdom was removed. Prison sentences were useless, for no town in Hungary possessed enough places of detention for the large numbers condemned. 150,000 troops had to be kept in Hungary to collect taxes which failed to pay for the upkeep of the occupying force.

Financial difficulties eventually undermined the Bach system and prevented it from supporting the foreign policy which Francis Joseph regarded as all-important. The enormous cost of occupying the Danubian Principalities during the Crimean War was followed immediately by the repercussions of the world-wide economic crisis of 1857. The monied classes lost confidence in the government and demanded cuts in expenditure, chiefly, of course, on the army and bureaucracy. Martial law was at last lifted from Lombardy-Venetia but no relaxation was possible in Hungary. German and Czech troops were still pinned down there when Austrian armies fought against Napoleon III in north Italy. Hungarian, Lombard, and Venetian troops naturally deserted in large numbers. In the midst of the war German capitalists refused to subscribe to further loans. In July 1859 Bach was dismissed, and Francis Joseph began to think of concessions.

His most effective opponents were the German financiers, who demanded parliamentary control over policy, and the Hungarian nationalists, who demanded the 1848 constitution. Characteristically, Francis Joseph would not yet compromise with these two groups, precisely because they were the most formidable. He always liked to think that his concessions might be withdrawn at some future date. At court two further groups, the aristocrats

and the bureaucrats, competed for his favour with offers to secure wide
support by making minimal concessions. Francis Joseph decided first to try
the aristocracy, the so-called Old Conservatives, of the various lands, who
hankered after a feudal system that had been dead in the rest of Europe for
half a century. A Polish aristocrat, Goluchowski, was appointed to replace
Bach, and some sixty representatives of the aristocracy were nominated to a
'Reinforced *Reichsrat*' or Privy Council to advise the Emperor on a change of
system. The most persuasive politician proved to be Count Széczen, leader
of the Hungarian contingent, and without further ado Francis Joseph commissioned him to draft a constitution, which was issued by decree on 20
October 1860. It provided for the old Diet and county committees to be
restored to Hungary, and for analagous institutions to be created in the other
'historic provinces'. The crown was to legislate with the co-operation of the
Diets in provincial matters, and of the *Reichsrat*, reinforced by members
from the Diets, in general matters. The whole complicated arrangement
(known as the October Diploma) satisfied hardly anybody. Széczen had
hoped that the Hungarian nationalists would accept it as a ground for
bargaining, but they rejected it outright. Slovaks, Serbs, and Roumanians
resented being sacrificed once more to the Magyars. Bohemian aristocrats,
who had supported the Magyars against the subject peoples in the *Reichsrat*,
were disappointed with their reward. The Germans were annoyed at the
loss of control over the empire, at the spurious liberalism of the Diploma,
and above all at the preferential treatment given to Hungary. If Hungary
could be regarded as a single constitutional entity, why not Austria? The
way was rapidly being prepared for dualism, but Francis Joseph would not
yet take it. He decided to try the bureaucrats, who assured him that they
could win support for their system with a few constitutional trimmings.
In December 1860 he dismissed Goluchowski in favour of Anton von
Schmerling.

Schmerling had a liberal record from 1848 but he was really a centralist of
the school of Bach. He believed that the German-Austrians would be
satisfied with a sham liberalism if he offered them also a policy of expansion –
the 'Empire of seventy millions'. A few weeks after his appointment, the
October Diploma was replaced by the February Patent (1861). The Diets
were no longer endowed with legislative powers: their chief function was to
send representatives to a *Reichsrat* of 343 members. This was to act as the one
legislative body for the whole empire. The electoral system was devised to
pack the Diets, and consequently the *Reichsrat*, in favour of the Germans.
The *Reichsrat* possessed none of the powers of a true parliament. Taxes
could be levied without its consent and ministers were not responsible to it.
Nevertheless the Germans accepted it, as Schmerling had anticipated they
would, deluding themselves into believing that the dynasty had been con-

verted to the liberal nationalism which alone could create a Greater Germany. The Czechs were taken in by the masquerade and joined the Bohemian aristocracy under Clam Martinitz in fighting for the 'historic' kingdom of St. Wenceslas. The Hungarian Diet met only to reject the February Patent. Schmerling had no course but to dissolve the Diet and send the Bach Hussars once more to Hungary. He could not appeal to the subject peoples because he was at loggerheads with his own Slavs in Bohemia. In any case the new leader of the Hungarian nationalists, Francis Deák, had softened old hatreds by promising the Serbs and Slovaks equality with the Magyars in a new Hungary. Nor could Schmerling appeal to the Croats, for the dynasty had never rewarded them for their help in 1848 by adding Dalmatia to Croatia as Jellačić had hoped. The Croats now accepted the 'clean sheet' on which Deák invited them to stipulate the conditions under which they would associate with Hungary.

Schmerling believed that the Hungarians would come to heel when his pro-German policy bore fruit, but the time never came. Francis Joseph would not give his full support to Schmerling lest the latter should be unable to control the liberal hopes his policy had aroused. He allowed his foreign minister, Rechberg, to work for a conservative alliance with Prussia over the affair of Schleswig-Holstein, thereby offending the liberal and national opinion to which Schmerling appealed. The German-Austrians in the *Reichsrat* thereafter criticized the military expenditure in Hungary and began to think that the only way they could secure real control over vital matters was by allying with the Magyars. They had thus moved away from imperialism towards dualism at the very time when Austria was committed to war against Prussia for supremacy in Germany. So too had Francis Joseph. Criticism from the *Reichsrat* had convinced him that he must never tie himself completely to German liberalism. In July 1865 he dismissed Schmerling, appointed a federalist government under Count Belcredi, and opened negotiations with Francis Deák. Some Hungarian nationalists believed that Hungary should take advantage of the defeat of Austria at Königgrätz to assert her independence, but this was not the opinion of Deák, who knew that Hungary had grown great only through association with Austria. Nor was it the opinion of Count Gyula Andrássy, who sprang into prominence during the negotiations. Andrássy believed that Hungary would remain great only if the Magyars predominated over the Slavs, and for this she needed the support of an Austria in which the Germans predominated over the Czechs. The Dual Constitutional Monarchy was arranged on this basis by the Compromise of 1867, and the nationalities were never able, for the rest of the century, to upset it.

CHAPTER XXI

The Clash of Empires

I. THE SECOND EMPIRE

NAPOLEON III had very little real knowledge of France when he became, at the age of forty-four, Emperor of the French. As a youth he had seen France through the peculiar medium of incurable Bonapartists in exile. As a man condemned to the rootless life of a cosmopolitan adventurer he had fixed his gaze upon the beckoning hand of his uncle's ghost and followed it with the heedless possession which reminded acquaintances of a sleep-walker. Throughout his life he had fed his mind on propaganda from the great man's lips. At some unknown point in his life he had become convinced that he was destined to rise to his uncle's eminence, and when his faith was fulfilled he naturally thought of France also rising to her former greatness. That he should copy the institutions through which the first Napoleon had governed France was expected by all who knew him, for in his generous and gullible way he would never have believed that his uncle's power rested from beginning to end on military conquest.

France in 1852 seemed to possess the resources necessary to become once more a leading power in Europe. Her population was second only among European nations to that of Russia: west of the Niemen, one in every seven Europeans was a Frenchman. Her chief need, to any Bonapartist mind, was a government which rose above selfish party interests and freed the nation's strength from crippling factional conflicts. 'I have taken as my model', wrote Louis Napoleon in a note which accompanied the constitution of January 1852, 'the political institutions which, at the beginning of the century and in similar circumstances, consolidated a shaken society and raised France to a high level of prosperity and greatness'. This constitution, which made its author President of the French Republic for ten years, needed only minor adjustments when the Second Empire was proclaimed. Dictatorship rested on Napoleon's power to appoint ministers responsible solely and individually to himself, and to nominate all officials from top to bottom of the administrative scale. The prefects were mostly inherited from the July Monarchy, for Napoleon III, unlike other new rulers of France in the nineteenth century, could not find a host of new agents, but they gave faithful service to a government which doubled their salaries and restored to them the power which their predecessors had exercised at the beginning of the century. The mayors, through whose activities government was brought to bear upon the remotest corners of the country, were rendered loyal to the régime less by fear of losing their jobs than by enjoyment of the petty authority and rights of patronage with which it endowed them.

Two legislative organs, without much power, completed the likeness to former Napoleonic times. A Senate, composed of Napoleon's nominees, was created chiefly to promulgate the emperor's decrees and to safe-guard the constitution. A *Corps Législatif*, elected by universal suffrage, could discuss and vote, but not amend, bills initiated by the emperor. The Senate could not admit the public to its sessions; the *Corps Législatif* could not report its debates to the newspapers. Napoleon III would never have admitted, however, even to himself, that these organs created a mere façade of representation. He instructed the prefects to secure the election of government candidates, but he advised them to bestow their favours not upon mere yesmen but upon men of real local standing. In the parliament of 1852 thirty-five of the government's elected candidates were ex-Legitimists and seventeen were ex-Orleanists. Napoleon III imagined that, by bringing such men into parliament, he was giving greater influence and prestige to the natural leaders of the countryside. He prided himself on creating a new ruling class consisting of 'the best men' from all political persuasions. They had, of course, sworn loyalty to the Emperor, but they remained aloof from the 'pure' Bonapartists. Similarly Napoleon liked to appoint as his ministers and high administrative officials men who could be said to have proved their capacity. Rouher, Baroche, and Magne were lawyers who had served both the July Monarchy and the Second Republic; Haussmann had been recognized as a promising career-bureaucrat; Fould came from a powerful banking family, friends of the Rothschilds. If they were not quite representative of all the élites, this was because the most notable members of the Legitimist, Orleanist, and Republican parties remained aloof from the Empire for a long time, and some of them to the end. Only Persigny, in the highest ranks, was totally lacking in pedigree and form, however; an adventurer, like his master. In the country at large the Bonapartist enthusiasts who had formed committees and organized elections for Louis Napoleon in 1851 were abandoned at the outset of the Empire. They were mostly small men, shopkeepers, notaries, apothecaries, and the like, whose support, it was felt, could do no good. The petty bourgeoisie had never been allowed to share political power with its wealthier brethren. Under the Empire its aspirations were to receive more sympathy from Prince Jerome Napoleon, Cousin 'Plonplon', than from the Emperor.

Napoleon III described his political system as a pyramid which former rulers had tried to balance upon its apex and which he had now set solidly upon its base. He meant that he regarded the wishes and needs of the people, the anonymous masses, as the fundamental concern of the reign, and their support as the basis of his power. The vast majority of the peasants remained loyal from beginning to end: some because Napoleon was the only political name they really knew, some because they expected the Man of December to save France from social upheaval, others because they wanted to shake themselves free from the old royalist notables who had dominated them for so long. Workers in the towns were more suspicious, but a considerable number were attracted by promises of plentiful employment, and during the boom of the eighteen-fifties they remained quiet if nothing else. Even in the 'sixties, when economic progress had slowed down and a higher cost of living had begun to swallow up the increased wages, the workers could sometimes be soothed by an Emperor who wanted so much to be loved by them and whose sympathy for all kinds of suffering was deep and sincere.

The only irreconcilables were minorities, and Napoleon was unfortunate in that they happened to be more articulate than the mass of his adherents. Paris as a city never forgave him for the blood shed in the course of the *coup d'état* and for 'baptizing himself' (as he is said to have put it) twice over in the votes of the ignorant peasantry. Paris was also the home of the intellectual élite – the literary and artistic salons, the Academies, the University – whose members found the Emperor and his court lacking in culture. Napoleon III was knowledgeable on scientific and especially military subjects but his taste in literature and art was said to be vulgar. In fact as far as painting was concerned his judgement was at least independent, for it was at his insistence that, from 1863, a Salon des Réfusés accommodated the pictures of Impressionists and others denied recognition by the official judges. The social élite of Paris continued to despise him. To the exclusive circles of the faubourg Saint-Germain the Imperial court seemed too fashionable to be dignified, and the Empress Eugénie (a Spanish lady whom the Emperor had married for love) too obviously beautiful to be quite well bred.

There were, of course, ways in which the régime could rightly be regarded as an insult to intelligence. The Second Empire in its authoritarian phase, and indeed for the greater part of its existence, imposed upon its subjects the petty restrictions typical of dictatorships in bureaucratic times. Political associations were forbidden to federate and political meetings could only be held in the presence of government officials. The University was humiliated; philosophy classes were abolished; teachers were forbidden to wear beards. A press decree of 1852 improved upon previous repressive systems to render newspapers, for seven years, more docile than they had ever been since the early days of Villèle. Government permission not only had to be obtained before a newspaper could be founded but renewed every time a member of the staff was replaced. Stamp duties were increased and huge sums of money had to be deposited with the Treasury as surety. New press offences were added to an already formidable list, and all were to be tried by correctional tribunals without jury. Moreover the Minister of the Interior in Paris and the prefects in the provinces were empowered to warn editors and, after three warnings, to suspend newspapers for activities displeasing to the government but not indictible at law. To facilitate the working of this unique and notorious device, daily reports on the contents of every newspaper published in France or admitted over the frontiers piled up in government offices. Napoleon III, like his uncle, believed in collecting information about persons in public positions great and small. His conspiratorial manner encouraged the feeling that he knew everything about everybody. The impression was wrong. The Second Empire was a police state only in a mild and relative sense. With so few whole-hearted supporters Napoleon III could not keep a check on all the people who accepted his régime with something less than enthusiasm. Nor could he reject their services. Rather than try, he pretended to respect honest reservations. The feelings of so silent and secretive a man are difficult to assess, but Napoleon III seems to have cared less about the existence of hostility, provided it was discreet, than about creating an impression of universal approval. For this reason, if for no other, he could not fill prisons with political prisoners.

The new Napoleon used his dictatorial powers to pursue, not military conquest, but economic development. Though he obviously thought mainly of bringing as much prosperity as possible to France herself, his horizon included a vision of France assuming the economic leadership of the continent. In this way she could aspire to some of England's prestige without attempting the hopeless task of challenging England's supremacy in the wider world. The foundation for French influence on the continent had been laid more than half a century before. The French Revolution had issued the first serious challenge to feudal concepts in western Europe, and Napoleon had made the first serious inroads into feudal land tenures. Napoleon's commercial code had been adopted in many parts of Europe, and the metric system, fully established in France by about 1800, had been gradually spreading to neighbouring countries ever since. The French language, long the language of diplomacy, had become the language of business to a generation of western Europeans brought up under French rule. France needed only to reinvigorate her own economy for her expansion to seem assured.

Napoleon III, who was extraordinarily receptive of other men's ideas when they were likely to contribute to his own ends, found intellectual support and scientific elaboration for his somewhat vague economic plans in the work of the Saint-Simonians. As long ago as 1821 Saint-Simon, among a profusion of slap-dash notions thrown out for the regeneration of mankind, had described the provision of material well-being as the true criterion of a healthy society, and had listed scientists, technicians, bankers, and industrialists as the men of the future. He had envisaged society arranged in a hierarchy dominated by businessmen and dedicated to the task of raising the standard of living among the poor. The vision had not appealed widely to Restoration society, and Saint-Simon's ideas had been discredited by the cranks who formed his only following after his death in 1825. A decade later, however, the scientific theory had been rescued from oblivion by the economist Michel Chevalier, who saw in it the blue-print for France's future prosperity and greatness. Worked upon by a number of enterprising men of the world, including notably the banker brothers Péreire, Saint-Simonism had become a systematic school of thought by the time Napoleon III needed it. The Saint-Simonians believed that the chief object of the future must be to liberate the forces of production. Napoleon III had prepared the way by putting an end to faction fights. The next step must be the growth of credit. Special banks were needed to scoop up idle capital and place it at the service of industry.

In 1852 Napoleon III gave a charter to a joint-stock investment bank, the Crédit Mobilier, which became the most characteristic institution of the Second Empire. The species was not new, but the éclat with which the Crédit Mobilier took the field under the management of the Péreires outshone the earlier achievements of the Société Générale in Belgium. The organization sought out investors large and small and poured their capital into every available enterprise. Some were important: railways, mines, steamship lines, gas companies, and a vast range of industrial developments. Some were almost bound to be dubious, for, as the more conservative bankers such as Rothschild pointed out, safe ventures could obtain backing from more orthodox sources; but the rot was slow to set in, and for some years the shares of the company paid handsome dividends. French concerns were soon found to be too narrow a field, and France was launched upon her important career of foreign investment. French capital went into credit banks in Germany, Spain, and Italy, into railways in Austria, Switzerland, and Russia, and into new industries everywhere. In 1869 French entrepreneurs completed their most important undertaking abroad, the cutting of the Suez Canal. Prominent Saint-Simonians, including Michel Chevalier, had been interested in the project since at least 1832, believing that it would regenerate the lands bordering on the Mediterranean and link East and West in peaceful association. Ferdinand de Lesseps, France's vice-consul in Alexandria and Cairo, was attracted to the idea at an early stage without seeing any means of carrying it out. Years later, two circumstances brightened his prospects: in 1853 his cousin Eugénie de Montijo married Napoleon III, and in 1854 his friend Said became Viceroy of Egypt. Said at once granted De Lesseps a concession to form a company to build a Suez Canal, but Napoleon III, though he would have liked to patronize so bold an enterprise, hesitated in face of opposition from the British government, which regarded the project as a threat to British interests in India. De Lesseps nevertheless floated a canal company, the shares being taken up mostly in France, and in 1859 work began. There were many set-backs, financial, practical, and diplomatic, but perseverence was finally rewarded. On 15 August 1869 the waters of the Mediterranean met those of the Red Sea. The opening ceremony three months later, at which all the rulers of Europe were represented, was the last spectacle of the Second Empire.

Credit played its part in completing for France a network of railways, which the Saint-Simonians rightly saw as an essential stimulus to production. In railway development the government intervened more directly than in most other economic spheres. A large number of small lines had been begun during the July Monarchy by speculators with an eye to the most profitable runs and by deputies desirous of political credit, but the construction of trunk lines had suffered from lack of adequate financing and lack of government direction. The Second Republic had excluded railway directors from the Legislative Assembly as corrupting influences, with the result that many of them had resigned from the boards. A proposal to nationalize the railways, though beaten off by Lamartine, had frightened promoters. France seemed destined to lag behind her neighbours in railway development, when Napoleon III took the field with long-term concessions to new companies and a guarantee of a minimum rate of interest on railway shares. A profusion of companies was soon seen to be inefficient and uneconomical: the state thereupon encouraged amalgamation into six companies, each serving a particular region of France. Dividends began to roll in from the northern system, which served the coalfields and manufacturing districts of Pas-de-Calais, and from the P.-L.-M. line (Paris-Lyon-Mediterranean). Railway shares began to appeal even to the most cautious investors and to rival the *rentes* in respectability. The depression of 1857 lowered confidence a little; the government was obliged to allow the companies to separate the accounts of the older and more profitable lines from the newer ones which ran through sparsely populated areas; and the guaranteed interest became a real charge on the taxpayer. By this time, however, railways had come to be regarded as a public utility, and government candidates at elections expected to be allowed to promise new lines to their voters. By 1870 France had almost as extensive a network of railways in operation as Prussia or Great Britain.

With progress on railways an industrial revolution at last got under way in France. Railways not only opened wider markets to goods of common utility, such as textiles, but created a market for manufactures of less obvious necessity, such as iron and steel products. The use of horse-power in industry quintupled between 1851 and 1870. The railways eventually brought about social changes also, by creating a more mobile labour force and by penetrating the rural isolation of the peasantry. Change in the countryside was very, very slow, however. The Second Empire could not promote anything like a revolution in agriculture. The pressure of population on the land remained very great in spite of the steady drift to the towns; holdings were small and divided, and the peasants resigned themselves to subsistence farming. If they could borrow a little money they used it not to improve their farming techniques but to buy more land, which brought too few returns to rescue them from debt. Facilities for borrowing were inadequate: the Crédit Foncier, founded in 1852 for the primary purpose of improving rural credit failed to operate satisfactorily over a countryside where property was so intricately divided, and the Crédit Foncier turned instead to investments in urban real estate, thereby facilitating the rebuilding of Paris and other large cities.

Napoleon III carried out so vigorous a programme of urban reconstruction that some city dwellers felt doomed to spend the rest of their lives among falling masonry, holes in the ground, and clouds of dust. Previous rulers had decorated their favourite towns with avenues and public buildings: Napoleon III altered the basic design of France's three major cities, giving them the wide boulevards, the parks, squares, quays, and bridges that became familiar to an increasing number of tourists. The complete transformation of Paris, Lyon, and Marseille was accompanied by more modest but still extensive development at Bordeaux, Lille, Le Havre, Toulon, Montpellier, Toulouse, Rouen, and Brest. Napoleon's task was different from that which would have faced planners in England, where industry had created new urban monstrosities such as Manchester and Leeds. France had some new urban agglomerations, such as Mulhouse and Roubaix, but they were too small to invite attention. French industry was still, in the eighteen-fifties, organized mainly on an artisan basis, and it had congregated in old towns of narrow alleyways and poky courtyards. With the coming of railways and better roads the chief need, as the Saint-Simonians had foreseen, was to create more space for the movement of traffic and the expansion of business. This need would not, however, in itself have stimulated the enormous activity which in fact took place. Napoleon III had other incentives. He was genuinely anxious to make towns healthier and pleasanter to live and work in. He wanted to create jobs for the unemployed workers in the big cities and to give the bourgeoisie more opportunities for investment. He saw a unique opportunity for advertising the strength and beneficence of his régime and for making France the cynosure of foreign eyes. He also without doubt felt the advantage that would be given by straight wide roads for moving troops quickly to strategic points in such radical cities as Paris and Lyon.

His building schemes caused much grumbling and some downright hostility. The officials who carried them out were accused of riding rough-shod over local opinion, of employing dubious contractors, and of spending money recklessly. Haussmann at Paris and Vaïsse at Lyon, occupying the unique position of mayor and prefect combined, came in for special criticism. The one was boisterous, cunning, and ambitious, the other cold, austere, and public-spirited, but both were ruthless in obtaining their ends. The need to evict and expropriate owners of condemned property brought inevitable complaints of hardship and unfairness; the building of new town centres caused bitterness among shopkeepers in old quarters: the construction of new roads and quays brought considerable expense to owners of adjacent property now at the wrong level or at an impossible angle. Workers who were turned out of their lodgings in condemned areas were obliged to crowd together in neglected quarters of the city or move out to squalid suburbs, for the new development was concerned with business premises and fashionable residences, not workers' dwellings. Even in the suburbs rents were higher, partly because men swarmed in from surrounding areas to get work on the new building sites. Reformers complained that in spite of vast expenditure on water supplies and sewers nothing was done to improve sanitation in the slums which lay behind and beyond the new façades. Many people regretted the obliteration of old haunts and historic buildings: some disliked the flashy scenes which replaced them. The urban developments without doubt created wealth, however. In Lyon, business men and railway companies invested more than three times the money Vaïsse had spent, and new enterprises came to make up for the declining silk industry. In Marseille, where new sea-walls sheltered new docks and warehouses on the made land, commercial firms exploited the trade with Algeria and looked forward to immense opportunities with the opening of the Suez Canal. In the capital, private enterprise lined the boulevards with smart shops; the first chain stores were opened; hotels and theatres proliferated; an atmosphere of carefree spending was deliberately cultivated; and Paris became the attraction of pleasure-seekers from all over the globe.

Frenchmen could certainly no longer be accused of lacking entrepreneurial drive. Their sudden display of initiative was such that Napoleon III needed only to co-operate. The upsurge of industry in the eighteen-fifties probably owed a great deal to general causes: the discovery of gold in California and Australia produced an inflationary effect throughout the world, and the discovery of new sources of energy and raw material stimulated industrial progress throughout western Europe. Napoleon III could claim to have given positive assistance at a few crucial points, however, even though, at one of these points, his intervention was widely criticized. His exile in

England had coincided with the repeal of the Corn Laws, and he had remained ever afterwards convinced of the value of free trade. Not so the majority of his countrymen, agriculturists and business men alike, who sheltered behind the tariffs set up in 1816 and boasted of an insular economy which gave them no need to employ the brutally competitive methods of the British. The deputies elected to the *Corps Législatif* in 1852 and 1857, docile in so many respects, successfully resisted a couple of attempts by the Emperor to loosen trade. At last in 1860 Napoleon took advantage of a clause in the constitution which allowed him to sign commercial treaties without reference to the legislature. The famous Cobden-Chevalier treaty substantially lowering tariffs between Britain and France was followed by similar agreements with Belgium, the Netherlands, the German *Zollverein*, Sweden, Switzerland, Italy, and Spain. Thanks to a 'most favoured nation' clause in each of these treaties, and to the negotiation of similar treaties by the other nations among themselves, France became the hub of an international network which gave Europe her nearest approximation to free trade. There was an immediate outcry from the French business world, and something like panic when a number of marginal firms in the iron and textile industries were forced out of business by British competition. Some 200 other firms obtained loans from the government to modernize their plant, emerging stronger than before, but unfortunately for Napoleon there was a general slowing down of industrial expansion in the eighteen-sixties. The American Civil War deprived France of nine tenths of her raw cotton; the silk industry suffered from a disease of the silk-worm; lack of confidence in the Emperor's foreign policy made the bourgeoisie less anxious to invest money. In the financial crisis of 1867 the Péreire brothers, who had always been disliked by more orthodox bankers, were deliberately allowed to go under. To many half-informed Frenchmen the sinking of the Crédit Mobilier, and its subsequent reorganization as an ordinary deposit bank, was an epilogue spoken by Providence to a venture based on reckless if not altogether discreditable principles. The Empire had been too closely associated with it to escape unscathed.

The year 1860 has been seen as a watershed in more than the economic history of the Second Empire. In November the Emperor suddenly announced that he was about to relax his authoritarian control, albeit by ever so little, and to 'give the great bodies of the state a more direct part in the formation of the general policy of our government'. Enemies did not hesitate to attribute the move to consciousness of a growing unpopularity and a desire to find new support in place of that lost through foreign and economic policies. The charge is difficult to substantiate. In the elections of 1857 the government polled just as many votes as in 1852, and the opposition was just as weak. Government candidates were returned in all but thirteen constituencies, and of the delinquents eight returned independents whose opposition to the régime was scarcely noticeable. The others (four in Paris and one in Lyon) elected republicans, but the mere fact that 'The Five', as their representatives were called, allowed themselves to be returned showed that they were disposed at any rate to collaborate with the régime. Napoleon III was pleased with the election results and thought that his ministers ought to have blazoned them across the front of the newspapers. Billault, the minister of the interior, was disappointed, rather, at the size of the opposition vote in the large towns. Far from advising concessions, however, he asked for a tougher attitude, especially in Paris, which should be reduced in size, he said, and deprived of its character as an industrial town. Haussmann in a long memorandum dilated upon the incurable wickedness of the working-class population of Paris and recommended the clearance of all the older parts of the city. What Napoleon thought of the advice cannot be ascertained. In 1859 he came nearer than ever before to obtaining popularity with the radicals through his Italian War. On 14 August the victorious Army of Italy marched into Paris amid popular acclaim. The Emperor felt secure enough to offer an amnesty to all political exiles save the notorious Ledru-Rollin.

True, the support of the Catholic hierarchy was shortly afterwards lost. As tension between Piedmontese policy and Papal intransigence drew towards a climax in Italy, Napoleon III tentatively suggested, in an anonymous pamphlet, that the independence of the Holy See might be guaranteed through possession merely of 'Rome and a garden'. The militant Catholic journalist Veuillot, more powerful as a spokesman than any bishop, called upon the French church to reject an Emperor who had betrayed the Pope. The loss to the Empire should not be exaggerated, however. The support given by the church in recent years had not been an unmixed blessing. Once the fear of godless revolt had subsided, the clergy had ceased to be grateful to the government for allowing the church to exploit the rights offered by the Loi Falloux, and for permitting an enormous growth of religious orders, and had become impatient with an Emperor who would not abolish lay control over the University or abandon the Organic Articles. The *procureurs* had been reporting for some time that under the influence of Veuillot the *curés* were growing more intolerant, and the government was glad of an opportunity to suppress his journal, the *Univers*. Radical Bonapartists such as Prince Jerome and Persigny rejoiced that the Emperor had escaped from the clutches of the church, and in areas where old-time Bonapartism was fairly strong the government gained in popularity. The break with the church came in time to save Napoleon III from some of the discomfiture which Pius IX meted out to worldly allies in the Syllabus of Errors in 1864, and to allow him to support a new minister of education, Duruy, in trying to make state schools as popular as those of the church.

Free trade certainly caused rancour among businessmen, and especially among those of the *Corps Législatif* whose repeated protests and obstructions had been circumvented. The Emperor's half-brother Morny, whose task as government-appointed President of the *Corps Législatif* since 1854 had been to seduce the deputies into thinking that they were playing a valuable part in public affairs, hinted that a mark of confidence in the deputies would help towards the better conduct of business. The ministers were all against concessions, however, and Napoleon must have arrived at his decision alone. His measures were as modest as they could well be. Once a year the members of the two houses were to be allowed to debate the speech from the throne in the presence of ministers who were to reply to them on behalf of the government. An official report of debates was to be published. As though to prove that these liberties had been granted willingly out of a plenitude of power Napoleon reappointed as minister of the interior the most rigid of Bonapartists, the faithful Persigny, the henchman of conspiratorial days, the accomplice of the *coup d'état*. Further concessions in the following year proved to be illusory. Newspapers were given the right to publish reports of parliamentary debates, but only if they could do so verbatim, a task which proved to be beyond the space of nearly all provincial and most national papers; and the *Corps Législatif* was allowed to vote the budget in sections instead of *en bloc*, a useless exercise whilst the Emperor retained the right to 'correct' the financial pattern which emerged. In 1863 Napoleon dismissed Persigny for failing, in spite of ruthless pressure, to prevent 15 Catholic and 17 radical opponents from winning seats. The liberal Morny could at last bring his influence to bear upon the Emperor's mind, but no further concessions followed. The Duc de Morny, shallow and unscrupulous but urbane and talented, had long despised the vulgarity, stupidity, and mediocrity of the men to whom a bureaucratic despotism inevitably gave authority. He believed that Napoleon had nothing to lose by sacking the lot and co-operating with men of intelligence in a qualified parliamentary system like that of the July Monarchy. His own skill at managing parliaments would doubtless have eased the transition if it had come in his time, but no move had been made when he died, at the age of 54, in 1865. A year earlier Napoleon had put out feelers in an opposite direction, allowing the workers the right to form trade unions and to strike.

Why Napoleon, after resisting liberal advice for so long, should have chosen to move further along the liberal path in 1867 is another of the many mysteries of the reign. The year saw the collapse, both ignominious and tragic, of the imperial adventure in Mexico, but the extraordinary ease with which the Empire shrugged off its failure should have illustrated the strength rather than the weakness of the régime. Apart from Mexico, French colonial activity owed little to the Emperor. A remarkable soldier and administrator, General Faidherbe, was alone responsible for extending French control over the hinterland of Senegal and laying the foundation of a prosperous colony. French missionaries led the way in the Far East, and army and navy spokesmen along with shipping firms and other special interests brought pressure to bear on the government to send expeditionary forces. Religious, humanitarian, economic, and nationalistic strains combined to produce co-operation with Britain in the Second Opium War, the annexation of Cochin-China, and the establishment of a French protectorate over Cambodia. Traditional interests in the Levant led to intervention on behalf of the Christians of Syria and the Lebanon in 1860, but nothing was done at this point to establish a colony. The Emperor positively tried to thwart colonialization of Algeria, describing himself sentimentally as the Emperor of the Arabs and protesting his desire to preserve Arab culture and society. Mexico was different because it had some bearing, though remote, upon Napoleon's determination to reassert France's rôle among European powers. The excuse for intervention in 1861 was to force the revolutionary republic of Mexico to honour debts owed to European financiers. When the British and Spanish governments withdrew their contingents the French stayed on to execute an ill-advised scheme of restoring Latin culture, clerical influence, and monarchical government to a people lacerated by anarchy and civil strive. Archduke Maximilian, brother of Francis Joseph, was persuaded to accept the throne, and Napoleon III dreamed of a client state which would bring France prestige and wealth. As usual the fighting proved to be tougher than he had expected. President Juarez was a formidable foe and the Mexicans were not as anxious to be 'liberated' as royalist exiles had suggested. Maximilian's well-meaning efforts to establish enlightened government were vitiated by the savagery of his partisans, and the affair dragged on, at a useless cost of men and money, until the American Civil War ended and the United States threatened France for her breach of the Monroe Doctrine. Napoleon III, like many other people, had not believed in 1862 that the North would win. By 1867 French troops had withdrawn from Mexico, leaving Maximilian to his death at the hands of a firing squad and his empress to sixty years of mental darkness. There was an outcry from the foreign visitors at the Great Exhibition; Thiers forecast overwhelming contempt for the Emperor; the lithograph of Manet's painting of the shooting at Queretaro had to be banned by the government. The ripples soon died away, however. The French public seemed anxious only to forget an episode in which it had been an accomplice.

On 17 January 1867 Napoleon III announced in an open letter to his minister of state that constitutional changes were about to be made. The decision probably owed something to the growth of a less intransigent opposition in the *Corps Législatif*. Groups of former republicans and monarchists, led by Emile Ollivier (one of The Five) and Adolphe Thiers (who had returned from exile to lead one of his usual centre parties) were ready to accept the Emperor if he would liberalize the Empire. In 1853 Napoleon III had suggested that liberty might one day 'crown the edifice': in failing health he seemed determined to complete his political triumphs by carrying out the most difficult of all political manoeuvres, the change from despotism to freedom. Characteristically he tried to give more to the public than to the politicians: controls on newspapers and public meetings were to be relaxed, but inside the Chamber deputies were merely to be allowed to interpellate ministers, who were to speak in support of their legislative proposals. Napoleon III still believed in himself and his mission, and he sent his minister of state, Rouher, into the *Corps Législatif* with new powers to explain it all to the politicians. He merely succeeded in baiting them. This stubborn, cunning, hard-working lawyer from Auvergne had been a devoted servant of the authoritarian Empire: like Persigny he believed that the Emperor would denature Bonapartism if not destroy himself by turning liberal. He conceived it to be his duty to save as much as possible from the wreck. Thanks largely to him the press bill was held up for more than a year, and when it came it held out on symbolic issues while making real concessions to freedom. Nobody thanked Napoleon III for it: the government majority voted for it only because the Emperor seemed to want it. The most important effects were in the provinces, where opposition journals were at last able to compete with government sponsored organs. Few of the new creations were hostile to the régime, however; they merely supported the dynastic groups which were working for a liberal empire. In Paris one wildly disrespectful journal, Henri Rochefort's *Lanterne*, created a nine days' wonder; a few new satirical journals received large sales; the republicans raked over old sores by starting a subscription for a memorial to a deputy Baudin killed on the barricades in 1851. The liberals made the most of these damp squibs as signs of real danger and flung themselves into an attack on ministerial despotism. Their main target, after Rouher, was Baron Haussmann, who had just asked the legislature for retrospective sanction of loans amounting to 400,000,000 francs, and who seemed to personify the kind of irresponsible government they were anxious to destroy. In 1869 Rouher fought the elections by all the old methods and lost two thirds of the seats to the dynastic opposition. The concessions which Napoleon III had long meditated were thus forced from him in the end. On New Year's day 1870 he appointed Ollivier head of a ministry responsible to parliament.

The liberal constitution was placed at the feet of the people in May 1870. The plebiscite was a resounding victory for the régime. While ultramontanes prepared to arm themselves with the dogma of Papal Infallibility and republicans exploited anti-clerical feeling, leaders on both sides admitted that the adversary was as strong as ever.

In an electoral manifesto to the people of Paris in April 1849 Louis Napoleon protested his devotion to peace in Europe. The British ambassador described the approval with which the posters were read on the hoardings. One of the reasons why opinion had turned against left-wing republicanism was the fear that it might lead France into expensive wars for idealistic causes. In 1851 Louis Napoleon assured the nation, in a speech at Bordeaux, 'The Empire means peace'.

Until the very last year of the reign Napoleon III was informed by his prefects and *procureurs* of the fundamental desire for peace. He could not lightly ignore the information, for he was, as Bagehot said, a 'democratic despot': lacking a party machine his power rested on a personal appeal to the people. At the same time no ruler bearing his name could ignore a deep emotional need of the French people for the reassertion of France's rôle among the Great Powers of Europe. In 1854 and again in 1859 Napoleon III shouldered the responsibility for war on the assumption that the diplomatic position gained would wipe out initial disapproval. The calculation was right the first time, wrong the second. The rectification of the south-eastern frontier by the annexation of Savoy and Nice placated those who feared a strong Italy, and the decision to take a stand over Rome, as alone necessary to Papal independence, satisfied Catholic lay opinion, but there had been times when criticism was acute. Thereafter Napoleon realized that the French people would not condone a war unless they received very great returns indeed. In subsequent years he tried to assert what he hoped and proclaimed to be a magisterial position in Europe without the sanction of war. He succeeded only in annoying the other Great Powers. In 1863 he protested against Russia's suppression of the Poles, thereby throwing away what was virtually an alliance with Alexander II, yet he did nothing to follow up the protest except to propose a congress, which aroused Britain's fears concerning his designs in eastern Europe. In 1864 he expressed sympathy with the Danes, but in view of the fact that the British government would only shout and not fight he could do nothing to secure the general European settlement after which he hankered. On both these occasions the French public, lavish in its sympathy for oppressed peoples but unwilling to act on their behalf, did not hesitate to blame Napoleon III for the loss of prestige. When war became inevitable between Austria and Prussia in 1866 Napoleon thought that he would have to intervene on the weaker side, but public opinion was dead against war. He thought, of course, that Prussia would be the weaker, and the miscalculation which led him to help Bismarck to secure an alliance with Italy seemed the less excusable afterwards from having been detected beforehand by Thiers. When the news of Sadowa informed Napoleon of his mistake he thought, for a moment, of ignoring public opinion and massing an army on the Rhine, as the Empress and the foreign minister Drouyn de Lhuys urged him to do, but moral courage failed him and he agreed with Rouher and La Valette (minister of the interior) to stick to peaceful mediation. Only Napoleon knew how little could be secured: the extent of Prussian aggrandizement in the Treaty of Prague and the total lack of any frontier rectifications for France came as a profound shock to the public. Napoleon III was inclined to accept a *fait accompli* and rely on Prussia to seek a 'natural' alliance with France, but the French people had been nurtured for too long in a sense of their own importance. Napoleon III was thus pushed into the fatal policy of seeking '*pourboires*' – the left bank of the Rhine, Belgium, Luxembourg – from Bismarck.

The policy was bound to lead to war at any moment when Bismarck wanted it, and Napoleon began, languidly and hopelessly, to seek for allies. Alexander II, disappointed in his hopes of assistance from France in revising the Treaty of Paris, offered Russian neutrality to Bismarck in return for a promise to annul the Black Sea Clauses. The English people had always been hostile, in spite of the Crimean War and the Cobden-Chevalier treaty: every other move, from Savoy and Nice to Suez, convinced them that Napoleon III was a menace. An approach to Francis Joseph, so much injured by France in Italy and cruelly hurt by the death of Maximilian, was received more courteously than Napoleon might have expected, but Austria dared not move without Italy, and this brought the negotiations to a standstill. The French public, indifferent in 1860 to the alarms of the clergy concerning the Pope, was determined now to keep Rome from the Italian nationalists, allies of Bismarck at Sadowa. The French garrison, withdrawn in 1866 after a guarantee from the Italian government to respect the integrity of Rome, was returned in October 1867 to help crush Garibaldi's assault at Mentana. There could be no alliance with Italy.

If Napoleon III was responsible, through the tergiversations of his foreign policy, for allowing France to approach the war of 1870 without allies, he was not responsible, unless from an inability to assert himself, for her lack of preparation. From 1866 Napoleon was only too well aware of the inferiority of the French army in numbers, training, weapons, and administration to that of Prussia. In theory all Frenchmen from the ages of eighteen to twenty-five were liable for military service, but in practice, under the army law of 1832, a small number, fixed by the legislature, was selected by ballot to serve for a period long enough to turn them into professionals, out of touch with the civilian population, and commanded by officers who were badly educated and routine-minded. In the autumn of 1866 military authorities estimated France's strength at 288,000 men, as against Prussia's 1,200,000. Napoleon set as a target a mobilized force of 1,000,000 men, and advocated a system of universal short-term military service on the Prussian model to achieve it. There was an immediate outcry from professional soldiers, who despised reservists; from politicians, who feared the strengthening of Napoleon's arm at home and abroad; from the public, which disliked conscription and shirked expense. The most radical politicians, precisely those who were insisting that territorial demands should be made upon Bismarck, advocated abolishing the standing army altogether and confiding the defence of France to a militia on the Swiss pattern. In 1867 Napoleon appointed a capable war minister, Marshal Niel, and backed him in plans to increase the potential size of the army by reducing the length of service to five years, creating a reserve, and training the National Guard to act in the same way as the Prussian *Landwehr*. Niel with much difficulty pushed a measure on these lines through the *Corps Législatif* in January 1868, but the proposal concerning the National Guard was so diminished as to be almost useless. During the next two years the deputies persistently knocked down the army estimates, and as late as June 1870 they reduced the annual contingent by 10,000 men. Napoleon's suggestions for creating a General Staff on the Prussian model and for mastering the Prussian technique of rapid mobilization met only with professional disapproval. Thanks to his insistence the breech-loading rifle which M. Chassepot had been working on for ten years was put into production for the whole army, but when 13 million francs had been spent on this the *Corps Législatif* refused to vote another 13 million to buy the breech-loading guns offered by the firm of Krupp. French politicians were too much concerned with the things that belong to peace, in a sense the French nation was too civilized, to prepare for war against Prussia.

The crisis which led France to declare war on Prussia on 19 July 1870 arose out of a very small incident. The King of Prussia allowed a Hohenzollern prince to accept an offer of the throne of Spain without informing the French government. When the news leaked out the French created such a furor that William I withdrew Prince Leopold's candidature. This was a great diplomatic triumph for France, and there need have been no war had not the French newspapers and the crowds in the cities insisted, as a revenge for repeated humiliations, on turning the knife in the wound. The King of Prussia must be asked for a personal guarantee that the candidature would never be renewed. The public sentiment was expressed by the Empress, supported by the foreign secretary Gramont (a career diplomat of no great understanding), and with the acquiescence of the Emperor, who was almost incapacitated through illness. William I could not accede to a request which seemed to impugn his good faith, but he behaved courteously to the French ambassador, and there still need have been no war had not Bismarck decided, apparently quite suddenly, to use this opportunity rather than wait for another to fight France for the sake of deciding which nation should lay down the law in Europe. 'I have conceived the vocation of the German people as great and dominating the world', Heinrich von Gagern had said in the Frankfurt Assembly: the dream was to advance a step nearer to fulfilment. Bismarck so edited the telegraphed report from the king that the whole of the French people believed their ambassador to have been insulted: when the 'Ems telegram' was published, both William I and Ollivier believed that it meant war. Ollivier was put into the picture by Gramont for the first time on 13 July: two days later he told the Chamber that he accepted responsibility for war 'with a light heart'.

The war minister Leboeuf, appointed after Niel's premature death in 1869, assured his cabinet colleagues that the French army was ready 'to the last gaiter button'. The statement was not a frivolous one, though it damned Leboeuf in the opinion of posterity. The *chassepot* was a better weapon than the Prussian rifle, and in plentiful supply. The Prussians had better guns but did not always know how to use them effectively. The Prussians had greater numbers, and their mobilization was quicker, but these were not decisive factors. The French failed most seriously in the matter of leadership. The Emperor, so ill that he could scarcely sit his horse, mishandled the opening campaign; small armies fought bravely but vainly without the support they needed; the Prussians, to their own surprise, were able to take the initiative almost at once. Napoleon III was pushed out of his supreme command by the generals in favour of Marshal Bazaine, a product of the Mexican adventure who turned out to be as unsatisfactory as a commander as he was peculiar as an individual. Withdrawing with combined armies upon the impregnable fortress of Metz, Bazaine found himself encircled and besieged there within a month. The Emperor, gathering an army under Marshal MacMahon at Châlons, was advised to retreat on Paris and take a stand outside the capital, but fearing the political consequences of such a plan he moved instead towards Metz in an attempt to relieve the strangely inactive Bazaine. MacMahon in his turn was encircled by the Prussians near Sedan. A brief battle fought on the next day (1 September) persuaded the Emperor that resistance to the Prussian guns was hopeless. After seeking death in vain in the firing line he surrendered with an army of 2,700 officers, 39 generals, and 84,000 men. It was one of the deepest humiliations in the history of warfare.

In Paris the news of invasion had already brought the downfall of the Ollivier ministry: with the news of Sedan the defunct Empire was brushed aside. The French nation in arms went on fighting heroically, desperately, but after several months even Paris was beaten to her knees. Bismarck's new

Germany succeeded to France's military pre-eminence and at once assumed a position of hegemony on the continent of Europe.

3. THE KINGDOM NOT OF THIS WORLD

As France and Germany moved towards their contest for supremacy Pope Pius IX prepared the citadel of the church for a siege by the forces of darkness. On 18 July 1870 the militant faithful received the word for which they had waited. With the approval of a General Council Pius IX promulgated the dogma of Papal Infallibility.

Since 1849 Pius had seen the world as growing in evil. His experiences during the revolutionary years had convinced him that liberalism and nationalism were inimical not only to the temporal power of the Papacy but to the spiritual authority of the Catholic church, and through this disillusioned gaze he came to regard new political creeds as but one branch of a modern trend of thought which challenged the very foundations of Christian faith. Developments in science seemed no less destructive than revolutions in government. At the beginning of the nineteenth century, readers of the Bible were able to believe that the story of the creation of the world was borne out by scientific knowledge. Gradually, however, scientists were obliged to abandon the theory that a series of catastrophes, reconcilable with the days of Genesis, had led to the formation of the earth's crust, until by 1830 they were ready to receive as authoritative the treatise of Sir Charles Lyell (*Principles of Geology*) which attributed the configuration of the earth's surface to a process of elevation and depression, deposition and erosion, operative for a million years and still continuing. Meanwhile Charles Darwin was steadily accumulating evidence to prove the theory (presaged 50 years earlier in the work of the French zoologist Lamarck) that the species into which the earth's flora and fauna were divided did not originate in separate creations but evolved from a common ancestry by a process of natural selection. The implications of the *Origin of Species* (1859) became obvious to the Christian public in a remarkably short time. By tracing the descent of man from the lowest animals, 'Darwinism' seemed not only to render untenable the Biblical account of the creation of life but to deprive man of the immortal soul uniquely bestowed upon the race of Adam. Many did not know what to think. Thomas Huxley, while helping to publicize Darwin's theories, coined the term 'agnostic' to describe the position of the searcher who could neither affirm nor deny the truth of Christianity. Among the scientists, almost all of whom were converted to evolutionary doctrine within a decade, the devout Christian faith of a Johann Mendel or Louis Pasteur became a matter for comment. Darwin himself, after a painful struggle, denounced the orthodoxy of his youth. The scientific discipline, involving as it did a refusal to accept any other authority, presented an intrinsic challenge to the churches. Popular interest in science encouraged the notion that scientific subjects held a monopoly of knowledge and that other activities of the human mind came in the realm of conjecture, myth, hallucination, or downright dishonesty. Less and less room was allotted to divine revelation.

The assumption that all phenomena ought to be submitted to rigorous, exact, 'scientific' investigation encouraged the critical studies of the Bible which had been proceeding in Germany since the eighteenth century. Attacks on the historical authenticity of the Old Testament gradually relegated most of the Pentateuch to a late date in Hebrew history. Critical onslaughts on the New Testament were even more disquieting. In 1835 a young lecturer at Tübingen, D. F. Strauss, published a *Life of Jesus* which rejected the historical validity of the Gospels and denied the virgin birth. Strauss's brilliant work, translated into English by George Eliot in 1846, presented a profoundly moving experience to some readers, for whom it liberated the eternal Christ from the deadwood of tradition. To Strauss himself the Gospels were at first no less valuable for being mythical embodiments rather than factual accounts of spiritual truth, but as his work came under fire from orthodox reviewers he grew more belligerent in his attitude and eventually denied the existence of a personal God. In France a fascination for German culture was the hallmark of intellectuals in the eighteen-thirties, and among those affected by German biblical studies was Ernest Renan, a boy from a devout Breton home who was sent to Paris to study for the priesthood. Eventually appointed to the chair of Semitic languages at the Collège de France, Renan published in 1863 a *Life of Jesus* which gave a stylish account of a gentle and altogether human Galilean preaching the Kingdom of God. The book was ridiculed by more ponderous German scholars but sold widely in France and was translated into many European languages.

Whilst faith in divine revelation weakened, faith in human endeavour went on from strength to strength. Science and history supported the belief that man and his works not only changed as time went on but changed for the better. Few doubted that technology and industry, in spite of all the incidental suffering which they brought, were on the whole beneficent and would increase in value. In politics the belief in progress expressed itself in the growth of liberalism and a variety of socialist creeds. Even Karl Marx, in calling upon the workers of the world to assist the forces of history, assumed that the inevitable trend moved upward. Doubtless the prevailing faith in progress played its part in Christian endeavour. Missionary effort, especially by Protestant churches, on a scale unprecedented since the early centuries of Christianity was supported by a conviction that European modes of thought and living would bring the people of Africa, India, China, and Japan nearer to the Kingdom of God. At the same time, however, faith in progress lent itself to a crude materialism which had nothing in keeping with Christian ideals.

The situation by mid-century was one of great anxiety for the leaders of all the Christian churches. Protestants had long prided themselves on the fact that their faith was demonstrable by reason: they were therefore obliged to grapple with the new knowledge and, after sore travail, they came to terms with Darwinism. To the Pope, who held a unique position as director of consciences, the problem presented itself in a different light. His duty seemed to be not so much to keep abreast of scholars as to see that the flock did not stray from the fold. In 1854 he recalled Catholics to an obedient faith by elevating the belief in the Immaculate Conception of the Virgin Mary to the status of dogma. In the ensuing decade he spoke out many times, in allocutions, encyclicals, and apostolic letters, against modern trends of thought. On 8 December 1864 he issued further denunciations in an encyclical letter *Quanta Cura*. At the same time his secretary of state Antonelli provided bishops with a handy list of errors condemned to date by Pius IX and his predecessors.

The *Syllabus Errorum* was launched upon the world three months after Napoleon III had agreed with the Italian government to withdraw his garrison from Rome. Though the agreement was conditional upon a guarantee from Victor Emmanuel to respect the Pope's remaining territory no-one could believe in the ability of the Italian government to stifle the determination of radicals such as Garibaldi to make Rome the capital of Italy. Relations between the Pope and the nationalist movement in Italy had deteriorated rapidly since 1849. Cavour had abolished most of the religious orders in Sardinia in 1855 and had extended his anti-clerical legislation over the rest of Italy as his annexationist policy gained ground. In 1860 he had laid hands on the Romagna, thereby rending, in Pius's metaphor, the seamless robe of Christ. Later in the same year he had extinguished the Papal States save for Rome. Thereafter he had offered Pius IX 'a free church in a free state', but since he had also pressed on with his anti-clerical measures in the centre and south Pius IX, like Montalembert, had seen in his promises nothing but the prospect of 'a despoiled church in a spoliative state'. Pius had embarked upon a holy war against the new Italian state: the Syllabus of Errors was to play a part in this war, but to describe it as a weapon designed chiefly to retain power over a few square miles of territory is to diminish its significance unwarrantably.

Not all Catholics believed in 1864 that the church needed to fight relentlessly against the modern world. In France Montalembert had carried the banner of liberal-catholicism for thirty years, with some success in the field of education. In Belgium Cardinal Sterckx had encouraged a Catholic group to co-operate with liberals in producing the constitution of 1831, and

AOP 2F

no ill-effects had as yet been seen. (It was not until 1868 that liberal governments with triumphant majorities embarked upon a secularizing programme
in education.) In Germany the theologian Döllinger had given scholarly
eminence to the liberal-catholic movement throughout the greater part of a
long career. In 1863 Catholic congresses at Malines and Munich had considered the attitude which ought to be adopted by the church to an age of
advancing unbelief, and Montalembert at the one and Döllinger at the other
had pleaded for freedom in all realms – religion, politics, and scholarship.
To Pius IX such manifestations were merely a proof of the insidious powers
of evil. In the Syllabus of Errors his strictest censures were reserved for
liberal-catholicism.

The Syllabus covered more or less the same ground as the encyclical
Quanta Cura, but whereas the latter was measured and conventional the
former was harsh and peremptory. Pius IX apparently paid little attention
to the form which the Syllabus should take. Speculation was afterwards
rife as to its authorship, but no-one could deny that it had been issued with
the Pope's approval. The Syllabus listed eighty errors as having been condemned in recent years. It began with pantheism, naturalism, and rationalism, with ancillary evils such as denial of revelation and assertion that the
Bible contains myths. A second section condemned indifferentism and
latitudinarianism, including the belief that God may be as well pleased in
Protestantism as in Catholicism. A single paragraph bore down upon socialism, communism, secret societies and Bible societies. A list of 37 errors concerning the respective rights of church and civil society included the opinion
that the state should control education and that church and state ought to be
separated. A further list of erroneous opinions on the subject of ethics was
particularly severe upon those who maintained that morality could be
achieved without the aid of revealed religion. Various forms of assault upon
Christian marriage were censured, and denial that the temporal power was
necessary to the independence of the Holy See was condemned. A few
errors connected with 'the liberalism of the day' brought the Syllabus to an
end with the resounding condemnation of the assertion that 'the Roman
Pontiff can and should reconcile and harmonize himself with progress,
liberalism, and modern civilization'.

The Syllabus was read with dismay by liberal-catholics, and the cleverest
politician among them, the French bishop Dupanloup, applied himself at
once to the task of minimizing its import. The Syllabus, he said, expressed
the 'thesis', the absolute truth which ideally should govern a Christian society;
this did not exclude recognition of the 'hypothesis', the adjustment which
might be necessary and even valuable to the church in particular circumstances. Thus, though the Pope could not allow religious toleration to be a
universal ideal he would accept it in countries where the Catholic church

might otherwise perish; and though he could not accept the claims of the rationalists to a monopoly of truth he would agree that reason allied to faith might be beneficial to Christianity. No less than 630 bishops thanked Dupanloup for the help given to consciences by his pamphlet (entitled *The September Convention and the Encyclical of 8 December*). The Pope congratulated him upon having confounded critics of the Syllabus, but without suggesting that his interpretation was the correct one. The leading publicist of the ultramontane school, Louis Veuillot, favoured a much more rigorous interpretation, and indulged the hope that in the near future the Pope would dogmatize the principles suggested in the Syllabus. The growth of ultramontanism not only in France, where the influence of Lamennais in this respect had outlived the liberal-catholicism of his latter days, but in the whole of the Catholic world was one of the most notable features of Pius IX's long pontificate. Moreover the prophets of the new ultramontanism were not content with a vision of the church freed from secular control; they wished to centralize authority within the church in the hands of the Pope and thereby create a church militant which might one day triumph over the state. It was in answer to their demands that the definition of papal infallibility became the sole topic of discussion at a General Council summoned by Pius IX to meet in Rome on 8 December 1869. To the dying Montalembert the ultramontanes had abandoned all hope of freedom 'in order to offer up justice and truth, reason and history, as a holocaust to the idol which they were erecting at the Vatican'.

Ultramontanes were not the only ones prepared to make a sacrifice of freedom, however. Liberal catholics in France, Germany, and even England hoped for interference by governments in the programme of the Council. The French emperor, as Bismarck pointed out, held the keys of the Council in his hands, for if his troops left Rome the Italians would enter. Napoleon III after a moment's hesitation was persuaded by Ollivier of the unwisdom of intervention, but the scare was serious enough for ultramontanes to petition the Pope to give priority to the discussion of infallibility. Dupanloup's efforts outside the Council to prefabricate opposition to the motion were unavailing. On 18 July the definition was accepted by 533 votes to 2, and Pius IX promulgated, amid the sounds of a great thunderstorm, the dogma that 'the Roman Pontiff, when he speaks *ex cathedra* to define a doctrine regarding faith or morals to be held by the universal church, is possessed of that infallibility bestowed by Christ on His church, and therefore such definitions are irreformable of themselves and not from the consent of the church'. Within the church, only Döllinger and his colleagues in Munich, Prague, and Bonn resisted the dogma, with shortlived success. In November 1870 Italian troops entered Rome, and the Pope, rejecting the Law of Guarantees offered him by a government which he could neither respect nor trust, retired as a voluntary prisoner within the Vatican. From here he directed the church in its most resounding conflict of the century: the *Kulturkampf* with Bismarck.

Bibliographical Note

There are three guides to further reading which can be used for this period:

A Select List of works on Europe and Europe overseas, 1715-1815, edited by J. S. Bromley and A. Goodwin (Oxford, 1956).

Ae Slect List of books on European history, 1815-1914, edited by Alan Bullock and A. J. P. Taylor (Oxford, 1957).

Modern European History, 1789-1945: a select bibliography, edited by W. N. Medlicott for the Historical Association (Helps to students of history, No. 60, 1960).

All three include works in the better known foreign languages. For Russia there is in addition the excellent *Select Bibliography of works in English on Russian history, 1801-1917*, edited by David Shapiro (Oxford, 1962). This is annotated, and includes articles in such learned journals as are likely to be available in public libraries.

The historiography of the French Revolution is discussed in *Historians and the causes of the French Revolution*, by Alfred Cobban (Historical Association pamphlet G.2 revised, 1958) and *Interpretations of the French Revolution*, by G. Rudé (Historical Association pamphlet G.47, 1961).

G. Wright: *France in Modern Times: 1760 to the present* (1962) contains bibliographical chapters and also discusses historiographical points in the body of the work.

Among the works which have appeared more recently than the guides mentioned above, the following are useful for this period:

E. J. Hobsbawm: *The Age of Revolution: Europe 1789-1848* (1962). An interpretation along Marxist lines, particularly interesting for its information on social and economic matters and for its excursions into little known parts of the world.

J. Godechot: *La Contre-Revolution, 1789-1804* (Paris, 1961). An attempt, stimulating though perhaps premature in the existing state of knowledge, to draw general conclusions about counter-revolutionary ideology and activity in many countries.

L. Gershoy: *Bertrand Barère* (1962). The definitive biography of this hitherto neglected revolutionary character.

G. Lefebvre: *The French Revolution from its origins to 1793* (1962). A translation of the first half of Georges Lefebvre's great history of the Revolution.

D. Silagi: *Ungarn und der geheime Mitarbeiter-Kreis Kaiser Leopolds II* (Munich, 1962). A brief and lucid account of the new historical viewpoint, from which Leopold appears as a truly progressive ruler.

J. C. Herold: *Bonaparte in Egypt* (1963). A lively narrative.

E. E. Y. Hales: *Napoleon and the Pope* (1962). A detailed but readable account of the great conflict between Napoleon and Pius VII, with emphasis on the personalities involved.

An article by A. N. Ryan on Britain's trade with the enemy (*Transactions of the Royal Historical Society*, 1962) and chapters on the Luddites in E. P. Thompson, *The Making of the English Working Class* (1963) offer supplementary and sometimes contrasting information to that given on these topics in F. Crouzet's magisterial work on the British economy and the Continental Blockade.

N. Botzaris: *Visions Balkaniques dans la préparation de la Révolution Grecque, 1789–1821* (Paris, 1962). A fascinating study of a little known subject; includes an account of social and political conditions throughout the Balkans at the end of the eighteenth century.

W. Carr: *Schleswig-Holstein, 1815–1848: a study in national conflict* (Manchester, 1963). Useful for the study of both German and Danish nationalism.

D. Johnson: *Guizot: aspects of French history, 1787–1874* (1963). A weighty piece of research which covers Guizot's ideas and activities in the realms of education, religion, history writing, and politics.

T. E. B. Howarth: *Citizen King: the life of Louis-Philippe* (1961). The first favourable biography of Louis-Philippe; scholarly and stylish.

C. M. Leonard: *Lyon Transformed: public works of the Second Empire, 1853–64* (1961). Scholarly and of much general interest.

R. F. Leslie: *Reform and insurrection in Russian Poland, 1856–1865* (1963). An invaluable companion to Dr Leslie's earlier work on the revolution of 1830; handles a mass of information in Polish.

M. Howard: *The Franco-Prussian War* (1961). The definitive military history.

H. Kohn: *The Mind of Germany* (1962). A survey of political ideas in Germany from the eighteenth to the twentieth century, tracing Germany's growing alienation from the West.

O. Pflanze: *Bismarck and the development of Germany* (1963). A sound and detailed account, up-to-date but pedestrian.

D. G. Charlton: *Secular Religions in France, 1815–70* (1963). Describes the many attempts made by French intellectuals to provide society with an ideological synthesis to replace Christianity.

N. Hampson: *A Social History of the French Revolution* (1963). A scholarly survey, based on original material, set in a political framework.

P. Tommila: *La Finlande dans la politique européenne en 1809–15* (Helsinki, 1962). An account in French by a Finnish historian of Finland's rôle in European affairs from the Treaty of Hamina, when she escaped from subjection to Sweden, to the Congress of Vienna, when she was confirmed in subjection to Russia. Contains a valuable section on Bernadotte.

F. Markham: *Napoleon* (1963). An up-to-date biography for the general reader. The economic history of the continent awaits its author. As an approach to it there is:

W. O. Henderson: *The Industrial Revolution on the Continent; Germany, France, and Russia, 1800–1914* (1961). A mine of information, much of it new.

R. E. Cameron: *France and the economic development of Europe, 1800–1914* (1961). A solid piece of research. Concentrates on France's rôle in investment and credit.

C. Cipolla: *The economic history of world population* (1962). An excellent introduction to the more solid work of M. Reinhard on population.

Two monumental pieces of research, at present suitable only for specialists, will need to be absorbed into more general accounts:

R. Cobb: *Les Armées Révolutionnaires. Instruments de la Terreur dans les Départements. Avril 1793 – Floréal An II* (Paris, 1963).

A. Daumard: *La Bourgeoisie Parisienne de 1815 à 1848* (Paris, 1963).

A beginning has been made on presenting Napoleon's correspondence to readers outside a narrow range of specialists:

Letters and Documents of Napoleon, selected and translated by J. E. Howard. Vol. I: The Rise to Power (1961).

The Historical Association has prepared a new atlas covering the period 1713-1948: Philips' *Atlas of Modern History* (1963).

Index

Bordeaux, 2, 33, 38, 69, 75, 238, 424, 231
Bornholm, 162
Bormida river, 131
Borodino, 211-12, 213
Borsig, August, German industrialist, 342
Bosporus, 193, 266, map V
Bouillé, Marquis de, 33, 35
Boulogne, 144, 146, 148, 325
bourgeoisie, bourgeois, 219, 269, 270, 273, 319-20, 358, 359, 363, 366, 367, 370; in Austria, 48, 321, 335, 336, 338, 341, 349, 414; in Belgium, 311; in Britain, 170, 318; in France, 1-4, 6-8, 10-12, 14-15, 21, 24-5, 26, 27, 31, 32, 35, 36, 39, 52, 71, 74, 81-2, 103, 104, 106, 110, 125, 126, 128, 140, 237, 241, 242, 272, 302, 305, 309, 310, 318, 321, 322-3, 326-7, 329, 330, 333, 419, 424, 426; in Germany, 59-61, 218, 223, 227, 231, 290, 317, 318, 321, 343-4, 345, 346, 349, 350; in Holland, 87, 123; in Hungary, 339; in Italy, 281-2, 351-2, 397; in Poland, 96, 218; in Russia, 201, 374, 390; in Spain, 178, 186, 280
Bourmont, Louis August Victor de, Comte, 310
Boyen, Hermann von, General, 230-1, 292
Brabant, 51, 52, 54
Braine-le-Comte, 243, map IV
Brandenburg, 230, 288, 405, map VII
Brandenburg, Count Friedrich von, 350
Brandes, Ernst, 60
Branicki, family, 95; Francis Xavier, 96-7
Bremen, 101, map IV
Brest, 85, 145, 158, 304, 424
Birenne, 9, 27
Bright, John, 382
Brissot, Jacques Pierre, 37-8, 39, 65, 71, 72, 73, 87
Brissotins, 38-40, 63, 65-70
Bristol, 170
Britain, British, in 1789-1802, 55, 58, 62, 72, 76, 79, 85, 87-91, 98-100, 101, 102, 106-7, 113, 114, 115, 116-17, 118, 119, 122, 131-2, 172, 181, 182, 270; in 1803-15, chapter IX *passim*, 142-4, 144-6, 149-51, 152, 154, 157, 172-3, 183, 184, 185, 187-8, 188-91, 192, 194, 195, 197, 207, 219, 235, 236, 238, 240, 243, 248, 282, 370-1; in 1815-70, 249-68, 270, 289, 301, 312, 313, 315, 316, 317-18, 320, 324, 326, 342, 349, 361, 362, 363-4, 367, 368, 369, 378-86, 394, 397, 400, 423, 426, 429, 431. See also England, Ireland, Scotland, Wales

Brittany, Breton, 5, 21, 27, 67, 98, 126, 237
Brougham, Henry, 170
Browers, De, Belgian patriot, 52
Browning, Robert, poet, 316
Broux, De, Belgian patriot, 52
Bruck, Baron Karl Ludwig von, 413
brumaire, *coup d'état* of, 120, 125, 130, 138
Brunswick, 58, map VII
Brunswick, Charles William Ferdinand, Duke of, 40, 65, 66, 67, 68, 69, 70, 154
Brussels, 33, 52, 53, 65, 71, 73, 99, 243, 244, 245, 270, 312, 316, 320, 351, maps II, III, and IV
Bucharest, 300, map VI; treaty of, 209
Büchner, Ludwig, scientist, 367
Budapest, 49, 340, 414
Buenos Aires, 165, 186
Buffon, Georges Louis Leclerc de, natural scientist, 176,
Bukovina, 41, 43, map I
Bulgaria, 297-8, 395, map VI
Buol, Count Karl von, 382, 384-5, 399
Buonarroti, Filipo, Italian patriot, 109, 123-4
Burgos, 182-3, 190
Burke, Edmund, 60, 88, 91, 273
Byron, Lord George, poet, 270, 274, 316-17

Cabanel, Alexandre, painter, 366
Cabarrús, Francisco, 177, 181
Cabet, Etienne, socialist, 319, 325
Cabezon, 184
Cadiz, 145, 149-50, 176, 179, 181, 184, 185-6
Cadoudal, Georges, Vendéan leader, 126, 134
Caen, 75, 76
cahiers de doléances, 4, 10, 14, 29, 31
Cairo, 117-18, 131, 422
California, 425
Calonne, Charles Alexandre de, 27, 38
Calvinist, 46
Cambacérès, J. J. Régis de, 129, 130, 138
Cambodia, 429
Cambon, Joseph, 26, 72
Camperdown, 117
Camphaussen, Otto von, 343
Campo-Formio, treaty of, 116, 131
Campomanes, Pedro Rodriguez, Conde de, 177
Canada, 164
Canning, George, 158-9, 183, 260-5, 268, 301
Cannizaro, Stanislao, chemist, 367
Canova, Antonio, sculptor, 270
Canrobert, François Certain, Marshal, 384

Ernest Augustus, King of Hanover, 344, 346
Ertholm islands, 162
Escher, Johann Conrad, Swiss patriot, 123
Essen, 342
Esslingen, 342
Estates General (France 1789), 1, 4, 5, 6, 7, 9, 21, 34
Esterházy, family, 43
Eugénie (de Montijo), Empress of the French, 420, 422, 432, 433
European Messenger (ed. Karamzin), 205
Execution of the Emperor Maximilian (painting by Manet), 366
Extremadura, 175
Eylau, 155

Faidherbe, Louis Léon César, general and colonial administrator, 429
Falloux, Frédéric, Comte de, 332
Far East, 163, 363-4, 394, 429
Faraday, Michael, chemist, 368
Fascist, 279
Fathers and Sons (Turgenev), 392
Ferdinand I, Emperor of Austria, 241, 334, 336-7, 340, 349, 350, 412
Ferdinand VII, King of Spain, 173, 182, 251, 260, 280-1
Ferdinand IV, King of Naples and Sicily, 121, 152
Ferdinand I, King of the Two Sicilies, 259, 281
Ferdinand II, King of the Two Sicilies, 352, 356, 357
Ferrara, 113
Ferrère, Bonapartist agent, 333
Ferrol, 184
Fersen, Axel von, Count, 35
Feuerbach, Paul Johann Anselm, Ritter von, jurist, 223
Feuillant, 37, 38, 63
Fichte, Johann Gottlieb, writer, 228, 231
Fidelio (Beethoven), 223
Filangieri, Gaetano, jurist, 176
Finkenstein, 155
Finland, 192, 209, 252
First Coalition, 97-101
Flanders, Flemings, 36, 52, 54, 99, 311
Flaubert, Gustave, writer, 365
Fleurus, 85, 100, map II
Flocon, Ferdinand, journalist, 330
floréal, *coup d'état* of, 119
Florence, 219, 279, 400, 403, maps III and VIII
Floridablanca, Joseph Moñino, Conde de, 177, 179, 181-2, 184

Flushing, 195
Foggia, 281, map VIII
Fontainebleau, 238, 239, map IV
Forckenbeck, Max von, 411
Forlí, 285, map VIII
Foscolo, Ugo, writer, 221, 279
Foster, Lady Elizabeth, 135
Fouché, Joseph, Duc d'Otranto, 82, 85-6, 137, 155, 235, 242, 247, 278
Fould, Achille, banker, 419
Foullon, J. François, 17
Fouquier-Tinville, A. Quentin, 79, 80
Fourier, François Charles Marie, socialist, 319, 392
Fourth Coalition, 235
Fox, Charles James, 88, 89
France, French, in 1789-99, chapters I, II, IV and VI *passim*, 44, 45, 46, 47, 48, 51, 52, 54, 55, 56, 57-8, 60, 61, 62, 63-4, 87, 88-9, 90-1, 92, 93, 96, 97, 99-100, 101-2, 125, 127, 129, 130, 134, 139, 140, 177, 179, 180, 202, 204, 207, 217, 222, 228, 237, 241-2, 270, 271-2, 273, 274, 279, 287, 295, 298, 302, 307, 309, 310, 317, 318, 319, 321, 330, 369, 407, 421; in 1799-1815, chapters VII and VIII *passim*, 143-7, 155, 158-63, 165-8, 171, 172-3, 179-81, 182-91, 192-7, 207, 208-15, 217, 220, 222, 225, 228, 231, 232, 233-5, 236-47, 270, 284-5, 373; in 1815-48, 247-8, 251-60, 261-3, 266-8, 272, 281, 283, 284, 287-8, 301, 302-11, 312, 314-16, 317, 318, 319-20, 321, 322-9, 343, 353, 378-9, 421-3, 436; in 1848-52, 329-34, 335, 355, 356-7, 358-9, 361, 379-80, 418-19, 423, 431; in 1852-70, 362, 364, 366, 367, 368, 370, 371, 380-3, 383-6, 393, 397, 401, 403, 404, 406, 409, 410, 411, 414, 418-35, 435, 438-9
Franche-Comté, 15, 241
Francis Joseph, Emperor of Austria, 335, 341, 381, 385, 400, 406, 407, 408-10, 412-17, 429, 432
Francis II, Holy Roman Emperor, later Francis I, Emperor of Austria, 41, 55, 63-4, 91, 92, 97, 113, 114, 116, 119, 131, 142, 146-7, 149, 151, 193, 194, 196, 269, 275-6, 278, 315, 316, 334, 339
François de Neufchâteau, 108, 116
Frankfurt, 64, 71, 162, 217, 218, 288, 349, 409, 410, 411, map VII; Diet of Princes at, 254-5; Frankfurt Assembly 338, 341, 345-50, 359, 360, 361, 433
Franz, Constantin, writer, 408